GIRLHOOD IN AMERICA

An Encyclopedia

Volume 2
J–Z

Miriam Forman-Brunell, EDITOR
Associate Professor of History
University of Missouri
Kansas City, Missouri

FOREWORD BY **Susan J. Douglas**
Professor of Communication Studies
University of Michigan — Ann Arbor
Ann Arbor, Michigan

A B C CLIO

Santa Barbara, California
Denver, Colorado
Oxford, England

Library of Congress Cataloging-in-Publication Data
Girlhood in America : an encyclopedia / Miriam Forman-Brunell, editor; foreword by Susan Douglas.
    p. cm. — (The American family)
Includes bibliographical references and index.
    ISBN 1-57607-206-1 (set : alk. paper) — 1-57607-550-8 (e-book)
    1. Girls—United States—Encyclopedias.   I. Forman-Brunell, Miriam.
II. American family (Santa Barbara, Calif.)
HQ777.G5745   2001
305.23'0973'03—dc21

                                                            2001001346

07 06 05 04 03 02 01   10 9 8 7 6 5 4 3 2 1 (cloth)

ABC-CLIO, Inc.
130 Cremona Drive, P.O. Box 1911
Santa Barbara, California 93116-1911

This book is also available on the World Wide Web as an e-book. Visit www.abc-clio.com for details.

This book is printed on acid-free paper ∞
Manufactured in the United States of America

46393648

THE AMERICAN FAMILY

The six titles that make up **The American Family** offer a revitalizing new take on U.S. history, surveying current culture from the perspective of the family and incorporating insights from psychology, sociology, and medicine. Each two-volume, A-to-Z encyclopedia features its own advisory board, editorial slant, and apparatus, including illustrations, bibliography, and index.

Adolescence in America

EDITED BY Jacqueline V. Lerner, Boston College,
and Richard M. Lerner, Tufts University;
Jordan W. Finkelstein, Pennsylvania State University,
Advisory Editor

Boyhood in America

EDITED BY Priscilla Ferguson Clement, Pennsylvania State
University, Delaware County, and Jacqueline S. Reinier,
California State University, Sacramento

The Family in America

EDITED BY Joseph M. Hawes, University of Memphis,
and Elizabeth F. Shores, Little Rock, Arkansas

Girlhood in America

EDITED BY Miriam Forman-Brunell,
University of Missouri, Kansas City

Infancy in America

EDITED BY Alice Sterling Honig, Emerita, Syracuse University;
Hiram E. Fitzgerald, Michigan State University;
and Holly Brophy-Herb, Michigan State University

Parenthood in America

EDITED BY Lawrence Balter, New York University

GIRLHOOD
IN AMERICA

An Encyclopedia

CONTENTS

A-to-Z List of Entries *vii*

Volume 1: Entries A to I *1*
Volume 2: Entries J to Z *383*

Bibliography *703*
Index *761*
About the Editor *773*

A-to-Z List of Entries

VOLUME 1, A–I

A

Acquaintance Rape
Adolescent Health
Adoption
Advice Books
African American Girls in the
    Twentieth Century
Allowances and Spending Money
American Girls Collection
Arts and Crafts
Asian American Girls

B

Babysitting
Barbie
Bat Mitzvah
Birth Control
Body Image

C

Camp Fire Girls
Captivity
Cars
Catholic Girls
Cheerleaders
Chicana Girls
Child Abuse
Child Guidance

Clothing
Collecting
College Girls
Comic Books
Communication
Consumer Culture
Cosmetics

D

Dance Classes
Dances and Dancing
Dating and Courtship
Daughters and Fathers
Daughters and Mothers
Depression and Girls
Diaries
Disabilities
Dollhouses
Dolls
Domestic Service
Domesticity

E

Eating Disorders
Education of Girls
Emotions
Enslaved Girls of African Descent

F

Fairy Tales
Fan Clubs

Female Sexuality
4-H
Free Girls of African Descent
Frontier Girls

G

Gifted Girls
Girl Gangs
Girl Power
Girl Scouts
Girls and Sweets
Girls' Culture
Girls' Fiction
Girls' Magazines
Girls' Rooms
Graffiti

H

Hair
Handbags
Home Economics Education
Hygiene

I

Immigration
Indentured Servants

VOLUME 2, J–Z

J

Jewish Education of Girls
Juvenile Delinquents

K

Kinaaldá

L

Latina Girls
Learning Disabilities, Reading Disorders, and Girls
Lesbians
Literacy
Little Mothers

M

Mathematics and Science
Mennonite Girls
Menstruation
Mill Girls
Movies, Adolescent Girls in

N

Nancy Drew Mysteries
Native American Girls

O

Orphans and Orphanages

P

Pets
Pickford, Mary
Play
Pocahontas
Prom
Psychotherapy
Punk Rock
Puritan Girls

Q

La Quinceañera

R

Radical Feminism
Reading
Red Diaper Girls
Relational Theory
Riot Grrrls
Rural Girls

S

Samplers
Saturday Evening Girls
Sexual Harassment
Slumber Parties
Sororities
Southern Belles
Sports
Substance Abuse
Suicidal Behavior in Girls
Summer Camps for Girls

Surfer Girls

T

Tea Parties
Technology
Teen Pregnancy
Teenybopper
Television
Temple, Shirley
Tomboys

W

Witchcraft
Work

Z

Zines

J

Jewish Education of Girls

The secular and religious education of Jewish girls, including their limited formal schooling, initially overlapped. But over the course of nearly three and a half centuries, Jewish girls' secular and religious instruction took separate paths. The secular education of Jewish girls has been tied closely to the emerging American educational system and has consistently expanded. The nature and scope of their Jewish education, however, have been inconsistent. It has been intimately related to the larger project of transplanting and sustaining Judaism in America and to the evolving roles of women within the various branches of American Judaism as these denominations have emerged since 1800.

Upon their arrival in the seventeenth century, the first Jewish settlers in North America provided rudimentary instruction to their own children, usually by employing tutors in the home. In the late eighteenth century, education began to move out of the home and the children of then-established Jews, boys and girls, went to dame schools (a combination child care and primary school run by women, often in their own homes) and private schools (a few linked to synagogues) where they received a general education.

Boys were tutored in Jewish subjects in preparation for bar mitzvah by religious leaders in towns having established synagogues such as New York, Newport, Philadelphia, and Charleston. Girls, unless a parent elected to provide tutoring, received virtually no formal instruction in Jewish subjects. A girl's Jewish knowledge was to be acquired by listening, observing, and modeling her own religious beliefs and practices on those of her mother. With an American Jewish population estimated to be scarcely 4,000 in 1830, these ad hoc arrangements appeared to suffice for both girls and boys.

When large-scale Jewish immigration from German lands got under way in the 1830s, girls in the northeastern United States were already well represented in coeducational common schools. By the middle of the nineteenth century, almost as many girls as boys attended elementary (common) schools, generally taught by women teachers, and by the 1870s the achieved educational level of girls had surpassed that of boys.

As did their Protestant counterparts, American Jewish women responded to the feminization of teaching that accompanied the development and growth of common schools. Unlike Catholics, who largely rejected the Protestant-controlled common schools as anathema to their religious beliefs, most Jews accepted the common school ideal. Jewish girls benefited from the expansion in educational

Rebecca Gratz (Library of Congress)

opportunities for all girls in the American common school, but the Protestant character of common schooling remained a problem.

Stimulated by the early-nineteenth-century Second Great Awakening, missionaries, many of whom were women staunchly committed to the evangelical religious movements of the age, directed their attention to the urban immigrant poor. Jews were particular objects of missionary zeal. Emblematic of the mission to convert, in 1820 the American Society for Meliorating the Conditions of the Jews was incorporated in Philadelphia. Especially following the panic of 1837, when economic conditions were unusually bleak and coinciding with the recent influx of Jewish immigrants from German-speaking lands, female missionaries in Philadelphia offered free food and clothing to immigrant mothers, infusing

the Gospel along with their charity and encouraging mothers to send their children to Sunday school. The ecumenical Christianity, moral instruction, and literacy training of the common school classroom could be brought by missionaries directly to the children of Jewish neighborhoods, boys and girls believed to be dwelling in ignorance and darkness. Philadelphia, home of the American Sunday School Union (1824), was a city well prepared to give these children a limited basic education linked to Protestant religious and moral instruction.

Led by Rebecca Gratz, a group of Philadelphia women rose to the dual challenge: the need to counter missionary efforts among Jews and the need for a Jewish education to supplement the general (and Christian-influenced) education received by most Jewish children. These women were themselves poorly schooled in Jewish subjects but were imbued with the American vision of women as pious, spiritual, and gifted at teaching the young. With years of public charitable activity behind them as members of the Female Hebrew Benevolent Society, they were prepared to publicly defend Jewish interests by founding a Sunday school in 1838 based upon the model of the Protestant Sunday school.

This may have been the first opportunity for American Jewish women to teach Jewish subjects. Lacking teaching materials, they adopted the Protestant Sunday School Union catechism as the basis of their religious and moral instruction, blotting out overtly Christian passages. Within two years, however, two sisters who helped found the Hebrew Sunday school produced the first instructional materials specifically intended for use in Jewish primary religious instruction: Simha Cohen Peixotto's *Elementary In-*

troduction to the Scriptures, for the Use of Hebrew Children and Mrs. Eliezar Pyke's Scriptural Questions for the Use of Sunday School for the Instruction of Israelites. The latter, known as "Pyke's catechism," became the basis of instruction in Philadelphia as well as in schools that were established shortly thereafter by Jewish women in Richmond, Charleston, Savannah, and Baltimore. The Philadelphia Hebrew Sunday school model rapidly spread by means of women's networks: Gratz and other Philadelphia women writing to relatives and friends in the still small, close-knit, interrelated American Jewish community.

In Philadelphia and elsewhere, Jewish women took up the challenge to sustain the children of Israel in the United States by educating them in the religion of their forbears. They usurped a traditional prerogative of males and in so doing redefined and expanded the woman's role in Judaism to include the Jewish education of children.

The Hebrew Sunday school enrolled boys and girls, American-born and immigrant. By providing formal Jewish teaching to girls, its instructors implicitly acknowledged that the mimetic process was insufficient for educating girls in Jewish traditions. The Hebrew Sunday school embraced the American practice of coeducation and placed women teachers at the head of the class. Since many of the Sunday school's pupils went to other schools during the week, the school's part-time curriculum reinforced the supplementary nature of Jewish education and legitimized the separate study of secular and religious subjects and "teacher" as a female role. It framed Judaism as an American religion that was compatible with and complementary to the American day school.

Americanized Jewish women also responded to the Protestant challenge by embracing some of its cultural features. The Sunday school curriculum presented Judaism as a religion with a catechism to master, Bible stories to mine for moral lessons, and religious practices compatible with American life. This Jewish education taught in English was worlds apart from European concepts of Jewish studies tied to Talmud and Torah, taught by men, and generally reserved for males.

In New York City in the 1840s and 1850s the course of Jewish education, for boys as well as girls, was tied to the relationship between the city's Jews and its public schools. German Jewish immigration in this period gave New York the largest Jewish community in the United States. The new arrivals found the city's schools divided by class and religious denominations. Parents with even modest means sent their children to private, usually church-related schools. Free public education, common throughout the rest of New York State and most of the northeastern United States, was not provided in New York City until 1842. Free education was available only at Protestant-imbued charity schools.

In the 1840s the city's small public school system had a decidedly Protestant cast that offended both Catholics and Jews. Many Jewish parents, especially among new immigrants, did not want to expose their children to Christianizing influences in either private or public school. The need of these parents to educate their children, coupled with the lack of viable alternatives, gave rise to pressures to found Jewish day schools. By 1854 there were seven day schools enrolling more than 850 boys and girls. Girls accounted for about one-third of enrollments, a proportion of Jewish school enrollments (day and supplementary) that, within a few percentage points of variation, has been relatively constant until the present. These schools offered both secular and religious studies at the elementary school level. Although it would appear that boys and girls followed a common curriculum, there was gender differentiation: girls received instruction in sewing and needlework and boys in cantillation of Torah and Haftarah. The presumed adult roles of men and women within the Jewish community seemed to permit, if not yet require, Jewish as well as general education for girls. But the presumed nature of adult participation, at least in the public religious realm, was still divided along gender lines, hence the differentiated studies.

At midcentury Max Lilienthal, then rabbi of New York's Congregation Ansche Chesed, introduced a new practice to the American Jewish community, a confirmation for both boys and girls. Lilienthal's Shavuot-linked confirmation ceremony, first held in 1846, was preceded by five months of twice-weekly classes for the participating twelve-year-old girls and boys. Criticized by more orthodox congregants and suspended because of unrelated congregational politics, the confirmation was adopted by Temple Emanu-El in 1852 and resumed by Ansche Chesed in 1860. It continues in many congregations to this day, especially in Reform Judaism, and was an early acknowledgment of the importance of educating Jewish women in their religious traditions.

Changes in New York State's education laws in 1851 and 1855 and changes in the nature of public education in the city addressed many of the concerns of Jewish parents. Local school boards were granted the powers to choose instructional materials, and reading from the Bible was made discretionary. Overt Christian religious influences were considerably diluted, especially in neighborhoods with concentrations of Jewish families. The vibrant congregational day school sector evaporated overnight. The seven congregational day schools that flourished in 1855 collapsed by 1856. Jewish parents in New York apparently were ready to accept the division of secular and religious instruction for their sons and daughters as had an earlier generation of Jewish parents in Philadelphia.

By the mid-nineteenth century, most Jewish children in New York City, like those throughout the United States, received their secular schooling in public schools. Jewish education, if received at all, was offered in supplementary schools or by private teachers who scheduled instruction after school hours. Since boys received more regular religious instruction outside public schools, the collapse of Jewish day schools affected the Jewish education of girls more than boys. Girls continued to receive a general education in the public schools, but the majority received little or no Jewish instruction. For those American Jews who embraced then-emerging Reform Judaism, the Reform Sunday school provided girls with a limited Jewish education.

For more orthodox Jews, especially newly arriving immigrants from eastern Europe, efforts were made to adapt European educational models of Jewish education. The first Talmud Torah school was opened in New York City in 1857, and by 1890 hundreds of chederim (a primary supplementary school usually run by a single teacher) had been established. A typical cheder enrolled forty to fifty boys, often in wretched physical quarters, after public school hours to learn mechanical reading of Hebrew-language religious texts.

As inadequate as the Jewish education was for boys, the state of Jewish education for girls was worse. With no eastern European models of Jewish girls' schools for adults to transplant, girls were largely neglected. In eastern Europe the mimetic tradition, coupled in many cases with home tutoring, provided girls with the knowledge, skills, and affective attachments they needed to live as Jewish women. Jewishness was as much cultural as intellectual. Hence the natural and informal process of cultural transmission for eastern European Jews carried along with it religious identity and beliefs, group attachment, lifeways, and gender-defined roles. Since Jewish women had few religious responsibilities outside the home and no obligation to study religious texts in Hebrew (although there was a considerable religious and later popular literature in Yiddish intended for a substantial female audience), little or no formal provision was made to educate girls. Immigrants seemed to assume that home and community in the United States would nurture the head and heart of Jewish girls as it had in the old world.

The opening of a Christian mission school in 1864 on New York's Lower East Side, home of many of New York's poorest immigrant Jews, spurred the Jewish community to action, as an earlier mission school had done in Philadelphia. Eleven congregations organized the Hebrew Free School Association, which opened its first school in 1865, a day school teaching general and Jewish subjects. Many in the established Jewish community opposed a day school, arguing that it segregated Jewish immigrant children and made it more difficult for them to assimilate into American society. Additional free schools were opened, all supplementary, and the day school closed in 1872. Public school atten-

dance became a precondition for enrollment at a Hebrew free school.

The free schools were more popular with girls than boys. Poor immigrant parents, many religiously orthodox, preferred the traditional instruction of the cheder for their sons to the free schools' lessons on morality, manners, vocational training, and Americanization. However, lacking a European precedent for daughters, these same parents seemed more disposed to experiment with a new curriculum when it came to their daughters' educations.

As the great wave of Jewish immigrants to the United States gathered force in the last decades of the nineteenth century, settled Jews became increasingly concerned with the poor Jews of the tenement districts. Out of a complex mix of self-interest and selflessness, established Jews greatly expanded their missionary and social work efforts. Charity work among the Jewish poor became a major expression of one's religiosity and identity as a Jew, especially among Reform Jewish women of the upper classes.

In New York City, Minnie Louis, president of the Sisterhood of Temple Emanu-El, led her colleagues downtown to make home visits to immigrant families. Out of these visits emerged the visiting trained nurses program (which, under Lillian Wald, became the Henry Street Settlement) and, in the early 1880s, the Down-Town Sabbath School, later called the Louis Down-Town Sabbath School. Initially, the school provided Jewish religious instruction one day per week to girls of the Lower East Side, but later it expanded to offer daily technical-vocational instruction for girls in 1887 and, after weathering several additional changes, became the Hebrew Technical School for Girls in 1899. What started as a school to bring religious education to Jewish girls who otherwise had few such opportunities was transformed into a vocational program to serve what came to be considered the more pressing need to help female Jewish immigrants adapt to a modern, enlightened, but economically demanding country.

Although there was considerable ambivalence about and much neglect of Jewish education for girls at the turn of the twentieth century on the part of parents as well as the Jewish charitable community, both Reform and Orthodox, there was a strong commitment to secular education for Jewish girls. Established Jews, often in close collaboration with American public schools, directed the children of immigrants into the public schools. By the time of World War I, more than 275,000 Jewish children attended New York City public schools, and fewer than 1,000 attended the city's three all-male yeshivas. Established Jews saw the public schools as their allies in efforts to transform immigrant children into model Americans. The public schools would have primary responsibility for making over the children of immigrants into true Americans, and a new, modern Jewish education would transform old world religious beliefs and practices into a modern Jewish religion better suited to the American milieu, one in which all citizens shared in a common secular-civic culture and individuals embraced compatible but separate religious denominations.

Jewish girls in American public schools, especially at the elementary level, were exposed to the potent model of the American woman teacher. The mimetic process, which traditionally had been relied upon to maintain Jewish religious and cultural lifeways, now was in the service of cultural transformation.

American life, observed and imitated in public schools, was reinforced in the streets; by public entertainment, magazines, and libraries; and by the casual processes of going window shopping on uptown outings, watching movies, and listening to the radio. Young Jewish women also acquired a new set of American aspirations that could be satisfied only by mastering American culture. American public schools could prepare them for modern women's roles. Many such women in New York, Philadelphia, Baltimore, Cleveland, and Boston followed a path from Ellis Island to public school, to a teacher's college, and back to the public school classroom.

Yet few Jewish children, especially girls, received any religious education in the period prior to World War I. As Alexander Dushkin reported in his study of Jewish education in New York City, published in 1918, fewer than one in four children in 1917 and only one in six girls received any Jewish education. More children would have received some Jewish education during their childhood than were enrolled in any given year, but it is clear that Jewish education was largely neglected.

The need to provide a modern Jewish education to American Jewish children was recognized early in the twentieth century by many Jewish leaders, especially those connected with the Kehillah of New York (an organization that represented New York City Jews from 1908 to 1922). Samson Benderly, the father of modern American Jewish education, was invited to New York to form the Bureau of Jewish Education in 1910. The dual task of Jewish educators, as he saw it, was to Americanize their students while simultaneously building a viable Jewish culture in the United States. Jewish education, he argued, should be "complementary to and harmonious with the public system" and should prepare Jewish youth for active participation in a bicultural world (quoted in Gorin 1970, 98).

The bureau recognized that modernizing the role of women in the American Jewish community was critical and set out to enlarge the Jewish educational opportunities of girls. Experimental programs for girls at the elementary level were developed, followed by Hebrew preparatory schools for girls (ages 11–14) and Hebrew high schools (the Marshaliah schools). By the 1920s the bureau had created what may have been the first Jewish school "system" for girls from elementary school to the Teachers Institute, a program that attracted more women than men. Based on American institutional models, the bureau actively embraced the American practice of training and employing young women as teachers. This new adult role for Jewish women who had been born into eastern European immigrant communities motivated many to pursue a Jewish education in the United States. And the growing presence of women educated in Jewish religious traditions helped to redefine roles for Jewish women. In 1922 the first bat mitzvah was celebrated by Rabbi Mordecai Kaplan's eldest daughter Judith, a ceremony that went beyond confirmation and opened possibilities for girls that became reality for many as the twentieth century progressed.

Upon the demise of the New York Kehillah after World War I, its young leaders scattered across the United States, helping to establish and run city bureaus of Jewish education. Between 1915 and 1938, bureaus were started in fifteen cities, and in four of these, Hebrew teachers' colleges were founded to train modern Jewish educators, both men and women.

Most Jewish children in the twentieth century, if they received a Jewish education, did so in congregational after-school programs or Sunday schools. But Orthodox Jews in New York and elsewhere grew increasingly concerned with the limited Jewish education available to their sons and daughters. Many felt that supplementary education was inadequate. In the 1880s Orthodox educators founded a boys' yeshiva that emphasized Torah and Talmud study but also offered secular studies to meet state education laws. New York's Orthodox Jews were first able to send their daughters to day school when the coeducational Yeshiva of Flatbush opened in 1928, followed shortly by the all-girls Shulamith School in 1929. These schools, along with the coeducational Ramaz School in Manhattan (1937), offered both secular and religious instruction, seeking to integrate the modern with the classical and Jewish with American. Although religiously orthodox, they supported cultural Zionism and the Hebrew language. In an important sense, within one Jewish institution they attempted to prepare students for the bicultural world envisioned by the new Jewish educators rather than splitting responsibility between public and Jewish schools.

In the 1990s Jewish day schools, which numbered about 600 in towns and cities throughout the United States, was a growing American Jewish phenomenon. Although about 70 percent are under Orthodox auspices, the Conservative and Reform branches of Judaism also sponsor day schools (Isaacs 1992, 66). In an American environment in which public education has been questioned by some and religious education

Torah reading at the Solomon Schecter Day School, White Plains, New York. (Shirley Zeiberg)

has become increasing relevant to many, the private religiously sponsored day school—Catholic, Protestant, and Jewish—is a common sight on the American educational landscape. Jews who at one time strenuously opposed Jewish day schools as a form of self-segregation and looked to the public schools as the best means of integrating Jews into American life are now confronted by a much more variegated educational-religious landscape. Modern-day schools are clearly distinguished from European yeshivas by their rejection of instruction in Yiddish and its replacement by English and Hebrew, the coeducational practice of many of these schools, the high level of Jewish instruction provided to girls, the employment of women teachers, and the

high regard for secular studies. Although most Jewish children still attend public schools, more than 11 percent attended Jewish day schools. And unlike at the beginning of the twentieth century, girls are now almost as likely as boys to attend day schools. In the 1990s an estimated 440,000 children were enrolled in Jewish schools, representing between 35 and 40 percent of all Jewish children: approximately 60 percent attended after-school programs and 40 percent day schools.

In addition to the modern Jewish day school, there is a second, potent, Jewish day school sector sponsored by the Ultra-orthodox Jews who arrived in the United States in small numbers before World War II and in larger numbers following the Holocaust. They brought with them models of settlement and education that conformed to their desire to separate themselves as best they could from the secular world. They rejected the models of American Jewish day schools developed by modern Orthodox Jews, schools that sought to synthesize the Jewish and the modern; established their own yeshivas that focused on Jewish texts and Jewish learning; and incorporated secular studies only to satisfy state laws.

For Ultraorthodox Jews, schools were integral to their efforts to protect their children from the perceived evils of secular America. Jewish education would do battle with the antireligious, assimilating, and secularizing forces of modern education, represented especially by public schools. And girls as well as boys had to be saved from public education. Ultraorthodox Jews who immigrated in the 1930s carried with them the Bas Ya'akov school model of girls' education created by Sara Schenirer in 1918 in Kraków, Poland. They established the first such school in Williamsburg, Brooklyn, in 1937.

Ultraorthodox girls, traditionally excluded from all study, were allowed to study the written law (Torah) and secular subjects, but not the oral law (Talmud). Secular study, lacking precedent in the Orthodox world for either men or women and considered to be of decidedly lesser value than the study of Jewish texts, was readily incorporated into the schooling of girls.

Whereas Jewish religious reformers saw schools as positive modernizing forces and modern Orthodox Jews saw schools as the arena within which modernity and tradition could be synthesized, the Ultraorthodox saw education as the means to conserve their beliefs and lifeways, a defense against the modern world, a way of ensuring separation rather than integration, and a way to reinforce stringent adherence to halakic prescriptions. For the first time in the history of Jewish settlement in the United States, a community of Jews sought to use schools as a defense against their new country and not as a means to incorporate Jews into American society.

The education of Jewish girls in the United States today is as heterogeneous as the Jewish community of which they are a part. By far the largest number attend public schools and secular colleges and universities. Many receive no Jewish education at all. But American Jewish girls now have Jewish educational opportunities broader than ever before and a full range of adult Jewish roles in which to actively employ their Jewish studies, including rabbi, cantor, Judaica scholar, and Jewish educator. The only limits to what women can study or the adult roles they can perform are set by the status of women in the branch of Judaism into which they are born or in which they choose to participate.

Stephan F. Brumberg

See also Bat Mitzvah; Domesticity; Education of Girls; Home Economics Education; Immigration; Little Mothers; Mathematics and Science

References and Further Reading
Ashton, Dianne. 1997. *Rebecca Gratz: Women and Judaism in Antebellum America.* Detroit: Wayne State University Press.
Brumberg, Stephan F. 1986. *Going to America, Going to School: The Jewish Immigrant Public School Encounter in Turn-of-the-Century New York City.* New York: Praeger.
Dushkin, Alexander M. 1918. *Jewish Education in New York City.* New York: Bureau of Jewish Education.
Gorin, Arthur A. 1970. *New York Jews and the Quest for Community: The*

Kehillah Experiment, 1908–1922. New York and Philadelphia: Columbia University Press/The Jewish Publication Society of America.

Grinstein, Hyman B. 1945. *The Rise of the Jewish Community of New York, 1654–1860.* Philadelphia: Jewish Publication Society of America.

Hyman, Paula E. 1995. *Gender and Assimilation in Modern Jewish History: The Roles and Representations of Women.* Seattle: University of Washington Press.

Isaacs, Leora W. 1992. "What We Know about Enrollment." Pp. 61–70 in *What We Know about Jewish Education: A Handbook of Today's Research for Tomorrow's Jewish Education.* Edited by Stuart L. Kelman. Los Angeles: Torah Aura Publications.

Kaestle, Carl F. 1983. *Pillars of the Republic: Common Schools and American Society, 1780–1860.* New York: Hill and Wang.

Pilch, Judah, ed. 1969. *A History of Jewish Education in America.* New York: Curriculum Research Institute of the American Association for Jewish Education.

Soloveitchik, Haym. 1994. "Rupture and Reconstruction: The Transformation of Contemporary Orthodoxy." *Tradition* 28, no. 4: 64–130.

Tyack, David B., and Elizabeth Hansot. 1990. *Learning Together: A History of Coeducation in American Public Schools.* New Haven, CT: Yale University Press.

Wertheimer, Jack. 1999. "Jewish Education in the United States: Recent Trends and Issues." Pp. 3–115 in *American Jewish Year Book, 1999.* Edited by David Singer and Ruth R. Seldin. New York: American Jewish Committee.

Juvenile Delinquents

The history of girls deemed delinquent by society is marked by a good deal of change, although themes from the past still affect current practices. Although ideas about "proper" gender roles for females have evolved, so too have societal images of girls in trouble. Despite some change, it is apparent that early theories and notions about girls continue to impact current treatment of delinquent girls. From the beginning, the etiology, processing, and treatment of female offending has been given low priority by delinquency theorists and researchers, particularly when compared to corresponding efforts to understand boys' delinquency. However, girls *have* received considerable attention regarding their morality, and historically there have been special attempts by the juvenile justice system to control their sexuality.

The formation of the juvenile justice system began with a concern to control the social and moral behavior of all juveniles. Within the context of a patriarchal society, this control has had unique application to the lives of girls. From the mid-1800s to the early 1900s, white, middle-class women reformers sought to address the social problems of the day. One of their concerns was the growing lower class, who in their estimation often failed to provide children with adequate moral virtues and a proper Christian upbringing. This perceived failing led to the belief that these young girls, largely from the lower class, were in danger of a life of vagrancy and sexual exploitation. Therefore, the problem of young, poor girls was given intense scrutiny, with the ultimate goal of establishing policies that would serve to maintain the existing social order.

The response of the reformers, the early courts, and correctional facilities clearly illustrated nineteenth-century attitudes about women. During this time period, "success" was defined as turning wayward girls into "respectable" women—a woman who would marry, have children, and live a domestic life. Ironically, however, it was frequently the family who would turn an incorrigible daughter over to the state in the hopes of providing a better life for her or the necessary training needed to transform her into a respectable young woman.

An additional concern of the reformers was protecting and controlling girls' sexual behavior because sexual chastity remained a crucial requirement of ideal femininity. Although sexual abuse in the home was ignored, the reformers focused their efforts on protecting women from more external threats like prostitution. There was concern that girls could use their sexuality as a way to survive if they had no one else to care for them.

Correctional efforts did little to change the social class of the girls, but they did strive to provide a family-style reformatory experience emphasizing Christian family life. It was the job of these correctional surrogate parents to help the girls realize their "natural" role as caretakers and homemakers. Although some of the intentions of the early developers of correctional institutions for girls were admirable, they often fell short of the high rehabilitative ideals they aimed for and all too frequently resulted in rigid training and punitive, custodial care. Along with the early institutional efforts, it is also important to examine the theories of delinquency for girls that shaped how the juvenile justice system responded to them. Like the reformers, theorists were influenced by the social beliefs of the day, and their ideas reflected this. Early studies of female criminality, though varied, found common ground in the assumption that girls' behavior was dictated by biological, hormonal, or genetic attributes (often conceptualized as weaknesses) that were believed to be unique to females. The most influential themes of early theories were the biolog-

ical and psychological inferiority of females, girls' sexuality as a main motivating factor toward delinquency, and the importance of females' adopting the culturally acceptable feminine role. Stepping out of that role was in and of itself defined as delinquent behavior.

It is important to note that the offenses for which girls came under correctional intervention were generally nonserious in nature; the overriding concern was guiding them toward appropriate moral and sexual behavior. This is one of the features of early responses to female juvenile delinquents that has had a long-lasting legacy on their treatment today. Using self-reported data from the youth themselves, delinquency researchers have highlighted and provided a critique of the juvenile justice system for operating under a double standard regarding the behavior of girls versus boys. Self-reported findings have suggested that girls and boys commit an equal number of status offenses (defined as violations only applicable to minors, such as running away, truancy, or violations of parental authority). However, girls are dramatically overrepresented for these offenses within the justice system, as seen in official statistics.

As noted, these practices have been shaped by early responses to female delinquency that relied on sexist and stereotypical ideas about girls. Arguably, minor offenses like status offenses have since been considered part of the normal maturational process for many adolescents. However, it is girls who run a higher risk of being identified and punished for what is more often considered normal behavior in boys, a practice that clearly discriminates against girls. Moreover, feminist reviews of processing studies have found that girls have been treated as or more harshly for status offenses than boys. In some cases, girls were found to be treated more harshly for status offenses than boys were for criminal offenses (Belknap 1996).

Several reasons have been offered to explain these current discrepancies in the treatment of girls and boys by the juvenile justice system. Consistent with the past, parents have been more likely to conform to gender-specific socialization patterns that require stricter standards of behavior for their daughters than their sons. Further, girls' sexuality has been key in determining how they are dealt with by law enforcement and the courts. For example, when girls were charged, particularly with minor offenses, their sexual reputation and how well they conformed to gender stereotypes influenced their sentences (Lees 1989). Even in cases in which the offense was not sexual, females were more likely to be given gynecological exams to assess their sexual behavior, and this evidence was sometimes used to charge girls with additional offenses (Chesney-Lind 1973).

Another way status offenses have had particular relevance for girls is through the criminalization of girls' survival strategies. For example, abuse may cause girls to run away from home to escape an abusive environment, which may in turn lead them to incorporate survival strategies on the streets that include theft and prostitution. In fact, the juvenile justice system has often treated girls similarly whether they were the victims of sexual abuse or engaging in sexual behavior. The focus on these status, or noncriminal, offenses has served to entrench girls in the system by mandating harsh punishments for behaviors that are in reality minor in nature. Stereotypical thinking about girls is so deeply embedded in U.S. culture that even legislation designed to

counteract unequal treatment has failed to correct the problems outlined above.

The "typical" female juvenile offender is a fourteen- to sixteen-year-old girl from an ethnic minority group, who is most likely a status offender living in poverty and instability with a family history of incarceration. In general, most juvenile offenses are minor. Girls make up approximately 26 percent of all juveniles arrested. Although the media portrays huge increases in violent offending by girls, it appears that any increases in girls' arrests have been mirrored by increases in boys' arrests—a fact that suggests more about changes in the behavior of all youths, or the processing of youths, rather than changes in the behavior of girls specifically. An examination of arrest trends in the United States for juveniles between 1958 and 1994 showed that although girls' arrest rates have increased more than boys', the arrest rates of girls for violent and serious crimes have not changed significantly (Chesney-Lind and Brown 1998). In fact, the proportion of girls arrested for the most serious crimes of murder and non-negligent manslaughter has been declining since 1985. These offenses made up approximately 6 percent of all arrests for girls in 1995. One of the most distinct differences between girls and boys in official arrest statistics was found in the status offense category of "running away," which made up 20 percent of girls' overall arrests and only 5 percent of boys' (Belknap and Holsinger 1998).

Although official statistics have led to the conclusion that females were more likely to be engaging in traditionally female crimes (e.g., status offenses and minor theft), self-reported studies have illuminated differential responses by the juvenile justice system based on gender.

First, self-reported studies have found no evidence supporting the contention that females are more involved in status offenses than males. In fact, their patterns of status offending, drug-related crimes, and less serious offenses were similar (Chesney-Lind and Shelden 1992). Self-reported studies have supported what is found in official statistics related to violent and serious offending. This area of offending represented the greatest difference between male and female delinquency patterns.

The 1980s and 1990s have brought a marked turnaround in the amount of research on female juvenile delinquents. Not only has this research been more plentiful, but it has identified gender differences in pathways to offending that continue to be explored. These new research initiatives promise to provide a more accurate portrayal and investigation of girls' delinquency etiology and experiences in the justice system. For instance, cycle of violence theories acknowledge the long-term consequences of childhood victimization (Widom 1989). It has been established that children who are physically harmed early in their lives are more likely than their nonabused counterparts to engage in juvenile delinquency, particularly delinquency that involves violence (Dodge, Bates, and Pettit 1990). Estimates of the rate of young women in the juvenile justice system who have been abused range from 40 to 73 percent (Chesney-Lind and Shelden 1992). Although neglect and abuse are also important issues in the delinquency of boys, studies have shown that these problems within families are more common, start at an earlier age, and last longer for girls.

Feminist perspectives offer a more sophisticated analysis of gender that includes a critique of how the structures of society and patriarchy have shaped the experiences of girls. Recently, feminist theorists have made significant advances in how female deviance is conceptualized and how pathways to crime often differ based on gender.

Some of the issues explored include the differential socialization of girls and boys, different motivations for crime, differences in contexts of offending, and differences in opportunities for crime and delinquency based on gender. A feminist perspective also requires paying close attention to the interaction of gender and sex with race and social class. This perspective emphasizes theorizing that is rooted in the realities of girls' lives, as opposed to stereotypical thinking. For example, feminists know that girls experience a double standard regarding sexual behavior, sexual objectification, and an expectation that they conform to the socially acceptable role for women.

As mentioned, one new area of exploration regarding gender differences in offending is differences in the "context of offending." This research suggests that, for example, a "typical" assault committed by a girl may look quite different than a "typical" assault committed by a boy. Initial research suggests there may be important gender differences in the level of seriousness, the role the offender played in the offense, the relationship between the victim and offender, the setting in which the offense took place, and the motivation or intent of the offense (Steffensmeier and Allan 1998). Research thus far has demonstrated that compared to males, females are less likely to inflict injury on their victims, more likely to hurt someone they know well, less likely to use weapons, and less likely to be on drugs when the offense was committed (Campbell 1986; Triplett and Myers

This fifteen-year-old juvenile delinquent was convicted of second-degree murder in New York for killing her grandmother in 1994. (Associated Press/Pool Times Herald Record)

1995). Girls' violence was also more likely to occur as a result of an interpersonal conflict with a relative or friend, whereas boys' violence was more instrumental and lethal (Chesney-Lind and Brown 1998). One of the most common reasons females are incarcerated is their involvement with significant others who are committing a crime. So far, the research has shown the greater effects of relationships for girls that may result in pulling females into crime.

Other gender differences are beginning to emerge as well. A review of literature on adolescent female development suggested that girls experience greater depression, more suicide attempts, and a decrease in self-concept during and after puberty, whereas young males experience *improved* self-concept and self-esteem. Self-injurious behavior is more common for girls than boys. Other findings suggest that girls, particularly in adolescence, perceive their relationships with their parents or guardians as more negative than boys. Indeed, this perception is strong enough to warrant more girls acting on the situation and running away. In addition, girls frequently have relationships with older boys and men and consequently have a unique vulnerability to involvement in the justice system as a result of these relationships.

In the area of substance use, many more girls than boys reported being addicted and experiencing withdrawal symptoms. Girls reported greater use of over-the-counter and prescription drugs, as well as younger initial use of crack and cocaine. Girls were more likely to report starting to use because of a boyfriend or because of depression, which is consistent with findings that girls use drugs and alcohol to self-medicate (Holsinger 1999).

With these newer, more gender-specific explanations of delinquency comes a prescription for change in which research informs policy and is used to improve the treatment of incarcerated girls. The correctional system has generally been developed for boys and is therefore less responsive to the unique needs of girls. Facilities serving girls are less likely to provide treatment for physical health problems, disruptive or violent behavior, mental health problems, and programs for sexual victimization than those serving boys. Facilities for girls also provided less aftercare, shorter programs, and fewer certified teachers on staff (Kempf-Leonard, Peterson, and Sample 1997). Similarly, another study found that girls received half as many treatment services as boys, had to wait longer for treatment services, and were offered services that were less intensive and of shorter duration than the programs provided for males and were "unisex" instead of "gender-specific" (Wells 1994). Some of the important needs of girls that have typically been ignored by the correctional system include issues of adequate medical care, substance abuse treatment, pregnancy and dependent children, mental health care, and a history of sexual and physical abuse.

Clare Feinman (1984) has argued that attempts to provide effective and helpful responses to girls will continue to fail as long as they are based on stereotypical gender roles rather than on the unique needs of the female population. Although girls and boys have some of the same problems, there are many that have unique application to girls "in a gendered society" (Chesney-Lind and Shelden 1992). Fortunately, there is a growing movement that seeks to provide more equitable treatment for girls in the juvenile justice system, although much more work needs to be done.

Kristi Holsinger

See also Female Sexuality; Girl Gangs; Graffiti; Movies, Adolescent Girls in; Substance Abuse

References and Further Reading
Belknap, Joanne. 1996. *The Invisible Woman: Gender, Crime, and Justice.* Cincinnati: Wadsworth Publishing.
Belknap, Joanne, and Kristi Holsinger. 1998. "An Overview of Delinquent Girls: How Theory and Practice Have Failed and the Need for Innovative Changes." Pp. 31–64 in *Female Crime and Delinquency: Critical Perspectives and Effective Interventions.* Edited by Ruth T. Zaplin. Gaithersburg, MD: Aspen Publishers.
Campbell, Anne. 1986. "Self-Report of Fighting by Females." *British Journal of Criminology* 26, no. 1: 28–46.
Chesney-Lind, Meda. 1973. "Judicial Enforcement of the Female Sex Role: The Family Court and the Female Delinquent." *Issues in Criminology* 8, no. 2: 51–69.
Chesney-Lind, Meda, and Marilyn Brown. 1998. "Girls and Violence: An Overview." Pp. 171–200 in *Youth Violence: Prevention, Intervention, and Social Policy.* Edited by Daniel J. Flannery and C. Ronald Huff. Washington, DC: American Psychiatric Association.
Chesney-Lind, Meda, and Randall G. Shelden. 1992. *Girls, Delinquency and Juvenile Justice.* Pacific Grove, CA: Brooks/Cole.
Dodge, Kenneth A., John E. Bates, and Gregory S. Pettit. 1990. "Mechanisms in the Cycle of Violence." *Science* 250: 1678–1683.
Feinman, Claire. 1984. "An Historical Overview of the Treatment of Incarcerated Women: Myths and Realities of Rehabilitation." *The Prison Journal* 63: 12–26.
Holsinger, Kristi. 1999. "Addressing the Distinct Experience of the Adolescent Female: Explaining Delinquency and Examining the Juvenile Justice System." Ph.D. diss., University of Michigan Dissertation Service.
Kempf-Leonard, Kimberly, Elicka S. L. Peterson, and Lisa L. Sample. 1997. *Gender and Juvenile Justice in Missouri.* Jefferson City: Missouri Department of Public Safety.
Lees, Sue. 1989. "Learning to Love: Sexual Reputation, Morality and the Social Control of Girls." In *Growing Up Good: Policing the Behavior of Girls in Europe.* Edited by Maureen Cain. London: Sage.
Steffensmeier, Darrell, and Emlie Allan. 1998. "The Nature of Female Offending: Patterns and Explanation." Pp. 5–29 in *Female Crime and Delinquency: Critical Perspectives and Effective Interventions.* Edited by Ruth T. Zaplin. Gaithersburg, MD: Aspen Publishers.
Triplett, Ruth, and Laura B. Myers. 1995. "Evaluating Contextual Patterns of Delinquency: Gender-Based Differences." *Justice Quarterly* 12, no. 1: 59–84.
Wells, Ruth Herman. 1994. "America's Delinquent Daughters Have Nowhere to Turn for Help." *Corrections Compendium* 19, no. 11: 4–6.
Widom, Cathy Spatz. 1989. "The Cycle of Violence." *Science* 244: 160–166.

K

Kinaaldá

A puberty rite for an individual girl, rather than a group ceremony, the *kinaaldá* occurs soon after the Navajo girl's first menstruation and traditionally lasts for five days and four nights. Except for some Hispanic girls who have a *quinceañera* on their fifteenth birthday or Jewish girls who are eligible for a bat mitzvah at twelve, very few adolescent girls in the contemporary United States undergo a puberty rite. Thus the Navajo are unusual in the attention they devote to a girl's first menstruation.

Many cultural critics insist that adolescents might benefit greatly from the special recognition such rites afford. Because puberty rites are so uncommon in the modern-day United States, anthropologists have gone to considerable length to explain why they do appear. It should not be assumed that all Indian tribes had puberty rites. First of all, there is the difficulty of defining exactly what one is—or was. Many Indian tribes practiced seclusion of menstruating women at the time of puberty, which appears to have arisen from fears of the polluting effect of women's menstrual blood. Menstrual blood was associated with spiritual power and had to be treated with care in order that a community survive and not fall victim to famine or devastating losses from war. Among those tribes that had puberty rites, the ritual varied from an individual vision quest to a ceremony attended by dozens of friends and family and held in the family's home. The kinaaldá belongs to this second category of ceremony.

Many anthropologists argue that the kinaaldá and other puberty rites for girls arose to serve three important functions: announce that a girl was eligible for marriage, protect the community from the dangers of a menstruating girl by secluding her, and initiate a girl into the responsibilities of being an adult. In addition, it should be noted that the two major Indian tribes today that have public ceremonies are the Apache and the Navajo. Both of these tribes traditionally had matrilocal residence rules and matrilineal kinship patterns. Thus there seems to be some connection between a history of maternal dominance of kinship and residence patterns and the presence of public ceremonies for girls. Perhaps a ritual is needed to mark a transition in status, since in respect to her residence, a girl essentially remains at home, living near her female kin. Anthropologist Judith Brown (1963) adds that the greater a woman's contribution to economic subsistence, the more likely her society will mark her passage from girlhood to adulthood. A girl in a matrilineal society, it is argued, needed to be prepared to assume her responsibilities in a female work group and was valued

Silver Horizons *by Nelson Tsosie. (AINACO/Corbis, 1996)*

more highly in a culture in which adult and older women had considerable power.

Advocates of puberty rites for girls insist that they provide a highly positive recognition of a girl's body and potential to be a mother. Indeed, to the Navajo, a girl's first menstruation was sacred and a cause for rejoicing, since it showed that she was ready to bear children. Closer examination of Navajo attitudes reveals, however, that the Navajo once segregated menstruating girls in separate huts, had powerful taboos limiting the activities a menstruating girl could undertake, and also frowned on telling boys that a girl was menstruating for the first time. To be sure, there is much evidence of respect for womanhood and motherhood in Navajo culture, as one might expect among a people who worshipped several female spiritual powers. Even so, the ritual, although respectful of women's ability to bear children, was intended to train a girl in her traditional female responsibilities and prepare her for marriage and motherhood.

It is best to think of the kinaaldá not as a girl's ritual but as a religious ritual in a religion that regarded women highly. The Navajo made no distinction between secular and religious—all life-sustaining activities demanded religious ceremony. Moreover, Navajo religion can be defined less as a unified system of doctrine and more as a series of ceremonial practices intended to uphold central beliefs. The audience looking for affirmation of its beliefs included not only kin but also spiritual beings who were dwelling in the midst of the living. Among Navajo spiritual beliefs the most important was the love of beauty, more liberally translated as the love of peace, harmony, and all that is good. A long list of rituals (called "Blessingway" ceremonies) were thought to express and realize this ideal of beauty. Of the many Blessingway ceremonies, from a wedding to the blessing of a house to the blessing of seeds, the kinaaldá was considered the most important.

The Navajo girl does not undergo any special advance preparation for the kinaaldá. Despite the importance of the mother-child bond and the common pattern of married women residing near the mother's kin group, the mother has no special role in the kinaaldá, either. Instead, there are two major roles for adults in the ceremony, one for an adult woman who acts as an instructor of the girl and the other for a lead singer at the all-night ritual of song and prayer on the last evening of the kinaaldá. An older woman, chosen to be the girl's lifetime companion and instructor, is selected to "mold" the girl's body because she has the physical strength and beauty to do it. The older woman sings sacred songs, washes and combs the girl's hair, and massages the girl's body. The girl's body is seen as pliable, similar to an infant's at birth. For that reason, her body can be reshaped so that it will be perfect and womanly, like that of Changing Woman. The other significant adult participant is the lead singer, the closest thing to a priest among the Navajo, who conducts religious rituals. The lead singer can be male or female, although males generally predominate. On the last night a lead singer directs the kinaaldá as well as the assembled group in the singing of special a cappella songs sung only at Blessingway ceremonies.

All puberty rites involve transformation of the youth into an adult, but in kinaaldá the girl is thought of as transformed not just into a woman but into Changing Woman, a central Navajo spiritual power of goodness who created the Navajo people. According to traditional teachings, Changing Woman had no parents but was raised in the hogan of the First Man and First Woman. As she grew up, she brought to the earth the single most valuable crop, corn, and gave fertility to women. Changing Woman had the first kinaaldá—presided over by Talking God. In repeating the same ritual Changing Woman underwent, it is thought that the female initiate takes on the qualities of goodness possessed by Changing Woman. Moreover, just as Changing Woman was fruitful (she mated with the Sun), so, too, a Navajo girl is seen as becoming able to have children not from her ability to menstruate but from having undergone the ritual of kinaaldá. After the ritual is completed, the girl acquires protection from misfortune and a guarantee of health and prosperity.

Despite a lack of standardization of the ritual or a written script, the kinaaldá has many standard elements, repetitive actions, and a standard costume. For a kinaaldá the girl wears an overblouse and skirt, a special sash and concho belt, and silver jewelry and turquoise beads. As part of the ritual the girl is secluded in her clan's hogan (originally a conical structure built out of mud and large sticks and later a multisided and sturdier log and mud house), where she takes instruction from an older woman in grinding corn. Since corn was the basic food of the Navajo, the girl was being taught through repetition so she would know how to make a meal effortlessly. The girl must leave the hogan and run clockwise three times a day for four days as a symbolic effort to chase the rising sun. After trying to catch the sun, she turns and runs back to the hogan. In an outdoor pit, she bakes an offering to the sun, a ceremonial cornmeal cake. The cake is served to the assembled community on the last morning of the kinaaldá.

The origin of the kinaaldá probably dates from 1650 to 1775, when the Navajo first became agriculturalists (Johnson Frisbie 1967, 9). Most crops were planted and tilled by female work groups, although the women might be assisted by men. Moreover, in the Southwest the Navajo came into contact with and were influenced by the Hopi and other southwestern Indian tribes. From the Hopi they borrowed the idea of making baked cornmeal into a ceremonial element. The costume of the kinaaldá, including the silver jewelry, reflects the impact of Navajo contact with the Spanish in the 1600s. The Spanish taught the Navajo blacksmithing, which the Navajo adapted in making silver jewelry.

Beginning in the nineteenth century, missionaries and teachers at boarding schools for Indians were largely successful in their efforts to stamp out coming-of-age ceremonies that had a decidedly sexual nature. Rites to initiate boys into secret societies were lost, as were vision quests of boys and sometimes girls sent to the wilderness to find a guardian's spirit. Moreover, missionaries and white teachers often sought to replace Indian rites with Christian ceremonies and encouraged speaking English at the expense of learning the native language. Many children were sent to schools far away from the reservations. Among some Navajo the kinaaldá must occur at the time of first menstruation; it cannot be postponed.

Because so many girls were away at boarding school, it was impossible for them to have a kinaaldá. The general assimilationist thrust in U.S. government policy also contributed to the decline of interest in Indian ritual. As a result, kinaaldá became rare by the 1940s and 1950s. Many girls openly refused to have one because they perceived it as hard work and resented having to wear "hot clothes and heavy jewelries" (Johnson Frisbie 1967, 28). In addition, quite a few elders had forgotten how to perform them.

The kinaaldá was rediscovered in the 1960s as younger Indians became more militant, grew more interested in their history and culture, and sought to revive cultural rituals that had fallen into disuse. As the largest Indian tribe, the Navajo had more elders who still had some memory of kinaaldá. Moreover, some teachers at community-controlled schools and community colleges established in the 1960s on or near the reservation sought to devise a school curriculum that included the teaching of long-lost ritual. Schools on the reservation began to teach the Navajo language and culture and used federal funding to publish guides on how to stage a kinaaldá. As the ritual was revived in the 1960s, it was shortened (from five days to two) so as to be compatible with the girls' school schedule. The number of times a girl had to run was reduced to twice a day. There used to be two kinaaldá, the second one a virtual repetition of the first, held when the girl menstruated for the second time. The second kinaaldá has disappeared in part because many modern teenage girls refuse to admit when they menstruate the second time so that they do not have to undergo the second ceremony. Thus, the ritual has been streamlined to accord with the unwillingness of modern teenage girls to undergo too strenuous an ordeal.

Although it is possible for a girl to have a kinaaldá in a city or town, most occur on the Navajo reservation, located in the region surrounding the Four Corners where the states of Arizona, Colorado, New Mexico, and Utah meet. For urban Navajos, having a kinaaldá means returning to the reservation where relatives, perhaps elderly grandparents, still live. Many girls postpone their kinaaldá until school summer vacation. Most hogans on the reservation are now used for ceremonial purposes rather than as dwelling units. The kinaaldá no longer announces availability for marriage, as it did as late as the 1940s, but instead serves as a symbol of a girl's interest in her Indian identity. There is more information about the history and evolution of the kinaaldá than any other Indian female puberty rite because it has been described by so many anthropologists.

Elizabeth Pleck

See also Bat Mitzvah; Menstruation; Native American Girls; *La Quinceañera*

References and Further Reading
Begay, Shirley M. 1983. *Kinaalda: A Navajo Puberty Ceremony*. Rough Rock, AZ: Navajo Curriculum Center, Rough Rock Demonstration School.
Brown, Judith K. 1963. "A Cross-Cultural Study of Female Initiation Rites." *American Anthropologist* 65: 837–853.
Johnson Frisbie, Charlotte. 1967. *Kinaaldá: A Study of the Navaho Girl's Puberty Ceremony*. Middletown, CT: Wesleyan University Press.
Keith, Anne. 1964. "The Navaho Girl's Puberty Ceremony." *El Palacio* 71: 27–36.
Lincoln, Bruce. 1981. *Emerging from the Chrysalis: Studies in Rituals of Women's Initiation*. Cambridge: Harvard University Press, 17–33.

L

Latina Girls

Latino is an umbrella term used to describe racially, linguistically, and culturally diverse ethnic groups from Latin American countries. Politically, *Latino* can serve as a useful term to unite such diverse groups for a common political agenda. Although the term *Latina girls* is not used in the political sense, it stresses the common experiences that Latina girls may have with one another as girls who live in a bilingual, bicultural world. Latino parents may have particular gendered expectations of their Latina daughters that are rooted in their cultures. For first-generation daughters, Latina girls may assume more responsibility within their families during the resettlement process in the United States. Advertisers have also begun to see Latina girls as an important segment of the consumer market. More commonly, however, if the media turns their attention to Latina girls, it is to portray them as teenage mothers. Beginning with civil rights movements in the 1960s, Latinas have become more successful in turning to sites of counter-cultural productions such as art, film, and literature to produce empowering images of Latinas. Studying Latina girlhood helps us understand how race is a central concept in the experience of girlhood, along with class and sexuality.

Demographic Overview
of U.S. Latinos

The U.S. Census Bureau counted 22 million Latinos in 1990 and predicted that the Latino population will double in size by the year 2020 to number approximately 43 million people. Latinos are the youngest ethnic group in the United States. With a median age of 26.2, they are nearly ten years younger than their non-Latino counterparts. At the current rate of growth, Latinos are expected to comprise 24.5 percent of the U.S. population in 2020, making them the largest ethnic minority population and almost half the size of the non-Latino white population (Kanellos 1997, 187).

Immigration and high birth rates together contribute to the rapid growth of the Latino population. In 1996 alone, over 300,000 people from Latin America and the Spanish-speaking Caribbean immigrated to the United States. Yet even without immigration, Latinos would remain the fastest-growing ethnic population because they are younger and have higher fertility rates than other groups. On average, Latina women bear children at a younger age than their non-Latina counterparts. Latina mothers between the ages of fifteen and twenty-four have 43 percent more children than non-Latinas of the same age. They continue to have

A Latina girl in Harlem, New York. (David Turnley/Corbis)

more children throughout their child-bearing years (Kanellos 1997, 187).

Invisible Family Workers
Although researchers have long understood that the presence of children in migrant households greatly influences parents' immigration and settlement strategies, only recently have they begun to recognize first- and second-generation children as active participants in the family settlement processes. Latino immigrant children and especially girls perform the mundane but essential labor that makes permanent settlement possible. As "invisible family workers"—babysitters, surrogate parents, part-time employees, housecleaners, errand runners, caretakers, translators, and family protectors and advocates—Latina daugh-

ters work to maintain the material and emotional well-being of their families. Although often overlooked in contemporary debates on poverty and immigration, Latina girls work to ensure the survival of Latino families in the United States. In order to understand how Latina girls fit into their families and their multiple cultures, we must look at the history of immigration and why their diverse families chose to migrate to the United States.

Mexican Americans' roots in the United States date back to before 1848, when the Southwest still belonged to Mexico. Single Mexican men emigrated to the United States in the late nineteenth and early twentieth centuries to obtain seasonal employment. By the 1920s, more Mexican families began to migrate to the United States. Studies of early-twentieth-century Mexican immigrants often tackle the issue of assimilation. Within these studies, examinations of Mexican girls deal with the theme of how issues of assimilation caused conflict between themselves and their parents. Parents lamented that as their daughters assimilated into American culture, they lost important values from their own culture (Monroy 1999). Many of these conflicts arose over issues of proper gender roles and parents' efforts to guard their daughters' sexuality. Parents viewed American popular culture as negatively affecting their daughters. Bobbed hair, red lipstick, and short skirts were often seen as the result of Americanization (Ruiz 1999). Yet Mexican film stars such as Dolores Del Rio and Lupe Velez were prominent figures, along with Clara Bow. Mexican daughters' position within the family also changed as they engaged in wage labor. As wage earners, many Mexican daughters contributed to the family income. Some young women were able to keep some of their paycheck and exert some economic independence. When young women exerted too much independence, as in the case of leaving home and moving in with a boyfriend, parents sometimes called in the police to bring their minor daughters back home (Odem 1995).

Politics and economics have been central to understanding the reasons behind Puerto Rican migration to the United States. Beginning in the early twentieth century, many Puerto Ricans moved to the mainland in search of employment. Puerto Ricans more easily migrated to the United States after 1917 when the United States extended citizenship to Puerto Ricans by making the island a U.S. commonwealth (Sánchez-Korrol 1994). Many of the second-generation Puerto Ricans who live in New York refer to themselves as "Nuyoricans." From 1948 to 1965, under "Operation Bootstrap," Puerto Rico underwent rapid industrialization and offered tax incentives and cheap labor to U.S. companies in an effort to attract them to the island. At the same time, many Puerto Ricans migrated to the United States in search of employment, a trend that continues today (Rodriguez 1989). Women are important actors in shaping family and community for Puerto Ricans, especially on the mainland. A large percentage of Puerto Rican women are employed, and many families are headed by single women.

Although Cubans can claim a longer history in the United States, large-scale Cuban immigration only occurred after 1959. Unlike Mexicans and Puerto Ricans, Cubans migrated as political refugees after the Cuban revolution in 1959, largely settling in Florida. A second large wave of Cuban immigration occurred in the 1980s. In a migration sanctioned by Fidel Castro, an estimated 10,000 Cubans left Cuba through the Mariel Harbor, and hence the refugees were known as *Marielitos*. Although the first wave of Cuban immigrants were mainly upper- and middle-class educated Cubans, the *Marielitos* were working-class and comprised more blacks and mulattoes. Many Cuban families remain very traditional, upholding ideals such as male authority in the family. However, women also play a strong role in the workforce. Cuban women have a higher rate of workforce participation than any other Latino group or Anglo women.

The passage of the Immigration and Naturalization Act of 1965 radically transformed immigration flows from Latin America and the Caribbean. This landmark legislation eradicated national origins quotas, which had favored applicants from western Europe. Congress instead established family reunification, refugee status, and human capital and labor skills as preferred categories for admission into the United States. After 1965, increased opportunities to migrate combined with economic and political turmoil led to a sharply increased immigration from the Dominican Republic, Central America, and Mexico. Women and children today comprise more than half of international migrants overall (Pedraza-Bailey 1991).

Gender and family formation is key to understanding contemporary Latino immigration and settlement processes. Not only do gender and familial ties influence decisions to immigrate, but also they differentially shape immigrants' settlement strategies and outcomes (Hondagneu-Sotelo 1994). In particular, the presence of children is an important factor influencing parental decisions to migrate and later decisions to remain in the United States. Research on undocumented Mexican immigration, for example, has shown that family formation is the first step in a lengthy process that leads to permanent settlement (Chavez 1991). Families composed of undocumented parents and U.S. citizen children often become binational, moving between the United States and their home country in coordination with employment cycles, school calendars, and holidays. Regardless of citizenship status, cyclical migration and binationalism are definitive characteristics of the family lives of Puerto Rican, Mexican, and most recently Central American and Dominican immigrants. Here again, the presence of children greatly influences decisions to migrate back and forth, as parents express

geographically conflicted desires for their children to receive formal schooling in the United States and to maintain close ties to the culture and language of their homeland. Within this context, binationalism also serves as a popular parental strategy to discipline "rebellious" Americanized daughters by entrusting them temporarily to the watchful eye and "traditional" influence of grandparents and other relatives back home.

Recent research on children in Latino immigrant households shows that girls contribute to family settlement and survival in several significant ways. First, they contribute monetarily by taking on full- or part-time employment; by assisting their parents in their work for little or no pay; and by performing unpaid labor at home such as child care, cleaning and cooking, and attending to sick relatives. Contrary to the prevailing view that children have become economically "useless" in postindustrial American society, demographic data suggest that working youth are essential to the economic survival of Latino households. Since the 1970s, declining real wages and the growth of part-time employment have increased the percentage of working poor in the United States, especially among Latinos, necessitating the growth of multiple-worker households.

Income and economic class is perhaps the starkest marker of diversity among Latinos. Relatively high levels of education, occupational status, and income reflect the middle-class status of the Cubans who migrated to the United States in the early 1960s. In contrast, both Mexican Americans and Puerto Ricans are overwhelmingly working-class populations with the lowest high school graduation rates of any U.S.-born ethnic group. Of these three groups,

Cubans have the highest average family income at $33,144 and Puerto Ricans have the lowest at $25,066 (Kanellos 1997, 388). Even more striking is a comparison of poverty rates. In 1998, approximately 26.7 percent of all Puerto Ricans and 24.4 percent of all Mexican Americans lived in poverty, compared to only 11 percent of Cuban American families (Ramirez 2000). In that same year, 34.4 percent of Latino children under the age of eighteen were living in poverty, compared to 10.6 percent of non-Latino white children. Although Latino children represent only 15.7 percent of all children in the United States, they make up over one-fourth of all children in poverty (Ramirez 2000).

In 1990, Latino youth were more likely to be employed year-round than white and black youths. Largely concentrated in low-wage service and manufacturing jobs, Latino youth also earn the lowest wages of all racial groups. In 1990, the median weekly earnings for full-time male workers ages sixteen to twenty-four were $238 for white males, $255 for blacks, and $238 for Latinos. Among female youths, the earnings were $250 for whites and $225 for blacks and Latinas (Kanellos 1997, 386). Although U.S. census data show that, as with all groups, Latino male youths are more likely to be employed than females, research on first- and second-generation Mexican immigrant households in Los Angeles suggests an opposite trend in which adolescent girls have higher employment rates than boys (Valenzuela 1998). In addition to paid work outside the home, Mexican American girls are significantly more likely than boys to perform unpaid domestic labor in their households. They are also more likely to assist their parents in complex financial transactions such as purchasing a home or automobile and filing tax returns. Similar findings are borne out in research on Puerto Rican and Dominican low-income families, which shows that, as with their white and black counterparts, Latina daughters perform the "girl's work" that is essential to the family economy among poor people in the United States (Dodson 1998). The girls in this Boston-based study reported responsibility for up to thirty hours per week of unpaid domestic labor, including caring for younger siblings and elderly or sick relatives, cooking and doing laundry, and shopping and running errands while their parents were at work. In households where parents worked two jobs to make ends meet, Latina girls as young as six or seven years old frequently became "surrogate parents," assuming primary responsibility for newborn babies and for caring for and raising younger siblings and cousins.

Research on low-income Latino households similarly points to the significant role that girls play as mediators and emotional caretakers in daily family life. In first-generation immigrant households, Latina daughters serve as the bridge between their Spanish-speaking homes and state institutions like public schools, medical clinics, the Immigration and Naturalization Service, and welfare offices. This involves not merely translating but learning to operate within complicated and often hostile institutional structures and to advocate for their parents and household in gaining access to public services and to their basic rights as workers and residents (Valenzuela 1998). In both immigrant and nonimmigrant households, Latina daughters also perform the very difficult emotional labor of "holding off the chaos" that often accompanies family life under the dual pressures of poverty and racism. Whether intervening in parental substance abuse, defending their mothers against domestic violence, or acting as a protector or confidante to a single parent, Latina girls learn at an early age to navigate through the world of adult problems and to assume responsibility for keeping their families safe and intact.

Latina Sexualities
As Latina girls in the United States, many girls live in bicultural, bilingual worlds. They may read Judy Blume books and listen to hip-hop but also watch *novelas* (soap operas) at night with their families. Because of the effects of globalization, transnationalism, and immigrant networks, Latina girls often experience American culture even before their families migrate to the United States (Rouse 1992). The shared experience of living in a bicultural world connects many Latina girls to Latina actors and singers, such as Tejana singer Selena (who herself did not learn Spanish until she began to perform for Mexican audiences). Latina girls often express their empowerment through their identification with other Latinas who are portrayed positively in the media.

During the 1980s, advertisers started targeting Latinos as a rapidly growing consumer market. Advertisers soon recognized the purchasing power of Latina girls. Latina teenagers, for example, purchase twice as many beauty products as other girls in their age group (*Los Angeles Times*, January 17, 1999). Consumer goods directed at Latina girls often emphasize their position as hyphenated Americans.

Although magazines directed at teenagers are not a new trend, a growing niche within this category now caters to Latina girls. Such magazines as *Latin Girl* cover wide-ranging topics, from sug-

gesting makeup products flattering to Latinas to topics Latina girls would presumably find interesting. Even *Latina Magazine*'s slogan, "When you miss *Latina*, you miss you" suggests that within the pages of this magazine Latinas can find images that reflect themselves and their needs. Yet since Latinas are physically and culturally heterogeneous, this often proves a formidable task. Many of the stories in these magazines focus on relationships between parents and daughters and especially issues of sexuality.

Sexuality has historically been a central issue in constructions of what it means to be Latina. Within various Latin American cultures, girls often grow up with their understanding of sexuality framed by the dichotomous symbols of virgin and whore. Many Latina girls themselves internalize these culturally rooted stigmas and therefore consider girls who use birth control promiscuous.

Latinas have stereotypically been labeled as irresponsible "breeders." These types of generalizations encouraged U.S. medical doctors to disburse experimental birth control pills to Puerto Rican women. During the 1960s, fueled by fears of a population explosion, the United States targeted Puerto Rican women in a massive sterilization campaign in which one in every three women on the island was sterilized, oftentimes without their knowledge. The sterilization procedure became so commonplace that Puerto Ricans simply referred to it as *la operación*. Similarly, in the 1970s, a group of Chicanas and Mexicanas sued Los Angeles County General Hospital for performing sterilizations without their consent or against their will (Velez-Ibanez 1980). Today similar controversy surrounds the disproportionate distribution of new birth control methods such as Norplant to Latina and African American teenagers through community clinics.

The dominant U.S. culture often stereotypes Latinas as hypersexual. Most news stories about Latinas focus on their lives as teenage mothers. Latinas and girls across ethnic lines who come into contact with the juvenile justice system often receive harsher punishments than boys for what juvenile officials consider excessive sexuality (Chesney-Lind 1997). Some argue that girls who come into contact with the court system are penalized for what some construct as their illicit sexuality. Even more taboo than heterosexuality is homosexuality. Authors such as Gloria Anzaldúa, Cherrie Moraga, Amelia Mesa-Baines, and Carla Trujillo have helped bring discussions of sexuality and lesbian experiences in Latino communities into the open, although they are still charged subjects for many. These authors discuss how as Latina lesbians, they challenge every aspect of prescribed gender roles for Latinas.

Coming-of-Age Narratives

Beginning with the 1885 publication of María Amparo Ruiz de Burton's *The Squatter and the Don*, the coming-of-age narrative (or bildungsroman) has been a benchmark of Latina fiction and autobiography. Ruiz de Burton's novel masterfully deploys the genre of the historical romance, as told through the tragic coming-of-age story of a young female protagonist, to pose a biting critique of Anglo racism, hypocrisy, and corruption in the years following the U.S. conquest of the Southwest. Nearly a century later, similar themes are powerfully articulated in the writing of New Mexican folklorist Cleofas Martinez Jamarillo. Most notable among Jamarillo's extensive list of publications is her 1955 autobiography,

Romance of a Little Village Girl (1955), which describes the brutal rape and murder of her seventeen-year-old daughter. Along with other Mexican American women writing during the period immediately after World War II—including *A Miracle for Mexico* and Fabiola Cabeza de Baca Gilbert in *We Fed Them Cactus* (1954)—Jamarillo's work reappropriates the pastoral style of the family memoir to dramatize the link between U.S. expansionism and sexual violence directed against Mexican American girls and women.

These early works set the stage for the explosion of and new directions in Chicana literature during the 1980s and 1990s. Authors like Sandra Cisneros and Ana Castillo shift the geographic and cultural discourse of Mexican American fiction through their stories and poems about young Mexican American girls growing up in the urban barrios of the Midwest. In her semiautobiographical *The House on Mango Street* (1985), Cisneros interweaves the life story of her preadolescent narrator, Esperanza, with the broader sociopolitical reality of Chicago's Mexican American community. Mary Helen Ponce's autobiography, *Hoyt Street* (1993), recounts similar memories of growing up as a Mexican American girl in the Pacoima barrio of northeastern Los Angeles. Immigration is another theme developed in the writings of contemporary Chicana authors. Most notably Helena Maria Viramontes's work, including *The Moths and Other Stories* (1995) and *Under the Feet of Jesus* (1996), dramatizes the experiences of undocumented Mexican families who migrate in search of seasonal agricultural employment.

Immigration also figures prominently in coming-of-age narratives written by Puerto Rican women. Most prolific among these authors is Nicholasa Mohr, a second-generation Puerto Rican, or Nuyorican, who was born in New York City's El Barrio (Spanish Harlem) to Puerto Rican immigrant parents. Among the first mainland Puerto Rican authors to publish in English, Mohr has documented the history of Nuyorican community formation in Spanish Harlem since World War II. Her first novel, *Nilda* (1973), is a series of vignettes about Puerto Rican girlhood in El Barrio. Mohr has also published many semiautobiographical works, including *El Bronx Remembered* (1975) and three books for juvenile readers, *In Nueva York* (1977), *Felita* (1979), and *Going Home* (1986). Mohr's writings testify to the presence of strong women in Puerto Rican community life and to the marginalization of Puerto Rican families in New York City schools, welfare offices, and public hospitals.

Another prolific Nuyorican writer is poet Sandra Maria Esteves. Her first publication, *Yerba Buena* (1980), explores the themes of self, community, and culture in a collection of poems about growing up Puerto Rican in the Bronx. As in her later publications, *Tropical Rains: A Bilingual Downpour* (1984) and *Bluestown Mockingbird Mambo* (1992), Esteves's poetry constructs a bilingual, bicultural notion of Puerto Rican identity. A similar portrait of Puerto Rican identity is developed in the writing of Judith Ortiz Cofer. Following three acclaimed books of poetry, Ortiz Cofer's first novel, *The Line of the Sun* (1989), portrays the migration from a Puerto Rican village to a multiethnic, working-class neighborhood in New Jersey. The success of this novel led Ortiz Cofer to publish her personal memoir, *Silent Dancing: A Partial Remembrance of Puerto Rican Childhood* (1990), a collection of vignettes and poems about her childhood experiences shuttling back and forth between Puerto Rico and New Jersey.

Other Puerto Rican women writers have also recently published coming-of-age memoirs. First published in Spanish in 1986, Magali Garcia Ramos's *Happy Days, Uncle Sergio* (English translation, 1995), recounts a middle-class girlhood in 1950s Puerto Rico, set against the panorama of suburbanization and ever-increasing U.S. influence on island politics and culture. Esmeralda Santiago's autobiography, *When I Was Puerto Rican* (1993), tells of her family's struggles to overcome poverty in Puerto Rico and later to adjust to the adversity of immigrant life in Brooklyn.

The coming-of-age experiences of Latina girls in the United States figure prominently in the work of Cuban American playwright and screenwriter Dolores Prida. Beginning with her first play, *Beautiful Senoritas* (1977), Prida's work has been produced in the United States, Puerto Rico, the Dominican Republic, and Venezuela. In *Coser y cantar* (Sewing and Singing, 1981) Prida created a bilingual text that reflects on the difficulties of growing up Latina in the United States. *Botanica*, which debuted in the Spanish Repertory Theater in 1990, develops these themes through its portrayal of intergenerational conflict within a family of Puerto Rican women in New York City. Prida has had more than twenty plays produced and has published several poetry collections, including *Treinta y un poemas* (Thirty-one Poems, 1967) and *Women of the Hour* (1971).

Achy Obejas is part of a younger generation of Cuban American women writers who reflect on their childhood within the exile Cuban community in the United States. In her collection of short stories,

We Came All the Way from Cuba So That You Could Dress Like This! (1994), Obejas relates her experiences of growing up in two cultures and two languages and of her sexual awakening as a lesbian. The conflict that young Cuban American girls experience between their own emerging sense of self and their parents' cultural norms and expectations is similarly explored in Cristina García's novel *Dreaming in Cuban* (1993). The novel's youngest protagonist is a teenage daughter of Cuban exile parents who, in a struggle to find an identity as a young artist in New York City, must imaginatively travel back to Cuba and bridge the emotional and political divide that has split her family in two.

Another notable contributor to Latina coming-of-age narratives is Dominican-born author Julia Alvarez. In her first novel, *How the Garcia Girls Lost Their Accents* (1991), Alvarez tells the story of the Garcia family, uprooted by the Trujillo dictatorship from their middle-class family life in the Dominican Republic to seek exile in suburban New York in the 1960s. As the four teenage Garcia sisters struggle for acceptance into American suburban culture, by straightening their hair, forgetting their Spanish, and dating boys unchaperoned, they come to realize that their new "American" identities are irrevocably tied to the island they left behind. Alvarez's semiautobiographical novel *Yo* (1997) presents a similarly complicated portrait of migration, acculturation, and Dominican-American girl- and womanhood.

Natalia Molina and
Alejandra Marchevsky

See also Chicana Girls; Female Sexuality; Immigration; *La Quinceañera*; Work

References and Further Reading

Aparicio, Frances R., and Susana Chavez-Silverman. 1997. *Tropicalizations: Transcultural Representations of Latinidad.* Hanover, NH: Dartmouth College Press.

Chavez, Leo. 1991. *Shadowed Lives: Undocumented Immigrants in American Society.* Fort Worth, TX: Harcourt Brace.

Chesney-Lind, Meda. 1997. *The Female Offender: Girls, Women, and Crime.* Thousand Oaks: Sage.

Dodson, Lisa. 1998. *Don't Call Us out of Name: The Untold Lives of Women and Girls in Poor America.* Boston: Beacon Press.

Hagan, Jacqueline Maria. 1994. *Deciding to Be Legal: A Maya Community in Houston.* Philadelphia: Temple University Press.

Hondagneu-Sotelo, Pierette. 1994. *Gendered Transitions: Mexican Experiences of Immigration.* Berkeley: University of California Press.

Horno-Delgado, Asuncion, Eliana Ortega, Nina M. Scott, and Nancy Saporta Sternbach, eds. 1989. *Breaking Boundaries: Latina Writing and Critical Readings.* Amherst: University of Massachusetts Press.

Kanellos, Nicolas, ed. 1997. *The Hispanic American Almanac: A Reference Work on Hispanics in the United States.* Detroit: Gale Press.

Mahler, Sara J. 1995. *American Dreaming: Life on the Margins.* Princeton: Princeton University Press.

Monroy, Douglas. 1999. *Rebirth: Mexican Los Angeles from the Great Migration to the Great Depression.* Berkeley: University of California Press.

Oboler, Suzanne. 1995. *Ethnic Labels, Latino Lives: Identity and the Politics of (Re)Presentation in the United States.* Minneapolis: University of Minnesota Press.

Odem, Mary E. 1995. *Delinquent Daughters: Protecting and Policing Adolescent Female Sexuality in the United States, 1885–1920.* Chapel Hill: University of North Carolina Press.

Pedraza-Bailey, Sylvia. 1991. "Women and Migration: The Social Consequences of Gender." *Annual Review of Sociology* 17: 303–325.

Perez Firmat, Gustavo. 1994. *Life on the Hyphen: The Cuban-American Way.* Austin: University of Texas Press.

Ramirez, Roberto R. 2000. "The Hispanic Population in the United States." In *Current Population Reports March 1999.* Washington, DC: U.S. Census Bureau.

Rebolledo, Tey Diana. 1995. *Women Singing in the Snow: A Cultural Analysis of Chicana Literature.* Tuscon: University of Arizona Press.

Rodriguez, Clara. 1989. *Puerto Ricans: Born in the U.S.A.* Boston: Unwin Hyman.

Romero, Mary, Pierette Hondagneu-Sotelo, and Vilma Ortiz, eds. 1997. *Challenging Fronteras: Structuring Latina and Latino Lives in the U.S.* New York: Routledge.

Rouse, Roger. 1992. "Making Sense of Settlement: Class Transformation, Cultural Struggle, and Trans-nationalism among Mexican Migrants in the United States." In *Towards a Transnational Perspective on Migration: Race, Class, and Nationalism Reconsidered.* Edited by Glick Schiller, Linda Basch, and Cristina Blanc-Szanton. New York: Annals of New York Academy of Sciences, vol. 645.

Ruiz, Vicki L. 1999. *From out of the Shadows: Mexican American Women in Twentieth-Century America.* New York: Oxford University Press.

Sánchez, George. 1990. "'Go after the Women': Americanization and the Mexican Immigrant Woman, 1915–1929." In *A Multi-Cultural Reader in U.S. Women's History.* Edited by Ellen DuBois and Vicki L. Ruiz. New York: Routledge.

Sánchez-Korrol, Virginia. 1994. *From Colonia to Community: The History of Puerto Ricans in New York City.* Berkeley: University of California Press.

Suarez-Orozco, Carola, and Marcelo Suarez-Orozco. 1995. *Transformations: Immigration, Family Life, and Achievement Motivation among Latino Adolescents.* Stanford: Stanford University Press.

Valenzuela, Abel. 1998. "Gender Roles and Settlement Activities among Children and Their Immigrant Families." *American Behavioral Scientist* 42, no. 4: 720–742.

Velez-Ibanez, Carlos. 1980. "Se me acabo la canción: An Ethnography of Non-Consenting Sterilizations among Mexican Women in Los Angeles." In *Mexican Women in the United States: Struggles Past and Present.* Edited by Magdelena Mora and Adelaida Del Castillo. Los Angeles: Chicano Studies Research Center UCLA.

Learning Disabilities, Reading Disorders, and Girls

Learning disabilities is one of the least understood diagnostic terms used in educational circles today. Because 10–15 percent of the U.S. population have been labeled "learning-disabled" and 80 percent of the learning disabled population have a reading disorder, most of the research has centered on reading problems rather than on general learning disabilities. The study of learning disabilities began around 1900 and focused on brain research until about 1930, when clinical study of the child became more important. From 1960 to 1980, legislative support for funding remedial programs increased, and rapid expansion of school programs occurred. During most of the twentieth century, educators and psychologists have assumed that reading disorders strike mostly boys and that females are consistently superior to males in all reading skills. Research has only recently begun to question these assumptions and to examine gender differences in reading disorders.

Some researchers have questioned whether there really are more boys than girls with reading disorders, citing the possibility that more boys are identified. Most of the previous research has been done with children who have been identified by their schools as having reading problems. Boys are more likely to receive special education and account for 80 percent of those being treated at reading clinics. These disproportionate statistics were investigated by Sally Shaywitz, codirector of the Center for the Study of Learning and Attention Disorders, and her colleagues at Yale University. They followed almost 500 Connecticut children from kindergarten through third grade and found that the schools identified more than four times as many boys as girls for diagnosis and treatment. However, when the research team independently tested the children, they found that *equal* numbers of boys and girls in both grades had reading difficulties. Other studies have corroborated that the disorder occurs at equal rates in males and females when careful diagnostic criteria rather than traditional school-based referral procedures are used.

A bias in sample selection rather than biological gender differences most likely accounts for the impression that more boys than girls have reading problems. Most school systems rely on the recommendations of teachers before testing students for underachievement rather than testing all the students. Teachers are far more likely to diagnose the condition in boys because boys are apt to act out and become troublesome to adults, whereas girls are more apt to withdraw and struggle quietly, drawing little attention to themselves. Girls are identified later than boys, and since it is well known that early identification makes a difference, they are deprived of appropriate help during critical years. This imbalance affects both boys and girls: too many boys are in special education and too many girls are struggling in silence.

One consequence of this pattern is that in the early grades, schools employ teachers for remedial reading classes, which are generally filled with boys. In contrast, by high school, girls usually fall behind in math, but fewer remedial math teachers are hired, since girls are *supposed* to be less proficient in math than boys.

Parental attitudes also contribute to the imbalance in identification and treatment. Because parents are attuned to the conventional wisdom and the information disseminated by the schools and the general press, they are more likely to *expect* reading problems in their sons than in their daughters. In addition, some parents believe that educational failure will have a greater impact on the future lives and careers of their sons than on their daughters. Boys are expected to be self-supporting, and although girls are expected to work for part of their lives, eventually they may be supported by husbands.

Other explanations for the gender imbalance of children identified as having reading disorders have been advanced. The causes of learning problems may vary because of physiological differences between boys and girls that begin at conception. Males are more vulnerable than females to a variety of developmental problems associated with abnormalities in neurological or psychological function that result in dyslexia, language disorders, stuttering, and autism. It has been suggested that males have more clusters of learning disabilities, manifested in both academic and behavioral difficulties, whereas females tend to have a single disability.

Another avenue of research has addressed the possibility of gender differences in the ways in which males and females use their brains in reading. With the development of high-tech imaging equipment, research into questions of brain anatomy and function has recently begun. Scientists have been able to identify specific brain malfunctions in reading disorders. It has been shown that the splenium of the corpus callosum is larger in dyslexic than in normal readers and larger in female than male dyslexics. Shaywitz and her colleagues at Yale University have found different areas of the brain become active during phonological processing. Individuals with reading disorders show very little activity in rear-brain areas (the angular gyrus and Wernicke's area), which are known to be important in linking written words with phonic components. Instead, individuals with reading disorders compensate by overusing a front-brain section called "Broca's area," traditionally associated with other aspects of language processing and speech.

In addition, it was found that different parts of the brain were used by women and men in arriving at the same solution. All the men in the study and some women used the left-side portion of Broca's area, but other women used both sides. The study strengthens the argument that the male brain is more asymmetrical than the female brain. These findings represent only a beginning; other researchers believe that there may be additional processes at work.

The social and emotional consequences for girls with learning disabilities are significant. All children with learning disabilities are likely to make negative attributions about their own ability and to show less effort following academic failure. Girls, however, have been found to be particularly vulnerable to the debilitating effects of perceived academic and social failure. Several stud-

ies have shown that girls with learning disabilities are at risk for developing and maintaining a sense of helplessness regarding academic tasks. They are likely to blame their own lack of ability for their failures and are less likely to persist in performing tasks they find difficult. Girls with learning disabilities also show adverse reactions to social failure. They tend to feel less well-liked, and this belief, together with a more passive social style, may result in more rejection and subsequent isolation and depression.

Learning disabilities have far-reaching effects in terms of employment. Follow-up studies of individuals with learning disabilities show that women tend to be steered into jobs consistent with sex-role stereotypes and that males are more likely to be employed full-time and to remain employed for several years after the initial study.

Clearly, reading disorders are disabling and interfere with academic progress. However, they also influence children's psychological and social development. Although the causes of reading disorders have yet to be definitively identified, the fact remains that girls with reading problems are not being identified as often and as early as boys. Girls who are not identified may not receive the appropriate remedial services they need to develop fully, which places them at risk for long-term academic, social, and emotional difficulties.

Anita Gurian

See also Disabilities; Education of Girls; Literacy; Reading

References and Further Reading
Lerner, Janet. 1985. *Learning Disabilities: Theories, Diagnosis and Teaching Strategies.* 4th ed. Boston: Houghton Mifflin.

Lubs, Herbert A., et al. 1999. "Familial Dyslexia: Genetic, Behavioral and Imaging Studies." *Annals of Dyslexia.*

Nass, Ruth. 1993. "Sex Differences in Learning Abilities and Disabilities." *Annals of Dyslexia* 43.

Settle, Shirley, and Richard Milich. 1999. "Social Persistence Following Failure in Boys and Girls with LD." *Journal of Learning Disabilities* 32, no. 3: 201–212.

Shaywitz, Sally E., Bennet A. Shaywitz, Jack Fletcher, and Michael D. Escobar. 1990. "Prevalence of Reading Disability in Boys and Girls: Results of the Connecticut Longitudinal Study." *Journal of the American Medical Association* 264: 998–1002.

Lesbians

Lesbians may be defined as those girls and women who find primary sexual and emotional satisfaction from other girls and women. It may appear odd to link the terms *lesbians* and *girls:* at the same time that contemporary heteronormative U.S. culture imagines childhood as "innocent," free from the encumbrances of sexuality, it assumes that children are always already heterosexual and that they possess an originary heterosexual identity. Thus it becomes almost impossible to imagine a "lesbian girl." Yet throughout the twentieth century, some girls (defined here as young women under the age of eighteen) in the United States have identified themselves as lesbians and have been identified by others as such.

The identity categories *homosexual* and *heterosexual* are relatively recent inventions that emerged in the latter half of the nineteenth century (Foucault 1978). Throughout history, people have experienced same-sex erotic attachments, but only recently was sexuality regarded as a central facet of identity and identification. Until the mid- to late nineteenth century, sexuality in the West was divided between natural and unnatural acts: sex for reproductive purposes inside marriage was thought to be natural, whereas all other sexual acts were considered "unnatural," regardless of who performed them. Gradually, in large part through the efforts of sexologists, who began to connect particular acts to deviant identities such as the onanist and later the homosexual, sexuality began to be regarded not as something someone did but as something someone had and was. Every person was thus expected to claim a sexual identity, and that identity was thought to transmit a particular set of truths about the self. Although this shift from acts to identities was widespread, it would be wrong to say that it was universal: not only did people persist in defining their sexualities through the acts they performed rather than through an appeal to an identity, but prior to the emergence of homosexual and heterosexual as dominant binaries of identity, other proto-identities existed, for example, the "sodomite" (Halperin 1998).

Prior to the late-nineteenth-century emergence of the identity category "lesbian," ways of defining female sexuality in the United States differed across race and class. White, middle-class girls and women could sustain lifelong "romantic friendships," passionate, intimate relationships, without suffering any social sanction (and even earning social approval) (Smith-Rosenberg 1975). In part because of the increased gender separation found in white, middle-class, Victorian culture, a spatial arrangement that was continued outside the home as girls began to enter the new semipublic spheres of the boarding school and the women's college, girls were able to form new intimacies with other girls and women outside the sphere of the family (Vicinus 1982). It would be wrong to claim, however, that these relationships were lesbian in the contemporary sense of the term. Not only was this label not available to these young women as a form of identification, but it is unclear from the evidence available whether whatever kinds of contact these girls and women shared would qualify as "sexual" according to contemporary understandings of the term. Yet it seems clear that in some, if not many, cases, "romantic friendships" included what we would now define as forms of female homoerotic sexual expression.

In the nineteenth century, white, middle-class girls might form relationships with other girls that lasted their lifetimes, often while also entering into heterosexual marriages, without attracting social censure as long as they did not transgress norms of gender, class, and race (for example, by acting "mannish" or by forming cross-class or interracial relationships) (Duggan 1993). "Masculine" women were often rejected by their families. In order to find employment, they were forced to conceal their biological sex because many occupations were closed to women or would not accept females who so obviously transgressed gendered norms. Such "passing women" were able also to court and sometimes even to marry other women (D'Emilio and Freedman 1988). It is harder to know how "feminine" working-class women who were attracted to other women fared because their stories have not been documented as well as those of women revealed to be passing as men.

As homosexuality and heterosexuality began to emerge as distinct identities inside the discourses of medicine and psychology, lesbian identities, as well as gay male ones, began to take on a distinctly deviant resonance. Homosexuality in general became the "unnatural" other to heterosexuality, the measure by which heterosexual norms of sex and gender could be maintained (Sedgwick 1990). Relationships between girls and between women that previously had existed without comment now began to be viewed with suspicion, not only by experts and educators but by the women within them. What had been previously viewed as harmless "crushes" or "smashes" between girls, for example, now were increasingly regarded as dangerous intimacies (Sahli 1979).

It is important to emphasize, however, that these were uneven developments: within various subcultures and regions, an older model of romantic friendship could exist unchallenged alongside newer models of lesbianism. Within same-sex organizations such as the Girl Scouts, for example, sometimes girls could still have intense crushes and express their love physically without fear of censure (Kent 1996). And in general, the space provided by "girlhood" remained for many a space of female-female erotic possibility, in part because theories of female sexual development argued that girls were asexual or innocent until the age of puberty and in part because the leeway afforded girls and women for same-sex physical expression and emotional intimacy in the twentieth century has been much greater than that afforded boys and men. Whereas normative masculinity often requires that boys and men repudiate same-sex emotional and physical intimacy, except in select, socially sanctioned contexts (on the battlefield, in sports), girls and women are often, although not always, allowed a much wider range of same-sex intimacies.

One should not romanticize this space, however: Freudian theories of female sexual development labeled homosexuality a "phase" that girls would and should grow out of, a step on the way to "mature heterosexuality." In the twentieth century, girls who continued into young adulthood to value female friendships over heterosexual romance suffered social stigma and worse. Furthermore, as in the nineteenth century, expressions of same-sex sexual desire, overt gender transgressions, and interclass and interracial same-sex relationships have often been cause for social approbation, as has been the increasingly common practice of "coming out," which by midcentury connoted not only entering the larger gay and lesbian community but also affirming publicly (to the community at large) one's homosexuality (Chauncey 1994). Girls who identified as lesbian or were identified as such by others (through rumor, because they were too "masculine," and so on) were and often still are at the mercy of their parents and guardians.

Lacking legal and often financial independence, they could not prevent their families from sending them to psychiatrists to be "cured" or from committing them to mental hospitals. It was not until 1973 that the American Psychiatric Association removed homosexuality from its list of mental disorders, and young women are still institutionalized for what is termed "gender-identity disorder," as Daphne Scholinski's recent narrative, *The Last Time I Wore a Dress* (1997), describes. Scholinski was committed to mental hospitals for three years solely because of her failure to conform to cultural ideals of femininity. Other young women were emotionally and physically abused or thrown out of their homes to make their way as teenagers on the streets, which made them more vulnerable to physical abuse. Currently, it is estimated that young gays and lesbians make up one-quarter of homeless teens in the United States (Singer 1993).

At the same time, the emergence of a movement for gay and lesbian civil rights has provided some young women with emotional, legal, and financial support, as have aspects of the feminist movement. However, stereotypes about the "recruitment" of youth into homosexuality have made connections between adult gays and lesbians and queer youth particularly fraught and dangerous, and the movement for gay and lesbian (and later bisexual, transgender, and queer) civil rights has also focused mainly on the rights of adults. Nonetheless, Sharon Thompson, researching the sexual lives of teenage girls in the United States, has found that what makes the most difference in the lives of young lesbians at the end of the twentieth century is not their sexuality per se but whether they have familial and social support networks to which they may turn. Unfortunately, it is still the case that gay and lesbian youth are at much greater risk of committing suicide (gay and lesbian children make up roughly 30 percent of all teen suicides). Yet in many major American cities, as well as in suburbs and even some rural areas, queer support groups have emerged not only through larger gay and lesbian organizations but within public and private schools in the United States. But with increased visibility has come increased vulnerability to attack because violence against gays and lesbians is also on the rise.

Cultural representations of lesbian girls have also increased dramatically. Within representations of lesbianism, girlhood often occupies an important position. Under intense pressure to combat various normative accounts of the formation of lesbian identity, many representations of lesbian girlhoods portray childhood as an originary space where the "clues" to one's sexual truth are already evident. Often writing against claims that homosexuality can be "cured" or that it is the result of abuse or seduction, lesbian authors portray childhood as revealing the hidden truth of the self, a truth that is often only realized later in life, a truth that has always existed and is immutable, natural, and innate. What may be disparate, unrelated childhood experiences find coherency only in retrospect, when the author or narrator discovers her lesbianism (Martin 1993).

Perhaps the first and most influential representation of what might be termed a lesbian girlhood is British writer Radclyffe Hall's 1928 account of the early life of Stephen Gordon in her novel *The Well of Loneliness*. In many ways, this text establishes the narrative tropes of lesbian girlhood, among them the main character's feelings of isolation and difference from the rest of society; her cross-gender identification; and her early childhood "crushes" on other girls and women. For Stephen, these differences become a curse rather than a source of pride or pleasure. More recently, Rita Mae Brown's *Rubyfruit Jungle* (1973) introduced an exuberant, brave young heroine, Molly Bolt, who experiences her difference from normative society not as a burden but as something eventually to be embraced and celebrated, something that gives her a more accurate view of the world. Although not the first novel since *The Well* to offer a happy ending, Brown's book has been hailed as a breakthrough in its celebration of lesbian identity and pleasure.

Despite their differences, both of these works describe their young heroines' conflicts with normative heterosexual society and their search for queer community. Since the 1970s, lesbians of color have described in both fiction and autobiography the ways in which queers of color are often caught between the homophobia of their "home" cultures and communities and the racism of the larger gay and lesbian community. In the short story "Johnnieruth" (1987), for example, Becky Birtha describes the specificities of a lesbian girlhood within a working-class African American community, as does Audre Lorde's "biomythography," *Zami: A New Spelling of My Name* (1992). Lorde narrates the conflicts with her family and, in particular, her mother that alienate her from her Afro-Caribbean community, but after coming out to the larger lesbian community, Lorde encounters racism and classism among her white lesbian peers. Ultimately, Lorde defines her own, racially specific homoerotics, linking her adult love for women to her early childhood passion for her own mother and the rituals of Afro-Caribbean culture she represents.

Specific cultural norms also provide different possibilities for female-female homoerotics as well as exerting different kinds of limitations upon them: as Catrióna Rueda Esquibel has argued (1998), the accepted practice of *comadrazgo* within Chicana/o culture allows young Chicanas to form intense female-female relationships without social sanctions. Esquibel points to such texts as Sandra Cisneros's *The House on Mango Street* (1984, 1991) and Denise Chávez's *The Last of the Menu Girls* (1987), which, while not offering representations of "out" young women, do eroticize young female friendships and describe what happens to these relationships as girls are forced into the heterosexual system.

A nineteen-year-old lesbian participates in the gay pride parade in Chicago. (Skjold)

Recent representations of lesbian girl-hood have also begun to appropriate the norms of popular romance for lesbians: Maria Maggenti's film, *The Incredible True Story of Two Girls in Love* (1994), co-opts many of the conventions of teen romance for a young lesbian, interracial, cross-class couple. Sadie Benning's semi-autobiographical videos, however, draw attention to the assumptions that lie behind the use of childhood in much of lesbian culture as a site for evidence of a "true" identity. Instead, as Mia Carter asserts, Benning stages her own identity as performance, as discontinuous and ambiguous. Similarly, other writers reject the nostalgia that often accompanies adult representations of childhood for rep-resentations of the sadomasochistic yet erotic cruelty of girls to other girls (Gait-skill 1992) and the brutal realities of queer teen desire (Lewis 1994). Regardless of how cultural producers use childhood—whether they see it as "proof" of an inher-ent sexuality or as a space of possibility, regulation, something to be nostalgically remembered or forever repressed—what is clear from all of these examples is that childhood itself is a site of struggle. As Elspeth Probyn has noted (1996), gays and lesbians have no choice but to enter into debates over its meaning when many other so-called experts claim to know what is best for children. Thus, childhood remains a crucial space for queer articula-tions of selfhood in the face of homopho-bic efforts to deny queer children access to sex education; safety from discrimination and abuse at home, at school, and in the workplace; social services; and basic emo-tional and material support.

In the face of such opposition, queer youth themselves have begun to organize and speak out about their experiences. For example, in the collection *In Your Face: Stories from the Lives of Queer Youth* (Gray 1999), lesbian-identified girls discuss topics such as knowing when they were lesbian, coming out to parents, being out at school, and falling in love. They also describe the communi-ties of queer teens they have found online, as the Internet provides new pos-sibilities for support and self-discovery. Increasingly, as the twenty-first century begins, in print, online, in music, and through grassroots community organiz-ing, girls themselves are claiming the right to define the terms by which they identify themselves as lesbian.

Kathryn R. Kent

See also Adoption; Body Image; Dating and Courtship; Female Sexuality; Girls' Fiction; Psychotherapy; Suicidal Behav-ior in Girls

References and Further Reading
Benning, Sadie. 1989a. *Living Inside.* Black and white, 4 min.
———. 1989b. *Me and Rubyfruit.* Black and white, 4 min.
———. 1989c. *A New Year.* Black and white, 4 min.
———. 1990a. *If Every Girl Had a Diary.* Black and white, 6 min.
———. 1990b. *Jollies.* Black and white, 11 min.
———. 1990c. *A Place Called Lovely.* Black and white, 14 min.
Birtha, Becky. 1987. *Lover's Choice.* Seattle: Seal Press.
Brown, Rita Mae. 1988. *Rubyfruit Jungle.* New York: Daughters, Inc., 1973. Reprint, New York: Bantam.
Carter, Mia. 1998. "The Politics of Pleasure: Cross-Cultural Autobiographic Performance in the Video Works of Sadie Benning." *Signs: A Journal of Women in Culture and Society* 23, no. 3: 745–770.
Chauncey, George. 1994. *Gay New York: Gender, Urban Culture, and the Makings of the Gay Male World, 1890–1940.* New York: Basic Books.

Chávez, Denise. 1987. *The Last of the Menu Girls.* Houston: Arte Público.

Cisneros, Sandra. 1991. *The House on Mango Street.* Houston: Arte Público, 1984. Reprint, New York: Vintage.

D'Emilio, John, and Estelle B. Freedman. 1988. *Intimate Matters: A History of Sexuality in America.* New York: Harper and Row.

Duggan, Lisa. 1993. "The Trials of Alice Mitchell: Sensationalism, Sexology, and the Lesbian Subject in Turn-of-the-Century America." *Signs: A Journal of Women in Culture and Society* 18, no. 4: 791–814.

Esquibel, Catrióna Rueda. 1998. "Memories of Girlhood: Chicana Lesbian Fictions." *Signs: A Journal of Women in Culture and Society* 23, no. 3: 645–682.

Foucault, Michel. 1978. *The History of Sexuality.* Vol. 1, *An Introduction.* Trans. Robert Hurley. New York: Pantheon.

Gaitskill, Mary. 1992. *Two Girls Fat and Thin.* New York: Bantam.

Gray, Mary L. 1999. *In Your Face: Stories from the Lives of Queer Youth.* New York: Huntington Park Press.

Hall, Radclyffe. 1928. *The Well of Loneliness.* Reprint, New York: Anchor Books, 1990.

Halperin, David. 1998. "Forgetting Foucault: Acts, Identities, and the History of Sexuality." *Representations* 63: 93–120.

Kent, Kathryn R. 1996. "'No Trespassing': Girl Scout Camp and the Limits of the Counterpublic Sphere." *Women and Performance: A Journal of Feminist Theory* 8, no. 2: 185–203.

Lewis, Heather. 1994. *House Rules.* New York: High Risk.

Lorde, Audre. 1992. *Zami: A New Spelling of My Name.* Freedom, CA: Crossing Press.

Maggenti, Maria, director. 1995. *The Incredibly True Adventure of Two Girls in Love.* Smash Pictures.

Martin, Biddy. 1993. "Lesbian Identity and Autobiographical Difference[s]." Pp. 274–293 in *The Lesbian and Gay Studies Reader.* Edited by Henry Abelove, Michèle Barale, and David M. Halperin. New York: Routledge.

Probyn, Elspeth. 1996. *Outside Belongings.* New York: Routledge.

Rupp, Leila J. 1999. *A Desired Past: A Short History of Same-Sex Love in America.* Chicago: University of Chicago Press.

Sahli, Nancy. 1979. "Smashing: Women's Relationships before the Fall." *Chrysalis* 8: 17–27.

Scholinski, Daphne, with Jane Meredith Adams. 1997. *The Last Time I Wore a Dress.* New York: Riverhead Books.

Sedgwick, Eve Kosofsky. 1990. *Epistemology of the Closet.* Berkeley: University of California Press.

Singer, Bennett L. 1993. *Growing Up Gay: A Literary Anthology.* New York: New Press.

Smith-Rosenberg, Carol. 1975. "The Female World of Love and Ritual: Relations between Women in Nineteenth-Century America." *Signs: A Journal of Women in Culture and Society* 1, no. 1: 1–29.

Thompson, Sharon. 1995. *Going All the Way: Teenage Girls' Tales of Sex, Romance, and Pregnancy.* New York: Hill and Wang.

Vicinus, Martha. 1982. "'One Life to Stand Beside Me': Emotional Conflicts in First-Generation College Women in England." *Feminist Studies* 8, no. 3: 603–628.

Literacy

In the colonial period, girls had limited access to education, with the literacy rate for adult women in New England at less than 50 percent (Lockridge 1974, 15). The establishment of public schools helped increase girls' access to instruction in reading and writing, and in the years after the Revolutionary War, an ideology of republican motherhood justified the education of young women so that they could appropriately instruct their sons in the virtues of citizenship. Educational opportunities for girls at all levels increased throughout the nineteenth century, and by 1870, European American girls ages ten to fourteen had surpassed

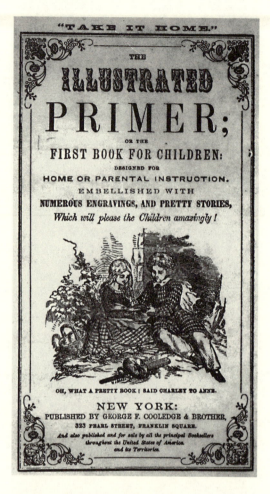

The Illustrated Primer, *published by George F. Cooledge and Brother, New York, intended to make learning to read fun for children. (Library of Congress)*

boys in literacy and academic achievement (Tyack and Hansot 1990, 46). African American children had far fewer opportunities for instruction in reading and writing, but in the years after the Civil War, African American literacy rates rose dramatically. By 1910, 85 percent of African American girls between the ages of ten and nineteen were literate (Tyack and Hansot 1990, 53). Although formal literacy instruction was largely denied African Americans until the final decades of the nineteenth century, it was often imposed on Native American children as a "civilizing" influence. Missionary and government schools were founded with the express purpose of teaching Native American children to reject the oral traditions and native languages of their families and tribes in exchange for education. Despite the educational limitations imposed upon them, girls of various ethnic and racial backgrounds have throughout U.S. history used their reading and writing skills in interesting, sometimes subversive ways.

Literacy rates are notoriously difficult to gauge, and scholars can draw only limited inferences based on the percentages of people who could sign their full names rather than merely make a mark (X) on public documents such as wills, deeds, and marriage licenses. For much of the population in the American colonies prior to 1700, it does seem that illiteracy was the norm. For girls in particular, literacy was not deemed necessary: they were schooled in cooking, spinning, sewing, and other domestic duties through face-to-face interactions with female kin and through direct experience. By the end of the colonial period, nearly universal male literacy had been achieved in New England, but perhaps only half as many women as men were literate (Tyack and Hansot 1990, 46).

This growth in literacy rates was due in part to the passage of laws that required parents to educate their children and townships to provide public education. In 1642, the Massachusetts General Court ordered selectmen in all towns in the colony to "take account from time to time of all parents and masters, and of their children, concerning their calling and imployment of their children, especially of their ability to read and understand the principle and capitall laws of this country" (quoted in Tyack and Hansot 1990, 15). This law that required that children be taught to read was soon replicated in other colonies: Connecticut in 1650, New York in 1665, and Pennsylvania in 1683. As the first legislation to mandate the use of public funds to support schools, the Massachusetts Bay Law of 1647 required townships of fifty families or more to "appoint one within their town to teach all such children as shall resort to him to write and reade, whose wages shall be paid either by the parents or masters of such children, or by the inhabitants in general" (quoted in Tyack and Hansot 1990, 16).

In response to such legislation, the private dame schools where many children learned the basic rudiments of reading, writing, and arithmetic slowly changed into more public institutions as towns began to pay "goodwives" to teach poor children. Originally, the typical dame school consisted of a few girls and boys under six or seven years of age who were instructed by a woman in her home. Parents paid a small fee for the supervision and instruction of their children. Over time, the dame school transformed into official public summer schools in which women taught boys and girls of various ages. The curriculum included learning the alphabet and basic spelling and mastering a few simple religious texts. Girls also learned to knit and sew, and boys sometimes received preliminary instruction in writing and oral arithmetic. Hornbooks served as students' introduction to reading in dame schools. Presenting the alphabet, the first few lines of a syllabary, and the Lord's prayer, the hornbook was a single page tacked on to a durable wooden paddle and covered with a pro-

tective layer of transparent horn. After mastering the hornbook, students would take up a primer, which usually contained several pages of instructional material, a more extensive syllabary, and words of increasing length. The final three stages of the reading curriculum consisted of mastering a Psalter, the New Testament, and the Bible.

Early in the eighteenth century, spelling books also became important texts for literacy education, and the "pronouncing-form method" of instruction was dominant. The instructor would call out a word, and the students, individually or in unison, would enunciate the letters of each syllable, pause to pronounce the syllable, then proceed to the next syllable until the word was completed (Gilmore 1989, 37). This method of repetition and rote memorization was considered appropriate since students would mainly devote their reading lives to religious texts. Schools and teachers were engaged in a shared intellectual project with religious leaders and parents to teach children the belief system of the dominant culture. Because the task of the reading teacher was so narrowly defined, instruction was often a female province. Throughout the colonial period, then, both girls and boys of European American ancestry learned to read through a patchwork system of dame schools, summer schools, charity schools, and town/district schools.

Writing, though, was largely a male domain. Defined in the colonial period as penmanship, good writing was viewed entirely in terms of formation of letters. For technical reasons, texts for writing instruction that featured various "hands" or scripts were not produced on colonial presses until after the American Revolution. Copybooks were thus the prized possessions of writing masters. Moreover, writing was considered a job-related skill necessary only for young men who would serve as clerks, lawyers, physicians, and ministers. Because girls were trained to be successful homemakers, penmanship was irrelevant to them. According to E. Jennifer Monaghan, the corresponding skill for girls was sewing (1989, 60, 64).

For elite girls who were more likely to acquire advanced literacy skills in their homes or through private education, literate activities such as letter writing and diary keeping could help nourish their developing sense of identity and emotional well-being. Letter writing allowed young women to craft their lived experiences into written artifacts to be shared with readers. Sending and receiving letters also created a sense of sociability with geographically distant friends and relatives and expanded the horizons of the world in which they lived. Keeping a diary similarly allowed a girl to assume editorial control of her life story as she encoded it in print. Although some girls viewed their diaries as a private space in which they could record intimate, personal information, other diary keepers viewed their writing as a record of personal, often spiritual development that could be shared with and evaluated by parents.

At the end of the eighteenth century, girls' opportunities for literacy education increased as a discourse emerged that positioned female education as necessary for women's newly politicized role as wife and mother. A new nation placed new demands on its citizenry, including women. In order to raise virtuous, well-informed sons who would be productive citizens of the new democracy, women would have to draw upon their capacities for rational, moral thought and give over their supposed tendencies toward the frivolous and sentimental. Terming this new conception of women's roles "republican motherhood," Linda Kerber has noted that advocates of education for women could now make a case that girls had a right to full educational experience. Both the demand for schooling for girls and the number of schools mushroomed after the American Revolution.

As the romanticism of the early nineteenth century took hold, the concept of childhood was redefined, and the literacy instruction received by girls in the burgeoning number of schools for young women began to change. Spurred in part by European educational reformers and thinkers like Johann Heinrich Pestalozzi, Friedrich Froebel, and Jean-Jacques Rousseau, the view that children were born into depravity and needed rigorous discipline gave way to a conception of childhood that foregrounded the essential goodness and innocence of young children. This revisionist thinking about childhood necessitated changes in the ways in which girls (and boys) were taught to read and write. As Lucille M. Schultz has noted, popular textbooks for literacy instruction that emphasized the parts of speech, types of sentences, and characteristics of style, and that provided students with an abstract list of topics for their own compositions (e.g., Richard Green Parker's *Progressive Exercises* [1832] and George P. Quackenbos's *First Lessons in Composition* [1851]) began to compete with texts that asked students to compose their own texts and write about their own lives. Using illustrations extensively, textbooks like Charles Morley's *Practical Guide to Composition* (1838) and John Frost's *Easy Exercises for Composition* (1839) helped students sharpen their observational and descriptive skills.

Even more importantly, as Schultz has argued, these new writing textbooks shifted the locus of authority. Previously, students had learned that authority resided in an unassailable repository of knowledge based largely on common religious principles and texts. Children were taught to use their literacy skills to demonstrate their comprehension of these shared cultural beliefs. During the nineteenth century, the locus of authority shifted, and the voice of the individual subject rose to prominence. By the end of the century, literacy instruction involved the composition of original, experience-based texts. For example, prize-winning essays at the Buffalo Female Academy in 1854 included "Our Home Wreath," "Visit to the Graveyard," "Pets," and "Trees" (quoted in Schultz 1999, 121).

Although the opportunities available to European American girls to acquire facility with written language prior to 1900 were often limited and tinged with assumptions about woman's proper sphere, girls of color faced additional educational challenges. In the hands of government-sponsored missionaries in the 1800s and in later federally funded schools for Native Americans, education was viewed as a way to "civilize" Indians and indoctrinate them in the norms of white society. Although many tribal leaders gradually came to accept the necessity of educating Native American boys so that they could better understand treaties and other documents written in English, accounts by Native American women and white missionaries indicate that there was less interest in educating girls well into the twentieth century (Coleman 1993, 67).

Girls who did attend day schools, reservation boarding schools, or off-reservation boarding schools often experi-enced a profound sense of dislocation. They were supplied with new clothing, forced to endure mandatory hair cuttings, and introduced to new foods and eating implements. Most significantly, they were given new, Christian names and were forbidden to use their native languages. The curriculum at schools like Richard Henry Pratt's multitribal school in Carlisle, Pennsylvania, the Hampton Institute, and the Phoenix Indian School were dominated by vocational training. Typically, students studied basic academic subjects (reading, writing, arithmetic, history) in the morning, and afternoons were devoted to learning job or domestic skills (e.g., sewing, laundry, and cooking for girls). Such a curriculum actually delayed the academic progress of many students. Helen Sekaquaptewa, a Hopi Indian who attended the Phoenix School, explained that the half-and-half curriculum (academic and vocational) prevented her from graduating (Coleman 1993, 114). Despite the emphasis on vocational training, oratorical competitions and school newspapers often flourished in schools for Native American students, suggesting that some students did become comfortable with the English language in both its printed and oral forms as a way to present themselves to the wider world.

In the nineteenth century, African American girls, particularly those dwelling in the South, were restricted by laws that prohibited teaching slaves to read and write. As the number of enslaved African Americans increased in the southern states during the early decades of the nineteenth century, the white population became more fearful of and resistant to the notion of literate African Americans. Between 1829 and 1835, various states passed laws making it illegal to teach slaves to read and write. There is little evidence that those who violated the laws were actually prosecuted, however. Such laws ran counter to the Protestant imperative that all persons have access to the Bible. Janet Duitsman Cornelius (1991) has powerfully documented the ingenious ways that slaves and free blacks learned to read, write, and share their literacy skills with other African Americans, often supported by religious societies and Protestant benevolent organizations. In northeastern, midwestern, and western states, free African American children were typically excluded from public schools. To counter such discrimination, African Americans established educational societies and opened schools in connection with their churches. Thousands of free African Americans learned to read and write in Sunday schools throughout the North prior to the Civil War.

As the United States moved into the twentieth century as an increasingly urban and industrial nation, progressive educators began drawing upon new scientific research in psychology and the social sciences as they sought to more directly address the vocational, health, family, and civic needs of diverse students and to prepare them to participate fully as citizens in a democratic society. At schools like John Dewey's University of Chicago Laboratory School and the Lincoln School of Teachers College in New York, the study of reading, spelling, penmanship, and grammar were all viewed as elements in the process of communication and textual production, and students were provided with opportunities to practice these skills in conversation, through letter writing, by keeping journals based on their personal observations, and in the production of student magazines and newspapers. Educa-

tors also looked for ways to link literacy studies with students' work in other areas of the curriculum. For example, if a class of sixth graders were studying farming in their science class, they might write letters to the Department of Agriculture requesting government bulletins on seed testing and then keep a lab journal as a means of recording the results of their own experiments with corn and soybean seeds.

The basic tenets of progressive education also had a positive impact on Native American girls through the Meriam Report (Institute for Government Research 1928). The eighty-three-page section of the report dealing with Indian schooling was authored by professional educator W. Carson Ryan, Jr. Ryan offered a well-reasoned and cogent critique of programs that removed Native American children from their homes, families, and tribes and instead insisted that Indian schools should draw upon tribal traditions as the basis for helping children creatively construct meaningful lives for themselves as citizens who brought a unique cultural heritage to modern society (Coleman 1993, 50–51).

In the world outside the classroom, American girls growing up in the early decades of the twentieth century were encountering a print culture in which forces of homogenization and diversification were operating simultaneously (Kaestle et al. 1991, 272). Regionalism, immigration, racism, sexism, and class stratification all contributed to diversity in print. The immigrant, religious, and radical presses thrived as printing and distributing periodical literature became less expensive, and such publications could play a role in the struggles of parents in immigrant and religious subcultures who often encouraged their chil-

A mentor and her five-year-old students read a book at a youth center in St. Paul, Minnesota. (Skjold Photographs)

dren to preserve their traditional values. Although on one level the broad literate public seemed to be splintering into smaller factions, forces of homogenization were also in play. The arrival of national wire services and syndicated features helped standardize newspaper content. Beginning in the 1890s, girls across the United States could read comics like "The Katzenjammer Kids." The radio and movie industry created popular heroes, and they spawned fan magazines and sponsored write-in contests that reached a nationwide audience. Literary "masterpieces" returned to prominence in American schools as the influence of progressive educators waned in midcentury, and more teenage girls were introduced to the same books at the same time (Kaestle et al. 1991, 272–293). Assessing the relationship between American society and the available reading and writing materials at midcentury, Carl F. Kaestle concluded, "society was not really homogeneous, but print culture was, to an unprecedented degree" (286).

Partly in response to the feminist, Black Power, and other radical movements of the 1960s and 1970s as well as an explosion in computer and media technologies, American girls at the beginning of the twenty-first century have access to an ever-increasing range of reading and writing materials. With the works of diverse authors available in paperback editions and textbooks that emphasize multicultural issues, teachers can introduce students to the works of writers like Langston Hughes, Maya Angelou, Sandra Cisneros, and Amy Tan. Moreover, the pedagogical emphasis on using reading and writing as a means to understand one's own life and to record personal experiences that first came into vogue in the nineteenth century and that was a central thread in the work of progressive educators largely remains in force for girls enrolled in American schools today. In her study of adolescent girls living in rural Iowa, Margaret J. Finders discovered that her subjects felt that expressive and narrative writing about personal experiences was what teachers valued as "good writing." As one girl explained to Finders, "It's what you have to write. It's the only thing they [teachers] count" (1997, 121).

For many young women, literacy events taking place outside the classroom—keeping diaries, signing yearbooks, passing notes, forging hall passes, reading teen zines, penning graffiti on bathroom walls, participating in home party retail ventures (e.g., Avon, Home Interiors), and entering extracurricular poetry contests—are a more vital means by which they use print to measure and control their growth into adulthood. Finders concluded that carrying and reading teen zines served as an act of self-presentation for early adolescent girls as they documented their interest in what they perceived to be adult material, and perhaps more importantly, they were demonstrating their willingness to challenge the authority of parents and teachers who did not deem teen zines to be appropriate texts for girls (1997, 57). Similarly, penning and reading bathroom graffiti about sexual orientation, physical desires, and bodily functions allow girls to explore and expose complex, adult issues. In her study of African American and Hispanic adolescent girls attending an urban junior high school, Amy Shuman found that young women often imitated the voices of adult authorities to serve their own playful ends. One young woman composed a "Constitution of Love" whose preamble began: "We the People young in heart [in] order to form more perfect kisses . . . ," and amendments attached to this amorous manifesto reminded adolescent readers that "Thou shalt not squeeze hard" and "Thou shalt kiss at every opportunity" (quoted in Shuman 1986, 87).

Although literacy can allow girls to begin negotiating more adult roles for themselves, they also use print to create strong bonds of solidarity and to define social boundaries. Finders found that by passing notes during class, girls established their membership within a network of friends, and the annual ritual of signing yearbooks served to mark hierarchies among groups of girls. According to Finders, students who could not compose a message deemed appropriate by others were marked as social outsiders, and permitting a girl of lesser status to sign one's book seemed to lower the status of the yearbook owner (1997, 43–44). Notes of apology and threatening letters left in student lockers are also forms of literate activity that circulate through girls' lives outside the classroom, binding them together and highlighting fault lines among them. For girls who feel alienated from social networks within their schools or communities because of socioeconomic status, sexual orientation, race, ethnicity, religion, personal appearance, or other reasons, literacy may involve deeply personal and private acts of reading and writing. By keeping a diary, writing poetry, or composing other types of texts that they protect from public view, some disenfranchised young women can safely use print to explore their frustrations and anxieties, vent anger, express sadness, and celebrate personal triumphs.

Jane Greer

See also Communication; Diaries; Education of Girls; Girls' Magazines; Graffiti; Learning Disabilities, Reading Disorders, and Girls; Reading

References and Further Reading
Coleman, Michael C. 1993. *American Indian Children at School, 1850–1930.* Jackson: University of Mississippi Press.

Cornelius, Janet Duitsman. 1991. *"When I Can Read My Title Clear": Literacy, Slavery, and Religion in the Antebellum South.* Columbia: University of South Carolina Press.

Finders, Margaret J. 1997. *Just Girls: Hidden Literacies and Life in Junior High.* New York: Teachers College Press.

Gilmore, William J. 1989. *Reading Becomes a Necessity of Life: Material and Cultural Life in Rural New England, 1780–1835.* Knoxville: University of Tennessee Press.

Institute for Government Research. 1928. *The Problem of Indian Administration* (The Meriam Report). Baltimore: Johns Hopkins Press.

Kaestle, Carl F., Helen Damon-Moore, Lawrence C. Stedman, Katherine Tinsley, and William Vance Trollinger, Jr. 1991. *Literacy in the United States: Readers and Reading since 1880.* New Haven, CT: Yale University Press.

Kerber, Linda K. 1988. "'Why Should Girls Be Learn'd and Wise?' Two Centuries of Higher Education for Women as Seen through the Unfinished Work of Alice Mary Baldwin." Pp. 18–42 in *Women and Higher Education in American History: Essays from the Mount Holyoke College Sesquicentennial Symposia.* Edited by John Mack Faragher and Florence Howe. New York: Norton.

Lockridge, Kenneth A. 1974. *Literacy in Colonial New England: An Enquiry into the Social Context of Literacy in the Early Modern West.* New York: Norton.

Monaghan, E. Jennifer. 1989. "Literacy Instruction and Gender in Colonial New England." Pp. 53–80 in *Reading in America: Literature and Social History.* Edited by Cathy N. Davidson. Baltimore: Johns Hopkins University Press.

Schultz, Lucille M. 1999. *The Young Composers: Composition's Beginnings in Nineteenth-Century Schools.* Carbondale: Southern Illinois University Press.

Shuman, Amy. 1986. *Storytelling Rights: The Uses of Oral and Written Texts by Urban Adolescents.* Cambridge: Cambridge University Press.

Tyack, David, and Elisabeth Hansot. 1990. *Learning Together: A History of Coeducation in American Schools.* New Haven, CT: Yale University Press.

Little Mothers

Little mothers was the term used at the turn of the twentieth century to describe girls who spent their time taking care of their younger siblings. Being a little mother was a common experience for many girls from immigrant and working-class families, an experience that taught girls from an early age to identify with their mothers and to share in their responsibilities.

Taking care of babies was only one of the ways in which girls helped out their mothers and contributed to the family. They also assisted with the cleaning, cooking, and daily marketing, bargaining with peddlers and shopkeepers to save a few pennies; worked alongside their mothers making artificial flowers, lace, or other kinds of "homework"; and helped out in family shops and peddled flowers or baskets to earn a little extra money. But taking on the care of babies and toddlers was probably the most important way a girl could contribute to her family and lighten her mother's heavy load of responsibilities. Too young

A girl sits on a doorstep in New York City with a baby on her lap in this photograph by Jacob Riis. (Bettmann/Corbis)

to do the heavy household work, girls were given the job of watching the little ones. Some started to be responsible for rocking babies and taking them out for air when they were as young as five years old and continued caring for them in the afternoons after school. Girls would sit together on the stoop with their babies or park their carriages next to each other in the street while they talked and played together. In some city neighborhoods, babies and small children were essentially raised by their older sisters, who fed, clothed, diapered, and bathed them and took personal pride in their appearance. Many girls reportedly came to see their charges as their own babies. When these babies got older, however, they some-

times resisted their older sisters' authority and could be difficult to control.

Girls' feelings about their child care tasks were often mixed, combining pride in "their" babies with regret and even resentment that their child care duties kept them from being able to play. Unlike the boys who ventured far from their homes to sell newspapers or peddle goods on other city streets, these girls stayed close to home with their babies. And of course, their work—like their mothers'—was unpaid, so they did not gain either the possibility of spending money or the increased status that their brothers' work might bring. Some may have resented their responsibilities as compared to their brothers' relative freedom to play in the streets, but most probably did not question their duty to help out their mothers.

In fact, when mothers became ill or died, daughters often felt responsible for taking over their duties and keeping the family together. One such girl in Philadelphia, whose mother was being treated for tuberculosis, tried to work and care for her three younger siblings. When a settlement house worker decided the children should be placed in foster homes instead, the girl broke down, becoming "melancholy on account of the illness of her mother and the breaking up of her home." Having taken on a mother's responsibilities, it became her personal failure when the family was split up (Rose 1999, 53). Girls who acted as little mothers might grow up to take on the role of "kin keeper," the woman who kept the family together, provided help in times of crisis, and remained at the center of family communication throughout her life.

Girls' experiences as little mothers clearly taught them to think of themselves as mothers, to share in their mothers' responsibilities and worries, and to remain closely tied to the family rather than venturing far into the outside world. Girls also learned—sometimes painfully, sometimes without much remorse—that their role in the family and their status as "good daughters" were much more important than their attendance at school. Some of these girls would grow into mothers who were determined that *their* daughters would not be kept out of school or lose their childhood independence to care for younger siblings.

Settlement house workers and other reformers often worried about these little mothers, who seemed to be carrying burdens they were not old enough to bear. Reformers were particularly troubled by the fact that children were staying out of school because they were needed to take care of their younger siblings. This concern partly motivated the establishment of charitable day nurseries that provided care for the children of poor working mothers. Settlement house workers referred to a "little mother problem," and newspaper reporters described these girls in detail. Many settlement houses and city public health departments sought to teach the little mothers modern baby care and hygiene, realizing that these girls were the ones in charge of most of the neighborhood's babies. Special classes or little mothers' leagues were organized, and settlement house workers often hoped that the lessons learned by the little mothers would also be communicated to the real mothers. Little mothers also acted as their mothers' link to expert child care advice when they took home economics at school or when they wrote letters to the U.S. Children's Bureau, asking for copies of child care manuals to translate for their immigrant mothers.

Although the phrase *little mothers* was used to describe immigrant girls in northeastern cities, the phenomenon was widespread in rural areas as well. Black girls growing up on farms in the South, for instance, started taking care of babies at a very young age and, as they grew older, learned to take on other household tasks, helping to sustain the household while their mothers worked as domestics in the homes of whites. Another farm daughter remembered her reluctance to be confined by her little mother responsibilities; she would give the baby's cradle a push and run out of the house before she could hear him cry (MacLeod 1998,

103). Not all little mothers were girls: if no older sister was available to care for the babies, boys were often pressed into service. This was true not only for working-class and immigrant families but also in middle-class households with many children. For instance, Benjamin Spock, the oldest of six children, remembered caring for his younger siblings, changing diapers, giving bottles, and jumping up from the dinner table to see why his baby brother was crying (Spock and Morgan 1985, 5). But child care and the role of the little mother were usually duties that parents and observers thought naturally belonged to girls, in which girls both helped their mothers and prepared for their own similar futures.

Elizabeth Rose

See also Babysitting; Daughters and Mothers; Domesticity; Immigration; Latina Girls

References and Further Reading
Hareven, Tamara. 1982. *Family Time and Industrial Time.* Cambridge: Cambridge University Press.
Macleod, David I. 1998. *The Age of the Child: Children in America, 1890–1920.* New York: Twayne Publishers.
Nasaw, David. 1985. *Children of the City at Work and at Play.* Garden City, NY: Anchor Press/Doubleday.
Rose, Elizabeth. 1999. *A Mother's Job: The History of Day Care, 1890–1960.* New York: Oxford University Press.
Spock, Benjamin, and Mary Morgan. *Spock on Spock: A Memoir of Growing Up with the Century.* New York: Pantheon Books.
Youcha, Geraldine. 1995. *Minding the Children: Child Care in America from Colonial Times to the Present.* New York: Scribner.

M

Mathematics and Science

Girls have historically been denied an education in mathematics and science. At the beginning of the nineteenth century, education was limited to private instruction in drawing, painting, and needlework. Mathematics and science were not part of the curriculum because it was generally believed that these subjects were a threat to girls' health and virtue. By mid-century, girls were attending elementary and high schools, but the debate about whether they should study mathematics and science continued. Despite the debate, more girls than boys were studying mathematics and science in high school as the nineteenth century came to a close. A reversal of this trend occurred in the first half of the twentieth century, when home economics and business education were introduced. These vocational tracks led to less rigorous mathematics and science courses for girls, and more rigorous courses were not reintroduced until after World War II, when mathematics and science finally became important school subjects. The status of these subjects led to the development of new curricula during the 1960s and 1970s, but these curricula did not address the perception that mathematics and science were male pursuits or promote girl-friendly teaching or testing strategies. The most recent standards-based reforms of the 1990s have increased the number of girls enrolled in mathematics and science, but barriers to participation still exist.

The Nineteenth Century and Elementary Education

In the first half of the nineteenth century, only the small segment of American society that was male, white, and upper-class received an elementary education. The curriculum was equally restricted and focused on reading, writing, and religion. Most people thought that this was sufficient and that teaching mathematics and science in elementary schools was inappropriate and unnecessary. Since elementary education was not free and a debate was raging over whether it was even appropriate to educate girls, it is not surprising that most girls in the early nineteenth century were not sent to school. The few girls who were sent to school did not stay more than a year.

From 1850 on, the efforts of reformers led to equal numbers of white girls and boys enrolling in elementary school. These students usually received poor instruction, and the curriculum continued to contain very little mathematics and science. In response to these conditions, reform-minded educators influenced by European thinkers such as Johann Heinrich Pestalozzi and Johann Friedrich Herbart began to argue for

435

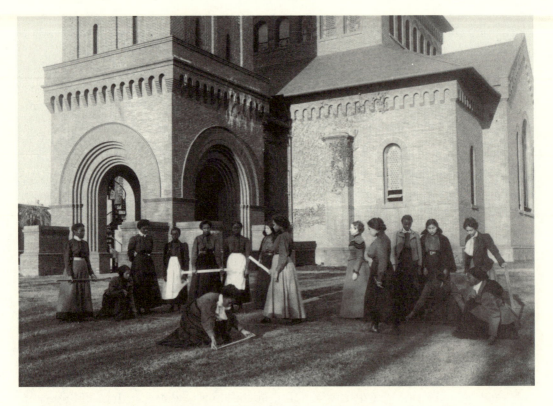

Girls measure a piece of ground in an arithmetic class at Hampton Institute, Hampton, Virginia. (Library of Congress, 1899)

teaching mathematics and science in elementary schools.

These educators further argued that young children should be manipulating physical objects rather than engaging in the mental manipulation of abstract symbols. Teachers who embraced this new philosophy taught science using nature. Teaching arithmetic emphasized activities such as measuring distances and counting real objects. These age-appropriate reforms, like those that would follow, had a limited impact. Most elementary schools continued to ignore mathematics and science or continued to emphasize memorization of facts, choral recitation, assignments from textbooks, and practice of arithmetic computations.

By the late nineteenth century, arithmetic had finally become part of the elementary school curriculum because of the downward movement of university mathematics into high schools, which in turn transferred the responsibility of teaching arithmetic to elementary schools. Science, however, was still not part of the elementary curriculum and would remain unimportant well into the twentieth century.

The Nineteenth Century and Secondary Education

Both private and public secondary schools existed at the beginning of the nineteenth century. Established for wealthy white males who were going to the university to become clergymen or to pursue literary careers, private academies and Latin grammar schools stressed a classical education in Latin and Greek. The curriculum did not include science or mathematics, although it was later modified to include some arithmetic.

Private academies for girls did not have a strong academic curriculum or include the study of the classics. Like the boys' academies, they eventually introduced a limited amount of arithmetic but not science. Most girls' academies emphasized needlework, drawing, and music. Some academies were even created to teach girls how to run a household well. This curriculum was called "domestic economy."

A notable exception to the typical academy for girls was the Troy Female Seminary, established by Emma Willard in Troy, New York, in 1821. The seminary required girls to study trigonometry, physiology, chemistry, and natural philosophy (an early term for science). Another exception was Mount Holyoke Seminary in Massachusetts, which was founded in 1837 by Mary Lyon and modeled after the Troy Seminary. These academically oriented schools provided girls with the preparation they needed to go on to the few universities that accepted women. However, the founders of these more rigorous institutions had to conceal their true intentions of providing girls with an education equal to that for boys. They publicly justified their curriculum as a way to create enlightened women who would become better wives and mothers.

As the nineteenth century progressed, more private schools for girls were established, but educational opportunities were still limited. There were fewer seminaries and academies for girls than for boys, and most were located in the eastern part of the United States. In addition, these institutions were costly to attend, and most did not have an academically rigorous mathematics and science curriculum.

Publicly funded secondary schools also began as single-sex institutions. Boston Girls High School, established in 1828, was the first high school for girls. Thereafter, the number of high schools for girls increased rapidly. Paying for two single-sex schools rather than one coeducational school made little sense to taxpayers, and coeducational schools soon became the norm. The argument that coeducation would compromise a girl's virtue fell on deaf ears in the face of economic realities.

The number of girls enrolled in high schools steadily increased throughout the century, and by 1870 they outnumbered boys. Enrollment continued to grow so much that by 1900 there were three times as many girls as boys in high schools. However, access to a high school education continued to be primarily limited to those who were white, urban, and living in the northeastern part of the country (Rury 1991).

Working-class girls attended high school at slightly lower rates than upper- and middle-class girls, but religion and immigration had a bigger impact on high school attendance than social class. Protestant girls were more likely to attend than Catholic girls, and immigrant families from Germanic and Scandinavian countries were more likely to send their daughters to school than families from eastern and southern Europe (Rury 1991).

The academies, seminaries, and high schools for girls were established by women reformers and liberal male educators who based their rationale for educating girls in the religious awakening of the early 1800s. They saw education as a way

Chemistry lab at St. Teresa's Academy, Kansas City, Missouri. (Library of Congress, ca. 1895)

to enlighten the minds of girls and women and to help them become more spiritual. However, the counterforce acting against the education of girls was a nineteenth-century fear that having girls study masculine subjects such as mathematics and science would be detrimental to society and lead to the destruction of the family.

Many people believed that females were physically and intellectually weaker than males and that education would make them incapable of bearing children, ruin their health, lead to depression, and make them unmarriageable. Opponents of publicly funded education were particularly vocal in their opposition to edu-

cating girls because they believed that girls should be educated at home to preserve their purity and delicacy. Nevertheless, by the mid-nineteenth century the debate about educating girls had moved from whether they should be educated to what subjects were appropriate for girls to learn.

This debate was temporarily resolved at the close of the nineteenth century. The coeducational public high school was dominated by what was called a male curriculum, which included mathematics and science. Public school educators argued for a male curriculum based on their belief that both sexes needed the same education and were equally capable. Government statistics for course enrollment patterns in 1889 indicate that girls also believed that they were capable of mastering a male curriculum (Rury 1991). More females than males were enrolled in high school algebra, geometry, physics, and chemistry. Furthermore, girls earned grades that were equal to or better than those earned by boys in all high school subjects, including mathematics and science. Girls were even winning mathematics prizes upon graduation based on their superior grades.

The situation was quite different in private single-sex secondary schools at the end of the nineteenth century. Although there were equal numbers of males and females enrolled, there was less equality in the curriculum. In particular, more boys than girls were taking algebra, geometry, and various sciences.

Even though by the late 1800s white girls had greater access to an education that included mathematics and science, many other girls remained uneducated. Black girls, girls from Asian immigrant families, Native American girls, and Chicana/Latina girls had fewer opportunities to obtain an education. Poverty, slavery, language, and culture all formed barriers to education for minority girls, but the greatest barrier of all was prejudice. The white majority believed that minority girls were intellectually inferior because of their sex and race or ethnicity.

The Twentieth Century
There were three waves of reform in teaching mathematics and science in the twentieth century. The first wave, built upon the ideas of Pestalozzi and Herbart, was led by John Dewey around 1920. Asserting that school should be enjoyable for children, Dewey and other Progressives emphasized a child-centered approach to teaching in the elementary school, mathematics and science topics that were socially relevant for young children, scientific and mathematical cognitive tools to solve everyday problems, developmentally appropriate tasks, and the social importance of knowledge. The elementary school mathematics curriculum was also driven by the idea of readiness to learn concepts and think mathematically. Consequently, formal mathematical instruction was postponed to later grades in the twentieth century than in the nineteenth century. Elementary science was hardly taught at all and continued to be limited to nature studies.

The Progressive movement was ahead of its time and foreshadowed many of the present-day recommendations for making mathematics and science more girl-friendly. Unfortunately for girls, most of Dewey's ideas were resisted by the public, and few were enacted in elementary schools. The history of girls taking mathematics and science in the twentieth century might have been very different if Dewey's ideas had been more popular.

Another innovation in the 1920s, which was the philosophical opposite of the Progressive movement, was the introduction of junior high schools. These schools served as an educational space maker for the mathematics and science curriculum. General science was moved from high schools to junior high schools to make room in the high school curriculum for the more rigorous sciences of biology, chemistry, and physics. In addition, general science was taught in junior high schools to compensate for the poor or nonexistent science curriculum in the elementary schools. The formal study of mathematics, delayed in elementary school, also began in junior high school. Educators felt that junior high school was both their last chance to provide mathematics and science to students who would drop out of school in a year or two and their first chance to prepare students for studying mathematics and science in high school. Girls and boys participated equally in the mathematics and science taught in the junior high school.

The high school mathematics and science curriculum took a step backward for girls in the early decades of the twentieth century. This period saw the introduction of vocational education. Girls were directed to a business (typing and stenography) or a home economics track, whereas boys were directed to a mechanical or university track. Then educators began to change the mathematics and science courses offered to reflect the vocational tracks of boys and girls. This led to a differentiated curriculum and a decline in the number of girls taking mathematics and science. Between 1900 and 1928 female enrollment in physics dropped 80 percent, and enrollment in algebra fell 33 percent (Rury 1991). Boys outnumbered girls in physics three to one and held a slight majority over girls in mathematics, even though the number of girls enrolled in high school was greater than the number of boys. Girls' chemistry classes were related to the home, cooking, and food adulteration. Boys' physics was more technical and scientific. Some educators even argued for limiting the mathematics taken by girls to arithmetic because that was all they would need for the home or office work.

Educating girls also became an economic issue in the 1930s. Science courses were more costly than other courses because they included a lab in which materials were consumed and had to be replaced. Consequently, principals and teachers actively discouraged girls from enrolling in science courses to reduce the number of students who would be consuming materials. Boys were not discouraged.

The decline in girls' participation in mathematics and science in the first half of the twentieth century caused little concern. Most young women still expected that they would be wives and mothers. Work was limited to the period before a young woman married, if she was middle-class or upper-class. Even women who wanted to work and had strong backgrounds in mathematics and science had difficulty securing university, government, or industry jobs that made use of their education.

At midcentury a dramatic change took place. President Truman was impressed by the inventions brought about by mathematics and science during World War II, such as the atomic bomb, radar, computers, and jets. He believed that Americans had to reform their educational system, especially in mathematics and science, in order to improve health, prosperity, and national security. The president's science advisers argued for a foundation that would fund research and improve science teaching in schools, and as a result the National Science Foundation was established. The foundation then funded for curriculum projects to improve mathematics and science instruction in kindergarten through twelfth grade.

These curricula took various approaches. The science curricula emphasized teaching through discovery, the learning cycle, and hands-on activities. They focused on understanding scientific processes and the structure of science and on making students scientists. The mathematics curricula emphasized teaching with manipulatives such as geometric shapes, counters, and blocks. They focused on concept formation, the structure of mathematics, and understanding of mathematical concepts. The content of the new mathematics curricula replaced algebraic, geometric, and trigonomic concepts with set theory, logic, Boolean algebra, and matrices.

Aspects of these curricula were successful in helping students learn, but they came under sharp criticism from teachers and parents and were replaced by the traditional lecture and textbook. Teachers objected because the curricula were elitist and too difficult for most students. Parents objected because they were too nontraditional in both content and pedagogy, especially when the textbook was eliminated. Some scholars objected because the curricula ignored the needs of girls and did not address the high attrition rate of girls from mathematics and science courses.

Educators were dismayed when these reforms failed girls, and researchers wanted to know why. They turned their attention to what happens to girls in schools and the nature of science instruction with regard to gender. Studies conducted from the 1970s through the 1990s painted a discouraging picture, but they also provided insights into what needed to be done. What follows is a brief review of this research and suggestions for ways to increase the participation of girls in mathematics and science.

Attitude and Self-esteem. Positive attitudes toward mathematics and science decline from the elementary school through high school, and at all grade levels girls' attitudes are less positive than boys. This decline is linked to the topics studied as well as the teaching strategies used. Girls also have lower self-esteem than boys, which is at the very lowest during the transition from elementary to high school (American Association of University Women 1999). Low self-esteem coupled with negative attitudes toward mathematics and science starts a chain reaction. Girls begin to lose self-confidence and believe that they are not smart enough to take mathematics and science courses. Less self-confidence leads to lower career aspirations. The end result is that fewer girls take noncompulsory mathematics and science classes. The combined effect of low self-esteem and low self-confidence is so strong that girls feel that they are not good at mathematics and science even when they make good grades.

Participation Rates. Most girls stop taking mathematics after algebra II. However, even when girls take the same number of mathematics courses as boys, they take lower-level courses such as basic and general mathematics. A similar pattern is found in enrollment in science courses. Girls enroll in biology and chemistry at comparable numbers to boys, but fewer girls than boys take physics. Enrollment for girls and boys in advanced placement classes for all areas of mathematics and chemistry is approximately the same. The number of girls exceeds boys in biology, but fewer girls than boys enroll in physics. Unfortunately, these high enrollment rates are not reflected in advanced placement testing. Fewer girls than boys choose to take the advanced placement tests, and when they do, they score lower than boys.

School Effects. Schools play a big part in promoting girls' participation in mathematics and science. For example, more girls than boys are identified and placed in gifted programs in the elementary school. Nevertheless, the selection and evaluation process appears to be biased because girls are not placed in gifted programs that focus on mathematics and science.

The way American schools teach also has a large impact on girls. Textbook-based instruction, competitive learning strategies, and mathematics and science activities that are not placed in a human context or linked to girls' concerns and interests (helping people, animals, and the world) do not promote interest in mathematics and science or high performance. These teaching strategies are more likely to match the learning styles and preferences of boys than girls.

Classroom interactions also favor boys. Teachers call on boys more than girls, ask them more thought-provoking questions, and give them more feedback for answers. Teachers praise boys more overall, especially for the quality of their work. In contrast, girls are more often praised for the appearance of their work. Teachers also tell boys, but not girls, that their failures are due to lack of effort. These interactions send a clear message to girls. It says that girls are not important in the classroom, that they are not as smart as boys, and that they fail because they lack ability.

Student-to-student interactions are dominated by boys and contribute to inequities in the classroom. This is especially true when students work in groups on hands-on mathematics and science activities. During group work boys hog materials and do the tasks. Girls watch or engage in stereotypical roles such as serving as secretary. Boys dominate the group discussions too. Boys ignore girls'

ideas, interrupt girls, or prevent them from speaking.

In addition, the standardized tests used by schools strongly favor boys. Boys are comfortable with a multiple-choice format, but girls are not and want more information to answer the questions. The test questions themselves are an additional source of bias because they are more likely to reflect male experiences than female experiences or to appeal more to boys than girls (Bateson and Parsons-Chatman 1981; DeMars 1998; Murphy 1996).

The Nature of Science and Mathematics. The general perception of the nature of mathematics and science also discourages girls. Boys, girls, parents, and society in general think of mathematics and science as more appropriate for males than females. A good example of the pervasiveness of this perception is the talking Barbie produced by Mattel. One version, which is no longer produced, had Barbie saying "Math is hard." Since schools are reflections of society, it should not be surprising to see that schools reinforce the message that mathematics and science are more appropriate subjects for boys.

Textbooks have also promoted the idea that mathematics and science are male professions. Until very recently, textbooks had few pictures of women scientists or mathematicians. There were fewer pictures of girls doing mathematics and science and almost no pictures of people of color.

Some teachers reinforce the masculine image of mathematics because they believe that boys are better mathematics students than girls. Others reinforce the masculine image of science when they allow boys to dominate science classes.

Even the makeup of the school mathematics and science faculty can contribute to a masculine image if there are few female teachers to serve as role models.

The Latest Reform. The wave of reform that took place at the end of the twentieth century emphasized national standards and systemwide change. The standards helped to increase the number of girls in mathematics and science because statewide testing was linked to the standards. To do well on these tests, girls had to take more than the minimum mathematics and science classes. They also had to take more mathematics and science to meet high school graduation requirements, which increased in response to the standards. These two changes led to more honors and advanced placement classes being offered. The cumulative effect of these changes was higher test scores and little or no gender gap in performance.

Research about how and what to teach to interest girls in mathematics and science also became part of the systemic reform effort in public schools and teacher preparation programs at universities. Although it is still very early to come to final conclusions, some positive effects have shown up in classrooms. Mathematics and science became more girl-friendly through the use of hands-on activities, carefully monitored group work, female role models, gender-sensitive textbooks, topics that interest girls, alternative assessments, long-term projects, and reduced competition.

Some coeducational schools are experimenting with single-sex mathematics and science classes to improve test scores, attitude, self-esteem, and participation for girls. Unlike changes in pedagogy and the effects of standards, these

Students learn about math from a tutor in an after-school program. (Skjold Photographs)

single-sex arrangements have not made much difference for girls. Achievement has not increased. Furthermore, girls in single-sex classes do not plan to take more mathematics and science than girls in coeducational classrooms. Nor has there been an increase in the number of girls considering a science or mathematics career. The only solid evidence is the impact on attitude. Girls in single-sex classrooms have a better attitude toward mathematics and science than girls in coeducational classrooms.

The Future
As the twenty-first century began, it remained to be seen whether the latest

reforms would translate into more girls liking mathematics and science, choosing to study these subjects, excelling on achievement tests, and embarking on mathematics and science careers. Parents must encourage their daughters to study mathematics and science and support their career goals. Everyone must be willing to invest in public education. Without paying for well-trained teachers, well-equipped laboratories, and access to computers, schools cannot provide girls or boys with a twenty-first-century mathematics and science education.

Dale Baker

See also Education of Girls; Gifted Girls; Jewish Education of Girls; Learning Disabilities, Reading Disorders, and Girls

References and Further Reading
American Association of University Women. 1991. *Shortchanging Girls, Shortchanging America: Executive Summary*. Washington, DC: American Association of University Women Educational Foundation.
———. 1999. *Gender Gaps*. New York: Marlowe.
Baker, Dale. 1998. "Equity Issues in Science Education." Pp. 868–895 in *International Handbook of Science Education*. Edited by Barry Fraser and Kenneth Tobin. Dordrecht, the Netherlands: Kluwer Academic Publishers.
Baker, Dale, and Michael Piburn. 1997. *Constructing Science in Middle and Secondary School Classrooms*. Needham Heights, MA: Allyn and Bacon.
Bateson, David, and Sharon Parsons-Chatman. 1981. "Sex-related Difference in Science Achievement: A Possible Testing Artifact." *International Journal of Science Education* 11: 371–385.
Campbell, Patricia. 1995. "Redefining the Girl Problem in Mathematics." Pp. 226–241 in *New Directions for Equity in Mathematics*. Edited by William Secada, Elizabeth Fenema, and Lisa

Adajian. Cambridge, UK: Cambridge University Press.
Deboer, George. 1991. *A History of Ideas in Science Education*. New York: Teachers College Press.
DeMars, Christine. 1998. "Gender Differences in Mathematics and Science on a High School Proficiency Exam: The Role of Response Format." *Applied Measurement in Education* 11: 279–299.
Eschbach, Elizabeth. 1993. *The Higher Education of Women in England and America*. New York: Garland.
Leder, Gerda. 1992. "Mathematics and Gender: Changing Perspectives." Pp. 597–622 in *Handbook of Research on Mathematics Teaching and Learning*. Edited by Douglas Grouws. New York: Macmillan.
Murphy, Patricia. 1996. "Assessment Practices and Gender in Science." Pp. 105–117 in *Gender Science and Mathematics*. Edited by Lesley Parker, Leonie Rennie, and Barry Fraser. Dordrecht, the Netherlands: Kluwer Academic Publishers.
National Council of Teachers of Mathematics. 1970. *A History of Mathematics Education. Thirty-second Yearbook*. Washington, DC: National Council of Teachers of Mathematics.
Oakes, Jennie. 1990. "Opportunities, Achievement, and Choice: Women and Minority Students in Science and Mathematics." Pp. 153–237 in *Review of Education Research*, vol. 16. Edited by Courtney Cazden. Washington, DC: American Educational Research Association.
Rury, John. 1991. *Education and Women's Work*. Albany: State University of New York Press.

Mennonite Girls

The Mennonites, a religious sect with origins in the sixteenth-century Anabaptist groups of the radical Reformation, take their name from their founder, Menno Simons. The Mennonites follow the Schleitheim Confession of faith, which calls them to adult baptism, separation from the world, and nonviolence. Today, a wide variety of Mennonites live in the United States and Canada. Each group embraces varying degrees of separation from the world, a fact that largely determines the lives of the girls in their communities.

Although Mennonites in the United States and Canada have traditionally lived agricultural lives, rapid modernization and urbanization have taken place in the twentieth century. This, too, has affected the lives of girls in Mennonite communities. More conservative Mennonite communities, including the Old Order and Holdeman Mennonites, as well as the Amish, are more visibly recognizable as living a life separate from that of mainstream North American society, whereas the Mennonite Conference, General Conference, and Mennonite Brethren groups have more fully integrated into mainstream society. For girls in such communities, the focus of Mennonite identity has shifted from separation to service in the broader community and more active witness to peace and justice concerns. As a result, women and girls have been able to participate more fully in the promotion of these ideals through various means, especially church-affiliated service organizations and educational institutions.

Restrictions on attire have long been an outward symbol of the Mennonites' rejection of worldliness that separates them from the broader American cultural landscape. Indeed, in some conservative Mennonite groups, especially those for which separation from mainstream society is still a central principle of group and individual identity, attire is a way to replace "the eroding function of social isolation and separate (German) language" long embraced by North American Mennon-

Frontispiece from Tillie: A Mennonite Maid *by Helen R. Martin (1904)*

ites (Juhnke 1989, 131). Mennonite girls in Old Order and Holdeman communities are still required to wear "modest" clothing that covers the entire body, and girls' heads must be covered by prayer caps (small bonnets worn on the back of the head). These restrictions on dress are designed to train girls in the biblical virtues of simplicity and social nonconformity and to teach obedience, specifically to Paul's command for women to cover their heads (1 Corinthians 11).

Clothing mandates differ from congregation to congregation. For example, prayer coverings vary "in size, material, strings, and color of string, and in whether

A modern Mennonite girl (Arne Hodalic/Corbis, 1991)

the strings were tied or hung loose" (Juhnke 1989, 130–131). In these communities, girls' attire is more restricted than that of boys. Indeed, girls' and "women's traditional clothing—cape dresses and head coverings—set them apart and forced them to bear the principal burden of separation from the world, a traditional Mennonite value" (Schmidt, Reschly, and Umble, forthcoming, 8). In more mainstream Mennonite communities, modesty is also encouraged, albeit in modern clothing. For example, makeup, jewelry, and revealing or economically ostentatious clothing are often implicitly, if not explicitly, discouraged for both girls and women.

The lives of Mennonite girls have been affected by the role that adult women have assumed in both the communities and the church. In the General Confer-

ence and Mennonite Conference groups, women have assumed new roles of leadership in the twentieth century, which in turn has opened up new avenues for girls. Mennonite colleges, such as Goshen College, Bethel College, and Eastern Mennonite University, are open to young women, predominantly from mainstream congregations, who wish to pursue a college education in a Mennonite academic setting. In addition, roles for women as ministers, professors, professionals, and leaders have also developed within the more progressive Mennonite communities. However, Mennonite women's and girls' "community practices, participation, and influence are often exercised through their husband's [or father's] place in the community or through female-centered activities, such as the Breadmaking ritual and kinship networks" (Schmidt, Reschly, and Umble, forthcoming, 9). This can limit the activities of girls and the opportunities available to them, both inside their communities and in the broader American culture.

Greta Grace Kroeker

See also Catholic Girls; Jewish Education of Girls; Rural Girls

References and Further Reading
Dyck, Cornelius J., ed. 1981. *An Introduction to Mennonite History: A Popular History of the Anabaptists and Mennonites.* Scottdale, PA: Herald Press.
Juhnke, James C. 1989. *Vision, Doctrine, War: Mennonite Identity and Organization in America.* Scottdale, PA: Herald Press.
Kraybill, Donald B. 1987. "Mennonite Women's Veiling: The Rise and Fall of a Sacred Symbol." *Mennonite Quarterly Review* 61 (June): 298–320.
Penner, Carol. 1991. "Mennonite Women's History: A Survey." *Journal of Mennonite Studies* 9: 122–135.
Schmidt, Kimberly D., Steven D. Reschly, and Diane Zimmerman Umble. Forthcoming. *Insider/Outsider: Women of Anabaptist Traditions in Historical Perspective.* Baltimore: Johns Hopkins University Press.

Menstruation

Menstruation in the modern United States has been shaped by a combination of biological and cultural changes over the past 200 years. On the biological side, the average age of menarche, or onset of menstruation, has dropped significantly since the eighteenth century. In the 1780s, the average age at which girls began menstruation was seventeen. Today, due to improvements in nutrition and health care, the average age of menarche is twelve, and it is not unusual for some girls to begin menstruating as young as eight or nine years of age (Tanner 1981). Cultural attitudes toward menstruation have also changed dramatically. In earlier historical periods, menstruation was viewed as a sign of a young girl's transition to womanhood. In modern times, menstruation is viewed as a "hygienic crisis," an attitude that emphasizes personal hygiene rather than rites of passage.

Studies of adolescent girls in different historical, geographic, and socioeconomic settings have demonstrated that the age of menarche is not fixed but is heavily shaped by numerous influences such as fatness at adolescence, physique, health status, genetics, degree of physical activity, and socioeconomic status. Since the reproductive process requires energy, reproductive ability is curtailed in times of food scarcity or when calories burned through physical exertion or exercise exceed the amount of food ingested. Researchers have clearly established that poorly nourished girls, female athletes, and girls with anorexia nervosa and other eating disorders reach menarche at later ages, have higher rates of amenorrhea, and have a greater frequency of menstruation without ovulation than well-nourished girls (Brumberg 1988; Brumberg 1997; Frisch 1978).

Physicians first began to notice a significant decline in the average age of menarche during the late 1800s but interpreted this phenomenon much differently than medical experts do today. Researchers now know that the declining age of menarche is due to improvements in nutrition and health care and the declining incidence of infectious disease. In the nineteenth century, however, most physicians endorsed racist ideas about human difference and looked for physical traits that would demonstrate that working-class Europeans and Africans, Asians, and Native Americans were inferior to white, middle-class Europeans. One of the physical signs that medical experts used to "prove" the inferiority of non-white and working-class individuals was early age of first menstruation, since this trait seemed to place these groups closer to animals. Doctors attributed the allegedly early age of puberty in nonwhite and lower-class individuals to two causes: precocious sexual activity and warm climate. Either or both of these factors, scientists argued, caused a buildup of heat in the body. Since many believed that heat was the engine of growth, anything that caused an accumulation of heat would lead to an early age of menarche. Anthropologists argued that peoples from tropical areas experienced earlier ages of physical maturity because of the hot climate and because these "primitive" cultures encouraged sexual experimentation and marriage at earlier ages than did Western countries (Russett 1989). Physicians noted that bodily maturation in American and European girls could be accelerated by indulging in conversations with men, kissing, or other sorts of sexual encounters. Some claimed that indulgence in sexual activity was why prostitutes and lower-class women had an earlier age of menarche than did gentlewomen (Tanner 1981).

As a result of these views, middle-class parents in the United States viewed declining ages of menarche among middle-class white girls with a certain degree of alarm. Medical advice literature in the nineteenth century advised mothers to prevent their daughters from masturbating, reading romantic novels, and indulging in any activity that might excite the sexual passions. Many physicians also believed that too much consumption of meat contributed to preco-

cious sexual longings and development in young girls and could even cause insanity and nymphomania. Doctors therefore advised mothers to restrict their daughters' intake of meat in order to prevent premature onset of menstruation. In retrospect, this advice may have contributed to the higher age of menarche in the late nineteenth century.

During the nineteenth and early twentieth centuries, doctors viewed menstruation as a pathological process that required close medical management. Most nineteenth-century physicians claimed that menstruation was a potentially dangerous, even life-threatening condition that required constant vigilance throughout a woman's reproductive life. Because of the alleged perils of puberty, menstruation, and menopause, physicians advised women to avoid strenuous mental and physical activities during their periods. These beliefs were closely linked to fears about "race suicide," the idea that the white, native-born, upper classes were dying out because of ill health, poor physical fitness, and lower birth rates compared to immigrants and African Americans. Many of these fears about race suicide focused on the health of college women, who married less often and, when married, had fewer children than women who did not attend college. These theories were used to restrict women's access to higher education. According to the noted Harvard physician Edward Clarke, excessive mental activity drew energy away from the developing reproductive organs, leading to menstrual disorders and infertility. Clarke and other medical experts recommended that girls should not be allowed to attend high school or college, since they believed that intensive studying during adolescence would damage their reproductive health.

Not everyone agreed with the medical theory, least of all women physicians who attempted to disprove the notion that education could damage women's health. Women physicians such as Mary Putnam Jacobi and Clelia Duel Mosher conducted studies of female students and observed that not only was rest not necessary during menstruation, but that physical and mental activity could actually alleviate menstrual pain (Brumberg 1997; Russett 1989). Nevertheless, women's colleges and coeducational institutions played it safe and protected female health by requiring women students to live on campus, hiring college physicians, and making physical education mandatory.

During the twentieth century, changes in women's roles and further medical studies gradually disproved the notion that menstruation was debilitating for women. Growing numbers of women entered higher education and the workforce without any apparent ill effects. Although some physicians undoubtedly clung to the notion of menstruation as pathology, this view gradually disappeared from mainstream medical opinion. The need to encourage women to enter the war production industries during World War II made the notion of menstrual debility increasingly untenable. Physicians combated the problem of "menstrual absenteeism" by emphasizing the normality of menstruation and stating that most women did not need to rest during their monthly courses (Lander 1988).

Popular knowledge appears to have lagged behind medical views, however, for the medical advice literature from the 1940s and 1950s is full of complaints that women were continuing to view menstruation as a "sickness" and "scaring their daughters to death" with lurid tales of the trials and tribulations women endured because of "the curse." Gynecologists may have been exaggerating the extent to which mothers failed to prepare their daughters in order to exalt their own medical expertise. However, historical studies indicate that as late as the 1960s, a significant number of girls felt ill-prepared for menstruation (Brumberg 1997).

At the same time, racist and elitist views about early menarche gradually disappeared. Medical studies of girls who had experienced famine, illness, and other harsh conditions during World War II demonstrated a definite link between poor nutrition and delayed menarche. These discoveries, combined with growing intolerance for racism in scientific theory, completely undermined earlier notions about the effects of climate or sexual activity on puberty and established once and for all that nutritional status is the determining factor in age of sexual maturation (Tanner 1981).

The growth of the sanitary products industry in the twentieth century also changed the ways in which girls experience menstruation. Until the late nineteenth century, most women and girls used scraps of spare cloth to absorb menstrual flow. By the 1890s, concerns about the spread of germs and the desire for disposable methods of menstrual hygiene among women workers and girls in schools and colleges led middle-class mothers and their daughters to make sanitary napkins out of gauze and surgical cotton. During the early 1900s, mass-produced sanitary napkins began to appear and were advertised in women's magazines starting in the 1920s. In 1933, Earle Cleveland Haas obtained the first patent for vaginal tampons, and the first manufactured tampons appeared on the market in 1936 under the brand name

Tampax. The product was an immediate sensation: working women and athletes in particular liked the product because it was less cumbersome and conspicuous than sanitary napkins. The popularity of tampons received an added boost during World War II, as women and doctors alike recognized the advantages of internal protection for female war workers and military personnel.

However, use of tampons by adolescent girls remained controversial well into the 1960s and revealed lingering anxieties about female adolescent sexuality. Many physicians and parents believed that using the product would corrupt girls by damaging or destroying the hymen, thereby paving the way for petting and intercourse. Others believed that tampons caused "erotic stimulation" in the genital area, thereby encouraging masturbation and other undesirable behaviors in young women. Despite these objections, adolescent girls continued to use tampons with or without parental knowledge or approval. Tampons gradually became part of adolescent girl culture in the years following World War II, as young women learned how to "put it in" from friends and older siblings. Using tampons allowed adolescent girls to become better acquainted with their bodies and their own sexuality in a context that was separate from either professional or parental control. The sanitary products industry responded to this growing teen market by offering "small" or "junior" size products designed especially for the adolescent vagina. Manufacturers of tampons also expanded their market by providing consumer education programs in public schools, guided by the philosophy that if "you sold them younger, you sold them longer" by devel-oping product loyalty at a young age (Brumberg 1997).

The transitions outlined above resulted in both gains and losses for adolescent girls. Menstruation has become a normal event, and girls are no longer advised to restrict their physical or mental activities when they have their periods. However, the growing prominence of the sanitary product industry and the emphasis on hygienic management have meant that adolescent girls equate menarche and menstruation with the use of a consumer product rather than seeing these events as part of a larger transition toward womanhood.

Heather Munro Prescott

See also Adolescent Health; Birth Control; Body Image; Female Sexuality; Hygiene; Teen Pregnancy

References and Further Reading
Brumberg, Joan Jacobs. 1988. *Fasting Girls: The Emergence of Anorexia Nervosa as a Modern Disease.* Cambridge, MA: Harvard University Press.
———. 1997. *The Body Project: An Intimate History of American Girls.* New York: Random House.
Frisch, Rose E. 1978. "Population, Food Intake, and Fertility." *Science* 199: 22–30.
Gould, Stephen Jay. 1981. *The Mismeasure of Man.* New York: W. W. Norton.
Horowitz, Helen Lefkowitz. 1984. *Alma Mater: Design and Experience in the Women's Colleges from Their Nineteenth-Century Beginnings to the 1930s.* New York: Alfred A. Knopf.
Lander, Louise. 1988. *Images of Bleeding: Menstruation as Ideology.* New York: Orlando Press.
Prescott, Heather Munro. 1998. "A Doctor of Their Own": The History of Adolescent Medicine. Cambridge, MA: Harvard University Press.
Russett, Cynthia Eagle. 1989. *Sexual Science: The Victorian Construction of Womanhood.* Cambridge, MA: Harvard University Press.

Tanner, James Mourilyan. 1981. *A History of the Study of Human Growth*. New York: Cambridge University Press.

Mill Girls

During the first half of the nineteenth century, the mill girls of New England became the first significant population of female factory workers in the United States. In response to the growing textile industry's need for factory operatives to work as bobbin-doffers, spinners, weavers, and dresser-tenders, large numbers of young women left their rural homes to take advantage of employment opportunities in expanding mill towns such as Manchester, New Hampshire; Chicopee, Massachusetts; Woonsocket, Rhode Island; and most famously, Lowell, Massachusetts. Working in the textile mills and participating in the communal life of the factories and the growing industrial towns afforded these girls a measure of economic and social freedom unavailable to women of previous generations. At the same time, the mill girls had to steer their way through profound social dislocations as they struggled to switch from the relative autonomy of work within a household economy to the regulated schedule of factory employment. In their attempts to reconcile their positions within a mechanized system of industrial labor with cultural ideals about feminine respectability and gentility, the mill girls used literacy and their literary productions in their attempts to forge sustainable identities for themselves as working girls.

In preindustrial America, women's work was an integral part of the household economy. More particularly, the spinning of yarn and weaving of cloth were primarily domestic activities that women and girls undertook within the home in order to meet the textile needs of their own families. In the early years of the Republic, Jeffersonian advocates of the household-based economy and agrarian lifestyle looked upon organized manufacturing with great distrust. As the Embargo Act of 1807 and eventual war with England interrupted foreign trade, the inconvenience of relying upon the domestic production of a rurally based population became all too obvious. For people who looked to promote the development of manufacturing interests in the United States, the making of cotton cloth seemed a promising venture: it was widely used; the raw material was grown on American shores; and though low in price, the sales volume was likely to be high.

The earliest spinning mills in southern New England had begun production in 1790 under the direction of an English immigrant and machinist named Samuel Slater, but these early mills relied on a "putting out" system that actually increased the demand for household labor (Dublin 1979, 15). Only the carding of cotton and spinning of yarn were fully mechanized. Home-based workers were still needed to clean the raw cotton and to weave cloth. Sheltered from the competition of English imports by the hostilities between the United States and Great Britain, the Slater mills initially prospered. But in 1813, Francis Cabot Lowell began to develop a power loom that would make it possible to integrate all the steps in the production of cotton cloth at a single location, thus eliminating the coordination and quality-control difficulties associated with Slater's system of putting out. In 1814, the Boston Manufacturing Company, comprising Lowell and a small circle of Boston merchants, began producing fabric at its Waltham, Massachusetts, mill and was poised to dominate the market for the inexpensive, coarse cloth used by the majority of Americans. By 1821, the Boston Manufacturing Company was paying average yearly dividends of 20 percent on its closely held stock and was looking to expand its operations beyond the limits imposed by the availability of water power along the Charles River in Waltham. Near the small village of East Chelmsford, Massachusetts, the Boston associates found sufficient water power where the Merrimack River dropped 32 feet in the space of 1 mile; in addition, the little-used Pawtucket canal could serve for power purposes, and the bigger Middlesex canal could offer freight and passenger access to Boston (Dublin 1979, 18–19). It was an ideal site to build a "city of spindles," and by 1850, Lowell, which was incorporated in 1826, was the leading textile center in the nation, with a population of 33,000 (Dublin 1979, 21).

Mill girls, most between the ages of fifteen and twenty-five, comprised a significant portion of the population of Lowell throughout its early decades. Needing a reliable pool of workers capable of handling the physical and mental demands of the power looms and other new machinery, the Boston textile magnates recruited the daughters of New England farmers to work in the mills. Typically, the families from which female mill workers came were the less propertied farmers in northern New England. These families did not face severe economic hardships, yet mill employment would have met a number of familial financial needs, for example, sending a brother to college, paying off a mortgage, making farm improvements, or providing a dowry. On average, the operatives worked for twelve hours a day, six days a week. In 1836, mill girls' daily earnings averaged 40 to 80 cents, with those workers employed in the dressing and weaving processes earning more based on their skills (Dublin 1979, 66).

To overcome the stigma attached to factory work and to address parental anxieties about their daughters leaving home to work, the mill owners adopted an attitude of corporate paternalism, which included building company-owned boardinghouses where mill girls could lodge, staffing those boardinghouses with reputable matrons, enforcing a 10:00 P.M. curfew, requiring church attendance, and strictly prohibiting alcohol and "games of hazard" on company property. Functioning as surrogate parents, boardinghouse keepers were expected to enforce these regulations and to report any infractions to mill agents. Although the corporations' efforts were regarded as responsible corporate stewardship, they also helped ensure a docile workforce. Providing their employees with accommodations afforded the mill owners an extra measure of control over the lives of the mill girls, and the company regulations were designed to ensure that workers were sufficiently well fed and well rested to meet the demands of factory work.

In addition to the corporate paternalism, broader kinship networks helped facilitate the movement of these farmers' daughters from their rural homes to the growing city of Lowell. As they sought employment in the mills, many girls were aided by sisters, cousins, in-laws, and hometown friends who were already working in the textile industry. Through these social networks, young women found places in the mills and were eased into their new duties as factory workers.

The experience of entering the mills and taking up wage labor for the first time could be profoundly disorienting for many young women. One writer in the *Lowell Offering* described the experience of a girl when she entered the factory for the first time:

> At first, the sight of so many bands, and wheels, and springs, in constant motion, was very frightful. She felt afraid to touch the loom, and she was almost sure that she could never learn to weave, the harness puzzled, and the reed perplexed her; the shuttle flew out, and made a new bump upon her head, and the first time she tried to spring the lathe, she broke out a quarter of the threads. It seemed as though the girls all stared at her, and the overseers watched every motion, and the day appeared as long as a month had been at home. (Eisler 1977, 180)

To help newcomers adjust to the demands of factory work, overseers used a system of "sparehands": that is, new workers assisted experienced operatives as a form of on-the-job training. In addition to the sparehands system of training, mill girls often helped each other by tending an extra loom, allowing a fellow operative to earn wages while taking a brief leave from work for illness or personal emergency. A mill girl's day was thus a social experience, not an individual servitude to industrial machines. Coupled with the kinship networks that facilitated their transition to factory towns and the fact that the mill girls were a homogeneous population in terms of age, ethnicity, and background, the

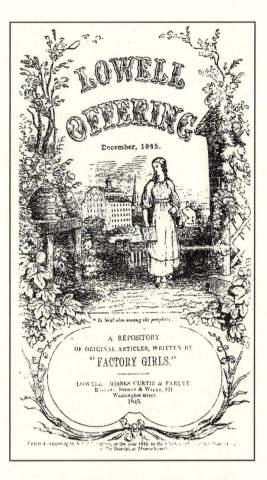

Cover of the Lowell Offering, *a periodical written and published by mill girls. (Lowell Historical Society, Lowell, Massachusetts)*

communal nature of work in the mills helped form a strong sense of solidarity among the factory operatives.

Once the closing bell rang signaling the end of the workday, the mill girls returned to their boardinghouses. Typically, each boardinghouse sheltered twenty-five young women, with four to six girls sharing each bedroom, and meals were taken in a common dining room. The boardinghouses afforded individual mill girls little privacy. One factory operative lamented the "bustle and confusion" of the "overflowing boarding-house," noting: "If there chance to be an intelligent mind in that crowd which is striving to lay up treasures of knowledge, how unfavorably is it situated! Crowded into one small room which contains three beds and six females, all possessing the 'without end' tongue of woman, what chance is there for *studying?* and much less for sober thinking and reflecting?" (*Factory Tract no. 1*, 1845, 3).

Outside the boardinghouses, the mill girls were able to take part in and help create a rich cultural life. Many young women availed themselves of local lending libraries. In her 1889 memoir of life as a mill girl, Lucy Larcom reported that she read the works of John Greenleaf Whittier, Washington Irving, John Milton, Alexander Pope, and Thomas Carlyle; Harriet Hanson Robinson (1976) similarly documented her reading of the novels of Samuel Richardson, Henry Fielding, Tobias Smollett, James Fenimore Cooper, and Sir Walter Scott. Periodicals such as *Godey's Lady's Book*, *Graham's Magazine*, *Blackwood's Magazine*, and the *Westminster* and *Edinburgh Reviews* were also widely read among factory operatives.

In addition to the popular lending libraries, Lowell was a frequent stop on the lyceum circuit, and lectures, concerts, and evening classes were well attended. Professor A. P. Peabody of Harvard recalled:

I used every winter to lecture for the Lowell Lyceum. . . . The Lowell Hall was always crowded and four-fifths of the audience were factory girls. When the lecturer entered, almost every girl had a book in her hand and was intent upon it. When he rose, the book was laid aside and paper and

pencil taken instead. . . . I have never seen anywhere so assiduous note-taking. No, not even in a college class, as in that assembly of young women laboring for their subsistence. (quoted in Robinson 1976, 45)

In addition to the opportunities for education offered by the lyceum and public lectures, many young women chose to affiliate with church-sponsored improvement circles or mutual self-improvement clubs, where they could meet to discuss commonly read texts and share their own writing with each other. These improvement circles ultimately gave birth to the much celebrated periodical publication, the genteel *Lowell Offering*. The Reverend Abel C. Thomas, a Universalist minister, helped launch the *Offering* in 1840, but by 1842 two factory operatives—Harriet F. Farley and Harriott Curtis—had assumed all editorial duties. With its cover illustration featuring a young girl with book in hand while a factory building, church spire, and schoolhouse arise in the background, the *Lowell Offering* featured poems, essays, short stories, and sketches that positioned factory operatives as contented workers whose extracurricular, literary activities marked them as equals to the ladies of the leisure class. After a visit to Lowell afforded him the opportunity to peruse several issues of the *Offering*, Charles Dickens remarked:

Of the merits of the Lowell Offering as a literary production, I will only observe, putting entirely out of sight the fact of the articles having been written by these girls after the arduous labours of the day, that it will compare advantageously with great many English Annuals. It is pleasant to find that many of its Tales are of the Mills and of those who work in them; that they inculcate habits of self-denial and contentment, and teach good doctrines of enlarged benevolence. A strong feeling for the beauties of nature, as displayed in the solitudes the writers have left at home, breathes through its pages like wholesome village air; and though a circulating library is a favourable school for the study of such topics, it has very scant allusions to fine clothes, fine marriages, fine houses, or fine life. (1842, 78)

For Dickens and many others who praised the *Offering*, the link between the literary talents of the mill girls and their claims to a feminine respectability usually reserved for the leisured class provided reassurance that factory work need not be degrading and would not promote female depravity. Although the texts in the *Lowell Offering* were by no means as wholly concerned with depicting the benefits of factory life as Dickens's reading suggests, the competing *Voice of Industry* staked out more radical ground.

Frustrated by the unwillingness of the *Offering*'s editors to acknowledge that workers' dissatisfaction with working conditions had been growing since the mid-1830s as the corporations increased the speed of work and chipped away at wages, Sarah Bagley and fourteen other mill girls formed the Lowell Female Labor Reform Association (LFLRA) in December of 1844 and joined forces with the *Voice of Industry*, a widely read labor newspaper of the day. In 1846, the LFLRA bought the printing press used to publish the weekly paper, and Bagley joined the three-person publishing board. Through

the *Voice*, the mill girls were able to articulate their demands for a ten-hour workday and improved working conditions. The *Voice* published operatives' poetry, sketches, essays, and fiction, which addressed topics as diverse as the dignity of labor and the exploitation of workers as well as subjects more typically labeled as feminine: fashion, courtship, and marriage. More obviously than in the *Lowell Offering*, the mill girls who contributed to the *Voice* were seeking to forge a diverse discourse in which feminine respectability and labor militancy could coexist. In calling attention to their literacy skills by publishing various types of texts in the *Voice*, reform-minded mill girls not only asserted the traditionally genteel prerogative of participating in the print culture but also insisted upon working conditions that would not be so debilitating as to silence their voices (Lutes 1993, 7–8).

Although the celebrated literary culture of the mill girls thrived in the first half of the 1840s, the textile industry and its workforce were already in a process of transformation, and by 1860 most of the farmers' daughters who had journeyed to Lowell had departed, to be replaced by a more fully proletarian immigrant workforce. The mill girls had first "turned out" of the mills to express their outrage over proposed wage reductions and hikes in rates charged by company boardinghouses in February 1934 and in October 1836. The factory operatives viewed these proposed changes as an assault upon their self-worth and dignity. Employing a republican rhetoric and invoking their heritage as daughters of Yankee patriots, the mill girls sought to assert their equality with overseers, agents, and mill owners. Their efforts met with mixed success: in 1836 the mills operated at reduced

This 1868 lithograph from Harper's Weekly titled Bell Time depicts mill girls leaving the Lowell Mill. (Library of Congress)

capacity for a number of months, and the proposed increases in boarding costs were largely rescinded. By the mid-1840s, though, a new labor movement had taken root in the textile industry. The failure of sporadic and isolated opposition to mill owners' attempts to speed up the rate of machines, to increase the number of machines each worker tended, and to establish a premium system that pitted overseers against operatives led workers to pursue legislative remedies against the mill owners. Lowell workers routinely sent petitions to the state legislature requesting a mandated ten-hour workday.

The efforts of the reform-minded workers to improve working conditions were undermined by a number of eco-nomic and demographic factors. By the 1840s, the mills along the Merrimack River had maximized their production capacities, and as the Waltham-Lowell patents expired, competition in the industry increased, driving down profit margins. Coupled with an influx of immigrants, mostly Irish, who were des-perate for employment under any cir-cumstances, work conditions in the mills deteriorated to the point that life as a mill girl was no longer an attractive option for the native-born daughters of New England farmers. Many of the mill girls left Lowell and other mill towns to become schoolteachers, missionaries, librarians, mothers, and wives. By 1860, nearly two-thirds of the mill workers were immigrants. No longer seeking to attract young women workers, owners stopped building and maintaining boardinghouses. The culture of the mill girls of the 1820s, 1830s, and 1840s had vanished from the scene by 1860.

Jane Greer

See also Immigration; Work

References
Dickens, Charles. 1842. *American Notes for General Circulation.* Leipzig: Bernard Tauchnitz.
Dublin, Thomas. 1979. *Women at Work: The Transformation of Work and Community in Lowell, Massachusetts, 1826–1860.* New York: Columbia University Press.
Eisler, Benita, ed. 1977. *The Lowell Offering: Writings by New England Mill Women (1840–1845).* New York: Harper Colophon.
Factory Tracts. 1845. 1982. Reprint, Lowell, MA: Lowell Publishing Co.
Foner, Philip S., ed. 1977. *The Factory Girls: A Collection of Writings on Life and Struggles in the New England Factories of the 1840s by the Factory Girls Themselves, and the Story, in Their Own Words, of the First Trade Unions of Women Workers in the United States.* Urbana: University of Illinois Press.
Freeman, Elizabeth. 1994. "'What Factory Girls Had Power to Do': The Technologic of Working-Class Feminine Publicity in *The Lowell Offering.*" *Arizona Quarterly* 50, no. 2: 109–128.
Larcom, Lucy. 1889. *A New England Girlhood Outlined from Memory.* 1996. Reprint, Boston: Riverside Press.
Lutes, Jean Marie. 1993. "Cultivating Domesticity: Labor Reform and the Literary Culture of the Lowell Mill Girls." *Works and Days* 11, no. 2: 7–26.
Robinson, Harriet H. 1898. *Loom and Spindle or Life among the Early Mill Girls.* 1976. Reprint, Kailua, HI: Press Pacifica.
Ware, Caroline F. 1931. *The Early New England Cotton Manufacture: A Study in Industrial Beginnings.* Boston: Houghton Mifflin.
Zonderman, David A. 1992. *Aspirations and Anxieties: New England Workers and the Mechanized Factory System 1815–1850.* New York: Oxford University Press.

Movies, Adolescent Girls in

Motion pictures have both shaped and reproduced adolescent femininity. Adolescent girls have been populating the screen from the inception of the medium, and moviegoing has been an important social activity of adolescence.

The necessity of appealing to a wide audience clearly dictated both the themes and tropes of the early cinema. The earliest representations of adolescence on film took their subject matter from nineteenth-century forms of popular culture, such as stage melodrama, vaudeville, burlesque, and pulp novels. Among the earliest actors were adolescent girls, partly because the stigma associated with acting in films deterred stage actors from film work. Moreover, these young actors needed little training—early films were very short. There was also a technical reason for the use of young women: because of their lack of wrinkles, adolescent girls photographed well in the harsh lights needed to expose the film used in the earliest movies.

The plots of one of cinema's earliest directors, D. W. Griffith, often turned on the exploits of adolescent girls. Griffith idealized his adolescent heroines and remained fairly consistent in his portrayals of innocent, prepubescent girls well into the 1920s. He cultivated a repertory company that included a number of adolescent girls, including Mary Pickford, Mae Marsh, Carol Dempster, and Dorothy and Lillian Gish.

The most enduring idealized representation of girlhood and adolescence from

1915 to 1930 was the one created by Mary Pickford. She began her film career in 1909 when she was sixteen, already older than most of the parts she would play, and would continue to play children until she was in her mid-thirties. Ultimately, she became a prisoner of her own image. Together, Pickford and Lillian Gish represented two extremes of the Victorian paradigm. Gish was either the victim or the redeemer, whereas Pickford was the plucky tomboy who triumphed over adversity in films like *Rags* (1915), *Rebecca of Sunnybrook Farm* (1917), *Pollyanna* (1920), *Little Annie Rooney* (1925), and *Sparrows* (1926).

Although the earliest representations of adolescent girls in film were idealized and took their content from nineteenth-century literary themes, by the early 1920s such films were of little interest to teenage girls. One theme that would emerge in the 1920s both on-screen and off was that girls' culture was built on both conformity and rebellion. The process of identity formation was tenuous, as girls tried to embrace standards set by the parent culture and struggled to conform to peers' expectations. Institutionalized secondary education, which would become widespread in the decade, encouraged peer conformity and adherence to group standards. By the 1920s, the peer group had become an important family substitute. Moreover, girls gained increased visibility as they began to carve out a cultural space that turned on their styles and fads. The cultural symbol of this new moral order was a teenage girl, the flapper. Although there were still idealized Victorian representations, increasingly the flapper began to replace the plucky orphan. The change also coincided with a shift from working-class to middle-class patronage of motion pictures. Flap-

per films like *Prodigal Daughters* (1923), *House of Youth* (1924), *The Plastic Age* (1925), *Campus Flirt* (1926), *Our Dancing Daughters* (1928), *Our Modern Maidens* (1929), and *The Wild Party* (1929) helped to perpetuate the popular image of wild adolescence and the revolt of youth.

As films about girls made clear, generational differences were more than superficial. Screen teens were clearly rebelling against the parent culture and attempting to assert their own autonomy. The breakdown of traditional forms of authority in both society and film appeared to spur an epidemic of sexual delinquency. There was a fine line separating the film flapper from the delinquent and increasingly Hollywood crossed it. By the late 1920s, the behavior of flappers was labeled as sexually delinquent in a number of screen treatments, such as *Road to Ruin* (1928) and *Port of Missing Girls* (1928). Sensationalist exposés and pseudodocumentaries produced by independent studios pandered to public perceptions and fears about "wild youth." Such depictions reinforced popular perceptions of delinquency while eroticizing female adolescent sexuality on the other. In both films and popular advice, the solution to a wayward daughter was a vigilant mother, so mothers were instructed to keep their daughters on a short rein.

In response to what they saw as the corrupting effects of such films, moral reformers, particularly female reformers, targeted motion pictures in the 1920s. They marshaled evidence to show that the new medium was responsible for the moral decline of youth. Filmmakers shot back not only by increasingly representing female adolescents as a problematic group but often by blaming female reformers for the problems of girls. One compelling feature of films of the 1920s, extending into the 1950s, was the trope of middle-class reformers and club women as "bad mothers." In fact, films have been fairly consistent in their condemnation of parental neglect as the cause of delinquency throughout the twentieth century.

Whether they were sexual delinquents or simply girls challenging traditional forms of authority, adolescent girls in film seemed intent on testing the boundaries of acceptable behavior. Girls themselves were seemingly unaffected by the exposés and exploitation films that were meant to serve as dire warnings to both parents and teens. Although parents might be worried by the delinquents portrayed on film, girls themselves favored representations of autonomous, independent teens like those created by Joan Crawford and Clara Bow, who offered new paradigms of behavior.

The Depression caused serious dislocation for American families, and adolescent girls on-screen were forced to solve their own problems without parental support or guidance. Increasingly, girls were represented as much more competent and resilient than their elders. Certainly, the tendency to mythologize teenage girls must be evaluated in the context of film censorship. Although films about teenage girls in the 1920s often challenged the censors, by the 1930s girls had become a safe topic again. For the first time, there were a large number of screen actresses able to portray distinct adolescent personas because they were themselves adolescents. Actresses such as Judy Garland, Bonita Granville, Anne Shirley, and Deanna Durbin offered clear characterizations that differed from those offered by child stars like Shirley Temple and Jane Withers. These representations coincided with the fact that female girls as fans also began to assert both their preferences and dislikes.

The exigency of war increased the market power of teenage girls in the 1940s. The emergence of a strong subculture and a subcultural icon, the bobby-soxer, was instrumental in the continuation of a public identity for girls. Their increased market strength involved new avenues of consumption, as whole industries, like music and clothing manufacturers, began catering to teenage girls. Bobby-soxers in films like *Janie* (1944), *Kiss and Tell* (1945), *Junior Miss* (1945), *The Bachelor and the Bobby-Soxer* (1947), *A Date with Judy* (1948), and *Father Was a Fullback* (1949) were self-absorbed and blissfully unaware of the world crisis. Although the trope was sometimes a foolish one, there was a kind of subversiveness about this teen symbol. In film, the bobby-soxer operated as a destabilizing figure because she had the power to subvert her father's authority (not to mention his sanity). Grown men seemed all but powerless in the face of the bobby-soxer's cultural practices.

The sexuality of teenage girls has consistently preoccupied filmmakers: it was problematized as delinquent in the 1920s, denied in the 1930s, and then made humorous in the 1940s. Particularly noteworthy were the ways in which girls were either the objects of adult male desire or the objects of continuous worry over their sexual behavior by adult men.

Filmic tropes of teenage girls began to change in the 1950s as the carefree bobby-soxer evolved into the conflicted teen. Representations of happy, carefree teens were hardly a feature of the 1950s adolescent film, and humor was strangely lacking in Hollywood's vision of screen teens. By this time, Americans were no longer laughing at the antics of

Cindy Williams with Ron Howard in American Graffiti. *(Photofest, 1972)*

youth. Films about adolescent girls increasingly began to reflect very liberal attitudes about sex, attitudes that are in many ways more liberal than their early 1960s counterparts. Films like *A Summer Place* (1959), *Blue Denim* (1959), and *Peyton Place* (1957) subtly warned against the double standard and adult hypocrisy and suggested not only that teenage sex was inevitable but that teenage girls had sexual needs.

As Hollywood's dependence on the youth market increased, it began to cater to them through a cycle of delinquency films. Exploitation and sensationalism were used to attract a teen audience.

Although films like *Rebel without a Cause* (1955), *The Wild One* (1954), and *The Blackboard Jungle* (1955) won critical acclaim, the mainstay of the genre was the cheaply produced films of American International Pictures (AIP). AIP was responsible for almost all films made about teens in the 1950s. In 1954, three independent producers, Sam Arkoff, James Nicholson, and Roger Corman, formed the studio to make inexpensive films that would cater specifically to teens. AIP set up shop when other studios producing low-budget "B" films were shutting down. Nonetheless, the AIP producers reasoned that exhibitors still needed B-fare that was topical, sensational, geared to youth, and, most importantly, cheap to make. During the 1950s, AIP released more than twenty films dealing with delinquency alone.

In the AIP product, there were only two kinds of girls—good and bad (or "thrill-crazy" as they were often called in these films). Female protagonists were either gang members, appendages to male gang members, or intent on reforming some boy (usually a gang member). The films featured large doses of sex, violence, hot rods, drag races, and rock and roll. They starred B-movie actresses such as Mamie Van Doren, Faye Spain, Anne Neyland, and Yvonne Lime in films like *Fast and Furious* (1956), *Reform School Girl* (1957), *Dragstrip Girl* (1957), *Hot Rod Girl* (1956), and *High School Hellcats* (1958). AIP films provided the perfect features for the new drive-in theaters that quickly became the province of teenagers.

In the 1960s, films began to center on what television could not—sex. Filmmakers started to go as far as the censors would allow. At least 70 percent of box office revenue continued to come from people between the ages of sixteen and twenty-nine, and studios continued to cater to the youth audience (Cohen 1969, 9). In the early 1960s, they did so by repackaging concepts and ideas about youth that had been successful in the 1950s. Juvenile delinquency was recycled in films like *Because They're Young* (1960) and *Kitten with a Whip* (1964), but by the mid-1960s, films detailing juvenile delinquency lost their relevance. Even the press abandoned the subject, and delinquents stopped being a marketable commodity. Something was needed to take the place of delinquents, and Hollywood found it on the beach instead of the drag strip. Once again AIP was at the forefront of the new teen craze by capitalizing on the increasing public fascination with the culture of Southern California. The cycle began in 1963 with *Beach Party* and would continue through *Beach Blanket Bingo* (1965), *Bikini Beach* (1964), and *How to Stuff a Wild Bikini* (1965). Former Mouseketeer Annette Funicello became the premier beach bunny in these silly, slapstick farces.

After the angst and teenage rebellion of the screen teens in the 1950s, Hollywood turned to more lighthearted, safer, and predictable themes about females in the 1960s. There was a return of the "harried father guarding his daughter's virginity" films of the 1940s, and once again teenage girls seemed sexually irresistible. The 1960s daughters were, in fact, much sexier than their bobby-soxer counterparts and thus more deserving of their fathers' concern in films like *Take Her, She's Mine* (1963), *I'll Take Sweden* (1965), and *The Impossible Years* (1968). Other films about teenage sexuality gave conflicting messages about the permissible boundaries of sexual behavior: *Susan Slade* (1961) warned of the hazards of teen sex, but *Splendor in the Grass* (1961) warned of the hazards of repressing sex.

Although the biggest audience for films well into the 1990s continued to be teenagers, in the 1970s Arkoff was not the only producer finding it increasingly difficult to track the tastes of adolescents. Sex continued to be a staple of films about adolescent girls in films like *The Last Picture Show* (1971), *Pretty Baby* (1976), *The Little Girl Who Lives Down the Lane* (1976), and *Manhattan* (1979). Moreover, the ways in which adolescent boys and girls were relating began to change in the 1970s as girls became sexual aggressors.

Angelina Jolie and Winona Rider in Girl, Interrupted. *(Kobal Collection/Suzanne Tenner/ Columbia Tristar)*

In the 1980s, films about adolescents introduced a new theme: teenage girls intent on losing their virginity in films like *Little Darlings* (1980) and *The Last American Virgin* (1982). The trend reached its apogee in 1984 with the remake of the 1960 classic *Where the Boys Are.* The original film centered on the exploits of four college women during their Easter vacation in Fort Lauderdale. Although the lead character, Merritt, played by Dolores Hart, mouths sophisticated platitudes about the importance of finding out about sexual compatibility before marriage, she is at heart a prude, holding out for true love. Unfortunately, one of her friends, played by Yvette Mimieux, takes Merritt literally, and loses her virginity to a young man posing as a "Yalie," who then shares her with one of his friends. In the film's climax, Mimieux tries to commit suicide because she is now "spoiled goods." The 1984 remake *Where the Boys Are '84* stands in sharp contrast as it follows four coeds, once again on spring break in Fort Lauderdale, who have a contest to sleep with as many men as possible. In the remake men become the objects of conquest and female sexual pleasure.

Another trend in teenage films, exemplified by *American Graffiti* (1972), *Grease* (1978), and *Back to the Future* (1985), was a nostalgia for simpler times. Nostalgia films allowed Hollywood to feature teenage virgins without seeming dated. For the most part, cinema teens were increasingly sophisticated as they came of age in films like *Sixteen Candles* (1984), *The Breakfast Club* (1985), *Risky Business* (1986), and *Ferris Bueller's Day Off* (1986), but they could be crude in films such as *Porky's* (1981) and *Fast Times at Ridgemont High* (1982).

The babysitter has been a destabilizing trope of female adolescence in films since the 1970s. In *Adventures in Babysitting* (1987), *The Babysitter* (1995), and *The Sitter* (1991), girls threatened the sanctity of marriage and family and the safety of children. Increasingly, girls also became victims of homicidal maniacs in a number of slasher films like *Halloween* (1978), *When a Stranger Calls* (1979), *Friday the 13th* (1980), and *Scream* (1996) (Forman-Brunell, forthcoming). The success of films like the cult classic *Heathers* (1989) and *Clueless* (1995) sparked a revival of the teen genre in the late 1990s. The renaissance is due in part to demographics because there are roughly 37 million ten- to nineteen-year-olds. Moreover, teen films are relatively inexpensive to make and do not require big-name stars. They continue to be a staple of the market.

Throughout the twentieth century, films about adolescent girls also commented on parents. Conflict with parents has been a consistent marker of films of female adolescence. Film parents, while sometimes well intentioned, more often have been preoccupied, absent, or simply inept. Teenage girls, however, have resented parental control and have struggled to assert their independence, particularly from their mothers. This theme pervaded two films released at the end of the century, *Anywhere but Here* (1999) and *Tumbleweeds* (1999).

Except for a brief period in the 1930s during which girls were idealized, for the most part they have represented both generational change and societal instability in times of flux or crisis. Although the dominant tropes of girls in film can be grounded in the historical and material conditions of the culture that produced them, this discursive construction is often at odds with the lived experience of female adolescents. Perhaps this discrepancy reveals that girls have been a tangible symbol of both the hopes and fears of the parent culture, which is particularly ironic because teen girls are thought to be a particularly powerless group. Their culture operates in private sites and certainly does not appear to be politically motivated. Yet in films, teenage girls have often been constructed as powerful, subversive, problematic, or in opposition to the parent culture. Girls, in turn, have often used the same destabilizing tropes to create a social identity and to affirm a cultural authority. In their struggle between conformity and autonomy, both on-screen and off, girls have commanded the attention of adults. Films about adolescent girls are not only a formative part of the nation's history in the early twentieth century but a formative part of becoming a girl.

Georganne Scheiner

See also Babysitters; Body Image; Fan Clubs; Female Sexuality; Girls' Culture; Pickford, Mary; Teenybopper; Television; Temple, Shirley

References and Further Reading

Clover, Carol. 1993. *Men, Women and Chain Saws: Gender in the Modern Horror Film*. Princeton: Princeton University Press.

Cohen, Larry. 1969. "The New Audience: From Andy Hardy to Arlo Guthrie." *Saturday Review* 27 (December): 9.

Considine, David. 1985. *The Cinema of Adolescence*. Jefferson, NC: McFarland.

Doherty, Thomas. 1988. *Teenagers and Teenpics: The Juvenilization of American Film*. Boston: Unwin Hyman.

Forman-Brunell, Miriam. Forthcoming. *Sitting Pretty: Fears and Fantasies about Adolescent Girls.* New York: Routledge.

Gateward, Frances, and Murray Pomerance, eds. 2000. *Sugar and Spice: Cinemas of Adolescence.* Detroit: Wayne State University Press.

Goldstein, Ruth M., and Edith Zorrow. 1980. *The Screen Image of Youth: Movies about Children and Adolescents.* Metuchen, NJ: Scarecrow Press.

Jackson, Kathy Merlock. 1986. *Images of Children in American Film.* Metuchen, NJ: Scarecrow Press.

Jowett, Garth, Ian Jarvie, and Kathryn Fuller. 1996. *Children and the Movies: Media Influence and the Payne Fund Controversy.* New York: Cambridge University Press.

McGee, Mark. 1995. *Faster and Furiouser: The Revised and Fattened Fable of American International Pictures.* Jefferson, NC: McFarland.

McGee, Mark, and R. J. Robertson. 1982. *The J.D. Films: Juvenile Delinquency in the Movies.* Jefferson, NC: McFarland.

Scheiner, Georganne. 2000. *Signifying Female Adolescence: Film Representations and Fans 1920–1950.* Westport, CT: Praeger.

Stacey. Jackie. 1994. *Star Gazing: Hollywood Cinema and Female Spectatorship.* London: Routledge.

N

Nancy Drew Mysteries

The Nancy Drew Mysteries (1930–) is the longest-running series of girls' books in American history. The first and most successful teenage detective heroine, Nancy Drew profoundly influenced twentieth-century series fiction by quintessentially defining a type that later became commonplace through many imitators. Independent and powerful, Nancy is hailed as an early feminist icon by some enthusiastic fans and scholars. Others, however, describe her as a champion of conservative social values. This paradox stems from the character's diversity; sculpted over several decades by an ever-changing team of artists and businesspeople, Nancy appeared in books, films, television series, foreign translations, spin-off series, and even computer games. Each of these incarnations presents a slightly different Nancy, so that ultimately the teen sleuth's most stable trait is the mercurial plasticity that allows multiple generations of readers to define her as they choose.

Nancy Drew was the last complete creation of Edward Stratemeyer, an author who revolutionized children's serial fiction at the turn of the twentieth century. A devotee of Horatio Alger's work, Stratemeyer wrote numerous boys' stories that he published widely as magazine serials and as hardcover books. In 1905 he estab-lished the Stratemeyer Syndicate, where he hired freelance writers to complete manuscripts based on his outlines. These ghostwriters received a flat fee and had to agree not to reveal their identities publicly; the books were then published under a variety of pseudonyms owned by Stratemeyer. Using this production method (for which some have dubbed him the "Henry Ford of children's literature"), Stratemeyer produced dozens of successful series, notably the Rover Boys (1899–1926), the Bobbsey Twins (1904–1992), Tom Swift (1910–1935), and the Hardy Boys (1927–).

But books for girls presented a different challenge. The years between 1900 and the onset of World War I saw an outpouring of girls' series fiction, much of which presented active, sporty heroines who spent more time with their peer groups than with their families. These girls at first seem a far cry from the docile, domestic girls of nineteenth-century books, yet they bore traces of residue from earlier conventions. The continued association between girls and a "softer" fictional aesthetic created hybrid heroines whose adventures were tamer than those of their male counterparts. Stratemeyer's early attempts at girls' series, like those of most other writers of the period, achieved only moderate success at best. The first truly successful girls' series produced by the

Stratemeyer Syndicate and Nancy Drew's direct foremother was Ruth Fielding (1913–1934). Ruth began in the tradition of many nineteenth-century sentimental heroines but evolved into a career woman in the film industry, producing and starring in her own films as well as traveling the globe and solving mysteries. Girls of the 1910s and 1920s, who grew up witnessing rather different options for women than their mothers had enjoyed, embraced this independent and accomplished heroine.

One of the ghostwriters whom Stratemeyer hired to write the Ruth Fielding books was a journalist from Iowa, Mildred Augustine (later Mildred Wirt). Her youth, vigorous style, and status as a career woman made her somewhat unusual among the syndicate's predominantly male, middle-aged stable of hired pens. When Stratemeyer devised the idea for Nancy Drew, Wirt was the ghostwriter to whom he offered the new series. Upon receiving Stratemeyer's outlines for the breeder set (the first three volumes, to be released simultaneously), Wirt set about creating a new kind of heroine; she would later say that she had wanted to depart from the "namby-pamby" fare, as she termed it, written for girls in her own childhood. Although Wirt had much freedom in crafting this character, certain of Nancy's characteristics were foregone conclusions. The son of immigrants and a firm believer in the powers of assimilation and hard work, Edward Stratemeyer made all his protagonists paragons of Anglo-American purity, vigor, and middle-class values. Nancy Drew, the blonde, blue-eyed only child of a prominent midwestern attorney, followed this formula, to which Wirt added her own ideals of the perfect heroine.

The series emerging from this collaboration found instant popularity because its central character satisfyingly embodied paradoxes not found in other heroines. Nancy was a self-directed and self-disciplined adult, although she was only sixteen years old (later she aged to eighteen, where she stayed). She was also capable of activities traditionally done only by male heroes in boys' books: she drove skillfully, fixed flat tires and outboard motors, and could single-handedly drag a fallen tree out of the road when it blocked her car. But she accomplished these feats without sacrificing her femininity, for Nancy was also an accomplished seamstress, cook, and pianist, demonstrating the traditional feminine graces. Indeed, one of the staples of the Nancy Drew Mysteries has always been her mastery of every skill imaginable, irrespective of traditional gender expectations.

Gender codes were further blurred in the portrayals of Nancy's clashes with criminals. Dressed in fashionable "frocks," she remained impeccably elegant even while fighting off the burly thugs twice her age and size who tried to eliminate her. The levels of danger and violence Nancy faced were unusual for a girls' series, and the ease with which she prevailed barely skirted absurdity. Commenting on Nancy's superhuman resilience, one author wryly noted that "Nancy is bludgeoned into unconsciousness . . . enough to reduce her to a lifetime of hanging around Stillman's Gym looking for odd jobs" (Prager 1971, 80). Her quick wits and physical strength are worthy of any male hero, and the structure of her stories has even been compared to that of the archetypal male quest myth (Caprio 1992). Perhaps the series' use of some traditionally masculine tropes explains the atypical phenomenon of its mixed readership—for, unlike her female literary forebears, Nancy counted boys among her audience. Her appeal was so wide and so pronounced that, by 1932, *Publishers' Weekly* reported that Nancy Drew was the single best-selling juvenile series in the United States.

Nancy's liminal gender status was matched by her liminal age status. Teenage girls are traditionally among society's least respected members, yet Nancy commanded the respect and occasionally the fear of every adult around her. Early volumes highlighted Nancy's duties in running the Drew household and supervising housekeeper Hannah Gruen, for Mrs. Drew had died when Nancy was a child. The absence of Nancy's mother has been hailed by many readers as a favorite element of the series. Free from the restrictions usually imposed by mothers, Nancy plays second fiddle to no woman. She is the lady of the house, the mother of her own identity, and the apple of her father's eye. Carson Drew, for his part, treats his talented daughter as an equal instead of a child. He gives her absolute respect and freedom, allowing her to embark on outrageous adventures with only a gentle warning to "be careful." When villains disable Nancy's roadster, either by sabotage or in harrowing car chases, Mr. Drew either pays for the repairs or simply buys his daughter a new car. The luxurious upper-middle-class accoutrements of Nancy's life contribute to her freedom and provided an escapist appeal to Depression-era children.

In addition to her famous father's wealth, Nancy enjoys the benefits of his reputation; when officious adults block her investigations she has only to mention his name to obtain her ends. If Nancy's physical prowess and freedom have led many to see her as a feminist role model, her reliance upon and identification with her father prompt others to disagree. Not only does Nancy share an unusually close relationship with Carson Drew, but she also upholds the values of the patriarchal society that he, as an officer of the court, represents. In volumes written throughout the 1930s and 1940s, Nancy Drew defends the property, traditions, and family structures of the white, moneyed classes. The victims of crime whom she aids are upright citizens from "good" families who have fallen upon hard times or have been swindled by nefarious—and often nouveaux riches—criminals whose dishonesty is coupled with a boorishness that signals their social inferiority. These villains frequently compound their lowly status with ethnic diversity. Often described as "dark" or "swarthy," they speak with foreign accents or, at the very least, terrible grammar. Asians, Egyptians, Jews, Hindis, and Gypsies are among Nancy's foes; African Americans are slovenly servants who shuffle their feet, abuse alcohol, and speak in broad dialect. Some feminists understandably hesitate to embrace the class-conscious, patriarchal, and stunningly racist early Nancy Drew as a role model. Others, however, point out that one must take one's heroines in their context. In her day, Nancy Drew was the first series heroine to provide an avenue of escape from the constrictions that circumscribed the lives of adolescent girls.

Stratemeyer's eye for popular trends led him to create some strong book heroines, but he was far from a feminist visionary. Believing that women should be wives and mothers, he forbade his daughters (he had no sons) to work outside the home. But his daughters had to assume control of the syndicate when Stratemeyer died suddenly from pneumonia less than two weeks after Nancy Drew's debut in 1930. Harriet Stratemeyer Adams and Edna Stratemeyer learned quickly to plot and edit manuscripts for their stable of series books. Almost immediately, the sisters added new characters to the Nancy Drew series: Nancy's friends, Bess and George (a girl with a boy's name), and her boyfriend, Ned. These characters somewhat dulled the quest-hero element of the stories, for Nancy no longer sleuthed alone. The new characters also heightened Nancy's femininity; the addition of a boyfriend endowed her with a chaste sexuality, and the extremes posed by her best friends—overweight, frilly Bess and athletic, tomboyish George—positioned Nancy as a golden mean of feminine behavior.

Under Harriet Adams's supervision, subtle changes in Nancy Drew's character became more pronounced over time. An East Coast, Wellesley-educated society matron, Adams had a far different worldview than that of Mildred Wirt, a middle-class midwesterner who worked in the rough-and-tumble world of newspaper reporting. Not surprisingly, the two women had different visions of Nancy Drew, and the chasm between these competing visions widened over time. After writing twenty-three of the first thirty volumes, Wirt stopped work on the series in 1953. Adams used other ghostwriters for a short time but soon began writing the manuscripts herself and continued to do so for the remainder of her life.

Starting in the 1950s, then, Nancy became a very different character. The decade's emphasis on conformity, strict gender divisions, and obedience to authorities mirrored Adams's conservative social values. Whereas the 1930s Nancy had been flippant with dimwitted policemen, the 1950s Nancy deferred to men in uniform. Whereas the 1930s Nancy had extricated herself from dangerous situations, the 1950s Nancy had to be rescued by her father and boyfriend. An even more radical change began in 1959, when Harriet Adams launched a massive project to update and revise all the earlier volumes. Spurred by complaints about the syndicate's representation of minorities and by her concerns that older books were now too outdated to hold children's interest, Adams and her staff cut every book by 20 percent of its length. The stories' pace became quicker and the action more streamlined, and offensively drawn minority characters either disappeared or were minimized.

The results were mixed. Much of the narrative charm that had leavened the series' formulaic rigidity was now erased, as were entire stories. Most volumes were merely "cut down," as Adams termed it, but several were completely rewritten, although the titles remained the same. Along with the outmoded technology and ethnic dialect, much of Nancy's independence and spunk disappeared as well. After the revision process was finally completed in 1977, Wirt's original texts could no longer be found in bookstores. This situation prevailed until 1992, when Applewood Books began publishing facsimile editions of the original Nancy Drew texts. These reprints are now widely available and very popular, particularly among adult collectors.

In 1979 Harriet Adams changed publishers, a decision that had long-term repercussions for Nancy Drew. Since the series' inception, it had been published exclusively by Grosset and Dunlap, but after a well-publicized court battle, Adams transferred all her series to Simon & Schuster. Within three years she died, and the remaining partners in the Stratemeyer Syndicate sold the company to the publisher. In addition to continuing the core series, Simon & Schuster launched a string of spin-off series that created multiple versions of Nancy Drew for multiple readerships. When the series debuted in 1930, it had been intended for girls between ten and fifteen years of age. Childhood got shorter during the next fifty years; by the 1980s, Nancy's primary readership was eight- to eleven-year-old girls. To recapture the teen market, Simon & Schuster released the Nancy Drew Files series (1986–1997), which emphasized romance and consumerism along with mysteries and depicted crimes more violent (including murder) than those used in the core series. The Nancy Drew/Hardy Boys Super Mysteries (1988–1998) joined the three detectives into one team, and Nancy Drew on Campus (1995–1998) sent Nancy to college, where she and her friends confronted issues like alcohol abuse, date rape, and fatal motorcycle crashes in addition to mysteries. (In one surprising plot development, George lost her virginity with a Native American boyfriend; Nancy herself remained chaste, however.) The Nancy Drew Notebooks (1994–), a series for younger readers, features the central characters as grade school children. The core series, meanwhile, also began to modify Nancy's personality slightly. Now written by a variety of ghostwriters from a younger generation than Harriet Adams's, the character Nancy recovered some of her former independence from male authority.

While children of the 1980s and 1990s were enjoying the plethora of new and diverse Nancy Drew personas, their elders were discovering a similar joy with the original Nancy Drew editions; during these decades, Nancy's value as a "collectible" shot skyward. Adults' nostalgic interest in Nancy Drew first began in the late 1960s, when upheavals among American youth led journalists across the nation to remark upon the continuation of a wholesome heroine like Nancy Drew. Considering that 1930s observers found Nancy revolutionary, it is significant that a mere thirty-five years later the same books were seen as embodiments of conservatism: the absence of any sex, drugs, or violence made mainstream journals interpret the series' continuity as a comforting sign that modern children still enjoyed old-fashioned values. At the same time, however, another thread of media discussion about Nancy Drew focused on her radical impact as a strong and self-determining heroine. The term *role model* began to circulate in discussions of children's culture, and the rise of second-wave feminism led to a celebration of Nancy Drew as an early feminist heroine. Articles and editorials expressing this perspective became staples of the popular press; literally hundreds of such pieces appeared locally and nationally during the 1960s, 1970s, and 1980s.

As she had with children, Nancy Drew fired the imaginations of adults through her deployment of paradox: now simultaneously an icon of nostalgia for the "good old days" as well as an icon of feminists' hopes for new and better days, Nancy enjoyed a massive surge of popularity among adult collectors. Original text editions became hot properties at flea markets and antique stores. Among established communities of series book collectors, Nancy Drew fans have grown to represent the largest contingent. In addition to the various editions of the books, collectors prize items reflecting Nancy's several incarnations in popular culture: she has been made into board games, a doll, a Halloween costume, a lunchbox, jigsaw puzzles, and coloring books, to name a few. In 1998 she entered the computer age when Her Interactive developed a series of role-playing mystery games about Nancy Drew on CD-ROM.

Several of these products were released in 1977 and 1978 in conjunction with Universal Studio's *Hardy Boys/Nancy Drew Mysteries*, a primetime television show that alternated episodes of the Hardy Boys and Nancy Drew weekly on the American Broadcasting Companies (ABC) network. Striking a balance that would attract family viewership—parents as well as children—proved a difficult task, however, and the series faltered. Nearly twenty years later, Nelvana/New Line television attempted to resurrect the Nancy Drew and Hardy Boys franchises; the series ran in syndication for only one season (1995–1996) before being cancelled.

These ill-fated television series were not Nancy Drew's first appearance on-screen. During the late 1930s, Warner Brothers Studios developed a string of B-movies based on the books. Although they received moderately good reviews, the films failed because they departed too sharply from the books' portrayal of Nancy. Using the formula of the screwball mystery, a hybrid genre popular at the time, Warner Brothers created a distinctly flighty heroine (Beeson 1994). Moreover, the studio conducted nationwide surveys of teens and social scientists to determine the characteristics of "the typical American girl of sixteen." This agenda, coupled with the conventions of the screwball comedy, resulted in an emotional, slightly bratty, and mechanically inept Nancy Drew whom readers of the books could not recognize. Four films were released from late 1938 through 1939; a fifth was in production when the series was cancelled.

Although the television incarnations of Nancy Drew did not violate the spirit of the books quite so drastically, there were sufficient differences to unsettle fans. Ultimately, all those who sought to bring Nancy to the screen faced similar obstacles: Nancy had a larger-than-life quality, even in the pallid revised texts; she was never simply a "girl next door." Also, because the books never emphasized descriptions of appearance or personality, Nancy remained a somewhat sketchy figure. Readers could thus project their own fantasies onto Nancy, imagining her however they liked. On-screen, Nancy had to be embodied in a real actress. Not only did this force viewers to assimilate concrete details of physical appearance, but also it meant that Nancy became merely life-sized instead of superhuman. Much of the books' potency lay in their offer of a semimagical alternative reality, retaining just enough "realism" to make Nancy's world seem almost attainable. Anchoring Nancy into the corporeality of a real actress destroyed this delicate balance. It also required a single, cohesive interpretation of the character, which presented a problem for a heroine who contained so many contradictions and underwent so many changes.

If Nancy's inability to be neatly pinned down has made her a poor film or television character, it has made her a superb candidate for co-optation by adult interpreters. Creative artists and academics of several different stamps have turned Nancy Drew into a growth industry. Critical attention began in the 1970s, contemporaneously with the encomiums in the mainstream press. While *Ms.* and *Vogue* published nostalgia pieces, the *Journal of Negro Education* and the *Journal of Popular Culture* published analyses of the series' Anglo ethnocentrism and its employment of dubious gender tropes. The 1980s and 1990s saw an increase in Nancy Drew studies by scholars in various academic departments. The watershed event came in 1993, when the University of Iowa—Mildred Wirt's alma mater—hosted a Nancy Drew conference to honor its distinguished alumna. This event produced a spate of scholarly papers later published in two collections and inspired other scholars to examine the series.

During the same period, artists began to acknowledge Nancy Drew's pervasive cultural influence. The teen detective has been translated into successful dramas for children's theater groups and into visual art by photographers and artists who play on the novels' themes. She has also been lampooned in satirical plays and fiction, some of which illustrate lesbian interpretations of Nancy's close relationships with George and Bess (seen as a butch/femme pair). Similar interpretations appear in several academic analyses by scholars of gender studies and queer studies. Nancy Drew's durable influence on American girls also attracts the attention of scholars in education, library science, youth culture, popular culture, and communications.

The qualities that made Nancy Drew such an unusual heroine in the 1930s have by now become common in children's fiction, and the question of how long she can hold a place on bookstores'

shelves is uncertain. But her flexibility bodes well for her future: for more than seventy years children and adults have found new ways to adapt this heroine to their recreational and professional needs. It is likely that Nancy Drew will continue to influence communities of readers, in some capacity, for years to come.

Ilana Nash

See also American Girls Collection; Girls' Fiction; Reading

References and Further Reading
Beeson, Diana. 1994. "Translating Nancy Drew from Fiction to Film." *The Lion and the Unicorn* 18, no. 1: 37–47.
Billman, Carol. 1986. *The Secret of the Stratemeyer Syndicate: Nancy Drew, the Hardy Boys, and the Million Dollar Fiction Factory.* New York: Ungar Publishing.
Caprio, Betsy. 1992. *The Mystery of Nancy Drew: Girl Sleuth on the Couch.* Trabuco Canyon: Source Books.
Chamberlain, Kathleen. 1994. "The Secrets of Nancy Drew: Having Their Cake and Eating It Too." *The Lion and the Unicorn* 18, no. 1: 1–12.
Dyer, Carolyn Stewart, and Nancy Tillman Romalov. 1995. *Rediscovering Nancy Drew.* Iowa City: University of Iowa Press.
Gardner, Julia D. 1998. "'No Place for a Girl Dick': Mabel Maney and the Queering of Girls' Detective Fiction." Pp. 247–265 in *Delinquents and Debutantes: Twentieth-Century American Girls' Cultures.* Edited by Sherrie A. Inness. New York: New York University Press.
Johnson, Deidre. 1993. *Edward Stratemeyer and the Stratemeyer Syndicate.* New York: Twayne.
Kismaric, Carole, and Marvin Heiferman. 1998. *The Mysterious Case of Nancy Drew and the Hardy Boys.* New York: Simon and Schuster.
Maney, Mabel. 1993. *The Case of the Not-So-Nice Nurse: A Nancy Clue Mystery.* Pittsburgh: Cleis Press.
Mason, Bobbie Ann. 1995. *The Girl Sleuth.* Athens: University of Georgia Press.

Plunkett-Powell, Karen. 1993. *The Nancy Drew Scrapbook*. New York: St. Martin's Press.

Prager, Arthur. 1971. *Rascals at Large; or, the Clue in the Old Nostalgia*. Garden City, NY: Doubleday.

Siegel, Deborah L. 1997. "Nancy Drew as New Girl Wonder: Solving It All for the 1930s." Pp. 159–182 in *Nancy Drew and Company: Culture, Gender, and Girls' Series*. Edited by Sherrie A. Inness. Bowling Green: Bowling Green State University Popular Press.

Native American Girls

The concept of community undergirds the traditional socialization of Native American girls, but Euro-American conquest and colonization attenuated that particular role of the extended family and kin network. The arrival of new authorities along with more individualistic values engendered conflict in Native American families and indigenous nations. Reconciliation has often come only with the "re-ethnicization" of girls, a process yet to be unencumbered in modern times by the influences of mass culture and the politics of race and gender. Reshaped by the consequences of war, surrender, relocation, and assimilation, American Indian cultures nevertheless have continued to mold Indian girls' worldview.

In the preconquest period, roughly before the early sixteenth century, an Indian newborn in North America joined a relatively separate and insular world. Girls and boys grew up in a homogeneous environment surrounded by "expanding concentric circles of people who cared for them" (Szasz 1985, 314). Besides the immediate family, relatives, friends, clan or lineage groupings, and secret societies shaped the worldview of the young child.

In most traditional Indian cultures, elders expected girls and boys to learn by application and imitation rather than by rote memorization of principles. Such training was considered pivotal for one to be accepted as a mature member of the tribe. Though training for survival was critical, knowledge of cultural heritage and spiritual awareness were hardly neglected. The instruction, often taking the form of play, reinforced girls' appreciation of Indian lifeways (Dejong 1993, 5, 10). Much of this traditional education came under attack in the wake of European colonization but did not necessarily disappear even in the twentieth century.

The instruction young girls received mirrored the sexual division of labor in the indigenous group. In most societies tasks defined gender; among the Cherokees, the question—"is it a bow or a (meal) shifter?"—inquiring after the sex of an infant was telling (Perdue 1998, 25). Girls were inculcated to respect the complementary nature of women's role that combined with the men's in a symmetry essential for the nation's survival. In Iroquois villages of present-day upstate New York, the "clearing," or human-made structures, food supplies, surrounding fields, and family life, was the woman's domain, but the "forest," or trade, diplomacy, and warfare, belonged to men (Richter 1992, 22–23). Catawba women of the southeastern United States impressed upon their daughters the seasonal nature of female labor; dependent on the land, women tended fields in the summer and in winter gathered edible wild plants, while men hunted for meat and skins (Merrell 1991, 37). Among the sedentary Pueblo Indians of the Southwest, girls learned about farming, pottery production, household construction, and

Two Crow girls on horseback, Crow Indian Reserve, Montana. (Library of Congress, ca. 1906)

basket making—skills they would require to function as wives and mothers in adulthood (Gutiérrez 1991, 8). Omaha girls of the Great Plains, in line with the mixed economy of their society, modeled their mothers' expertise in dressing skins and drying bison meat but also became conversant with planting and harvesting corn (Fletcher and La Flesche 1911, 330). Even in the twentieth century, the centrality of work in girlhood remained paramount; Kaibah (Kay Bennett), a Navajo who grew up during the interwar years, was kept away from Euro-American schooling for a number of years so that she could help her single mother with sheep herding, the mainstay of the Navajo economy (Bennett 1964, 62, 204). Girls also had gender-cum-age-specific chores; for example, among Inuit people, preteen

girls carried toddlers, which freed adult women for work with seal and caribou skins (McElroy 1989, 298). Omaha girls unpacked horses returning from a hunt, and their male peers led them to water and food (Tong 1999, 26).

Surviving the landscape would have been hopeless if the young woman was bereft of cultural knowledge that framed the individual's life within a constellation of human relations. Most Native American societies imparted the culture to children via storytelling. Esther Burnett Horne, part Shoshone and part white and born in 1909, remembered her Indian mother telling her about the coyote, a trickster who represented the perversity, ambiguity, and contradiction of life. Trickster tales conveyed to Horne and her siblings tribal values without the tedium of direct instruction (Horne and McBeth 1998, 18; Szasz 1988, 12–13). Elders also told their young relatives creation accounts or stories that related the origins of their group. Through such instruction, the children came to understand the time-honored belief that their people belonged to the land on which they lived.

To understand the meaning of life, girls and boys had to attain spiritual awareness. Young girls absorbed spiritual lessons through human relationships as well as through ritual and ceremony. When a girl reached puberty, she would have to undergo certain rituals to mark her entry into adulthood. Among the Yakima, Nez Perce, and Puget Sound Salish, both boys and girls went on guardian spirit quests, designed to secure a living creature who could aid and guide the youth for the remainder of his or her life (Szasz 1988, 17). Madonna Swan (Lakota), raised on the Cheyenne River reservation in the early twentieth century, like so many other Indian girls went through rituals commemorating the arrival of her first menstruation, a female life cycle associated with inordinate power. After a four-day period of isolation and many lessons imparted by her grandmother, she was declared a young woman, notwithstanding her biological age of thirteen (St. Pierre 1991, 43). The Iroquois puberty ritual involved retiring into the woods. The girl could return to the natal family after the end of the menstrual period, but thereafter whenever she menstruated, she would live apart from others (Wallace 1969, 38).

Girls in Native American societies also enjoyed play. Like work, play was sex-segregated. Until the process of urbanization in the twentieth century gradually introduced mass culture to Indian lifeways, female youngsters, in the absence of factory-produced toys, depended on nature to amuse themselves. Madonna Swan remembered that her carefree upbringing included playing with homemade beaded buckskin dolls. She and her friends fashioned tents out of full-sized blankets and played moving these "tipis" from one place to another, replicating the seasonal cycle of mobility when families used to hunt the buffalo for food and hide (St. Pierre 1991, 27). Omaha girls also imitated life by shaping dishes out of clay and building houses out of mud (Fletcher 1896, 892).

Regardless of whether it was related to labor or leisure, each aspect of precontact native girlhood involved reciprocity, either in the form of exchange of gifts or bonds of obligations for services rendered or gifts received from elders. But European colonization disrupted the generational lines of authority and eventually destroyed the dyadic status relationship between givers and receivers. Through overt displays of authority, Spanish Franciscan padres in seventeenth-century New Mexico convinced Pueblo children that their fathers and gods were impotent before the friars. The padres reassigned gender roles for men and women, "emasculating" the men in the process. The padres then moved into the parental role by presenting themselves as benevolent fathers and nurturing mothers who deserved the gift of Indian baptisms and obedience of God's laws (Gutiérrez 1991, 77).

In the eighteenth century, unequal power relations also played out in Spanish California. Given the Spaniards' belief in a code of honor that rewarded sexual conquests, Indian women and girls were targeted for seduction, a phenomenon that persisted long after the end of the chaotic

Native American children in front of an adobe church. (Corbis)

Gold Rush of the mid-nineteenth century. The need to dominate the general native population played a role in the assaults and rapes of Indian females by the Spaniards. Indian families, in an attempt recover lost bride-price (which was the exchange for the "loss" of daughters upon marriage), might have encouraged their daughters to engage in prostitution so as to enhance their productive value. Girls and women took this up in the most desperate circumstances of starvation, Indian wars, and sexual assaults (Hurtado 1999, 15–16, 87).

A more common fate for Indian girls (and boys) before the nineteenth century was their status as forced labor, one partly shaped by the demands of an economy tied to mercantilist European powers. As early as the 1610s, English families in Virginia took in Indian children to rear. Motivated by a philanthropic desire to "civilize" the "savages," this practice became a pretense to expropriate native labor when Virginia expanded its lucrative tobacco-growing plantations within the next few decades. Because of Indian parents' opposition, children were often kidnapped or stolen and then sold to other interested parties. Though legally considered servants, most children were nothing less than slaves in spite of the laws passed to protect them (Roundtree 1990, 69–70, 92, 137).

In this context of physical coercion and political disempowerment, Indian girls attempted to control their fate in several ways. Older girls, given the lopsided sex ratio of some war-torn societies, sometimes in the name of self-protection sought to marry Europeans; perhaps the best documented were the cross-cultural marriages between Cree, Ojibwa, and Chippewan young women and fur traders in western Canada in the first half of the nineteenth century (Van Kirk 1984, 9). Given Europeans' indifference to reciprocity, such unions did not necessarily secure free access to provisions or respect for Indian rituals (Merrell 1991, 63–64; Van Kirk 1984, 9–13). Others chose to embrace Christianity—which offered empowering rituals and was to some degree conceptually akin to native beliefs—so as to subvert Indian patriarchy and control the social turmoil of diseases, increased warfare, and dispossession. Kateri (Catherine) Tekakwitha was one of the many late-seventeenth-century Iroquois who accepted the teachings of itinerant Jesuits and, later, like other neophytes, had to flee the harassment of the native non-Christian majority by joining a Catholic-influenced village in lower Canada. Rejecting marriage, Tekakwitha, in a career of almost pathological piety, dedicated herself to virginity, female-oriented Christian societies, and self-mortifications (Richter 1992, 115–116, 126–128; Shoemaker 1995b, 52–54, 66).

A far less widespread response on the part of girls to European colonization was participation in the pan-Indian revitalization movement that gathered momentum after the mid-eighteenth century. Centered around the Great Lakes region, this movement involved nativism and was often spearheaded by the spiritual guidance of prophets, who cajoled Indi-ans of all societies to see their common history of oppression and the need to rise up against their white colonizers. Several of the prophets were late adolescent females; one of the earliest to challenge Anglo-American dominance was Wyoming Woman (real name unknown) of the Delawares, who claimed receiving a vision from the Great Power demanding that all Indians resist accommodationist Indians and Anglo-Americans. Another seer, known only as Delaware Woman, warned her people in 1806 that if rituals were neglected then a whirlwind would soon wipe them out completely (Dowd 1992, xxii, 30, 128).

This revitalization movement did little to stymie the Anglo-American advance beyond the Appalachian range. In the early nineteenth century, especially after the War of 1812, the pressure for removal of Native American groups in the Southeast and Old Northwest to the inhospitable West so as to meet the insatiable demand for lands gathered momentum. The justification for this removal hinged on the assumption that Indians were "uncivilized" and could never assimilate into American life.

Ironically, by the time the U.S. Congress debated the Indian Removal bill, which passed in 1830, many southeastern groups (such as Choctaws, Cherokees, Creeks, and Chickasaws) had already imitated the Euro-American lifeway so as to find acceptance from the white-dominated society. The Cherokees, for example, had by then raised crops for sale, adopted a constitution and a written law code, and impressed education upon their children (Ehle 1988; Foreman 1932). While their elders lobbied and even sued to ward off the threat of removal, young Cherokee girls attending mission schools, of mostly mixed blood and from acculturated families, played the role of cultural brokers. In their correspondence with white benefactors of the schools, they sought to convince Euro-Americans that removal would divest the Cherokees of their homeland and retard the progress of Christian endeavor. Even as they exhibited enthusiasm for the outside world and were contemptuous of traditional ways, they felt they could be as good as whites, thus expressing nascent tribal patriotism (Coleman 1994, 126–128, 132). Choctaw girls, however, resisted mission schooling since it alienated them, given its emphasis on manual labor and physical discipline that ran headlong into a clash with the Choctaw learning-by-example approach to childrearing. Furthermore, their attendance was intermittent because parents used them for manual labor or domestic chores (Kidwell 1995a, 54; Kidwell 1995b, 122–124).

Neither resistive nor accommodationist strategies blocked the process of removal. The various, seemingly endless journeys west told the same story: fatigue, disease, privation, and the humiliation of capitulation took a toll, especially on children (Perdue and Green 1995, 160, 168–169). But the forced displacement of Native American groups to the West did not end Indian-white tensions. After the mid-nineteenth century, Indian nations of the western United States came under siege as American expansion gathered pace, motivated by the spirit of Manifest Destiny. Plains wars raged on for decades, exacerbating the deadly impact of epidemics of smallpox and other diseases along with existing intertribal hostilities. After the end of the Civil War, settlers moved west in increasing numbers into and across Indian homelands. In response to the land

hunger, the federal government coerced Native American nations to sign unequal treaties that required the latter to confine themselves within reservation lands. A dwindling buffalo population, hunted for sport and hide, weakened Indian opposition to this loss of autonomy. With Apache warrior Geronimo's capture in 1886, the American military conquest of the West was complete (Calloway 1999, 281–292).

Even before the wars came to an end Indians were subjected to intense "Americanizing," designed to remake them in the image of white American citizens. To that end, all vestiges of tribal life and culture had to be eradicated, to be replaced by Protestantism, individualism, and citizenship. The Dawes or General Allotment Act of 1887 introduced the allotting of lands to Indians as private property, which white authorities deemed would weaken tribalism and push Indians into mainstream society. Education, however, was key in the attempt to prepare Indians for their new privileges and duties. White reformers and the government preferred to place Indian girls and boys in off-reservation boarding schools so that they could be isolated from "contaminating" native influences. Although education to "civilize" the Indian was nothing new, having existed since early English conquest of the eastern seaboard, what took place beginning with the establishment of Carlisle Indian School in Pennsylvania in 1879 was far more intensive and had far-reaching consequences on Indian children and their indigenous nations (Adams 1995).

Government officials and concerned humanitarians aimed to transform Indian girls into middle-class, Victorian ladies who were domestic, pious, and chaste in line with the "true womanhood" ideology

Native American girls were often forced to replace their traditional dress with Anglo-American clothing and to speak English instead of their indigenous languages, as in this classroom scene at the Carlisle School, Carlisle, Pennsylvania. (Library of Congress)

of the late nineteenth century. Female graduates, government officials predicted, would promote a Christian, "civilized" lifeway and support their husbands in the transition from hunters to farmers. To prepare for that fate, the curriculum for girls at boarding schools emphasized domestic chores, relegating academic learning to a secondary role. Since school officials believed in the educational value of manual labor, by the mid-1880s they relied on student labor for school operations. In many schools, girls washed and mended clothing, cooked daily meals, and cleaned dormitories. Another form of exploitation that grew out of this training for domesticity was the "outing" system, which involved the placement of girls in white homes for the purpose of improving their domestic and English-language skills. The system, however, evolved into a source of cheap labor for white households (Lomawaima 1994, 82, 86–87; Trennert 1982, 271–277).

Because authorities deemed Indians to be lacking in discipline, the entire school routine was highly regimented. Students' adaptation to this new environment varied according to their families' level of acculturation, students' age when entering school, and the presence of siblings. Anna Moore Shaw, of a Christianized, Pima family background, had attended a reservation day school before she was sent off to the Phoenix Indian School in Arizona at the age of ten. Her previous exposure to Euro-American culture along with her cognitive immaturity prepared her to accept without rancor the discipline meted (Shaw 1974, 132–136). In contrast, Helen Sekaquaptewa, whose Hopi people had had a long, conflict-ridden relationship with European colonizers, recalled how mothers attempted to pass their daughters off as older offspring so that soldiers would not take them away to the Phoenix School. And in 1906, when she and other children were finally taken from their families under military escort, she remembered that they were a "group of homesick, lonesome, little girls" (Sekaquaptewa 1969, 96, 121).

Gender also differentiated the experiences of those who attended this forced assimilationist experience. Unlike boys who had more freedom, girls came under heavy scrutiny. At the Chilocco Indian School in Oklahoma, girls could play only within the yards of their dormitories, but boys could freely roam the large campus. Mingling with the opposite sex was restricted to chaperoned Saturday night dances (Lomawaima 1994, 60, 95). Although some girls accepted the limits of movement and socialization, those who came unwillingly to the school or had to separate from traditional families often resisted these impositions. The writer and activist Zitkala-Ša (Gertrude Simmons Bonnin), a Sioux of the Yankton band and the daughter of a tradition-bound mother, was outraged when told that she would have to forsake her long hair on her very first day in school. Since "short hair was worn by mourners, and shingled hair by cowards," she recalled, her only recourse was to hide from the authorities. When later discovered, she

"resisted by kicking and scratching wildly" (Zitkala-Ša 1921, 54–55). Some girls even ran away from school. Other, less overt means of resistance included huddling in the dormitory rooms after lights out to share ghost stories; passing notes to boys in class or communicating with winks, waves, and sign language; and conspiring to outwit matrons so as to avoid wearing regulation bloomers (Lomawaima 1994, 115).

Available evidence points to a failure in attaining the goals of the educational program. Because there were few job opportunities on the reservation and their education was irrelevant in an environment devoid of modern technology, most young women returned to traditional life upon returning home. Moreover, the young women discovered a conflict of values—their elders did not necessarily appreciate their educational achievements. Polingaysi Qoyawayma, a Hopi woman, recounts the tale of how her family rejected the cakes and pies she made in place of traditional food and even treated her as an outcast. Some young women who refused to accept the traditional lifeway returned to the cities, eking out a living as domestics or prostitutes (Qoyawayma 1964, 74; Trennert 1982, 389). The sense of displacement continued to haunt the lives of these young women well into the post–World War II years. Edna Manitowabi, an Ojibwa, dropped out of school in the 1950s at the age of fifteen. Alienated from her family—an emotional estrangement fueled by her resentment over being sent away to boarding school and by the cultural gap that ensued—Manitowabi moved to the city, drifted in and out of manual labor, became a single mother, and eventually landed in a mental hospital because of a suicide attempt (Manitowabi 1971).

But in their adulthood some girls did use their schooling experiences to reshape their lives and those of others. They learned to adapt to a changing world, fused a bicultural identity, and functioned as cultural mediators. The Omaha sisters Susan and Suzette La Flesche parlayed their knowledge of the non-Indian world into efforts to champion Indian rights and improve socioeconomic conditions on the reservation (Tong 1999). Zitkala-Ša penned published essays about the negative impact of American education on her ethnic consciousness, and eventually headed her own political organization, mobilizing the oratorical skills she honed while in school to lobby on behalf of her people.

The arrival of cultural relativism in the early twentieth century somewhat reshaped the lives of Native American girls and boys. The Indian New Deal in the 1930s speeded up the effort to close boarding schools in favor of reservation day schools. Students were also encouraged to attend mainstream public schools. Federal funds were set aside for bilingual instruction and courses in native cultures. But residual prejudices on the part of officials, along with federal-state rivalry, undermined these idealistic goals (Szasz 1974).

Even though forced assimilation via education has petered out, Native American girls in the late twentieth century still suffer from government interference in their lives. Beginning in the late 1940s, the government initiated a program of urban relocation as a means of ending reservation poverty and accelerating the pace of assimilation. Thousands of Indians who moved found the adjustment to city life difficult. Wilma Pearl Mankiller, who in 1987 became the first female chief of the Cherokee nation, recalled that she and her siblings were terrified of the impending move from Oklahoma to San Francisco. In San Francisco they encountered a bewildering range of noises. A confused Mankiller hated her new school, where the students poked fun at her surname and southern accent. Without the support of the extended family or kinfolk, urban Indian girls endured poverty, emotional suffering, substance abuse, and poor health, the last generated in part by fetal alcohol syndrome (defects that stemmed from alcohol abuse during pregnancy) (French 2000, 41; Mankiller and Wallis 1993, 69–73).

Against the backdrop of the civil rights movement, the rise of the counterculture, and unremitting poverty on the reservation, Indian girls who grew up in the 1960s and early 1970s faced the threat of cultural loss when raised by acculturated elders who had received Euro-American educations. Mary Crow Dog, a mixed-blood Sioux, was raised by her mission school–educated grandmother, having been abandoned by a materialistic mother. When she had her first menstruation, her grandmother offered reassurance, but the ritual celebrating that passage of life had long been neglected. Crow Dog recalled that the "whole subject was now distasteful to them [Sioux Indians]" (Crow Dog and Erdoes 1990, 67). The neglect of such a ritual, which symbolically reminded the Sioux of how potent femininity was, suggests a devaluation of women's status in the Sioux nation. Adrift, Crow Dog became a juvenile delinquent, engaging in violence, drinking binges, theft, and drug abuse. Her later involvement in the American Indian Movement would finally offer her the opportunity to reconcile with her ethnic identity.

Native American girls in contemporary times are victims of a long history of racial oppression, which engendered self-hatred among some Indian elders and a generational gap with the young. And yet Native American girls like Yvonne Thomas (Lummi tribe, Washington State) appreciate that history also provides lessons in survival; these lines from Thomas's student writings suggest Indian identity endures amid marginalization: "echoing spirits / you, my people / who have gone / and left upon / ancient canoes / one day you shall / return to your people" (Thomas 1992, 99–100).

Benson Tong

See also Education of Girls; *Kinaaldá*; Play; Pocahontas; Work

References and Further Reading

Adams, David Wallace. 1995. *Education for Extinction: American Indians and the Boarding School Experience, 1875–1928.* Lawrence: University Press of Kansas.

Bataille, Gretchen M., and Kathleen Mullen Sands. 1984. *American Indian Women: Telling Their Lives.* Lincoln: University of Nebraska Press.

Bennett, Kay. 1964. *Kaibah: Recollections of a Navajo Childhood.* Los Angeles: Westerlore Press.

Calloway, Colin G. 1999. *First Peoples: A Documentary Survey of American Indian History.* Boston: Bedford Books/St. Martin's Press.

Coleman, Michael C. 1994. "American Indian School Pupils as Cultural Brokers: Cherokee Girls at Brainerd Mission, 1828–1829." Pp. 122–136 in *Between Indian and White Worlds: The Cultural Broker.* Edited by Margaret Connell Szasz. Norman: University of Oklahoma Press.

Crow Dog, Mary, and Richard Erdoes. 1990. *Lakota Woman.* New York: HarperPerennial.

Dejong, David H. 1993. *Promises of the Past: A History of Indian Education in the United States.* Golden, CO: North American Press.

Dowd, Gregory Evans. 1992. *A Spirited Resistance: The North American Indian Struggle for Unity, 1745–1815.*

Baltimore: Johns Hopkins University Press.

Ehle, John. 1988. *Trail of Tears: The Rise and Fall of the Cherokee Nation.* New York: Doubleday.

Fletcher, Alice C. 1896. "Glimpses of Indian Child Life." *The Outlook* (May 16): 891–892.

Fletcher, Alice C., and Francis La Flesche. 1911. *The Omaha Tribe.* Bureau of American Ethnology Twenty-seventh Annual Report, 1905–1906. Washington, DC: Government Printing Office.

Foreman, Grant. 1932. *Indian Removal: The Emigration of the Five Civilized Tribes of Indians.* Norman: University of Oklahoma Press.

French, Laurence Armand. 2000. *Addictions and Native Americans.* Westport, CT: Praeger.

Gutiérrez, Ramón A. 1991. *When Jesus Came, the Corn Mothers Went Away: Marriage, Sexuality, and Power in New Mexico, 1500–1846.* Palo Alto: Stanford University Press.

Horne, Esther Burnett, and Sally McBeth. 1998. *Essie's Story: The Life and Legacy of a Shoshone Teacher.* Lincoln: University of Nebraska Press.

Horsman, Reginald. 1967. *Expansion and American Indian Policy, 1783–1812.* 1992. Reprint, Norman: University of Oklahoma Press, 1992.

Hurtado, Albert L. 1999. *Intimate Frontiers: Sex, Gender, and Culture in Old California.* Albuquerque: University of New Mexico Press.

Kidwell, Clara Sue. 1995a. *Choctaws and Missionaries in Mississippi, 1818–1918.* Norman: University of Oklahoma Press.

———. 1995b. "Choctaw Women and Cultural Persistence in Mississippi." Pp. 114–134 in *Negotiators of Change: Historical Perspectives on Native American Women.* Edited by Nancy Shoemaker. New York: Routledge.

Lomawaima, K. Tsianina. 1994. *They Called It Prairie Light: The Story of Chilocco Indian School.* Lincoln: University of Nebraska Press.

Manitowabi, Edna. 1971. *An Indian Girl in the City.* Buffalo, NY: Friends of Malatesta.

Mankiller, Wilma, and Michael Wallis. 1993. *Mankiller: A Chief and Her People.* New York: St. Martin's Press.

McElroy, Ann. 1989. "Ooleepeeka and Mina: Contrasting Responses to the Modernization of Two Baffin Island Inuit Women." Pp. 290–318 in *Being and Becoming Indian: Biographical Studies of North American Frontiers.* Edited by James A. Clifton. Chicago: Dorsey Press.

Merrell, James H. 1991. *The Indians' New World: Catawbas and Their Neighbors from European Contact through the Era of Removal.* New York: W. W. Norton.

Perdue, Theda. 1998. *Cherokee Women: Gender and Cultural Change, 1700–1835.* Lincoln: University of Nebraska Press.

Perdue, Theda, and Michael D. Green. 1995. *The Cherokee Removal: A Brief History with Documents.* Boston: Bedford Books.

Pettitt, George A. 1946. *Primitive Education in North America.* Berkeley: University of California Press.

Prucha, Francis Paul. 1984. *The Great Father: The United States Government and the American Indians.* 2 vols. Lincoln: University of Nebraska Press.

Qoyawayma, Polingaysi. 1964. *No Turning Back: A Hopi Indian Woman's Struggle to Live in Two Worlds.* 1992. Reprint, Albuquerque: University of New Mexico Press.

Richter, Daniel K. 1992. *The Ordeal of the Longhouse: The Peoples of the Iroquois League in the Era of European Colonization.* Chapel Hill: University of North Carolina Press.

Roundtree, Helen C. 1990. *Pocahontas's People: The Powhatan Indians of Virginia through Four Centuries.* Norman: University of Oklahoma Press.

St. Pierre, Mark. 1991. *Madonna Swan: A Lakota Woman's Story.* Norman: University of Oklahoma Press.

Sekaquaptewa, Helen. 1969. *Me and Mine: The Life Story of Helen Sekaquaptewa.* Tucson: University of Arizona Press.

Shaw, Anna Moore. 1974. *A Pima Past.* Tucson: University of Arizona Press.

Sheehan, Bernard W. 1973. *Seeds of Extinction: Jeffersonian Philanthropy and the American Indian.* Chapel Hill: University of North Carolina Press.

Shoemaker, Nancy. 1995a. "Introduction." Pp. 1–25 in *Negotiators of Change: Historical Perspectives on Native American Women.* Edited by Nancy Shoemaker. New York: Routledge.

———. 1995b. "Kateri Tekakwitha's Tortuous Path to Sainthood." Pp. 49–71 in *Negotiators of Change: Historical Perspectives on Native American Women.* Edited by Nancy Shoemaker. New York: Routledge.

Szasz, Margaret Connell. 1974. *Education and the American Indian: The Road to Self-Determination since 1928.* 3d ed. Albuquerque: University of New Mexico Press, 1999.

———. 1985. "Native American Children." Pp. 311–342 in *American Childhood: A Research Guide and Historical Handbook.* Edited by Joseph M. Hawes and N. Ray Hiner. Westport, CT: Greenwood Press.

———. 1988. *Indian Education in the American Colonies, 1607–1783.* Albuquerque: University of New Mexico Press.

Thomas, Yvonne. 1992. "Untitled." Pp. 99–100 in *Rising Voices: Writings of Young Native Americans.* Selected by Arlene B. Hirschfelder and Beverly R. Singer. New York: Charles Scribner's Sons.

Tong, Benson. 1999. *Susan La Flesche Picotte, M.D.: Omaha Reformer and Tribal Leader.* Norman: University of Oklahoma Press.

Trennert, Robert A. 1982. "Educating Indian Girls at Nonreservation Boarding Schools, 1878–1920." *Western Historical Quarterly* 13 (July): 271–290.

Van Kirk, Sylvia. 1984. "The Role of Native Women in the Fur Trade Society of Western Canada, 1670–1830." *Frontiers* 7, no. 3: 9–13.

Wallace, Anthony F. C. 1969. *The Death and Rebirth of the Seneca.* New York: Vintage Books.

Zitkala-Ša. 1921. *American Indian Stories.* 1985. Reprint, Lincoln: University of Nebraska Press.

O

Orphans and Orphanages

Although early European Americans considered an orphan to be any child who had lost her father, today, strictly speaking, an orphan is a child who has lost both parents and who therefore depends for her sustenance either upon other relatives or various public or private institutions. Orphanages, which emerged in the early-nineteenth-century United States, fell out of favor, though not entirely out of use, in the twentieth century. *Orphan* has since proved a powerfully evocative term to various American "child-saving" philanthropies and their advocates. *Orphan* has been thus used to designate impoverished children separated from their families for any number of reasons, including separations that happened only after the children had been "saved" by charity workers and sent to live elsewhere. Today, social welfare agencies typically use the term *dependent child* to include orphans, foster children, and other impoverished children who need more support than their parents or guardians can provide.

But beyond the strict definition of the term, orphan is also an ancient literary category. A character type that recurs in many Native American, African, Asian, Middle Eastern, and European cultural traditions, the orphan embodies the resiliency, heroism, ingenuity, and self-reliance that all human spirits need to develop as they come of age in an often explicitly unwelcoming world. From the songs of slavery, various Native American oral stories, and European fairy tales to Jane Eyre, Little Orphan Annie, Dorothy Gale, and the heroines of Disney films, *orphan* evokes an image of an isolated child—lonely and sorrowful, perhaps, but still special, even sacred. Deprived of parents and stripped of overt cultural support, the literary orphan makes her own way in the world, finding people or animals to support, advise, and assist her on her journey to independent adulthood.

Cinderella is the classic example of an "orphaned" girl in the Western folk tradition carried to America by European settlers. In this tale, the princess-in-disguise is trained in the concept of "noblesse oblige" by her long, trial-filled period as an abused daughter of a wicked stepmother and weak father, waiting to be discovered by the prince who will rescue her from poverty and degradation. Literary critics have argued that the orphan at the center of the romantic tradition inherited from Europe represents not only real fears of the loss of parents but also the anxieties of American colonists separated from family, tradition, and "fatherland"— as well as expressing thinly disguised class-based ideals in an ostensibly "classless" society. Among the first and most popular children's novels to be published in America was *Little Goody Two-Shoes* (1787), a didactic story of an orphan girl who eventually becomes a wise, virtuous schoolmistress.

This exaltation of the literary orphan, however, has not protected real dependent girls from various widely held suspicions about their family origins, sexual lasciviousness, and even criminal tendencies. Hence, these potential heroines of romance have also long been recognized as a potential drain on the culture at large—not to mention public monies. In the New England colonies and the South, even young children were expected to provide cheap, much-needed labor, usually as an apprentice, in return for room, board, secular and religious education, and instruction in vocational skills. However, particularly in the case of orphaned or illegitimate children, it was frequently in the master's interest to pay little attention to the provision of any of these rewards. The child might perform only menial tasks and remain illiterate, poorly clothed, and malnourished. Social welfare statutes were directly transported from the English poor laws (ca. 1601), which required local communities to provide support for orphans, usually through village "selectmen." As Nathaniel Hawthorne's most famous novel, *The Scarlet Letter* (1850), would later demonstrate, these men were authorized to oversee the town's kinship structures, mediate all indentures, act in loco parentis for illegitimate children (like Pearl in Hawthorne's novel), and later supervise and fund poorhouses. Sometimes their "charity," however, took the form of auctioning off poor, unconnected women and children to the person who agreed to take them in for the least amount of money. Later, impoverished parents sometimes paid a minimal fee to a service, usually a woman in her private

home, to take infants "off their hands." These children did not generally live long. In contrast to the twentieth century, orphaned infants were long the least desirable candidates for informal adoption or early versions of foster care because their care consumed time and money when they could not yet work.

The primarily family-based structure of northern colonies did not, then, readily care for orphans or other dependent girls, but in the South, the Virginia Company explicitly sought orphans for use as indentured laborers in the New World in its earliest days. Indentured servants accounted for more than half of all people who came to the colonies south of New England, and most servants were under nineteen years old. Labor was especially critical to the large plantations, including domestic labor, so the City of London deliberately transported several groups of children in the early seventeenth century "from their superfluous population" (quoted in Mason 1994, 1) to Virginia. Many of those children did not live to see their freedom. In addition, at one point a group of young women were transported to Jamestown and sold as brides for a specified quantity of tobacco. The use-value of children was so high that strict new laws had to be enacted in England against "spiriters" who would kidnap children, regardless of their familial situation, and sell them to the colonizers for a fee.

All children in both the North and the South were in dire risk of losing one or both of their parents while growing up. However, given the large number of indentured servants that were imported into the South, orphaned girls there were more likely to lack any kinship connections than girls in the North. As a result, these southern girls had greater freedom to determine their own marriage partners than their peers with living relatives, but it also made them ripe for severe exploitation, as has been particularly documented in the Chesapeake colonies. Girls and boys there were viewed as passing from infancy to childhood at age three; children orphaned at infancy were so likely to die and yet demanded so much time and effort that caregivers had to be paid to take them in. After surviving to age three, orphaned girls were expected to earn their own keep—doing domestic labor, caring for livestock, and so on.

Poorer mothers who had lost their husbands were often forced to place their children out with other families in exchange for food or livestock. Wealthier widows, however, also had to act quickly and carefully to preserve the inheritances of their children from first marriages before remarriage because stepfathers controlled all finances from the moment of the wedding and could readily strip stepchildren of any wealth or entitlements. Children without a parent nearby were likely to be worked harder than other children and to receive less education, particularly if they were impoverished or illegitimate children. And even if they did have property, it was in danger of embezzlement by desperate or unscrupulous caretakers. A girl whose father died when she was still a minor was, moreover, also more likely to become pregnant before marriage.

To further complicate matters, in all the European colonies, north and south, enslaved children were, legally speaking, akin to orphans. If the child's mother was classed as property, only the tie to the child's master held legal sway. The system thus sought to create a child who was legally and emotionally without parents by invalidating slave marriages and regularly separating parents from chil-

dren. Although its legal architecture was derived from other European social institutions designed to deal with orphans, especially involuntary indentured servitude, unlike even that asymmetrical power relationship, slavery actively and legally resisted many forms of education, particularly literacy training, in a way incomparable to any other "child care" institution. The lifelong servitude of slavery attempted a complete transformation of human beings into property from earliest childhood. *Uncle Tom's Cabin* (1851) has been credited by some scholars with attempting almost single-handedly and perhaps arrogantly to reverse that dehumanization by sentimentalizing enslaved people for an Anglo-American audience, particularly through such problematic but highly compelling female orphan stories as those of Eliza, Cassy, and Topsy.

Slave narratives and modern histories of slavery, however, suggest that kin-based networks of grandparents, aunts and uncles, and cousins still often managed to adapt to the vagaries of the system and counteract the powerful antifamily force of the institution. The narrative produced by Harriet Jacobs, *Incidents in the Life of a Slave Girl* (1861), in particular, challenges and complicates the stereotypical views of enslaved girlhood, demonstrating a complex social welfare structure within slaves' extended kin networks, sometimes extending to members of the white community and providing care for Jacobs after her parents died and for her children after she escaped north.

As the nineteenth century progressed, the wage-based, industrializing, and increasingly capitalistic international economy—which was thoroughly entangled with slavery—also further broke down traditional European responses to dependent, nonenslaved children. Wage-based

Mealtime at the New York Foundling Hospital. (The Byron Collection, Museum of the City of New York, 1900)

workers were required to move to wherever their labor was demanded, which caused not only waves of immigration to the United States but massive movements within the American states, straining kinship networks and breaking apart families. At the same time, ideals regarding the purity and innocence of children emerged in the broader American culture, popularized by a wide variety of magazines and novels. Little Eva from *Uncle Tom's Cabin* remains the exemplar of this innocence, although she was not herself an orphan. A novel published one year earlier, Susan Warner's *The Wide, Wide World* (1850), was also one of the first American "best-sellers." It features Ellen Montgomery, a middle-class child who loses both her parents. Ellen, like Cinderella, must endure a period of toil and misfortune before being rescued to a life of opulence by her own "Prince Charming," John Humphreys, a middle-class American minister.

Sentimental notions about childhood thus retained their strongest connection to the earliest childhood of the white middle class but nevertheless helped to make the use of child labor, particularly in purely industrial settings, more problematic, even as they increased the urgent need to remove poor children from the streets. Orphanages, reformatories, and houses of refuge were thus created specifically for the care and custody of dependent or delinquent children during the early nineteenth century, to remove them from the influences of the adults on the streets and those in nonsegregated institutions like county poorhouses. And the

orphanages were themselves further segregated, typically on the basis of such categories as gender, religious identification,
ethnicity, age, and especially race.

Such institutions were designed to provide systematic, careful, and regimented
training to counteract the chaotic life
that reformers believed they saw in ethnic communities, urban and otherwise.
Native American children, including
Sioux writer and civil rights activist
Zitkala-Ša (Gertrude Simmons Bonnin),
were regularly removed from kin groups
on reservations and placed in orphanages
or boarding schools in order to be trained
to "American" standards of industry, fru-
gality, and patriotism. City-based reformers feared especially for the virtue of
immigrant girls working and living on
the streets and thus sought to "save"
them from poverty and "degeneracy" and
to reform them to domesticity and obedience. These girls were typically bound
out to domestic service positions or factory work at the age of fourteen, under
involuntary indentures that would last
until age eighteen or marriage, whichever
came first.

Many such institutions, operating on a
combination of both public and private
funding sources, had to market themselves both to governments and individual, wealthy donors. The white male
heads of these groups needed to transfer,
in the minds of would-be donors, the sentimental qualities of little Eva or Ellen
Montgomery to the seemingly less immediately appealing, rough-talking street
waifs and even to potentially "fallen"
girls, since life on the streets was often
equated with rape or prostitution. Indeed,
Horatio Alger's stories of the orphan boy
rising from rags to riches often were set in
children's charities like the Newsboys'
Lodging House and the Children's Aid

Society (CAS) in New York. E. D. E. N.
Southworth, also an extraordinarily popular writer of the period, created a cross-
dressing New York street waif/southern
belle in disguise, Capitola Black, at the
center of her novel *The Hidden Hand*
(1859). Capitola's roguish voice is used to
criticize the limited options for poor girls
on the street who want virtuous employment and emphasizes the difficulty of
avoiding sexual assault and harassment
on the street.

The term *orphan* was thus ripe for
exploitation. Commentators from the
late nineteenth century noted that the
term was often used very loosely, describing half-orphans, illegitimate children,
and others who, for reasons of "moral
depravity," abusiveness, or, most common of all, just plain poverty, were not
able (or willing) to remain with their relations. When used as a marketing term,
orphan thus avoided a direct confrontation with middle-class anxieties about
poverty and sexuality, let alone the rights
of poor families to remain together. It was
thus almost guaranteed to evoke a sentimental response in the mass culture generally—and in wealthy and middle-class
donors specifically—to support private
social welfare programs for impoverished
children. The term allowed people with
power to view those children in isolation,
easily separable from the taint of poverty
that often engulfed their families and
communities. Systemic cultural problems, which many social scientists would
argue were at the root of mass poverty,
could be more easily overlooked, and the
children's group connections could be
disregarded when benevolent, middle-
class administrators made decisions
about their care.

However, it is important to mention
that poor children and adults were never

Orphan train on the Atchison, Topeka and Santa Fe Railroad. (The Santa Fe Collection, Kansas State Historical Society)

simply inert pawns in these systems. Girls and boys sometimes sought help from "child-savers" themselves. Parents in dire economic straits, cut off from kin because of immigration, poverty, or death, would use whatever means they could to care for their children, even if it sometimes meant turning them over to an orphanage or other children's philanthropy. Even the so-called orphan trains plan, an emigration scheme used most prominently by the CAS, sometimes helped to underwrite the costs of transporting adults and families west despite being overtly devoted to "rescuing" street waifs.

The CAS was also in the vanguard of efforts that criticized orphanages, arguing that the best "institution" for raising children was the "Christian family," ideally in a rural, Protestant setting. This anti-institutional rhetoric generally became stronger over the course of the twentieth century, and the CAS's industrial-scale transportation plan, which itself ended in 1929, thus provided a model for the modern foster care system.

Additionally, an increased acceptance of both adoption, which was legally streamlined in most states during the mid- to late nineteenth century, and much later, abortion, legalized in the 1970s, finally led to a decline in the number and population of U.S. orphanages over the course of the twentieth century.

At the end of the twentieth century, the desire of wealthy parents from the United States to adopt children from abroad led to an increasing market for the adoption of orphaned children from poorer nations. Indeed, cultural preferences for male children in countries like China, which instituted serious population control measures beginning in 1979, increased the numbers of girls in orphanages there. Their plight was described in controversial news stories, including a British television documentary entitled *Return to the Dying Rooms* (1999), which described the institutions as cruelly neglectful and maliciously abusive to these girls. This publicity gained the attention of adoption agencies and of adults in the United States to the point that thousands of

Americans and Europeans now adopt orphans from other countries each year. Many agencies and adopting individuals as well as the Chinese government believe that the abuses in the orphanages were exaggerated in the film, which they say played to Western stereotypes about Chinese people, and they cite the government's requirement that anyone adopting from the orphanages must make a mandatory financial contribution to the care of the children left behind.

In the eyes of many critics, orphanages and adoption agencies, originally designed to serve the needs of children, have increasingly come to serve the needs of childless adults. The "blank slate" of healthy orphaned infants holds an especial power in American culture: an innocent victim completely cut off from any potentially still-interested parent, available to be rescued from appalling living conditions and to be given a chance at a better life, is a kind of American dream. Older children with family ties or those with special needs, meanwhile, are much more likely to remain within institutions or trapped in the troubled American foster care system. Many modern dependent children thus lack consistent homes and suffer emotional and physical problems, which are often inadequately addressed by the resources made available to them. And despite the occasional roar of anger, millions of children orphaned by acquired immunodeficiency syndrome (AIDS) remain in dire straits in Africa. Despite the continued sentimental power of the orphan in storytelling traditions, from the ancient oral genres to today's electronic formats, contemporary response to these children remains, all too frequently, inadequate and sometimes even abusive.

Lori Askeland

See also Adoption; Child Abuse

References and Further Reading
Bellingham, Bruce. 1986. "Institution and Family: An Alternative View of Nineteenth-Century Child-Saving." *Social Problems* 33, no. 6: S33–S57.
Bremner, Robert A., John Barnard, Tamara K. Hareven, and Robert M. Mennel, eds. 1970–1974. *Children and Youth in America: A Documentary History.* 3 vols. Cambridge, MA: Harvard University Press.
Gutman, Herbert G. 1976. *The Black Family in Slavery and Freedom, 1725–1925.* New York: Random House.
Holt, Marilyn Irvin. 1993. *The Orphan Trains: Placing Out in America.* Lincoln: University of Nebraska Press.
Katz, Michael. 1986. *In the Shadow of the Poor House.* New York: Basic Books.
Mason, Mary Ann. 1994. *From Father's Property to Children's Rights: The History of Child Custody in the United States.* New York: Columbia University Press.
May, Elaine Tyler. 1997. *Barren in the Promised Land: Childless Americans and the Pursuit of Happiness.* Cambridge, MA: Harvard University Press.
Pazicky, Diana Loercher. 1998. *Cultural Orphans in America.* Jackson: University of Mississippi Press.
Rothman, David J. 1971. *The Discovery of the Asylum: Social Order and Disorder in the New Republic.* Boston: Little, Brown.
Trattner, Walter I. 1994. *From Poor Law to Welfare State: A History of Social Welfare in America.* 5th ed. New York: Free Press.

P

Pets

Mary had a little lamb,
Its fleece was white as snow,
And every where that Mary went,
The lamb was sure to go.

When Sarah Josepha Hale, author and editor of *Godey's Lady's Book*, published "Mary's Lamb" in 1830, she offered her young readers a concise story that connected little girls, kindness to animals, and keeping pets in a manner that reflected changing attitudes toward all three. At the time, middle-class culture was actively redefining what it meant to be a child generally and how little girls and boys should be socialized to their appropriate adult roles. A broad debate on society's obligations to animals also took place in the popular print media of the time, articulating a "domestic ethic of kindness." This ethic viewed the family as the front line for training children into self-consciously kind behavior, and it argued that animals were the first subjects through which children learned to be benevolent toward all dependent beings, including human ones. It also argued that animals were capable of recognizable feelings like love and were exemplars for the values a rapidly changing society needed, particularly loyalty and willing service. Thus pet keeping (selecting an individual animal for special attention and care), which had

been practiced in some American families before the nineteenth century, was transformed from a personal indulgence to an act of high moral purpose, and it became inextricably linked with the course of childhood. In the nineteenth and early twentieth centuries, published advice for children about pets was usually directed explicitly to boys, but girls were active pet keepers, caring for a wide range of small animals and livestock.

The rest of "Mary's Lamb" is less well known today. Turned outdoors, the lamb waits patiently for his little mistress until school ends and greets her with joy. When her classmates ask why, their teacher replies that the girl's love for the animal leads to affection returned:

And you each gentle animal
To confidence may bind,
And make them follow at your call,
If you are always kind. (Hale 1830)

"Mary's Lamb" could theoretically have been called "Harry's Lamb," but that would have been unlikely. In antebellum children's literature, girls were almost always the untutored voices of kindness. This reflected the era's assumption that girls were innately predisposed toward gentleness and nurturance, qualities that would achieve their full expression when they had families of their own. Fictional

The Playful Pets, *colored lithograph. (Courtesy Harry T. Peters "America on Stone" Lithography Collection, National Museum of American History, Smithsonian Institution, ca. 1850s)*

boys, however, seemed to have a propensity to inflict thoughtless cruelty on animals. They destroyed animal families by stealing birds' nests and baby squirrels out of trees; they carelessly tortured and killed toads, turtles, and cats; and they hunted and trapped small mammals just for fun. This did reflect some common forms of play by boys, but popular authors such as Hale, Lydia H. Sigourney, Lydia Maria Child, and Harriet Beecher Stowe worried that such antics were a strong predictor of violence by adult men and had difficulty distinguishing unlovely but guileless acts from truly sociopathic behavior.

Having made the diagnosis, however, authors recommended the cure: pet keeping. Almost forty years after "Mary's Lamb," Hale published an essay titled "Pets and Their Uses," which argued that pets actually "humanized" boys and offered "a great preventative against the thoughtless cruelty and tyranny they are so apt to exercise toward all dependent beings!" (Hale 1868). For little girls, pet keeping simply reinforced their feminine qualities; it was useful but unnecessary.

A double meaning in the very word *pet* also reflected on little girls. The noun was first used for coddled, spoiled children in the late sixteenth century; it was not applied to favored animals until the seventeenth century, when it was first associated with orphan lambs (like Mary's pet). By the nineteenth century, however, *pet* had evolved to suggest a third related meaning, a "compliant, yielding creature" that could be easily bent to a superior (adult) will (Oxford English Dictionary). As popular prints of the time suggested, girls could themselves be seen as pets.

Hence most nineteenth-century advice literature on pet keeping was directed to

boys. A comparison of *The American Boys Handy Book* (1882) by Daniel C. Beard with *The American Girls Handy Book* (1887), a companion volume written by his sisters Lina and Adelia H. Beard, is revealing. Beard provided his readers with instructions on how to make, stock, and care for both freshwater and marine aquaria; he devoted two chapters to rearing young birds taken from the nest as pets; and he insisted that a boy without a dog was "almost incomplete . . . an unfinished story" (Beard 1983, 223). Lina and Adelia B. Beard's ideal girl gardened and played tennis, gave parties, and painted, stitched, and modeled decorative accessories for her home; she did not, however, take care of pet animals.

Given the assumptions of people who wrote advice literature for children, what was the actual experience of girls in the nineteenth and early twentieth centuries? Girls were in fact enthusiastic pet keepers: they kept aquaria, bred canaries and gave young birds as gifts, created elaborate pretend games that included beloved cats and dogs, raised chickens and sold the eggs to their mothers, and wrote poetry and letters to their favorite animals. Although the archived papers of children are relatively rare, the voices of little girls from the past can be found in places like the letters column of *St. Nicholas* magazine, which published scores of enthusiastic letters reporting on pets. In 1877, Annie Curtis Smith wrote about her Maltese cat Pussine, who "rides in my doll-carriage, and don't jump out. She climbs on the shelf outside the door, and rattles the door-knob to be let in. Papa has taught her to jump through our arms and to stand up in the corner" (Smith 1877).

Enough letters, diaries, and memoirs do survive to indicate that, for middle-

and upper-class girls, pets could be an important part of their emotional and play lives through early and middle adolescence. In 1850, Helen Kate Rogers of Philadelphia wrote a poem to her squirrel Chickey, a parody on a popular verse titled "Beautiful Spring," asking: "How shall I woo thee dear little chick / What shall my offering be?" (Furness 1850). Alice Stone Blackwell, the only child of suffragists Lucy Stone and Henry Blackwell, also wrote an "ode" to her cat Toby (she described it as "very dripping") and was much put out when her mother published the poem in the *Women's Journal* in 1872 without her permission (Merrill 1990, 37). As teenagers in the late 1850s, Ellen Tucker and Edith Emerson enjoyed the company of a small green parrot; Ellen reported in a letter that their father Ralph Waldo Emerson called Polly their "green cat" (Gregg 1982, 132). Emily Marshall Eliot of Boston relied on her dog Bounce as playmate and walking companion through the streets of Boston. In 1869, twelve-year-old Emily recorded dressing him up in "my old red plaid shawl, and then I tied a handkerchief on his head and tied an old veil anon and then we played organ grinder." Bounce was a member of the "Free and Easy Club" (Emily, the family cat, her doll Nina, and her brother Willy were the others) (Eliot 1869). In 1870, Kitty B. Putnam of Albany, New York, began her adventures in aquarium keeping with goldfish purchased in Brooklyn during a family visit. By 1871, the fourteen-year-old girl was so fascinated by her aquatic world-in-miniature that she filled several pages of her composition book discussing the aquarium decor (which included "caves" and a small statue of Memmon, an Ethiopian king killed by Achilles in the Trojan War), her care for the popula-

tion of goldfish and minnows, and her active efforts to obtain more captives in a nearby stream. She was pleased that "my fish know me for when ever [*sic*] I come to the globe they all come out from their hiding places in the caves and sometimes they will take things out of my fingers they are so tame" (Putnam 1871).

As the letter from Annie Curtis Smith suggests, pets also provided a medium for playful interaction between parents and children, especially toward the end of the nineteenth century when new ideas about more companionable marriage and family life gained favor in middle-class households. In the 1880s, the three daughters of Samuel ("Mark Twain") and Olivia Clemens allowed their father to name all their pets, along with their dolls, because his suggestions were so amusing. This led to cats with names like Sour Mash and Famine; three collies received as a gift were dubbed I Know, You Know, and Don't Know.

Girls had very large, demanding pets, too. Nan Hayden Agle, a children's author who published an entire memoir structured around the animals on her parents' suburban property outside Baltimore in the 1910s, had as her own particular pet a donkey named Peanuts; she not only drove a cart but rode him saddled and bareback. Elizabeth Wood, daughter of the Pennsylvania artist George B. Wood, also had a donkey for a time, but she and her brother preferred harnessing the family dogs to draw their sleds in winter. Looking back, many people assume that all Americans knew how to ride horses before the 1920s, but in fact, few urban or suburban families could afford to keep them. Riding and driving for pleasure were elite recreations, and women and girls were further hampered from enjoyment by the requirement that they ride sidesaddle. Families that did own horses often treated them as pets, but the association of young girls with special love for horses seems to be a product of the twentieth century. The publication of books like *National Velvet* and increasing middle-class prosperity following World War II meant that the elite hobby spread as some families could afford riding lessons and even a horse or two for their daughters. Before the automobile, fast horses were something about which boys and young men fantasized. When tinkering with cars became a common hobby for teenage boys, some girls turned to horses instead. Recreational riding is now a predominantly female activity.

The demise of a pet was often a little girl's first self-conscious encounter with death, and it provided an opportunity to practice adult mourning customs. Children held funerals for animals that often included improvised coffins and tombstones, but some families had real pet cemeteries where several generations of four-footed friends rested. When Alice Hughes's dog Dick was shot by a policeman for biting the postman, she commemorated the event with a poetic eulogy that included the lines: "And they laid him to rest / With his paws on his breast / Far, far from his own sunny home" (Neupert 1977, 88).

Although girls from middle-class and elite households probably had more pets and certainly had more time to play with the ones they did have, the families of little girls in frontier communities and in working-class urban settings did cherish some animals, and families set aside time and resources to care for them. Ann Ellis, who grew up in hardscrabble Colorado mining towns in the 1880s, recalled that

her mother always kept canaries, no matter how tough times were, and that if one died, "all of us cried at the funeral" (Ellis 1990, 60).

By the twentieth century, then, pet keeping was an unquestioned part of the experience of growing up for both boys and girls. The activity received an additional boost in the post–World War II era, as families with more disposable income to spend began to keep more animals and to spend more money on supplies and equipment; by 1995 the "pet industry" was worth $20 billion each year. In addition to earlier merit badges associated with animals in the 1920s that encouraged girls to raise poultry or other livestock, the Girl Scouts of America acknowledged the expanded role of pets as both childhood companions and a medium for teaching responsibility by creating national merit badges called "Cat and Dog" (1947), "First Aid to Animals" (1947), and "Pets" (1963).

Katherine C. Grier

See also Domesticity; 4-H; Girls' Culture; Rural Girls

References and Further Reading
Agle, Nan Hayden. 1970. *My Animals and Me: An Autobiographical Story.* New York: Seabury Press.
Beard, Daniel Carter. 1882. *The American Boys Handy Book: What to Do and How to Do It.* 1983. Reprint, Boston: David R. Godine.
Beard, Lina, and Adelia B. Beard. 1887. *The American Girls Handy Book: How to Amuse Yourself and Others.* 1987. Reprint, Boston: David R. Godine.
Eliot, Emily Marshall. Diaries for 1869–1871. Entry for March 2, 1869. In Schlesinger Library, Radcliffe College.
Ellis, Ann. 1929. *The Life of an Ordinary Woman.* 1990. Reprint, Boston: Houghton Mifflin.
Furness, Helen Kate Rogers. Letter to "Miss K. C. Brush" (the squirrel), dated

April 25, 1850. Philadelphia: Historical Society of Pennsylvania.

Gregg, Edith E. W., ed. 1982. *The Letters of Ellen Tucker Emerson*. Kent, OH: Kent State University Press.

Grier, Katherine C. 1995. "Animal House: Pet Keeping in Urban and Suburban Households in the Northeast, 1850–1900." Pp. 109–129 in *New England's Creatures: 1400–1900*. Dublin Center for New England Folklife Annual Proceedings, 1993. Edited by Peter Benes. Boston: Boston University Press.

———. Forthcoming. *Pets in America: A History*.

Hale, Sarah Josepha. 1830. "Mary's Lamb." *Juvenile Miscellany* 4, no. 1 (September–October): 64.

———. 1868. "Pets and Their Uses." In *Manners; or, Happy Homes and Good Society All the Year Round*. 1972. Reprint, New York: Arno Press, 244.

Merrill, Marlene Deahl, ed. 1990. *Growing Up in Boston's Gilded Age: The Journal of Alice Stone Blackwell, 1872–1874*. New Haven: Yale University Press.

Neider, Charles, ed. 1985. *Papa: An Intimate Biography of Mark Twain by Suzy Clemens, His Daughter, Thirteen. With a Foreword and Copious Comments by Her Father*. Garden City, NY: Doubleday.

Neupert, Alice Hughes. 1977. "In Those Days: Buffalo in the 1870's." *Niagara Frontier* 24, no. 4 (Winter): 77–89.

Putnam, Catherine Bonney. 1871. Composition Book. In collection of Historic Cherry Hill, Albany, New York.

Serpell, James. 1996. *In the Company of Animals: A Study of Human-Animal Relationships*. 1986. Reprint, Cambridge University Press.

Smith, Annie Curtis. 1877. "The Letter-Box." *St. Nicholas* 4, no. 11 (September): 765.

Pickford, Mary

Known first as "America's Sweetheart" and then as the "World's Sweetheart," Mary Pickford was the premier film star of the silent film era. For a generation she was held up as the ideal of American girlhood. Pickford's typical character was an energetic young girl who grew up by the end of the film and married the hero. Pickford's small size and long golden curls allowed her to play young characters well into her thirties. In a career that lasted into the sound era, Pickford acted in 196 films, 52 of which were feature films. Although she was not the very first movie star, Pickford was unquestionably the most successful. She was beloved internationally, and her hold on moviegoing audiences was unchallenged for a decade.

Pickford started making films in 1909 with D. W. Griffith, one of the great silent film directors. In 1913 she joined Famous Players, the organization that would become Paramount Pictures. For years she was the most powerful woman in Hollywood. Pickford was one of the first actresses to have creative control over her films and by 1918 earned $1 million a year. In 1919, Pickford became one of the founding members of United Artists, along with Douglas Fairbanks, Charlie Chaplin, and D. W. Griffith. In 1920, she married Fairbanks, the other premier star of their generation. For the next ten years the couple were the unquestioned social leaders of Hollywood and arguably the most famous couple in the world. Their marital difficulties and divorce in 1935 were watched with as much interest as their marriage had been. Although Pickford's popularity was challenged by younger stars starting in 1925, she retained a loyal following, and her films continued to earn a profit. She decided to retire in 1933 so that she could leave the screen while she was still a great star.

Although she amassed a considerable fortune, her impoverished childhood was an important part of Pickford's star appeal. Mary Pickford was born Gladys Smith in Toronto, Ontario, in 1892. The story of her impoverished childhood after the abrupt death of her father was well known to her fans. Gladys went onstage as a child along with her sister and brother. Of the three, Gladys was the most successful and was often the sole financial support of her family. The hardship of the life in a touring stock company and Gladys's determination to rise in her profession were the stuff of legend. Eventually, she would join the company of the most important Broadway impresario of his day: David Belasco. It was Belasco who changed Gladys Smith's name to Mary Pickford and gave her the prestige that she later parlayed into stardom and wealth. Many of the roles Pickford played imitated her rags-to-riches story. In the publicity that surrounded those films, Pickford's poor childhood was often cited as proof of the sincerity of her performance. Pickford herself frequently claimed allegiance with working girls.

Pickford's ability to control a great fortune and yet convincingly identify with poor working girls was one example of the way she could embrace seemingly incompatible ideals. For her fans, Pickford reconciled the profound changes in the culture with older, more traditional values. She did this in a number of ways through different aspects of her life. The characters that Pickford played appealed particularly well to the film audiences of the 1910s and 1920s. They combined strength and vulnerability in a way that was modern without being too risky. They were rebellious and tender by turns. In character Pickford could ride bareback, clear a saloon, or take on a crowd of small boys. Yet even at their most mischievous, Pickford's characters

Mary Pickford. (Library of Congress, ca. 1911)

were always sweet: she could adopt small animals, care for invalids, and gather flowers. These coming-of-age stories followed the heroine as she developed from an unruly child into a lovely young woman. Her characters were notably physically active and independent throughout most of each film and challenged conventional expectations of girlish behavior. However, by the end of the story, the heroine's energetic spirit was tamed: she matured and fell in love.

Pickford managed to play characters that were rebellious without being shocking because she played little girls; their youth meant that the characters were sexually innocent and relatively unthreatening to bourgeois culture. By the time the little girls grew up and fell in love, they had learned their manners.

Pickford's stardom fell at a time when women were becoming more financially and politically independent. Within two generations, women had gained the right to own property, to retain their own earnings, to divorce their husbands, and ultimately to vote. Although some of these changes had developed gradually over time, for many middle-class families at the turn of the twentieth century, it must have seemed that the culture was transforming before their eyes. Pickford's characters provided her fans with a kind of compromise between older values of hearth and home and newer attitudes toward marriage and women's work and leisure. She created an image of female independence that challenged some conventions while adhering to others. Although it is impossible to re-create the experience of Pickford's fans, both her film roles and the publicity that surrounded her off-screen life suggest that she responded to both her audience's longing for change and their fear of going too far.

Pickford carried this ability to be both innovative and conventional into the publicity of her off-screen life. She was a shrewd businesswoman and wielded enormous power over her own career, the film industry, and the Hollywood community. She accomplished all this before she had the legal right to vote. With her astute understanding of her value to Famous Players, Pickford negotiated salaries that stunned the world. As early as 1915, a caption that accompanied a portrait of the star published in *McClure's Magazine* commented that she earned more money than the president. By the 1920s, Pickford had become famous for her business acumen and was identified as a woman who managed both her fortune and her production company successfully. She was an independent and successful woman.

Yet Pickford was also strongly associated with domesticity. She was often photographed with her mother and credited her success in large part to that relationship. Although Pickford had no children of her own, the fan magazines often provided her with surrogate children. Her work with a Los Angeles orphanage was widely publicized, as was her relationship with her niece, Mary Pickford Rupp. In fact, Mary Pickford was photographed more often with young Mary than was the child's mother, Lottie Pickford, who also had a film career. During the 1910s, Pickford and her first husband Owen Moore were often identified as one of the many happy couples of the film industry, although they lived together only sporadically and separated definitively in 1917.

In her public image, Pickford managed to combine the image of an independent and powerful businesswoman with that of a good daughter, wife, and mother at a time when these two images of womanhood were considered basically incompatible. She succeeded in this uneasy compromise in part because of the roles she played and in part because of the consistent publicity of her moderate lifestyle in the bosom of her family. The respectability of Pickford's off-screen life matched the innocence of her characters. When Pickford married Douglas Fairbanks in 1920, her image in the popular press and movie fan magazines changed subtly. Pickford was able to hide her separation from Owen Moore for several years and kept most details of her personal life from her fans. In fact, the scandal that surrounded Pickford's divorce from Moore and subsequent marriage to Fairbanks was the first time that the star really faced adverse publicity or even publicity that she herself could not control. Pickford hesitated for several years before divorcing Moore and marrying Fairbanks, for fear that the scandal would ruin her career. She and Fairbanks both rode out the storm and were welcomed back into public favor mostly because they were the two most successful stars at that time and because they both avoided vulgarity or any hint of sexual suggestion in their films.

Following her marriage with Fairbanks, Pickford rarely escaped the glare of publicity. She and Fairbanks were both important celebrities in their own right. Moreover, because theirs was the first marriage between major stars, the marriage itself was the focus of public attention. They were the first great celebrity couple of the twentieth century and attracted enormous crowds wherever they went. On their honeymoon tour in Europe, Fairbanks had to carry Pickford on his shoulders on one occasion to protect her from being crushed by the crowd. The scrutiny into their private lives also meant that Pickford and Fairbanks spent several years before their official separation denying rumors that they were on the verge of divorce. Everything in her life, from her home furnishings to the status of her marriage, was analyzed exhaustively in the press. Some of the attention Pickford invited, but some of it she could not avoid.

Even before her marriage with Fairbanks, Pickford was conscious of her potential as a role model, and the advice she gave her fans corresponded to many elements of her film roles. Starting in late 1915, a daily advice column was published under her name. The column was syndicated across the country and ran until May 1918. From the beginning, the column had an intimate tone. Pickford referred to readers as her friends and told them often how much she enjoyed their letters and photographs. The columns ranged over a variety of topics, including anecdotes from Pickford's work in the film industry, discussions of her close family relationships, and advice on beauty, clothing, or work. At the end of each column were replies to letters that readers had sent in to their local newspapers. Several themes recurred consistently. When consulted about romantic affairs, Pickford advised that her readers confide in their mothers. She discouraged her readers from using cosmetics or dying their hair. She repeatedly assured readers that she considered homemaking and motherhood the highest calling for all women and would sometimes express regret that she herself was not a wife and mother. This advice was entirely consistent with the culture of domesticity that was prevalent during the nineteenth century. However, Pickford often encouraged readers to find work that interested them outside the home and gave detailed, practical advice about how to get into the film industry. The column was actually written by Pickford's close friend and screenwriter Frances Marion, but fans were repeatedly assured that Pickford wrote it all herself.

In later years, after the termination of the column, Pickford would advise her fans in interviews and magazine stories along much the same lines. She continued to valorize work outside the home and domestic work alternately. She could discuss her work passionately and then voice regrets at not having had children, two roles that Pickford herself described as incompatible. This suggests that, like her fans, Pickford was ambivalent about the many changes in women's lives during her lifetime. It was her ability to express this ambivalence so beautifully that fueled her success at the height of her career. By the end of her acting career, film audiences had become more accustomed to women having active careers outside the home and more comfortable with expressions of female sexuality. Pickford ultimately ceded her place as queen of Hollywood to younger stars like Clara Bow, Gloria Swanson, Norma Shearer, and Joan Crawford.

As the most important star of the early silent era and, moreover, a star who avoided scandal, Pickford was an important asset to the entire film industry. She lent the industry respectability when it most needed to prove its worth to political and moral leaders. Pickford not only brought prestige from her early experience acting on Broadway, but she also made decent, wholesome films. From early on in its history, the film industry fought attempts at local, state, and national levels to censor, regulate, and control motion pictures and their theaters. Most famously, on Christmas Day in 1908, the mayor of New York ordered all the movie theaters closed. The theaters reopened the next day, but it was just the first in a long series of battles that continue to this day. The industry attempted to raise the prestige of the films as one strategy to reassure reformers and avoid censorship. In the 1910s, film producers began to hire prominent theater and opera stars to make films. They also adapted famous novels and plays to film or hired well-known authors to write scenarios. The industry began to make longer films that allowed them to tell more complicated stories and to imitate more closely the experience of going to the theater.

The opening of the 1914 film *Tess of the Storm Country* reveals how Pickford served the industry in this quest for respectability and prestige. The film was a huge success for Pickford, arguably the film that made her a star. *Tess* was an adaptation of a best-selling novel that told the story of a squatter village struggling to survive on the shores of Cayuga Lake. Tess was the high-spirited heroine who ultimately saved the village from wealthy landowners who were determined to destroy it. The film opened with a prologue in which Pickford emerged from behind a stage curtain and arranged a large bunch of roses in a vase. She was beautifully dressed, and her hair was arranged in long curls down her back. She looked every inch the Broadway star. The prologue served no narrative purpose in the film, but it did remind the audience of Pickford's association with prestigious theater productions. The prologue further reminded viewers that when not in character, Pickford was a very demure young woman. In contrast, the role of Tess required Pickford to spend the entire film barefoot and in rags. Her famous hair was a tangled mess, and she was generally very grubby. Tess was a hoyden and a mischief maker. Although she ultimately learned her manners and married the hero, Tess spent most of the film defying authority. When the story was introduced with the short scene of Pickford arranging flowers, the audience could see her as both the dainty young lady and the defiant spitfire. Pickford had it both ways: her character's high spirits were daring and appealingly modern, and the prologue reminded readers of the star's association with high culture. Pickford could appeal to audiences' desire for new and exciting images of femininity while reassuring them that she continued to embrace middle-class values of gentility and sexual respectability.

Anne Burri Wolverton

See also Movies, Adolescent Girls in;
   Temple, Shirley

References and Further Reading
Basinger, Jeanine. 1999. *Silent Stars*. New
   York: Alfred A. Knopf.
Beauchamp, Cari. 1997. *Without Lying
   Down: Frances Marion and the
   Powerful Women of Early Hollywood*.
   New York: Scribner.
Bowser, Eileen. 1990. *The Transformation
   of Cinema, 1907–1915*. Vol. 2, *History
   of the American Cinema*. Berkeley:
   University of California Press.
Brownlow, Kevin. 1999. *Mary Pickford
   Rediscovered: Rare Pictures of a
   Hollywood Legend*. New York: Harry
   N. Abrams, in association with the
   Academy of Motion Picture Arts and
   Sciences.
Eyman, Scott. 1990. *Mary Pickford: From
   Here to Hollywood*. New York: Donald
   I. Fine.
Koszarski, Richard. 1990. *An Evening's
   Entertainment: The Age of the Silent
   Feature Picture, 1915–1928*. Vol. 3,
   History of the American Cinema.
   Berkeley: University of California
   Press.
Pickford, Mary. 1956. *Sunshine and
   Shadow: The Autobiography of Mary
   Pickford*. London: William Heineman.
Whitfield, Eileen. 1997. *Pickford: The
   Woman Who Made Hollywood*.
   Lexington: University Press of
   Kentucky.

Play

Girls' play over more than 400 years of
America's past has been culturally constructed. In Puritan New England with
its subsistence economy, play and playthings were widely regarded as unproduc-
tive distractions to adults and children
alike. By the end of the colonial period,
however, leisure invigorated laborers,
and play became the work of children.
Since the acceptance of play in the second half of the eighteenth century, adults
have used toys, especially dolls and
miniature household equipment, to

socialize girls according to prevailing
notions of gender. As the material culture of play, girls' toys have been shaped
as well by changing economies, philosophies, ideologies, demography, technology, and fashion. In response to the narrow
limits imposed on their play, girls of all
ages, classes, races, and regions over the
past 300 years have contested play's
socializing purposes with the games,
dolls, and toys given to girls or appropriated by them.

For centuries before the arrival of Europeans, Seneca girls spent much of their
infancy entertained by lavishly decorated
hoops attached to fur-covered cradle
boards to which they were swaddled.
When they could walk, girls were free to
play and pry and even indulge in early sexual experimentation. Seneca parents
praised their daughters' achievements and
did not punish them for their wrongdoing,
according to the many Euro-American
trappers, traders, colonists, and missionaries who chronicled their observations.
Despite the many differences between
tribes, girls' play aimed to teach cultural
beliefs and traditions and to serve as
instructional models of mothers' work.
According to one Jesuit missionary,
"Whenever they begin to put one foot in
front of the other, [girls] have a little stick
put into their hands [in order] to train
them and teach them early to pound corn,
and when they are grown somewhat they
also play various games with their com-
panions, and in the course of these small
frolics they are trained to perform trifling
and petty household duties" (quoted in
Axtell 1981, 34).

Seventeenth-century Puritan girls,
however, were allowed few indulgences.
There were no nurseries, and what little
baby furniture there was, such as walking stools, served to inhibit toddlers'

movements and force them to imitate their "upstanding" elders. In her study of American portraits of children, Karin Calvert found no playthings before 1750, though girls in the middle and southern colonies raced, wrestled, played tag, and played with tops. Doll "poppets" symbolized the presence of dangerous demonic forces in New England, whereas rag babies were the only dolls durable enough for little girls in places like Pennsylvania. But everywhere in the seventeenth century, the word *toy* simply referred to something that was amusing to anyone, regardless of age. In Puritan New England, "Toys were temptations to idleness, reverie, and fantasy" (Calvert 1992, 50). And play at any age was generally discouraged, "lest they should think diversion to be a better and nobler thing than diligence," explained colonial minister Cotton Mather (quoted in Pollock 1987, 148).

Like their elders, Puritan girls' ability to play was restrained by custom and also constrained by clothing. Swaddled in strips of linen and shoved into airless, hooded cradles, baby girls could do little but lie still. Puritan girls wore stiffened petticoats until the age of six, when they donned similarly restrictive garments also worn by adult women. Regardless of what they wore, there was little time to play in Puritan households, where girls spent their days assisting mothers and other females in an endless routine of household activities and farm chores. Aimed at lightening their labors were the spontaneous games played by siblings and teenage servants who tossed swaddled babies like footballs.

It was not until the end of the seventeenth century that girls in Andover, Massachusetts, challenged community customs by "night walking." At taverns,

the "licentious" daughters of both elite and laboring-class families kept company with neighborhood youth, caroused, drank, danced, frolicked, fought, and fornicated. Also influenced by social, cultural, economic, and political transformations in New England were preadolescent and adolescent girls in Salem, Massachusetts, who played a dangerous game with fatal consequences. Using egg whites, water, and the supernatural, they attempted to decipher the identity of their future husbands. Their divining game caused unprecedented alarm among their religious elders, who were deeply troubled by fears of demonic possession.

The play of girls and the recreations of their older sisters changed over the course of the eighteenth century because of the gradual decline of paternal control, the rise of prosperity, and the importance of privacy. For older girls, this meant greater choices in whom to spend their time with and how. Increasingly, young women could avoid adult surveillance by going to another room instead of having to share cramped domestic space typical of seventeenth-century dwellings. More young women clearly indulged in unsanctioned activity with young men as the percentage of pregnant brides rose to more than 40 percent in some eighteenth-century New England towns.

Over time, John Locke, Jean-Jacques Rousseau, and other Enlightenment thinkers led parents to view their daughters as innocent individuals with age-appropriate needs and abilities. Although reading material remained as limited as girls' access to it, sex- and age-appropriate toys became acceptable when play was viewed as a learning process crucial to childhood development. Toys became the province of childhood and dolls the exclusive domain of girls now encouraged to practice the domestic and maternal activities of women. That is why George Washington ordered dolls and doll furniture for his stepdaughter Patcy Curtis from a London toymaker in 1760 and why New England sea captains brought back dolls to daughters in Salem and Boston. Using string, straws, rags, and water, girls pretended to spin yarn, wash clothes, and scrub floors.

Whether playing with dolls or other gender-appropriate toys, girls in the eighteenth century were able to move their bodies in less restricted ways as loose-fitting dresses replaced the stiffened stays of a bygone era. Rousseau had recommended that the "limbs of a growing child should be free to move easily in his clothing; nothing should cramp their growth or movement; there should be nothing tight, nothing fitting closely to the body, no belts of any kind" (1762, 91). Nor were hairstyles to constrain girls, as an androgynous shoulder-length haircut with bangs replaced tight, hairpinned coifs.

In South Carolina and elsewhere in the South, elite girls played more than had seventeenth-century indentured servants and hardworking daughters of planters. A higher standard of living (related to the rise of slavery) and family stability (because of decreased death rates and increased rates of life expectancy) led to a more child-centered family life. Members of the gentry experienced more parental intimacy, affection, and tenderness and were given more toys. Parents celebrated births and christenings and gave their children nicknames, and mothers in particular forged lifelong friendships with their daughters. But increasingly rigid gender-role expectations—that girls be compliant beauties with feminine charms—inhibited girls' development. Acceptable play became those activities that imbued girls with the cardinal virtues of southern femininity: modesty, meekness, compassion, affability, piety, and passivity. Their brothers' games and play encouraged autonomy, self-reliance, honesty, virtue, obedience, and self-control. But girls *themselves* were expected to be the precious, frivolous, and amusing playthings of their families. The aim of pleasing others was reinforced in the music, drawing, dancing, needlework, and poetry curriculum that comprised an elite girl's education.

In Victorian prints, pictures, portraits, and poetry, frail and fair girls dressed in their best clothes cradled exquisite dolls. These nineteenth-century representations had been influenced by Enlightenment philosophy, the doctrine of republican motherhood, and Victorian gender ideology that aimed to train daughters to assume their allotted role as middle-class wives and mothers. Girls' play in particular was to instill such newly devised bourgeois values as restraint, regularity, self-control, and discipline and to nurture such feminine virtues as purity, piety, domesticity, and submission. In order to teach girls how to assume their proper role, they were to serve an informal apprenticeship in a female world sheltered from the corrupting influence of the masculine public sphere.

The mastering of requisite feminine skills and sensibilities shaped girls' play activities and vice versa. Widely represented as winged angels, shepherdesses, and gardeners, Christian girls were to find satisfaction in Bible reading and hymn singing and to observe the Sabbath by not playing. Books such as *Anecdotes for Girls* (1854) emphasized the importance of feminine submission and devotion to duty. Others taught deportment and decorum to future wives of businessmen, professionals, or statesmen. Lydia Maria Child's *The Girl's Own Book* (1833) encouraged girls to practice polite social rituals while "visiting" and at tea parties and dances. Diary keeping was intended to record the development of a girl's moral character, and fancy work and playing the piano were windows into the purity of their souls. Domesticity, consisting of a great variety of household skills and feminine accomplishments that built character, was to be mastered through sewing samplers, painting, making dolls, and participating in other leisure activities that signified middle-class status.

Inventors and entrepreneurs responded to the concerns of middle-class families and the suggestions of domestic experts for sex-segregated toys that promoted utility, morality, and gender stereotyping. Girls' toys—an increasing assortment of dolls, dollhouses, doll clothes, and miniature furnishings and housewares—were intended to nurture their inherent domestic and maternal nature. Made of china, wax, and other fragile materials, commercially produced dolls required delicate motions and careful play. Daughters received fewer toys than did sons, whose toys were also more varied and durable. The gradual proliferation of toys of all kinds over the course of the nineteenth century was due to the rise of international trade and the growth of a domestic toy industry. Although few toys were intended for both girls and boys, printers and publishers did produce games such as Mansion of Happiness for parlor entertainments.

In the American popular imagination, shaped in large part by prolific images and iconography, Victorian girls were all white, middle-class, and uniformly angelic. In the words of one contemporary poet, girls were "sugar and spice and all things nice." But this idealized portrait reflected how things *ought* to be rather than representing a reality that was far more complex and contested. Through both sanctioned and unsanctioned play, Victorian girls resisted and rebelled against narrow definitions of acceptable feminine activities. For example, instead of making dolls or playing in the parlor with the expensive ones their mothers kept under lock and key, rural girls preferred more vigorous play. With little encouragement given to girls like Lucy Larcom by adults and experts, they nevertheless actively explored fields, rivers, quarries, and cemeteries where they rolled hoops, jumped rope, tossed snowballs, skated, sled, raced, and enjoyed other activities that inadvertently challenged gendered norms. With friends, they put on plays, and in attics girls secretly played cards with decks they created.

The new "Brutus" or "Titus" haircut, which required no hairpins or small combs, contributed to girls' ability to engage in unfettered play. Such changing fashions as loose-fitting and short frocks (hemmed well above the ankles) worn over "pantalettes" (later called "bloomers") also freed girls from constraints. The introduction of "pantaloons" enabled girls to romp, roll, and run without embarrassment, though they were strictly forbidden from straddling hobbyhorses, rocking horses, or seesaws due to fears about sexual arousal. Yet once they started to wear undergarments, girls appropriated the game of jump rope from boys.

How girls negotiated cultural prescriptions in their play can also be gleaned from the copious letters, diaries, and memoirs they wrote as well as from the books they read. Often inexpensive juvenile periodicals, dime novels, and numerous domestic novels were filled with girl heroines who posed challenges to the patriarchal social order. Girls read "unsanctioned" works on their own and at raucous "reading parties," even though mothers tried to supervise their daughters' reading habits. Chagrined critics expressed their fears about the detrimental effect that reading "worthless" novels and magazines would have on girls, especially those on the brink of womanhood.

In an effort to tame a rebellious nature and enforce conformity, parents typically curtailed the freedoms of girlhood during adolescence. "I can never jump over a fence again, so long as I live!" cried Frances Willard, the future founder of the Woman's Christian Temperance Union (quoted in Green 1983, 10). This was a popular theme in Victorian girls' books like Louisa May Alcott's *Little Women* (1868), in which Jo gradually sheds her assertive masculinity and accepts prevailing standards of feminine modesty and propriety. It was a painful process experienced by many *real* girls as well. "Mother insists that at last I must have my hair done up woman-fashion," complained Frances Willard. "My back hair is twisted up like a corkscrew; I carry 18 hairpins; my head aches miserably; my feet are entangled in the skirt of my hateful new gown" (quoted in Green 1983, 10). For most girls, a change in appearance marked their entrance into young womanhood. But the perception that Victorian marriages offered women little else but confinement, dependence, and vulnerability led many adolescent girls to perpetuate their largely unchaperoned courtships spent skating, biking, hiking, dancing, and attending country fairs, carnivals, and traveling circuses.

Those girls and young women who worked for wages found ways to incorporate leisure into their labors. In the Northeast, mill girls pasted strips of poetry near their looms, read the latest fashion magazines, visited the library, and attended Lyceum lectures. In the plantation South, African American girls forced to care for the infants and children of white masters and slave parents rambled through woods, swam in streams, gathered nuts and berries, played with corncob dolls, played house, played hopscotch, and jumped rope. According to David Wiggins, "ring games" or "ring dances" were the most popular group activity of slave girls, who sang familiar songs with such coded lyrics as:

My old mistress promised me,
Before she dies she would set me free.
Now she's dead and gone to hell
I hope the devil will burn her well.
(1985, 177)

Play activities such as these provided girls with a venue to express deeply felt ideas and strong feelings.

In the slave quarters, girls' play activities also included singing secular and religious songs as well as telling stories. Grownups told survival tales such as the well-known "Tar Baby" story in order to impart wisdom to slave girls. This tale, in which the dark girl made of tar has no voice of her own, taught girls to endure physical mistreatment by masking their feelings.

From slave children, nurses, and other house slaves, white girls who were largely shielded from work learned songs, folklore, religious principles, ghost stories, and African tales. The southern belle's typical day consisted of playing with Topsy-Turvy and other dolls, reading, writing letters, visiting, shopping, fixing hair, gathering flowers, arranging flowerpots, arranging the bedroom, and mending kid gloves. On some days, older girls did nothing at all, but on others, they frolicked with friends and flirted with beaus at parties and balls. Until girls married, however, their leisure activities were typically chaperoned.

For girls on the frontier, play activities were often integrated into work responsibilities. While collecting "cow chips" for fuel, girls transformed buffalo dung into weapons. While herding cattle, girls raced on horseback, and while picking berries they played "hide and seek." With greater freedom from the gender-role prescriptions that shaped girlhood in the North and South, the collections girls assembled often consisted of snakeskins, fossils, and tarantulas. One girl who lived in Oklahoma bagged a dozen snakes for fun in 1872. Another girl recorded in her diary that she spent Thanksgiving Day riding 55 miles in a futile effort to catch coyotes. Frontier girls' play was less likely to have been monitored, and their toys were less likely to have been manufactured. Until the widespread circulation of Sears Roebuck catalogues ("the farmer's Bible") that brought commercial toys to the Midwest, tree branches served as weapons, horses, and brooms, and inflated pigs' bladders became balls and balloons. Melon rinds on wooden floors worked as well as ice skates on frozen ponds. Fox and geese, red rover, ring-around-a-rosy, ante-I-over, and other games that were transported from other regions and countries bridged gaps and forged cultural bonds between frontier girls of different nationalities, social classes, and races. In the frontier town of Deadwood, South Dakota, Estilline Bennet went sledding with black and Chinese

children. Native American girls in Indian boarding schools, however, were forced to renounce traditional games for Americanized ones befitting their sex.

In the last quarter of the nineteenth century, mass production and distribution gave rise to a consumer culture that made dolls and other toys widely available to daughters of the expanding middle class. But parents who indulged their daughters with imported fashionable lady dolls from France and Germany were disturbed to find that when girls played, they were more likely to stage doll funerals than white weddings. Often girls preferred to play with paper dolls, toy soldiers, or wagons. When someone asked two girls pretending to be a horse and its driver if they would rather play with some dolls, they explained that they would rather run instead (quoted in Formanek-Brunell 1998, 30). Changing clothing fashions around the turn of the century provided greater freedom of movement for girls who loved sledding, jumping rope, playing tag and hide-and-seek, walking fences, roller skating, flying kites, and indulging in other rough-and-tumble play. *Youth's Companion, St. Nicholas,* and book-length compendia such as *The American Girls Handy Book* (1887) provided girls with useful information for making toys, playing games, and exploring nature.

Though overworked, underpaid, and often exhausted, working-class girls of immigrant and migrant families pursued their own pleasures in play. Perpetually strapped for cash, however, working-class girls were unlikely to have the latest doll, teddy bear, bicycle, or ice skates they saw displayed in department store windows. Instead of playing with toys, any girl with a nickel could attend an inexpensive neighborhood movie theater with friends

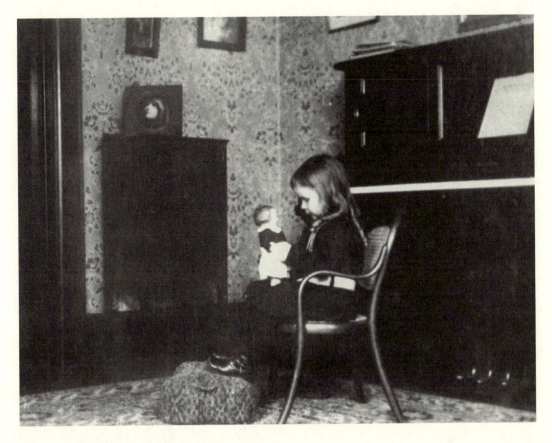

Girl plays with a doll. (Library of Congress)

and family. Alarmed Progressive reformers and vice commissioners strategized about how to secure girls' innocence in the "house of dreams." They joined scholars and playground promoters determined to combat the evils of industrial capitalism.

When not doing chores and watching siblings on front stoops, working-class girls played jacks on sidewalks and ball games on city streets. One study conducted in 1906 revealed that balls were the fourth most popular toy among girls by the age of thirteen (Ellis and Hall 1896). Whenever they could, girls also frequented penny arcades where older sisters flaunted authority, respectability, and conventionality as they reinvented standards of female adolescent virtue. Working-class adolescent girls shopped for colorful clothes they wore to dance halls, vaudeville shows, movie theaters, amusement parks, and other new forms of commercialized leisure. In places like Coney Island, adventurous, stylish, thrill-seeking, and pleasure-loving girls indulged in heterosexual experimentation with young working-class men on weekends.

By the early twentieth century, a new ideal of girls as energetic, handy, and healthy, promoted by the Girl Pioneers, Camp Fire Girls, and Girl Scouts, replaced the image of the pale and passive, docile and domestic Victorian girl. Between 1900 and World War I, girls could read about active and adventurous college girls and other heroines in new series fiction. In domestic novels of the period, motherless heroines such as Rebecca in *Rebecca of Sunnybrook Farm* by Kate Douglas Wiggin (1903) were plucky, young tomboys. The emerging image of modern girlhood was also given substance by toy, doll, and clothing manufacturers in the process of standardizing an American girlhood ideal for a national market. Doll producers replaced the vapid-looking French fashion dolls of the older order with girl dolls that sported bobbed haircuts and wore ready-to-wear jumpers. Business-sponsored mass-marketing events and product advertising aimed to make consumption (not production) an important part of twentieth-century girls' play culture. Though the dolls and other playthings American manufacturers promoted would embody domestic and maternal ideals, girls continued to jump rope, play hide-and-seek and tag, ride bikes, and play hopscotch.

Although the Girl Scouts championed the "new girl" ideal, they nevertheless opposed the teenage cultural icon of the flapper, who represented the new moral order in the post–World War I period. Adolescent "new girls" who explored the boundaries of acceptable standards of behavior in their play petted in cars, where they enjoyed privacy and freedom from scrutiny. Although small-town black girls and white girls were held to strict moral codes by parents, middle-class girls in the 1920s took to smoking and dancing just as working-class adolescent youth had in the prewar era. That young women wore shorter dresses and bobbed their hair enabled them to move their bodies in ways that the Victorian hourglass ideal had prevented. When not dancing, adolescent girls joined younger

ones at feature-length movies, which became an acceptable form of middle-class family entertainment in the 1920s. Alarm about the threat that "ill-bred young hoydens" posed to the social order, however, led experts to write books and magazine and newspaper articles (quoted in Goodsell 1924, 263). *Ladies' Home Journal* was one among many that provided subdebutantes (known as "sub-debs") with advice and information about hosting house parties. School officials did what they could to discourage the sensuality, style, and spending of female adolescents who threatened traditional sensibilities of purity, restraint, and thrift. But in truth, students had already begun to enforce conformity to conventions.

The Great Depression imposed financial hardships on families, but girls nevertheless went to the movies along with other Americans. Girls who saw Shirley Temple movies might have yearned for a Shirley Temple doll, which grossed millions of dollars despite curtailed budgets. Depression-era girls also read books such as *Caddie Woodlawn* by Carol Ryrie Brink (1935), in which the youthful heroine triumphs over other challenges in our nation's past. Girls between the ages of ten and fifteen were drawn to Nancy Drew's gender-bending heroism and catapulted book sales of the soon-to-be-best-selling children's series.

With fathers abroad and mothers at work, wartime girls had more responsibilities but also less supervision. When not in school, girls watched newsreels, read magazine stories, listened to radio shows, played war games (despite the disapproval of adults and most boys), and devoured the newly created Wonder Woman comic books with origins in turn-of-the-century cartoon strips. Their older sisters, many of whom had left small towns for employment, lodging, and sociability, participated instead in a youthful urban subculture. For excitement, comfort, and escape, "bobby-soxers" explored the growing consumer market of fashions, fads, hairstyles, music, movies, and magazines (e.g., *Calling All Girls* and *Seventeen*). Girls' freedom from economic constraints and parental supervision led many adults at the time to worry about teenage immorality, delinquency, and truancy. Casual heterosexual experimentation increased rates of teen pregnancy as many adolescent girls became "war brides," soon thereafter giving birth to the "good-bye" babies that ushered in the baby boom.

Approximately 38 million girls were born between 1946 and 1964 to war-weary parents eager to shelter their daughters in newly developed suburban neighborhoods. At a time when black girls' play was limited by poverty, discrimination, segregation, and violence, "child-centered" middle-class families nurtured their daughters' material, emotional, and educational well-being. Stay-at-home mothers supervised and scheduled girls they shuttled to and from after-school activities. Unlike previous generations, white girls born after World War II were more likely to play board games and read comic books indoors than play games outdoors. Urban black girls, however, were in the process of making the city sidewalks arenas for double-Dutch jump roping (transformed into a sport by adults to contain them in the 1970s). Television and toys, such as a new generation of dolls and miniaturized modern household equipment, promoted a reconstructed ideology of maternity, domesticity, and fantasy. Teenage girls participated in the growing consumer culture in teen goods that catered to the power of the purse. An evolving teen culture fueled by rock and roll, however, had many adults worried about delinquency and dissent.

The sexual revolution, second-wave feminism, and 1960s youth culture changed how girls of all ages would spend their leisure. Although dolls like Barbie and TV shows like *Gidget* reflected changing roles for girls and women (albeit ambiguously), the popular movies teenage girls saw on weekends increasingly explored the continuum of adolescent female sexuality by both exalting virgins (e.g., *American Graffiti* in 1973) and rewarding teenage girls for their sexual exploits (e.g., *Where the Boys Are* '84). Slasher films (e.g., *Halloween*) of the 1970s and 1980s, however, punished girls who threatened to destabilize the social and sexual order. The 1980s discourse about adolescent female sexuality led to a broader spectrum of representations in the books girls read by authors such as Judy Blume, author of *Are You There, God? It's Me, Margaret* (1970), and Louise Fitzhugh, *The Long Secret* (1965).

Mary Pipher, a clinical psychologist and author of *Reviving Ophelia: Saving the Selves of Adolescent Girls* (1994), was among many in the 1990s who argued that the "girl poisoning" culture limited "girls' development, truncate[d] their wholeness and [left] many of them traumatized" (12). Attempts to counter the consumer culture images and messages about appearance, fashion, romance, and consumption were initiated by underground grrrl zines and cyberspace Internet sites such as Echick and Chickclick. These have been followed by cultural products—*Buffy the Vampire Slayer*, *Power Puff Girls*, and *Discovery Girls*, as well as the American Girls

Friends playing on a tire swing. (Skjold Photographs)

malls or online has become a leisure-time activity for the roughly 37 million ten- to nineteen-year-old girls. Girls spend their allowance and leisure shopping for dolls, toys, accessories, electronics, and computer programs, often coded in hot pink and marketed "just for girls." But whether it is dressing dolls, watching TV, sitting in front of a computer screen, or listening to compact discs on headphones, girls' play has become more solitary and fantasy-oriented. The accessorizing and sexualizing of girls of all ages at play have also bridged a gap between little girls and their adolescent sisters. But for most American girls and young women, whether they are studying in extended day programs, participating in after-school activities, doing chores, or working as salesgirls, there is now simply less time to spare for play.

Miriam Forman-Brunell

See also African American Girls in the Twentieth Century; American Girls Collection; Asian American Girls; Barbie; Chicana Girls; Dollhouses; Dolls; Domesticity; Girls' Culture; Latina Girls; Nancy Drew Mysteries; Native American Girls; Pets

References and Further Reading
Axtell, James. 1981. *The Indian Peoples of Eastern America: A Documentary History of the Sexes.* New York: Oxford University Press, 34.
Beard, Lina, and Adelia B. Beard. 1887. *The American Girls Handy Book: How to Amuse Yourself and Others.* 1983. Reprint, Boston: David R. Godine.
Calvert, Karin. 1992. *Children in the House: The Material Culture of Early Childhood, 1600–1900.* Boston: Northeastern University Press.
Child, Lydia Maria. 1833. *The Girls' Own Book.* New York: Clark Austin.
Clinton, Catherine. 1982. *Plantation Mistress: Women's World in the Old South.* New York: Vintage.
Cross, Gary. 1997. *Kids' Stuff: Toys and the Changing World of American*

series of dolls—all aimed to provide girls with positive images, useful information, emotional support, and opportunities for self-expression. Like the new girl-friendly TV shows, cartoons, magazines, and dolls, advice books written by girl writers and published by companies staffed by all-girl editorial boards utilize feminist notions about empowerment and autonomy to construct a more feminist girlhood.

Although in the 1990s The Spice Girls promoted "girl power" among young girls, they also contributed to commercialization of an ideology. There is no doubt that in the twenty-first century, girlhood has become a vast commercial frontier where shopping for goods at

Childhood. Cambridge, MA: Harvard University Press.

Ellis, A. C., and G. Stanley Hall. 1896. "Study of Dolls." *Pedagogical Seminary* 1, no. 2 (December).

Farrar, Eliza Ware. 1837. *The Young Lady's Friend*. Boston: American Stationers' Co.

Fass, Paula S. 1975. *The Damned and the Beautiful*. New York: Oxford University Press.

Formanek-Brunell, Miriam. 1998. *Made to Play House: Dolls and the Commercialization of American Girlhood, 1830–1930*. Baltimore: Johns Hopkins University Press.

Fox-Genovese, Elizabeth. 1988. *Within the Plantation Household: Black and White Women in the Old South*. Chapel Hill: University of North Carolina Press.

Gaunt, Kyra D. 1998. "Dancin' in the Streets to a Black Girl's Beat: Music, Gender, and the 'Ins and Outs' of Double-Dutch." Pp. 272–292 in *Generations of Youth: Youth Cultures and History in Twentieth-Century America*. Edited by Joe Austin and Michael Willard. New York: New York University Press.

Goodsell, Willystine. 1923. *The Education of Women: Its Social Background and Its Problems*. New York: The Macmillan Co.

Green, Harvey. 1983. *The Light of the Home: An Intimate View of the Lives of Women in Victorian America*. New York: Pantheon, 10.

Grover, Kathryn. 1992. *Hard at Play: Leisure in America, 1840–1940*. Amherst: University of Massachusetts Press.

King, Wilma. 1995. *Stolen Childhood: Slave Youth in Nineteenth-Century America*. Bloomington: Indiana University Press, chap. 3.

MacLeod, Anne Scott. 1984. "The 'Caddie Woodlawn' Syndrome: American Girlhood in the Nineteenth Century." Pp. 97–120 in *A Century of Childhood, 1820–1920*. Edited by Mary Lynn Steven Heininger et al. Rochester, NY: Strong Museum.

Mergen, Bernard. 1980. "The Discovery of Children's Play." *American Quarterly* 32 (Fall): 399–420.

———. 1982. *Play and Playthings: A Reference Guide*. Westport, CT: Greenwood.

———. 1992. "Made, Bought, and Stolen: Toys and the Culture of Childhood." In *Small Worlds: Children and Adolescents in America, 1850–1950*. Edited by Elliott West and Paula Petrik. Lawrence: University of Kansas Press.

Norton, Mary Beth. 1980. *Liberty's Daughters: The Revolutionary Experience of American Women, 1750–1800*. Ithaca, NY: Cornell University Press, 102–103.

Peiss, Kathy. 1986. *Cheap Amusements: Working-Class Women and Leisure in Turn-of-the-Century New York*. Philadelphia: Temple University Press.

Pipher, Mary. 1994. *Reviving Ophelia: Saving the Selves of Adolescent Girls*. New York: Ballantine.

Pollock, Linda. 1987. *A Lasting Relationship: Parents and Children over Three Centuries*. Hanover, NH: University Press of New England, 148.

Pursell, Carroll W., Jr. 1979. "Toys, Technology, and Sex Roles in America, 1920–1940." In *Dynamos & Virgins Revisited: Women and Technological Change in History*. Edited by Martha Moore Trescott. Metuchen, NJ: Scarecrow Press.

Rousseau, Jean-Jacques. 1762. *Emile*. 1974. London: J. M. Dent & Sons, Ltd. Reprint.

Thompson, Roger. 1984. "Adolescent Culture in Colonial Massachusetts." *Journal of Family History* (Summer): 127–144.

Vallone, Lynn. 1995. *Disciplines of Virtue: Girls' Culture in the Eighteenth and Nineteenth Centuries*. New Haven, CT: Yale University Press, chap. 5.

West, Elliott. 1989. *Growing Up with the Country: Childhood on the Far Western Frontier*. Albuquerque: University of New Mexico Press, chap. 5.

———. 1996. *Growing Up in the Twentieth Century: A History and Reference Guide*. Westport, CT: Greenwood Press.

Wiggins, David K. 1985. "The Play of Slave Children in Plantation Communities of the Old South, 1820–1860." In *Growing Up in America: Children in Historical Perspective*. Edited by N. Ray Hiner and Joseph M. Hawes. Urbana: University of Illinois Press.

Pocahontas

Pocahontas, the legendary Native American girl, saved the life of Englishman John Smith, who faced execution by her father, a powerful seventeenth-century Algonquian chief. Her legendary staying of his execution, conversion to Christianity, and marriage to an Englishman named John Rolfe enabled successive generations to reinterpret her narrative within the context of changing American ideals.

Born in the mid-1590s, Pocahontas was the daughter of Chief Powhatan, who in the 1570s had united diverse bands of Algonquian bands into a loose confederation. During the sixteenth century, Spanish and English traders and explorers traveled to the southeastern region of the North American continent inhabited by the Powhatans. In June 1607, newcomers established Jamestown, named after the English king, and called the land "Virginia" after the virgin queen, Elizabeth I. For the next six months, Pocahontas interacted with the Englishmen. Through a system of trading frequently carried on by females, she learned the language and about English culture.

Over the next half-year, however, conflict and tensions increased between the newcomers eager to expand and the indigenous Powhatans. In an effort to protect his tribe from encroachment and seeking retribution for the murder of two Powhatans, Chief Powhatan captured John Smith. According to the English captain's own published narrative, he was about to be clubbed to death when eleven- or twelve-year-old Pocahontas forcefully intervened. Unable to entreat her father to halt the execution, Smith recalled that she cradled his "head in her arms, and laid her owne upon his to save him from death." His brave daughter's devotion moved Powhatan to grant

Pocahontas, a Native American girl, dressed in colonial attire after she married Englishman John Rolfe. (Library of Congress)

Smith clemency, declaring that the prisoner "should live" (Kamensky 1995, 13).

For the next six years, Pocahontas served as a translator between the English and Algonquian peoples, who otherwise lived in uneasy proximity. By 1613, however, tensions erupted between the Jamestown settlers and the Powhatans. Pocahontas was captured by the Virginians, who held her captive in an attempt to improve their bargaining position with her father. Incarcerated for months, Pocahontas re-created herself as a Christian woman. She "renounced the religious traditions of her birth," converted to Christianity, and was christened a member of the Church of England, changing her name to Rebecca. Just days after her release in April 1614, she married John Rolfe, an English tobacco planter she had known during her captivity.

In June 1616 she traveled to London for seven months with her husband and son, where she "was presented at the court of Queen Anne and honored at palace balls and affairs of state as Lady Rebecca, a symbol of the promise of the 'new' world." The former Indian princess now impressed all as a proper Christian woman with a strong command of the English language and customs. However, Pocahontas, who became ill with pneumonia or tuberculosis while living in London, died on board the ship bound for home. She was "eulogized by an English preacher, buried in English soil, and entombed under her English name" (Kamensky 1995, 15).

Much of what we know about Pocahontas derives from Smith's own *Generall Historie of Virginie* (1624). But historians and other scholars in various disciplines have cast doubt upon the veracity of Smith's published recollection. Was it fact or fiction? Is it possible that Smith misunderstood the nature of the stay of execution that is at the center of the Pocahontas story? Research on Iroquoian women (also Algonquian) reveals that stopping executions was one way in which Native American women exercised their political power. Another method was the right to call for an "adoption." The Algonquians achieved retribution for a slain family member (and inadvertently added to their population) through an adoption process. It was often women who called for adoptions that led to raids. A recent anthropological interpretation maintains that Smith possibly misunderstood the nature of Pocahontas's actions, casting it in romantic rather than demographic terms. Her real intention was, perhaps, to adopt Smith into the tribe.

The "new" social history of Native American women further reveals that "a Pocahontas-like figure [was] at the center of virtually every major encounter between natives and Europeans from the 15th century through the 19th" (Kamensky 1995, 15). Other Native American women elsewhere also served as translators, emissaries, and guides to Euro-American men they occasionally married. However, scholars of Scottish ballads have demonstrated that even before 1300, narrative tales of the oral tradition are remarkably similar to the Pocahontas story. For example, in "Lord Bateman and the Turkish King's Daughter," the American version of "Young Beichan," a man is captured by a ruler and then rescued by his daughter (who converts to Christianity). It would seem, then, that Smith's story was informed by traditional literary conventions with which Europeans were already familiar.

Because Smith's story drew upon older European traditions, it was easily adapted by the British to express their concerns about colonization and by successive generations as well. The centuries-old icon of the preadolescent Native American girl has reflected concerns and shaped perceptions about a wide variety of issues: race, gender, class, sexuality, liberty, culture, and national identity. Pocahontas has been the subject of paintings, poems, plays, and prints that romanticize our past and contribute to a historical mythology. Whether as exotic and sexual or maternal or virginal, powerful iconographic metaphors of the Native American princess (in contrast to the degraded dark-skinned "squaw") have been used widely, even to sell products such as tobacco, perfume, cigars, and flour.

Just as she reinvented herself in her lifetime, Pocahontas has symbolized nobility, Christianity, Otherness, femininity,

Disney's historically inaccurate version of Pocahontas offended many Native Americans. (Kobat Collection)

and most recently, Disney's view of bourgeois feminism. In this postfeminist animated movie version, Pocahontas is not only physically precocious but is also superhuman. Though she was only about eleven or twelve years of age when she "saved" John Smith, Disney's Pocahontas is a towering titan with Barbie-doll proportions. Pocahontas also has the same romantic devotion that Barbie has to Ken. To heighten the devotion (and simplify the plot), the animated Pocahontas falls in love with John Smith and not John Rolfe, the Englishman she, in fact, did marry. Typically, the movie tied into a consumer market of Pocahontas clothing, accessories, toys, and books, makes shoppers out of little girls who can imagine themselves as gorgeous, independent, courageous, and deeply romantic.

Miriam Forman-Brunell

See also Native American Girls; Puritan Girls

References and Further Reading
Green, Rayna. 1975. "The Pocahontas Perplex: The Image of Indian Women in American Culture." *The Massachusetts Review* 16 (Autumn).

Kamensky, Jane. 1995. *The Colonial Mosaic: American Women 1600–1760.* New York: Oxford University Press, chap. 1.

Woodward, Grace Steele. 1969. *Pocahontas.* Norman: University of Oklahoma Press.

Young, Philip. 1962. "The Mother of Us All." *Kenyon Review* 24 (Summer): 391–441.

Prom

As a little girl, I always fantasized about this famous night where I would resemble Cinderella in my gown.
　　　　　　　　—Female prom attendee

The high school prom is an iconic event in American culture. One need only take a cursory look at the profuse media images that depict the prom to gain a sense of this event's importance, not only to lives of teens but also to American culture. Many teen prom films are Cinderella-inspired tales of transformation. As the story unfolds, the central female character, usually a wallflower, submits to a series of changes culminating in her emergence as a beauty queen at the prom. In these Hollywood productions, the process of getting ready for the prom is a privileged space where bodies are magically reworked and identities refashioned.

Predictably, the popular construction of the prom as a moment to reinvent the self is a gendered one; this story is usually told through the voice of a girl, and the transformation that occurs is mapped through her body. This is because the prom belongs to "the feminine." Again and again, girls are told that going to the prom is fundamentally important to being and becoming feminine. In prom magazines, "making a statement" is the very promise of the prom—"the prom is your night to shine." The message is that a carefully fashioned feminine self is the ticket to a memorable prom. This packaging of the prom virtually ensures girls' participation in the consumption of goods and in feminine bodywork. There is tremendous pleasure in the project of self-change, in becoming someone else, even if for only one night.

But even as girls are expected to take up the work of becoming feminine at the prom, they also are confronted with the inherent contradiction in doing this kind of work. The very practices in which girls are expected to invest and to find pleasure are also dismissed as trivial. The basic paradox can be summarized in this way: the project of becoming feminine is defined as frivolous, and that which is frivolous is also feminine. This contradiction, articulated by so many girls, reveals an ongoing tension many girls experience as they become women in a consumer culture that at once idealizes and trivializes those practices conventionally tied to femininity. Drawing from interviews with and narratives written by young women and observations of four high school proms, this entry explores how girls struggle to make sense of what it means to be feminine in American culture as girls prepare for and then attend their proms (Best 2000).

Despite the tensions some girls felt initially about investing in an event that had been defined as superficial and silly, many young women looked forward to the prom as a moment to be seen. One young African American woman wrote, "When I stepped out of the limo I remember thinking that I was just the princess of the night. All lights were on me and this was my night."

Because of the importance of being seen in this setting, preparations are extensive and often expensive. A significant number of American girls spend what many would consider an extraordinary amount of money on their prom. According to one prom website, an average of $500 is spent to go to the prom (www.proms.net). A 1996 poll featured in *Your Prom*, one of the many prom magazines available for purchase each spring, reported that $188 is the average cost of a prom dress. These estimates are not surprising when one considers that many young women enlist the help of beauty professionals, even if their financial situation might prevent them from doing so on a more routine basis. One girl reported that she and her

A couple going to their high school prom. (Urban Archives, Temple University, Philadelphia, 1947)

friends rented a limo to take them to the hair salon, and another girl and her friends hired a cosmetic representative to come to her home before the prom. Certainly, the availability of money determines the ease with which girls are able to engage in the extravagances of the prom, but economic circumstances do not seem to ultimately determine their willingness to do so. Girls whose economic situation might otherwise preclude their participation also manage to engage in the work of the prom.

For many girls, the process of preparing for the prom was as important as the end product, if not more. As a young white woman wrote, "I don't remember any-thing eventful about the prom itself. I remember the major preparation that went into it. FINDING THE DRESS" (her emphasis). Several girls declared that getting ready for the prom was an entire day's commitment. Hair was plucked, worked, and cajoled into shape, and faces were magically transformed; many girls attended tanning salons, some joined gyms, and others reported that they had dieted to lose weight before the prom. One young white woman wrote, "All I can remember was that the prom wore me out. From half a day at school, to a morning appointment to get my hair done, I was literally exhausted." For a number of girls, how they transformed their bodies directly related to their having a successful prom. "When the day started off I thought it would be the best day. I had the perfect dress (no one had anything else like it) and my hair was done beautifully," one young African American woman wrote.

An important part of getting ready for the prom is finding the "perfect" prom dress. One local dress boutique, where a number of girls from one school bought their prom dresses, kept a detailed record of who bought which dress in an effort to prevent the unthinkable—two girls at the same prom wearing identical dresses. After all, an unforgettable dress secures an unforgettable night. Perhaps this also explains why one young woman never made it to her prom because her dress, which she had specially designed for the event, was not ready.

Although preparations for the prom are fundamentally about setting oneself apart, these preparations were a collective process. Talk about how they intended to prepare for the prom began months in advance. Girls drew sketches of their dresses during study hall for friends to admire, and their discussions about who was wearing what echoed through school halls. These conversations often transformed their initial ambivalence about the prom into excitement about the prospects of working on their bodies for the upcoming event.

It was not uncommon for family and friends to assemble at one girl's house as girls dressed for the prom. Even at the prom, girls talked openly about the work they undertook to achieve what some might call an idealized feminine image. Their discussions about their bodies, dresses, and preparations were not only an obvious source of pleasure but were also an integral part of the actual prom,

as important as the first dance and the crowning of the prom queen. This kind of talk helps girls make sense of what it means to be female in a culture that treats the body as the consummate canvas to express the feminine self.

To transform themselves for the prom, girls depend on an almost endless consumption of products; makeup, dresses, hair accessories, shoes, and handbags are all products marketed as tools for feminine display at the prom. Since the expansion of a distinct teen commodity culture during the post–World War II 1940s, the prom in general has been heavily marketed, but it is the particular market emphasis on feminine consumption that is most striking. Today, the prom is a multimillion-dollar industry (www.proms.net). Popular girls' beauty magazines, including *Seventeen* and *Young and Modern*, now dedicate entire monthly editions to preparing for the prom, and department stores host yearly prom fashion shows.

Engaging in the work of becoming "beautiful" for the prom represents a struggle to stake a claim to one's identity. For many girls, participating in beauty work enables them to occupy a position within a public space, a significant fact when considering women's historical relegation to the private sphere. These young prom-goers occupied hair salons, nail salons, and dress shops in the same way middle-class women in the 1920s, just after winning the right to vote, proudly (and paradoxically) announced their new freedom: they wore shorter skirts, bobbed their hair, and smoked cigarettes in public.

Not only are these girls able to demonstrate a public commitment to feminine practices, but they can also express their competence as beauty practitioners. Many young women are willing to endure what might be understood as the burdens of beauty for the prom in order to express their heterosexual desirability. But young women also do this work to please themselves (Radner 1989). The prom presents itself as an opportunity to indulge themselves in ways that many of them cannot do every day. Part of what made the body-work of the prom worth doing, then, stems directly from how they experience everyday life as young women.

Teenage girls are often denied control over their bodies, their desires, and their self-definition. Engaging in this elaborate consumption-oriented bodywork enables them to craft a space of self-control, self-definition, and self-pleasure that is experienced immediately. Of course, the consequence is that the pleasure of excess conceals the ideological workings of the prom; proms structure girls' investments in upholding gender and heterosexual norms, ensure their participation in commodity culture, and focus their attention toward the all-consuming project of the body.

The prom is a space where young women can play with a range of identities, many of which are closed off to them within what Nancy Lesko (1988) refers to as the "body curriculum" of schools, which operates to regulate girls' sexuality and desire. Without romanticizing the practices of dressing up, one could argue that the prom represents a safe, playful space for many girls to negotiate cultural representations of adolescent girls' sexuality. Girls repeatedly drew upon sexual codes as they discussed the dress they had selected for the prom. A Latina wrote: "I'm such a tomboy. The prom was an experience. Everyone kept commenting on how beautiful I looked, 'You have a great figure; you shouldn't hide behind jeans and a T-shirt.' My

friends barely recognized me. People who've known me all my life stared at me." Most girls wore long fitted dresses, many of them black, often with exposed backs and deep slits running up one leg. As one girl described her dress, what seemed most important was what it revealed: "It's got spaghetti straps and a scoop neck. It's got a slit up the mid-thigh and the back is completely open. It kind of comes in at the sides so your sides are showing."

When understood within the context of schooling that emphasizes modesty in dress for girls, a sexy and often revealing prom dress symbolizes a way to negotiate the sexual terrain of school. Girls have very few spaces in which they can claim sexual agency. Through what they wore, many girls seemed to claim a visible sexual identity that countered a racially based, middle-class image of the adolescent girl as the bearer of sexual innocence (Haug et al. 1987). Although the activity of dressing up binds girls to an unequal order of gender, they can nevertheless generate alternate meanings that enable them to exert some control over those sexual struggles that shape their everyday lives.

Can girls resist the prom as a space to solidify their feminine identities without rejecting the prom fully? The discourses on beauty, pleasure, and consumption that take shape around this event secure girls' investment in femininity, but girls also negotiate and at times refuse their total influence. For example, some girls wear tuxedos, instead of the expected prom dress. Wearing a tuxedo to an event that is profoundly tied to conventional femininity reveals nothing less than a struggle to distance themselves, if not physically, then symbolically, from the trappings of the feminine ideal. For other girls, resistance to these feminine conventions, if it could be called that, often arises because of budgetary constraints. Many girls simply do not have the money to buy expensive dresses; others think it too indulgent to spend considerable money on one night, unless they found that "perfect prom dress." Rejecting the pressures to invent themselves anew, some girls bought their dresses at second-hand consignment shops or simply wore a dress they already had. Several girls had their dresses made by their mother or a friend. In short, they refuse the snare of the consumer market, but making their own dresses also set them apart from other girls by virtually guaranteeing that their dresses would be originals. These girls did not reject the project of inscribing images of femininity on their bodies; they welcomed this project but challenged its direct connection to a commodity market.

Interestingly, many girls indicated that they were willing to go to extraordinary lengths to transform themselves for the prom. A number reported that they do not usually wear makeup and only periodically visit the hair salon. If young women invest in feminine bodywork for the prom but not necessarily daily, what, then, is the connection between gender and this cultural scene? Proms secure girls' complicity in maintaining prevailing feminine forms. As a result, resistance seems to be possible for only a few. The limits of resistance to these gender precepts seem to be determined by the very social organization of this space— proms are the domain of the feminine, where girls' desire to make a statement about themselves is especially pronounced. Perhaps this also explains why race and class seemed to exert little influence over how girls came to invest in the prom. Although one might expect meaningful race and class distinctions to be more prevalent, curiously, it was not the case. The cultural influence of gender appears to be so overwhelming that the differences across race and class lines, which are apparent elsewhere, are more or less subsumed.

What girls wore to their prom and the activities they participated in tied them in many ways to gender structures that concentrate their energies on their bodies. At the same time, the prom emerges as a space for girls to respond to how their schools and culture have defined adolescent femininity, and thus them. Understanding what girls are responding to is important for understanding why they invest in these activities, the pleasure they derive from them, and the meanings they attach to them. Ironically, the very practices that seem to solidify their place in the culture also become a means for them to respond to that culture. As girls make sense of becoming women in a society where gender continues to operate as a pervasive force, they negotiate a slippery slope. These girls must find meaning in a cultural context that all too often limits the possibility for meaningful self-representation for them as girls.

Amy L. Best

See also Body Image; Clothing; Dances and Dancing

References and Further Reading
Best, Amy L. 2000. *Prom Night: Youth, Schools and Popular Culture*. New York: Routledge.
Brown, Lyn Mikel. 1999. *Raising Their Voices: The Politics of Girls' Anger*. Cambridge, MA: Harvard University Press.
Brumberg, Joan Jacobs. 1997. *The Body Project: An Intimate History of American Girls*. New York: Random House.

Fine, Michelle. 1993. "Sexuality, Schooling and Adolescent Females: The Missing Discourse of Desire." In *Beyond Silenced Voices: Class, Race and Gender in United States Schools.* Edited by Michelle Fine and Lois Weis. Albany: State University of New York Press.

Fiske, John. 1989. *Reading the Popular Culture.* Boston: Unwin Hyman.

Haug, Frigga, et al. 1987. *Feminine Sexualisation: A Collective Work of Memory.* London: Verso.

Inness, Sherrie A. 1998. *Delinquents and Debutantes: Twentieth-Century American Girls' Cultures.* New York: New York University Press.

Leadbetter, Bonnie, and Niobe Way, eds. 1996. *Urban Girls: Resisting Stereotypes, Creating Identities.* New York: New York University Press.

Lesko, Nancy. 1988. "The Curriculum of the Body: Lessons from a Catholic High School." In *Becoming Feminine: The Politics of Popular Culture.* Edited by Leslie G. Roman and Linda Christian-Smith. London: Falmer Press.

McRobbie, Angela. 1991. *Feminism and Youth Culture: From Jackie to Just Seventeen.* Boston: Unwin Hyman.

Radner, Hillary. 1989. "'This Time's for Me': Making Up and Feminine Practice." *Cultural Studies* 3: 301–321.

Roman, Leslie G., and Linda Christian-Smith, eds. 1988. *Becoming Feminine: The Politics of Popular Culture.* London: Falmer Press.

Tolman, Deborah L. 1994. "Doing Desire: Adolescent Girls' Struggle for/with Sexuality." *Gender and Society* 8, no. 3: 324–342.

Walkerdine, Valerie. 1990. *Schoolgirl Fictions.* London: Verso.

www.proms.net (accessed March 1999).

Psychotherapy

Troubled and troublesome girls have always gone to the adults in their communities for help. Teachers, midwives, religious leaders, older sisters, babysitters, and aunts have provided comfort, counsel, and limits when a girl's parents could not do so. Beginning in the mid-1800s, this kind of help became the domain of medical specialists, and with the development of psychoanalysis at the end of the century, the practice of child psychotherapy began. Throughout the twentieth century, the field of psychotherapy was influenced by developments in child analysis and other theories of personality and technique and by social movements such as the American child guidance movement. Currently, girls receive psychotherapy from licensed practitioners in a number of fields. New ideas from therapists interested in family relationships, trauma and abuse, and feminist theory shape the therapies girls undertake today.

Psychoanalysis is a theory of personality development and psychotherapeutic technique created by Sigmund Freud in fin-de-siècle Vienna. Freud's work with women and girls played a crucial role in the early ideas and methods he developed. Like that of many nineteenth-century physicians, Freud's career as a neurologist soon took him to the study of hysterical illnesses. Girls and women of this period often developed dramatic psychosomatic symptoms such as paralysis, coughing or stomach pain, inability to speak, amnesia, or anorexia, and these problems were increasingly understood as a manifestation of emotional conflicts rather than of neurological damage. Freud studied hysteria with Jean-Martin Charcot, whose large sanitarium, Salpêtrière, housed hundreds of girls whose behavior or social problems led to their separation from their families. Charcot believed that their hysterical symptoms stemmed from suppressed sexuality. Freud recalled this notion when his friend and teacher Joseph Breuer shared with him a story about a remarkable patient, Bertha Pappenheim.

Bertha was twenty years old when she began seeing Breuer for severe symptoms of hysteria. She had first begun to cough while nursing her dying father and over a period of months developed paralyses, anesthesias (where parts of her body became numb), hallucinations, and dissociative states. After her father's death, she had difficulty seeing and recognizing people, speaking in her native language, and keeping track of time. Breuer met with her daily, and together they developed what she called her "chimney sweeping" technique. She talked and talked, telling him stories and fantasies and tracing her symptoms back to the traumatic events in which they originated. Although Breuer's treatment with Bertha ended painfully in her delusion that she was pregnant with his child, and although she required several subsequent periods of treatment in sanatoriums, Bertha Pappenheim went on to become a pioneer in social welfare. She provided homes for teenage mothers and their children, saved young Jewish women from sexual slave traders, and wrote and spoke about international efforts to improve the lives of disadvantaged girls.

Freud learned much from her story, which Breuer published using the pseudonym Anna O. Freud too began to treat teenage girls, and Bertha's "chimney sweeping" developed into the method of free association. Among his first patients was "Katharina," a young girl he met during a mountain vacation whose depression followed sexual molestation by her uncle, and "Elisabeth von R," whose chronic leg pain and difficulty walking were traced to painful losses and disappointments in love. Both girls found relief in his understanding of the unconscious meanings of their symptoms.

His work with eighteen-year-old "Dora" was more difficult. She shared with him a complex history involving her awareness that her father was condoning his friend's making propositions to her in order to facilitate his own affair with the friend's wife. When Freud responded to this story by turning his attention to her own sexual knowledge and urges, Dora left treatment abruptly. Freud learned a great deal from this, both about the role of transference in psychoanalysis and about Dora's love for the women in her life, especially for her father's lover. Another adolescent patient who became suicidal when her father prohibited her romantic relationship with an older woman taught him more about female homosexuality.

Freud's work with these young patients was heavily influenced by his early theories of sexuality. By the early 1920s, his theory and technique had developed further. He became more aware of the importance of relational and developmental factors in normal and troubled personalities and came to place more emphasis on the analysis of the ways in which people protect themselves from anxiety and pain than on a search for hidden sexual memories. During the years Freud was studying ego psychology, defenses, and anxiety, his daughter Anna undertook her own training in psychoanalysis, and she played a pivotal role in extending his therapeutic work to children.

The first child analyst was Hermine Hug-Hellmuth. Shortly after she began using play to work with young children, Anna Freud and Melanie Klein extended the field of psychoanalysis by applying it to their own work with troubled girls. Throughout their adult lives, these women were rivals, each claiming to be more true to the essence of Freud's work. Klein emphasized Freud's theory of sexuality and his work in the late 1910s on the death instinct. She worked with very young, very ill children, a number of whom had what would now be seen as pervasive developmental disorders. She interpreted their early fears about working with her as stemming from very primitive anxieties and used play and drawings to explore these girls' fantasies about their own and their parents' bodies. Aspects of her work were carried on by Donald Winnicott. In his case history *The Piggle* (1977), he described how a little girl responded to the birth of a younger sister by withdrawing into frightening fantasies. In contrast, Anna Freud, who had originally been trained as a teacher, emphasized the adaptive defenses girls used during different stages of development. She introduced therapy to them by teaching them something about how the mind works. She helped them become aware of and curious about their conflicts, proposing that the girl join with the analyst to understand the feelings behind her problems. Anna Freud worked with well-to-do youngsters in Vienna but also helped establish clinics and preschools for poor children. After the Freuds moved from Vienna to London to escape the Holocaust, she set up the Hamstead Nurseries, in which girls fleeing the bombings in London and refugees from the Holocaust were cared for and treated.

In the 1940s and 1950s, students of Anna Freud began to work in the United States and made important contributions to the practice of child analysis. Bertha Bornstein and Edith Buxbaum continued Freud's work on the importance of exploring girls' feelings and the ways they protect themselves from anxieties. They explored problems corresponding to the early development of the conscience and threats to girls' self-esteem. They studied girls' development at different stages and developed therapeutic techniques appropriate to different ages. In the 1960s and 1970s, their work was carried on by Selma Fraiberg, who wrote compelling case histories about her work with young girls with fears, psychosomatic problems, and obsessive-compulsive disorder. She developed modifications of classical psychoanalytic techniques especially for children (such as the "what pops into your mind game" to approximate free association), wrote about how to begin a therapy process with young adolescents, and did sensitive work on the effects of family trauma, which she referred to as "the ghosts in the nursery."

Although child analysis in the United States was developed primarily by the students of Anna Freud, play therapy was developed by followers of analysts or therapists with different orientations. The neo-Freudians (Karen Horney, Alfred Adler, Erich Fromm, and Harry Stack Sullivan) influenced a generation of child therapists who were more active and direct than classical analysts, who focused less on conscious material, and who emphasized girls' family and peer relationships. A compelling fictionalized portrayal of a psychotherapy process with Frieda Fromm-Reichman, an early relational therapist, is offered in the popular autobiographical novel *I Never Promised You a Rose Garden*. Followers of Otto Rank, who based his psychoanalytic ideas on the concept of birth trauma, stressed conflicts involving separation and individuation. Therapists like Jessie Taft and Frederick Allen frequently worked with shy or inhibited girls and used play therapy to help them work through significant losses. These therapists emphasized the importance of working through interruptions and terminations in therapy for helping girls master separation anxieties. Carl Rogers's nondirective psychotherapy was applied to work with girls by Virginia Axline. She used a warm, accepting relationship to encourage girls' own strivings for growth and development.

Child therapists who worked from the 1930s through the 1950s struggled with the question of how to manage freedom and limits in the therapy setting. Earlier therapists such as David M. Levy and Joseph C. Solomon tended to give girls free rein to express their impulses and emotions. They saw this as a way to help girls abreact traumatic experiences or to express repressed impulses. They might structure the play situation by selecting toys or play themes to allow girls to work on selected issues. By the late 1940s and through the 1950s, the importance of limit setting in therapy was recognized by such therapists as Roy H. Bixler and Haim Ginnott. Setting appropriate limits was seen as a means of helping girls feel safe, trust adults, and learn to manage impulsive acting out. Therapists did not allow children to hurt themselves, the therapist, or things in the office; did not extend the time limits of the therapy session; and did not allow children to remove toys from the playroom. The child guidance movement helped make psychotherapy available in community centers to children whose families might not have been able to afford it on their own.

From the 1960s through the present, specific play techniques have been developed to help girls work on particular issues. Anatomically correct dolls are often used to help young girls express memories and feelings about sexual abuse. Structured games and storybooks help girls verbalize and explore feelings, learn assertiveness skills, and work through issues caused by bereavement, divorce,

abuse, court appearances, and body image. Cognitive behavioral techniques have been applied with children to treat depression, and other behavioral techniques are used to treat phobias, obsessive-compulsive disorders, and behavior disorders.

Contemporary therapy with girls has been influenced by the findings of feminist psychologists. Following Carol Gilligan's work on girls' patterns of learning, moral development, and relationships, feminist therapists have explored girls' tendencies to sacrifice their autonomy and "voice" for the important motive of preserving relationships and minimizing interpersonal conflict. Feminist therapists work with patients' "resistance" to change by examining their ties to family members and friends; exploring their positive and negative identifications with their mothers and other women; and encouraging their ability to articulate their thoughts, feelings, and conflicts. Feminist therapists are sensitive to the importance of class, ethnic, and religious identity in girls' development and explore sexual orientation and gender issues in terms of the difficulties girls with these issues encounter in society and in their families rather than as solely internal problems.

Contemporary feminist therapists are also sensitive to the impact of social pressures on girls' development. A rising divorce rate; the pressure of two-career families; community violence and media depictions of violence; uninhibited sexuality; sadomasochism; and the encouragement of intense competition around beauty, money, status, and academic or career success can create such intense distress for girls that they develop problems ranging from perfectionism and poor self-esteem to eating disorders, suicidal tendencies, self-mutilation, drug abuse, and profound depression. Treatment involves making girls and their families more aware of the ways that these external forces have become intertwined with personal issues and strengthening family ties, intergenerational mentoring, and supportive friendships.

Whatever a therapist's theoretical orientation or technique, the therapy process takes on a life of its own. If the therapist is attentive and receptive, the girl patient will feel safe enough to play or talk about her life. Soon a mutual language and set of references develop. Therapist and patient become familiar with each other's temperament and style, and with growing spontaneity and mutuality they can recognize and create new ways of understanding the girl's experience. The therapist will notice and comment on patterns in the girl's play or talk and will address her resistance to their work. Gradually, the therapy relationship itself becomes the focus of the work. The girl patient may experience with the therapist feelings and conflicts that have been troubling in previous relationships. The therapist's ability to notice and reflect on this, instead of reacting in ways that might feel insensitive, punitive, or seductive, allows the girl to take a new perspective herself on her ways of being with others. Sometimes she will be sad or angry as she recalls and reexperiences past disappointments, but this necessary mourning will allow her to move on to more satisfying relationships in the future. Her progress is facilitated by the therapist's willingness to acknowledge mistakes or lapses in empathy without becoming defensive or losing perspective. This honesty allows the girl to be more comfortable with her own imperfection, to see adults as both fallible and responsible, and to identify with the therapist's capacity to reflect on the relationship.

The therapy process must take into account a girl's developmental stage; value her family and community relationships; and support her developing competence, autonomy, and relatedness. The therapist must be aware of the ethical issues involved in psychotherapy and must respect the patient's right to appropriate confidentiality, personal boundaries, and safety from dangerous behavior of her own or of other people. The therapist must work carefully with her family and be responsible in matters of payment.

Therapy will move toward a termination when the girl's symptoms have been resolved and she has been able to resume her progressive development. During the termination process, important themes will be revisited, and problems may temporarily intensify. New skills and ideas will be appreciated, and the patient may leave therapy feeling a poignant mix of sadness and pride, doubt and confidence.

Many girls today think about becoming psychotherapists. They might have been in therapy themselves or have friends or family members who have been. They may have read about therapy or seen depictions of it on television or in films. Often, they are aware of their own unaddressed problems, take pleasure in thinking about their inner lives, or sympathize with other people's suffering.

The best preparation for becoming a therapist is a broad educational and cultural background. Although taking psychology courses is important, so are reading fiction and poetry; cultivating exposure to art, music, and drama; and learning about history and the social sciences. As the interaction between emotional and physiological problems is increasingly understood, gaining an education in the life sciences becomes more and more important to the therapist's effectiveness. Knowing how to play and to express feelings and thoughts clearly is crucial.

A young woman can take a number of professional routes to a career in psychotherapy, and the profession she chooses may depend on her interests and on what kind of training is possible and available. Psychiatrists, psychologists (clinical, counseling, or educational), and social workers provide most psychotherapy in the United States, but increasingly, nurses, pastoral counselors, and marriage and family counselors also offer psychotherapy. Professional therapists must be licensed by the state in which they practice, which requires a degree from an accredited university or professional school, a specified period of supervised practice, and passing written or oral examinations or both. Periodic relicensure ensures that therapists behave ethically and keep up with current knowledge.

Sharon H. Nathan

See also Adolescent Health; Body Image; Child Abuse; Child Guidance; Daughters and Fathers; Daughters and Mothers; Depression and Girls; Eating Disorders; Female Sexuality; Lesbians; Relational Theory; Substance Abuse; Suicidal Behavior in Girls

References and Further Reading
Axline, Virginia. 1947. *Play Therapy.* Boston: Houghton Mifflin.
Breuer, Joseph, and Sigmund Freud. 1895. "Studies in Hysteria." In *The Standard Edition of the Complete Psychological Works of Sigmund Freud.* Edited by James Strachey. London: Hogarth Press.
Coppolillo, Henry P. 1987. *Psychodynamic Psychotherapy of Children.* Madison: International Universities Press.
Fraiberg, Selma. 1987. *Selected Writings of Selma Fraiberg.* Columbus: Ohio State University Press.
Freud, Anna. 1946. *The Psychoanalytical Treatment of Children.* London: Imago Publishing.
Gil, Eliana. 1991. *The Healing Power of Play: Working with Abused Children.* New York: Guilford Press.
———. 1996. *Treating Abused Adolescents.* New York: Guilford Press.
Gilligan, Carol, Annie G. Rogers, and Deborah L. Tolman. 1991. *Women, Girls, and Psychotherapy: Reframing Resistance.* New York: Haworth Press.
Green, Hannah. 1964. *I Never Promised You a Rose Garden.* New York: Holt, Rinehart, and Winston.
Klein, Melanie. 1932. *The Psychoanalysis of Children.* London: Hogarth Press.
O'Conner, Kevin John. 1991. *The Play Therapy Primer: An Integration of Theories and Techniques.* New York: John Wiley and Sons.
Schaefer, Charles, ed. 1976. *The Therapeutic Use of Child's Play.* New York: Jason Aronson.
Winnicott, D. W. 1977. *The Piggle.* New York: International Universities Press.

Punk Rock

Because of the do-it-yourself (DIY) approach to music making and the theoretically tolerant ethics in the punk rock community, the emergence of the punk subculture in the late 1970s marked the first time in popular music that a large number of girls were involved as instrumentalists and that many all-girl bands were formed. In the mid-1970s, punk rock developed in the United Kingdom and the United States. The ethics and aesthetics of punk were specifically targeted at rewriting the history of music in order to critique social injustice and the perceived banality of 1970s mainstream music. Girls' involvement in punk rock was crucial to expanding their limited role in popular music.

As a community of youth focused on politics, independent production, and the deconstruction of social roles, punk allowed young (mostly) white women to spurn the gender codes that restricted women's social interaction and music making. The freedom girls claimed in punk opened a space for the female instrumentalists, feminist performances, and girl-positive fan communities that have occupied the arena of popular music ever since. The ethics of punk were the catalyst for the creation of a new generation of female musicians, a generation in which girls' voices can be heard loud and clear. Through the work of the women of 1970s punk, the voices of the 1980s female pop sensations who learned their tactics in punk, and the explicitly feminist riot grrrl movement in the 1990s, girls have self-consciously rebelled against the historical position of women in music, making way for female musicians with sophisticated political messages, large audiences, and a canon of female rock role models. Opening new spaces for women in popular music required this kind of critical voice from female musicians who were traditionally limited to "appropriately feminine" roles in music making. The deconstructionist project of women claiming a place in punk rock engendered a riot against the structure of the recording industry and musical traditions, as well as women's subordinate position in this tradition. Questioning the expected activities of women in popular music and the generically restrictive framework of the recording industry opened the door for women to trade in their eyeliners and hairspray for electric guitars and the authorial pen.

Historically, women in popular music have been singers. The connection of the voice to the body falls in line with women's "biologically determined" social roles and the pressure for these singers to conform to white standards of beauty and sexual attractiveness. Because of the connection of singing with the body, vocalists were not seen as skilled musicians. Mavis Bayton notes that "even [jazz singer] Billie Holiday's singing was discussed in terms of an emotional response to her life history of personal suffering, rather than in terms of learnt craft" (Bayton 1998, 13). Vocalists in the big band era were paid less than instrumentalists and were often used only to give the "real musicians" a rest or as sequin-clad eye candy for audiences.

This image of the woman in music carried through to the birth of rock and roll. A few female figures, like influential country guitarist Maybelle Carter and the racially integrated all-girl big band International Sweethearts of Rhythm, were able to make significant instrumental contributions to popular music. But these women, with the exception of the celebrity singers, have been all but written out of the history of popular music.

Rock and roll, which emerged in the mid-1950s, further restricted roles for women. At the time some women were very important in popular music: for example, rhythm and blues (R&B) singer Ruth Brown's popularity single-handedly carried the Atlantic label in the early 1950s. Until the early 1960s, there were no female voices in rock. In the late 1940s, as many as one-third of top-selling pop singles were by female vocalists; in 1957, only two of the top twenty-five were by women. Neither of these were rock and roll musicians.

In the early 1960s, a new phenomenon called the "girl group" became important. In December 1960, the Shirelles' "Will You Love Me Tomorrow" became the number one hit on the pop charts. This was the first time a girl group, notably one composed of four black teenagers, had hit number one. From 1960 to 1966 many of these girl groups,

The Ronettes, precursors to punk rock bands of the 1980s. (Hulton Getty/Archive Photos, 1964)

which descended from R&B, charted dozens of hits. Their music, characterized by thick vocal harmonies and orchestration, focused on girl talk—boyfriends, friendships, and teen angst. Despite—or perhaps because of—the popularity of the girl-oriented messages in the girl groups' music, they have also been dismissed from the canon as cookie-cutter groups created by genius male producers. At the time, the focus was on the producers' talent and the girls' bodies. In 1968, a *Rolling Stone* magazine article described the Ronettes as "tough whorish females of the lower class, female Hell's Angels who had about them the aura of brazen sex. The Ronettes were Negro Puerto Rican hooker types with long black hair and skin tight dresses revealing their well shaped but not quite Tina Turner behinds. . . . Ronettes records should have been sold under the counter along with girly magazines and condoms" (quoted in Garofalo 1997, 190). As the girl groups died out in the mid-1960s, attitudes like these about women became common in rock music itself.

The rise of the rock supergroups like the Beatles and the Rolling Stones refocused attention on male musicians and instrumental virtuosity in popular music. The girls' place was in the audience, chasing and dreaming of male performers. In 1963, at the height of the girl groups' popularity, female artists recorded 32 percent of the records on the year-end singles chart. By 1969, only 6 percent of the year-end singles were by groups with female vocalists. Despite the moderate success of women in folk and the strong pro-woman statements of some female soul artists (like Aretha Franklin's "RESPECT"), the mainstream of rock was often extremely offensive toward women. Songs like the Rolling Stones' "Stupid Girl" and "Under My Thumb" created a culture of hypermasculinity as the standard in rock. As a result, the few women, like Janis Joplin and Grace Slick, who were able to break into this boys' club necessarily developed wild, masculine personas, conforming to the norm for men in rock. As in the pre-rock period, there were female artists like Goldie and the Gingerbreads and Fanny, two of the first all-girl rock bands, but the existence of these musicians has not been institutionalized in the rock canon or the history of popular music.

The fragmentation of popular music in the 1970s into many genres and subgenres, which were divided along more than just racial lines, created more opportunities for women in music. Folk and soft

rock had many female voices, and out of the folk movement a specifically feminist genre called "womyn's music" developed. Folk musicians like Cris Williamson and Holly Near recorded feminist albums on woman-oriented independent record labels. Even though these musicians were still mostly associated with the role of singer, womyn's music successfully created new opportunities and a new market for women's music at a time when the sexist music industry presented few female role models. However, the niche market nature of the separatist womyn's music scene focused on women already involved in the feminist movement who were mostly middle-aged, educated, and white. Young women were still the focus of mainstream bubblegum groups like the Osmonds and the Partridge Family. A change in girls' roles in popular music would come from neither the mainstream structure that limited girls to the feminine roles of singers, sex objects, and fans nor the feminist womyn's music movement that paid little attention to young women and concentrated on a folk style that lacked mass appeal.

Instead, the emergence of punk rock in the United States and United Kingdom broke open the music world for women. Punk music's genealogy includes strains of early 1970s art rock, Britain's androgynous glam/glitter rock, and U.S. garage/surf bands. The convergence of these rock influences created a community that criticized social injustice, restrictive social roles, and the mainstream music industry with a particular focus on cultural satire. The term *punk* describes the subculture of youth that created and consumed the music that resonated from these American and British roots as well as a genre of music—punk rock—and the style of dress associated with the subculture. It was contradictions that were most important to the creation of a punk community, and for this reason, it is almost impossible to universalize and extremely difficult to define. Punk ideals questioned prejudice, social injustice, and vicious circles of inequality. Punk tactics attacked the assumed naturalness of the structures and attitudes that perpetuate voicelessness, oppression, and institutionalized lack of opportunity, or "no future." In punk, every aspect of the community—music, clothing, politics, lifestyle—is inseparable from the others. Each is designed to intensify the ideological basis for the movement. Penelope Houston of the Los Angeles punk band The Avengers explained, "The original concept of the band was the musical concept. The music is still important, but it's like the music is a Tool. Rock & roll is easy to play. Anybody can learn to play, so you have to take it farther" (Vale 1996, 40). Greil Marcus goes further: "What remains irreducible about this music is its desire to change the world" (Marcus 1989, 5).

The punk ethics system stood in opposition to the politics perceived in adult culture by the mostly white, working-class teenagers involved in making punk music and style. Tolerance and openness were the crux of punk ideology. Although not practiced universally, the *idea* that punk was open to everyone was central to the rhetoric of punk rock, politics, and identity. Antiracism was also a central plank in the punk platform. A theme of lyrics, writing, and images, antiracism was addressed in music and in political activism. The creation of the Rock Against Racism (RAR) program, a series of concerts that featured high-profile punk bands paired with Jamaican reggae groups

with an explicitly political agenda, reacted against the racial tension in the United Kingdom in the 1970s and laid down the punk community's stance on the issue. Punk also criticized sexism on an ideological level through political songs on abortion, women's oppression, compulsory heterosexuality, and other gender issues. Soon after the creation of RAR, a Rock Against Sexism (RAS) concert series was created to critique women's roles in society and music, sexual assault, and mainstream attitudes about sexuality.

These ideals were backed up through the tactics punks used to fight the "politics of boredom." By challenging the everyday, punks attacked boredom as a form of social control. According to punk "theory," boredom prevented massive uprisings among disgruntled and oppressed peoples by creating and enforcing a consensus around the mundane and expected. For punks, rebellion against boredom, no future, and unquestioned assumptions was essential to reinvigorating the ailing British state and the pathetic American culture. Rather than focusing on traditional political avenues, punks politicized and organized the disempowered, the young people who looked forward to no future. Punk youths turned every aspect of their lives—music, appearance, and behavior—into political fighting words.

By wearing garbage bags as shirts, tearing apart clothing and putting it back together with safety pins, inscribing radical style on the body through tattoos and piercings, and idealizing extreme hairstyles that could not be covered or just put on for the weekend, punks strove to create category confusion. Class lines blurred when "appropriate" styles were discarded. Chronology and meaning became jumbled when vintage clothing

Two punk girls. (Michael T. Sedam/Corbis)

was renovated and consumer products were used as sartorial accessories.

There was a coherence between punk dress and the punk style of music making—it was all DIY. Flying in the face of the rock culture that required virtuoso skill in playing instruments, punk youth denied that technical ability on guitar or drums was necessary to make good rock music. The DIY ethic encouraged punks with no musical experience to start their own bands. Punk rock became a space where *anyone* could begin to play guitar, write songs, and perform in public. Anyone could learn along the way. For the first time in popular music, musical incompetence was aesthetically and politically valuable to further the deconstruction of mainstream ideas of "good"

and "valuable" music. Being a musician was no longer a goal but a *means*.

Because of the tolerant, antisexist ideals of punk and the DIY ethic, girls became an early and important part of the punk scene. From the mid-1970s, artists like Patti Smith rewrote the trope of the female singer to include the role of the poet, activist, and critic. For the first time, women were able to learn to play electric guitar, bass, and drums because already knowing how to play was not required for them to enter the music scene. The open interrogation of femininity and gender roles among female and male punk musicians facilitated this—the electric guitar was divorced from its presumed masculine connotations. Punk also deconstructed the masculine meaning of the band and public performance, allowing girls to form bands and play in public spaces, de-gendering the space of the stage and the position of musical authorship. By refusing the history of popular music and the baggage of traditional gender roles, punk addressed girls' needs where mainstream popular music, the feminist movement, and womyn's music had failed.

The importance of punk to girls in popular music and girls consuming popular music is enormous. Punk created the first canon that was inclusive of female artists—some of the most famous bands, like the Slits, X-Ray Spex, Blondie, and Siouxsie and the Banshees, were female-driven. In addition, the beginnings of a specifically female canon of popular musicians emerged. Punk artists like Joan Jett rediscovered forgotten female musicians, often covering their songs and publicizing their names through the network of punk fanzines. The most significant legacy of punk for girls is what punk has added to this female canon. Not only are 1970s punk bands like Penetration and the Avengers a part of this influence, but so are all the female musicians that were jumpstarted into popular music by punk and the DIY philosophy. Punk allowed women to learn to play and write music, and in the 1980s, the promise of a large audience and professional status led many of these punk women to the pop mainstream.

Female artists who learned to be musicians in the punk culture thrived in the 1980s mainstream. The latent punk ethic these women carried into the top forty brought feminism, strong female role models, and DIY musical tactics to the large audience of young white girls targeted by the pop industry. In 1981, the Go-Go's, members of the Los Angeles

Cyndi Lauper, a punk idol in the 1980s, in concert. (Corbis, 1984)

punk scene since 1977, became the first all-girl band in history to hit number one on the pop charts. Throughout the decade, strong female figures like Cyndi Lauper, Chrissie Hynde, Joan Jett, and Madonna changed the face of popular music by bringing glimpses of feminism to mainstream audiences.

Having grown up with the strong yet unapologetically female voices and images of musicians like the Go-Go's and Cyndi Lauper, in the 1990s a group of punk girls were able to reinscribe female voices and feminism into punk, refiguring it as a platform for feminist political, musical, and social change. "Riot grrrls," a movement centered around feminism and punk rock, was formed in 1991 to criticize and create an alternative to both punk culture, which had become extremely male-dominated and violent during the 1980s, and mainstream pop culture, which by that time was focusing on violence, male angst, and women's bodies as marketing tools. DIY tactics and teamwork characterized the strategies these girls used to accomplish their goals: to create a feminist-punk community, to make girl-positive punk rock music, to politicize the position and the lives of girls, and to change the world. Not only were these bands (for example, Bikini Kill, Heavens to Betsy, Excuse 17, and Bratmobile) influential among punk girls, but their influence was also felt when explicitly feminist, pop-oriented artists like Alanis Morrissette, No Doubt, and The Spice Girls co-opted riot grrrl attitudes into the mainstream.

Rebecca Daugherty

See also Body Image; Girl Power; Hair; Zines

References and Further Reading
Bayton, Mavis. 1998. *Frock Rock: Women Performing Popular Music.* New York: Oxford University Press.
Gaar, Gillian. 1992. *She's a Rebel: The History of Women in Rock and Roll.* Seattle: Seal Press.
Garofalo, Reebee. 1997. *Rockin' Out: Popular Music in the USA.* Needham Heights, MA: Allyn and Bacon.
Gottlieb, Joanne, and Gayle Wald. 1994. "'Smells Like Teen Spirit': Riot Grrrls, Revolution, and Independent Rock." Pp. 250–274 in *Microphone Fiends: Youth Music and Youth Culture.* Edited by Andrew Ross and Tricia Rose. New York: Routledge.
Hebdige, Dick. 1979. *Subculture: The Meaning of Style.* New York: Routledge.
Juno, Andrea. 1996. *Angry Women in Rock.* Vol. 1. New York: Juno Books.
LeBlanc, Lauraine. 1999. *Pretty in Punk: Girls' Gender Resistance in a Boys' Subculture.* New York: Routledge.
Marcus, Greil. 1989. *Lipstick Traces: The Secret History of the Twentieth Century.* Cambridge, MA: Harvard University Press.
O'Brien, Lucy. 1999. "The Woman Punk Made Me." Pp. 186–198 in *Punk Rock: So What? The Cultural Legacy of Punk.* New York: Routledge.
O'Hara, Craig. 1999. *The Philosophy of Punk: More Than Noise!* San Francisco: AK Press.
Vale, V., ed. 1996. *Search and Destroy #1–6, The Complete Reprint.* San Francisco: V/Search Publications.

Puritan Girls

Puritans girls were the daughters of religious dissenters from the Church of England who established the Massachusetts Bay colony in the early seventeenth century. Puritan girls' lives were shaped by Old Testament notions, English traditions, and New World experiences. In seventeenth-century New England, a Puritan girl was born at home within a circle of women. Her birth was the culmination of a female social ritual attended by female family and friends and facilitated by a midwife. The mother-to-be ate "groaning cake" and drank "groaning beer" to facilitate labor. Her daughter was raised in a large nuclear family with many siblings (from six to eight). Healthy living conditions, early marriage, and no birth control were all factors that contributed to the large size of Puritan families. In rural New England where the vast majority lived, nine out of ten infants were likely to survive to at least age five. In bustling seaport towns like Salem or Boston, however, infant mortality rates were high; three out of ten infants were unlikely to survive their first year of life.

Puritan infants swaddled in strips of linen and laced with staybands were held to adult standards. By the age of two, Puritan girls (and boys) were likely to face the arrival of another sibling and a very sudden weaning. Thereafter, it was up to the father, the central authority within the patriarchal Puritan household, to break the child's will. Stern fathers inflicted physical and psychological punishments on their young children who exhibited signs of original sin or "infant depravity." The task was to overcome self-assertion and aggression and become pious and submissive like their devout elders.

Between the ages of six and eight, Puritan children abandoned their gender-neutral frocks, or "petticoats." Instead they donned clothing that resembled adults', a sartorial marker of a new relationship to the economy and society. Because the Puritan family was the main unit of production, each member of the family was expected to be economically useful. Sons followed their fathers from fields to pastures and from barns to workshops, where they built and maintained fences, forged tools and repaired utensils, tended livestock, hoed, plowed, planted, weeded, and harvested. Daughters shared another domain with their mothers and other female kin. They did the "indoor work," assisting mothers in an unceasing routine of daily, weekly, seasonal, and annual chores: hoeing gardens; tending orchards; caring for animals; making soap, candles, and cloth; churning butter; baking bread; salting meats; stoking the fires; and milking the cows. Three times a day daughters assisted their mothers with meals. Since wives milked the cows early each morning, the first meal of the day consisted of leftovers: toasted bread, cheese,

An idealized Puritan family scene depicted in a nineteenth-century print. (Library of Congress)

meat, turnips, cider or beer in the winter, and milk in the summer. "Dinner," which was the main meal of the day, was a one-dish "pottage" prepared in cavernous hearths. "Supper" was a simpler meal of bread, cheese, and beer.

At adolescence girls—along with boys—were "fostered out" to learn a trade, as was the custom in England. Until the eighteenth century, Puritan daughters were routinely placed in the families of others. Unlike boys, however, girls learned housewifery and needlework. Girls received no formal education: they were taught how to read (so as to study the Bible) but not how to write; that was for males, considered their superiors. Woven into the fabric of Puritan theology, society, customs, and culture was the belief that females were physically, intellectually, spiritually, and morally inferior.

In all these ways, girls were raised to assume their allotted place as good wives and mothers in Puritan society. Marriage, especially between families of means, was an economic arrangement largely based on property. (Sometimes marriages resulted from sexual transgressions.) Fathers, who assumed central authority in marital negotiations, provided their daughters with a dowry when they could. Land inherited by married daughters (*feme covert*, or "covered woman," that is, after marriage her rights became one with her husband's) became the legal possession of their husbands under English common law. Sons customarily received two times as much land, though property titles were only relinquished after a father's death, thereby prolonging a filial devotion born of dependency. Daughters received equal portions of an estate only if their father died intestate (not having left a will) and they had no brothers.

Over several generations of families with large numbers of sons and daughters, the continuous division of land according to inheritance gradually diminished the size of inheritances; the consequences for young women were enormous. Unable to provide either "movables" (e.g., linens) or a cash dowry, fathers lost some of their authority, and eighteenth-century daughters became more able to do as they pleased. To begin with, young women were more likely to engage in premarital sex than had their ancestors. By 1750, as many as 40 percent of the young women in a number of New England towns were already pregnant by the time they were married. Many also began to marry without parental consent. A growing number of younger sisters also wed before their older sisters, whereas others elected not to marry at all.

Miriam Forman-Brunell

See also Daughters and Fathers; Daughters and Mothers; Witchcraft

References and Further Reading
Calvert, Karin. 1992. *Children in the House: The Material Culture of Early Childhood, 1600–1900.* Boston: Northeastern University Press.
Demos, John. 1970. *A Little Commonwealth: Family Life in Plymouth Colony.* New York: Oxford University Press.
Earle, Alice Morse. 1899. *Child Life in Colonial Days.* New York: Macmillan.
Greven, Philip. 1979. *The Protestant Temperament: Patterns of Child-Rearing, Religious Experience, and the Self in Early America.* New York: Meridian, chaps. 2–3.
Morgan, Edmund. 1944. *The Puritan Family: Religion and Domestic Relations in the Seventeenth Century.* 1966. Reprint, New York: Harper and Row.

Q

La Quinceañera

Many families of Mexican American and other Latin American backgrounds celebrate the fifteenth birthday of their daughters with a special coming-of-age ceremony called *la quinceañera*. The name *quinceañera* derives from the Spanish words *quince*, meaning "fifteen," and *años*, meaning "years," and may refer either to the girl or to the ceremony itself. In Mexican American communities, the *quinceañera* celebration marks the change from adolescence to womanhood.

Scholars have long questioned the historical roots of the *quinceañera*, believing it has dual origins. Sister Angela Erevia, a Catholic nun in San Antonio, Texas, and an authority on the religious *quinceañera*, argues that it dates back to Mayan and Toltec customs in which fifteen-year-olds of both sexes were presented to their tribal communities in festive religious rituals (1980, 3). She suggests that the rite honored the childbearing capacity of the young woman's body, thereby enhancing her relationship with her community, and explains the significance of this ritual as a time when the young woman recognizes the power of her womanhood. For the ancient Mayan and Toltec cultures, the *quinceañera* symbolized the power to procreate.

Some historians argue that the Aztec celebration of a girl's puberty signified a social shift in her status in society. At the age of twelve or thirteen, the girl could attend two types of preparatory schools, the *Calmacac* or the *Telpucucali*. Young women who entered the *Calmacac* school were prepared to commit their lives primarily to religious service, whereas those attending the school of *Telpucucali* were primed for marriage (King 1998, 12). The selected daughters of nobles went to the *Calmacac* school, where they were taught by priestesses. As part of their rite of passage, the young girls participated in several nightly offerings of incense to the gods, practiced celibacy, and embroidered fine clothing. The daughters of commoners went to the less formal *Telpucucali* where women known as *ichpochtlatoque*, "mistresses of the girls," prepared them for marriage. By fifteen the Aztec girl was ready to leave her parents and teachers and enter the life of adulthood either as a wife or priestess (King 1998, 40).

In addition to its indigenous origins, the *quinceañera* may have European influences. Erevia indicates that, after the Spanish colonization in the Americas, the celebration took on variations of the religious, patriarchal, and colonial representations that were imposed on the early Indian civilizations (1980, 3). Incorporating Catholicism into the native ceremonies was an attempt by the Spanish to indoctrinate the Aztec into Christianity. The Spanish imposed their religious faith onto the Aztec ceremonies, which had created rigidly defined roles for young women in their society. Now the native young women had a choice of dedicating their lives to the church (most likely the modest life of a nun) or to motherhood (a similar choice, just under a different religion).

In *Quinceañera: Celebrating Fifteen,* Elizabeth King documents a Mexican American *quinceañera* in Mission Hills, California. She argues that European cultural influences had an impact on Mexican celebrations, which reached a cultural zenith during the reign of Emperor Maximilian and his wife, the Empress Carlota (1998, 40), and included courtly European social customs such as elaborate ball gowns and ballroom dancing.

Scholars of the *quinceañera* agree that there is no definitive way to conduct or administer the ceremony. Many factors may influence how it is celebrated, including the young woman's socioeconomic status, Latina ethnicity, religion, geography, and individual preferences. As in other important Latino celebrations, families often spend several months or longer preparing for a *quinceañera.* Ethnographer Norma Cantú (1999), who has researched the *quinceañera* along the Texas-Mexico border, and anthropologist Karen Davalos (1996), who has written about the *quinceañera* in the U.S. Midwest, assert that in Mexican American culture most *quinceañera* celebrations have two distinct components, the religious ceremony that takes place at church and the secular celebration.

The religious ceremony may be conducted by a Protestant minister or a Catholic priest. At the ceremony, the *quinceañera* usually wears an elaborate dress (*el vestido*), comparable to a debutante's or bride's gown. She is accompanied throughout the ceremony by an honor court of friends and their escorts (*damas y chambelanes*), her godparents (*padrino y madrina*), family, and friends. There are multiple ways of conducting a religious ceremony, whether it is a Catholic mass or a Protestant service. Generally, the services include moments when the young woman reaffirms her faith by reading from the Bible and takes an oath to assume new responsibilities in her adult life.

The religious ceremony includes various symbolic objects such as a metal cross necklace, a finger ring, crown, Bible, pillow, and flowers. Erevia documents the meaning of each symbol in her book *A Religious Celebration for the Quinceañera.* The metal cross represents the young woman's Christian faith, and the ring symbolizes her responsibility to community and God. Worn during the ceremony to represent her success in leading a virginal life, the crown is her reward for maintaining purity against worldly temptations. Finally, the flowers signify a renewal of her commitment to continue a responsible, mature, and virtuous life (Erevia 1980, 9).

During the religious ceremony, the symbols or images are presented to the young woman by the priest or minister, her parents, and her godparents. Cantú underscores that the religious ceremony may include other significant images and objects, such as a pillow (*cojín*), which is placed at the altar where the *quinceañera* will kneel; a rosary; and a Bible (1999, 88, 93). Priests or ministers conducting the religious ceremony take this opportunity to educate the *quinceañera* and other young members of the congregation on the teachings of the church and moral values.

The secular part of the celebration usually includes a reception for family and friends, and a dance (*la fiesta*) oftentimes concludes the event. The dance may include a highly choreographed procession with formal introductions of the honoree, her parents, her godparents, her court of honor and their escorts, family, and friends. Cantú points out that there are often specified moments during the secular festivities when the young woman dances with her father, her escort, and other significant members of the celebration. A great variety of music and food characterize *quinceañera* customs, depending on region, ethnicity, social class, and financial resources (1999, 83, 84).

For most ceremonies, food is an important element in the festivities. In Mexican American culture, traditional foods such as beans, tamales, chicken mole, flour or corn tortillas, and enchiladas are customary. According to Cantú, food preparation is one of the most significant changes in the celebration of the *quinceañera* dance or reception. The "traditional celebratory foods" have evolved into whatever the caterer offers or the family provides (1999, 83). In some *quinceañera* ceremonies, catered cold platters, finger foods, and buffet-style dishes have been substituted for a Mexican traditional menu. However, in most instances, family friends and community members still offer to cook traditional dishes and serve the food and cake to the honoree and the participants in the *quinceañera*.

In contemporary practices, *la quinceañera* is celebrated in various forms. In less affluent and less traditional families, a simple birthday party suffices. However, a full-fledged *quinceañera*, featuring elaborate attire, grand decorations, specialized catered food, colored photographs, video recordings, special gifts, and a live musical band, can add up to an expensive affair. Although such an elaborate party has become a standard way of celebrating a *quinceañera*, many young women choose to commemorate their *quinceañera* in different ways. For example, Anna Maria Padilla from Santa Fe, New Mexico, interpreted this celebration as an opportunity to commit herself to a career in music. As a guitarist, she opted to record her first compact disc, which included a repertoire of classical and flamenco music, instead of a formal *quinceañera* (Salcedo 1997, 215). Other ways that young women celebrate their *quinceañera* are by having a surprise party, studying abroad, planning a cruise, and going dancing at a nightclub with family and friends.

In modern discourse, *la quinceañera* is certainly not without its critics. Michele Salcedo, author of *Quinceañera! The Essential Guide to Planning the Perfect Sweet Fifteen Celebration*, notes that priests, ministers, and educators are concerned that the traditional *quinceañera* emphasizes a girl's sexuality at a time when there are too many teen pregnancies. In some cases, priests have criticized the celebration as "advertising a young woman's sexual availability," which promotes a stereotype that young Latina girls are sexually permissive (1997, 6, 9).

In addition, scholars of the *quinceañera* point out that religious officials construct a limiting view for young ladies. In particular, Davalos argues that the ceremony encourages the girl to take on a subservient role in life and to subject her wants and needs to those of her family

A Cuban American girl celebrates her quinceañera *celebration, Miami, Florida. (Patrick Ward/Corbis)*

and the church. She claims that embedded in the ceremony is the religious doctrine that limits the girl's future role to one of motherhood (1996, 111, 121, 122). The *quinceañera* presents a limiting view of a young girl's position in life and constructs a narrow image of the roles played out in womanhood.

Catholic officials contend that this rite of passage must be celebrated in order to preserve Catholic traditions. Priests claim that the event should be a public expression of religious devotion and commitment to the church and society (Davalos 1996, 111). As the issues of gender roles and sexuality are being debated among scholars and church officials, literary critics are beginning to use the *quinceañera* as a framework for discourse and analysis

in the coming-of-age experience in young Mexican American women.

As a whole, the religious and secular celebrations provide general enjoyment and community goodwill. The coming-of-age rituals reinforce the young woman's personal and spiritual identity and social position. Cantú asserts that after a young girl has gone through a *quinceañera*, she may be perceived by her community, family, and even herself as a young adult. Following the *quinceañera*, the young woman gains new privileges at home, including oftentimes the opportunity to begin dating. Most importantly, the consensus among young women who have gone through this ceremony is that it has a positive spiritual transformative effect in their lives (1999, 90). For many Mexican American young women, it is a time when they leave their girlhood behind and join the ranks of womanhood. Among Mexican Americans in the United States, the *quinceañera* event is a thriving and evolving ritual and celebration. Whether young Mexican American girls decide to have a *quinceañera* or not, these adolescents face different dynamics and anxieties based on their rite of passage into adulthood in a traditional culture. Ultimately, the *quinceañera* is an opportunity for young women to learn about their cultural identity and commemorate their Mexican ancestry.

Today in Mexican *barrios* (neighborhoods), it is common to find a specialty store geared toward providing the essential material elements needed to prepare and conduct a *quinceañera;* there are also multiple websites that cater to families and young women who are preparing for the *quinceañera*. Scholars are optimistic about the future of the tradition. Cantú notes that the *quinceañera* tradition is now serving as an inspiration for new life-cycle ceremonies, for instance, the *quinceañero* (a *quinceañera* for boys) and the *cinquentañera*, which is the celebration of a woman's achievements in her life as she reaches the age of fifty (1999, 98). At the dawn of the twenty-first century, for many Mexican Americans the *quinceañera* is an old Aztec ritual tradition that connects modern young women to their Mexican cultural roots—it is a way of preserving history.

Cecilia J. Aragón

See also Chicana Girls; Latina Girls

References and Further Reading
Cantú, Norma E. 1999. "La Quinceañera: Towards an Ethnographic Analysis of a Life-Cycle Ritual." *Southern Folklore* 56, no. 1: 73–101.
Davalos, Karen Mary. 1996. "La Quinceañera: Making Gender and Ethnic Identities." *Frontiers* 16, nos. 2–3: 101–127.
Erevia, Sister Angela. 1980. *A Religious Celebration for the Quinceañera*. San Antonio, Texas: Mexican American Cultural Center.
King, Elizabeth. 1998. *Quinceañera: Celebrating Fifteen*. New York: Dutton.
Salcedo, Michele. 1997. *Quinceañera! The Essential Guide to Planning the Perfect Sweet Fifteen Celebration*. New York: Holt.
Vigil, Angel. 1998. *Una Linda Raza: Cultural and Artistic Traditions of the Hispanic Southwest*. Golden, CO: Fulcrum.

R

Radical Feminism

Proclaiming that gender, not class, constituted the primary category of analysis for any critique of American society, for a time in the late 1960s and early 1970s radical feminism became the heart and soul of the women's liberation movement. Upon breaking with the New Left over the subordination of women's issues within "the movement" in the 1960s, radical feminists rejected both the socialist perspective that the rising tide of a class revolution would inherently lift all women and the liberal feminist commitment to integration. Instead, radical feminists concluded that women made up a "sex class" in American society, thereby necessitating the need to reconsider all gender relations from a political perspective if equality of condition was ever to be achieved. Variously described as the most vital and creative wing of the women's liberation movement, radical feminists sought to walk the point in a broad assault against patriarchy and a misogynist culture. Ultimately they facilitated many of the earliest and most comprehensive analyses of women's roles within the family and marriage, as well as of sexuality, domestic violence, rape, birth control, day care, and sexual objectification.

Radical feminism, whether manifested on urban streets or college campuses, grew out of several key debates precipitat-ed by the genesis of second-wave feminism during the Vietnam era. From its inception, activists within the women's liberation movement were divided over what issues were most salient, how to effectively organize, or even what to call their nascent movement; "feminism" was discredited among many due to its association with the reformist first-wave feminism from the mid-nineteenth century through 1920, when women gained the vote. According to historian Alice Echols, much effort in the first years of the women's movement was spent trying to reconcile these problems among participants who eventually split into so-called politicos and feminists, the latter becoming known as "radical feminists." Both camps essentially offered the common leftist critique of the American system (including but not limited to its paternalistic foreign policies, racism, sexism, poverty, and the military-industrial complex) as inherently corrupt and in immediate need of a complete overhaul. Likewise, each believed the true enemy was not so much the overt manifestations of this diseased political and social system but instead the core institutions and people who served them. At the heart of their schism, however, were critical debates over whether women were primarily oppressed by capitalism (politicos) or men (feminists) and whether women should remain in the movement and help men tear down the system first before building a new one with greater gender equality (politicos) or organize outside the movement around women's issues (feminists).

Where radical feminists fundamentally broke with other male and female leftists was over the intractable nature of sexism and the ability of any type of revolution led by men, socialist or otherwise, to bring about liberation for all groups, women included. Although class, race, and sexual orientation divided radical feminists, the one common denominator they shared was the basic premise that women comprised a sex class in the United States and that issues of gender, not class, would be primary in restructuring society. Thus by subordinating class and race issues to gender, the achievement of women's liberation could undermine male supremacy and capitalism at once.

After making the determination to organize separately from men, the visionary core of radical feminism consisted of women in their twenties and thirties on the East Coast who organized groups such as the Redstockings, Cell 16, the Feminists, New York Radical Feminists, Women's International Terrorist Conspiracy from Hell (WITCH), and the Furies. At a time when men and women were attempting to renegotiate nearly every facet of American society, each of these groundbreaking groups helped to shape the character, look, and nature of women's activism while revealing the ongoing dialectics of the modern struggle for women's liberation. Like those in the New Left and counterculture, many radical feminists rejected mainstream American cultural sensibilities, announcing their political orientation by sporting faded jeans, long natural hair, and various elements of the hippie aesthetic. Yet what often set them apart in fashion and lifestyle was that these women openly celebrated their femininity and sexuality, all the while rejecting male definitions of sexual liberation.

Founded in 1969 by Ellen Willis and Shulamith Firestone, Redstockings is an excellent example of the radical feminist's pioneering commitment to "consciousness raising" as the primary vehicle for meaningful change. Perhaps the hallmark of the women's liberation movement, these often informal grassroots assemblies afforded women of all ages space to renegotiate gender roles and debilitating stereotypes, dispel feelings of inferiority, and forge new bonds of sisterhood. Although Redstockings—so named by Willis and Firestone because it appropriated the derisive term for early feminists (*bluestockings*) by combining it with the traditional color of revolution—focused chiefly on abortion, their early application of the truism "the personal is political" helped situate the confrontation with sexism firmly within existing social, familial, and marriage structures. Likewise, the Feminists, founded by radical feminist pioneer Ti-Grace Atkinson, and later New York Radical Feminists utilized consciousness raising as a vehicle through which they could create new self-conceptions and definitions of femininity and thereby deny men this historical tool of oppression.

Different groups like the more radical WITCH, Cell 16, and the Furies also epitomized radical feminism's original and creative forms of activism and highlighted other internal debates. Although still regarding personal experience as a sound foundation on which to base a movement, many radical feminists nevertheless labored over the importance and role of consciousness raising, fearing that by itself consciousness raising potentially impeded direct action. To address this concern, the 1968 Miss America pageant in Atlantic City was targeted for radical feminism's first "zap action." Inspired by the recent politically confrontational actions of the Youth International Party (Yippie) at the Chicago Democratic National Convention, radical feminists engaged in various productions of guerrilla theater, the countercultural method of using avant-garde theater to express dissent. Some of the more inspired productions included crowning a pig Miss America to decry the way women were judged; chaining themselves to a life-size "Amerika-Dollie" puppet to symbolize women's subjugation to artificial beauty standards; and disposing of various items of oppression such as bras, high heels, false eyelashes, and *Playboy* magazine into a "freedom trash can."

Building on this precedent, Robin Morgan, Florika, Peggy Dobbins, and others formed WITCH in 1968 as an action-oriented group dedicated to tweaking corporate America. On a national level, WITCH garnered modest media attention with their zap actions at the United Fruit Company, Chicago Transit Authority, several bridal fairs, and the financial district in New York. Outside the East Coast, the acronym was often altered by numerous local "covens" to reflect local concerns, such as Women Incensed at Telephone Company Harassment, Women Inspired to Commit Herstory, and Women Intent on Toppling Consumer Holidays. On college campuses, WITCH covens disrupted fraternity and sorority parties, homecoming queen contests, and certain faculty functions to draw atten-

tion to the systemic objectification of coeds. Eschewing guerrilla theater, Cell 16 simply chose to remove themselves physically and politically from male-dominated society, living communally and adhering to celibacy while training in martial arts for an eventual clash with American society. Taking Valerie Solana's decidedly separatist *SCUM Manifesto* to heart, Cell 16, founded in 1968, developed the reputation as the vanguard of militancy among feminist groups, even influencing movement style with their distinctive short hair, khaki pants, work shirts, and combat boots. The Furies, a lesbian-feminist collective founded in 1971, rivaled the others in radicalism but because of their presumption that heterosexuality buttressed sexism, advocated lesbianism as the only viable method for toppling American patriarchy. The growing prominence and visibility of the Furies and other lesbian groups within the women's movement eventually forced all female activists to address the "heterosexual presumption" and the political desirability of lesbianism.

On college campuses, radical feminism manifested itself in a variety of ways. Throughout the Vietnam era, college women of all ages, both students and faculty, tentatively organized around such issues as university restrictions on female freedom, sexual objectification, birth control, women's health, day care, equal employment opportunities, and equity in pay. Yet prior to 1968 the only formal organizations exclusively for women and dedicated to addressing these issues were dominated by NOW-style liberal feminists, and despite their efforts, most universities proved unresponsive or unyielding on most of these issues. In part, the suppression of women's issues on campus resulted from the uproar then being created by male militants and the determination on the part of the nation's universities not to reward dissent. Likewise, at a time when competition for publicity was intensifying among university and community dissenters, the actions of the nascent women's movement were often carried out without fanfare or media attention, and thus it was comparatively easier to place them on the back burner.

By the late 1960s, radical feminism developed on campus in response to these conditions and changes within the women's movement in general. Countless young coeds flocked to local consciousness-raising groups to begin to, as a young woman at a large midwestern university explained, "face the fact of yourself as exploited—as a worker, as a 'sex object,' as a political unit." For many young women coming of political age in the era, consciousness raising became the vehicle for them to "start thinking about obvious things like why women's wages are low" and "why sex is used to sell everything." Moreover, as the aforementioned coed concluded, the experience of talking and listening to various female perspectives instilled in them the conviction not to "let men's systems of thought—new left men as well as old right ones—replace thinking for yourself" (*Vortex* 1970, 1).

Aside from organizing thousands of consciousness-raising groups, radical feminists, disgusted with being perceived as "hot-pantsed groupies" to New Left men, joined the battles first begun by liberal feminists while articulating their own agenda. In many cases they demanded their universities create autonomous women's studies programs or, at the very least, begin teaching courses on the subject of women's liberation to institution-alize the newfound emphasis on the uniqueness of women and their growing solidarity. They led protests ranging from "speak-outs" to brief occupations of campus buildings, with the aim of compelling schools to hire more female faculty, make the pay scale more equitable, and promote female administrators. On some campuses young activists organized "women's centers" as clearinghouses for various women's activities, including libraries, switchboards, self-defense classes, abortion counseling, birth control and child care information, and women's education courses. Besides these genuine achievements that fundamentally altered college campuses, ultimately radical feminism unified a number of women and afforded an occasion to become more demanding and more visible.

By the early 1970s, radical feminism was weakened by its own inherent debates and contradictions. With more radical women alienated by lesbian-feminists, cultural feminism—similar in many ways to cultural nationalism within the Black Power movement—grew out of radical feminism and supplanted it as the dominant wing of the movement. The exclusive dedication to the creation of autonomous female space at the expense of social confrontations, which was inherent in cultural feminism, ultimately allowed more active liberal feminists to regain their position as the most visible and therefore most widely acknowledged leaders of the women's movement.

Joel P. Rhodes

See also College Girls; Girl Power; Red Diaper Girls

References and Further Reading
Cott, Nancy. 1989. *The Grounding of Modern Feminism*. New Haven: Yale University Press.

Echols, Alice. 1989. *Daring to Be Bad: Radical Feminism in America, 1967–1975.* Minneapolis: University of Minnesota Press.

Eisenstein, Zillah. 1981. *The Radical Future of Liberal Feminism.* New York: Longman.

Evans, Sara. 1979. *Personal Politics: The Roots of Women's Liberation in the Civil Rights Movement and the New Left.* New York: Vintage Books.

Freeman, Jo. 1975. *The Politics of Women's Liberation: A Case Study of an Emerging Social Movement and Its Relation to the Political Process.* New York: Mayfield Publishing.

Harrison, Cynthia. 1989. *On Account of Sex: The Politics of Women's Issues, 1945–1968.* Berkeley: University of California Press.

Millett, Kate. 1971. *Sexual Politics.* Garden City, NY: Doubleday.

Morgan, Robin. 1970. *Sisterhood Is Powerful: An Anthology of Writings from the Women's Liberation Movement.* New York: Vintage.

———. 1978. *Going Too Far.* New York: Random House.

Vortex, Women's Issue. 1970. Lawrence: University of Kansas Libraries, 1.

Reading

Early Americans imported most of their books from England. American girls' reading materials in the seventeenth and eighteenth centuries consisted primarily of the Bible, Puritan tracts, educational texts like the *New England Primer,* and manuals written to teach young ladies how to behave properly. In the late eighteenth century, British authors like Maria Edgeworth and Anna Letitia Barbauld had a great effect on young female readers by providing a shift in emphasis away from Puritanism toward a more secularized didacticism. However, children's magazines probably provide the most significant markers of the emergence of a distinct form of literature for children.

Children's magazines became popular in the 1800s and provided young readers with a greater variety of reading material than ever before, including short fiction, nonfiction, poetry, and artwork all wrapped up in one inexpensive package just for kids. More than 130 juvenile periodicals were launched between 1840 and 1870 and 105 between 1870 and 1900 (Avery 1994, 146). *The Juvenile Miscellany,* edited first by Lydia Maria Child and later by Sara Josepha Hale (1826–1836); *The Youth's Companion,* originally published by Nathaniel P. Willis (1827–1929); *The Riverside Magazine for Young People,* edited by Horace Scudder (1867–1871); and *St. Nicholas,* edited by Mary Mapes Dodge (1873–1940), each provided a showcase for American women authors who made names for themselves through their magazine contributions. But it was the nineteenth-century division between the domestic novel and the adventure story that really marked the development of gender-specific literature.

Susan Warner's *The Wide, Wide World* (1850) and Louisa May Alcott's *Little Women* (1868–1869) were among the most popular domestic novels, exceeding even the sales of British favorites by Sir Walter Scott and Charles Dickens. Domestic novels emphasized the home as the most important site for moral development that would penetrate the public realm. These texts took the roles of girls and women seriously as saviors of their culture and also offered distinctly American heroines who were independent, sturdy, and practical. Girls' books were generally expected to reinforce the importance of women's roles in society as private and domestic. However, the power of girls' stories seemed to be in their allowance of moments of power beyond the home. The development of literature for girls was linked to the creation of characters who allowed girls to act out fantasies of power that may have been stifled in their real lives. Domestic novels often focused on a "naughty girl" who was reformed through the course of the story into an "ideal woman."

Ellen Montgomery, the heroine of *The Wide, Wide World*, is just such a girl. Ellen suffers a great loss with the death of her mother and is forced to live with her cruel aunt, who continually thwarts her desires. Despite the fact that Ellen is ultimately "tamed," her wildness and rebelliousness provided girls with an acknowledgment of their own often denied or unsatisfied desires. Even Ellen's frequent crying spells represent her ability to act out against patriarchal outrages for which she has no other recourse, and her eventual moral conversion allows her to influence and convert male figures of authority in the novel (Foster and Simons 1995, 49–51).

Alcott's *Little Women* is a less overtly religious story that, nevertheless, emphasizes a kind of moral conversion from tomboy to wife. Jo March cuts her hair off like a boy and acts in ways that are traditionally masculine. She disobeys authority, expresses dissatisfaction with accepted feminine roles, and launches her own career as a writer; eventually, however, she does marry (though not the typical hero) and settle down into some form of domesticity. Barbara Sicherman discusses at length the self-authorizing effect Jo's assertive behavior has had on female readers for more than a century in her essay "Reading *Little Women*: The Many Lives of a Text" (1995). Overall, though, domestic novels suggest that growing into womanhood "is a learned and often fraught process, not an instinctual or natural condition of female development (Foster and Simons 1995, 87). As Anne MacLeod notes, "The child who read late-nineteenth-century books could hardly avoid the conclusion that the end of childhood was also the end of the best part of life. Certainly, a girl was unlikely to miss the message that puberty would be for her the beginning of imprisonment in a 'woman's sphere'" (MacLeod 1994, 29). Though the rebelliousness of the domestic novel is typically contained at the end, the possibility was open for girls to focus on and remember the subversiveness of the characters' behavior and the regret felt by the girl who must "shape up" and prepare to enter adulthood.

During the nineteenth century, the subject of girls' reading became a hot topic of debate. John Ruskin's emphatic warning to parents in *Sesame and Lilies* to "keep the modern magazine and novel out of your girl's way" (1864, 66) exemplifies the nineteenth-century conception that popular literature could be detrimental to female readers. The widespread concern about the dangers of girls' reading was intimately linked to the explosion of the publishing industry in the mid-1800s, which made periodicals and novels inexpensive commodities easily obtained by middle-class readers.

Technological advances in printing and paper production, along with the expansion of the railroads and the patriotic desire of Americans to create their own national literature, contributed to this publishing boom. By 1850 the United States was a full-fledged capitalist economy that was beginning to carve out distinct market niches. Thus, the publication of books that targeted the emerging audience of youthful readers became a central—rather than a marginal—part of the publishing industry. As M. E. M. Blake observed in 1891, one publishing firm alone produced 1,250,000 children's storybooks, 100,000 bound literary annuals, and 75 novels. In addition, the "bewildering array" of magazines for juveniles constituted "not less than 1,200,000 individual volumes, with reprints in the shape of miscellaneous collections that would count at least 5,000,000 more" (475–476).

The overwhelming abundance of reading material was seen as a particular problem for parents, librarians, and critics, who noted the need for strict regulation of children's reading practices because "the readers of this worse than worthless literature mount every year into hundreds of thousands, and publishers are found reckless and vile enough to sow those seeds of death for sake of the filthy profits they receive" (Blake 1891, 477). Although the expression of fears about the proliferation of "bad literature" was standard critical fare, such hyperbolic language was most often used in relation to girls' reading.

Girls—especially those who were on the verge of womanhood—were conceived of as a special problem. At the turn of the century, girlhood was a vague category that included "any unmarried female of genteel family background between the ages of, say, five and twenty-five" (Nelson and Vallone 1994, 9). No longer playing with dolls but not yet marriageable, on the verge of sexuality and subjectivity, girls were liminal figures who floated between boundaries and resisted categorization. Girlhood, therefore, was potentially subversive of patriarchal values. Sally Mitchell notes that although most girls lived traditional, domestic lives that coincided with the values of the dominant culture, there was a consciousness of a particular "girl's culture." It was most evident in books

and magazines that actually invented the word *girl* itself as a replacement for the outdated term *young lady* (1995, 3–6).

The comparative freedom of girlhood combined with the free range of printed texts available to girls inspired responses such as F. M. Edselas's "What Shall We Do with Our Girls?" (1895) and Lutie E. Stearns's "The Problem of the Girl" (1906). These articles conceptualized girls' reading as a particular conundrum that was vital to solve in order to produce women who would be good wives and mothers. Edselas pinpoints the problem by asking what one should do with the girl so that she may "become a truer, nobler woman? . . . Perilous beyond human ken is that transition state called maidenhood" (1895, 538–539). Stearns likewise reports that "there is no more perplexing problem that confronts the modern librarian, teacher and parent, than the selection of books for the girl . . . who is separated from womanhood by such a brief span that her ideas, acts and ideals are rapidly taking on the aspects of maturity" (1906, 103). Despite the efforts to improve librarians' and teachers' skills in directing girls' reading, the burden weighed most heavily on mothers:

The influence of home teaching is enormous; all the school can do pales before it. Let the mother add to the poet's rhyme the music of her soft and beloved voice; let great fiction be read to the breathless group of curly heads about the fire; and the wonders of science be unrolled, the trilling scenes and splendid personalities of history displayed. Children thus inspired may be trusted to become sensitive to literature long before they know what the word means. (Burton 1898, 286)

This mid-nineteenth-century lithograph shows a mother teaching her daughter how to read. (Library of Congress)

A girl's proper reading of the right literature was seen as an antidote to the dangers of modern life and a sign of an effective mother. As Stearns's survey of girl readers indicated, "Many girls whose reading showed contact with good, healthful literature showed also the influence of a refined home" (1906, 104). The influence of mothers on their children's reading was deemed so essential that it was equated with their influence over their children's cleanliness; just as mothers must coax their children into seeing the "intrinsic merit of soap and water" by "forced application three times daily for at least six to eight years," so must they coax their girls into reading properly (Blake 1891, 482).

As more and more dime novels, sensational tales, and series books were published, critics called for a return to the days when children and adults consumed the same great literary texts, when they were interested primarily in "classic" British novelists like Jane Austen, Sir Walter Scott, and Dickens:

> Fashion in reading has changed and it must be confessed, for the worse. . . . After girls satiate their minds with the second-rate, the insipid, or the ultra-sentimental, they have lost the key to the great kingdom of the good and the beautiful. . . . The modern parent, teacher, and librarian cannot escape blame for the present state of affairs. The modern mother exercises far less supervision over her daughter than did the mother of a generation ago. (Stearns 1906, 105)

Thus, mothers were called upon to play a more active role in guiding their daughters in the selection of literature. Renewing the habit of reading aloud, which formerly united the family around the hearth, was frequently suggested as "the greatest safeguard" for "sobriety and carefulness in the matter of approaching a book" (Blake 1891, 481). Containing girls' reading within the domestic sphere would, it was hoped, eliminate the potential of girlhood rebellion.

According to Nancy Tillman Romalov, the assumption among librarians was that with more extensive and fast-paced reading, the benefits of reading were lost. Romalov's study of girls' own letters to authors of the popular books they read indicates "the ways in which girls literally inscribed themselves into the books" and "engaged in this mass-marketed and consumer-oriented fiction in intensely public and meaningful ways" by creating communal reading experiences and joining together in collective fantasies that affected how girls saw themselves socially (1996, 93). So to a certain extent, the fears about girls' were well founded: reading could further separate girls from traditional society and allow them to live in a liberating world of their own, if only for a short time.

Although the moral lessons of domestic novels made them acceptable reading choices for girls, nineteenth-century dime novels and their offspring, twentieth-century series books, presented greater cause for concern among adults. As Romalov argues,

> girls' reading of series books was a noisy, . . . public and communal activity rather than one characterized as quiet, private, or passive. When girls read non-sanctioned series books, they were engaging in a mild form of protest against those authorities who,

believing the books not only inferior but dangerously habit-forming, would keep the books from them. . . . In contrast to mainstream literature, the series books did not attempt to woo the adult through their language, subject, or pedagogical value but were addressed exclusively to female readers. (1996, 90)

Series books in particular inspired fear and disdain among librarians and critics, who saw the series as a fully capitalistic venture that was characterized by poor writing and sensational plots. Series books symbolized the plummeting taste of Americans. The most successful publisher of these books was the Stratemeyer Syndicate. Stratemeyer created girls' series such as the Motor Girls, which exemplified girls' independence and escape from traditional domesticity through their technological know-how and adventurousness, as well as the most famous of all series books, the Nancy Drew Mysteries. Nancy Drew books conveyed girls' intellectual abilities, assertiveness, and practicality. Nancy's dominance over her boyfriend Ned and her father, a lawyer, provided powerful wish fulfillment for girls who were used to seeing female characters demur to males. Nancy is essentially a female character who is allowed to fulfill a masculine role, though this is hidden beneath a conventional sense of propriety: "Autonomy is her *right*, won by her responsible and intelligent management of practically everything" (MacLeod 1994, 39–40). The independence of Nancy Drew and the series heroines was followed up by a return to domesticity in the 1950s stories that focused on accepting oneself and becoming a wife and a mother. However, series books have continued to thrive and are still an important part of girls' reading

today. Sherrie A. Inness's collection of essays, *Nancy Drew and Company* (1997), emphasizes the cultural importance of girls' series books throughout the twentieth century.

The increasingly consumer-oriented culture of the prosperous postwar 1940s and 1950s spawned a new wave in girls' reading practices, with the birth of teen magazines such as *Seventeen Magazine*, which debuted in September 1944. The growing influence of school and peers on teens proved instrumental in creating an even more differentiated youth subculture that included its own fashions, music, and attitudes capitalized on by teen magazines. But *Seventeen* proved popular because it made girls feel that they fit in somewhere, that they were doing something more than just lurking on the borderline between girlhood and womanhood. As one girl reader of the magazine wrote: "some of these so-called magazines for the high school crowd . . . either have us in the Fifth Grade having our pigtails pulled or seated at a bar in some swanky night-club, fluttering our eyelashes at some Navy lieutenant" (quoted in Schrum 1998, 140). Although *Seventeen* defined the teenage girl as a means of promoting and selling products, Teena, the magazine's mascot, was attractive to readers because of her sassy attitude, fashion sense, and consumer skills. Still, letters from readers indicate teenage girls' willingness to resist the fashion, beauty, and dating advice provided by the magazine. Girls were particularly vocal about their objections to girdles, which the magazine pushed in its advice columns and advertising campaigns (Schrum 1998, 135, 151). This early example of the marriage between girls' culture and marketing is taken even further today by a plethora of teen magazines, including *Sassy* and *YM* (formerly *Young Miss*), and fashion catalogues aimed specifically at girls like *Delia's*, which has its own bedroom decorating products as well as a clothing line. And the Pleasant Company's *American Girl* magazine features tie-ins to the American Girls Collection of dolls, including a line of historical books about girls, a matching catalog of dolls and doll accessories, and girl-sized clothes that match those for the dolls.

Nevertheless, reading—in whatever form it takes—is considered a positive activity for girls, far preferable to watching television, the latest target of critical outcry. Today, the concerns adults have about girls' reading have shifted from its ability to corrupt girls' taste and values (which is now the primary venue of the media) to the effects of reading on a girl's self-worth and development of an independent identity. As Angela Hubler's recent study of adolescent readers shows, girls often ignore repressive endings and resist sexist stereotypes, instead engaging with and remembering the strong, independent, and heroic qualities of the girls about whom they read. In other words, girls often take from their reading what best suits their needs. Hubler calls this "liberatory reading," an act that allows readers to imagine alternatives to traditional gender roles. Such "reading strategies suggest that [girls] are actively engaged with the literature they read: they participate with the author in the construction of the text" (1998, 270–271). Hubler further asserts that the "status of many classics for girls may, in fact, be based on their ability to foster this awareness of, and thus resistance to, repressive female gender roles" (1998, 282). Thus even as concerns about girls' reading have changed, it seems that girls' responses to

A nine-year-old girl reads in her backyard garden. (Skjold Photographs)

their reading experiences have always been—to some extent—selective and potentially empowering.

Jennifer Phegley

See also Advice Books; American Girls Collection; Girls' Culture; Girls' Fiction; Girls' Magazines; Literacy; Nancy Drew Mysteries; Zines

References and Further Reading
Avery, Gillian. 1994. *Behold the Child: American Children and Their Books 1621–1922*. Baltimore: Johns Hopkins University Press.
Blake, M. E. M. 1891. "Literature and the Formation of Character." *Catholic World* 53 (July): 475–484.
Burton, Richard. 1898. "Literature for Our Children." *North American Review* 167: 278–286.

Edselas, F. M. 1895. "What Shall We Do
with Our Girls?" *Catholic World* 61
(July): 538–545.

Foster, Shirley, and Judy Simons. 1995.
*What Katy Read: Feminist Re-Readings
of "Classic" Stories for Girls.* Iowa
City: University of Iowa Press.

Hubler, Angela E. 1998. "Can Anne
Shirley Help 'Revive Ophelia'?
Listening to Girl Readers." Pp. 266–284
in *Delinquents and Debutantes:
Twentieth-Century American Girls'
Cultures.* Edited by Sherrie A. Inness.
New York: New York University Press.

Inness, Sherrie A., ed. 1997. *Nancy Drew
and Company: Culture, Gender, and
Girls' Series.* Bowling Green: Bowling
Green State University Popular Press.

MacLeod, Anne Scott. 1994. *American
Childhood: Essays on Children's
Literature of the Nineteenth and
Twentieth Centuries.* Athens:
University of Georgia Press.

Mitchell, Sally. 1995. *The New Girl:
Girls' Culture in England, 1880–1915.*
New York: Columbia University Press.

Murray, Gail Schmunk. 1998. *American
Children's Literature and the
Construction of Childhood.* New York:
Twayne Publishers.

Nelson, Claudia, and Lynne Vallone.
1994. *The Girl's Own: Cultural
Histories of the Anglo-American Girl,
1830–1915.* Athens: University of
Georgia Press.

Romalov, Nancy Tillman. 1996.
"Unearthing the Historical Reader, or,
Reading Girls' Reading." *Primary
Sources and Original Works* 4 (1–2):
87–101.

Ruskin, John. 1864. *Sesame and Lilies.*
1965. New York: Everyman's Library.

Schrum, Kelly. 1998. "'Teena Means
Business': Teenage Girls' Culture and
Seventeen Magazine, 1944–1950." Pp.
134–163 in *Delinquents and
Debutantes: Twentieth-Century
American Girls' Cultures.* Edited by
Sherrie Inness. New York: New York
University Press.

Sicherman, Barbara. 1995. "Reading *Little
Women*: The Many Lives of a Text."
Pp. 245–266 in *U.S. History as
Women's History: New Feminist
Essays.* Edited by Linda Kerber et al.
Chapel Hill: University of North
Carolina Press.

Stearns, Lutie E. 1906. "The Problem of
the Girl." *The Library Journal* 31:
103–106.

Red Diaper Girls

Red diaper girls are female "red diaper babies": they are the daughters of communists, former communists, or so-called fellow travelers, nonparty members who regularly participated in political, social, or cultural activities sponsored by the Communist Party (CP) and its affiliated organizations. Although red diaper girls are still being born, the term generally refers to a mid-twentieth-century experience of girlhood because the CP was most able to attract a following between 1920 and 1956.

According to Judy Kaplan and Linn Shapiro, the term *red diaper baby* originated in the 1920s, coined by CP activists who scorned those attempting to use birthright to move up in party ranks. In the 1960s the John Birch Society revived the label when they published a list of red diaper babies enrolled at the University of California at Berkeley in an attempt to intimidate student activists. That effort backfired because the list actually enabled politically minded students to find one another. By the 1970s, adults who had grown up in the communist milieu began identifying themselves as "red diaper babies." The waning of anticommunist fervor in the United States made it possible for them to begin assessing the ways in which the political culture of the party had shaped their sense of identity, values, ambitions, and life choices.

Red diaper babies have had enough in common to make the label meaningful, but their experiences have varied in sig-

A labor protest on May Day in New York City. (Courtesy of the Tamiment Institute Library, New York University, John Albok Collection, 1936)

nificant ways, not only from family to family but more generally according to generation, region, class, race, ethnicity, religion, and gender. Children growing up in cities with relatively strong radical traditions—such as New York or Los Angeles—were more likely to be part of a supportive left-wing community than those growing up in rural areas in the South or the Midwest. Jewish red diaper babies often took part in a vibrant, secular Jewish culture that combined radical politics with Jewish traditions. Children of immigrants—that is, most of the first generation of red diaper babies—experienced unique issues around assimilation. Perhaps more than others, African American red diaper babies experienced the struggles against economic oppression and against racism as inseparable objectives. And red diaper *girls*, from varying backgrounds, had to reconcile a heightened political consciousness with contradictory messages about women's roles, messages that came not just from American society in general but also from the insular world of the left. But whether from New York or Birmingham; whether Jewish, African American, or first-generation Italian; whether a child of the Depression or the Cold War, red diaper babies grew up conscious of their status as "outsiders" in American culture.

Most fundamentally, their parents questioned a core American belief in capitalism, but their childhoods were unusual in other ways as well. These children, forced to disguise their family's politics in their everyday lives, led a split existence: at home they said "People's Republic of China" and "Soviet Union," though at school they were careful to say "Red China" and "Russia." At school they learned that communists were destroying "the American Way of Life"; at home they were told that textbooks, teachers, newspapers, and movies were full of lies. The sense of having a split identity was often worse for girls than for boys, though their outsider status may have made it easier to question society's constrictive gender norms. Red diaper girls tended to grow up with strong female role models, and they recognized gender equality as an ideal (if not always a practice in their own homes). This ideal of equality, coupled with their forced or chosen status as outsiders, meant that red diaper girls often saw norms governing femininity, fashion, and popularity as in conflict with many of the values they learned at home; thus girlhood itself was fraught, especially for red diaper girls growing up in the 1950s at the height of the "feminine mystique." But whether a girl was mortified or proud when her date saw the *Daily Worker* on the coffee table had much to do with the particularities of her temperament and family situation. Those children who felt

nourished and nurtured by their parents' commitments tended to relish their outsider status; those more keenly aware of their parents' limitations often had a more difficult road.

Girls and boys raised in the CP milieu and trained to identify social contradictions were quick to notice when parents did not put their "progressive" and democratic ideals into practice at home. One woman whose strict Marxist father forbade her religious Jewish mother from teaching the children any prayers or religious rituals remembers her father's rigid control extending over the friends she chose, the books she read, and the clothes she wore; she even recalls being forced to change a school essay to conform with her father's economic interpretation of history. Other girls felt that their parents spent so much time fighting for the world's oppressed peoples that they had little left for their own children. But at least as many girls and boys had positive experiences: their parents were open-minded, thoughtful, and willing to take their questions and opinions seriously.

In either case, girls raised in the CP milieu grew up perceiving a clear moral universe that distinguished right from wrong and "progressive" from reactionary. They understood commitment to social change as a moral imperative and passive acceptance of injustice as a sin. Their oppositional identity and sense of solidarity with an international, multicultural working class were often sources of pride for girls. "As children of the left we had always known we had a meaningful place in the Communist vision," Kim Chernin notes. "We were the hope and promise; it was we who carried the hope of the revolution they had expected in their youth" (1983, 243). For some girls that hope was a burden; others resented their families' oddities and longed to be "normal."

Identification with the communist movement was all-encompassing. During the years that the CP was most able to expand its ranks (the 1930s and 1940s), members and related groups sponsored a wide variety of activities and created an array of cultural forms to socialize children. Activities included summer camps, after-school programs, singing societies, sports, theater, and even a special unit of the party for children, the Young Pioneers. Party-influenced secular-Jewish, ethnic, and fraternal organizations such as the Yiddish *shules*, Finnish social halls, and the International Workers Order had special programs and publications for children. Centers of Marxist education like the Jefferson School of Social Science and the California Labor School had story hours, dance, music, and other activities for girls and boys; communist publications from the *Daily Worker* to the *Fraternal Outlook* had children's pages; and the CP published dozens of children's books that openly or subtly criticized capitalism, racism, and nationalism, discussing history, science, and everyday life from a "working-class" perspective.

Beyond party-sponsored culture was a less formal but perhaps even more significant "progressive" universe. For girls as well as boys it was characterized by certain children's books (usually by radical authors) like the interracial picture book *Two Is a Team*; certain "progressive" schools like the Downtown Community School in New York; certain communities and community centers like the cooperatives in the Bronx or the Unitarian Church in Los Angeles (especially in the McCarthy era); and certain kinds of music: Pete Seeger, Paul Robeson, and

anything from Folkways or the Young People's Record Club. Hazy as the latter emblems of "progressive" childhood were, many recalling their red diaper girlhoods insist that most of the "communist" values and ideas they learned came more via "osmosis" than through formal party activities.

There was no "party line" on parenting, although the CP discourse around childhood and socialization reflected the party's changing relationship to American society and institutions, as well as more general trends in childrearing and education. During the 1920s and early 1930s, the CP attempted to develop a "proletarian perspective on childhood"; to do so it "focused on the poverty and social crisis that were part of so many working-class children's lives, and on the ways these conditions were created by capitalism" (Mishler 1999, 20). Thus in the early 1930s when the Children's Bureau was distributing a pamphlet that asked, "Are You Training Your Child to Be Happy?" the CP was distributing one on "Children under Capitalism" and urging children themselves to become militant activists. In addition to marching in May Day parades, Young Pioneers in the early 1930s protested child labor and run-down schools and called for free lunches and more playgrounds. The CP's "proletarian" perspective on childhood included girls but was notoriously gender-blind, if not biased toward boys. Though party literature recognized the special burdens faced by working *mothers*, it rarely differentiated between boys and girls. Moreover, frequent criticisms of organizations like the Boy Scouts were rarely matched by attention to organizations serving girls or to typical girl activities.

This began to change as the CP, attempting to enter the American mainstream in the mid-1930s, developed a rhetoric of inclusivity. Parenting advice in organs of the CP left became almost indistinguishable from the "progressive" or "democratic" childrearing approach characteristic of Arnold Gesell or Benjamin Spock. For the left, family "togetherness" meant that children were more likely to participate in left-wing activities with their parents, rather than through separate children's organizations (although left-wing summer camps also proliferated during this time). The inclusive rhetoric of the "popular front" against fascism emphasized racial and ethnic diversity, but there developed as well in CP publications for children at least some attention to gender issues. Perhaps Sasha Small's book for children, *Heroines*, was most striking in this respect: it contained portraits of Mollie Pitcher, Lucretia Mott, Frances Wright, Clara Zetkin, Nadezhda Krupskaya, Elizabeth Gurley Flynn, Mother Jones, Ella Reeve Bloor, Harriet Tubman, and "women under fascism."

The informal "movement culture" characteristic of the CP milieu became more important as McCarthyism eroded formal party structures and party membership dwindled. When anticommunism became a national preoccupation in the 1950s, the children of communists experienced McCarthyism as a threat to their own families. How much children were told about their parents' activity varied, but all understood that there were secrets, that being "different" involved a risk. Even those children kept ignorant of their parents' work in the party might not have been saved from the fear and anxiety parents communicated along with their beliefs and values. The fear was greatest, of course, for children whose parents were investigated, black-

listed, arrested, or moved "underground" by the party. Several red diaper babies spent their entire childhoods in exile; others lived apart from one or both parents for months or even years. All children of the left understood that their parents were at best unusual and at worst in grave danger. Those who grew up in the 1950s inevitably recalled the execution of Julius and Ethel Rosenberg for espionage as a traumatic event: if the "innocent" Rosenbergs could be imprisoned and put to death, so might their own parents be. For red diaper *girls* growing up during the Cold War, the feminine mystique and McCarthyism were mutually reinforcing forces that contributed to profound anxiety and confusion.

The obvious question to ask of red diaper girls is whether their experience in the CP milieu was more likely to make them feminists. Although communists typically dismissed "feminism" as a bourgeois movement that failed to consider the primacy of economic oppression, the "woman question" was regularly raised in party discourse in terms of the ways in which women (and especially women of racial minorities) faced a double burden under capitalism. Women were encouraged to take active roles in the party, and even the gendered division of labor within households was increasingly critiqued (at least in principle) by the late 1940s as part of a broader attack on "male supremacy." Party discussions of children often arose in the context of discussing the "woman question"—thus reifying some of the very categories these discussions sought to counter—but this meant that concerns about children's socialization might encompass, at least subconsciously, some attention to gender norms.

Girls growing up in the communist milieu often had mothers who worked full-time, who took an active interest in politics and culture, and who played important roles in party organizations. Most red diaper girls were told by their parents that they were equal to boys and that all paths in life were open to them. But in their own households mothers tended to be in charge of housework and child care, whether they worked outside the home or not. Even in homes where domestic labor was shared, many girls understood that their fathers were the intellectual authorities and recognized that their mothers' views—and the realm of the "feminine" in general—were less important. But other girls grew up in homes where mothers were even more committed activists than fathers. And if talk of the "woman question" subsided under the pressures imposed by McCarthyism, women nevertheless continued to show their daughters the importance of activism, even if that was by acting in a traditionally feminine capacity, for instance by serving on the "families committee" for the Smith Act prisoners or by joining Women Strike for Peace. (The Smith Act, passed in 1940, made it "illegal to teach or advocate the overthrow of the government or to join any organization that did" [Schrecker 1994, 15]. The United States government filed Smith Act charges against nearly 150 people, including most of the CP's top leaders).

As primary caretakers, women were perhaps the most important purveyors of the left's values. Moreover, scholars have uncovered direct links between the Old Left and second-wave feminism (as well as other postwar social movements). Still, to the extent that the CP left enforced a division between public (political) and private (personal), red diaper daughters who joined the New Left, civil rights, women's liberation, or gay liberation movements sometimes did so partly in *reaction* to their upbringing.

Red diaper girls have come to terms with their political legacies in very different ways. A minority followed in their parents' footsteps and joined the CP themselves; more often, young women translated their upbringing to fit a different kind of political activity and engagement. Some eschewed political involvement completely. Though many, if not most, red diaper babies retained a commitment to social justice and activism in some form, they often experienced a devastating loss of faith when they came to recognize the flaws in their parents' vision. This was especially so for those whose adolescence coincided with the 1956 report by Nikita Khrushchev admitting to atrocities committed under Joseph Stalin's rule in the Soviet Union. But however and to whatever degree it might occur, loss of political faith was in some ways a loss of childhood. As Kim Chernin puts it, "When for some of us the vision had collapsed, it left an emptiness that reached back into the earliest experience of childhood and shook the very fundamentals of memory" (1983, 243). In the post-Soviet, post–Cold War era, in which communism seems to many more like an anachronism than a threat, it is possible to romanticize childhood in the all-encompassing world of American communism. But in fact that experience, though different for every girl, was characterized by a complex combination of pride and shame, public activity and secrecy, a sense of specialness and a sense of alienation. The complexity of that experience and the full impact of red diaper girls on American society remain to be assessed.

Julia Mickenberg

See also Radical Feminism; Work

References and Further Reading

Belfrage, Sally. 1994. *Un-American Activities: A Memoir of the Fifties*. New York: HarperCollins.

Chernin, Kim. 1983. *In My Mother's House: A Daughter's Story*. New York: HarperCollins.

Evans, Sara. 1979. *Personal Politics: The Roots of Women's Liberation in the Civil Rights Movement and the New Left*. New York: Vintage Books.

Horowitz, Daniel. 1998. *Betty Friedan and the Making of the Feminine Mystique: The American Left, the Cold War, and Modern Feminism*. Amherst: University of Massachusetts Press.

Kaplan, Judy, and Linn Shapiro. 1985. *Red Diaper Babies: Children of the Left. Edited Transcripts of Conferences Held at the World Fellowship Center, Conway, NH*. Somerville, MA: Red Diaper Productions.

———. 1998. *Red Diapers: Growing Up in the Communist Left*. Urbana: University of Illinois Press.

Kimmage, Ann. 1996. *An Un-American Childhood*. Athens: University of Georgia Press.

Lieberman, Robbie. 1989. *My Song Is My Weapon: People's Songs, American Communism, and the Politics of Culture, 1930–1950*. Urbana: University of Illinois Press.

Meyers, Joan. 1999. "Secret Lives: The Making of Feminist Red Diaper Daughters." Master's thesis, San Francisco State University.

Mickenberg, Julia. 2000. "Educating Dissent: Children's Literature and the Left, 1935–1965." Ph.D. diss., University of Minnesota.

Mishler, Paul. 1999. *Raising Reds: The Young Pioneers, Radical Summer Camps, and Communist Political Culture in the United States*. New York: Columbia University Press.

Schrecker, Ellen. 1994. *The Age of McCarthyism: A Brief History with Documents*. Boston and New York: Bedford Books of St. Martin's Press.

Small, Sasha. 1937. *Heroines*. New York: Workers Library.

Weigand, Kathleen A. 2001. *Red Feminism: American Communism and the Making of Women's Liberation*. Baltimore: Johns Hopkins University Press.

Relational Theory

Traditional Western developmental psychologies have emphasized a trajectory of growth for all people characterized by movement toward autonomy, separation, and independence. These models of growth and maturity are based on a dominant value system that privileges highly individualistic human beings. Self-sufficiency and autonomy are seen as desirable characteristics in North American Eurocentric culture. By these standards of development, girls and women are often viewed as lacking because they are seen as too dependent, too emotional, too needy, and not cognitively abstract and linear enough. Thus the psychology of "human beings," based on values held for adult males, judges girls and women as "lacking." New understandings of the psychology of girls and women, however, suggest that girls in American culture organize their sense of meaning and feelings of worth in relationship with others.

Most theorists agree that gender differences arise from an interplay of biology and socialization and that there is considerable overlap between male and female psychological development. The core sex differences appear to revolve around the greater frequency of direct aggression and rough-and-tumble play among boys and greater attention to relationships among girls. And furthermore, it is likely that the primary gender differences that are reliably reported in social behavior occur in the context of exposure to different cultures in childhood: a boy culture and a girl culture. Boy cultures emphasize competition, power, and separation from others, whereas girl cultures emphasize cooperation, relationality, and nonaggression as gender ideals.

More traditional models promoted the ideas that anatomy was destiny, that penis envy heavily influenced a girl's sense of worth, and that girls were destined to be objects to serve male subjectivity (Freud 1959; Beauvoir 1971). But there is abundant evidence that parents and teachers treat boys and girls differently, with boys accorded more status and encouragement for agency. Power differentials may be essential to the sex differences that have been observed and may also figure importantly in differences among girls and women in terms of race, class, sexual orientation, and other sources of "diversity." Failure to acknowledge the white, middle-class, heterosexual bias of most gender theories leads to a major misrepresentation of everyone's experience.

Contemporary theories of girls' development increasingly emphasize the centrality of relationships in girls' lives and suggest that girls grow through and toward relationships (Miller 1976; Gilligan 1982; Jordan et al. 1991). These relational theories point to the inevitable interdependence that human beings experience but, in particular, note that girls in most Western cultures are socialized to create relationships that foster growth. Although all people undoubtedly yearn for connection and a sense of meaning in relationships, the emphasis on connecting is especially cogent for girls and women. In growth-fostering relationships, both people create a relationship that is characterized by mutual empowerment and mutual empathy and that encourages a sense of zest, clarity, mutual growth, productivity, and a desire for more connection. This model moves away from a psychology that overemphasizes autonomy.

Mutual empathy is at the heart of growth-fostering relationships. All people are born with a certain readiness to develop empathic skills; in fact, there may be a neurological basis in the limbic system of the brain for the evolution of empathy (Maclean 1958). Modern Western cultures tend to encourage empathy in girls and discourage it somewhat in boys; boys are taught to control their emotions, whereas girls are taught to be responsive, tuned in, and "caring." Individuals and relationships grow and flourish when there is an interactive, mutual empathy between people. People in such relationships gain confidence, feel good about themselves, and contribute to the well-being of the other person.

This relational understanding of girls' and women's development is at odds with the prevailing models of development that emphasize an increasing capacity for separation, the development of the self, and the individual's role as an autonomous and independent being. These more traditional models of development pertain to the valued socialization for boys in this culture: "the boy code" indicates that boys and men should be tough, autonomous, and abstract and linear rather than emotive and intuitive in their thinking; they most definitely should not show vulnerability or a need for connection (Pollack 1999). Thus the traditional sex-role prescriptions for boys suggest that boys need to separate firmly and early from mothers and fathers, control emotions that might make them vulnerable (sadness, fear, sensitivity, tenderness), and develop their aggressive potential. Control and independence have been celebrated as indicative of maturity for all people in Western culture (Broverman et al. 1970). The mature individual and the mature man are seen as possessing overlapping characteristics. When standards of maturity that were developed to explain male development are applied to women, however, women are seen as deficient.

In Western cultures, little girls are encouraged to learn the empathic skills that are ultimately involved in mothering. They are supported in their expressions of care for others, allowed a wide range of emotional expression and awareness of their own vulnerability, and given permission to ask for help. Until adolescence, little girls can try out a variety of behaviors without regard to gender expectations (e.g., girls can be active, assertive, competitive, angry, instrumental and caring, or fearful). Young girls are often seen as sturdy, resilient, confident, and caring about connection. Using Carol Gilligan's metaphor, they speak in clear, strong voices (Gilligan 1982). Girls are also relatively free to behave in ways that are stereotypically masculine; that is, they can be "tomboys," athletic, assertive, and even competitive.

Much of girls' energy is devoted to making relationships that are characterized by dyadic pairings in which sharing, self-disclosure, and mutual support constitute the main "activity." Gilligan (1982) reports research by Lever that suggests in play situations, when conflict arises, young girls stop the game to preserve the relationship, whereas boys head into the conflict with the aim of winning. Maccoby (1990) has also shown that in same-sex peer groups, boys tend to vie for positions of power and hierarchy and are directed toward activity rather than connection. Girls tend to talk, listen, and seek help and are motivated toward making good connection rather than establishing positions of power or advantage. Studies suggest that in schools, girls are shortchanged by systems that reward the more assertive and

sometimes impulsive style of many boys (Sadker and Sadker 1994). Boys get more "air time" because they raise their hands faster, blurt out answers, and exude a kind of confidence. Boys tend to attribute success to personal effort and failure to chance, whereas girls do the opposite (Dweck and Repucci 1973). But girls excel in school in the early years and show fewer behavioral problems than boys do. In the elementary years, boys are referred for mental health counseling at a much higher rate than girls.

In most developmental theories, adolescence is seen as a time of great change, bridging the worlds of childhood and adulthood. It is commonly portrayed as a period of rapid and dramatic body changes brought about by hormonal shifts; psychologically, it is often seen as a tumultuous, conflict-filled period. Much that is written about adolescence suggests that the biological alterations and the appearance of overwhelming and peremptory sexual urges create havoc in the adolescent's life. Until recently, the psychology of adolescence was often written as if what happened in adolescence for boys and girls had parallel antecedents and was experienced in similar fashion. An individualistic bias in most traditional developmental theories suggested that the teen years were the time for separation, for becoming one's "own man" (Levinson 1978), for autonomy. Portrayals of parent-child relationships often referred to conflict, anguish, and the necessary separation between parent and child.

Recently psychologists working on the development of girls and women have cast doubt on some of the traditional narratives about the development of adolescent girls. They have suggested that for girls the "crisis of adolescence" is not so much caused by hormones, body changes, and the push to separate from family but may have more to do with the social context and debilitating messages girls begin to receive as they move into the adolescent world of heterosexual pairing, where socialization includes learning to be an object to another's (male person's) subject. During this time of transition, the hardiness, robustness, zest, and confidence of the prepubescent girl are often replaced by accommodating others, pretending not to know things, and keeping large aspects of self out of relationship ("staying out of relationship in order to stay in relationship," Gilligan's prototypical adolescent girl dilemma). Girls in adolescence learn that the rules of success in the world are made by men. They learn that they are to play a subordinate role, that they are not to be too angry, too bright, too big, or too outspoken. In the course of learning these "rules," girls often lose their "voices" and sense of self-worth (Wellesley 1992). They lose a sense of authentic connection with themselves and with others. That is, they do not feel they can fully represent themselves in important relationships.

In adolescence, girls are taught to close down on behaviors and emotions that are not sex-role appropriate. This process of disconnecting from certain aspects of their own experience may be similar to what happens to boys at about the age of three or four, when they are encouraged to disconnect from feelings suggesting vulnerability. A dilemma, and sometimes crisis, for girls in early adolescence occurs when the culture begins to give the message that girls must adopt prototypically feminine qualities. They learn that certain feelings, behaviors, and experiences are unacceptable for women in this cul-

ture and that in order to be in relationships, notably with boys, they must begin to present themselves in certain ways and keep certain aspects of themselves out of the relationship. Just as boys at the age of three or four are pushed toward disconnecting from their feelings of fear, sadness, or desire for comfort from others, girls in adolescence begin to disconnect from their feelings of personal ambition, direct expressions of anger, and sexual initiative. They fear being "too bright," "too assertive," and "too strong." They understand that this culture rewards power, individual achievement, independence, assertiveness, and abstract intelligence, and they learn that these are all qualities that are thought to be appropriate for boys but not girls.

In adolescence these two modes of being tend to converge and collide. That is, boys socialized to be in control, instrumental, nonemotional, rational, and independent come into more intimate contact with girls who are taught to be loving, caring, and empathic. Furthermore, heterosexual intercourse is a rite of passage to manhood in our culture (where there are few rituals marking the movement from boyhood to manhood), and the girl sometimes gets objectified in the boy's developmental step. In general, girls in adolescence struggle with this sense of objectification. Advertising and the media tend to capitalize on the female as object, and girls often learn to objectify their own bodies, trying to achieve impossible standards of thinness, beauty, and receptivity to males. The differences that show up in heterosexual dating relationships for boys and girls also continue to be manifest in same-sex groups. Thus groups of boys and men tend to organize around patterns of dominance and hierarchy. Girls and women tend to engage in self-disclosure, establishing bonds of closeness through sharing and helping one another.

Much of this research on the loss of voice in adolescent girls has been carried out on white, middle-class girls, but girls of color and girls from different classes may experience the passage of adolescence differently: the study by the American Association of University Women and Wellesley College that showed that white girls experience a dramatic drop in self-esteem in early adolescence failed to find such a shift for African American girls (Wellesley 1992). Tracy Robinson and Janie Ward have suggested that African American girls face particular challenges in adolescence that do threaten their belief in themselves. These authors suggest several pathways for the "development of a belief in self far greater than anyone's disbelief" (1991). These include the capacity for critical thinking vis-à-vis the values of the dominant culture.

The relational model does not suggest that gender differences are essential, biological, or inborn. Rather, there is a clear emphasis on context and the importance of learning. Power issues shape gender differences, as well as race, sexual orientation, class, and so forth. In order to be resilient and maintain their authenticity, all girls must develop the capacity for "resistance" that Robinson and Ward delineated for African American girls. Girls and women from the dominant white, middle-class culture have much to learn from girls and women who are marginalized about the development of courage, resistance, and resilience.

Judith V. Jordan

See also Communication; Domesticity; Emotions; Girl Power; Girls' Culture; Psychotherapy; Radical Feminism; Riot Grrrls

References and Further Reading

American Association of University Women. 1992. *The AAUW Report: How America's Schools Cheat Girls.* Washington, DC: AAUW Educational Foundation.

Beauvoir, Simone de. 1949. *The Second Sex.* 1971. Reprint, New York: Alfred A. Knopf.

Broverman, I., D. Broverman, F. Clarkson, P. Rosenkrantz, and S. Vogel. 1970. "Sex-role Stereotypes and Clinical Judgments of Mental Health." *Journal of Consulting and Counseling Psychology* 43: 1–7.

Comas-Diaz, L., and B. Greene, eds. 1994. *Women of Color: Integrating Ethnic and Gender Identities in Psychotherapy.* New York: Guilford Press.

Dweck, C., and N. Repucci. 1973. "Learned Helplessness and Reinforcement Responsibility in Children." *Journal of Personality and Social Psychology* 25: 1090–1116.

Freud, Sigmund. 1925. "Some Psychological Consequences of the Anatomical Distinction between the Sexes." Pp. 252–272 in *The Collected Papers of Sigmund Freud.* Edited by J. Strachey; translated by J. Riviere. Vol. 5. 1959. Reprint, New York: Basic Books.

Gilligan, Carol. 1982. *In a Different Voice.* Cambridge, MA: Harvard University Press.

Greene, B. 1990. "Sturdy Bridges: The Role of African American Mothers in the Socialization of African American Children." *Women and Therapy: Motherhood, Feminist Perspectives* 10: 205–225.

Hoffman, M. 1997. "Sex Differences in Empathy and Related Behaviors." *Psychological Bulletin* 84, no. 4: 712–722.

Jordan, Judith. 1987. "Clarity in Connection: Empathic Knowing, Desire and Sexuality." *Work in Progress no. 29.* Wellesley, MA: Stone Center Work in Progress Series.

Jordan, Judith, Alexandra Kaplan, Jean Baker Miller, Irene Stiver, and Janet

Surrey. 1991. *Women's Growth in Connection.* New York: Guilford Publications.

Levinson, D. 1978. *The Seasons of a Man's Life.* New York: Alfred A. Knopf.

Maccoby, E. 1990. "Gender and Relationships: A Developmental Account." *American Psychologist:* 513–520.

———. 1998. *The Two Sexes: Growing Up Apart, Coming Together.* Cambridge, MA: Harvard University Press.

Maclean, P. 1958. "The Limbic System with Respect to Self-preservation and the Preservation of the Species." *Journal of Nervous and Mental Diseases* 127: 1–11.

Miller, Jean Baker. 1976. *Toward a New Psychology of Women.* Boston: Beacon Press.

Pollack, William. 1999. *Real Boys.* New York: Owl Books.

Robinson, T., and J. Ward. 1991. "A Belief in Self Far Greater Than Anyone's Disbelief: Cultivating Resistance among African American Female Adolescents." *Women and Therapy:* 81–103.

Sadker, M., and D. Sadker. 1994. *Failing at Fairness.* New York: Charles Scribner.

Riot Grrrls

Riot grrrl is an underground feminist youth movement committed to empowering girls through self-expression and to combating sexism, homophobia, and misogyny. Initially coined in 1991 by members of the female punk music communities in Olympia, Washington, and Washington, D.C., *riot grrrls* are a call to action or to "Revolution Girl-Style Now!" in the words of their most well-known rallying cry. Including girls and women from all over the United States, Great Britain, and elsewhere, riot grrrls resist being defined by one particular code of beliefs and, in fact, proclaim that "every girl is a riot grrrl." They do share some common traits, however: the aspiration to create all-female spaces where girls can express themselves and their experiences; a do-it-yourself (DIY) ethos in which girls and women are responsible for their own modes of production, both musically and editorially; the call to embrace a pro-female, proactive stance; and the desire to oppose, even playfully mislead, members of the media and academe who would try to define and commodify them as the newest and hippest example of a vibrant youth culture. Although initially framed within the context of the underground music "scene" (as opposed to the more mainstream and capitalist music "industry"), riot grrrl quickly spread well beyond its musical roots to create a vibrant "zine" and World Wide Web–based movement, complete with local meetings and grassroots organizing to end ageism, homophobia, racism, sexism, and, especially, physical and emotional violence against women and girls.

Various accounts claim that riot grrrl was born in 1991 when members from the bands Bratmobile and Bikini Kill sought to challenge the sexism of the underground music scene and empower girls and women to do the same. Kathleen Hanna, singer for Bikini Kill, claims that the phrase *riot grrrl* was coined when a musician friend of hers, Jean Smith, commented on the 1991 Mount Pleasant riots in Washington, D.C., by saying, "we need a girl riot too." According to Hanna, members of the band Bratmobile then decided that they were going to start a fanzine called "Riot Grrrl" (Leonard 1998, 103). The idea that girls are angry about the treatment they receive in their daily lives, rebellious, and ready to do something about it quickly caught on to create a vast riot grrrl network. The message, forwarded through song lyrics, musical production and performance, and various manifestos included in the numerous riot grrrl zines, spoke to girls from Alabama to Alaska and from London to Dyfed, Wales.

Contrary to the opinions of many music critics, who define riot grrrl solely in aesthetic terms as a subgenre of punk music—as "women in punk"—the movement from its inception was something much more far-reaching than a group of musicians with a penchant for a certain musical style. Riot grrrls also wanted self-definition through the written word and promoted a female-centered version of punk's DIY politics.

For riot grrrls, DIY is an attempt to short-circuit capitalist, exploitative, and frequently male-identified modes of production while also claiming the authority of self-definition. Riot grrrls exemplify this ethos on many different fronts—from women-run record labels and untraditionally structured musical performances to assertive bodily styles that attempt to disrupt traditional notions of "fashion" and "femininity." In these ways riot grrrls can be placed in a historical trajectory not just with punk but also with another group from the 1970s: second-wave feminists and, specifically, lesbian separatists who developed alternative and pro-woman modes of living, both personally (outside heterosexual marriage) and professionally (through their own women-run businesses).

So even as DIY as a political statement does align riot grrrls with members of the punk movement, riot grrrl's version of DIY has the added twist of gender awareness. Punk rockers used thrift store fashions, body piercing, and unconventional haircuts in an overt attempt to define

themselves over and against a dominant adult culture that ignored their particular needs and concerns. Similarly, in the early 1990s many riot grrrls adopted overtly feminine modes of dress but then used markers to write derogatory words like "whore" on their arms or stomachs, a gesture that pointed directly to the ways in which femininity is often an oppressive social construction. By using articles of clothing from mainstream sources and then altering them in specific ways, riot grrrls were able to invest them with new and subversively gendered meanings.

Also like the punks, riot grrrl is a *youth* movement—but unlike the punks who were typically quite suspicious of girls, riot grrrl is an overtly female youth movement. As the first youth culture to claim the word *girl* as a political identity and therefore the first to claim that adolescent girls' subjectivities are *different* from women's, riot grrrls are interested in exposing the fact that adolescent "girlhood" today brings with it more media objectification and consumer overload and perhaps even more physical and emotional violence than in previous generations. Riot grrrls are highly self-conscious of the negative forces affecting girls, and they want to talk about them in order to fight them. In other words, even as riot grrrl is like punk in that it is partially about subversive "style," it has more to do with political activism. Even though many riot grrrl musicians do share the loud, hard, and fast musical style associated with punk, the aggressive in-your-face attitude of its performers, and a similar desire to do-it-yourself, their message is their mission, and that message has everything to do with empowerment for girls.

Perhaps the most significant aspect of the DIY approach for riot grrrls can be seen in their complicated network of "zines," or independent, self-published texts that are written informally, produced inexpensively, and then distributed in a bartering or not-for-profit system to other grrrls via mailing lists. With names like *Fat Girl, Hotskirt!, Girl Luv,* and *Housewife Turned Assassin,* zines possess several qualities that make them a particularly powerful medium for youth grassroots activism. First, because zines are usually handwritten or hand-drawn, photocopied, and mailed, they are inexpensive to produce and require very little technological savvy, characteristics that make them widely accessible to young girls without large financial resources as well as those in relatively isolated rural communities. Second, they represent the primary mode of communication within riot grrrl networks, communities dispersed from Leeds to Little Rock to Los Angeles. As a result, zines are generally intimate in tone and wide-ranging in topic. They offer girls the opportunity to discuss anything that concerns them: hobbies, music, books, film, or more seriously, racism, queer politics, abuse, rape, and other personal traumas. Third and most important, zines form a kind of conversation among girls in that the writers consistently invite comment and feedback from the others in the network; in fact, they expect it. As the Riot Grrrl Press Catalogue puts it, "I want to encourage people not to just order zines like they were any commodity but to write to anyone whose zine you feel inspired by or have a critique of. It would truly bumm [*sic*] me out if this turned into a commodification of 'girl zines' where if you have the cash you can have access to whatever you want" (Leonard 1998, 108). Accordingly, zines are more about encouraging dialogue than self-pro-

motion. And finally, the act of producing their own texts allows riot grrrls a certain amount of control over their own representation. Teens are usually targeted as consumers who will willingly buy into the latest trend as a means to form an identity for themselves, but zines allow girls to become producers in the most basic sense and thus achieve a kind of cultural agency.

This sense of agency translates to the riot grrrl music scene as well. In early riot grrrl musical performances, like those in the Bikini Kill–Huggy Bear 1993 joint tour, musicians attempted to dismantle the male domination of the physical concert space. At the beginning of shows they passed out flyers asking the girls in the audience to move to the "mosh pit," or the space in front of the stage. Well aware that girls and women avoid the pit for fear of violent slam dancing or harassment by male concertgoers, the flyers made clear the bands' intention of creating a safe space for girls when they wrote: "[We] really want to look at female faces while [we] perform. [We] want HER to know that she is included in this show, that what we are doing is for her" (Bikini Kill–Huggy Bear Flyer, quoted in Leonard 1997, 234). In addition to rearranging the gig space, riot grrrl performers broke down other concert conventions based on unequal power relations when they handed the microphone to girls at the front of the stage and asked them to voice their opinions or when they engaged in conversations with hecklers from the audience. Again, these shows put a premium on dialogue and debate instead of mere passive viewing.

This desire to create safe spaces—both physically and editorially—where girls can articulate their own version of reality drives the riot grrrl community. Although some have critiqued the movement for its white, middle-class orientation, others have praised it for its earnest desire to understand, tolerate, and make room for difference. Media and academic accounts aside, however, it is clear that those involved in the riot grrrl community prefer to remain part of an underground movement. They are highly critical and suspicious of the media accounts describing their network and, in fact, went so far as to issue a press blackout in 1993. Riot grrrls are well aware that in defining them, even in an encyclopedic entry, writers run the risk of containing their dynamism. As one group of zine writers put it: "We are aware of the media . . . that crush anything it [sic] discovers. . . . Seeing all that, we use *their* media whilst we sneakily construct girl lines of communication" (Leonard 1997, 245).

Kimberley Roberts

See also Girl Power; Girls' Culture; Punk Rock; Relational Theory; Zines

References and Further Reading
Gottlieb, Joanne, and Gayle Wald. 1994. "'Smells Like Teen Spirit': Riot Grrrls, Revolution, and Independent Rock." Pp. 250–274 in *Microphone Fiend*s. Edited by Andrew Ross and Tricia Rose. New York: Routledge.
Kearney, Mary Celeste. 1997. "The Missing Links: Riot Grrrl—Feminism—Lesbian Culture." In *Sexing the Groove: Popular Music and Gender*. Edited by Sheila Whiteley. London: Routledge.
———. 1998a. "'Don't Need You': Rethinking Identity Politics and Separatism from a Riot Grrrl Perspective." Pp. 148–188 in *Youth Culture: Identity in a Postmodern World*. Edited by Jonathan S. Epstein. Oxford: Blackwell Publishers.
———. 1998b. "Producing Girls: Rethinking the Study of Female Youth Culture." Pp. 285–310 in *Delinquents and Debutantes: Twentieth-Century American Girls' Cultures*. Edited by Sherrie A. Inness. New York: New York University Press.
Leonard, Marion. 1997. "'Rebel Girl, You Are the Queen of My World': Feminism, 'Subculture' and Grrrl Power." In *Sexing the Groove: Popular Music and Gender*. Edited by Sheila Whiteley. London: Routledge.
———. 1998. "Paper Planes: Travelling the New Grrrl Geographies." In *Cool Places: Geographies of Youth Cultures*. Edited by Tracey Skelton and Gill Valentine. London: Routledge.
Rosenberg, Jessica, and Gitana Garofalo. 1998. "Riot Grrrl: Revolutions from Within." *Signs* 23, no. 3: 809–842.
Wald, Gayle. 1997. "Just a Girl? Rock Music, Feminism, and the Cultural Construction of Female Youth." *Signs* 23, no. 3: 585–610.

Rural Girls

Although they are a demographic constant, rural girls are infrequently part of any historical narratives except as casual beneficiaries of institutional services designed primarily for their brothers or parents. The dearth of literature makes defining the category a historian's first challenge. For the purpose of this entry, rural girls will mean twentieth-century girls whose primary residence was a farm.

The term *rural girls* presumes a distinctive context for girlhood, and as long as rural residence remained normative, it would be difficult to isolate significant elements of the experience or to differentiate between small-town residents and girls who were members of farm households. Two other groups whose experiences, at least temporarily, had common elements with the rural girls were Native American girls sent to off-reservation boarding schools and orphans put out for adoption into farm families. These girls are discussed in other entries.

Even with this narrowing, generalizations about rural girls must be formulated

Farm girls carry supplies on a horse-drawn wagon, in the foothills of the Ozarks, Arkansas.
(Library of Congress)

cautiously. Regional variations were undoubtedly more significant for farm girls than for small-town and urban girls throughout most of the twentieth century. Crops, for example, establish work patterns, each having a logic of its own. Beyond that, regional demographic characteristics shaped daily life and social contexts. Race and ethnicity are obvious variables. Family composition, birth order, and economic cycles also influenced the content of rural girls' daily lives.

For twentieth-century girls, the dominant regional settlement pattern must also have mattered. In states like Rhode Island with more than 80 percent urban settlement by 1880, the experience would have been more distinctive than in Maine, Vermont, North and South Dakota, West Virginia, or Mississippi, which remained more than 50 percent rural in the 1980 census.

Rural girls participated in a family economy in which all labor was integral to the farm and each member's contributions had real economic value. Class, commodity specializations, and family composition all influenced girls' tasks within the family enterprise. For young girls, most of whom started "helping out" at about the age of five, tasks easily crossed gender lines. As age and strength made them capable of more skilled chores, the work assignments gradually became more differentiated. Girls worked with their brothers in the garden and fields but also became responsible for chores in the henhouse and garden. Most simultaneously assisted with baking, caring for younger siblings, cleaning and filling lamps, sewing, and housecleaning. After the age of twelve, midwestern girls added canning and churning to their responsibilities, but did fieldwork only when extra hands were needed. Girls without brothers who could assist, however, often remained involved in field labor.

The labor intensity of the family crops was an important factor in the amount of fieldwork expected of girls. Tobacco demanded more hands; thus daughters remained heavily involved. For hybrid corn crops, tassels had to be removed from all female stocks to ensure proper cross-pollination. This labor-intensive process, which needed to be completed in a two-week window, looked like fun to an Iowa farmer's young daughters in the early 1940s as they watched the teens hired from a nearby town. By the time they reached the requisite 5 feet, 2 inches and twelve years of age, the process lost some of its magic in the afternoon sun, but they remained members of the crew nonetheless.

Girls who lived on wheat farms rarely did fieldwork because most tasks were mechanized. Instead, they worked with the livestock. Harvesting and threshing grain were tasks normally accomplished by men, at least until combines eliminated the need for a large crew of neighbors or hired hands to assist with the process. However, girls were involved in feeding the fieldworkers. One remembered looking forward to threshing so she could "wait on tables." Even after the automobile shortened the travel time for neighbors and only two meals needed to be served during threshing, noon dinner and an afternoon lunch, much of the women's days went to cooking. Younger girls refilled bread and butter plates in the kitchen, and older daughters brought serving dishes and iced tea and lemonade refills to the eating area. By the time the women and girls ate their own dinners and finished the dishes, it was time to carry afternoon lunch to the field.

Girls from less prosperous farms frequently turned to off-farm wage work as their contribution to the economically interdependent family unit. Housework, teaching, clerical jobs, nursing, and cannery work all provided monetary resources for farm family survival. This became a more common experience as commercial agriculture disrupted traditional work patterns. In 1939 the U.S. Department of Agriculture reported that farm families accounted for more than 50 percent of the annual increase in working population. The juxtaposition resulted in an increase in subsistence agriculture in locations that permitted combining farm and nonfarm work. In this configuration, other family members joined rural daughters in contributing off-farm earnings to the family economy.

Rural girls' school experiences varied widely, but there are some identifiable national patterns. Most attended one-room schoolhouses staffed by female teachers for grades one through eight. High school attendance required boarding or being able to get to the nearest town each day. Normal schools provided training for girls who wanted to become teachers. Many schools, especially in the early 1900s, were staffed by young women who needed to complete their preparation during summer school sessions. State licensing requirements gradually mandated normal school certificates or four-year degrees prior to appointment. How much schooling rural girls received depended primarily on family labor patterns, geographic location, and race. Like their urban counterparts, however, girls seem to have been both more likely to attend school and to be kept home for family emergencies than their brothers.

For those able to attend, the length of the school year depended on weather and local families' needs for help with crops. In general, rural girls experienced shorter school years than urban students. This was particularly true in Appalachia and the South. Kentucky had no public schools in the mountains until 1918. Travel was difficult, and one young woman who came as the first teacher in the area found that the creek beds flooded each January. Because there were no other roads, school could not resume until these routes became passable. In North Carolina, the rural school year lasted less than six months until 1919, when legislation specified a 120-day minimum. Mississippi, the last state to do so, had passed its first compulsory school attendance law just the year before. In contrast, communities in the Midwest and West tended to establish accessible elementary schools quickly, often due to laws requiring that new schools be provided when a threshold number of students lived outside a specified radius of an existing facility.

Except for anecdotal evidence from girls' diaries and teachers' memoirs, readily accessible contemporary studies of early-twentieth-century rural schools primarily documented their perceived inadequacies. The country life movement, a loose coalition of politicians and social service professionals that was particularly active in the Midwest from 1900 until 1920, decried the "absolute inadequacy" of rural schools in 1915. Much as they insisted that larger, scientific farms were more efficient, the reformers promoted school consolidation. They wanted several one-room school districts merged and the area served by a larger, graded school. Parents resisted, and after 1920 the movement subsided, with most rural children still attending local one-room or small graded schools until a renewed consolidation movement emerged in the 1950s.

Some reformers also wanted to make materials more relevant to rural youngsters' lives. Textbooks were rewritten so that math problems, for example, used crop-related details. One wonders if the changes made much difference to rural girls, whose activities and interests were still missing from assignments. The exception to this pattern was introduction of home economics courses as vocational education for girls after passage of the Smith-Hughes Act in 1917.

Overlooking the network of socializing agencies that provided education for rural youth within the context of family life, reformers visualized the modern school as a centralized institution with total responsibility for preparing competent rural adults. In isolated areas the school building often served as the center of community life as well as a classroom. In more accessible and prosperous areas, however, it was one of several existing institutions, and parents frequently resisted educators' expanded view of their role.

Churches, subjected to similar recommendations that they consolidate for economic and practical reasons, also played a formal role in communities. Unfortunately, here again, written sources are primarily sociological studies of the "rural problems" or suggested denominational responses written for ministers. Except in areas where isolation precluded any institutions beyond family and neighborhood networks, churches were often in place before schools were built and provided a multipurpose gathering place for communities. Consistent with the organization of daily life, rural churches were family-centered institutions. After the 1940s ministerial associations encouraged some emphasis on providing recreational opportunities for youth, particularly for young men. Reform-minded adults hoped to counteract the attractions of urban life and secular amusements. Though church leaders focused on boys, the initiative provided new peer-group social opportunities for some rural girls.

Recreation also combined families and strengthened community networks. Early in the 1900s, farm families in one Oregon community came to town to dance at the Grange Hall every other Saturday night. County and state fairs linked recreation and work as girls were encouraged to prepare contest entries. The excitement of these annual outings, particularly to the state fair, then became part of girls' play as they recreated rides and "showed" their cats and dogs for siblings and local playmates.

Innovations in transportation and technology increasingly brought farm families in contact with nearby towns or urban areas and national affairs. Between 1900 and 1940, the first purchases of midwestern households were an automobile and a telephone. Although much has been written about the mobility and independence automobiles afforded youth, neither purchase automatically altered girls' family-centered patterns of work and recreation. In 1988 Joanne Meusburger recalled family vacations as the primary benefit of their beloved "Old Mere." Rural electrification proceeded unevenly, even after adoption of the Rural Electrification Act (1936).

Although only 30 percent of southern tenant family households contained radios in 1940, the U.S. Housing Census revealed that nationwide almost three-fourths of U.S. farm owners and almost half of tenant families nationwide owned one. Telephones came much more slowly: only 29 percent of farm families nationwide had them in 1940. Many girls' lives remained bounded by the local community.

Rural girls had other routes to participation in activities that created contacts beyond the family circle. The Girl Scouts of America created a "Lone Scout" program for those who lived in isolated areas. Until 1926 this membership category never had more than 103 registrants; but after an article appeared in the March issue of *The Farmer's Wife*, almost 6,000 girls applied. As one twelve-year-old Ohio girl wrote, "I have no brothers or sisters. . . . I get lonesome." Letters, cards, and booklets sent from the Lone Scout Bureau, designed to give farm girls a sense of companionship with others, apparently succeeded. One girl wrote that belonging had given her "a new friend." Others sent away for membership in the Junior Audubon Society. Technology and the consumer culture both influenced rural girls' lives, but neither force quickly altered consumption practices or removed recreation from the family setting.

Although much has changed about growing up female on a farm, which is strikingly epitomized in the U.S. government's decision to eliminate discrete categories for nonfarm rural and farm residents within the census, it remains a distinctive experience. Children across the country currently attend 400 one-room rural schools. Agricultural labor remains a categorical exemption from child labor laws, and girls still do fieldwork on southern family tobacco farms.

Even when farmers' daughters have automobiles of their own, many retain family and community as their primary units of identification.

Kathleen C. Hilton

See also Education of Girls; 4-H; Home Economics Education; Mennonite Girls; Puritan Girls

References and Further Reading
Bremner, Robert A., et al., eds. 1971. *Children and Youth in America: A Documentary History.* Cambridge, MA: Harvard University Press.
Danbom, David B. 1979. "Rural Education Reform and the Country Life Movement, 1900–1920." *Agricultural History* 53, no. 2: 462–474.
Hagood, Margaret J. 1939. *Mothers of the South: Portraiture of the White Tenant Farm Woman.* Chapel Hill: University of North Carolina Press.
Hargreaves, Mary W. M. 1979. "Rural Education on the Northern Plains Frontier." *Journal of the West* 18, no. 4: 25–32.
Inscoe, John C. 1988. "Memories of a Presbyterian Mission Worker: An Interview with Rubie Ray Cunningham." *Appalachian Journal* 15, no. 2: 144–160.
Lindstrom, David Edgar. 1946. *Rural Life and the Church.* Champaign, IL: Garrard Press.
Martin, William C. 1948. *The Church in the Rural Community.* New York: Board of Missions and Church Extension of the Methodist Church.
Meusburger, Joanne. 1988. "Farm Girl." *The Palimpsest* 69, no. 1: 34–48.
Neth, Mary. 1995. *Preserving the Family Farm: Women, Community, and the Foundations of Agribusiness in the Midwest, 1900–1940.* Baltimore: Johns Hopkins University Press.
"One-Room Schoolhouses in the United States." http://www.laca.org/Johnstown/Cornell/states.html. Accessed July 29, 2000.

S

Samplers

The earliest European settlers brought with them the girlhood tradition of sampler making, that is, exercising skills in embroidery by decorating a piece of cloth with rows of letters and numbers, pictures, and edifying verses. Sewing samplers was a common feature of girlhood education but began to decline in popularity in the 1840s. Whether under the instruction of a private sewing teacher or as part of other various forms of private and public education, a girl sewed her sampler to gain a repertoire of embroidery stitches and designs that would have a practical use when she became a homemaker. A girl as young as six years old began her first sampler on a small rectangle of cloth, most often using silk thread on linen fabric to form alphabets and rows of numbers. This would create a "marking sampler," primarily composed of one stitch: the marking stitch, now more commonly known as the "cross-stitch," one tiny "X" sewn beside another to form lines and curves. The term *marking sampler* suggests one application of a girl's embroidery: to mark valuable household linen and family garments with identifying letters, numbers, or symbols. Through age fourteen or fifteen, as her skills increased, a girl moved on to create larger and more complex samplers. Under her teacher's tutelage, she might complete a

succession of accomplished samplers, ornamenting her cloth with borders, figures, pictures of houses or flora and fauna, and lines of poetry, or she could move on to other sampler variants. The genealogical sampler incorporated names and life dates of family members. This type of sampler might begin as a wedding sampler that the bride would then add to as children were born and relatives died. The map sampler depicted the continents and nations of the world in embroidered outline, and the globe sampler did the same in three dimensions as a stuffed spherical model of the earth. Akin to the needlework mourning picture, the mourning sampler featured a suitable design and verse in memory of a departed loved one.

As an early form of values education in America, sampler verse promoted ideals of femininity of the period: virtue, industry, piety, friendship, and a humble awareness of human mortality. Samplers sometimes included the girl's name and the date she worked on her sampler and occasionally her birth date, the town where she lived, or even her teacher's name. In addition to marking items for identification purposes, the sampler maker would use her embroidery skills throughout her life to ornament clothing and household textiles. Her sampler also served as a model of stitches she might refer to in the future. Thousands of samplers were pro-

Mothers often had their daughters make samplers before they were allowed to participate in a quilting bee such as this one in colonial times. (Library of Congress)

duced by girls throughout America, and the custom moved westward with settlement, remaining popular well into the nineteenth century. However, sampler making was most common in the eastern states. Though practical in their original purpose, samplers eventually became decorative objects to be displayed in the family home. After its decline as a teaching medium for budding homemakers, sampler making continued through the nineteenth century, though never with the enormous popularity it had until 1850. Today adult women continue to sew samplers as ornamental handiwork; many of their designs derive from the samplers of early America.

The Sampler's History

Although sampler makers in America developed distinctive styles, the sampler itself had a long history before its arrival in the New World. Probably developing in the Middle Ages in Europe, samplers were well established by the 1500s, and Shakespeare mentioned them in his plays *A Midsummer Night's Dream* and *Titus Andronicus*. Although sampler making thrived in several European countries, the traditions in Great Britain, Holland, and Germany were the most influential in America (Harbeson 1938, 43). As in America, the original purpose of the sampler in Europe was practical: to practice embroidery skills and to prepare a reference catalogue of stitches. In fact, the earliest European samplers merely featured rows of blocks or horizontal stripes, each exemplifying a different stitch. These were sewn upon a long, narrow rectangle of cloth, the width limited by the narrow looms of the period. As a girl gained skill, she added new examples of stitches (hence the name *sampler*). She would then store the cloth until she needed to consult it for future projects. This process would continue through her adulthood.

The earliest extant American sampler is sewn on such a long narrow strip of cloth. Now on display in Plymouth, Massachusetts, it was embroidered by Loara Standish (1633–1656), daughter of Miles Standish, the well-known member of the Plymouth colony. Probably made about 1643–1646, Loara's handiwork shows us that when the sampler came to America it had become more complex in design and, as hers does, often included a verse. As time passed, American samplers continued to evolve, acquiring a short, squarer shape; employing new preferences in thread colors; and using a finer woven cloth and new designs.

Sampler Making as a Girlhood "Accomplishment"

Sampler making was considered to be one of the girlhood "graces" or "accomplishments," along with drawing; painting on glass or on ladies' fans; making pictures out of shells, hair, wax, feathers, or quills; "japanning" (like present-day decoupage); performing a variety of other needlework skills; practicing elocution; and singing, playing musical instruments, and dancing. This curriculum might be pursued after a short, early period of study in the rudiments of reading, writing, and "ciphering."

From the earliest settlement period, education of the young took many forms. Mothers often gave children their earliest lessons, and local clergymen provided some instruction. Women took in pupils for the community, creating what were called "dame schools," "penny schools," or "reading schools" that offered the basics of literacy and arithmetic. Here a girl might receive instruction in sewing. Girls were often taught the feminine "accomplishments" by private teachers, women who advertised their services to teach girls sewing or other things that were thought to add polish to a girl's education. There are numerous extant advertisements of such teachers, and the samplers themselves tell us about these schools and their instructors. Samplers made in a certain time and place sometimes include the teacher's name and use the same verses or design features, showing us that the teacher's influence was strong in determining the sampler's content. We can also see by the quality of the girls' handiwork and, by the improvement in successive pieces by the same girl, that some instruction must have been excellent. There were a few pattern books available for inspiration, but clearly each teacher developed her own favorites in design, verse, and style. The evidence of these sewing schools also suggests the social element that sampler making provided for young girls. Not uncommonly, sisters, cousins, and friends attended these schools together.

Even in the early settlement period, as communities grew, schooling was an official concern. For example, Nieuw Netherland, now New York, made provision for public schooling in the 1660s, and in 1647 Massachusetts required that schools be established in communities of fifty families or more. Of course, the development of regular educational institutions took time. Some families were able to hire private tutors, which was especially suitable for prosperous families who lived far from town, such as those who lived on the plantations of the South. In the eighteenth century, girls' boarding schools became common, but by whatever means a girl's education was received, it was widely true throughout this era that after her early education in the rudiments, a girl's education took a different direction from a boy's. The "graces" a girl went on to learn were intended to bring charm, beauty, taste, and refinement to her character and her home.

Of course, embroidery was of practical use, too. As an adornment it was widely used on quilts and coverlets, bedhangings, tablecloths, sheets and pillowcases, purses and pinholders, as well as on garments for all members of the family— from baby's christening gown and cap to Mama's best dresses, Papa's waistcoat, and Grandmother's shawl. The marking of family linen was no trifle either. A family's linen was costly and was given a prominent place in wills and estate inventories. The marking of it served to identify ownership and to record the extent of the collection and the origin and acquisition of each piece.

Yet even in the eighteenth century, there was criticism of the lack of academic content in girlhood education, with its emphasis on handicrafts rather than intellectual development. It should not be forgotten, though, that sampler making encouraged patience, discipline, self-confidence, and aesthetic sensitivity. Remaining samplers from this period are often stunning specimens of needlework, precision creations that must have demanded care and concentration from a young girl to a degree that amazes people living today.

A Source of Wisdom

Like the emphasis on the "graces" in girlhood education, the verses girls inscribed on their samplers give us insight into what were thought to be the ideals of femininity. Since samplers made by several girls in a teacher's school sometimes featured the same verses, we know that teachers influenced the choice of poetry. Other evidence tells us that parents sometimes chose the verses, and certainly girls themselves had their influence. Of those samplers that include poetry or mottoes, universally the verses of this period encourage aspects of ethical personal conduct and belief. Of all qualities they promote, the lines a young seamstress would learn as she sewed most frequently spoke of virtue:

> *See here the Youth by Wisdom led*
> *The paths of life securely tread*
> *The dangerous lures of folly shun*
> *And virtue's course serenely run.*

In pursuit of girlhood virtue, verses warned against vanity and worldly temptations. "Favor is deceitful and Beauty is vain," they reminded these girls. "The joys of earth" should be spurned, for "youth and beauty fade away." Time is ever flying, they counseled, and "life is like a summer's day," quickly passing by. Sampler poetry encouraged humility, diligence, and piety. Parents were duly honored, and the "guiding hand of Parent fondness" was welcomed because it "prunes every fault and every worth improves." Reverence for God was a girl's first concern: "Duty, Fear and Love / We owe to God Above," a common motto proclaimed. The poem Loara Standish inscribed on her seventeenth-century sampler incorporates many of these concepts:

> Lord, guide my Heart that I may do
>   thy will
> And fill my hands with such conven-
>   ient skill
> As will conduce to Virtue void of
>   shame,
> And I will give the Glory to thy Name.

The patience, care, and usefulness this needlework encouraged and the virtues its verses promoted reflect the role of womanhood up until about the 1840s. In this world, infant mortality was high and life expectancy was low; women were economically and legally dependent on fathers and husbands; and a woman's role as a "domestic being," to use Abigail Adams's famous phrase, included educating children, nursing the sick, attending births and keeping deathbed vigils, performing laborious household chores, assisting in a family business or farm, raising large families, and providing strength and guidance in a precarious, difficult world. Virtue, duty, faith, friendship, usefulness—these were the qualities a girl would need to survive. The sampler "craze" of an earlier era invites provocative questions about our own preparation of girls for womanhood and about the ethical framework accompanying that preparation.

The accomplishment of these young seamstresses has also had an effect on modern needlework and on the practice and study of needlework in art and textile programs in colleges in many parts of the world (Edwards 1983, 18–20). Samplers by American girls through the mid-nineteenth century are a resource in the study of needlework and provide an authoritative model of excellence in its development.

Girls and Their Samplers
The many historic American samplers in museums, historical and preservation society collections, private collections, and homes of sampler makers' descendants testify to the popularity of sampler making in the past. The large number of surviving samplers suggests, as well, the value placed on them by the individuals, families, and communities preserving them. These collections also show us that the girls who made these samplers valued them. Many a museum donation or heirloom sampler is accompanied by a note from the maker or testimony passed down from descendants stating that this was a treasured souvenir of the maker's childhood. Diaries and memoirs recall the pride girls took in their samplers and the admiration they brought from others (Swan 1977, 52–53). Of course, there must have been girls who rebelled at the long, painstaking labor of needlework, girls who longed to be at play or engaged in another favorite pleasure. One such disgruntled little girl sewed her dismay right on her sampler with these words: "Patty Poke did this and she hated every stitch she did in it. She loves to read much more" (Bolton and Coe 1973, 96).

Yet most evidence shows that girls took pride in their samplers. Sampler makers passed down their samplers in their wills, often leaving them to a favorite child or grandchild. These women regarded their girlhood embroidery as a precious accomplishment. By the late seventeenth century, families began to frame their daughters' samplers for display, as the markings and fade patterns show. Increasingly, girls placed their own names in the embroidery, and sometimes their verses included their names, especially in this popular pattern: "Betsy Browne is my name / And with my needle I wrought the same." To this was usually added the humble declaration: "And if my skill had been better / I would have mended every letter." Another common name pattern cites the child's home and declares her faith: "Hannah Wilcox is my name / New England is my nation / Springfield is my dwelling place / And Christ is my salvation." The most touching evidence of a girl's relationship to her needlework lies in those samplers that show she knew that what she created with her needle would outlive her. Many a sampler proclaims, with varying lines, the idea that "the twining texture of this thread / Will speak of me when I am dead" and asks us to "look at this and think of me / When I am quite forgotten."

The Sampler's Decline

Several factors led to the decline of girl-hood sampler making. In the 1840s indelible ink was developed, which provided a simpler means of marking garments and linen. In that same decade Elias Howe patented his first sewing machine, and the invention was so popular that Howe was hard-pressed to protect his patent.

The key factor, though, in the decline of this craft lay in the movement to reform education for girls. The year 1825 saw the opening of the first public high schools for girls, one in Boston and one in New York. Advocates urged that girls be prepared for adulthood by studying more academic curricula. Although sampler making declined both in popularity and artistry throughout the nineteenth century, it continues to this day, but as a pastime for women rather than girls. Yet the sampler's heyday as a girlhood enterprise has left us with a vision of American girlhood and femininity important in the history of American culture.

Luise van Keuren

See also Arts and Crafts; Domesticity; Education of Girls; Girls' Culture; Literacy

References and Further Reading

Bolton, Ethel S., and Eva J. Coe. 1921. *American Samplers*. 1973. Reprint, New York: Weathervane.

Edmonds, Mary Jaene. 1991. *Samplers and Samplermakers: An American Schoolgirl Art, 1700–1850*. New York: Rizzoli.

Edwards, Joan. 1983. *Sampler-making, 1540–1940*. Surrey, UK: Bayford Books.

Harbeson, Georgiana. 1938. *American Needlework*. New York: Bonanza Books.

Ring, Betty. 1993. *Girlhood Embroidery, American Samplers and Pictorial Needlework, 1650–1850*. 2 vols. New York: Alfred A. Knopf.

Swan, Susan Burrows. 1977. *Plain and Fancy: American Women and Their Needlework, 1700–1850*. New York: Routledge.

Saturday Evening Girls

The Saturday Evening Girls' (SEG) Club was established in 1899 through the combined efforts of two working women, Edith Guerrier, a librarian, and Edith Brown, an artist, and their upper-class patron, Helen Osborne Storrow. Frustrated by the lack of opportunities for the intellectual advancement of young immigrant women and girls, they conceived of a library club program to provide educational, cultural, economic, and social resources for the growing numbers of poor young Jewish and Italian girls and women living in the North End of Boston. Initially held on Saturday evenings for young women who worked during the week, this club soon expanded into eight library clubs, identified by the days of the week on which they met, each day holding meetings for girls and young women of different age groups. At their peak in the mid-1910s, the clubs supported approximately 250 members, published a newspaper called the *S.E.G. News*, operated the Paul Revere Pottery, and struggled to improve their community and their own lives. For almost twenty years the library clubs offered girls a refuge and an alternative to work, domestic, and familial responsibilities.

It was Edith Guerrier's early frustration with the continual neglect of girls' and women's intellectual and social lives that resulted in her establishing the Saturday Evening Girls' Club. Guerrier originally began work in the day nursery at North Bennet Street Industrial School (NBSIS) in the early 1890s. Within a few years, she was appointed head librarian for North Bennet's reading rooms, which became a station of the Boston Public Library. Through the library, Guerrier was able to establish a new class of clubs for girls and young women that addressed their intellectual needs. Burdened by the directive to "draw these girls in, from the perils of the street" (NBSIS Archives, *Annual Report, 1897–1898*, 4), Guerrier sought instead to organize the clubs along the same lines as the more literary and educational clubs that already existed for boys. The emphasis on "perils of the street," a constant theme throughout the reform literature of the time, reflected middle-class observers' assumption that all poor, immigrant women needed to be morally and physically protected. The reformers' language was, therefore, typical of the time and low expectations of immigrants' moral character but did not reflect the reality of these young women's lives.

During the fall of 1899 Guerrier began her Saturday evening meetings for the benefit of young unmarried working women of the neighborhood. Guerrier successfully enticed prominent political, professional, educational, and reform leaders of the day to come speak to the SEG Club on a variety of classical and contemporary issues. In the meantime, while taking evening courses at the Museum School of the Museum of Fine Arts in Boston, Guerrier became close friends with a talented young artist named Edith Brown, who was hired by NBSIS to teach drawing and, later, clay modeling to the various clubs. Brown and Guerrier moved in together and started a lifelong personal and professional relationship that would span forty years of dedication to each other.

As a result of her work in the library, Guerrier met Helen Osborne Storrow, who had joined the board of managers of NBSIS in 1898 and was a member of the board of visitors of the Boston Public Library. Storrow was the granddaughter of Martha Coffin Wright and grandniece of Lucretia Coffin Mott, who, together with Elizabeth Cady Stanton, were among the small group that organized the first women's rights convention in 1848 in Seneca Falls, New York. Married to James Jackson Storrow, Jr., a prominent Boston lawyer and banker, in the early 1890s, Helen Storrow was just emerging as an important philanthropic figure in the Boston community when she met Guerrier and became interested in her work in the library. It was through Guerrier that Storrow began to learn of the difficulties facing poor and immigrant young women. Although Storrow was instrumental in establishing new programs at NBSIS for both boys and girls, her involvement with the Saturday

Evening Girls developed into a more personal and lifelong relationship. Storrow would later draw upon her experiences with the SEG when she became involved with the fledgling Girl Scout movement in the 1910s.

In 1906, Storrow purchased an acre of land at Wingaersheek Beach in West Gloucester, Massachusetts, where she built a cottage with fourteen bedrooms, a living room, and a kitchen for the club members. Monitored by a camp director, who was often a professional social worker, the girls were scheduled for one- or two-week vacations of fresh air, swimming, hiking, playing, and resting. To accommodate the different religious and cultural customs of the club members, no meat was served at the camp. Only fresh fish, which the girls occasionally caught themselves, and fruits and vegetables that Storrow had delivered weekly were served.

These clubs for girls and young women became an important part of the Americanization process, not only because of the programs that focused on civic and educational agendas but also because of their self-governing organizational structures. A governing body of ten members was elected yearly by the most senior group, the Saturday Evening Girls. A house committee was formed that met on a weekly basis to generate policies and rules concerning the running of the clubs, which were then voted on by the entire body of the clubhouse once a month. The girls and young women learned on a microlevel the concepts of democratic government. They found discipline and confidence in a system whereby they could create an organization with rules and laws, resolve problems, and reach decisions based on a vote of the majority. By participating in the everyday running of the clubs, the members learned valuable lessons about responsibility and the use of power, lessons particularly important for young women and girls who lacked opportunities in the public sphere as well as the private sphere to govern their own lives.

Guerrier, Brown, and Storrow recognized that immigrants girls' need to contribute to family income conflicted with the pursuit of education beyond grammar school. Although settlement houses and other reform organizations were providing educational, vocational, and Americanization programs, very few addressed the fact that many immigrant youths could not fully take advantage of the opportunities because their financial contribution to the family far outweighed the importance of higher education. Establishing a commercial industry to provide financial resources rather than just skills training was a step toward resolving that problem.

By 1906, Edith Brown had been teaching clay modeling for more than five years at North Bennet Street, so her artistic training and background played a major role in the decision to start a pottery. With Storrow's approval and her donation of funds to purchase the equipment, Guerrier and Brown started training in the specifics of pottery making. By the summer of 1907, a few library club members began to learn pottery making at Guerrier and Brown's Chestnut Hill home. They proudly signed their pottery "SEG," for Saturday Evening Girls, along with their own initials and date; and the pottery works, or Bowl Shop as it was first known, was established.

In early 1908 Storrow purchased a four-story brick building at 18 Hull Street in the North End to house the pottery and the eight library clubs. The building was located near the Old North Church where Paul Revere had hung his famous lantern, and therefore the pottery was named the Paul Revere Pottery. Guerrier and Brown moved into the fourth-floor apartment of this building to continue directing the activities of the clubs and the pottery. Many of the girls worked a few hours on Saturday mornings, if only to sweep, clean, pack, assist, work off their weekly or monthly dues, pay for summer camp, or earn a few extra dollars to help them pursue higher education. A few worked either full-time or on a more regular part-time schedule. The pottery became known for its children's dish sets, which were decorated with Brown's designs of children, witches, chickens, roosters, rabbits, ducks, flowers, trees, camels, squirrels and other animals, and nursery rhymes or mottoes that could be personalized with a child's name and birth date.

Shock and surprise have often characterized the response of reformers and native-born privileged classes to demonstrations of intelligence and eagerness to learn by immigrants and the poor. Still, these attitudes informed the establishment of educational and training programs and were used to social reformers' advantage when trying to raise support. Exhibitions were held every year to showcase NBSIS programs and individual craft pieces made by the students, not only to celebrate their achievements but also to raise badly needed funds. Although the students were proud of their work, there was some resentment over these expectations of inferiority. When tourists came to view the remarkable work these supposedly illiterate and ignorant immigrant girls were doing at the pottery on Hull Street, the girls sometimes acted out by pretending to be deaf and mute or feigned ignorance of English and exhibited a general lack of intelligence, all for the visitors' benefit.

Over the next few years the pottery continued to expand, gaining national recognition. SEG wares were sold across the country in gift shops; in department stores; in their own stores in New York, Washington, D.C., Chicago, San Francisco, and Martha's Vineyard; and on Boylston Street in Boston. By 1914 the pollution from the kilns was adding to the dirt and filth in an already highly congested area, so the pottery was relocated to nearby Brighton, Massachusetts. Though its products were artistically acclaimed, financial success for the Paul Revere Pottery remained elusive. Not only did Helen Storrow subsidize the pottery, but the SEGs were expected to help raise funds as well. Throughout the history of the library clubs, the girls performed Shakespearean plays, operettas, recitals, and folk dances to raise funds for their club work, the pottery, and summer vacations in West Gloucester. They performed at North Bennet Street, the open-air theater at the Storrows' home in Lincoln, the Vendome Hotel in Boston, Isabella Stewart Gardner's Fenway Court, and many other Boston locations.

The SEG Club was originally conducted at the North Bennet Street Industrial School (NBSIS), a charitable institution founded by Pauline Agassiz Shaw in the early 1880s to provide social services, industrial and vocational training, and "Americanization" programs to the immigrant population of the North End. By 1895 the North End of Boston had become a crowded settlement point for a new wave of eastern European Jews and southern European immigrants. Crowded together in old, dilapidated tenement neighborhoods where poverty was pervasive, many immigrants kept within their own ethnic spheres, separated by a street corner from another ethnic enclave. Reformers of the Progressive era recognized the perils of overcrowded neighborhoods and the stress placed upon cities and their residents, both native-born and immigrant. Organizations such as NBSIS sponsored many Americanization programs in their own building and in the public schools. Viewed as agents of socialization, these programs also provided many services to immigrants to help mediate the effects of poverty, displacement, and unemployment. Heavily burdened with thousands of young immigrant children speaking dozens of languages from eastern and southern Europe, Boston educators scrambled to accommodate and teach them. In horribly overcrowded schools, children struggled to learn English and the basics of compulsory elementary education. Significant language barriers, poorly educated parents, and economic need also forced many children out of public schools and into the labor force prematurely.

During this period NBSIS developed and refined a variety of manual and industrial training programs to augment the public school programs in the city. NBSIS represented a new trend in the development, use, and ideology of industrial and manual training during the late nineteenth century. In addition to a kindergarten and nursery school, it provided classes and manual training programs in woodworking, printing, clay modeling, metalsmithing, sewing, and leatherworking. A library and a kitchen where girls were instructed in housework were also established. Completely supported by private donations, the school maintained programs for Boston's public school children throughout the early part of the twentieth century.

Through club work at the North Bennet Street facility, many new ideas of social reform were played out. Here reformers capitalized on opportunities for "social intercourse" and "good citizenship" (NBSIS Archives, *Annual Report, 1904–1905*, 24). Through the multitude of literary, debate, and athletic clubs for boys and young men and the sewing, cooking, and occasional literary clubs for girls and young women, reformers and immigrants often experienced their first cross-class and cross-cultural exchanges. Library clubs, manual training, and other activities for boys flourished and dominated most efforts directed toward immigrants. Education, self-improvement programs, vocational training, and clubs for girls were much slower in coming, and most, if not all, efforts were centered around domestic training and related skills such as needlework, cooking, and cleaning. According to popular social work magazines of the day, teaching young girls Latin and Shakespeare did not help them keep a cleaner home. As one Saturday Evening Girl noted, "the girls were the drudges in housework and chores" (*Story of the Saturday Evening Girls* 1929, 4).

By 1915 there were more than 250 girls and young women in eight different library clubs from grades four through adult. The library club programs included courses in literature, history, sociology, economics, science, civics, music, art, and current events. The Monday Afternoon Girls group was for eighth graders; Monday Evening Girls, third and fourth years of high school; Tuesday Afternoon Girls, seventh graders; Wednesday Afternoon Girls, fifth and sixth graders; Thursday Afternoon Girls, first and second years of high school; Thursday Evening Girls, high school seniors and some working girls; and

Saturday Evening Girls folk dance at a Library Club story hour. (Boston Public Library, ca. 1914)

Friday Evening Girls, eighteen- to twenty-year-old working young women. The oldest group, the Saturday Evening Girls, monitored and conducted many of the younger library club groups. They also spent time investigating community organizations to foster cooperation among different agencies for improved housing, education, and urban planning. The goal of most young library club girls was ultimately to become a Saturday Evening Girl. In June of each year, the Friday Evening Girls who were over twenty years old were formally invited to join the SEGs.

From 1912 to 1917 the library clubs published a newspaper entitled the *S.E.G. News*, which focused on contemporary issues such as immigration, education, the library, social reform, democracy, employment opportunities, literature, religion, community features, and social news. For the most part, the newspaper avoided controversial issues such as woman suffrage and trade unionism, but an underlying tension was evident in editorials about women's roles in society, social workers, and life in an immigrant community. The editors were particularly irritated by the criticism that "education and social work among the poor retard marriages" among the social workers (*S.E.G. News*, February 12, 1916, 2–3). They admonished social workers whose desire to "uplift" was derived from a sense of superiority, and they were particularly resentful of the reformers who spent all their time making "microscopic studies . . . of the children of the slums" but who ignored the voices of the children themselves (*S.E.G. News*, December 11, 1914, 5).

Although it was never financially stable, the pottery continued to operate until 1942, providing refuge and employment for some of the SEGs hardest hit by the consequences of the Depression. The financial importance of the pottery to the girls varied: some earned their livelihood from it, whereas others earned enough to enable them to stay in school. They supported the pottery as a collective effort for the benefit of all. Without it, their eager pursuit of economic independence would have taken on a different meaning. Making marmalade or fruitcake and hemming napkins and dishtowels were domestic chores and typical female fundraising venues, but for the SEG the pottery represented a new identity, as women and as workers, and offered them greater economic opportunities.

In the aftermath of World War I, as the SEGs aged and moved out of the North End, the structure of the clubs weakened. The individual library clubs consolidated, and thereafter they were all identified as Saturday Evening Girls. Edith Brown, artistic director of the pottery for twenty-five years, died in 1932. Helen Storrow died in 1944 after forty-five years of personal involvement with the SEGs and thirty-five years of providing financial support for the Paul Revere Pottery. Guerrier retired from the Boston Public Library in 1940 after forty-six years of library service. She died in 1958 at the age of eighty-eight.

The SEG Clubs were a successful response to the new urban industrial order that also provided an alternative to the cult of domesticity, which offered only one image for women, particularly poor and immigrant women. The richness of their experience in the library clubs enabled the majority to complete high school at a time when that was often not possible for immigrant and poor girls and young women. An unusually high number attended college, and many went on to inspire and educate others. They became teachers, librarians, office and clerical workers, social workers, saleswomen, secretaries, artists, musicians, and other professionals. These working-class Jewish and Italian women negotiated native-born white middle-class ideologies and expectations into a cultural framework within which they could identify themselves. In the process they were all changed into active participants in the forging of a new ideal of womanhood. The bonds that were created motivated many Saturday Evening Girls to continue meeting in the Boston area on an irregular basis. They finally voted to dissolve in June 1969.

Kate Clifford Larson

See also Camp Fire Girls; Education of Girls; 4-H; Girl Scouts; Home Economics Education; Immigration; Little Mothers; Summer Camps for Girls

References and Further Reading
Boris, Eileen. 1986. *Art and Labor.* Philadelphia: Temple University Press.
Boston Public Library. 1890–1920. *Records of the Corporation.*
Lazerson, Martin. 1971. *Origins of the Urban School: Public Education in Massachusetts, 1870–1915.* Cambridge: Harvard University Press.
Matson, Molly, ed. 1992. *An Independent Woman: The Autobiography of Edith Guerrier.* Amherst: University of Massachusetts Press.
McCarthy, Kathleen D. 1991. *Women's Culture, American Philanthropy and*

Art, 1830–1930. Chicago: University of Chicago Press.

Muncy, Robyn. 1991. *Creating a Female Dominion in American Reform, 1890–1935*. New York: Oxford University Press.

North Bennet Street Industrial School (NBSIS) Archives. Manuscript Collection 269, Schlesinger Library, Radcliffe College, Cambridge, MA.

Paul Revere Pottery Gallery File. Fine Arts Department, Boston Public Library.

Personal interviews with descendants of Saturday Evening Girls, by author, 1995–1999.

S.E.G. News (Boston). November 1914–May 1917.

S.E.G. News: 1899–1952. 1952. Boston.

S.E.G. News, Cherry Tree Edition, 1899–1954. 1954. Boston.

Solomon, Barbara Miller. 1985. *In the Company of Educated Women: A History of Women and Higher Education in America*. New Haven: Yale University Press.

———. 1989. *Ancestors and Immigrants*. Boston: Northeastern University Press.

The Story of the Saturday Evening Girls' Reunion. 1929. Boston: Privately printed, December 12.

Ware, Leonard. 1970. *Helen Osborne Storrow, 1864–1944: A Memoir*. Northhampton, MA: Privately printed.

Sexual Harassment

The practice of sexual harassment is an old one, but one without a recorded history. As a result, this entry draws upon recent results of surveys and other empirical research. At first, most of the literature on sexual harassment pertained to the workplace, usually confined to women's harassment by men, but more recently the focus has been on sexual harassment in schools.

Sexual harassment began to be discussed in the 1970s when feminist activists sought a way to address the unwanted sexual attention that women faced in the workforce. The concept originally included the many types of offensive behaviors that women considered as impeding their job performance and making them vulnerable to retaliation. The 1980 definition by the U.S. Equal Employment Opportunities Commission (EEOC) elaborated on two main types of sexual harassment: the coercive quid pro quo (i.e., pressure for sexual favors as a condition of employment) and the more common "hostile environment." As a form of sex discrimination, sexual harassment thus became illegal. Public attention focused on sexual harassment in the workforce with Anita Hill's 1991 testimony before the Senate Judiciary Committee's hearing on the confirmation of Supreme Court nominee Clarence Thomas, whom she described as having harassed her in the workplace.

Sexual Harassment in the Schools

In school settings, the hostile environment form of harassment is the most common type. In contrast to work settings, sexual harassment in school often occurs in public; thus it may be more damaging because of its potential for public humiliation and damage to one's reputation. When public sexual harassment occurs and is not condemned by the school authorities, it may be viewed as encouraging a hostile environment. Title IX of the Education Amendments of 1972 had outlawed discrimination on the basis of sex in education programs receiving federal aid. A landmark 1992 Supreme Court decision heightened public awareness of sexual harassment, coming the year after the above-mentioned Senate hearings. *Franklin v. Gwinnett County Public Schools* directed that schools could be held liable for compensatory damages if they fail to provide a school

More than 80 percent of girls report experiencing sexual harassment in school. (Sue Ficca)

environment free from sex discrimination. Although the victim's gender was not specified in sexual harassment cases, in the popular view harassment was thought to occur between female and male students. However, harassment is not confined to heterosexual students, and several states (Massachusetts, Wisconsin, Connecticut, and Rhode Island) now have laws that specifically protect gay and lesbian students.

Bullying is a troublesome behavior that resembles sexual harassment and is common in schools. Moreover, teasing and bullying may be the antecedents of sexual harassment and should not be accepted or ignored by parents and teachers (Stein 1999b). Bullying in western European schools and measures taken to stop it have been investigated, particularly in England (Whitney and Smith 1993) and in Norway and Sweden. Dan Olweus states that "a student is being bullied or victimized when he or she is exposed, repeatedly and over time, to negative actions on the part of one or more other students. An additional criterion of bullying is an imbalance in strength (an asymmetric power relationship)" (1995, 196). Name-calling is a common type of bullying, as are extortion, physical violence, rumors, exclusion from groups, damage to belongings, and threats. Boys tend to bully more often than girls. In studies, boys are reported to bully both girls and boys, but girls bully only girls. Boys and girls also use different types of bullying behavior.

Boys engage in more physical forms of attack, whereas girls give and get more indirect forms such as being ridiculed or victimized by rumors. Although bullying is more common among boys, girls and boys can be both bullies and victims. However, boys are more likely to be attacked by boys, whereas girls may be attacked by girls, boys, or mixed groups (Schuster 1996). The incidence of bullying in U.S. schools has been reported to range from a high of 80 percent, with only 20 percent of students reporting no bullying behavior in a thirty-day period (Bosworth, Espelage, and Simon 1999), to much lower estimates. Barry Thorne (1993) has reported that, in U.S. elementary schools, boys use sexual insults against girls and regard girls as a source of pollution. Her example is the game of cooties, which highlights the social status of children and is a way of keeping children outside a given group. The rules are that boys do not give cooties (i.e., by touching) to boys. But when girls give cooties to boys, they are acting aggressively, not in keeping with their female social role. The cooties game is found among prepubescent children and may be interpreted as a precursor of later sexual harassment.

Surveys of Sexual Harassment in Schools

The first survey was large but not systematic, appearing in *Seventeen* magazine in 1993. Three major themes emerged from the girls' responses. Sexual harassment in the schools was public; the targets were not passive when harassed, and when girls informed school officials of the harassment, their reports were often trivialized or dismissed. Although much was learned from this survey, it was neither systematic nor random, and findings could therefore not be generalized.

In 1993 the American Association of University Women (AAUW) published the results of a survey in a book titled *Hostile Hallways*. The AAUW report concludes that sexual harassment is very pervasive in high schools; that students consider harassment unwelcome and problematic; that, as the *Seventeen* survey found, sexual harassment occurs in public places; and that students have difficulty receiving help from teachers and administrators despite their requests. The AAUW survey aimed to provide a profile of the problem of sexual harassment in public high schools. The sample included 79 randomly selected schools across the country with 1,632 students in grades eight to eleven participating. Because the sample was large and students were randomly selected, findings may be generalized to all U.S. public school students in eighth through eleventh grades.

Sexual harassment was defined by the survey as unwanted and unwelcome sexual behavior that interfered with a student's life, and students were queried about their experiences with fourteen different forms of sexual harassment. Sexual harassment in the schools was found to be widespread: four in five students (81 percent of 1,632 students from 79 schools) said they had experienced some form of sexual harassment. Overall, 83 percent of girls and 60 percent of boys reported experiencing unwanted sexual attention in school. Twenty-five percent of the girls and 10 percent of the boys reported being harassed by a school employee. African American girls reported suffering more harassment from school employees than girls in other ethnic groups. Students did not usually report harassment incidents to teachers or other authorities or even to their families. That schools often constitute a hostile environment was emphasized by the finding that 66 percent of the boys and 52 percent of the girls admitted to sexually harassing someone in a school setting.

Janet Sawyer's interviews with students illustrate types of sexual harassment. Seventy-five high school girls told of being harassed on a daily basis in school. In fact, "over 90 percent of the girls reported incidents of verbal abuse, and 10 percent reported physical abuse" (1994, 70). "Boys call girls fat. Girls who are pretty and have lots of boyfriends are called 'sluts.' If a girl goes out with a guy for a while, guys start a rumor called 'haunting.' They make up a story about the girl having sex, and keep the story going for weeks until they 'haunt' another girl" (72). According to Sawyer, although a girl is called a "slut," a guy is called a "stud" and feels complimented. But the girl's reputation is hurt. Even though they felt angry, frustrated, violated, and powerless, the girls did not confront their harassers or tell them to stop. They reported that harassment goes on everywhere, even in the presence of other students and sometimes teachers. Teachers often ignore verbal abuse and do not reprimand students who engage in it.

A large and in-depth study drew its subjects from the AAUW sample of high school students reported in *Hostile Hallways*. V. E. Lee et al. (1996) searched for students who could verify their experiences of harassment by identifying a school-related location for the harassment, reporting a school-related person associated with their experience, and indicating that the experience upset them. Based on these criteria, 425 respondents were dropped from the sample because their experiences with sexual harassment were considered ambiguous. Results based on the remaining 1,203 students showed that 83.4 percent of girls and 60.2 percent of boys said that they had received unwanted sexual attention in school. These results confirm the results of the AAUW survey.

Lee et al. state that sexual harassment is strongly related to gender; that neither the occurrence nor the severity of harassment is related to either family social class or race and ethnicity. Although students' academic performance is unrelated to the probability of being harassed, those with lower academic performance report more severe harassment experiences. The study authors express concern over the "environment of harassment" because more than half of all students reported having both experienced harassment and harassed others in school. Harassment by school employees was found to be more severe than that from other students. In an examination of different theories that might have a bearing on sexual harassment, only the "abuse of power" theory, particularly the abuse of organizational power, seems applicable. That is, individuals have differing amounts of power in organizations, depending on their roles: principals have power over teachers; teachers over students. Males typically occupy higher authority roles in school and are therefore in positions to abuse that authority. Females in such roles could of course be equally prone to such abuse. While this formulation does not explain peer harassment in schools, abuse of power might contribute to the climate of harassment. Researchers on bullying have reached the same conclusion.

Because the existence and pervasiveness of sexual harassment in schools are well established and no longer controversial, research has leveled off. Research does exist, however, on methods to stop harassment. Nan Stein states that her research since the 1970s "on peer-to-peer sexual harassment has confirmed that schools may well be the training grounds for domestic violence through the practice of and permission for sexual harass-

ment" (1999b, 213). Between 1995 and 1998, Stein surveyed nearly 500 sexual assault and domestic violence organizations concerning their work in kindergarten through grade twelve in regard to gender violence. She has also developed a teaching guide for grades seven through twelve, entitled "Gender Violence/Gender Justice." Despite the work of community organizations in the schools, their skills are inadequately used because they are rarely allowed to see the same group of students more than 2.7 times. This reduces the impact of their presentations, also minimized by their materials, which are frequently of inferior quality. Stein recommends the following to reduce and prevent sexual harassment in schools:

1. Heightened awareness among all school staff about the problems of sexual violence in schools.
2. Cooperation between the schools and domestic violence or sexual assault groups in working to eliminate or reduce the problem.
3. Redesigned and readministered sexual harassment surveys that probe the relationship between the harasser/perpetrator and the target.
4. School-based restraining orders.
5. Expansion of restraining orders, also called orders of protection, to include noncohabiting minors in abusive relationships. Most states exclude orders of protection for either minors and/or noncohabitants. Thus adolescents remain in danger until all states permit them to request orders of protection from the violence of a dating partner.
6. Permission for domestic violence and sexual assault organizations to apply for more government funding to be used in the schools.

7. A more unified definition of sexual violence.

8. The inclusion of gender-based and gender-motivated hate crimes in the national and state definitions of hate crimes. (Stein 1999, 214)

The 1999 Supreme Court Decision

In 1999, efforts to eliminate sexual harassment in public schools accepting federal funds received considerable encouragement from a five-to-four Supreme Court decision. In a *New York Times* front-page report on May 25, 1999, entitled "Sex Harassment in Class Is Ruled Schools' Liability," reporter Linda Greenhouse writes: "School districts can be liable for damages under Federal law for failing to stop a student from subjecting another to severe and pervasive sexual harassment." Justices opposed to the ruling stated that the issue represented an unwarranted federal intrusion into the classroom and into the "routine problems of adolescence." The majority decision was based on an interpretation of Title IX and was a response to the Court's review of one of many sexual harassment lawsuits. The lawsuit considered by the Supreme Court was brought by Aurelia Davis of Forsyth, Georgia, to help her daughter LaShonda, who had been harassed for months by a boy in her fifth-grade class. The school had done nothing to stop the boy, who had become increasingly provocative. LaShonda, upset and despondent, talked of suicide and had a difficult time in class. LaShonda's mother, who under the ruling is now eligible to sue, poignantly stated, "They make you send your kids to school, right? So don't you think they should protect them while they're there?" (Greenhouse 1999, A25).

Ruth Formanek

See also Acquaintance Rape; Body Image; Child Abuse; Depression; Education of Girls; Female Sexuality; Psychotherapy; Relational Theory; Suicidal Behavior in Girls

References and Further Reading
American Association of University Women (AAUW). 1993. *Hostile Hallways. The AAUW Survey on Sexual Harassment in America's Schools.* Washington, DC: AAUW.
Bosworth, K., D. L. Espelage, and T. R. Simon. 1999. "Factors Associated with Bullying Behavior in Middle School Students." *Journal of Early Adolescence* 19: 341–362.
Greenhouse, Linda. 1999. "Sex Harassment in Class Is Ruled Schools' Liability." *New York Times* (May 25): A25.
Lee, V. E., R. G. Croninger, E. Linn, and X. Chen. 1996. "The Culture of Sexual Harassment in Secondary Schools." *American Educational Research Association Journal* 33: 383–417.
Olweus, Dan. 1995. "Bullying or Peer Abuse at School: Facts and Intervention." *Current Directions in Psychological Science* 4: 196–200.
Sawyer, Janet. 1994. "What Could You Possibly Learn by Studying Us? A Qualitative Study of the School Lives of High School Girls." Ph.D. diss., Hofstra University.
Schuster, B. 1996. "Mobbing, Bullying, and Peer Rejection." *Psychological Science Agenda* (July–August): 12–13.
Stein, Nan. 1995. "Sexual Harassment in School: The Public Performance of Gendered Violence." *Harvard Educational Review* 65: 145–162.
———. 1999a. *Classrooms and Courtrooms: Facing Sexual Harassment in K–12 Schools.* New York: Teachers College Press.
———. 1999b. "Gender Violence in Elementary and Secondary Schools." *Women's Studies Quarterly* 27: 212–217.
Thorne, Barry. 1993. *Gender Play: Girls and Boys in School.* New Brunswick, NJ: Rutgers University Press.
Whitney, I., and P. K. Smith. 1993. "A Survey of the Nature and Extent of Bullying in Junior/Middle and Secondary Schools." *Educational Research* 35: 3–25.

Slumber Parties

Slumber parties are a composite of folk rituals, festival practices, and girls' cultural activities that enable preadolescent girls to behave in ways that are generally considered both inappropriate and unacceptable. In the absence of restraining routine and the monitoring of teachers and parents, slumber parties serve to provide girls with a wide variety of opportunities: to safely engage in gender-role subversion, define female identity, and transmit girls' culture. Whatever meanings slumber parties have for girls, they have been appropriated by adult experts and entrepreneurs. Pornographic portrayals eroticize slumber parties, and manufacturers and marketers have commercialized and commodified them.

Slumber parties are most typically unisex sleep-overs with three or more girls and are often given to celebrate a birthday or other event. Slumber parties usually begin among elementary school girls and continue into adolescence. They consist of storytelling (often involving horror), pillow fights, pranks, jokes, and late-night snacks. Although the origins of the slumber party are unclear, sleeping over at a friend's house dates back to the nineteenth century. In Louisa May Alcott's *Little Women,* Meg spends a fortnight with her friend Annie Moffat. References to slumber parties do not appear in popular magazines, however, until the early 1950s. The postwar emphasis on a childhood free from adult responsibilities like work and the perceived importance of peer groups were factors that gave rise to slumber parties. So did suburbanization. The new houses provided children with more room and parents with access to quieter parts of the house.

Slumber party activities can be understood as a series of age- and sex-appropriate developmental tasks. For example, pillow fights provide girls with "an opportunity to grow in muscular coordination within a nonthreatening environment" (Oxreider 1977, 128). Although failure can lead to unhappiness and societal disapproval, a successful party can lead to personal happiness and social success: "Having mastered most of the problems of childhood within the slumber party framework, the girl gains confidence in her ability to direct her own life, and in so doing she discovers who she is and what she is becoming" (133). According to this view, a girl will learn "socially sanctioned behaviors appropriate to her sex" (130).

In addition, slumber parties can challenge prevailing gender norms. Though slumber parties are a composite of various folk practices, they function much like festivals, carnivals, and holidays that enable participants to behave in ways that are usually considered both inappropriate and unacceptable. Although some holidays aim to assert the authority of the dominant culture, still others tolerate riotous challenges to political dominants and social elites. Female peasants in early modern France, for instance, created a topsy-turvy world in which women dominated, if only for a short time. With no one to restrain them, girls at slumber parties behave much like boisterous carnival participants.

In the protection of the slumber party, girls can misbehave as boys have greater license to do. Girls temporarily contest gender-role norms as obedience is replaced with ritualized defiance. Slumber parties allow girls to be uninhibited and unself-conscious; to indulge in scatological and sexual jokes and songs and not patrol the borders of decency; to express aggressive feelings (pillow fights) and be

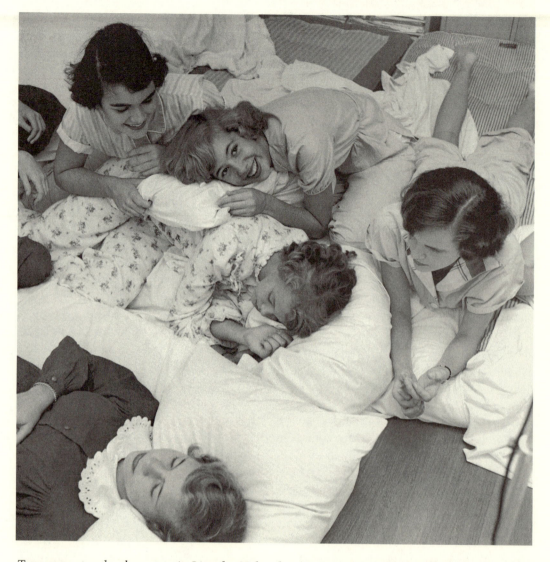

Teenagers at a slumber party in Lincoln, Nebraska. (Genevieve Naylor/Corbis, 1953)

assertive; and to behave subversively and mischievously (pranks, phony phone calls), not conscientiously. Levitation (where a group of girls levitate another with only their fingers) enables participants to feel the thrill of remarkable strength. Séances, a popular activity that involves invoking the spirits of great leaders (e.g., Elizabeth the First, Mary Queen of Scots, or Martha Washington), suggest girls' interest in exercising extraordinary power in the present and over the past. (Séances also have deep roots in nineteenth-century girls' culture. Many schoolgirls who pioneered the spiritualist movement acted as mediums who contacted the spirit world.)

The subversion of modern girls' slumber parties derives from a variety of factors. First, as time is held in abeyance, ordinary life is suspended and is replaced with an alternative reality. Second, staying up late and indulging in hilarious laughter add to a giddy intoxication that extends the oblivion of their "day out of time." One mother in the late 1950s described the "fever of delight" her daughter experienced as a result of the raptures of her slumber party. Third, slumber parties are tolerated because everyone knows that order will be restored in the end. Thus, the expression of transgressive actions is safely contained. Fourth, slumber parties (like other kinds of festivals) generate solidarity and provide cohesion and integration, especially so in the midst of unsettling developmental changes. Fifth, slumber parties are similar to other festivals that serve to define identity (e.g., female identity) and transmit culture (e.g., girls' culture).

Adults' anxiety about slumber party subversion has led to a growth in books and gadgets meant to provide redefinition. In *The Berenstain Bears and the Slumber Party* (1990), a prescriptive story about appropriate behavior for girls and their mothers, the daughter rhetorically recites a mantra about privilege and responsibility as she prepares for a slumber party. But in her excited anticipation, the well-behaved cub forgets all about her mother's prescription and thoroughly enjoys herself when things at the party get out of control. Although overreactive Mama bear responds punitively, Papa bear proffers insightful advice. Lessons are learned.

Elsewhere in the culture, slumber parties have been appropriated by an entrepreneurial ethos that markets feminine submission rather than female subversion. The pornography industry has not only contributed to the commercialization of the slumber party but also to the eroticization of girls and this all-female cultur-

al ritual. "Teen Sluts Slumber Party" is one of many titles with links to hard-core pornographic websites. *Slumber Party 2* and *The Last Slumber Party* are among a number of pornographic movies currently available that sexualize (and slash) teenage girls whose all-girl ritual is presented as the ultimate male sexual fantasy.

To other businesspeople, slumber parties incorporate feminine indulgence in romance, adornment, cosmetics (games such as "Blind Makeover" and "Rainbow Nails"), and consumerism. Like other holidays that have been commercialized, slumber parties have been commodified by makers of "Slumber Party Dolls" and "Pillow Buddies." In a company's cyberspace handbook, "The Ultimate Slumber Party Survival Guide," girls are informed that they will *want* to hold on to their pillow-sized stuffed animal while watching a scary horror movie. Not surprisingly, this website also promotes Blockbuster Video's choice of the "Top 10 Recommended Slumber Party Movies."

In the new juvenile advice or self-help books—some of which are allegedly written by girl authors—slumber party activities center around food. "How to Have the Greatest Slumber Party of All Time," the chapter on slumber parties in *Girls Know Best 2: Tips on Life and Fun Stuff to Do* (1998), is modeled after a cookbook. Books such as *Super Slumber Parties* (1977) aim to provide girls with advice, guidance, and tips on making their next slumber party a big success. To be a successful hostess depends upon following a recipe that identifies "the main ingredients" of party planning. For example, rule number three suggests girls provide an abundance of food for games and hide the rest for "Midnight Madness," the forbidden late-night snack. Girls compete over food in such recommended party games as "M&M Master" and "Hanging Doughnuts."

Miriam Forman-Brunell

See also Advice Books; Consumer Culture; Eating Disorders; Girls' Culture; Sororities

References and Further Reading
Berenstain, Stan and Jan. 1990. The Berenstain Bears and the Slumber Party. New York: Random House.
Manson-Burton, Marianne, comp. 1998. Girls Know Best 2. Hillsboro, OR: Beyond Worlds Publishing, 25–32.
Oxreider, J. W. 1977. "The Slumber Party: Transition into Adolescence." Tennessee Folklore Society Bulletin 43, no. 3: 128–134.
Paulsen, Susan B. 1988. "Sociable Speech in the American Slumber Party: An Ethnographic Study." Ph.D. diss., University of Washington.
Simons, Elizabeth Radin. 1980. "The Slumber Party as Folk Ritual: An Analysis of the Informal Sex Education of Preadolescents." Master's thesis, University of California at Berkeley.

Sororities

A sorority is a society of young women or girls who typically join organizations that are most active in colleges or universities. Aiming to foster friendship among members and sponsor group activities, the majority of sororities are social in nature. Since their origins in the latter half of the nineteenth century, sororities have been a major part of the college experiences of many American girls. The first sororities evolved in response to the male fraternal societies that excluded women during the early development of higher education. The avowed goals of these early groups were to promote the academic and social development of the female minority of students. Through the years, they have continued to provide a source of fellowship and community for women but have also sparked controversies. Sororities have been criticized for emphasizing the social side of university life over academics, for fostering elitism through their exclusivity, and for racial and religious discrimination. In recent years, sorority leaders have striven to address these aspects of their organizations and reassess the ways that sororities shape campus culture and influence members.

When a college student decides to become a sorority member, she determines how she will experience many aspects of her university life. To join a sorority, a college woman participates in a process called "rush." During rush, potential members visit the different sororities and, by a process of mutual selection and rejection, may accept an invitation to join a specific group. A new member may then participate in a pledge program filled with activities designed to forge bonds of friendship between members and teach new members about the sorority's history and rituals. Pledging has been controversial because new members are sometimes asked to perform dangerous or demeaning activities before achieving full membership. Once initiated, most sorority women live together in a house or specified sections of dormitories. The sorority provides a steady schedule of social events, typically including formal dances, parties, hayrides, and homecoming celebrations. Sorority members also participate in charity projects, administrative meetings, study hours, and group retreats. To cultivate unity and loyalty among members, sororities have developed rituals, symbols, and mottoes. Members often refer to each other as sisters and wear jewelry and clothing inscribed with the sorority insignia.

Both sororities and fraternities can trace their roots to the university literary and debating societies that formed around the time of the American Revolution. The typical college curriculum emphasized rote memorization and the indoctrination of a canon of knowledge rather than encouraging thoughtful debate or discussion among students. As a result, students formed their own forums to address literary and social issues. Phi Beta Kappa, founded at the College of William and Mary in 1776, was the most prominent of these societies. Although Phi Beta Kappa evolved into an honorary society that recognized members for academic accomplishments, other social fraternities developed during the early 1800s. They adopted many of the attributes of the fraternal societies that existed outside universities, such as the Freemasons, and created secret rituals, handshakes, and Greek letter acronyms from which they took their names. Fraternity life came to be characterized by a sense of rebellion against both the social and intellectual regulation of universities. Campus officials opposed the existence of fraternities because they seemed to undermine discipline, threatened school loyalty, and because the selectivity and the rivalries that existed among them were antidemocratic. But fraternities continued to grow on college campuses and developed national organizations with affiliate chapters throughout the young nation. By the Civil War, these groups were a major force in social and extracurricular life at American universities.

Until the 1830s, women were excluded from universities and from participation in Greek letter societies. But in 1836 the Georgia Female College (now Wesleyan College) was founded, and in 1837 Oberlin became the first coeducational institution. As other colleges followed this trend, higher education became a real option for women but one that Victorian social norms discouraged. The first female students were rebels who challenged the doctrine of separate spheres, which encouraged "proper" women to devote themselves to their homes and families rather than to intellectual ambitions. During the nineteenth century, female students were often viewed as social misfits and were resented by their male classmates, who vastly outnumbered them. Excluded from extracurricular activities such as student government and publications and ostracized socially, women students struggled to cultivate intellectual and social communities for themselves.

In 1851, nineteen women at Wesleyan Female College formed the Adelphean, a secret sisterhood and literary society. A year later, they had a rival, the Philamathean. Like fraternities, each group had secret rituals and mottoes but did not form chapters on other campuses until the 1900s, when they adopted the Greek names Alpha Delta Pi and Phi Mu. The first sisterhood to pattern itself directly after fraternities and establish chapters on campuses throughout the country was founded at Monmouth College in Illinois in 1867. It began under the name I. C. Sorosis before adopting the Greek name Pi Beta Phi twenty-one years later. The first women's societies to officially adopt Greek letter names were Kappa Alpha Theta at DePauw University in Illinois and Kappa Kappa Gamma at Monmouth College, both founded in 1870. The woman who founded Kappa Alpha Theta was first offered a token membership in her brother's fraternity, but she demanded full membership. Her request was met with a gift, a silver cake basket, rather than real membership. Her father suggested that she start her own group, and Kappa Alpha Theta was formed in direct reaction to women's exclusion from all-male organizations.

The founders and earliest members of sororities defied social convention to pursue higher education and occupied a precarious position on the outskirts of male-dominated college campuses. This situation prompted them to place academic development at the forefront of their sorority agendas. Female students were concerned with proving themselves worthy in the classroom, as well as with demonstrating that women could be both feminine and intellectually vigorous. Sorority founders enshrined the ideals of scholarship and intellectual achievement in sorority mottoes and rituals. Sororities provided these pioneering students with camaraderie and encouragement.

Women's position on campuses became more secure around the turn of the century, and by the 1920s higher education had become more of a socially acceptable option for middle- and upper-class women. As females from these groups streamed into universities, they brought new sets of values, often prizing social and economic enrichment over academic achievement. Like education itself, sorority membership became an index of class status. By the early twentieth century, students could view their sororities as social networks rather than expressions of solidarity against a hostile academic environment. These later generations of sorority women focused more on social activities than had their scholarly predecessors. They transformed the goals of sorority life to emphasize the cultivation of traditionally "feminine" attributes—grace, poise, social charm—and began to use appearance and sociability as their criteria for selecting new members.

This era also saw the emergence of an autonomous youth culture in the United States, which fueled sorority members' enthusiasm for socializing. During the 1920s, youth was increasingly defined as a distinct life stage, separate from both childhood and maturity. Young people assumed distinctive ways of dressing and speaking, created their own dances, and adopted common tastes, all of which distinguished them as a group from their elders. Increasingly, they constructed their own social worlds, subverting adult supervision and regulation to plan their own parties and outings. As sorority girls bobbed their hair, did the Charleston at homecoming dances, and wore short skirts to fraternity parties, Greek organizations provided social venues for the propagation of youth culture on college campuses.

As the Greek system grew more elaborate, it influenced social life in more subtle ways as well by organizing students into "cliques" and defining their social status. These functions invited critics to note that sororities and fraternities chose only the more socially favored as members and then encouraged a conformist style of thought and behavior among them. School administrators and state legislators campaigned against the Greek system and abolished sororities and fraternities at some schools. But nationwide, the organizations continued to expand throughout the 1920s. Only the Great Depression slowed the growth of Greek organizations during the 1930s, and after World War II sororities and fraternities gained in popularity throughout the 1950s.

One pernicious aspect of the Greek system during these years was exclusion based on class, race, and religion. The selection process, which emphasized social graces and outward appearances, discriminated against those whose class backgrounds had not provided them with the leisure or opportunity to cultivate such attributes. Meanwhile, both sororities and fraternities typically excluded blacks, Jews, and other minority groups. Christian, Anglo-Saxon ideals and symbolism were embedded in the rituals of most sororities and fraternities, and some organizations even had "Aryan clauses" overtly forbidding the membership of nonwhites or non-Christians. Surveys done in the 1920s at Syracuse University revealed the depth of prejudice: less than 6 percent of non-Jewish students indicated that they would willingly admit a Jew to their Greek organization. Group photographs of fraternities and sororities that excluded blacks and Jews made prejudice explicit and visible.

Just as the founders of sororities had responded to the gender discrimination of fraternities by establishing their own organizations and patterning them after those that had excluded them, the African Americans and religious groups who found themselves cut out of Greek life created their own groups. The early twentieth century saw the development of predominantly African American, Jewish, and Roman Catholic sororities and fraternities. Students also founded organizations dedicated to promoting tolerance and diversity through which minority students could have access to Greek life, but these groups remained outside the mainstream sorority and fraternity systems.

Sororities have played a particularly significant role in the history of African Americans' struggles to gain political and social equality. Although they developed many of the same problems as their white counterparts, including intense

rivalries among groups and an emphasis on social status, black sororities were also strongly committed to uplifting the race. In 1919, the black sorority Alpha Kappa Alpha pioneered efforts to promote education in the African American community with a nationwide campaign aimed at high school students that urged them to "Go to High School, Go to College," and featured the dissemination of literature to younger students as well as speeches and workshops. By the 1930s, "Go to High School, Go to College" had been replaced by the "Education for Citizenship" campaign that embodied the hopes of many black leaders that education would help African Americans challenge their disenfranchisement by preparing them to make informed voting decisions. Black sororities also organized social welfare programs aimed at improving health conditions and developing job skills within impoverished black communities. Throughout the twentieth century, black sororities have shown greater commitment to social and political causes than most Greek organizations, participating in the movements for woman suffrage and civil rights. Sororities were important among the array of voluntary organizations that provided institutional structure and common meeting grounds where middle-class blacks could develop critiques of racial prejudice in American society and devise methods for combating political and social inequality.

After World War II, in the shadow of Nazism and the Holocaust, a self-segregated system of Greek organizations for different races and religions seemed inadequate to many people. The majority of students, administrators, and lawmakers began to believe that student organizations should represent democratic ideals

Sorority sisters pack into a tiny Renault to try to set a car packing record in Sioux City, Iowa. (Bettmann/Corbis, 1959)

and that all groups should be equally open to all students. As the United States became entrenched in a Cold War mentality, these efforts to distinguish American organizations as democratic institutions in opposition to "totalitarian" structures intensified. Universities pressured national fraternities and sororities to remove discriminatory restrictions based on race or religion. Although surveys indicated that most students applauded these efforts, efforts to abolish prejudicial practices incited conflicts within fraternities and sororities, as small sectors of students tried to continue informal discrimination and resist efforts toward integration. Even without formal rules, some groups simply neglected to invite nonwhites or non-Christians to join.

In the late 1960s, college campuses became hotbeds of political activism where students held demonstrations to protest the Vietnam War, demand equal rights for women, and denounce racism. In this atmosphere, Greek organizations that emphasized social life and had histories tainted by elitism and prejudice seemed out of step with the social and political causes that many students were championing. Although the original sorority founders, in their efforts to empower an oppressed female minority at universities, had shared some of the sentiments of twentieth-century feminists, decades of sorority experiences that emphasized feminine rather than feminist virtues left the organizations ill prepared to become potent participants in the women's rights movements of the

1960s and 1970s. For the first time in history, sororities and fraternities began to decline in membership and popularity. In 1972, less than 5 percent of students belonged to Greek organizations.

The 1980s brought renewed enthusiasm for fraternities and sororities, and their membership numbers began to climb again. As sororities have regained popularity and influence in campus culture, leaders and members have shown an increasing level of awareness about the dangerous tendencies inherent in the structure and history of their organizations, as well as their potential to make positive contributions to university communities and enrich members' educational experiences.

Some of the social structures traditionally established by sororities have made members particularly vulnerable in certain areas that are problematic for college women. By organizing "happy hours," "champagne brunches," and other festivities involving drinking, sororities have placed alcohol at the center of social life. Excessive consumption of alcohol, especially at fraternity parties, also contributes to a social environment in which women may be more vulnerable to sexual pressures or harassment. Sorority culture emphasizes social life and includes rituals such as "pinning ceremonies" for members with boyfriends, thus celebrating romantic and sexual relationships and encouraging members to focus on socializing and dating, sometimes at the expense of other aspects of college life. Perhaps because sororities have tended to emphasize outward appearances in their selection processes and encourage conformity among members, eating disorders have been a particular problem for many sorority women. The close living quarters and communal aspects of sorority life also provide an environment in which behaviors and attitudes toward food and weight are quickly transmitted. Although problems with alcohol, sexual harassment, and eating disorders are not endemic to sororities, some educators have pointed to the organizations for establishing conditions in which these issues may have a greater potential of emerging.

Contemporary sororities' newsletters are filled with articles describing the organizations' efforts to mitigate these problems and highlighting the positive contributions that sororities can make. These publications are a central means by which sorority leaders and members consciously represent their agendas to themselves and others. They demonstrate participants' ongoing efforts to reevaluate the meaning of all female societies in changing campus environments. The educational campaigns that sororities have launched to confront these issues feature an abundance of articles on eating disorders, alcoholism, and sexual harassment that describe ways in which various chapters have addressed these problems through lectures, seminars, and support groups. Newsletters note the changed policies of national sorority organizations, which have recently initiated programs to monitor and limit alcohol consumption at Greek events, instilled antiprejudice clauses into their bylaws, and issued statements forbidding chapters from "hazing" new members. Articles laud the philanthropic projects of various sororities, which raise money for causes ranging from children's cancer hospitals to rape crisis centers. Sororities also offer scholarships for both undergraduate and graduate students to pursue higher education. By including stories and articles that discuss the goals and structures devised by their founders, sororities use their publications to keep their traditions intact and reinterpret them in modern contexts. In their attention to these issues, sorority leaders and members are demonstrating a current awareness that the meaning of all female societies for university students shifts in changing historical circumstances and that participants are engaged in a continual process of redefining the place of sororities in modern campus culture.

Mary Miles

See also Acquaintance Rape; African American Girls in the Twentieth Century; College Girls; Eating Disorders; Education of Girls; Relational Theory; Sexual Harassment; Substance Abuse

References and Further Reading
Beach, Mark. 1971. "Fraternities and Sororities." Pp. 93–98 in *The Encyclopedia of Education*. Edited by Lee Deighton. New York: Macmillan.
Horowitz, Helen. 1987. *Campus Life: Undergraduate Cultures from the End of the Eighteenth Century to the Present*. New York: Alfred A. Knopf.
Lee, Alfred McClung. 1955. *Fraternities without Brotherhood: A Campus Report on Racial and Religious Prejudice*. Boston: Beacon Press.
Palmieri, Patricia. 1995. *In Adamless Eden: The Community of Women Faculty at Wellesley*. New Haven: Yale University Press.
Schilling, Peter, and Daniel Soyer. 1996. "Fraternities and Sororities." Pp. 1047–1052 in *Encyclopedia of African American Culture and History*. Edited by Jack Salzman, David Lionel Smith, and Cornel West. New York: Macmillan.
Solomon, Barbara. 1985. *In the Company of Educated Women: A History of Women and Higher Education in America*. New Haven, CT: Yale University Press.
Turk, Diana. 1999. "Bound by a Mighty Vow: Sisterhood in Kappa Alpha Theta, 1870–1920." *Kappa Alpha Theta Magazine* (Summer): 6–7.

Southern Belles

Southern belles, the adolescent white daughters of wealthy slave owners in the antebellum South, were a unique phenomenon of the American South. Unlike slave girls in the South or free white girls in the North, the white daughters of elite plantation masters were shaped by dominant Victorian ideologies in regard to race, gender, and class. The representation of the belle was a deliberate creation of southern aristocratic male culture heavily invested in maintaining a patriarchal society and slave economy. The ornamental southern belle placed on a gilded pedestal was extolled by southern writers for her unsurpassed propriety, purity, and piety. Symbolizing her father's wealth, status, and power, her ultimate purpose was to cloak the violence, vices, and immorality of fathers, brothers, and other plantation males whose sexual abuse of female slaves was widespread. The southern belle was culturally constructed in order to mask the violence and inhumanity of slavery.

Though often initially disappointed by the birth of a daughter whom they regarded as inferior, parents sheltered southern girls within the family circle. Indulgent parents, especially mothers, guided their daughters according to the precepts of the prevailing nineteenth-century ideology of domesticity. According to this ideology (also referred to as "separate spheres"), females were to cultivate gendered characteristics that contemporaries believed were biologically determined. From their mothers, southern white girls learned how to be modest, pious, humble (not vain), proper, presentable (e.g., maintaining a light complexion), and fashionable (accomplished by lacing corsets tightly).

Southern girls received very little practical training useful in their future capac-

In this scene from Gone with the Wind, *based on Margaret Mitchell's famous novel, Vivien Leigh portrayed the ultimate southern belle. (Photofest, 1939)*

ity as plantation mistresses. Despite the centrality of motherhood among southern women, girls were not taught how to care for children, even though most had numerous siblings. (Because they often married early, southern women had fertility rates that were 20 percent higher than the national average.) White girls learned little about how to care for children because that was the responsibility of enslaved girls and women, not of plantation mistresses. Generally speaking, toddlers and infants were left in the care of nurses and other house slaves, from whom young girls learned songs, folk-

lore, religious principles, ghost stories, and African tales.

Although older siblings accompanied their mothers on daily rounds of tasks and trips, they learned little more than how to supervise gardens, put up preserves, and sew. According to Elizabeth Fox-Genovese, "The primary household responsibilities of slaveholding daughters included the care of their own rooms and clothing. . . . Gertrude Clanton's day normally consisted—beyond reading, visiting, and shopping—in dressing and fixing her hair for the evening, gathering flowers to dress flower pots, arranging her room, gathering roses and putting the leaves up to dry, and mending her kid gloves. Occasionally she passed a whole day in doing nothing at all" (1988, 114).

Instead of assuming ever-greater responsibilities of household management as she got older, the belle focused on acquiring the rules of rituals. It was largely mothers—as opposed to mammies—who supervised daughters in regard to manners. Daughters learned about deportment from their mothers, whom they accompanied (along with a male chaperone) as they made social visits and attended church services and frequent parties and balls. Daughters also learned about the proper forms of letter-writing etiquette from their mothers, who corrected drafts, making sure that forms of address were as appropriate as the sentiments expressed. Elizabeth Morrow Nix (1996) has explored the variety of responses of young girls to their role in southern society. In novels, diaries, and periodicals, adolescent girls were depicted as resisting the limitations imposed upon the belle by means of restraint and decorum. Although Morrow Nix also found evidence of their culture's simultaneous tolerance of their resistance, unrefined behavior could be dealt with harshly when southern girls challenged the boundaries of their tightly regulated upbringing. Mothers were a formidable force in the plantation household and occasionally meted out punishment with a slap of a face or a crack of a whip.

Whether stern, indulgent, or somewhere in between, it was fathers who exercised ultimate authority. They assumed control over their daughters' formal education, though usually not until their daughters reached adolescence. Because of the daughter's financial dependence, her father's will usually prevailed. Around age thirteen, most upper-

class girls could attend one of the South's female academies or boarding schools, which emphasized the importance of the "polite arts" in a fundamentally ornamental education. They learned grammar, composition, music, languages, literature, and geography but neither science nor mathematics. At school (and accompanied by a servant), schoolgirls also had more opportunities to socialize with friends than was often the case on remote plantations. Nevertheless, they maintained close relationships with siblings and especially with sisters.

"These few years between puberty and marriage were the closest that most women came to freedom," according to Catherine Clinton. "The great decision of their lives—the choice of when and whom to marry—lay ahead, and their time to choose was filled with fun and frivolity. This period—when women were most carefree, most hopeful—was therefore cherished by planter-class females. Young girls anticipated being a belle. Belles themselves conveyed a sense of exhilaration" (1982, 61–62). But belles also faced certain constraints. It was often mothers who selected, supervised, and chaperoned suitors, whether at home or at parties. One contemporary observer noted: "In the South it is deemed indecorous for them to be left alone, and the mother or some member of the family is always in the rooms; and if none of these, a female slave is seated on the rug at the door" (63).

Despite the presence of others, however, flirting was an acceptable—even expected—form of behavior for the adolescent southern belle. According to one historian, "many belles raised it to an art form" (Goldberg 1994, 27). To be a "reputed belle," coquettish girls like Cary Bryon aimed to engage as many men as she could in playful banter, but absolutely no sex: "Southern planter society placed an absolute premium on the bride's 'purity'" (28). In the event that a young woman's sexual purity (or "honor") was transgressed by an overly amorous suitor-turned-seducer, he could find himself a mere ten paces from her paternalistic father or protective brother. But more often than not, courting ended with a pen, not a pistol, as families forged the financial bonds of matrimony. Most southern daughters married by the time they reached twenty; some by ages fifteen or sixteen, when parents agreed to solid marriage proposals from insistent bridegrooms.

Miriam Forman-Brunell

See also Dating and Courtship; Daughters and Fathers; Daughters and Mothers; Domesticity; Enslaved Girls of African Descent; Girls' Culture

References and Further Reading
Clinton, Catherine. 1982. *Plantation Mistress: Women's World in the Old South.* New York: Vintage.
Farnham, Christine Anne. 1994. *The Education of the Southern Belle: Higher Education and Student Socialization in the Antebellum South.* New York: New York University Press.
Fox-Genovese, Elizabeth. 1988. *Within the Plantation Household: Black and White Women in the Old South.* Chapel Hill: University of North Carolina Press.
Goldbert, Michael. 1994. *Breaking New Ground: American Women 1800–1848.* New York: Oxford University Press.
Morrow Nix, Elizabeth. 1996. "An Exuberant Flow of Spirits: Antebellum Adolescent Girls in the Writing of Southern Women." Ph.D diss., Boston University.

Sports

American girls have encountered a mixture of opportunities and obstacles over the past century as they have sought entry into a modern sports world dominated by men. Historically, sport has been not only a site of male recreation and competition but an arena in which boys and men learn or display "masculine" skills. In this capacity, the sports world has served as a major proving ground for masculinity, with female athletes often perceived as unwelcome intruders. Consequently, girls and women seeking to participate have met institutional and ideological roadblocks that have discouraged female athletic involvement and success at almost every turn. Despite these impediments, however, girls and women have consistently sought out athletic opportunities, taking advantage of school, municipal, and elite amateur and professional sports programs whenever they were available. The history of girls' sports is not, therefore, a history of discrimination so extensive as to stifle all interest in competitive athletics but rather an uneven patchwork of avid female athletic participation set within a broader context of pervasive discrimination. Discrimination typically has taken two forms: explicit prohibitions on or criticism of female athleticism and implicit discouragement through lack of opportunity or support.

By the 1910s, popular magazines had begun to note a new phenomenon called the modern "athletic girl," who loved outdoor sports and play just as much as men did. The excitement about this new type of athlete reflected both the growing popularity of sport in American society and a profound shift in gender ideals. Nineteenth-century Victorians had praised women only in their domestic role as mothers and wives while emphasizing their purity and frailty. By 1900 this image began to fade before the far more robust image of the "new woman," noted for her bold, adventurous spirit and her eagerness to embrace public activities like business, education, politics, and sports. The break from Victorianism toward modernism was often represented by the figure of the physically liberated girl emancipated by bold new dress styles, liberalized sexual mores, and a heightened interest in sports. By the 1920s, female tennis players and aquatic champions—many of them girls in their teens—rivaled movie stars for celebrity status as the popular press and advertisers featured them in stories and photos celebrating modern womanhood.

National attention bestowed upon teenage stars like swimmers Aileen Riggin, Helen Wainright, and Gertrude Ederle capped a much broader and deeper expansion of girls' and women's sports at the grassroots level. Girls' sports blossomed through the efforts of recreation leaders and physical educators who believed that athletic activity was an important part of female physical and social development. In urban working-class neighborhoods, sports developed through service-based organizations like the Young Women's Christian Association, Catholic Youth Organization, or newly formed municipal parks and recreation departments. Teenagers and young women also found opportunities in industrial leagues sponsored by businesses interested in promoting goodwill among workers and within local communities. Concurrently, middle-class girls and women seized upon a growing array of athletic opportunities in high school and college athletic programs. Schoolgirls frequently competed in intramural sports programs and newly created interscholastic basketball, baseball, field hockey, or track competitions. The pop-

ularity of girls' sports prompted the Amateur Athletic Union (AAU), which governed men's amateur sport, to establish national championships in women's swimming, track and field, and basketball during the 1920s. The capstone of women's new athletic freedom came during the international Olympic Games where, by the 1920s, girls and women competed for medals in skating, swimming and diving, and track-and-field events.

The enthusiasm for the "new type of athletic girl" did not go unchallenged. Critics viewed sports as an inherently masculine activity appropriate for men only and thus unsuitable for girls who, by this logic, could succeed only by sacrificing their natural femininity for masculine qualities of body and mind. They also complained that vigorous athletic activity exposed the female body to public view and would inevitably damage a girl's reproductive organs, possibly ruining her chance for future motherhood. Moreover, opponents predicted that aggressive physical competition would unleash physical, sexual, and emotional passions that put girls at risk of bodily injury, sexual impropriety, and nervous collapse.

Oppositional forces succeeded in limiting or altering competitive opportunities for girls in at least three ways. First, forced into a defensive posture, female physical educators adopted a philosophy of "moderation," which sought to stamp out all interscholastic competition. Under this policy, educators modified girls' athletic rules for the purpose of reducing physical strain and containing competitive impulses. At many high schools and colleges, rigorous interschool competition gave way to exclusively intramural sports with the occasional exception of a "play day," which brought together different schools for a single round of friendly competition and socializing. These policies lasted until the 1960s in many regions, limiting girls' competitive opportunities and sending the message that "real sport" was an activity suited for boys or men alone.

Anticompetition forces also succeeded in banning girls and women from certain athletic events. For instance, in the 1920s International Olympic Committee (IOC) officials refused to allow college student Sybil Bauer to swim against men in the Olympic backstroke competition, despite the fact that she had previously broken the world (*men's*) record for her event. In another move, the IOC eliminated all long-distance running events for women after 1928, so that women ran no race longer than 200 meters until 1960, when the IOC restored the 800-meter race.

Finally, opposition to girls' sports manifested itself through foot-dragging and inequitable distribution of athletic resources. Recreational leaders and school officials regularly slighted girls' sports in favor of extensive programming for boys, channeling girls into arts or crafts activities deemed more appropriate for their gender. Similarly, despite sponsoring national championships for women's swimming, track, and basketball, the Amateur Athletic Union did little at the local, district, or state level to support girls interested in pursuing these sports.

Countervailing forces for and against women's athletics created a complex picture in which certain female athletes achieved great stature, modeling a positive image of liberated, assertive, and alluring new womanhood, whereas the great masses of girls and women found

Child dressed for tennis. (Hulton-Deutsch Collection/Corbis)

only limited opportunities for athletic competition and were as likely to reap scorn as to earn praise if they pursued athletic excellence.

This pattern persisted in the 1930s and 1940s as the team sports of softball and basketball became the most popular activities among athletic girls. Typically, a girl might first get involved in informal neighborhood play, then join a team through the local recreation program, and as she entered her late teens or twenties,

Mildred "Babe" Didrikson breaks the record in hurdles at the Olympic Games in Los Angeles, California. (Library of Congress, 1932)

play for an adult recreational team sponsored by her employer or some other local business. The most skilled might, as a teenager, join a semiprofessional team that competed regionally before traveling to the national championship tournament. However, the axiomatic assumption that sporting ability and success were fundamentally masculine continued to pose obstacles to girls and women's participation.

The mixed reception that women's sports received during the Depression and World War II eras is best illustrated by the two most high-profile events of these decades, the 1932 Olympic performance of Babe Didrikson and the establishment of the All-American Girls Professional Baseball League (AAGPBL) in the early 1940s. Mildred "Babe" Didrikson grew up in a working-class Texas community, excelling at every sport she tried. In the summer of 1932 the eighteen-year-old Didrikson took the Olympics by storm, winning two gold medals and a silver in track-and-field events. Didrikson's astounding abilities made her an instant national celebrity among reporters and fans. Appreciation for her abilities, however, went hand in hand with more derisive comments about Didrikson's appearance and personality, described in wholly masculine terms. Criticisms of track athletes as "manly women" gained momentum in the succeeding years, so that by the late 1940s women's track and field occupied such a marginal position that to any observer it would appear that girls and women simply had no interest in the sport. Only in black communities and a few other ethnic enclaves did girls' track continue to receive support. African American girls who grew up competing for positions on local track squads and black college teams eventually became the backbone of postwar national track teams of the 1950s and 1960s.

Softball, unlike track, continued to thrive throughout the Depression and war years. In 1942, enterprising midwestern businessmen launched a professional women's softball league, which they quickly converted to baseball. The AAGPBL demonstrates, paradoxically, both the strength of girls' and women's sports in the 1940s and the persistence of attitudes that discouraged female athletic activity. The league operated for twelve seasons from 1943 to 1954, thriving in midsize cities like Rockford, Illinois, and South Bend, Indiana. It received press coverage in major national magazines and became the subject of a 1947 Movietone newsreel film, *Diamond Gals.* League players, many of them girls in their late teens, thrilled at the chance to play professional baseball and regularly held clinics to encourage the next generation of girls to take up competitive ball.

Yet the league's male leadership never trusted that athletic skill could by itself draw the crowds necessary for financial success. League directors conceived of their product as a dramatic contrast of "feminine girls" with "masculine skill."

The league required players to wear skirted uniforms, keep their hair long, and attend preseason charm and beauty classes. Such policies sent a mixed message to players and the public: athletic skills were essentially masculine, and femininity existed outside—and in contrast to—athletic ability and passionate commitment to sports. The notion that femininity and athletic skill were contrasting attributes served, in the long run, to reinforce the axiom that sport was inherently masculine and that girls and women, therefore, would always remain a sideshow to the "real" game of men's baseball.

In the conservative post–World War II years, a renewed emphasis on family, marriage, and conventional femininity caused a gradual erosion of support for girls' and women's sports. For instance, as burgeoning Little League programs enrolled more and more boys, fewer girls grew up playing neighborhood baseball on mixed sandlot and playground teams. Those girls who wanted to play were excluded by the Little League's boys-only policy. In high schools and colleges intramural activities vastly outnumbered the few interscholastic and intercollegiate sports programs for girls. In municipal settings, recreation programmers put new emphasis on activities that occurred away from athletic fields or gymnasiums, including classes in "beauty culture," baking, and sewing. Recreational leaders commented that their task had changed from one of discouraging the competitive zealot to stimulating interest among the majority of nonathletic girls who did not want to sweat, mess up their hair, or, worst of all, be accused of being masculine.

A general climate of suspicion surrounded female athletes, causing a decline in the number of girls' and women's leagues and the number of female athletes willing and able to devote time to sports. Girls who continued to seek high-level sporting opportunities faced a set of stereotypes that described female athletes as "grotesque," "ugly," "unnatural," and "masculine." Rumors associating female athletes with lesbianism, behavior also stigmatized as "masculine," underpinned more open criticisms and created a powerful disincentive for girls' athletic involvement.

Even in this chilly climate, an undercurrent of more sympathetic views of girls' and women's competitive sports slowly gained momentum, emerging in the 1960s along with the first stirrings of a reborn feminist movement. In the field of physical education a younger generation of professionals, many of whom had grown up playing competitive sports in their local communities, pressed conservative leaders to relax their stand against intercollegiate competition. This approach gained institutional ground with the founding in 1966 of the Commission on Intercollegiate Athletics for Women (CIAW). Established to govern and promote major intercollegiate tournaments for women, the CIAW was the direct predecessor of the Association for Intercollegiate Athletics for Women (AIAW), which from its founding in 1971 became the sole sponsor and chief advocate of women's intercollegiate sports during the 1970s. For younger girls, the decade of the 1960s began to see a more favorable attitude develop toward athletic activity, influenced in part by the nationwide fitness campaign initiated during the Kennedy administration through the President's Council on Physical Fitness. The expansion of suburban parks, athletic facilities, and recreation programs created more space for athletic activity in general, with girls reaping a portion of these benefits.

The subtle changes of the 1960s opened the door to more dramatic changes to come. Responding to momentum from within the sports world and external demands by feminists for gender equality, girls' and women's sports underwent a sea change in the 1970s and 1980s. For the first time, female athletes successfully challenged traditional beliefs in the masculinity of sport, positing instead that athletic play was a human endeavor appropriate to any girl, boy, woman, or man.

The U.S. Congress set this process in motion in 1972 by including in the Education Amendments Act a section, Title IX, that outlawed sex discrimination in any educational setting receiving federal assistance. Since almost all schools, from elementary through college institutions, receive some federal monies, the law had enormous implications, especially in the field of sports. At the time of Title IX's passage, the most generous college and university athletic programs allocated only 1 to 2 percent of their funds to women's athletics. Twenty-five years after the passage of Title IX, girls and women received approximately one-third of athletic scholarships, and one-quarter of operating budgets for collegiate sports went to women's teams (Sklover 1997, 12–16).

Although the National Collegiate Athletic Association, which governs intercollegiate sport, has recognized that this figure falls far short of full gender equity, the enormous shift in resources that has occurred has meant opportunities for girl and women athletes that earlier generations could only have wished for in their wildest dreams. In 1972, only 300,000 high school girls—or one of every twenty-

Two thirteen-year-old friends playing basketball in a city park. (Skjold Photographs)

seven girls—participated in interscholastic sports. By 1997 the number had reached 2,400,000, about one of every three girls, compared to a steady rate of one of every two boys. The number of women in intercollegiate athletics has more than tripled in the same time span, from 32,000 in 1971 to more than 110,000 in 1997, or just under 35 percent of college athletes.

Women's current standing in professional and Olympic sports, as with interscholastic and intercollegiate sports, has not reached parity by any definition. But the phenomenal changes in both the numbers and skill levels of highly competitive female athletes have put a permanent, deep dent into long-standing discriminatory practices and the corresponding belief in women's athletic infe-

riority. Schoolgirls report that athleticism is a source of popularity and seem unfamiliar with the idea that female athletic ability carries any sort of stigma. Parents express a similar attitude, with a vast majority now maintaining that sports are as important for daughters as for sons.

A dramatic increase in girls' involvement in community-based sports has underwritten many of these changes. Since interscholastic sports do not begin until junior high school at the earliest, athletic programs for younger children offered through public recreation departments or independent athletic bodies provide an important avenue for early female athletic involvement. Joining a local soccer, softball, or basketball team is often a girl's first encounter with organized sports. Between the ages of six and twelve girls gain the fundamental athletic skills—how to run, jump, kick, throw, and slide; how to swing a bat or racket; and how to practice, learn from coaches, and get along with teammates—necessary for later success. At this time they also gain the initial confidence and pleasure that will ensure later participation in athletics, whether oriented toward health, recreation, or high-stakes competition.

Opportunities for girls still fall short of the number and variety of opportunities offered to boys. In the absence of equal opportunities, girls miss out on formative athletic experiences, placing them a full step behind boys (or other girls from localities where opportunities do exist) who grow up participating in informal playground sports and organized athletics. This in turn makes the achievement of gender equity in intercollegiate, Olympic, or professional sports more difficult to attain.

As girls bid for full equality in sports as well as other arenas of American life, they raise a critical question, one with both legal and policy implications: What constitutes "equality"? Under Title IX, the abolition of sex discrimination has been interpreted to mean an equitable—but not identical—allocation of resources with the goal of establishing equivalency in the number of sports and scholarships offered, athletic budget size, training facilities and travel arrangements, and the number and salaries of athletic staff positions.

The exact meaning of *equity* has been somewhat loosely defined in schools and even more so outside the schools, but it remains the goal toward which most athletic programs claim to strive. Yet some have asked whether girls and women want to follow along the same path as male competitive athletics. Responding to the prevalence of eating disorders and serious injuries in sports like gymnastics; the emphasis on competitive success over participation and pleasure; and a system that rewards winning, playing through pain, and individual excellence at the expense of health, cooperative learning, and well-rounded physical and emotional development, some advocates for girls' and women's sports have begun to explore "partnership" models of sport that encourage mutual respect, competitive striving, and shared enjoyment at all levels of ability.

We can expect that struggles over gender equity and the culture of sports will continue in the courts and on the playing fields. But in the meantime, more and more girls play organized sports, considering themselves fully entitled to physical strength, athletic skill, and the pleasure and confidence that sports can bring. Even though gender equity is currently a goal to strive toward rather than an achieved reality, already girls have reaped enormous benefits from their increased participation. Researchers have found that athletic activity correlates with higher graduation rates, lower rates of teenage pregnancy, stronger body image, and higher self-esteem.

Susan K. Cahn

See also African American Girls in the Twentieth Century; Play; Surfer Girls; Tomboys

References and Further Reading
Acosta, Vivian, and Linda Jean Carpenter. 1994. *Women in Intercollegiate Sport.* Brooklyn: Brooklyn College Press.
Cahn, Susan. 1995. *Coming on Strong: Gender and Sexuality in Twentieth-Century Women's Sport.* Cambridge: Harvard University Press.
Festle, Mary Jo. 1996. *Playing Nice: Politics and Apologies in Women's*

Sports. New York: Columbia University Press.

Guttmann, Allen. 1991. *Women's Sports: A History.* New York: Columbia University Press.

Nelson, Mariah Burton. 1991. *Are We Winning Yet? How Women Are Changing Sports and Sports Are Changing Women.* New York: Random House.

Sklover, Beverly. 1997. "Women/Sports." *AAUW Outlook* (Winter): 12–16.

Women's Sports Foundation. 1989. "Minorities in Sports: The Effect of Varsity Sports Participation on the Social, Educational, and Career Mobility of Minority Students." New York: Women's Sports Foundation.

Substance Abuse

Substance abuse among girls appears to be a growing problem in American society. Many Americans believe that only "bad" girls indulge in drinking, smoking, and drug use, activities that seem fundamentally "unladylike" and have often been linked with "promiscuous" or "deviant" sexual behavior. Although it is probably impossible to determine with precision how many girls used and abused alcohol, tobacco, and other substances in the past—especially since many people tried desperately to keep such habits secret—girls' consumption rates appear to have been generally lower than boys' throughout American history. Even as conformity to conventional gender roles has made girls less likely to use alcohol and other drugs, cultural assumptions about femininity have brought a double standard of judgment down on those girls who do. Further, although fewer girls than boys consume such substances recreationally, medical experts and social scientists have maintained that individual females may be *more* vulnerable than males to substance abuse, especially addiction to drugs or alcohol used medic-

inally. Since addiction has been linked with biological and psychological turning points, it is not surprising that adolescence has been seen as an especially dangerous time; in particular, substance use can complicate the development of girls' sexual identities, frequently bringing an increased level of vulnerability. For some substances, particularly alcohol, the line between moderate, recreational use and addiction is not clear, especially in the case of girls, for whom *any* consumption can be perceived as a violation of fundamental gender norms.

Drinking, smoking, and drug use have been adopted as features of a "youth culture," especially in the 1920s (during Prohibition), the 1960s, and afterward. Girls' participation in these behaviors has alarmed many social critics because it seems to represent the most radical break with the past. Indeed, the fear that girls' consumption rates are "converging" with those of boys, or "closing the gender gap," has been expressed frequently by such critics as part of widespread concern about the direction of social change. Although rates of adolescent substance use and abuse have become increasingly similar across gender lines over time, the motivations for and consequences of these behaviors still demonstrate important differences for young men and women. In addition, patterns of substance use and abuse diverge significantly *among* girls, with important variations by age, race, class, region, and other factors. Finally, experts agree that more research on substance abuse among adolescent girls is needed to ensure better prevention efforts and treatment programs.

Examining patterns of substance use and abuse throughout American history reveals many changes in girls' habits. During the colonial era, alcohol consumption in general was more widespread than it is today, due in part to an unreliable water supply. Girls might consume alcoholic cider or other beverages, but strict community standards shaped their drinking practices and brought dire consequences for intoxication. By the nineteenth century, although many young women, especially immigrant women, continued to enjoy liquor, the increasingly heated temperance debate cast women and girls as symbols of innocence, purity, and domesticity—and as antidotes to the saloon. Reflecting the presumed connection between alcohol consumption and "deviant" sexual behavior, moreover, many people assumed that young women who spent time in saloons were prostitutes. Reformers argued that such young women had often been "seduced" by drink and unscrupulous men; trapped in a life of prostitution, these women often relied on alcohol and other drugs to cope with their difficult lives. In fact, the link between prostitution and saloons shows that young women who drank were considered sexual threats to "respectable" society even as these women were themselves sexually most vulnerable.

During the late nineteenth and early twentieth centuries, then, the alleged connections among public drinking by young women, prostitution, and the saloon provided powerful ammunition for temperance campaigners. At the same time, though, girls and women did use liquor, as well as highly alcoholic "patent medicines" and other drugs as medicine for "female complaints," a catch-all term for gynecological difficulties or any other health problems linked with the female condition. Believing that female physiological processes rendered women especially vulnerable to addiction, doctors warned girls and women against consum-

ing alcohol or other drugs to relieve the discomforts of menstruation and to aid recovery from childbirth. Many women who developed addictions to alcohol or other substances such as morphine later recalled that their addiction had begun this way. Since it followed from private, medicinal use, however, this consumption pattern seemed more appropriately "feminine" and generally attracted less attention than did young women's public drinking.

By the middle decades of the twentieth century, both the youth culture and patterns of substance use and abuse underwent fundamental changes. During the 1920s, the increasing number of young people in high school and college, as well as the general affluence of many Americans and the availability of new technologies such as the automobile, fostered the development of a modern youth culture focused on leisure and consumer goods. At the same time, the Eighteenth Amendment to the Constitution ushered in national Prohibition in 1920, making the manufacture and sale of alcoholic beverages illegal. Many young people, attracted by the additional excitement of violating Prohibition, responded by drinking more than their predecessors had. Drinking and smoking became increasingly glamorized in the images of popular culture; young people explained that they engaged in both to demonstrate their freedom from previous restraints. The behavior of girls, especially the "flapper" who bobbed her hair, wore short skirts, and drank and smoked, represented one of the most significant breaks with the past. At least some young women smoked and drank in the belief that doing so represented "equality" with young men. Liquor consumption also played a major role in dating customs, and many female alcoholics later recalled that they had begun drinking in their teens or early twenties in order to feel less inhibited in social situations. Drinking and smoking in these circumstances, however, did not necessarily mean abuse in a clinical sense, although conservative experts did portray these new consumption patterns, especially by young women, as evidence of a general breakdown in social standards and gender roles.

The repeal of Prohibition with the Twenty-first Amendment to the Constitution in 1933 lessened the symbolic significance of alcohol consumption for young people, and the Great Depression and American involvement in World War II ended or at least greatly curtailed the affluent, carefree lifestyle that had shaped the youth culture of the 1920s. The unsettled conditions of the war years, however, contributed to new fears about juvenile delinquency, especially among girls who drank, smoked cigarettes and even marijuana, and engaged in sexual activity with soldiers. Criticism directed at these girls demonstrated that a double standard continued to influence assessments of substance use and of sexual behavior.

Although drinking and smoking had symbolized the glamorous youth culture of the Roaring Twenties, a wider constellation of drugs characterized the "hippie" culture of the post–World War II era, particularly the 1960s. Marijuana and psychedelics, especially lysergic acid diethylamide (LSD), became drugs of choice for young Americans who sought to demonstrate the breadth of the "generation gap." As with previous drug and alcohol use by American youth, this consumption did not necessarily qualify as clinical addiction, but it was heavy enough to bring a host of associated medical, emo-

A young hippie girl smokes a cigarette at a "love-in" in Los Angeles. (Henry Diltz/Corbis, 1967)

tional, and social problems. Girls partook alongside boys, but for them, as in earlier periods, the sexual "freedom" that accompanied drug use frequently meant sexual vulnerability.

As a result of a renewed focus on addiction among women more generally and the perception that drugs are an increasing problem among young people, substance use and abuse among girls have received more attention since the 1970s. Despite this increased focus, however, adolescent girls still fall through the cracks in research designs and treatment programs. Their unique motivations for—and patterns of—substance use as well as their special needs in treatment, distinct from those of both adolescent boys and adult women, are too frequently overlooked. Since the 1970s, as in earlier periods in American history, patterns of substance use and abuse among girls resemble those among boys but in important ways continue to differ from them. Numerous researchers and commentators have insisted that girls' consumption rates are approaching those of boys or even, in some cases, surpassing them. Adolescence is a time of strong peer pressure for both genders, and both boys and girls are experimenting with various substances at younger ages. Yet important differences remain between young men and women in consumption patterns; substance preferences; motivations for using; and the consequences, especially those related to sexuality, that result from substance use and abuse.

Prohibition and its repeal and the recent "tobacco wars" illustrate continuing American ambivalence about alcohol and cigarettes. Legal for adults but forbidden for children, the two substances remain popular among many teenagers who argue that age restrictions represent hypocrisy and discrimination. Although recreational drinking and experimental smoking have often been dismissed as youthful indiscretions, a substantial number of adolescent girls and boys find themselves struggling with drinking problems or smoking "habits"—or both—that are extremely difficult to break. Surveys and other research indicate that fewer girls than boys drink heavily, but girls' consumption rates do seem to be catching up to those of boys. In addition, some studies suggest that girls require fewer drinks than boys to reach a given level of intoxication. Gender differences in alcohol metabolism have been attributed to girls'

generally lower body weight, smaller amount of body fluid, and lower levels of enzymes implicated in the breakdown of alcohol by the body. Whatever the reasons behind it, this gender difference has important ramifications in the recognition and treatment of alcohol-related problems among females. Although girls may be influenced to drink less since they experience intoxication sooner, for that very reason they may also be more vulnerable to alcohol-related medical, psychological, and social problems.

For the moment, girls' rates of liquor consumption continue to lag behind those of boys. When it comes to smoking, however, young females have apparently closed the gap. Indeed, research indicates that smoking is the most significant substance abuse problem among young women. Girls seldom use smokeless tobacco—a substance that presents a growing problem among males—but girls' rates of cigarette smoking equal and in some cases even exceed those of adolescent boys. Beginning in the 1920s, cigarette smoking among women was increasingly glamorized in advertisements and the media, and by the 1960s and 1970s, the number of girls who smoke cigarettes had grown significantly. Although incidence rates have declined somewhat since then, the smoking rate among boys has decreased more quickly, thus narrowing or even eclipsing the gender gap. One reason for the prevalence of smoking among girls is the belief that cigarettes aid weight control efforts. Some girls report that they rely on cigarettes in order to avoid other behaviors that they consider even more destructive, such as overeating. Many girls thus apparently believe that the positive cultural value placed on being slender compensates for the health risks associated with cigarette smoking, and their tobacco use today is linked with concerns of sexuality and body image.

Like alcohol and cigarettes, prescription drugs and narcotics are considered acceptable for some sectors of the population, even as they are considered illicit among others. In general, females are more likely to use drugs in a medicinal, therapeutic context, whereas males are more likely to consume drugs recreationally. This long-standing historical pattern echoes conventional gender roles. In the late nineteenth century, for example, women who would never have entered a saloon nevertheless partook freely of high-alcohol patent medicines. Similarly, girls today are more likely than boys to use amphetamines, which also can be rationalized as a tool for weight control. Addiction to substances that were initially prescribed by a physician is more of an issue for women, who take more such medicines than do men. Further, many young women attempt to "self-medicate" with alcohol and other drugs, using them in addition to or instead of prescription medications such as psychotherapeutics to cope with depression and stressful life events.

When it comes to illicit drugs that are consumed primarily for recreation, however, rates of use are lower among girls than boys, although here too girls seem to be closing the gap. Marijuana is the most commonly used illicit drug among adolescents of both genders, but even though overall prevalence rates are similar, boys are more likely than girls to be heavy or frequent users. Female adolescents are less likely than boys to use or abuse other drugs, including cocaine, hallucinogens, inhalants, opiates, and phencyclidine (PCP), although the trend appears to be toward convergence.

The deep and abiding connections between issues of substance use and abuse and sexuality and reproduction have very different implications for adolescent females and males. For both sexes, substance use often accompanies dating; young men and women turn to alcohol and other drugs to alleviate shyness and overcome inhibitions. Girls frequently acquire substances or gain access to them through young men, often in exchange for some kind of sexual activity. This sexual barter might range from girls engaging in kissing or petting with dates who buy beer to young women prostituting themselves in order to feed a cocaine habit. Recent research indicates, in fact, that female adolescents who use alcohol and other drugs are also more likely to become involved in sexual activity at an early age.

Discussion of these issues in recent years shows that the double standard continues; girls' sexual activity, like girls' substance use, is still judged more harshly than boys'. The consequences of sexual experimentation, especially when combined with alcohol and drug use, can be much more severe for girls. When substance use impairs their faculties, girls too easily become victims of sexual assault; binge drinking and certain drugs sometimes given to girls without their knowledge have been linked with date rape. Girls who have sexual intercourse while under the influence of alcohol or other drugs are less likely to use contraception, increasing their chances of getting sexually transmitted diseases, including acquired immunodeficiency syndrome (AIDS), and of becoming pregnant. Pregnancy and early motherhood frequently diminish the educational and occupational opportunities young women enjoy. At the same time, clinical research suggests that addiction to alcohol and other drugs among women has reproductive consequences, threatening the long-term health of babies born to mothers who abuse these substances. Indeed, the powerful image of the "crack baby," allegedly born disproportionately to young, unwed, especially African American women, demonstrates further the confluence in modern American culture of ideas about substance abuse, teen pregnancy, poverty, and race.

Michelle L. McClellan

See also Acquaintance Rape; Body Image; Dating and Courtship; Depression and Girls; Eating Disorders; Female Sexuality; Girl Gangs; Juvenile Delinquents; Psychotherapy; Suicidal Behavior in Girls; Teen Pregnancy

References and Further Reading
Bodinger–de Uriarte, Cristina, and Gregory Austin. 1991. "Substance Abuse among Adolescent Females." *Prevention Research Update* 9 (Fall).
Burnham, John C. 1993. *Bad Habits: Drinking, Smoking, Taking Drugs, Gambling, Sexual Misbehavior, and Swearing in American History.* New York: New York University Press.
Fass, Paula S. 1977. *The Damned and the Beautiful: American Youth in the 1920s.* New York: Oxford University Press.
Kandall, Stephen R. 1996. *Substance and Shadow: Women and Addiction in the United States.* Cambridge, MA: Harvard University Press.
Sandmaier, Marian. 1980. *The Invisible Alcoholics: Women and Alcohol Abuse in America.* New York: McGraw-Hill.

Suicidal Behavior in Girls

This entry examines suicidal behavior in adolescent girls from a contemporary perspective. Suicidal ideation and behavior are serious problems among girls in the United States. Suicidal thoughts and behavior are far more common in girls than in boys in this country, and during adolescence, depression is also more common in girls than in boys.

The term *suicidal ideation* refers to thinking or talking about killing oneself. A behavior is defined as suicidal when a girl intends that behavior to end her life, or when she engages in a life-threatening act and does not care about surviving it. This definition includes intentionally suicidal acts that are interrupted before any harm occurs, such as the behavior of a girl or boy who intentionally lies across railway tracks but is rescued before the train arrives. A suicidal act may be fatal or nonfatal. The outcome of the suicidal act is not a reliable measure of intent. Not every suicidal death is planned, but conversely, some suicidal acts intended to be fatal do not result in death.

A range of suicide methods may be used, including cutting one's wrists, deliberately ingesting medication in excess of the therapeutic or generally recognized dosage, deliberately crashing a car, hanging oneself, or shooting oneself with a firearm.

In addition, the suicide method does not accurately measure intent. The same method may be used with different intentions. Some individuals survive what they may have thought of as a lethal suicidal act, for example, a car crash. Others will die of an action they did not think would kill them (e.g., an overdose of Tylenol). Suicide methods tend to be culturally specific. Methods common in one culture may be unusual in another culture. Females and males tend to use the methods that are permissible for them in their community. In some communities, young women and men use different suicide methods; in other communities they use the same methods.

In the United States, adolescent girls are two to three times more likely than adolescent males to report suicidal ideation. It appears to be particularly common among Mexican American youth. Adolescent girls are also more likely than adolescent boys to engage in nonfatal acts of suicidal behavior by an average ratio of 3 to 1. Approximately one in ten adolescent girls reports having engaged in some form of suicidal behavior. Gender differences in nonfatal suicidal behavior are not found in all ethnic groups in the United States. For example, among native Hawaiians and Native Americans, adolescent girls report similar rates of nonfatal suicidal behavior as adolescent boys. Rates of nonfatal suicidal behavior appear to be particularly high among Mexican American girls. Adolescents who engage in nonfatal suicidal behavior seem to come from lower socioeconomic strata. For example, low levels of parental education are associated with higher adolescent suicidal risk (Canetto 1998).

Adolescent females in the United States, however, are less likely to die as a result of a suicidal act than are adolescent males, by a ratio of 5 to 1. The gender difference in mortality holds across ethnic groups, although suicide rates vary greatly from group to group. Native American girls have lower rates of suicide than Native American boys but higher rates of suicide than European American boys. Gender differences in suicide mortality among adolescents are not universal. For example, in Mauritius, young females and males have the same rates of suicide mortality. In other countries, the gender trends in youth suicide mortality are reversed relative to the United States. For example, in several Asian and South American countries, including Brazil, Cuba, the Dominican Republic, Ecuador, Hong Kong, Paraguay, the Philippines, Singapore, and Thailand, young females' suicide mortality exceeds that of young males.

In the United States, suicidal behavior, both nonfatal and fatal, is uncommon in childhood and early adolescence, when it is seen almost as often among girls as among boys. No differences in rates of depression are recorded until adolescence. The incidence of suicide increases less rapidly among females than among males during adolescence and young adulthood. In recent decades, the gender gap in suicide mortality has been widening, especially in some U.S. ethnic minority groups. Rates of suicide mortality among girls of all U.S. ethnic groups have tended to remain stable. However, rates for U.S. ethnic minority boys have increased markedly.

It is important to remember, however, that the majority of adolescent suicidal acts are nonfatal. Very few adolescents actually take their own lives. At the same time, they engage in a very high number of suicidal acts. At no other time in the life span is the ratio of nonfatal to fatal suicidal behavior as high as during adolescence.

Why are adolescent girls in the United States more depressed and more likely to engage in suicidal behavior but less likely to kill themselves than boys? What protects girls from dying of suicide, despite the fact that they engage in more suicidal acts than boys? Many explanations have been proposed for the gender paradox of suicidal behavior, but it seems to be a culturally specific and historically fluid phenomenon, which suggests that it needs to be understood in light of cultural variables.

A promising theory is that of cultural scripts, which is based on the observation of a correspondence between social expectations and actual behavior in different cultures. Individuals tend to engage in the behaviors (including suicidal behaviors) that are meaningful and permissible in their community. In each cultural community, there are scripts of suicidal behavior, that is, specific conditions under which suicidal behavior is expected and specific ways to commit suicide. Cultural scripts define the scenario of the suicidal act, including the actor, method, precipitating factors, and themes. In each culture there are also common reactions to and consequences of suicidal behavior.

In the United States, girls' high rates of nonfatal suicidal behavior make sense in light of the fact that these behaviors are viewed as feminine. Studies show that nonfatal suicidal behavior in females receives less disapproval than the same behavior in males. However, killing oneself is viewed as masculine behavior and is thus less acceptable in females than in males. Among the young, female suicide is judged as more wrong, more foolish, and weaker than male suicide. Girls who kill themselves are viewed as less well adjusted than boys who kill themselves, independent of what caused the suicide. These cultural scripts of gender and suicidal behavior may be particularly powerful for adolescents, since they are in the process of defining their identity and may take messages about gender-appropriate behavior more seriously and more literally than adults.

The fact that nonfatal suicidal behavior is viewed as feminine does not mean that suicidal females are treated in a caring manner. Studies suggest that young persons respond negatively to their suicidal peers. They view them as cowardly and tend to avoid them out of a mixture of shock, anger, repulsion, and helplessness. In one study, young suicidal persons reported that their peers had made fun of suicidal ideas that they expressed. Caregivers also tend to respond in a critical and even hostile manner to suicidal persons, especially when they perceive them as "not serious" in their intent to die. For example, caregivers tend to interpret nonfatal suicidal behavior as manipulative, despite evidence that most persons describe their suicidal act as motivated by despair rather than by the desire to influence someone. Similarly, mental health clinicians have little empathy for their (overwhelmingly female) suicidal clients and often dismiss them as immature and hysterical.

Gender differences in method probably account in part for girls' higher rates of survival from suicidal behavior. In the United States, girls are more likely than boys to use poisoning and cutting as suicide methods, although the use of firearms is growing among girls. Poisoning is a method that allows for more possibilities for rescue, at least in the United States. The rescue potential of a suicide method depends on a number of individual and community factors, including the immediate lethality of the method, the place of the suicide, the likelihood of being found quickly, and the likelihood of quick and effective care once found. The more rapidly lethal the method and the less public the suicidal act, the lower the likelihood of survival. In developing countries, suicide by poisoning, even one that is carried out in a public area, carries a high death potential because of the toxicity of the poisons used (e.g., agrochem-

High school students comfort each other outside a mortuary in San Pedro, California, as they mourn the suicide of two female classmates who jumped to their deaths from a 15-foot cliff. (Associated Press AP, 1996)

icals) and the likelihood that good medical care may not be available quickly enough to make a difference.

The question of whether U.S. girls' choice of suicide methods reflects their lesser intent to die is difficult to assess because adolescents' knowledge of the lethality of suicide methods is often limited. It is likely that more female suicidal acts than males' are intended as nonfatal. Most suicidal acts are in some ways planned. There is also evidence of a correlation between intent and lethality. At the same time, it is important to remember that in the United States, girls' choice of suicide method and scenario takes place against a cultural script that prohibits girls from taking their own lives.

The search for causes of suicidal behavior, fatal and nonfatal, spans many fields of study, from biochemistry to psychology to sociology to astronomy. A sampling of proposed risk factors includes genetic markers, the menstrual cycle, mental disorders, sexual and physical abuse, parental divorce, parental education, rates of unemployment within families, cognitive style, coping skills, low self-esteem, and phases of the moon. Information on risk factors and dynamics unique to suicidal females, however, is limited because most researchers do not focus on questions of gender and do not separately analyze data for females. In addition, information on risk factors has not advanced enough to help predict suicidal behavior at the individual level. Many young persons experience some or many of the risk factors and never become suicidal.

Among mental disorders, depression, alcohol and substance abuse, and antisocial behavioral disorders have been most commonly associated with risk for suicidal ideation and behavior, both fatal and nonfatal, among adolescents. For girls, depression appears to be a stronger predictor of suicidal behavior than for boys. Drug abuse for suicidal girls may involve the abuse of over-the-counter medications rather than illegal substance abuse. Adolescent girls with eating disorders constitute another risk group for nonfatal suicidal behaviors. Suffering from more than one disorder increases the risk for all suicidal behavior. Disease and impairment may also play a role in nonfatal suicidal behavior. In the late twentieth century in the United States, sexual abuse has increasingly been recognized as a factor in girls' nonfatal suicidal behavior. There is considerable debate about whether sexual orientation is a risk factor for suicidal behavior among lesbian and bisexual girls. Low self-esteem, low academic achievement, peer difficulties, and social isolation have been identified as factors in nonfatal suicidal behavior. In addition, experience with suicidal behavior, including a family history of suicidal behavior, recent suicidal behavior by a friend, or a girl's own past suicidal episodes, has been found to increase the risk of all suicidal behavior. Stressful life events, including turmoil and instability in key relationships, particularly with parents, seem to be typical precipitants of suicidal behavior in adoles-

cents. In general, the more difficulties a girl has or has had, the more likely she is to engage in suicidal behavior. At the same time, although adversities increase the risk for suicidality, they are particularly potent in those adolescents whose thoughts and coping strategies are dysfunctional. The impact of these risk factors in terms of probability of nonfatal suicidal behavior is stronger for females, which suggests the influence of a facilitating cultural script for girls.

In the United States, the risk for death by suicide is predicted by a similar set of factors as nonfatal suicidal behavior. At the same time, the availability of firearms seems to be less of a risk factor for suicide in girls, possibly because guns are still perceived as a more masculine method. The main fact is that U.S. girls are far less likely to kill themselves than boys. Relative to boys, girls are protected from suicide. Thus, in the case of suicide, the impact of the risk factors is lower in girls than in boys, suggesting the influence of an inhibiting cultural script.

Many questions about girls and suicidal behavior remain unanswered. At the same time, the data on gender, culture, and suicidal behavior suggest some important new directions for primary prevention. In the United States, given the gender differences in patterns and meanings of suicidal behavior, suicide prevention programs should consistently address questions of gender. Educational programs should evaluate the participants' beliefs about femininity and nonfatal suicidal behavior. They should also be prepared to engage girls in challenging the idea that nonfatal suicidal behavior is an acceptable feminine way of coping. Suicide prevention programs should also consider the implications of girls' empathic attitudes toward suicidal persons. Although these sympathetic responses are usually taken as a sign of maturity and a protective factor, in girls they may signal an acceptance of nonfatal suicidal behavior as a way to deal with difficulties.

Awareness of girls' socialized behavior also matters in evaluating the impact of secondary prevention services such as crisis lines. Girls are high users of crisis lines. This has traditionally been taken as an indication that these services benefit suicidal girls. In reality, the fact that young women are the highest users of crisis services simply tells us that many girls are suicidal and that they are willing to disclose their suicidal thoughts to a stranger—a behavior that is understandable in light of the fact that talking about one's suicidal feeling or behavior is considered more acceptable for females than for males. Whether or not crisis services actually meet suicidal girls' needs and reduce girls' suicidal behavior remains to be tested.

Finally, evaluations of the effect of suicide prevention programs should not measure outcomes solely by changes in suicide mortality records, since death by suicide is a relatively rare outcome, particularly among girls. Program evaluations should include assessments of changes in suicidal ideation and nonfatal suicidal behavior because these are the most common forms of suicidality among adolescents and are uniquely epidemic among girls. Information on depression, suicidal ideation, and nonfatal suicidal behavior is particularly important in testing the impact of these programs on girls. Finally, program evaluations should include measures of cognitive styles and coping behaviors, as these seem to mediate the risk of suicidal behavior.

Silvia Sara Canetto

See also Acquaintance Rape; Adolescent Health; Body Image; Child Abuse; Depression and Girls; Eating Disorders; Lesbians; Psychotherapy; Substance Abuse; Teen Pregnancy

References and Further Reading
Canetto, Silvia Sara. 1998. "Meanings of Gender and Suicidal Behavior among Adolescents." *Suicide and Life Threatening Behaviors* 27: 339–351.
Canetto, Silvia Sara, and David Lester. 1995. "Gender and the Primary Prevention of Suicide Mortality." *Suicide and Life-Threatening Behavior* 25: 58–69.
Garland, Ann F., and Edward Zigler. 1993. "Adolescent Suicide Prevention: Current Research and Social Policy Implications." *American Psychologist* 48: 169–182.
King, Cheryl A. 1997. "Suicidal Behavior in Adolescence." Pp. 61–95 in *Review of Suicidology*. Edited by Ronald W. Maris, Morton M. Silverman, and Silvia Sara Canetto. New York: Guilford.
Lewinsohn, Peter M., Paul Rohde, and John R. Seeley. 1996. "Adolescent Suicidal Ideation and Attempts: Prevalence, Risk Factors, and Clinical Implications." *Clinical Psychology: Science and Practice* 3, no. 1: 25–46.

Summer Camps for Girls

Since the late nineteenth century, American girls between the ages of four and eighteen have left their families and neighborhoods behind, if only temporarily, to attend camps during the long summer vacation. These child-centered leisure institutions were first organized on behalf of elite white Christian boys. By the turn of the century, adults were establishing camps for girls of similar backgrounds— and later, as the industry extended and diversified its reach, an increasingly wide spectrum of girls and boys. These camps attested to the intensifying social value of childhood, the rise of supervised, age-specific activities (including playgrounds and high schools as well as camps), and the

Summer camps have been a bonding and learning experience for girls, as this photo from Camp We-Ha-Ha on the New York–New Jersey border shows. (Courtesy of Hyman Bogen)

expanding market in children's recreation. The rise of girls' summer camps more particularly and their growing success in the twentieth century have also highlighted gender shifts flowing across generations. Summer camps for girls have provided access to adventurous and athletic outdoors experiences, many of which had once been near-exclusive male prerogatives.

Prior to industrialization, rural American children often played significant roles in the family economy. But by the late nineteenth and early twentieth centuries, increasing numbers of urban middle- and upper-class children were no longer helping their parents on farms during the summer. For a cohort of white Protestant men working with youth, this long vacation was an opportunity in the making. Worried about the effects of "artificial"

leisure in the city and of modern urban life more generally, these men decided to provide physically strenuous vacations to the elite boys whom they believed would grow up to lead the nation. For "muscular Christians," camping vacations for both men and boys were antidotes to the "softness" of the modern work regime and of vacations at resort hotels. A "primitive" sojourn into savagery, as contemporary psychologist G. Stanley Hall contended, was particularly critical to the development of white boys, providing, amid the safety of select peers and adult supervision, a kind of inoculation against the feminizing effects of civilized culture. The first camping experiment for boys took place at the Gunnery Camp in Connecticut (1861–1879) and the North Mountain School of Physical Culture in Pennsylvania (1876–1878). The first church-sponsored camp was established by George Hinckley during the summers of 1880 and 1881 in Rhode Island, and Ernest Balch's Camp Chocorua, which operated from 1881 to 1889 in New Hampshire, was the first commercial organized camp for boys.

Most early camps served boys, but a few pioneers started camps for elite girls as well. The Nature Science Camp, established in 1890 by Albert Fontaine, originally served New York boys. By 1891, Fontaine had started a separate girls' camp, which ran for five seasons. Also in New York, Arey's Natural Science Camp, established in 1890, accepted girls from 1892 onward; in 1902, renamed Camp Arey, it began to serve girls exclusively. In 1896, the French Recreation Class for Girls on Lake Placid, New York, offered outdoor exercise, walking and rowing, daily French study, optional classes in botany and sketching, and special college preparatory courses. Other pioneering girls' camps included New Hampshire's Redcroft (1900), Kehonka (1902), and Pinelands (1902) camps, and the Wyonegonic Camps in Maine (1902). In Vermont, Camp Barnard (1903) and Camp Aloha (1905) were the pioneering camps in a cohort that would become particularly active in the upper Connecticut valley.

From their inception onward, American camps were never spread out equally across the nation. Some clusters developed in the upper Midwest, the southern Appalachians, and the Rocky Mountains. Because camps responded so directly to anxieties about urbanization, they achieved their greatest popularity close to the cities of the densely settled Northeast, in New England, New York, and Pennsylvania. The populations that they served, however, were increasingly diverse. By the turn of the twentieth century, private camps were joined by organizational camps sponsored by the Young Men's Christian Association (YMCA), Young Men's Hebrew Association (YMHA), and settlement houses, all of which originally served middle- and working-class boys. After all, a greater number of city-based organizations focused on boys and their leisure needs, including camping, and traditional ideas about boys' purportedly greater need for "primitive" experience and adventure persisted well into the twentieth century. Meanwhile, the Young Women's Christian Association's (YWCA) first camp, which opened in 1898 at Altamont, New York, benefited somewhat older "working girls" of limited means rather than younger girls.

Only in the 1910s did girls' camps achieve the beginnings of parity. The network of private girls' camps expanded rapidly, and several new youth groups for girls offered camping opportunities. Shortly after the Boy Scout movement was imported from Britain to the United States (1910), two similar organizations for girls were founded: the Camp Fire Girls (1911) and the Girl Scouts (1912). Both walked a fine line between traditional domestic ideology and new modes of adventure. The first, the Camp Fire Girls, was modeled on Luther and Charlotte Gulick's private Maine camp, Wo-He-Lo, where the Gulick daughters and a few paying friends had been spending their summers. Charlotte Gulick's sister-in-law, Harriet Farnsworth Gulick, and her husband Edward Leeds Gulick had founded Camp Aloha in 1905, and in 1908 Harriet's brother Charles Farnsworth and his wife Ellen had started the Hanoum Camps, also in Vermont. At Camp Wo-He-Lo (named for "work, health, and love"), the girls adopted Indian names and made ceremonial dresses

A group of girls learn to light a safe campfire at a church camp in Jamesport, Long Island, New York. (Hulton Getty/Archive Photos, 1955)

with Indian-style symbols. But for the Gulicks, camping and Indian ritual were meant to buttress traditional female skills, not to explore, as Boy Scouts might, the regenerative possibilities of "savagery." This popular girls' organization provided thousands of its mostly middle-class members the opportunity to attend affordable local camps.

The Girl Scouts, founded in 1912 in Savannah, Georgia, by Juliette Gordon Low, provided similar kinds of camping opportunities. Like the Camp Fire Girls, whom they would outnumber by the 1930s, the Girl Scouts blended traditional and modern gender expectations; girls acquired badges for laundry as well as for outdoors pursuits. Still, at Girl Scout camps, girls experienced rugged camping. Low's Savannah troop first went camping in 1912 dressed in long bloomers, which they decorously covered in skirts until they were out of town. Out of the public eye, they swam, cooked for themselves along the Savannah River, and slept on the sand. By the late teens, a number of Girl Scout troops were, like their male counterparts, going camping: sleeping in tents, saluting the flag, marching in unison, knot tying, and swimming. Vigorous and active, Girl Scout camping exemplified new possibilities for girls in outdoor recreation and more generally as active players in American life.

Many of the directors of girls' camps (sometimes called "directresses") were college-educated women who worked during the school year as teachers and social workers. In 1916, a number of girls' camp directors, male and female, banded together to form the National Association of Directors of Girls' Camps (NADGC). This organization was the professional counterpart to the Camp Directors' Association of America (CDAA) that had been organized in 1910 by the directors of boys' camps. In 1924, the CDAA and the NADGC merged into a new Camp Directors' Association, a manifestation of the increasingly important role of girls' camps in the industry. To a significant extent, the earlier rhetoric of "muscular Christianity" gave way to more secular ideals of leisure for its own sake and healthy outdoor living for both sexes. Still, girls' camps remained ideologically and materially distinct from their male counterparts. Girl campers had increased access to "the primitive life," but their camps were likely to offer crafts and dancing, while boys' camps gave lessons in carpentry or riflery. Girls' camps often had a higher staff-to-camper ratio

than did similar camps for boys, meaning that girls were under greater adult supervision and protection than their brothers.

Gender has, however, been only one of several factors in play where camping is concerned. The parents of middle- and upper-class children have been able to choose among many options, whereas working-class parents have relied on local settlement house and charitable camps. And some ethnic groups have supported camping more fervently than others. For example, Jewish camps, serving both religiously observant and acculturated families, have been particularly successful. In the early twentieth century, native-born Protestant and Jewish girls were somewhat more likely than Catholic girls to attend camps. And only in the late 1930s and early 1940s would many northeastern organizational camps move toward racial integration. Until then, only a few American camps accepted African American girls: organizational camps such as Camp Atwater in Massachusetts and Camp Guilford Bower in New York and segregated YWCA and Girl Scout troop camps. A small number of self-consciously progressive and politically radical interwar camps, such as the Pioneer Youth Camp in New York and Camp Wo-Chi-Ca in New Jersey, made racial integration central to their programs. Only in the postwar era would interracial camping become more common.

The postwar era also saw the expansion of coeducational camping. At their inception, most camps were spaces of real, although not total, gender separation. Some girls never saw boys during the camp season. Others had a nearby "brother" camp, often under the same management, with which they socialized. Most of the first coed camps, in which boys and girls lived on opposite sides of a single camp, only served preadolescents rather than teenagers of "dating age." The earliest camp leaders tended to believe that gender segregation of campers was natural and appropriate. By the interwar years, however, child-study experts began increasingly to suggest that late childhood and adolescence represented a necessary time of heterosexual development. Girls' camp crushes on one another became more controversial. In other words, the larger culture's intensified emphasis on heterosexuality affected girls' leisure institutions as well. From the 1930s onward, more camps went coed (and doubled their potential clientele in the process). At many of those camps that remained single-sex, social encounters with similar kinds of boys from neighboring camps constituted increasingly important seasonal or even weekly rituals, particularly for older girls.

At the turn of the twenty-first century, girls and boys attend camps in fairly equal numbers. Along with boys, girls attend day camps and overnight camps, single-sex camps and coed camps, and even specialty camps with emphases ranging from computers to horseback riding to weight loss. The traditional eight-week private camp is no longer as popular as it was during the postwar era, when the baby boomers were of camping age. Now, the significant majority of camps are run by organizations rather than individuals. Each summer, more than 8 million children and adolescents between the ages of five and seventeen attend a wide variety of camps. Regardless of their specialty or orientation, most camps draw on traditions that are a century old, including swimming, camp songs, campfires, overnight hikes, and learning to live apart from one's family. Here, they prom-

ise, girls can take social risks and learn new skills within protected and sheltering environments. Attending summer camp is no longer the challenge to gender conventions that it once was, but it remains, for many girls, a formative rite of passage.

Leslie Paris

See also Camp Fire Girls; 4-H; Girl Scouts; Play; Saturday Evening Girls

References and Further Reading

Bederman, Gail. 1995. *Manliness and Civilization: A Cultural History of Gender and Race in the United States, 1880–1917.* Chicago: University of Chicago Press.

Buckler, Helen, Mary F. Fiedler, and Martha F. Allen. 1961. *Wo-he-lo: The Story of the Campfire Girls 1910–1960.* New York: Holt, Rinehart, and Winston.

Cavallo, Dominick. 1981. *Muscles and Morals: Organized Playgrounds and Urban Reform, 1880–1920.* Philadelphia: University of Pennsylvania Press.

Cohen, Daniel. 1990. "For Happy Campers, Nothing Beats the Old Rites of Passage." *Smithsonian* 21 (August): 86–94.

Deloria, Philip J. 1998. *Playing Indian.* New Haven: Yale University Press.

Eells, Eleanor. 1986. *Eleanor Eells' History of Organized Camping: The First 100 Years.* Martinsville, IN: American Camping Association.

Gibson, H. W. 1936. "The History of Organized Camping." *Camping* 7 (January–December).

Gutman, Richard J. S., and Kellie O. Gutman. 1983. *The Summer Camp Memory Book: A Pictorial Treasury of Everything, from Campfires to Color Wars, You Loved about Camp.* New York: Crown.

Joselit, Jenna Weissman, ed., with Karen S. Mittelman. 1993. *A Worthy Use of Summer: Jewish Summer Camping in America.* Philadelphia: Museum of American Jewish History.

Mishler, Paul C. 1999. *Raising Reds: The Young Pioneers, Radical Summer*

Camps, and Communist Political Culture in the United States. New York: Columbia University Press.

Palladino, Grace. 1996. *Teenagers: An American History.* New York: Basic Books.

Paris, Leslie. 2001. "The Adventures of Peanut and Bo: Summer Camps and Early Twentieth Century American Girlhood." *Journal of Women's History* 12, no. 4 (Winter).

———. Forthcoming, 2001. "'A Home Though Away from Home': Brooklyn Jews and Interwar Children's Summer Camps." In *The Jews of Brooklyn.* Edited by Ilana Abramovitch and Séan Galvin. Boston: University Press of New England/Brandeis University Press.

West, Elliott, and Paula Petrik, eds. 1992. *Small Worlds: Children and Adolescents in America, 1850–1950.* Lawrence: University of Kansas Press.

Zelizer, Viviana. 1985. *Pricing the Priceless Child: The Changing Social Value of Children.* New York: Basic Books.

Surfer Girls

Though female surfers have been around since the kings and queens of Hawaii rode waves at Waikiki, the symbolic figure of the energetic, naive, but determined surfer girl emerged only during the affluent postwar years. In the summer of 1956, surfer Kathy "Gidget" Kohner told her screenwriting father about her days on the beaches at Malibu. Frederick Kohner fictionalized these into the novel *Gidget* (1957), which was made into a 1959 film starring Sandra Dee. Both attracted huge audiences and created lucrative new markets for water sports products as well as for novels, movies, television shows, and popular music detailing the lifestyle of surfing. Over the next ten years, the original *Gidget* novel spawned six sequels reprinted in ten languages: *Gidget Goes Hawaiian* (1961), *Gidget Goes to Rome* (1963), *The Affairs of Gidget* (1963), *Gidget in Love* (1965), *Gidget Goes Parisienne* (1966), and *Gidget Goes New York* (1968). A series of well-known films followed the original as well, as did about thirty "spin-off" beach blanket movies featuring, most famously, Elvis Presley. By the mid-1960s, American families were on first-name terms with Gidget. The beach sounds of Dick Dale and the Del Tones and the Beach Boys cinched the craze, making "Surfer Girl" and "Surfin' USA" American musical classics.

Because of the overlap between the fictional promotion of surfing and the actual surf community that promotion described, facts and fictions about surfer girls cannot be entirely disentangled. To determine which came first, the fact or the fiction, is impossible. But if Hollywood's beach movies exaggerated the frequency of luaus or the warmth of the southern Californian night air, they remained true to the fact that the "girl surfer" represented by Gidget had begun to be noticed in the waters of the Pacific by the summer of 1950. Linda Benson from Encinitas, the best woman surfer in the world by the time the Gidget craze struck, doubled for Deborah Walley during the actual surfing scenes portrayed in *Gidget Goes Hawaiian* (1961). A decade earlier, Mary Ann Hawkins Morrissey had been recruited by Hollywood to work as a stuntwoman precisely because of her legendary reputation, during the 1940s, as an expert Malibu surfer and all-around water woman. Of course, male surfers of this period, Mickey Dora being the most colorful, boasted relatively extensive Hollywood connections. And Hollywood stars—including Peter Lawford, Marilyn Monroe, Jackie "Butch" Jenkins, Richard Jaeckel, Robert Walker, and Red Grange—

Female surfboarders form a star as they lie on the beach in Santa Monica, California. (Hulton Getty/Archive Photos, 1935)

nurtured surfing connections. But Benson and Morrissey were surfing *women*, and the money they received was Hollywood money. Compared to dime-store work, a principal employment option for white women in the 1950s, Hollywood money was "real" money.

Though the history of women's surfing in California during the 1950s is sketchy, there is evidence of a Malibu "girl crowd" surfing as early as the summer of 1950. Vicki Williams Flaxman, Aggie Bane Quigg, Darilyn Zinc, Marge Gleason, Robin Grigg, Patty O'Keefe, and others formed the "Hele Nalu" Girls' Surf Club—adopting a Hawaiian name that translated as "going surfing" to christen their efforts. Most of these girls already

were capable young tennis players or skiers before they took to the water, and surfing struck them as a new, better kind of sport because it brought them in touch every day with the sea, sand, wind, and tides, and it gave them deep pleasure. O'Keefe, Quigg, and Flaxman later became champion canoe paddlers in Hawaii and continue to surf today. This group of girl surfers figures largely in the history of the sport because to please them (especially Aggie Bane, who later became his wife), Malibu board shaper and surfer Joe Quigg designed "girl boards," a lighter-weight, more dynamically shaped, balsawood surfboard. Quigg combined tail and rail rocker end to end, permitting a new range of motion and control. This retooled board served as the template for all future board innovations and ultimately paved the way for surfing's short board revolution.

Malibu was not the only place on the California coast that had breaking surf in the 1950s, and membership in surfer girl clubs probably proved more the exception than the norm for the surfer girl in search of waves. Then as now, surfing attracted into its ranks very independent, persevering personalities. If it required of its young men considerable body strength, agility, and mental composure (imagining an approaching 10-foot wall of water provides a good idea of the mentality needed for surfing), it required all of that and more for the young woman who wanted to learn. For in no way was surfing considered "normal" for a girl. Though by most accounts relations between the sexes enjoyed a profound cordiality in this period, suggesting why the era goes by the name of "surfing's golden age," nonetheless the standard expectations for women during the 1950s suggested girls' time was better spent preparing themselves to be future mothers—not combing the beaches, day and night, marching to an entirely different drummer.

That "difference" can be seen in the life histories of women like Claire Cassidy and Shelly Merrick of Malibu, Rosemari Reimers Rice of Hermosa Beach, and Marge Calhoun of Laguna Beach—all embodiments of the original independent surfer ideal. Cassidy, Reimers Rice, and Merrick report surveying the coastline looking for surf, sometimes from San Onofre to the Ventura County line (more than 200 miles in the days before interstates). Calhoun, as did Linda Benson, found her way to the big waves at Makaha in Hawaii, and handed on an enormously powerful legacy to the surfing

world in general and to her two surfing daughters in particular, Candy and Robin. Unlike most female surfers of the period, Calhoun and Reimers Rice continued their daily searches for waves even with young children in tow. Reimers Rice remembers packing small children and playpen into her station wagon, along with a nice young babysitter and, of course, always her surfboard.

If Malibu was not the only breaking surf, neither were Gidget or primarily blonde "California girls" the exclusive inspirations for the surfer girl mythology. The mainland surfing community had, for most of the twentieth century, evidenced a deep regard for Hawaiian peoples and cultures. Many books and magazines produced by surfers report that as early as the 1400s, Polynesian chants and legends remembered a volcano goddess who surfed named Pele. In the early nineteenth century, before missionary incursions into Hawaii convinced natives of surfing's supposed evils, courtship rituals of royal Hawaiian families demanded that young women signal their choice of husband by riding a wave with the chosen man. By the 1890s, in defiance of missionary teachings, Hawaiian queen Emma, *Surfer* magazine reports, ruled the royal waters at Waikiki (George 1999, 112). Certainly, most surfers in the United States eventually learn of Duke Kahanamoku, the Olympian swimmer from Hawaii who in the 1920s introduced American audiences to surfing. They are also likely to learn about Rell Sunn, "Queen of Makaha," another all-around water woman named first president in 1976 of Women's Professional Surfing (WPS). When she died of breast cancer in 1998, she left behind a community in mourning.

If surfers look upon the "aloha" spirit of surfing with fondness and reverence, many are also aware of the more complicated relationship between the surfing industry and Hawaiian culture and history, a relationship that some locate within the colonial tradition. Since the early 1900s, Americans have visited the Hawaiian islands, both imaginatively and literally. As tourist industries became increasingly important to the economies of the western United States in particular, Hawaii's image as a landscape of sublime peoples and nature grew and with it the profits such an image promised. The question of whether Hawaiian culture is truly respected within surf culture, or is instead "lifted" out of its historical roots in order to serve profit-making ends, is a fair one asked by many longtime surfers.

The aloha spirit has undergone yet another test as women surfers, in the years during and after the craze, took to the water in record numbers and with less apology. Many report that the gentlemanly behavior of men changed during the mid-1960s. On her very first time out in 1963, Jericho Poppler reports to *Wahine* magazine, the guys suggested she come back when her "tits were bigger" (Douglas 1999, 25). In an era of social revolution, antiwar protests, and civil rights agitation, on the threshold of the sexual revolution, tensions between men and women in the water might be understood as reflecting the growing pains of American society. Poppler herself, emblematic of changing times, went on to become a world-class surfer, a woman of many talents, and founder in the 1970s of the first women's professional tour. But as early as the 1950s, the bohemianism of surf culture served to affirm female physical strength, pleasure, and fun, while it simultaneously challenged the expectation that women of the period should give

their lives wholly to the reproduction of Cold Warriors.

By the mid-1960s, some surfer girls clearly were more than mere "Gidgets." Accomplished and risk-taking athletes who surfed far better than did the vast majority of men, young women like Joyce Hoffman from Capistrano Beach emerged as the first female star surfer, winning world titles and leading female surfing worldwide. In the Hoffman era, many other women rose to public prominence: Gail Cooper and Phyllis O'Donnell from Sydney, Australia; Gerry Stewart of New York; Linda Merrill, the first girl ever on the cover of *Surfer* magazine; Joey Hamasaki; Little Mimi Monroe; and at the end of the 1960s, Margo Godfrey Oberg, who at sixteen won the world championship while riding the new, radical short board—ending the reign of Joyce Hoffman and changing the women's surf scene forever.

During the 1970s, surfer girls "grew up," so to speak, formulating the organizational structure that supports women's professional surfing today. The Women's International Surfing Association (WISA) was founded; contests like the Hang Ten Women's Pro at Malibu showcased new talent; and International Professional Surfing (IPS) named, for the first time, a female world champion, Margo Godfrey Oberg. After the mid-1970s, the names of able new stars grew too numerous to list. Some came from newer places, like Jane "from the Lane" Mackenzie, whose home break is Steamer's at Santa Cruz, or Wendy Botha, who hails from South Africa. Others included Mary Lou Drummy, Linda Davoli, Lynne Boyer, Kim Mearig, Australia's first professional surfer Pam Burridge, and the overnight sensation Frieda Zamba.

Though much is known about "the best" surfer girls in the water from the mid-1970s to the 1990s, a mystery hangs over the majority of surfer girls, who did or did not surf competitively or did not live in areas where surfing was a high-visibility sport. About these young women, we can only wonder. Does the surfer girl mythology live on? How has it met up with changing rules circulated by the contemporary women's movement and women surfers themselves, about women's abilities, "rightful" community roles, and potential?

The enormous commercial boom of surfing in the mid-1990s has fostered a renewed interest in women's surfing and its history. First, the unprecedented accomplishments of stars like Lisa Andersen, Rochelle Ballard, Layne Beachley, Pauline Menczer, Megan Abubo, and Serena Brooke suggest this truly is a new age for women's surfing. At the same time, the commercial potential of surfing has undergone a massive renaissance—a watershed not unlike that inspired by Gidget in the late 1950s. In 1991, Quiksilver debuted its new surfwear made for women, especially girls' board shorts, creating a huge market of new female surfers and surfer-wannabe women consumers, whose purchases account for most of its sales. As in the 1950s, magazines and books that detail the world of surfer girls are again popular: *Wahine* is in its fifth year, and regular spreads on women's surfing appear in other sports magazines. Joy Nicholson's first novel, *The Tribes of Palos Verdes*, is slated to be a major motion picture. But unlike in the 1950s, women business owners are now principals in the new industry, heading up women's surf shops, schools, film companies, photography studios, equipment manufacturers, tours and vacations, and competitions. The notion of "girl power"—the power of girls to excel in sports and in life, as well as the consumer power of girls and women—is a central tenet of the renaissance. At the time of this writing, girl power remains one of the most intriguing forces for change in recent memory.

Krista Comer

See also Girl Power; Girls' Culture; Movies, Adolescent Girls in; Sports; Television; Tomboys

References and Further Reading
Comer, Krista. Forthcoming, 2003. *From Gidget to Surfergrrrls: Cultural History and Gender Formation in an Era of Globalization.* (See for oral histories with Rosemari Reimers Rice, Linda Benson, and Jane Mackenzie.)
Douglas, Theo, and Elizabeth Glazner. 1999. "The Real Gidget." *Wahine* 5, no. 2: 20–25.
Duclos, Jeff. 1999. "In Trim: Women of Malibu." *LongBoard Magazine* (May–June): 50–58.
Finney, Ben, and James D. Houston. 1996. *Surfing: A History of the Ancient Hawaiian Sport.* San Francisco: Pomegranate Art Books.
Gabbard, Andrea. 2000. *Girl in the Curl: A Century of Women's Surfing.* Seattle: Seal Press.
George, Sam. 1999. "500 Years of Women's Surfing." *Surfer* 40, no. 3: 112–113.
Nicholson, Joy. 1997. *The Tribes of Palos Verdes.* New York: St. Martin's Press.
Warshaw, Matt. 1997. *Surfriders: In Search of the Perfect Wave.* New York: HarperCollins.

T

Tea Parties

Since the nineteenth century, tea parties have been an encouraged form of play for girls by grownups concerned with promoting genteel feminine behavior. Tea parties were encouraged by nineteenth-century middle-class mothers committed to raising daughters to assume their allotted role as wives and mothers. The widespread production of miniature tea tables (some painted to represent marble) and porcelain tea sets (including doll-sized ones) enabled girls, friends, and their dolls to imitate adult lavishness as they practiced the social rituals of polite society. Fewer household responsibilities and increased leisure—a consequence of industrialization—led to more play activities that imitated work. Mothers hoped that ritualized girls' teas would cultivate civility, a central feature of bourgeois domestic values promoted by middle-class advisers. An elaborate code of table manners required girls, along with others, to achieve discipline over the body, emotions, and appetite.

Tea drinking as a marker of civility began as an upper-class English custom that spread to the colonies. Because both tea and tea sets were expensive, it was an activity that only the well-to-do could afford to enjoy until 1750, when increasing availability lowered the cost of tea and tea equipment. This new material indicator of refinement was often among the very first household acquisitions for those colonial families with social aspirations toward gentility. Only certain kinds of tables, tablecloths, trays, teapots, cups, and saucers were regarded as acceptable among the genteel. Using coded equipment, eighteenth-century elites mastered the etiquette of the highly disciplined social ritual of the tea ceremony. Those who achieved mastery of the elaborate performance of steeping, serving, and sipping acquired prestige and the social acceptance of a powerful elite. Those unfamiliar with the rules and roles of the ceremony, however, were marginalized.

Portraits of refined-looking girls with tea set props were painted in the late eighteenth century, when teatime became a family ritual (except during the Revolutionary War, of course). It was customary for the mistress or her eldest daughter to serve the tea. Tea parties at home provided adolescent girls and boys an opportunity to socialize and for parents to scrutinize potential suitors. Courtship might also include dancing, singing, and playing. For younger children, diminutive ceramic and China tea sets were sold in cities like Boston and Philadelphia, where little Peggy Livingston received a complete tea set from her uncle so that she could hold tea parties for her dolls (Roth 1988, 450).

Two little girls have a tea party with a stuffed panda. (Lambert/Archive Photos, 1950s)

It was not until the nineteenth century, however, that children's tea parties became more widespread because of the greater availability of less expensive pottery along with the increased purchasing power of the middle class. Numerous stereographs, advertising trade cards, illustrations, and postcards portrayed girls reenacting the elegant social performances of their elders with child-sized tea sets. Doll-sized china tea sets cost between 25 cents and $2 at the 99-cent and variety stores. There were even children's books such as *The Dolls' Tea Party* (1895) that codified the ritual for little ones. Whether in the Midwest or Northeast, tea parties were staged with great

regularity. One late-nineteenth-century study revealed that out of 242 girls who played with tea sets, 73 considered it their "favorite" activity (Croswell 1899, 354).

Believing that all girls "longed for" tea nooks or tea tables (preferably with two lower shelves for extra cups), turn-of-the-century interior decorators recommended them as standard furnishing for girls' rooms. "No girl's room can be complete," one decorator wrote, "without its little tea table which makes her realize, perhaps more than anything else, that here she is responsible for the comfort of her guests; and so she will soon learn to dispense hospitality gracefully" (Tachau 1915, 10). But not all girls delighted in the conventions of teatime. One study conducted in 1899 suggests that far fewer girls preferred tea parties to other play activities. Out of 929 girls in Worcester, Massachusetts, 687 preferred sledding, jumping rope, and playing tag, hide-and-seek, and other games to playing with dolls' tea sets. Some clearly objected to the intentions of adults who sought to inculcate gender roles through ceremony. Seeing her brother having fun with a pack of friends, one girl (who later became a feminist and a writer) wreaked havoc on her tea party by smashing her unsuspecting dolls to bits. One woman in her memoir described the raucous tea parties of her girlhood. Instead of sedately sipping tea, the girls took turns sitting on top of the tea tray and sliding down the hall stairs.

That is probably not what Italian educator Maria Montessori had in mind when she incorporated tea sets into her curriculum to teach poor children middle-class mores. After all, pouring tea from one vessel into another could have functional uses; its fine motor control has appealed to progressive preschool educators ever since. (Tea sets are a standard part of the Montessori equipment in preschools today.) At home, tea parties became more formalized shortly after World War II. *House Beautiful* recommended tea parties for Valentine's Day and *Good Housekeeping* promoted the Christmas tea. Some tea parties in the extravagant 1980s were conspicuously ritzy. Mother-and-daughter teas also became a popular form of entertainment. Still considered within the domain of girls, tea parties are as popular as ever among birthday party planners, many of whom market theirs as old-fashioned, Victorian-style high teas. Little Princess Tea Parties by Lynda is one of many busi-nesses nationwide that offer elegant tea parties with lace and frills for girls ages four to eleven. At formal tea parties, girls dress up in long lacy dresses, don large hats, nibble small sandwiches, and drink tea served on a silver service. For presents, girls are likely to receive inexpensive and less fragile china tea sets or safer plastic ones. Tea parties held in cyberspace—such as Hello Kitty's interactive tea party—provide children with social opportunities, even in the absence of friends.

Miriam Forman-Brunell

See also Consumer Culture; Dollhouses; Dolls; Domesticity; Girls' Culture; Play

References and Further Reading

Calvert, Karin. 1992. *Children in the House: The Material Culture of Early Childhood, 1600–1900.* Boston: Northeastern University Press.

Croswell, T. R. 1899. "Amusements of Worcester School Children." *Pedagogical Seminary* 4 (September): 354.

Roth, Rodris. 1988. "Tea-Drinking in Eighteenth-Century America: Its Etiquette and Equipage." Pp. 439–462 in *Material Life in America 1600–1860.* Edited by Robert Blair St. George. Boston: Northeastern University Press.

Tachau, Nina. 1915. "The Girl's Room." *House Beautiful* 38 (June): 10.

Technology

When Pocahontas, Abigail Adams, Harriet Tubman, and Amelia Earhart were girls, *technology* did not mean computers and the Internet. In fact, a girl growing up during the Revolution or the Civil War would not have used the word *technology*—the word can be found during the 1800s but did not become common until the 1930s. When we talk about girls and technology in American history, we have to think about technology as "knowing how" and examine all the ways of making and doing things girls learned at different points in time. This view of technology is used by historians and anthropologists to understand the tools and techniques of widely varying cultures.

Thus "girls and technology" includes grinding corn and growing squash, mending clothing, tending fires, churning butter, and even playing with dolls as well as using sewing machines, riding bicycles, and surfing the Web. Just as modern toddlers practice grownup work by playing with small pots and pans or trucks or toy cash registers, children in earlier times learned how the technologies of their cultures worked by playing with a small horse and wagon or making doll clothes. Learning about technology is part of how girls learn to be women and boys learn to be men. In some places and times, girls and boys learn about the same technologies: for example, a child who has the job of taking out the garbage learns about garbage cans and garbage trucks. In other cases, grownups expect girls to know about some technologies and boys to know about others, as in the days when girls took home economics in school and boys took shop.

Before the Word Technology

Girls in Native American communities, the British colonies, and the new United States learned all about the tools and techniques of women's work as they grew up. Among Native Americans, girls learned to tend and harvest crops, cure meat and fish, cook food, and make clothing and leather goods, depending on where they lived. Among European Americans, most girls lived on farms, so while their brothers were out in the fields helping their father, girls learned all the household and garden jobs that kept the family going. Families often made the things they used from day to day: clothing, soap, candles, bread, and furniture. African American girls in this period grew up in enslaved families, often on farms growing cash crops such as tobacco, so they learned all the work of farms but also knew more about fieldwork—hoeing and keeping bugs off tobacco plants and drying the leaves for sale—than their free counterparts. Their parents did not have much say in what slave children did all day. In all these communities, even small children learned to be careful of fire, and older girls would be taught to tend the hearth. The big cooking pots might be too heavy for her to lift, but she would be instructed in making stews and how to make a hotter fire, find the warm spots away from the flames, and keep the temperature even while cornbread was cooking.

In European American communities, fieldwork—except at harvesttime when everyone's help might be needed—was mostly for boys and men, but vegetable gardens were planted and tended by women. Girls learned how to pick vegetables when they were ready, save seeds for the following year, and plant and tend seedlings at the right time in the spring. Seasonal tasks like salting meat or pickling vegetables preserved food through the winter, and in northern areas, potatoes and beets and apples stored in a root cellar had to be checked every now and then to remove any items beginning to go bad. Families with a dairy cow had milk and cream, and girls and women churned butter and processed cheese. Sometimes such goods could be traded at the local store for items not made at home. In the modern days of the World Wide Web, a butter churn seems quaint—but more than 1,000 patents had been issued for different kinds of churns by 1873 when the U.S. government tallied all the patents since 1790.

In the days when family members might make all their own cloth and then all their own clothes, mothers and daughters had very important jobs. Little girls practiced sewing scraps together until they had learned to sew straight seams, and then they could help make underwear and shirts and help with the mending. Making clothes took so much time and effort that only the oldest and most worn-out clothes went into the rag basket. Even then, the fabrics were recycled: girls pieced patchwork quilts from good scraps or sewed rags together in long strips so they could braid the strips and then coil them to make a rug. When they were between seven and ten years old and were good at sewing, in many families or schools they sewed a sampler using all the stitches they knew and pretty colored threads, if they could afford them. Older girls often learned to spin linen or wool and eventually to weave, and teenagers set up the loom with warp threads so their younger sisters could do simple weaving. Spinning and weaving were useful activities in households with older girls or teenagers, and sometimes these girls worked for neighbors; a mother with very small children would usually trade some of her squash or beans for having her weaving completed. Then, of course, there was the laundry. Girls learned to make soap as they helped their mothers, as well as how to wash and hang the clothes. Ironing had to be done using a solid metal "iron," heated in the fire (or, later, on the stove). The iron was heavy, and if it was too hot it might scorch the clothes, but if it was too cool it would not smooth out wrinkles.

Thus even very young girls knew about many important technologies, and by the time they were teenagers they were very helpful people to have around the house. Often a teenage girl from a family with other sisters would go live with a neighbor's or relative's family for a while, so she could learn from a different woman and help in a different household before she began her own. Sometimes her family set up the arrangement as a formal apprenticeship, with a contract called "indentures" signed by both sides, especially if one of her parents had died or if an older woman had particular skills. A town girl learning fancy dressmaking or mantua making (coat making) usually did so under formal indentures, promising to serve her mistress faithfully until she was eighteen years old in return for food and lodging and clothing provided in her new mistress's household.

Industrialization and New Machines
During the first 150 years of U.S. nationhood, Americans changed the technologies for almost everything they did. In the early days of the republic, the vast majority of Americans lived on farms and worked in agriculture, but by World War I more than half of all Americans lived in towns, and increasingly they expected that food would be purchased rather than grown. This long, slow process of industrialization meant that many of the tasks girls and women had learned and performed changed dramatically—slowly at first but more and more noticeably as Americans thought theirs a nation of "progress" and tied "progress" to expanding production of all kinds of material goods. When we think about girls and technology, it is important to remember that someone had to buy all the things the new factories were making: consumption is the other side of the coin of production.

Even by the early nineteenth century, items like soap and candles were being made in small factories, and families could purchase them in local stores. Girls might have some extra time, but buying goods meant the family needed extra money; many farm families added tasks such as making extra butter or plaiting straw for bonnets as part of their household routines. Some families could acquire a stove for cooking, and girls and women learned new techniques for keeping fires going and for cooking and baking.

New technologies brought major changes early on for enslaved girls as well. Most important, perhaps, was the cotton gin: with a machine to pick the sticky seeds out of cotton, landowners could make large profits from growing and selling the soft fibers. But more cotton fields meant more people picking cotton, and the number of slaves in the United States grew from less than 700,000 in 1790 to 4 million by 1860. A girl on a cotton plantation helped care for the smaller children until she was old enough to help with household chores for her owners or with the cotton picking in the fields.

The cotton was the raw material for the new textile mills in the North that got under way by the 1820s, for by that time fewer people were making cloth at home. The factories turned out yards and yards of standardized cotton and also woolen fabric, all of it carded, spun, and woven by large, fast, noisy machinery. Factory owners thought teenage girls would be good at tending machines like looms, watching for bobbins near empty, or tying broken threads. They also found that girls were good at making craft-based items for the stores, such as cardboard boxes or artificial flowers. In this period many people,

African American and European American and new European immigrants, were moving to cities, and by the middle of the century and especially after the Civil War, girls who lived near factories often worked long hours doing repetitive jobs for cash wages, a new kind of contribution to the family economy. Or they worked in wealthier households, cleaning and cooking, learning all about the new household technologies even though they were too expensive for many working people to have at home.

For most of the nineteenth century, even with factory-made cloth, making clothing and household linens was a job for women and girls at home, or, for fancy dresses, for dressmakers and their apprentices. Girls learned to sew just as consistently in the 1800s as they had in the 1700s, although the new coeducational public schools meant sewing was a home activity rather than a school one for many children. But this task, too, changed with the new machines: besides machine-made cloth and machine-made thread, in the second half of the century families with enough money could buy sewing machines to help with straight seams. By the end of the nineteenth century, sewing machines and paper patterns were common tools in many households.

Girlhood in Industrial America

By World War I, a wide range of ready-made household items were available: flour was sold in packages by national distributors, prepared food was sold in cans, and clothing could increasingly be found already sewn. Besides underwear and men's shirts, in cities the new department stores sold entire gowns and suits to middle-class customers. Meatpacking plants in the Midwest packaged hams and sausages and shipped them by train to the cities, and railroads brought factory-made goods out to the new towns in the western states. By the turn of the century, even rural people could choose items from thick catalogues—Sears Roebuck and Montgomery Ward—and order them by mail, getting a taste of all the items people in big cities could find in the stores. For women and girls, being consumers was one of the jobs of running the household, along with old jobs like cooking and cleaning and gardening. But the old jobs changed as more and more houses had hot running water, gas hookups, and even electricity for washing, cooking, lighting, and eventually running small motors. Girls' roles changed as public schooling became not only more widely available for more of the year but mandatory by state and local law.

Industrial society meant everyone in the family had new roles to play and new technologies to learn. When Americans imagined their ideal family, many of them thought of a married couple with children, in a household managed by the mother (possibly with the help of a servant), using money earned by the father. In this image, children went to school and played until sometime in their teenage years. And when Americans thought about machines and progress and engineering and modern cities, they thought of these things as good but also as so noisy and so fast that everyone needed a break from them—and they imagined that "home" was a peaceful place in comparison to work, school, travel, and commerce. In fact, many technologies and even many modern machines could be found inside this cozy peaceful place, but people came to think of machines as belonging somewhere else. More importantly for girls in the twentieth century, many people came to think of home as a place of consumption, not production. Making, designing, producing, and repairing things—these activities were seen as industrial, not domestic. And so they also came to be seen as boys' and men's activities, not girls' and women's.

We can see these differences in the kinds of indoor toys children played with in the first half of the twentieth century. Girls had not only dolls but toy kitchens, small versions of household appliances installed once electricity or natural gas was available to run them. Most of these toys were not designed to be taken apart and reassembled but to serve as props in role-playing games. Girls played at home-making and shopping—but they also practiced using the new technologies and came to understand grown-up versions of gas stoves and electric appliances. This period was one of much technological change in the kitchen, so a girl who learned to bake or to help her mother put up tomatoes was, as in past periods, acquiring significant technological knowledge even if she did not think of it in those terms. Meanwhile, the building toys of the period were marketed to boys, who were encouraged to play at designing, constructing, and repairing the material world. These activities were the ones regarded as "technological" as the word came into use in the 1930s. And these differences in expectation were reflected in the adult world, as well, for example in the ways auto manufacturers marketed to women (via color, upholstery, comfort) and to men (through design, engine type, mechanical innovations) from the 1920s on.

These ideas also played out in schools. Educators reintroduced technological

Girls investigate a phonograph made for children. (Hulton-Deutsch Collection/Corbis).

activities into schools, partly because they believed children should learn from activities as well as books but also because it seemed that children from immigrant families and children who would grow up to work in factories needed different kinds of schooling from children who might go on to college. The new "progressive" education for girls meant cooking and sewing, starting in the 1880s and becoming more popular with the home economics movement of the early twentieth century. Home economics meant incorporating scientific ideas about nutrition and public health into girls' education, but it also focused girls' learning on domestic issues. For boys, who were thought to suffer from city life, progressive lessons meant basic carpentry and sometimes metalwork, a standard class often referred to as "shop" or sometimes "industrial arts." In the later decades of the twentieth century, these classes became coeducational and then, in many towns, obsolete, but they were standard fare for well over fifty years. Some boys learned drafting and advanced metalwork in preparation for careers in engineering; girls in high school could learn clerical tasks, including the use of typewriters and bookkeeping machines. In these school activities, too, girls were taught in terms of *using* machines, whereas boys were taught about either building them according to someone else's design or designing machines themselves. Even when they were mostly users, boys were taught to believe they should understand and interact with machinery—for nice girls, messy dishes and diapers were appropriate, but greasy overalls were not.

Nonetheless, as machines became more ubiquitous, everyone acquired new knowledge of the changing material world. Girls growing up with radios, televisions, refrigerators, washing machines, and curling irons acquired mechanical understanding under the rubric "housework." Just as girls had learned to churn butter or make soap in the past, twentieth-century girls learned about wash cycles, thermostats, circuits, and fuses. But in the age of steel mills and fighter-bombers, this knowledge was not labeled "technological." Most twentieth-century households depended on large technological systems supplying electricity, gas, or drinking water, and those who ran the households made technological choices on a regular basis, but the technological nature of domestic spaces was invisible in the common understanding of where technology might be located.

Girls did have a few daring role models, women who defied stereotypes: to drive cars, early on, and soon to fly airplanes. The publicity on "first women" such as Amelia Earhart or Bessie Coleman and then the women pilots of World War II, who ferried every type of military aircraft used during the war, showed girls that women could handle machines reserved mostly for men. The wartime campaigns to persuade women to enter heavy industry, known now by the emblematic "Rosie the Riveter," also taught girls that the rules were not steadfast. Despite the home-and-family ideology of the baby boom decades, for most of the century girls had a widening range of role models skilled at manipulating machines everyone came to recognize as technology, as well as role models knowledgeable about technologies.

But being publicly technological took real courage, and even these unusual women had to remind everyone that they were still feminine. By a broad historical definition those reminders can be called "technologies of identity": shoes with high heels, hosiery made of the finest silk or the latest laboratory-made fibers, and makeup designed to provide a range of pigments in convenient and safe powders, creams, and solids. Aviator Jacqueline Cochran sold her own lines of cosmetics, and women's events like the All-Women's Transcontinental Air Race were commonly known, from the 1930s through the 1960s, as "powder puff derbies." Similarly, most girls learned how to "dress up," and in doing so they learned not only to choose among the many products of the mass production economy but to design their own external identity using a range of tools: colors, fabrics, chemicals, and fasteners. Similar options—with a larger apparent budget—could be exercised in the world of Barbie and other fashion dolls, as well. By the end of the century such choices were treated more generally as choices, but beginning by the 1920s and continuing at least into the 1970s, girls most often learned that without performing such feminine rituals they might jeopardize their access to a proper place in society.

Girls of the Information Age

Girls in what is now called the "information age"—the recent decades when computers and chips and wireless communications have been changing what the older mechanical machines can do—are also girls growing up after the major changes in men's and women's roles of the 1960s and 1970s. The rigid differences between boys' work and girls' work, men's work and women's work, along with many legal distinctions in property rights and economic controls, have given way to greater choice about who learns how to do what and what kind of adult life a child can imagine seeking. Meanwhile, girls assume they will be able to see pictures of the other side of the world almost instantly and that they will be able to purchase a wide range of items on the telephone or the Internet; kids and parents keep in touch via cell phones or beepers. Food often comes ready to eat or at least ready to heat, and restaurant chains sell standardized meals to people who are, accordingly, producing fewer meals at home. These behaviors and expectations can be attributed to the combination of technological, political, social, and economic changes that have shaped modern American society.

Thus, in the middle of the twentieth century, a girl wanting to be a veterinarian, an engineer, or a race car driver might have been told, "That's for boys, dear"; in the beginning of the twenty-first century, she is more likely to be encouraged. Even Barbie rollerblades and flies an airplane. Girls meet women doctors, see women on highway construction crews, and learn about women astronauts. Both girls and boys take home economics and shop, or else such subjects are left out of the curriculum entirely. The budding female electrician will probably find supportive adults who will say, "Of course you can," in addition to discouraging ones who say only that it is difficult, that there will be mostly boys in her classes, or even that boys will not like girls who do jobs like repairing air-conditioning systems. In other words, many of the activities though of as "technological"—heating soup in the microwave, calling home on a cell phone—are now performed by men and women and learned by boys and girls. Nonetheless, despite all the changes, girls and boys continue quite frequently to be assigned different kinds of technological tasks. When women in fields like engineering tell girls about how much they love their exciting jobs, they wonder whether or not to reveal the stories of fighting for the opportunity or the other obstacles they faced along the way.

A trip through the aisles of any large toy store at the turn of the twenty-first century reflects these examples of change and continuity. Boys and girls both will find computer chips and electronic enhancements in their toys; grow up familiar with the possibility that inanimate objects talk, move, and even respond in lifelike ways; and assume that images move, morph, and portray unreal scenes in very realistic ways. These features can be found in toys for toddlers—cheerful dinosaurs, monsters, and other creatures—as well as for older children. But on the aisle where most of the plastic and packaging are pink, lavender, and white, most of the toys re-create homes and fashion choices; on the aisle where most of the plastic and packaging are black and green, most of the toys emphasize transportation, adventure, and combat. "Pink" technological choices are most often about consumer activities and

A sixteen-year-old girl working on a computer. (Skjold Photographs)

domestic settings; pink technological design focuses on how bodies look and on domestic settings. "Black and green" technological choices are most often about making machines go places, dig holes, build things, or kill imaginary enemies; black and green technological design focuses on mechanical, architectural, or military capabilities. Girls and boys both learn to use computers, but the "Barbie" computer, in pink and white floral casing, comes with a digital camera and fashion design software, and the "Hot Wheels" computer, in blue and flaming yellow casing, comes with a steering wheel, foot pedal, and racing scenario software. The users of both computers learn about graphics and the capabilities of computer processing. But the uses of the tool in these color-coded packages encourage different kinds of technological knowledge and portray interaction with different technologies: pink technological knowledge includes fabrics and colors and the visualization of how things look; blue and yellow technological knowledge includes engines and speed and the visualization of what things do. It can still be quite difficult to cross these lines, in either direction.

But knowing there are computer chips in things or knowing what computerized tools and toys are likely to be able to do is not the same as knowing how to make them work. The earliest computer programmers, including Navy Rear Admiral

Grace Hopper, were mostly women, but the field of computer science, as it developed, became a terrain populated mostly by men. Girls today often do not think of programming as a career option. Teachers report boys are more interested in how computers work, whereas girls work with them as tools for other tasks. Books teaching computer programming often compare a program to a recipe, a set of instructions to follow using particular "inputs," and Web design depends on visualization of how things look, so perhaps in the twenty-first century women will be heavily involved in these areas based on what they learned as girls.

In general, the trends since 1800 have resulted in less difference in what girls and boys know and what work men and women do and greater difference in what machines do versus what people do. This pattern can most easily be seen in the food we eat, if we think about who grows it, who harvests it, and how it is processed, cooked, heated, and eaten. Consider potatoes. Instant mashed potatoes and fast-food French fries are industrial products just like cars and disposable diapers. But machines doing more work affect areas far beyond consumer choices. Large jets now have automatic controls, for example, so pilots make fewer minute-to-minute decisions about flying the plane.

In this technological world, some people are learning how to use devices, while others are deciding how to design them. Who will learn which approach? In some schools students can study computer science, and in general right now more boys than girls choose to do so. But in other schools there are not enough computers or even electrical outlets for all the students to get a chance to use the word processors. At various points in our nation's past, adults debated how to prepare their children for adulthood partly in terms of what technologies they should learn. Nobody can predict the future, but what girls (and boys) learn now shapes what choices they will make about technology later, when they grow up and teach technology to children of their own.

Nina E. Lerman

See also Consumer Culture; Domesticity; Education of Girls; Mathematics and Science; Mill Girls; Work

References and Further Reading
American Association of University Women. 2000. *Tech-Savvy: Educating Girls for the New Computer Age.* Washington, DC: AAUW Educational Foundation.
Calvert, Karin. 1992. *Children in the House: The Material Culture of Early Childhood, 1600–1900.* Boston: Northeastern University Press.
Canel, Annie, Ruth Oldenziel, and Karin Zachmann, eds. 2000. *Crossing Boundaries, Building Bridges: Comparing the History of Women Engineers, 1870s–1990.* London: Harwood Academic Publishers.
Cassell, Justine, and Henry Jenkins. 1998. *From Barbie to Mortal Kombat: Gender and Computer Games.* Cambridge, MA: MIT Press.
Cowan, Ruth Schwartz. 1983. *More Work for Mother: The Ironies of Household Technology from the Open Hearth to the Microwave.* New York: Basic Books.
Douglas, Deborah G. 1990. "United States Women in Aviation, 1940–1985." *Smithsonian Studies in Air and Space* no. 7. Washington, DC: Smithsonian Institution Press.
Douglas, Susan. 1994. *Where the Girls Are: Growing Up Female with the Mass Media.* New York: Times Books.
Dublin, Thomas. 1994. *Transforming Women's Work: New England Lives in the Industrial Revolution.* Ithaca, NY: Cornell University Press.

Jellison, Katherine. 1993. *Entitled to Power: Farm Women and Technology, 1913–1963*. Chapel Hill: University of North Carolina Press.

Jensen, Joan. 1986. *Loosening the Bonds: Mid-Atlantic Farm Women, 1750–1850*. New Haven: Yale University Press.

King, Wilma. 1995. *Stolen Childhood: Slave Youth in Nineteenth-Century America*. Bloomington: Indiana University Press.

Lerman, Nina E., Arwen Mohun, and Ruth Oldenziel, guest eds. 1997. "Gender Analysis and the History of Technology." *Technology and Culture* 38, no. 1 (January).

McGaw, Judith, ed. 1994. *Early American Technology: Making and Doing Things from the Colonial Era to 1850*. Chapel Hill: University of North Carolina Press.

Peiss, Kathy. 1998. *Hope in a Jar: The Making of America's Beauty Culture*. New York: Owl Books.

Scharff, Virginia. 1991. *Taking the Wheel: Women and the Coming of the Motor Age*. Albuquerque: University of New Mexico Press.

Spector, Janet. 1993. *What This Awl Means: Feminist Archaeology at a Wahpeton Dakota Village*. St. Paul: Minnesota Historical Society Press.

Stanley, Autumn. 1995. *Mothers and Daughters of Invention: Notes for a Revised History of Technology*. New Brunswick, NJ: Rutgers University Press.

Ulrich, Laurel Thatcher. 1990. *A Midwife's Tale: The Life of Martha Ballard, Based on Her Diary, 1785–1812*. New York: Alfred A. Knopf.

Teen Pregnancy

Teen (or *teenage*) *pregnancy* is a term that emerged in the 1970s and has been used since then by politicians, policymakers, educators, the medical community, and others to refer to a social problem: the consequences of what many Americans consider the inappropriate sexual behavior of unmarried girls younger than twenty. Since the 1980s, the term has been commonly used to refer particularly to the pregnancies of young women who are poor, unmarried, nonwhite teenagers.

The relatively short history of the term *teenage pregnancy* reflects a long-standing concern in the United States with youthful, unmarried female sexuality, pregnancy, and motherhood. Since at least the early nineteenth century, families, communities, and government authorities have mounted strategies to define, assign responsibility for, and respond to the unsanctioned sex and pregnancies of adolescent girls. State legislators have, over time, crafted many kinds of laws and policies to constrain female sexuality, some particularly targeting youthful sexuality and its consequences. Among these laws have been slave laws, age-of-consent laws, antiprostitution laws, eugenics laws, anticontraception and antiabortion laws, various welfare regulations, and "parental notification" laws. In general, champions of such legislation have claimed that the incidence of youthful, unmarried female sex and pregnancy is an index of social disorganization. Laws and policies, they have claimed, have been necessary to regain sexual control of youthful females and set society and social relations right again. Crucial to an understanding of social, political, and legal responses to youthful female unmarried sex and pregnancy in the United States is that, across the centuries, private and public strategies to deal with what we now call teenage pregnancy—and the ideas fueling these various strategies—have always been inflected by race and class.

No data survive from the early decades of the young republic to indicate accurately the incidence of unmarried sex and pregnancy among young women. Historians have argued, however, that when such women had babies, "bastardy," the consequence of unmarried pregnancy, was more an economic than a moral problem. Young white women at the end of the eighteenth and beginning of the nineteenth centuries were unlikely to be ejected from their family homes or ostracized from their communities for this misstep. A nonconforming young woman would typically remain with her family. She would eventually marry, and in the meantime, both parents would be responsible for the child born out of wedlock.

Young African American girls and women were, of course, at this time almost all enslaved. Often they were forbidden to marry, and their sex and reproductive experiences were frequently under the control of "owners." Throughout the nineteenth century, age-of-consent laws (in the tradition of British common law) were meant to protect only very young girls and to inconvenience few males. In 1886, twenty-five states had laws that set the age at which a girl could rationally agree to engage in sexual relations at ten years old.

By the late nineteenth century, adolescence was defined as a discrete and increasingly important phase of girlhood. Class status came to define life more and more, and reformers around the country built various kinds of female-rescue institutions to save the victims of urbanization, industrialization, and immigration. All these developments shaped the ways white Americans experienced and responded to the pregnancies of young white unmarried women. Again, it is important to stress that most African American young women remained enslaved for two-thirds of the nineteenth century, and after-

ward, most lived under apartheid in the American South. Youthful out-of-wedlock sexuality and childbearing were family and community matters for African Americans. Historians have argued that for most women in this group at the end of the nineteenth and beginning of the twentieth centuries, youthful pregnancy was premarital; marriage generally followed soon after the birth.

Among native white and white immigrant populations, unmarried youthful pregnancy rates doubled between the middle of the nineteenth century and 1910, with the largest increase occurring among urban, working-class girls. In response, evangelical, social purity, and temperance organizations created institutions to provide refuge for "fallen girls" and pushed for vice commissions and state laws to protect "innocent victims." In the 1880s, for example, the Woman's Christian Temperance Union mounted crusades to convince state legislators to raise the age of consent for girls to sixteen. At the same time, child labor laws, compulsory education laws, and child protection laws all drew attention to the vulnerability of the young and helped define a new upper limit of youth: adolescence. Adolescence was defined as a time when girls, in particular, needed protection against victimization, especially by sexually predatory males. The new life stage was generally defined as a phase through which young women should properly pass before entering into the adult activities of sex, marriage, and childbearing.

Social commentators and reformers found many girls at this time who violated the new norms of adolescence. They pointed to the sexual behavior—and unwed pregnancies—of some young girls as evidence and symbols of social disintegration. Assertion of control over urban, working-class girls was posited as the most potent antidote to family and community breakdown. Rescue homes, such as those under the National Florence Crittenton Mission, affirmed their commitment to girlhood innocence in part by sorting their target population into redeemable girls and others who represented fatally compromised innocence. A poor, pregnant, resourceless, immigrant girl, for example, might be more likely to end up in court for adjudication as an "incorrigible" or a prostitute than in a rescue home.

Distinguishing between categories of young, pregnant girls continued to be important to doctors, moral reformers, and others into the twentieth century. As more white girls had access to education and more were attached to the middle class, many had much to lose by engaging in premarital sex and risking unmarried pregnancy. For girls from "respectable" families, a mistake could be so consequential that secret pregnancies and relinquishments and secret criminal abortions became crucial strategies for many.

From the turn of the century through the 1930s, white, working-class girls who became pregnant while unmarried were often treated by professionals schooled to believe that unmarried pregnancy was symptomatic of environmentally induced disease, for example, low intelligence quotient (IQ) or parental alcoholism, the wages of slum living. In these early decades of the twentieth century, most in this group kept their babies since adopters were not clamoring to take the offspring of girls whose pregnancies were believed to indicate biological inferiority.

By the 1920s, when more Americans lived in cities than in rural areas for the first time, many adolescent girls—both working and middle-class, both white and

The Young Women's Christian Association (YWCA) was founded to help girls lead "moral lives." (Library of Congress, 1919)

black—experienced aspects of what has been referred to as "sexual emancipation." Many lived away from family and religious controls, and many young women earned their own wages. At this time, social commentators under the influence of Sigmund Freud and other emergent sexologists did not strongly associate youthful female sexuality with pregnancy. After all, being a modern girl meant protecting oneself, using birth control and illegal abortion. Even so, fears flourished about weak young girls who lacked the strength of character to protect themselves. Influential commentators claimed only the state was strong enough in the new urban context to maintain distinctions between good girls and bad ones, between moral and deviant behaviors.

Whatever state-sponsored or private institutional solutions were devised to this end—Young Women's Christian Associations (YWCAs), maternity homes, or "white slavery" laws, for example—were sure to be racially segregated, thus preserving the distinctions between white girls and girls of color, as well.

For about a generation after the 1940s, the experience and assessment of youthful pregnancy cut along two well-defined axes. First of all, youthful pregnancy embraced large numbers of married as well as unmarried teenage girls. After World War II, increasing numbers of teenagers gave birth; in 1950 27 percent of all first births were to teenagers. And by 1965, 39 percent were to married teenage girls.

Second, for a number of reasons, public policies and community institutions racialized the treatment of unwed teen mothers and their babies more formally than before in this era. In what was promoted as a generous reform, white unwed mothers (the term *teenage pregnancy* had still not yet been coined) were pressed to hide their pregnancies, which were now defined by professionals as the result of psychological maladjustment, and relinquish their babies—now seen as valuable commodities—at birth. This way, teenage girls who erred could preserve the public appearance of purity and the possibility of proper marriage and motherhood in the future.

Politicians and policymakers treated the youthful pregnancies of African American and other young, unmarried, pregnant girls of color (all members of populations struggling to overthrow apartheid in the second half of the twentieth century) as occasions for punishment. These pregnancies also became justifications among whites for resisting both the dismantling of apartheid and the enfranchising of people of color as full citizens. Resisters used the specter of the unwed pregnancies of some young women of color to argue for blocking integration of public schools and public housing and to stimulate hostility to young mothers of color who collected welfare benefits for their babies (who were tarred simultaneously as too costly to white taxpayers and as valueless children). The very fact that poor young mothers of color were newly eligible for welfare benefits in these decades stimulated white hostility to the welfare system itself. In this hostile context, African American girls who gave birth kept their babies and struggled with or without government assistance to be mothers. By the mid-1960s, it was clear that the state's and community's determination to control youthful sexuality and its consequences, including controlling which girls got to be mothers of their children and which did not, gave authorities the "right" to treat different groups of girls differently, depending on race.

During this same era, the development of the birth control pill gave millions of young women significantly more ability to manage their own sex lives and fertility. The Pill also gave medical and social work professionals a tool many defined as the best method for fighting poverty (again, linking youthful female sexuality to a rise of massive social problems and the venue for controlling those problems). In the 1960s and 1970s, poor girls and girls of color were pressed to fulfill their duty to avoid pregnancy by using birth control, dispensed at one of the quickly growing number of publicly funded family planning clinics. Liberals tended to champion these clinics for their contribution to the antipoverty

Teenage pregnancies have been treated differently by society depending on race and class. (Shirley Zeiberg)

effort, whereas conservatives began to speak out against them as government-supported facilitators of illicit, youthful sex. Birth control represents yet another area in which politicians and various experts constructed the experiences of girls according to race and class scripts.

The term *teenage pregnancy* emerged in the 1970s in several government documents. In this decade, the teenage population was very large in relation to the adult population, and increasingly, adults defined adolescence as a problem-fraught life stage. Politicians, government officials, birth control advocates, educators, and others routinely referred to the "epidemic" of teenage pregnancy in the 1970s, despite the fact that the rate and

ratio of adolescent pregnancy had been much higher in the 1950s than they were in the 1970s. Between 1955 and 1977, the rate dropped 44.8 percent.

A number of factors account for the intense public attention to and concern about pregnant teenage girls. For one thing, it is notable that the "epidemic" was named during a period when teen pregnancy rates were rising dramatically among whites, in fact, four times more rapidly than among black teenagers. Also, many of the teenage girls who had babies in the 1950s, but not those who gave birth in the 1970s, were married. By the 1970s, significant numbers of teenage pregnancies could no longer even be considered premarital. Many Americans were alarmed at the rise of youthful single motherhood. In addition, teenagers' access to sex education in public schools and to birth control and abortion—their new "privacy right" to make choices about such matters—alarmed some parents, who felt they were losing the ability to transmit values to their daughters.

A number of Supreme Court decisions and other federal government actions in the 1970s underwrote teenagers' reproductive autonomy. In *Ordway v. Hargraves* (1971) public school girls were granted the right not to be expelled from school because of pregnancy. In 1972 Congress required welfare offices to offer birth control services to teenagers who were sexually active. In the same year, the Supreme Court, in *Eisenstadt v. Baird*, ruled that unmarried persons had a right to birth control access, and five years later, in *Casey v. Population Services International*, this right was explicitly extended to unmarried minors. And, of course, *Roe v. Wade* (1973) legalized abortion for all women, including teenagers. In 1978, Congress passed the Adolescent Health Services and Pregnancy Prevention and Care Act. All these developments and the explosion of data and media coverage available about teenagers and their sexual behavior transformed teenagers' sexual secrets, even their "shameful" pregnancies, into common knowledge.

Not surprisingly, there was a swift backlash against the sexual empowerment of teenagers and against the new federally sanctioned supports for pregnant teenagers and their "choices." The Reagan administration, which assumed office in 1981, set to work at once to restigmatize and politicize teenage pregnancy and limit the options and benefits available to pregnant teenage girls. President Ronald Reagan and others began to name teenage pregnancy (and its association with welfare and "welfare queens"), along with the crack cocaine epidemic and inner-city violence, as the chief causes of poverty and other social ills in the United States. Despite the fact that black rates of teenage pregnancy continued to fall in relation to white rates in the 1980s, New Right politicians and political commentators boldly defined teenage pregnancy as a black problem at this time. Also, despite the fact that myriad studies could not prove the charge, politicians accused black teenagers of getting pregnant in order to collect welfare. Public attacks on this vulnerable population were frequent, strident, and counterfactual. In response, advocates and young women themselves raised questions about the New Right agenda as one that cast the teen pregnancies of African American girls as a deeply unacceptable assault on male power and white authority.

During the 1980s, policy initiatives regarding teenage pregnancy turned away from focuses on personal empowerment and choice or public health. Instead policy initiatives embraced abstinence-only education and the importance of economic self-sufficiency for poor young mothers. Abstinence education revived a 1950s theme—that teenage sex was dangerous physically and mentally—and partly because sex and marriage were so frequently uncoupled, youthful sex was also cast as dangerous financially for teen mothers. This retro sex education also drew on the 1950s idea that vulnerable females made bad choices; they were pre-rational "babies having babies."

Meanwhile, Reagan-directed policies cut federal support for a number of programs that could have assisted pregnant teenagers toward self-sufficiency, includ-

Abstinence-only sex education dominated public policymaking regarding teen pregnancy during the 1980s and 1990s. (Associated Press AP)

ing child care, birth control, job training, and public housing programs. Reigning antistatism attitudes in the 1980s mandated that the government minimize its interference in the economy, especially regarding efforts to help vulnerable young mothers and their children. In the 1970s, teen pregnancy was often cast as a result of insufficient access to birth control and abortion. In the 1980s, however, sexual permissiveness (symbolized by teenagers' access to birth control and abortion), welfare programs, and the weak cultural values of minorities were cast as the causes of teen pregnancy.

Tellingly, at this time more than ever before, the sexual activities of young women were becoming more like the sexual activities of young men and youthful white sexual patterns more similar to

youthful black patterns. Far more young white mothers were keeping and raising their babies, as African American young mothers had always done. These new developments were startling and disturbing to many white adults. Yet the willingness to blame and try to constrain young women for their "bad choices" and for causing the worst problems in American society had the effect of deflecting attention from the larger social and economic forces that caused and sustained poverty.

A number of progressive commentators and scholars began to point out in the 1980s that, in the United States, poverty caused teenage pregnancy (80 percent of babies born to teenagers were born to poor teenagers), not the other way around. These voices were typically drowned out by voices demonizing poor, black teen girls who had sex, got pregnant, and sometimes became mothers.

Racialized and politicized concern about teenage pregnancy continued into the 1990s and the era of "welfare reform." During this period, studies showed that 80 percent of the American public and 80 percent of U.S. senators agreed that teenage pregnancy was ruining the country. As before, this heightened concern did not seem to incorporate the news that teenage pregnancy rates were declining steadily, as were teen abortion rates. In 1991, almost two-thirds of teen births were to girls eighteen or nineteen years old. More teens than ever were using birth control, including long-acting contraceptives. By the late 1990s, the teen pregnancy rate was at its lowest level since 1973. Still, teenage pregnancy remained the focus of public worry about abortion, out-of-wedlock births, and sex among unmarried young girls.

It also remained the focus of public hostility to welfare, despite the fact that studies in the 1990s showed that at any given time, more than 90 percent of the women on welfare were not teenagers. (Many women on welfare did enter the rolls as teenage mothers, but three-fourths of the teenagers who have been welfare recipients collected benefits for less than three years.) Crafters of welfare reform foregrounded the problem of teenage pregnancy by featuring abstinence-only sex education, limited access to abortion, and cuts in family planning support but giving scant support for programs focusing on young males. The introductory sections of the Personal Responsibility and Work Opportunity Act of 1996 (welfare reform) presented a raft of statistics indicating that teenage mothers produce inferior children; little attention is given to the impact of poverty and lack of educational and employment opportunities on the decisions of young girls to achieve adulthood via the only available route: motherhood.

Recent legislation and public relations campaigns have emphasized educating teenagers about the financial responsibilities and consumerist aspects of motherhood. The motto of the government's National Strategy to Prevent Teen Pregnancy is, "Don't become a parent until you are truly ready to support a child." A Baltimore anti–teen pregnancy program's slogan is "A baby costs $474 a month. How much is your allowance?" Scholars have shown, however, that because young people, minorities, and women are victims of wage discrimination in the United States, many girls and women could never become mothers without some kind of government assistance. These writers have pointed out that for poor women, delaying motherhood has not helped them avoid poverty. They have also raised questions about the fairness of excluding significant groups of females from motherhood because of their poverty and inability to earn a living wage.

The changing behavior of teenagers over time has pushed the development of public policies that recognize and respond to teenagers' needs. Teenage girls, through their changing relation to sex and reproduction, have forced Americans several times to redefine their notions of respectability, deviance, self-determination, and girlhood itself. At the same time, however, large segments of the American public continue to believe that teenage girls should not have sex, should not get pregnant, and should neither have abortions nor become mothers, especially if they are poor.

Rickie Solinger

See also Adolescent Health; Adoption; Birth Control; Body Image; Female Sexuality; Indentured Servants; Menstruation; Orphans and Orphanages

References and Further Reading
Kaplan, Elaine Bell. 1997. *Not Our Kind of Girl: Unraveling the Myths of Black Teenage Motherhood.* Berkeley: University of California Press.
Ladner, Joyce A. 1971. *Tomorrow's Tomorrow: The Black Woman.* New York: Doubleday.
Luker, Kristin. 1996. *Dubious Conceptions: The Politics of Teenage Pregnancy.* Cambridge, MA: Harvard University Press.
Nathanson, Constance A. 1991. *Dangerous Passage: The Social Control of Sexuality in Women's Adolescence.* Philadelphia: Temple University Press.
Solinger, Rickie. 1992. *Wake Up Little Susie: Single Pregnancy and Race before* Roe v. Wade. New York: Routledge.
Thompson, Sharon. 1995. *Going All the Way: Teenage Girls' Tales of Sex, Romance and Pregnancy.* New York: Hill and Wang.

Teenybopper

A teenybopper is, in the most general terms, a girl in her very early teens with a predilection for popular music and the boys who play it. The word was coined and popularized in the United States sometime in the mid-1960s and is most likely a modernized form of *bobby-soxer*, the name given to the young female admirers of Frank Sinatra. A versatile term, *teenybopper* can be used not only to describe musical artists and genres but also to define an entire subculture of adolescent female fandom.

Teenyboppers were not primarily associated with the performance of pop music until 1968 or 1969. Prior to that time the word was also used to describe any high school–age girl who followed cultural fads. Initially the term possessed a neutral tone; a 1966 *Australia Telegraph* arti-

cle proclaimed that the "teenybopper is aptly named because her two distinguishing features are her teeny size and her cool boppy with-it attitude to life" (quoted in Simpson and Weiner 1989). One year later the term was eroticized in the novel *I Was a Teeny-Bopper for the CIA*, which depicted adolescent Lolly Popstick as a "sizzling teeny-bopper" whose miniskirted body danced seductively at the wrap party for a local drama club. Although these references are admittedly outdated and obscure, the sentiment behind them remains static: teenyboppers are often equated to "little Lolitas" at pop concerts, adolescents who dress with the intention of attracting the attention of a particular teen idol and inadvertently capture the gaze of other men.

In 1968, *teenybopper* was defined by the editors of *Current Slang* as a "young person trying to be a hippie," a change that indicates that the word was derogative even before it became associated with the music industry (Dill and Burkholder 1966, 124). This stigma has persisted ever since. Being called a teenybopper has negative connotations regardless of the context in which it appears; if the reference is positive or neutral the word will often be shortened to "bopper."

It is important to note that the creation of the category "teenybopper" roughly coincided with the rise of bubblegum music, a subgenre of pop that was manufactured specifically by studio-based musicians for preteens. Intending to capitalize on an audience for whom the Beatles were already too advanced, this development reflected the increasing importance of the teenage demographic within the music industry. With more economic capital at their disposal than ever before, girls were able to influence trends in popular culture for the first

Teenyboppers at a Herman's Hermits concert in Washington, D.C. (Wally McNamee/Corbis, 1967)

time. As a result, music groups were created to appeal specifically to this population, a practice that eventually demonstrated a strong connection between age, gender, and musical preferences.

Bubblegum music was generally enjoyed by girls ages ten to fifteen. The genre, pioneered by producer Neil Bogart, is characterized by male teen vocals and a basic lyric structure that revolves around juvenile sexual innuendo. The Monkees are one of the first examples of a bubblegum-influenced marketing phenomenon. Hired to *play* a rock band in the 1966 television show of the same name, the actors eventually *became* a band who recorded and released albums. The group is representative of the entire genre: manufactured, studio-based recordings performed by attractive young

men who were engineered to be the next teen idols.

In one of the earliest references to the word, fans of the Monkees were called "teenyboppers" and "pre-teenyboppers" in an edited collection of their love letters. Although this reference is not necessarily derogatory, it marks the Monkees' fans in another way: teenyboppers are girls who are excessive, unable to control their emotions or distinguish between fantasy and reality. The sentiments expressed in many of the letters indicate that fans believed that they each had a special relationship with Davy Jones, Michael Nesmith, Peter Tork, and Mickey Dolenz. This fantastical belief, that the members of the band were to be considered friends and potential boyfriends, was created and reinforced by the scores of teenybopper fan magazines that were published while bubblegum dominated the radio airwaves. Gloria Stavers's teenybopper publication, *16 Magazine*, achieved its peak circulation during the Monkees' reign.

Bubblegum music is significant because it not only pioneered early conceptions of teenybopper fandom but set the precedent of style over substance in the musical consumption of teenage girls. Bubblegum groups such as Ohio Express, Tommy James and the Shondells, and the 1910 Fruitgum Company flourished in 1968 and 1969 before the genre was transformed into what is today more commonly referred to as "teenybop pop."

In the 1960s and 1970s, radio broadcasters referred to the evening hours as "teenybop drive" because teenagers driving around with friends were thought to make up the majority of the listening audience. Although that term is most likely obsolete, the relationship between youth and pop music has remained solid. Teenybop pop has become synonymous with Top 40 radio. Much like bubblegum music, the genre is primarily a commodity to be marketed and sold to teenage girls. Pop utilizes a specific formula to turn a profit, leaving many to believe that the fans who consume the product are cultural dupes, unsuspecting victims of the machinery of commercialization. This tenet has important repercussions for adolescent girls, for whom the style is specifically created. Pop music and teenyboppers are inexorably linked, and criticisms of the genre are automatically transposed onto its fans.

Distinguishing between "cock rock" and "teenybop," Simon Frith (1981) and Angela McRobbie and Jenny Garber (1975) maintain that males are regarded as active participants in the former,

whereas females are seen as passive consumers of the latter. The melodies themselves are a blend of pop and soft rock, and the lyrics are characterized by frustrated tales of adolescent loneliness. In teenybop ballads, the male teenage performer has either been scorned in love or is seeking a meaningful relationship with a soulmate. Accepted cultural stereotypes are often inverted within this context: teenage girls are portrayed as sexual predators, whereas the boys they heartlessly abandon are looking for serious emotional commitment.

The use of sexuality within teenybop pop is representative of the larger themes of the subculture. Fans are encouraged to believe that they have an individual relationship with the performer and are not merely part of the collective. The vast majority of teenybop songs are sung in the first person; through his words and actions onstage, the performer positions his audience as potential friends or lovers. Despite the glitter of fireworks and pyrotechnic light displays, concerts are framed as intimate gatherings. This paradox obscures the manipulation that lies at the heart of every teenybop phenomenon: these are musical acts that claim sincerity and often attempt to bolster the self-esteem of adolescent girls, yet their primary motivation is financial gain.

Teenybopper fandom is essentially a subculture of consumption, and nothing is more valuable to an adolescent girl than the simulated possession of a teen idol. Teenybop fan magazines help facilitate this fantasy. The earliest and most widely imitated publication was *16 Magazine*. It presented teen idols in a way that readers could understand; articles never focused on music. Editor Gloria Stavers knew that teenyboppers were more interested in what their "fave rave" ate for dinner or what qualities he found most attractive in a girl than the actual songs he sang. The magazine's favored style of prose facilitated an intimate, imagined relationship between fan and performer; much like teenybop songs, features were written in the first person, often resembling personal correspondence.

Teenybop idols are marked by their nonthreatening, feminine mannerisms and appearance. Although there are successful formulas that are typically followed, performers are often cast in response to generational and marketing trends. Each idol enjoys an approximate three-year span of popularity; this cycle makes sense within the context of the subculture. If it is assumed that girls as young as ten become teenyboppers as a safe way of exploring their sexuality, then the idol would logically be abandoned after the girl reached adolescence and was ready for a "real" relationship. Fandom, therefore, is perceived to be innocent. The prepubescent girls who proclaim their love for the teenybop act of the moment do so, it is assumed, without knowledge or experience of the sexual implications of their actions. Although their appearance may at times be similar, teenyboppers and groupies have different intentions.

In contrast to the celebrity singers of the previous decade, the teen idols of the mid-1960s consisted primarily of male music groups. Reflecting the Beatles-initiated British invasion, Herman's Hermits and the Doors were topping charts and stealing the hearts of teenage girls on both sides of the Atlantic. The early 1970s were dominated by family acts, many of whom garnered fan bases from both television and live musical perfor-

mances: the Partridges, Bradys, Osmonds, and Jacksons. That era also produced what some consider to be the three biggest teenybop idols of all time: David Cassidy, Donny Osmond, and Bobby Sherman. However, a teenybopper backlash could be detected by the end of the 1970s. For the first time, potential teen idols resisted the label that had been applied to similar acts for more than a decade. Being associated with teenyboppers was tantamount to professional suicide, and performers with aspirations toward adult singing or acting careers went to great lengths to avoid this stigma.

In the early 1980s, an era marked by heavy metal bands like Bon Jovi, Twisted Sister, and Poison, developing a fan base of adolescent girls was the surest way to lose artistic legitimacy. Singer George Michael declared: "There's nothing wrong with teeny-boppers. They're great kids, but the minute you're lumped with teeny-bopper bands, no one listens to the music anymore" (quoted in Pareles 1985, 24). The development of Music Television (MTV) fostered this belief. Teenyboppers have always been characterized as cultural grazers, fans who follow the hippest band only to move on to the next a few weeks later. The advent of the music video provided exposure for a wide variety of artists, and teenage girls soon began appearing in droves at concerts they would not have otherwise attended, most notably the performances of Duran Duran. However, by the end of the 1980s, the phenomenal success of New Kids on the Block reacquainted teenyboppers with their bubblegum roots.

Newspapers and music industry publications lamented the "dying scream of the teenybopper chorus" just a few years later. With mainstream popular musical styles more representative of the emerging Seattle grunge scene, there was no room on the Billboard charts for the lighter sounds of pop. Scores of fan magazines, both in England and in the United States, reported sagging subscription rates; Britain's teenybopper television show "Top of the Pops" recorded its lowest ratings in thirty-two years. President George Bush, running for reelection in 1992 against Arkansas governor Bill Clinton, briefly returned attention to the word when he rejected an MTV campaign appearance, explaining, "I'm not going to be a teeny-bopper at 68" (quoted in Cummings 1992, 4). Five years later, the trend would reverse itself.

The 1997 success of Hanson instigated the resurgence of bubblegum pop. Music industry insiders credited the reversal to the inherent negativity of grunge. "Angst is tiring after a while," one marketing manager for Virgin Music remarked (quoted in Monk 1997, D9). Following the boy band formula created by Maurice Starr and popularized by New Kids on the Block almost a decade before, groups like the Backstreet Boys and N'Sync inspire a new generation of teenyboppers. This demographic has begun to attract the attention of academics and marketers alike; it is estimated that by 2010, there will be 35 million teenagers living in the United States, the largest number in the nation's history. That projection, combined with the growing scholarship on adolescent girls, marks teenybop as an important new topic for cultural analysis.

Teenybop is considered one of the most accessible subcultures for adolescent girls because membership is not contingent upon location, socioeconomic, or class status. For many preteen girls, teenybopper fandom is thought to facilitate the transition from childhood to adolescence. Frith and McRobbie and Garber have all prefaced their analyses of girls and subcultures with the assumption that girls do not have, for varying reasons, the same access to public spaces as their male counterparts. This limitation is precisely the element that makes teenybopper fandom so attractive; it can be, for the most part, carried out within the girl's bedroom. As a subculture, teenybopper fandom is located primarily within the girl's home and can be picked up or discarded at will. This practice, called "bedroom culture," is essentially commercial in nature and involves the purchase of inexpensive fan magazines and merchandise. Bedroom culture remains prevalent today, despite increasing opportunities for girls in sports or after-school activities. The most obvious exception to this is, of course, the pop music concert. Within the context of this venue girls possess, for at least a couple of hours, a freedom to express themselves that is unmatched in any public space besides the local shopping mall.

There are indications that teenybopper fandom is evolving. Frith's assertion that girls grow out of the fantasy sexuality of teenybop as they begin to date and go out with boys more seriously is negated by the fact that many bands maintain an active fan base for years, sometimes even decades, after reaching peak popularity. A recent Monkees reunion tour sold out venues across the country; an annual New Kids on the Block convention is bringing fans together ten years after the teenybopper group stopped touring and releasing albums.

This phenomenon can be credited, in part, to the nostalgic quality of pop music. Bands are revived to conjure the feelings, fantasies, and memories of their fans' youth. Yet there is paradox building within the subculture that cannot be ignored: in an effort to maximize profits, producers of teenybop pop have begun to target younger and younger audiences. Originally, the subculture encompassed girls ages ten to fifteen; that market has spiraled downward with each succeeding generation. Girls as young as five years old are now encouraged to become teenyboppers. It has become common for groups like N'Sync and the Backstreet Boys to have both preschool and adult fans.

The transgenerational attraction of teenybop bands might be related to the fact that today's adolescents most likely had mothers who loved the Beatles or the Monkees and can therefore identify with, or at least appreciate, their daughters' hysterical fandom. This wide range of popularity obviously leads to increased profits, so record labels are happy to indulge the nostalgia factor by manufacturing more groups in their image. Yet there are larger implications to this practice that must be considered.

One of the benefits of teenybop subculture is that membership carries few risks involving personal humiliation or degradation and provides emotional benefits that come with the vicarious expression of sexuality. This idea can be extended to the culture as a whole. Teenyboppers are inherently placed in a subordinate position in society. To be marked in such a negative way at the onset of adolescence could have lifelong repercussions for girls whose sense of self is defined by this affiliation, a phenomenon that Ien Ang (1998) terms "the ideology of mass culture." In her study of *Dallas* viewers, Ang found that a fan's sense of self-worth was connected to the perceived value of the popular culture products that he or she consumes. Therefore, individuals who derive pleasure from "inferior" texts like soap operas or pop music risk not only their position in the cultural hierarchy but their self-esteem as well. Teenage girls are particularly vulnerable to this classification.

The exact ways in which girls use pop music, the ways in which they recode it for their own purposes, have not yet been completely identified. There is, however, causal evidence that suggests that teenyboppers might use the concert venue as a site of cultural rebellion. Usually the object of what Laura Mulvey (1989) calls "the male gaze," girls have the power to subvert this phenomenon for two hours during a pop music performance. Within the frame of the concert, girls have the power to actively consume a male image, a privilege traditionally denied to them by the dominant culture.

The prognosis for the genre and its fans is good. After dominating the airwaves and concert halls for nearly half a century, teenybop pop is likely never to go out of style. The adolescent girls who classify themselves as teenyboppers increasingly do so with a sense of affiliation and agency.

Kristen Kidder

See also Consumer Culture; Fan Clubs; Girl Power; Girls' Magazines; Movies, Adolescent Girls in; Punk Rock; Riot Grrrls; Television

References and Further Reading
Adler, Bill, ed. 1967. *Love Letters to the Monkees*. New York: Popular Library.
Ang, Ien. 1998. "*Dallas* and the Ideology of Mass Culture." Pp. 265–274 in *Cultural Theory and Popular Culture: A Reader*. Edited by John Storey. Athens: University of Georgia Press.
Cummings, Jeanne. 1992. "Election '92 TV's Starring Role." *Atlanta Journal and Constitution* (November 1): C4.

Dill, Stephen H., and Clyde Burkholder, eds. 1966. *Current Slang.* Vol. 1. Vermillion: University of South Dakota.

Ehrenreich, Barbara, Elizabeth Hess, and Gloria Jacobs. 1986. "Beatlemania: Girls Just Want to Have Fun." Pp. 84–106 in *The Adoring Audience: Fan Culture and Popular Media.* New York: Routledge.

Fiske, John. 1989. *Reading the Popular.* Boston: Unwin Hyman.

Frith, Simon. 1981. *Sound Effects: Youth, Leisure, and the Politics of Rock 'n' Roll.* New York: Pantheon Books.

Mark, Ted. 1967. *I Was a Teeny-Bopper for the CIA.* New York: Berkley.

McRobbie, Angela, and Jenny Garber. 1975. "Girls and Subcultures." Pp. 209–222 in *Resistance through Rituals: Youth Subcultures in Post-War Britain.* Edited by Stuart Hall and Tony Jefferson. New York: Holmes and Meier.

Monk, Katherine. 1997. "Resurgence of Bubblegum Pop Takes Music Industry by Surprise." *Ottawa Citizen* (April 7): D9.

Mulvey, Laura. 1989. *Visual and Other Pleasures.* Bloomington: Indiana University Press.

Pareles, Jon. 1985. "The Pop Life: Wham Facing Up to New Popularity." *New York Times* (February 13): C24.

Reisfeld, Randi, and Danny Fields. 1997. *Who's Your Fave Rave?* New York: Boulevard Books.

Simpson, J. A., and E. S. C. Weiner, eds. 1989. *The Oxford English Dictionary.* New York: Oxford University Press.

Television

Since television was first mass-marketed to Americans in the late 1940s, girls have been included in its various programs, appearing primarily in prime-time situation comedies (sit-coms) and, to a lesser extent, in dramatic series and made-for-TV movies. Girls have also appeared in morning cartoons and in prime-time animated series. Although television programs focusing on young people traditionally have privileged boys over girls, there have been many shows that feature female youth as lead characters, a trend particularly noticeable in the 1960s and 1990s.

Most girls in television programs are white, heterosexual, middle-class suburbanites between the ages of eight and eighteen. Television plots involving female youth usually center on their moral, social, and physical development, and many place them in activities stereotypically associated with female youth, such as obsessing about boys. More recently, however, television series featuring girls are including contemporary concerns of female youth, such as sports, sexual initiation, and preparing for college. As in real life, girls on television have relationships primarily with family members, friends, schoolmates, and teachers and are depicted typically in the homes of families and friends (especially girls' bedrooms), schools, and teen hangouts, such as fast-food restaurants. Older girls are also shown in after-school jobs and other extracurricular activities.

The history of girls on television goes back to the introduction of this medium. In an attempt to attract audiences during the early years, many successful radio programs were adapted to television. Early sit-coms like *The Goldbergs* (CBS/NBC; 1949–1954) and *Mama* (CBS; 1949–1957), which featured ethnic, working-class, urban-dwelling families with children, connected audiences to a collective memory of U.S. history and explained transformations occurring in postwar American society. New values, such as the privileging of consumerism, were associated on these shows primarily with younger characters. As postwar prosperity encouraged the pursuit of the American Dream via suburban life, a distinct transformation in television programming began to develop by the early 1950s. In contrast to televi-

Mia Farrow in a scene from Peyton Place.
(Photofest)

sion's original family shows, the sit-coms that emerged during the mid- to late 1950s—*The Adventures of Ozzie and Harriet* (ABC; 1952–1966), *Father Knows Best* (CBS/NBC; 1954–1962), *Bachelor Father* (CBS/NBC/ABC; 1957–1962), *Leave It to Beaver* (CBS/ABC; 1957–1963), and *The Donna Reed Show* (ABC; 1958–1966)—focused on white, middle-class, nuclear families living in suburbia. These shows established many of the conventions still used in domestic sit-coms today.

Although the gender politics of the immediate postwar period contributed to the privileging of male youth in many early sit-coms, often at the expense of exploring girls' experiences, female youth had considerably more representational space in programs introduced in the late 1950s, such as *Father Knows Best, The Donna Reed Show,* and *Bachelor Father.* As with earlier shows, the girls on these sit-coms often functioned as romantic interests of male characters, yet they also served as the center of story lines that explored the transformation of female roles in the postwar United States. For example, these shows often depicted girls as having nondomestic ambitions in addition to their primary objectives of being wives and mothers. *Father Knows Best* was unique in its portrayal of two sisters of different ages, a technique that allowed audiences to experience the many stages of girls' lives, especially the androgyny of prepubescent girlhood.

As female youth received greater recognition during the late 1950s and early 1960s for their important place within our consumerist economy, five sit-coms were introduced that centered specifically on teenage girls: *Too Young to Go Steady* (NBC; 1959), *The Patty Duke Show* (ABC; 1963–1966), *Karen* (NBC; 1964–1965), *Gidget* (ABC; 1965–1966), and *Tammy* (ABC; 1965–1966). As their titles suggest, the keystones of these sit-coms were the female adolescents who held together narratives exploring the unique experiences of modern girlhood. *Too Young to Go Steady,* television's first girl-centered series, dealt with the sexual awakening of fourteen-year-old Pam Blake (Brigid Bazlen). *The Patty Duke Show,* the longest running of the 1960s' girl sit-coms, revolved around the teen exploits of Patty Lane and her identical Scottish cousin, Cathy (both played by Patty Duke). *Karen* focused on the experiences of urban adolescent Karen Scott (Debbie Watson), and *Gidget* involved the adventures of Frances "Gidget" Lawrence (Sally Field), a trendy teen who lived in California. *Tammy,* like *Gidget,* was adapted from a popular film series and focused on eighteen-year-old Tammy Tarleton (also played by Debbie Watson), who lived with her relatives on a houseboat in the rural South and worked as a secretary for a plantation owner.

As the first television programs to focus specifically on the experiences of female youth, *Too Young to Go Steady, The Patty Duke Show, Karen, Gidget,* and *Tammy* crystallized many of the representational and narrative strategies relied upon in future programs about girls, including the use of voice-over narration and direct address to convey girls' thoughts. These sit-coms regularly included story lines about girls' obsessions with their appearance, as well as their assimilation into the world of heterosexual relations, especially their "first crushes" and initial dating experiences. However, given the difficulty of representing sexuality on television during the 1960s, these shows devised several ways of depicting girls' emerging sexuality without offending morally conservative audiences and advertisers. For example, by privileging the girls' relationships with other female youth above those with boys, these sit-coms reinforced the primacy of same-sex friendships during girlhood. In addition, these shows often portrayed the strong relationships the girls had with their families. As much as these shows, like earlier sit-coms, reproduced the traditional notion that "a woman's place is in the home" and their characters often spoke of marriage as one of their primary goals, the girls' independent and assertive attitudes suggested that as they aged they most likely would pursue additional goals, including college and work outside the home.

Unfortunately, the success of the 1960s girl shows was short-lived, as Americans became more enamored of young adults and the social and political conflicts of the time. During the late 1960s to the late 1980s, many family and school shows included girls in their mixed-sex, multigenerational casts; however, female youth were seldom the focus of such programs. Girl characters during this period often reproduced stereotypes about the primary interests of female youth: their appearance, shopping, and boys. Although both *The Brady Bunch* (ABC; 1969–1974) and *The Partridge Family* (ABC; 1970–1974) featured their girl characters in episodes about feminism, most television shows shied away from exploring such controversial issues. Fortunately, there were several series that emerged during the 1970s and 1980s that signaled transformations occurring in American girlhood, including *One Day at a Time* (CBS; 1975–1984), *Family* (ABC; 1976–1980), *The Facts of Life* (NBC; 1979–1988), *The Cosby Show* (NBC; 1984–1992), and *Roseanne* (ABC; 1988–1997).

One Day at a Time focused on a divorced mother and her two daughters, a premise that allowed the show to address the difficulties women and girls were facing at a time when gender norms were changing dramatically in American society. Although the younger sister Barbara (Valerie Bertinelli) represented an old-fashioned type of girlhood, her older sister Julie (MacKenzie Phillips) signified a liberated form of female identity by exhibiting qualities typically associated with male adolescents, such as rebelliousness and independence. The two sisters' emerging sexual identities received considerable attention on this show, which was the first to candidly approach the subject of girls' premarital sexual activity.

Marcia and Cindy Brady in a scene from The Brady Bunch. *(Photofest)*

Another television show that explored contemporary social issues was *Family*, a dramatic series that revolved around a Californian working couple and their children. The younger daughter, Buddy (Kristy McNichol), was the center of many episodes, and as she aged, several plots focused on issues of concern to contemporary youth, such as homosexuality and substance abuse. As an assertive and physically confident tomboy, Buddy became a role model for many female youth who identified with her nontraditional approach to girlhood.

Of the several school-oriented shows that emerged during the late 1970s and early 1980s, *The Facts of Life* was the only sit-com to feature girls. Centered on a prestigious girls' boarding school in New York, the show originally included seven girl characters, several of which were cut in its second season so as to focus more specifically on a smaller group. The primary girl characters on the show were Blair Warner (Lisa Whelchel), a rich, attractive girl; Tootie Ramsey (Kim Fields), a gossip and television's first middle-class African American girl; Natalie Green (Mindy Cohn), an impressionable girl; and Jo Polniazek (Nancy McKeon), a tough, independent girl. *The Facts of Life* was one of the first television shows to portray girls outside the family home. In turn, it was one of the first to depict girls moving from high school to college and, finally, into adult life.

Another program to feature several girls transitioning from girlhood to womanhood was *The Cosby Show*. Although this series was known best for resurrecting the happy, wholesome nuclear family of earli-

A scene from The Facts of Life. *(Photofest)*

er sit-coms, *The Cosby Show*'s focus on middle-class African Americans was groundbreaking. With several girl characters between the ages of five and twenty, the show allowed viewers to experience the full spectrum of female subjectivity, particularly from an African American perspective. Although several of the Cosby daughters displayed traditional forms of femininity through their primary interests in dating and shopping, one of the daughters, Denise (Lisa Bonet), represented an independent and assertive personality more in keeping with contemporary women. When Denise left home to attend college, a spin-off series called *A Different World* (NBC; 1987–1993) was created, making it the first television show to focus on a black woman in college.

Although most shows featuring girls on television have depicted middle-class families, several series from the 1980s focused on the difficulties working-class families faced during the Reagan era. *Roseanne*'s primary focus was on the mother character (played by Roseanne Barr/Arnold), who, along with her two daughters, sister, mother, and female friends, constructed a matriarchal family environment. In keeping with the show's alternate view of American families, the younger daughter, Darlene (Sara Gilbert), was an intelligent and cynical young woman into sports, vegetarianism, and horror comic books who eventually left home to pursue a college education and prepare for her career. With witty, sarcastic repartee that rivaled that of her mother, Darlene became a role model for many girls who identified with her independent and assertive personality and nontraditional interests.

Since 1990, female youth have been featured in more than ten television series, the largest number of girl-centered shows since the mid-1960s. Many transformations have occurred in television's representations of girlhood in recent years. Although girls still appear primarily in family and school sit-coms, several shows feature girls as lead characters in action dramas. In addition, programs that focus on girls no longer present marriage and motherhood as their primary objectives, and girls often discuss their nondomestic plans for life after high school, including college and careers. This does not mean that these girls are no longer interested in boys; in fact, many female youth in contemporary television still give romance and male attention high priority in their lives. Although girls are typically not explicitly as sexually active, several shows have made a point of exploring the conflicting emotions girls have over their first sexual experiences. Perhaps most significantly, the worlds in which today's television girls live are more culturally and racially diverse than ever before. Shows like *Sister, Sister* (ABC/WB; 1994–1999), *Moesha* (UPN; 1996–present), and *The Mystery Files of Shelby Woo* (Nickelodeon; 1996–1999) have pushed the traditional boundaries of television by privileging nonwhite characters and cultures. (*The Mystery Files of Shelby Woo* is the first television program to star an Asian American girl.) In turn, an increasing number of shows featuring white girls include nonwhite youth as secondary characters. Unfortunately, the experiences of working-class girls continue to be underrepresented,

and adolescent lesbians are rarely depicted in prime-time television.

Contemporary shows featuring girls can be broken down into three main genres: sit-coms, dramatic series, and animated cartoons. The first girl sit-com of the 1990s was *Blossom* (NBC; 1991–1995), which starred Mayim Bialik as Blossom Russo, a smart, responsible white teen growing up in a dysfunctional, male-dominated family in a Los Angeles suburb. *Clarissa Explains It All* (Nickelodeon; 1991–1994) focused on Clarissa Darling (Melissa Joan Hart), an assertive blonde teen who attempted to educate young people about how to grow into responsible and confident individuals. *The Baby-Sitters Club* (HBO; 1991) was a short-lived attempt to adapt for television Ann M. Martin's popular book series about a group of adolescent girls who work part-time as babysitters. One of the first shows to tap into the increasing number of girls participating in sports was *Phenom* (ABC; 1993–1994), a sit-com that focused on the experiences of Angela Doolan (Angela Goethals), who struggled to balance her extraordinary talent as a tennis player with her desire to grow up as a normal teen. *Sister, Sister*, the first television program to star African American girls, borrows its premise from the film *The Parent Trap*. The show features Tia Landry and Tamera Campbell (Tia and Tamera Mowry), identical twins who were separated at birth and reunited during adolescence. Another show to feature a black girl is *Moesha*, which focuses on Moesha Mitchell (played by music star Brandy Norwood), a teenager who lives with her family in Leimert Park, a multicultural neighborhood in Los Angeles. Like many other girl sit-coms, this show focuses on Moesha's dilemma of remaining loyal to her family and friends while struggling to find an independent identity. In the fantasy sit-com *Sabrina, the Teenage Witch* (ABC; 1996–present), adapted from the comic book series by the same name, Sabrina Spellman (Melissa Joan Hart) struggles with growing up as both a "mortal" and a witch. *Clueless* (ABC/UPN; 1996–1999), adapted from the blockbuster film by the same name, focused on a group of overprivileged teens living in Beverly Hills, including Cher (Rachel Blanchard), the show's protagonist and narrator; Dionne (Stacey Dash), her best friend; and Amber (Elisa Donovan), their catty rival.

One of the most popular dramatic series of the 1990s to include girls as primary characters was *Beverly Hills, 90210* (Fox; 1990–2000), the first prime-time serial to feature teenagers since *Peyton Place* (ABC; 1964–1969). By relying on strategies used in the prime-time soap operas of the 1980s, this show appealed to its audiences through a combination of melodrama and realism as it attempted to present the various problems facing contemporary teens and, more recently, young adults. Although *Beverly Hills, 90210* was transformed considerably over its lengthy run, it always included a variety of girl characters, including Brenda Walsh (Shannen Doherty), who at the show's start had recently moved with her family to Beverly Hills; Kelly Taylor (Jennie Garth), a snobbish rich girl who became Brenda's best friend; and Donna Martin (Tori Spelling), Kelly's and Brenda's naive friend.

The first dramatic series of the 1990s to feature a girl in the starring role was *My So-Called Life* (ABC; 1994–1995), which focused specifically on the coming-of-age experiences of an introspective fifteen-year-old named Angela Chase (Claire Danes). In this show, Angela dealt with conflicts in her own family as well as among her friends and schoolmates, particularly Rayanne (A. J. Langer), who exposed her to the less conformist experiences of contemporary girlhood. Like many other television shows featuring sisters, *My So-Called Life* contrasted the increasingly independent Angela with her younger, less experienced sister, Danielle (Lisa Wilhoit).

Although *My So-Called Life* portrayed the internal experiences of contemporary female adolescence, *The Mystery Files of Shelby Woo*, *The Secret World of Alex Mack* (Nickelodeon; 1994–1998), and *Buffy the Vampire Slayer* (WB; 1997–present) focus on the chaos of girls' external worlds and their abilities to bring order to those spheres. Although there are many differences between these three action-oriented dramatic series, especially in terms of their target audiences and production budgets, they each represent an alternative to other girl-centered programs previously (and currently) on the air, which tend to reproduce stereotypes about female youth. Most significantly, each of these dramatic series features a girl in the traditionally male role of action hero and in doing so embraces the concept of "girl power," the idea that female youth are intelligent, confident, assertive, and powerful. In turn, each of these shows privileges the qualities of loyalty and support by teaming its lead girl character with another girl and boy, who help her to solve mysteries, track criminals, or fend off demons.

Many contemporary cartoons include girl characters in their casts, but several recent animated programs make a more direct appeal to female viewers by featuring girls as lead characters. *The PowerPuff Girls* (Cartoon Network; 1998–present) focuses on a group of young girls who are action heroes, whereas *Pepper Ann* (ABC; 1997–present) and *Daria* (MTV; 1997–present) have more realistic portrayals of older female youth. *Pepper Ann* focuses on Pepper Ann Pearson, a junior high student who is undergoing the transformation from childhood to adolescence. Significantly unlike other cartoons, *Pepper Ann* has themes more common to real girls' experiences, such as developing acne and purchasing a first bra. Produced for an older teen/young adult audience, *Daria* (a spin-off of *Beavis and Butt-head* [MTV; 1993–1997]) focuses on the experiences of sixteen-year-old Daria Morgendorffer, a disaffected yet highly intelligent girl who, along with her best friend Jane Lane, has little respect for the conformist members of her community.

The proliferation of girls on television in the 1990s is no doubt due both to the increasing number of women involved in the television industry today and to commercial attempts to appeal to the female youth audience. In addition, the increase in programming slots made available through cable and satellite delivery systems has made room for numerous shows that specifically focus on and are produced for girls. Indeed, with the Fox Family Channel's introduction of the Girlz Channel, we may see more portrayals of girls in the twenty-first century than ever before.

Mary Celeste Kearney

See also Consumer Culture; Movies, Adolescent Girls in

References and Further Reading
Denis, Christopher Paul, and Michael Denis. 1992. *Favorite Families of TV.* New York: Citadel Press.
Kearney, Mary Celeste. 1998. "Girls, Girls, Girls: Gender and Generation in Contemporary Discourses of Female Adolescence and Youth Culture." Ph.D. diss., University of Southern California.
Leibman, Nina C. 1995. *Living Room Lectures: The Fifties Family in Film and Television.* Austin: University of Texas Press.
Lipsitz, George. 1992. "The Meaning of Memory: Family, Class, and Ethnicity in Early Network Television." Pp. 71–108 in *Private Screenings: Television and the Female Consumer.* Edited by Lynn Spigel and Denise Mann. Minneapolis: University of Minnesota Press.
Luckett, Moya. 1997. "Girl Watchers: Patty Duke and Teen TV." Pp. 95–116 in *The Revolution Wasn't Televised: Sixties Television and Social Conflict.* Edited by Lynn Spigel and Michael Curtin. New York: Routledge.
Taylor, Ella. 1989. *Prime-Time Families: Television Culture in Postwar America.* Berkeley: University of California Press.

Temple, Shirley

A child motion picture star in the 1930s, Shirley Temple continued making movies until 1949. After signing her first contract with Educational Studios in 1932, she performed in twelve short films. By 1934 she had signed with Twentieth-Century Fox and made seven feature films, including *Little Miss Marker* (Paramount, 1934, loan), one of her greatest triumphs. During the next five years, Americans of all ages found inspiration in the way Shirley Temple acted, danced, and sang her way through the Great Depression. In 1940, at the age of twelve, her mother bought out her contract with Fox, and Shirley signed with Metro-Goldwyn-Mayer. During the 1940s "the World's darling" grew up, got married, had a daughter, and got divorced. In the 1950s, after marrying Charles Black and becoming an ordinary housewife, she had two more children. She returned to show business in 1957, ran for Congress in 1967, and in 1974 became the U.S. ambassador to Ghana.

Temple is significant to the history of American girlhood because she influenced many young girls to pursue their dreams. By creating an on-screen image of hope, she allowed girls to overcome insecurity. She represented positive and animated energy at a time of great despair and gave girls a respite from an economically and socially tumultuous world. Little girls as well as teenage girls identified with her.

Shirley Jane Temple was born on April 23, 1928, to George and Gertrude Temple in Santa Monica, California. Her parents adored their only daughter: Gertrude described her daughter as a "sunny and pretty child" (Basinger 1975, 19). According to her mother, Shirley was given an extra amount of attention even before she was born. George was able to pay for dance lessons for Shirley by the time she turned three years old. At the dance school, she was discovered in 1934 by Charles Lamont, a director and talent scout at Educational Studios.

Lamont cast Shirley in a series of movies called the "Baby Burlesks" and paid her $10 a day and, later on, $50 a picture. The series included *War Babies* (1932), *The Runt Page* (1932), *Pie Covered Wagon* (1932), *Glad Rags to Riches* (1932), *Kid's Last Fight* (1933), *Kid in Hollywood* (1932), *Polly-Tix in Washington* (1933), *and Kid in Africa*. She met all the Baby Burlesk requirements, which included height, curly hair, bright teeth, infectious smile, and a distinctive personality. She was cast in old comedy favorites that featured kids in satires on the popular movies of the day. In short films such as *Glad Rags to Riches* (1932) and *War Babies* (1932), the children were dressed in adult costumes on the top and diapers on the bottom. The combination of adult and baby attire appealed to both young and teenage girls in the audience. Shirley made four major films outside of her work on the "Bay Burlesques" series in 1932, six in 1933, and three in 1934 for Educational Studios, and was loaned out to Tower Productions in 1933 to play a small roll in *Red-Haired Alibi.*

By this time, Gertrude Temple had figured Shirley could get good work as a child actor and took her to casting offices. Shirley appeared in small parts for Paramount's *To the Last Man* (1933) and Universal's comedy *Out All Night* (1933) while under contract to Educational Studios. In 1934, she was given a roll in Paramount's *New Deal Rhythm.* Because of the strong public reaction to her performance in *New Deal Rhythm,* Paramount planned for her to star in *Little Miss Marker* after completing her contract with Educational. Paramount waited patiently for Fox to loan Shirley to them for their production of *Little Miss Marker.* In 1934 the film paid off, not only in dollars, but it made Temple a star. Because of its success Shirley Temple became a gold mine for her home studio. Fox was more than happy to bring her home and star her in *Baby Take a Bow* (1934), where, with James Dunn, she sings an audience-pleasing duet, "On Accounta I Love You."

From 1934 until 1940, Shirley acted in seventeen films for Fox and in Paramount's *Now and Forever* (1934), with Gary Cooper and Carole Lombard. During the Great Depression, films such as *Curly Top* (1935), *Poor Little Rich Girl* (1936), and *Rebecca of Sunnybrook Farm* (1938) featured an "overcoming all odds" theme that allowed moviegoing girls and other audience members to forget their troubles for a mere 10 cents.

Curly Top, in which Shirley appears with Easter Dale, John Boles, and Rochelle Hudson, allowed girls in the audience to look into the life of the wealthy, with a home in Southampton, silk pajamas, and a bedroom for the former orphans (Hudson and Temple) decorated in an expensive nautical motif. The theme of poor little orphans escaping poverty and cruelty hit close to home for those trying to survive hard times. *Rebecca of Sunnybrook Farm*, the story of an orphan who becomes a radio performer, also proved to be a hit with audiences down on their luck. It includes everything audiences learned to love about a Temple film. Shirley sings "If I Had One Wish to Make" and "Come and Get Your Happiness," and panders to the power of the box office in one scene in which she sings songs from past movies like "On the Good Ship Lollipop," a favorite number from *Bright Eyes* (1934), and "Animal Crackers in My Soup" from *Curly Top*.

In *Poor Little Rich Girl* (1936) Shirley played in the now-familiar story of the lonely only child with the workaholic father, played by Michael Whalen. The first scene opens with Shirley singing to her expensive doll collection "I Want to Make Mud Pies (Then I Know I'd Find Happiness)." When her father comes home, she snuggles in his lap to sing a romantic ballad, "When I'm with You." Other songs include "But Definitely" and "You've Got to Eat Your Spinach, Baby," sung by Alice Faye. The movie's story line progresses when an automobile strikes Shirley's nanny, who is taking her to boarding school. Shirley then stumbles on two hopeful radio performers, Alice Faye and Jake Haley. The audiences loved the story, and Shirley's performance encompassed everything they had come to see: great timing, excellent dancing, and a charming theme.

Because of her successful acting career, Shirley became a national commodity and helped sell everything from soap to toys. It is estimated the family grossed over $10,000 every ten days, a handsome sum during the Depression. There were Shirley Temple dolls, sheet music, jewelry, clothes, sewing items, and playing cards, to name just a few of the products bearing her name during the 1930s and 1940s.

In 1940 Gertrude Temple bought out the rest of Shirley's contract with Twentieth-Century Fox and announced her daughter's retirement from films. It appears that Gertrude Temple spoke too soon concerning Shirley's retirement, however, because in a short time a contract was signed with Metro-Goldwyn-Mayer (MGM). In 1941 *Kathleen* was released starring Laraine Day, Herbert Marshall, and Gail Patrick. Shirley, appearing as Kathleen, wore her first long dress on-screen and, at age twelve, remained poised and pretty. *Kathleen* did not fare well with the critics, however, and the MGM contract was canceled by mutual consent. Shirley ended her childhood career with an Edward Small Production released through United Artists entitled *Miss Annie Rooney* (1942).

Shortly thereafter, Shirley took two years off from making movies. She attended Miss Westlake's school for girls, where she was popular with her classmates. After graduating, she announced her comeback by signing a personal contract with David O. Selznick. Shirley starred with Claudette Colbert, Jennifer Jones, and Joseph Cotten in *Since You Went Away* (1944), her first Selznick production released by United Artists. In this movie she portrayed some of the childhood charm seen in her earlier performances. Now sixteen years old, she gave her first interview without the presence of her mother. The transition from childhood actor was a success, and Shirley made several other adult movies before announcing her engagement to John George Agar.

The couple married September 19, 1945, at the Wilshire Methodist Church with 15,000 fans waiting outside. Shirley continued to work after the wedding and released *Honeymoon, The Bachelor and the Bobby-Soxer*, and *That Hagen Girl* in 1947 and *Fort Apache* in 1948. After *Fort Apache*, Shirley's daughter was born on January 30, 1948. Although Shirley and her husband starred in several pictures together, the marriage fell apart, and on December 5, 1950, the couple divorced.

Just two weeks after her divorce was finalized, Shirley married Charles Alden Black, a San Francisco businessman. They had met in Hawaii while Shirley was on vacation recovering from her divorce. Black, "a solid citizen," war hero, and the son of a prominent California businessman, held his own next to "the world's darling." He admitted never having seen a Shirley Temple movie. Shirley retired from the screen and became a suburban housewife during the post–World War II period when domesticity and maternity were exalted for women. Black adopted Linda Susan, and together he and Shirley had two more children.

In Atherton, California, Shirley was active in groups such as the Allied Arts Guild, the Peninsula Children's Theatre, and the Sierra Club. By 1957 she agreed to do a television series called *Shirley Temple's Storybook*. The series, sponsored by Breck Hair Products, ran from 1957 through 1961 and was shown on NBC. Shirley continued to act until 1965, when she decided to work instead for the Republican Party as a speaker and fund-raiser.

In 1967 she ran for a seat in Congress after discovering that Representative J. Arthur Younger of California was too ill to run again. Ronald Reagan and George Murphy were among those advising her to run. She lost the seat to Democrat Roy Archibald but went on to make more than 200 speeches that year. In 1969, President Richard Nixon appointed her the U.S. delegate to the United Nations, and President Ford named her ambassador to Ghana in 1974.

In 1972 Shirley discovered she had breast cancer and decided to share her experience with the public. She discussed her operation and her recovery in a *McCall's* magazine article, on the radio, and on television. Her autobiography, *Child Star*, was published in 1988. Shirley Temple Black is a mother and grandmother and lives with her husband of more than fifty years in northern California.

Rita Papini

See also Dolls; Movies, Adolescent Girls in; Pickford, Mary

References and Further Reading
Basinger, Jeanine. 1975. *Shirley Temple: Pyramid Illustrated History of the Movie*. New York: Pyramid Publications.
Black, Shirley Temple. 1988. *Child Star: An Autobiography*. New York: McGraw-Hill Publishing Company.
Smith, Patricia R. 1979. *Shirley Temple Dolls and Collectibles*. 2d series. Paducah, KY: Collectors Books.
Zierold, Norman J. 1965. *The Child Stars*. New York: Coward-McCann.

Tomboys

Tomboys in American fiction provide valuable lenses through which to consider gender identities and autonomy in both public and private. Tomboys appear in stories before and after the Civil War as athletic, often masculine or cross-dressed, female children and adolescents who resist conventional ideals and practices of femininity and obedience to institutional authority. Many of these stories warn that masculine and often dark-complected tomboys, if allowed to reach adulthood unchecked, could refuse feminine behaviors or even engage in public sex (prostitution). Twentieth-century texts add the threat of lesbianism. Tomboy narratives often answer such challenges with abrupt and improbable shifts to "feminine" dress and behavior, Christian obedience to authority, and sudden interest in heterosexual relationships and marriage. These last-minute capitulations seem designed to reassure readers that sex and gender conventions will survive all challenges. The shifts also illustrate the arbitrary nature of the conventions themselves. Tomboy stories—from the etymological origins of the term *tomboy* to the impressive variety of tomboy characters in American literature—illustrate the complexity of cultural work literally "at play" in seemingly straightforward stories of childhood and adolescence.

The *Oxford English Dictionary* (OED) lists a 1553 reference to "whiskyng and ramping abroad like a Tom boy" and another, in 1622, that links masculinity to tomboys through its mention of "short-haired Gentlewomen." Tomboyism has been associated with 1860s theatrical and Beadle dime-novel burlesque conventions, with female cross-dressing and performances of masculinity "a central feature" (Habegger 1982, 173). By 1876, the OED states, Charlotte Mary Yonge's *Womankind* provides a description of the tomboy: "What I mean by 'tomboyism,'" she says, "is a wholesome delight in rushing about at full speed, playing at active games, climbing trees, rowing boats, making dirt-pies, and the

like." The OED also provides a clear connection between the ubiquitous term *tom* in British and American culture ("often a generic name for any male representative of the common people") and working-class promiscuity. A measure of the term's depth as a marker of class and sexuality is that it serves as a prefix for more specialized terms denoting both consumers of sex ("tomcats") and the objects of that consumption ("tomrigs"). *Tom-rig* is synonymous not only with "strumpet" (used since the fourteenth century to denote "prostitute") but also with "romping girl" and "tomboy." The linkage between uncontrollable girls and bad women is explicit in a phrase from Tomson's *Calvin's Sermons* (1579): "Women must not be impudent, they must not be tomboyes, to be shorte, they must not be unchast" (OED 211).

There is an additional etymological layer to the prefix *tom* and its relevance to *tomboys*. The term *tomfool*, used since the fourteenth century to denote a simpleton or buffoon, introduces the element of liminality to the concept of tomboys. "Liminal" figures elude categorization because they invert conventional identities and relationships. Young girls—tomboys—who possess no social or economic power acquire that power by functioning as disobedient, athletic, heroic, entrepreneurial, eccentric, or masculine "bad girls." Whether they appear as major or minor characters, tomboy presences are usually marginalized, enabling them to speak the truth about rigid gender-role expectations.

Since the term *tomboy* itself fuses associations with masculinity, promiscuous sexuality, prostitution, and lesbianism, the figure of the tomboy is more complex than is commonly supposed. The physicality of masculine girls links girls' bodies with physical labor, even when they are engaged in "play." The class anxieties this suggests are complicated by the darkness of tomboys' skin, hair, and eyes, typical features of literary tomboys. Fears of racial contamination and miscegenation also sexualize these figures. Tomboy masculinity is characteristic of most stories about tomboys. In Louisa May Alcott's *Little Women* (1868), Jo March calls herself a "business man" (51) and despises tears as an "unmanly weakness" (76). In E. D. E. N. Southworth's novel *The Hidden Hand* (1859), the orphaned Capitola Black cross-dresses as a newsboy to survive, regretting only "what a fool I had been, not to turn to a boy before, when it was so easy!" (47). Hellfire, protagonist of Mark Twain's short story "Hellfire Hotchkiss" (1897), could swim, skate, fish, boat, hunt, trap, run, and break horses and is described as "the only genuwyne male man in this town" (187). She illustrates the liminality so typical of tomboys: "Hellfire kept the community in an unrestful state; it could settle to no permanent conclusion about her. She was always rousing its resentment by her wild unfeminine ways, and always winning back its forgiveness again by some act or other of an undeniably creditable sort" (196). Hellfire's behavior causes a female moral guardian, Betsy Davis, to warn Hellfire that this has made her the object of "reports" (presumably, rumors of promiscuity).

Gypsy Breynton, another masculine child, receives a similar warning from her mother in *Gypsy's Year at the Golden Crescent* by Elizabeth Stuart Phelps (1867). This female guardian's rebuke addresses gender transgression and, potentially, lesbianism. Mrs. Breynton disapproves of the influence of Jo Courtis, Gypsy's cross-dressing friend, and threatens to send Gypsy to a school "where they will make a boy of you." When Gypsy expresses horror, her mother replies, "Well then, my dear, don't *try* to be a boy. . . .

If you decide to be a woman, be a woman" (184). Meg March reproves Jo in the opening pages of *Little Women:* "You are old enough to leave off boyish tricks, and behave better, Josephine. It didn't matter so much when you were a little girl; but now you are so tall, and turn up your hair, you should remember that you are a young lady" (3). Nearly 500 pages later, Jo finally accedes to class and gender conventions.

In Susan Warner's novel *The Wide, Wide World* (1850), Nancy Vawse receives a more spiritually pointed message from her moral guardian, Ellen Montgomery. Ellen warns Nancy that if she doesn't read the Bible Ellen has given her, she "may have to go where you never can read it, nor be happy nor good neither" (334). The full punitive force of Christian culture, threatening prison, prostitution, and hell, is all implicit in Ellen's warning. Tomboys were often orphaned, and the surrogate moral control imposed by older girls and women provided comfortable reassurances of national self-governance and benevolence.

Pairings of tomboys with sissies are a frequent occurrence in tomboy stories. These linkages seem designed less to correct gender excess than to demonstrate that it *can* be corrected. Pairings of Jo March and Laurie Laurence in *Little Women,* Tommy Shirley and Jay Harper in Willa Cather's "Tommy, the Unsentimental" (1896), Hellfire Hotchkiss and Thug Carpenter in "Hellfire Hotchkiss," Georgiana Isham and a French baron in Phyllis Duganne and Harriet Gersman's story "Tomboy!" (1928), Kerry and Mick in Hal Ellson's *Tomboy* (1950), and Fannie Lou Babcock and Russell in Allyn Allen's *Lone Star Tomboy* (1951) illustrate a near-century of cross-gendered pairs. Tomboys successfully masculinize sissy girls and prevent them from becoming domestic invalids (Ellen is checked by Nancy in *The Wide, Wide World,* and Clara Day is checked by Capitola Black in *The Hidden Hand*), but they are less successful in masculinizing sissy boys. In numerous instances of gender Darwinism, sissy boys simply drop out of their texts.

Tomboy stories present girls and young women as capable of challenging the erotic limitations of sisterly love. Studies of romantic love by several feminist historians suggest that sexuality between girls and women may best be viewed as occurring within a "continuum" of nineteenth-century American homosocial and spiritual cultural relationships (Faderman 1981, Smith-Rosenberg 1985, 75–76). Same-sex desire is unambiguously presented in many texts, however (Willa Cather's "Paul's Case" and "Tommy, the Unsentimental," for example).

Most tomboys are described as dark or strange in some way. Jo March in *Little Women* is "very tall, thin and brown"; Georgiana Isham in "Tomboy!" has a "brown" face and hands; twenty-year-old Val Wakefield in Wenona Gilman's *Val, the Tomboy* (1891) has a "sun-browned face" and "great dark eyes"; Nancy Vawse possesses "bold black eyes"; and Nell Gilbert in Jeannette Gilder's *The Tom-Boy at Work* (1904) has "burning black eyes." Dark or strange girls threaten institutional order with ungovernable play, contempt for authority, working-class indifference to conduct, and a failure to aspire to motherhood.

One of the reasons that the slave child Topsy becomes one of the most memo-rably individuated figures in Harriet Beecher Stowe's *Uncle Tom's Cabin* (1851–1852) is that she uses her body radically—not to work but to *play*—just out of reach of the social, spiritual, and economic systems that govern the St. Clare family and most of their other slaves. Indeed, Topsy's work is, precisely, to play—to deflect authority by bungling the work that defines her as a slave. In this, she resembles Nancy Vawse and many other literary tomboys who cannot be controlled and whose play threatens the most basic assumptions of adult guardians: that the girls in their charge will want, someday, to become like their adult mentors. At first, Topsy seems an unlikely tomboy. Her body is property, and her gender identity—as girl or as woman—is nullified by that status. But what Topsy and many white tomboys share in common is a capacity to reinvent themselves so that throughout most of their narratives, until the intervention of a sudden transformation, institutions of race, class, or gender cannot quite fix on, identify, and harm or destroy them.

An idealized balance between physical and mental exercise proves to be a complex class balancing act, as well, as too little attention to the body can be fatal. Ellen Montgomery's severe Aunt Fortune in *The Wide, Wide World* diagnoses Ellen's mother's illness as having originated from a class-produced imbalance of physical and mental activity: "If she had been trained to use her hands and do something useful instead of thinking herself above it, maybe she wouldn't have had to go to sea for her health" (Warner 1850, 140). Activity that exceeds its value as exercise and is therefore willful, however, exceeds class ideals. When Ellen befriends the lawless "bad girl" Nancy Vawse and returns home dirty and wet from a day with Nancy in the fields and a spill in the creek, Ellen's "exercise" signals intransigence for Aunt Fortune.

Stories about tomboys, along with women's political writing and serialized women's romances, often debate notions of "true womanhood" and the necessity of preserving rigidly polarized men's and women's "spheres." Much of what is assumed about "domesticity," that its most essential features are piety, submission, charity, and the like, is belied by many nineteenth- and twentieth-century women's texts, both fictional and nonfictional. They often promote the following principles: athleticism over invalidism (*The Hidden Hand*) and economic self-sufficiency over reliance upon husbands, fathers, and brothers (*Little Women*; *Ruth Hall* by Fanny Fern, pseudonym for Sarah Parton, 1855). The importance of devaluing artificial gender identities when they limit the capabilities of both men and women is emphasized in contemporary treatises (Margaret Fuller's *Woman in the Nineteenth Century*, 1845; Charlotte Perkins Gilman's *Women and Economics*, 1898).

Few writers of tomboy fiction are listed in encyclopedias of women's writing, and the category "tomboy" is usually missing, as well. These exclusions may signal an editorial policy that distinguishes between "adult" and "children's" literature. In an 1867 article entitled "Books for Young People," Horace E. Scudder noted that "the ordinary classification of 'books for young people' is a very recent one" and that he would "pay no very close attention to the line which divides books written for the young from books written for the old" (quoted in Haviland 1973, 23–24). The line has remained blurred, and tomboy narratives remain unclassified. Some tomboy literature is identifiable through titles, as in George Baker's *Running to Waste: The Story of a Tomboy* (1875) and Jeannette Gilder's *The Autobiography of a Tomboy* (1901), or through categorization as girls' adventure series literature (Gypsy Breynton, Outdoor Girls, Motor Girls, Girl Flyer, and Nancy Drew, for example). The term *tomboy* in a title does not, however, guarantee a tomboy in the text. Anne Pence Davis's *Mimi at Camp: The Adventures of a Tomboy* (1935) features Mimi Hammond, who, because she experiences no gender cross-identification, engages in no significant challenge to authority, and does not represent a problem that her text needs to resolve, is not a tomboy.

More often, tomboys are simply where their readers find them, creating counter-narratives as minor characters (usually) within the master narratives that dramatize the coming-of-age stories of other, more spiritualized girls who are closer to becoming "good women." Thus Topsy counters the story of Eve St. Clare, and Nancy Vawse contests Ellen Montgomery's story. Tomboys dramatize the artificial necessity of requiring girls who usually behave as "boys" to begin to behave, often reluctantly, as "girls" instead.

In the space of a few lines, the tomboy character often sheds masculinity, puts on a dress, becomes a "lady," finds a mate, and marches to the altar. Her gender, class, and sexual ambiguities are thus resolved within a narrative instant. Jo March in *Little Women*, America's best-known tomboy, is forced to abandon her commercially successful Gothic thrillers to write conventional stories with pathos and "heart" instead and to marry paternalistic Professor Bhaer. Alcott's readers have loved Jo not because she married a benevolent figure but because during

Tomboys often cross gender lines in their dress and activities. (Skjold Photographs)

incompetent sissy Jay Harper and then comments (unconvincingly) of men: "They are awful idiots, half of them, and never think of anything beyond their dinner. But O, how we do like 'em!" (Cather 1994, 242). Topsy drops out of Stowe's narrative at Eve's deathbed and only reappears 200 pages later, toward the end of the novel. She is transformed from a child who lies, blackmails, steals, and manipulates to a mature, devout missionary in the space of one paragraph.

The category "tomboy" continues to trouble sex, gender, and class equilibrium. Debates over whether tomboys will become lesbians are still featured in women's magazines, and "makeovers" of masculine girls and women are a staple of television talk shows, demonstrating the continued elusiveness of "true womanhood."

Mary Elliott

See also Body Image; Lesbians; Play; Sports; Surfer Girls

References and Further Reading
Alcott, Louisa May. 1868. *Little Women.* 1989. Reprint, New York: Penguin.
Cather, Willa. 1905. "Paul's Case." Pp. 149–174 in *Willa Cather: Five Stories.* 1956. Reprint, New York: Vintage.
———. 1896. "Tommy, the Unsentimental." Pp. 234–242 in *Chloe Plus Olivia: An Anthology of Lesbian Literature from the Seventeenth Century to the Present.* Edited by Lillian Faderman. 1994. Reprint, New York: Viking/Penguin.
Faderman, Lillian. 1981. *Surpassing the Love of Men: Romantic Friendship and Love between Women from the Renaissance to the Present.* New York: William Morrow.
Gilman, Wenona. 1891. *Val, the Tomboy.* Cleveland: A. Westbrook.
Habegger, Alfred. 1982. "Funny Tomboys." Pp. 172–183 in *Gender, Fantasy, and Realism in American*

most of the novel, she was unique, powerful, independent, and fearless.

Like Jo, tomboys such as Nancy Vawse in *The Wide, Wide World*, Capitola Black in *The Hidden Hand*, Gypsy Breynton in *Gypsy's Year at the Golden Crescent*, and Tommy Shirley in "Tommy, the Unsentimental" all learn their lessons by the end. Nancy is subdued with a Bible, and Capitola perfunctorily marries the noble Herbert Greyson at the close of their respective texts. Gypsy follows her mother's advice to "be a woman," whereas Tommy forfeits her love Jessica to the

Literature. New York: Columbia University Press.

Harris, Susan K. 1990. *Nineteenth-Century American Women's Novels: Interpretative Strategies.* Cambridge: Cambridge University Press.

Haviland, Virginia. 1973. *Children and Literature: Views and Reviews.* Glenview, IL: Scott, Foresman.

Koppelman, Susan, ed. 1994. *Two Friends and Other Nineteenth-Century Lesbian Stories by American Women Writers.* New York: Meridian.

Phelps, Elizabeth Stuart. 1867. *Gypsy's Year at the Golden Crescent.* 1897. Reprint, New York: Dodd, Mead.

Smith-Rosenberg, Carroll. 1985. "The Female World of Love and Ritual: Relations between Women in Nineteenth-Century America." Pp. 53–76 in *Disorderly Conduct: Visions of Gender in Victorian America.* New York: Oxford University Press.

Southworth, E. D. E. N. 1859. *The Hidden Hand, or, Capitola the Madcap.* Edited by Joanne Dobson. 1988. Reprint, New Brunswick, NJ: Rutgers University Press.

Twain, Mark. 1897. "Hellfire Hotchkiss." Pp. 88–133 in *Mark Twain's Satires and Burlesques.* Edited by Franklin R. Rogers. 1967. Reprint, Berkeley: University of California Press.

Warner, Susan. 1850. *The Wide, Wide World.* 1987. Reprint, New York: Feminist Press.

W

Witchcraft

On Halloween many girls today dress up as witches or as one of their familiars, though one that is more sweet than satanic, usually the black cat. But during the most extensive witch hunts in America's past, most notoriously in Salem, colonial girls acted as accusers, not as the accused. Only one little girl, four-year-old Dorcas Good, was ever accused of doing the devil's work. Adolescent girls, many of whom were among the most powerless in communities in the throes of transformation, attributed their afflictions to the demonic spells of adult women.

European folklore and religious beliefs about the supernatural were transported from the old world to the new world by European immigrants. Because colonists lacked the scientific knowledge of later generations, they often attributed strange occurrences to supernatural causes. The sudden death of apparently healthy children or farm animals, an unexplained miscarriage, or other mysterious events could lead one suspicious neighbor to accuse another of witchcraft. Bad luck for some led to rumors that ruined the reputations of others.

In seventeenth-century New England, witchcraft accusations and prosecutions—which began in the 1630s—had been sporadic. Historians have not reached a consensus about why the vast majority of accused witches were female or why some women became scapegoats and others did not. Early interpretations have been challenged by newer findings. For example, initially scholars believed that mostly poor and needy women were the likeliest targets of witchcraft accusations. But in Salem, only a small number among the accused were poor. Instead, a significant proportion of accused witches actually increased their share of family resources by defying accepted principles of inheritance. Scholars also believed that it was unruly women who became victims of male supremacy. Social deviants offended neighbors angered by abrasive, argumentative, assertive, or aggressive behavior. But only one of the accused in Salem fits this description. In the eyes of her suspicious neighbors, pitiful Sarah Good—pregnant, poor, and homeless—could also be quite difficult.

Further research has revealed a complicated picture of the past. For instance, recent findings suggest that those women who became easy targets lacked the protection of a husband—either because he was abusive (as was the case with Bridget Oliver Bishop), dead, or too poor to initiate a legal suit against slander. But *not* having children or having too few could have similar dire consequences. Because Puritans valued fertility, childless, infertile, and menopausal women were also

A bewitched girl in Salem, Massachusetts reveals demonic possession before Puritan ministers and an accused witch. (Hulton Getty/Archive Photos)

suspected of cavorting with the devil. (The vast majority of witches were middle-aged.) Such might have been the case, especially after an inexplicable illness afflicted a child. But even women healers, many of whom used charms, incantations, and herbal potions to cure the sick, were also targeted. Although there is still no uniform profile, all agree that those accused of witchcraft challenged the patriarchal standards of Puritan society in one way or another.

Such was the case in early January 1692, when girls between the ages of nine and nineteen became the principal witchcraft accusers in Salem, Massachusetts, an old farming town in the midst of dramatic transformation. In the colonial kitchen, nine-year-old Betty Parris, the daughter of the minister of Salem Village; her cousin, eleven-year-old Abigail Williams; and their friends used supernatural powers to predict the identity of their future husbands. Their queries about the future occurred against a backdrop of profound political, economic, cultural, and social change in New England. The declining Puritan commonwealth was becoming a royal regime. Salem itself was in the process of transition. Salem Village, where the accusers lived, was inhabited by those ill at ease with the new and nearby commercial and secular culture of Salem Town. This bustling seaport was the home of, but not a haven for, accused witches. Samuel Parris's daughter Betty spent her time with Tituba, the Parrises' slave. On occasion when Parris was away, Tituba taught Betty, Abigail, and other neighborhood girls about divining. She told them African voodoo tales and instructed them in how to bake "witch cakes." (All that is known about Tituba is that she was married to a Native American, John Indian, and that she was from Barbados, an important sugar-producing region and a central stop on international trade routes.)

Not long after their divining activities, however, the girls began to experience nightmares, have violent fits and convulsions, become disoriented, bark, spit, and refuse nourishment. Nor were they alone; other young girls in other towns (as far away as Boston) also revealed strange symptoms and exhibited mysterious behavior in private as well as in public.

Gripped by fears of a demonic conspiracy, Samuel Parris and others in Salem suspected the girls of being bewitched. An avalanche of charges led to the jailing of dozens of villagers from twenty-four different towns over the next four months. In court, the girl accusers described their torment at the hands of witches. All but one of the accused maintained their innocence. Tituba vividly described witches' Sabbaths, spectral yellow birds, and night flights on broomsticks. Indeed, helping the victims required the discovery of the guilty: "Possession by the devil might be cured by a regimen of prayer, fasting, and repentance; victims of bewitchment, however, could not be cured until the guilty were found—and punished or destroyed" (Berkin 1996, 48–49). In all, 156 people were accused; 14 of the 19 hanged on "Witch Hill" were women.

Although historians of the "new" women's history have broken ground in their examination of witches, they have overlooked their juvenile accusers. What factors and forces led adolescent girls to challenge their elders? How can the deadly conflict between generations of females be understood?

Perhaps no residents of Salem felt greater insecurity about their future than did the female adolescent accusers. The status of women in colonial New England—constricted and constrained—had become even more precarious by the late 1600s. Specters of spinsterhood or widowhood were all around them. Some of the afflicted girls had been recently orphaned in Indian attacks in Maine. Without families to provide for them, they worked as domestic servants in local Salem households. Without dowries, they were less competitive in the marriage market. As orphans, domestic servants, children, and females, they were among the most powerless in Puritan society. Even though the Puritan experiment was reaching an end, the society and culture still placed strict limits on girls' lives and opportunities for the future.

Such was also the case for three of the afflicted girls whose future dowries and inheritances were in the process of litigation. Moreover, there were increasingly fewer eligible or desirable bachelors in Salem because many were migrating to other parts of New England and New York State in search of land; the frequent division of ancestral holdings among Puritans had left them with too little to support a family. Prospects in Salem were even bleaker for vulnerable unmarried girls whose anxious uncertainty was probably a contributing factor to extreme psychological stress (a condition today referred to as "hysterical conversion").

Miriam Forman-Brunell

See also Puritan Girls

References and Further Reading

Berkin, Carol. 1996. *First Generations: Women in Colonial America.* New York: Hill and Wang, chap. 2.

Boyer, Paul, and Stephen Nissenbaum. 1974. *Salem Possessed: The Social Origins of Witchcraft.* Cambridge, MA: Harvard University Press.

———. 1993. *Salem Village Witchcraft: A Documentary Record of Local Conflict in Colonial New England.* Boston: Northeastern University Press.

Hall, David D. 1991. *Witchcraft in Seventeenth-Century New England: A Documentary History, 1638–1692.* Boston: Northeastern University Press.

Kamensky, Jane. 1995. *The Colonial Mosaic: American Women 1600–1760.* New York: Oxford University Press, chap. 5.

Karlsen, Carol. 1987. *The Devil in the Shape of a Woman: Witchcraft in Colonial New England.* New York: W. W. Norton.

Work

Idealized conceptions of girls sheltered from toil and productive economic activity have cloaked the fact that girls in America have always worked. True, much of their labor has been disguised as "chores," the unremunerated duty of daughters, the economic benefits of which have yet to be calculated. But whether they earned appreciation, a wage, or its equivalent (room and board), girl workers have played an indispensable role in American economic development. For many thousands of years before European settlement, for example, Native American girls worked as agriculturists in a variety of subsistence economies. So did seventeenth-century Anglo-American girls, who worked as indentured servants in the colonial South or as apprenticed or bound servants in the Northeast. Born into a lifetime of service, African American girls were forced to contribute to the plantation economy by providing day care for white children as well as enslaved ones. At the beginning of the nineteenth century, swarms of farmers' daughters who worked in the new nation's textile mills became first proletariat, and working-class girls in the street trades contributed to the development of the urban industrial economy. As scavengers, girls also fueled informal economies, and as thieves and prostitutes, they participated in underground economies.

Immigrant Jewish and Italian girls who worked as pieceworkers and factory operatives contributed to the urban industrial economy at the turn of the twentieth century. As babysitters and defense workers during both world wars, girls worked for the good of the country; they grew Victory gardens and recycled scrapped goods that benefited the war industry. The expansion of the service economy since World War II has benefited from girls who have labored often as part-time workers in low-wage, sex-segregated jobs. That girls' work has continued into the twenty-first century has been fueled by high divorce rates, immigration, the feminization of poverty, second- and third-wave feminism, a consumer culture targeted at teens, and changing ideals about childhood, youth, girlhood, and female adolescence. "What do you want to be when you grow up?" we ask girls as if it were entirely up to them. Although women in the twenty-first century have a far greater range of career choices available to them, what most girls do not realize is that their first job is likely to be a feminized one, dominated by low-paid female workers doing low-status work with little opportunity for upward mobility.

Before 1800

Long before Euro-Americans settled in North America, Native American girls and their families inhabited the region. Over 20,000 years, Native American girls helped their families and communities adapt to the seven geographic areas they inhabited in the Southeast, Southwest, the plains, Great Basin and California, Pacific Northwest, Arctic coast, and eastern woodlands. Although the Europeans would regard "Indians" as a single undifferentiated people, there were several hundred distinct groups, each with their own political structure, language, economy, family, kinship styles, and girlhoods.

Although little is known about what life was like for girls among most Native American tribes, limited information exists on the role of work in the lives of some. Jesuit priest Gabriel Sagard observed that "whenever they begin to put one foot in front of the other, [they] have a little stick put into their hands to train them and teach them early to pound corn . . . and in the course of these small frolics they are trained to perform trifling and petty household duties" (quoted in Axtell 1981, 34). Other observers noted that Seneca girls began work at eight or nine when their play was modeled after their mothers' work. Because fathers, brothers, and other male kin were away for months at a time hunting or fighting, it was women and girls who maintained the extensive agricultural economy upon which the tribe depended. Working together in small groups, Seneca girls helped produce corn, beans, squash, and tobacco and gathered nuts, berries, and insects. They were assigned the lighter duties in the longhouse and in the garden plots located around the villages. Similarly, Catawba girls in the Southeast learned by imitating their mothers, who taught them how to hoe and plant, butcher and cook, and braid and sew. Pueblo girls who farmed in the Southwest also helped construct adobe houses, make pottery, and weave baskets. In the Great Plains, Omaha girls planted and harvested, dressed skins, and dried meat.

Although there were no girls among the newcomers to Jamestown in 1607, they did set sail after settlement became the goal of the Virginia Company in 1618. Believing that family life would bring stability to the region, the company had advertised for "maids." Although the majority of newcomers continued to be young men, Alice Pindon was not the only teenage girl who left England for Virginia. Approximately one-third of all settlers were young, unmarried girls. Most came by choice, but some were "orphaned apprentices," kidnapped from the streets of London by profit-seeking "spiriters." Colonial documents reveal that the Virginia Company regularly requested shiploads of boys and girls ages twelve and up. Those children who resisted faced imprisonment; those who perished were replaced.

Because the majority of girls who came voluntarily could not afford the cost of the transatlantic journey, they contracted to serve for between four and seven years as "indentured servants" to tobacco planters. As adolescents and young women, they planted crops, enriched seedbeds, transplanted seedlings, stripped leaves, harvested tobacco, and helped run the domestic economy that enabled the South to eventually prosper. But the difficult and repetitive work, warm weather, poor diet, vitamin-deficient foods, high rates of mortality, and limited sociability on scattered farms in the countryside made many long for home. Daughters and sons of indentured servants born out of wedlock in a land unsupervised by male kin were put to work at age three.

Until the end of the seventeenth century, however, agues and fever, typhoid, smallpox, and malaria plagued most marriages, leaving widows with daughters and sons to support in the same type of small wooden shacks they had lived in as servants. Young women who survived their "seasoning" (a bout with malaria) and served out their indenture became planters' wives, eventually replacing themselves and enabling successive generations to expand by reproduction, not immigration. As in England, fears about a poverty-stricken population shaped colonial laws, customs, and practices in which poor children were bound to service. Daughters of widows who had no options or opportunities took their place in the impermanent households made up of "complex families" (successions of stepparents and stepsiblings), where they received erratic supervision and sometimes abuse.

The labor of girls was essential to the subsistence economies elsewhere in North America. The utilitarianism of the farm family economy shaped the material culture of Puritan life, where at age six girls donned garments that were miniature versions of their mothers'. The change marked girls' new relationship to the family and household economy, which depended upon the labor of everyone. In the gendered domains of the colonial New England household, sons took their place next to their fathers in fields, pastures, barns, and workshops. Daughters shared the domestic domain with their mothers, sisters, and other females. The Puritan family household was the main unit of production, where girls were obliged to assist mothers in unceasing routines. Even little ones—such as five-year-old Eliza and her seven-year-old sister Hannah Sewell—assisted mothers with meals and other household tasks (Fass and Mason 2000, 288). Daily, weekly, seasonal, and annual chores consisted of spinning, carding, sewing, knitting, baking, brewing, planting, hoeing, harvesting, milking, churning, and cooking. In dark and drafty colonial households that were centers of production and reproduction, swaddled infants were also cared for by older siblings and servants.

The daughters of Caucasian, Native American, or African American midwives and healers were apprenticed to help their skilled mothers, but it was an opportunity that came to very few. More typically, young workers were exchanged between colonial goodwives who relied heavily on their services. When they reached adolescence, the Sewell sisters were "fostered out" as indentured servants or apprentices, as were others regardless of family wealth and status (Morgan 1944, 77). Under another's roof, adolescent girls like Sarah Gibbs of Plymouth, Massachusetts, received vocational and religious training and lessons in the dangers of idleness (Morgan 1944, 79). Unlike boys, however, girls learned housekeeping and little else. "Helps" learned as they assisted in the domestic production of candle and soap making, spinning, weaving, gardening, cooking, and preserving. By the eighteenth century, however, girls were no longer fostered out for vocational training.

White girls in the eighteenth-century South were drawn into the sex-segregated world of their mothers when they were about six years of age. Girls generally assisted their mothers and other female kin in daily chores on the plantation, where they tended gardens, cared for dairy and poultry yards, cooked, cleaned, spun, sewed, and knitted. Girls of the southern gentry, like Thomas Jefferson's daughter Maria (a.k.a. Polly), learned how to "manage the kitchen, the dairy, the garden, and other appendages of the hous[e]hold" (Norton 1980, 28). White girls were also taught how to command slaves, including those older than themselves. Eliza Lucas, the teenage daughter of a plantation owner, was fairly unusual among her contemporaries. In her father's absence, the well-educated adolescent managed his three plantations, where she introduced new crop varieties and invented indigo, the soon-to-be leading southern export (Kamensky 1995, 132). More typically, elite daughters worked on perfecting such feminine skills as modesty, meekness, compassion, affability, piety, and passivity in order to make themselves attractive to suitors and thus secure their financial future.

But in the New England farm household where the vast majority of American girls lived, the labor of daughters was critical. Spinning, according to New Jersey Quaker Susanna Dillwyn, was "a very proper accomplishment for a farmer's daughter" (quoted in Norton 1980, 17). By 1750, the widespread availability of looms enabled many families to acquire one for their daughters' use. The time-consuming, monotonous task of spinning wool or flax fiber threads was done by young women, who had more time than married ones. But girls as young as six, who stood on footstools in order to reach the great wheel, also spun wool and flax into skeins of yarn. Other primary chores performed by farmers' daughters included sewing and weaving. Rural daughters' activities were much like those of fifteen-year-old Elizabeth Fuller, who baked pies, made candles, cleaned floors, minced meat, made cheese, washed the laundry, and ironed the clothes.

Sewing—taught to girls at a young age— was beneficial to the family wardrobe and, in urban areas, the purse. In colonial cities, adolescent girls often contributed to family welfare by working as paid seamstresses. However, city daughters from wealthy families were at the forefront of a leisured lifestyle soon to be idealized by the "new" middle class for their daughters. Girls of well-to-do families often spent their days together making, mending, and altering shirts, aprons, and caps at a relaxed pace. Without the pressing demands shouldered by other girls at the end of the colonial period, the white daughters of the urban elite rose late, spent hours with friends, and read the latest novels.

1800 to 1900

Industrialization, urbanization, immigration, migration, and ideologies of race, class, and gender were among the many factors that transformed the nature of work for girls in the nineteenth-century United States. There was no shortage of work to be done in the four- and five-story Federal-style and elaborate Victorian homes of the "new" middle class, despite the increasing production and consumption of industrialized goods. Though the domestic economy was declining, native-born girls found employment as live-in domestics. Many routinely complained about the unrealistic expectations of their mistresses, who scrutinized their efforts and criticized their work, demanded long hours, paid low wages, provided substandard accommodations, treated "their" help with little respect, and gave little "time off." Some girls went from one household to another in pursuit of a less demeaning, demanding, and degrading position, but many chose to work in factories and workshops and to live in board-inghouses with other girls and young women.

The commercialization of agriculture that adversely affected family farms led farmers' daughters as young as ten years of age to take advantage of newly emerging employment opportunities. In 1793, two girls were among the seven children who worked at Samuel Slater's Rhode Island mill, and they were followed by numerous farmers' daughters who became bobbin-doffers, spinners, and weavers in Lowell or one of the other new mill towns in Mass-achusetts and Rhode Island. In autobio-graphical works and in literary magazines, mill girls (ages fifteen to twenty-five) described the experiences they shared with other unmarried girls who helped each other adjust to the new economic and social order. Ten-year-old Harriet Hanson Robinson and eleven-year-old Lucy Larcom worked as doffers, fourteen hours every weekday and eight hours on Saturdays, for $1 per week. Relatively well-paid young women who lodged in company-owned and -controlled boarding-houses supervised by widows and other matrons spent their days tending looms and their nights attending lyceums and borrowing books from libraries. Competi-tion led labor and living conditions to deteriorate by the mid-1830s, however. Eleven-year-old Harriet Robinson was among the 2,000 mill girls who went on strike in 1836. Mill girls formed the Low-ell Female Labor Reform Association in 1844 and published their grievances in the *Voice of Industry*. Despite strikes and state petitions, however, most left the mills and were replaced by desperately poor Irish immigrant women, their daugh-ters, and other family members.

Many white, native-born mill girls joined others who became teachers, one of the better jobs available to middle-class young women, especially the graduates from one of the many female seminaries and academies that flourished in the new nation. These institutions prepared young women to pursue careers as teachers in public schools established during the 1840s. In the Midwest, however, "Bo-hemian and Scandinavian girls could not get positions as teachers, because they had no opportunity to learn the language," according to novelist Willa Cather (1918, 128). But teaching, like all other female employments in the nineteenth century, was shaped by a powerful gender ideology. Teaching was an acceptable occupation for young women only because it was a temporary caregiving activity that pre-pared its practitioners for marriage and maternity. Though imbued with the con-fidence and independence that academic training and salaried employment could engender, the vast majority of young women were nevertheless forced to end their teaching careers upon marriage.

Middle-class adolescent girls raised in rural areas in the Northeast were expect-ed to sacrifice their own needs for those of others within the family circle. In Brattle-boro, Vermont, Mary Palmer Tyler's daughter spent her days cooking, clean-ing, washing, ironing, and sewing, as had generations of girls before her. But over the course of the nineteenth century, the need for domestic production would be gradually curtailed by the industrial pro-duction of consumer goods. In place of the utilitarian fundamentals of house-keeping, daughters of the "new" middle class were urged to master such feminine accomplishments as sewing samplers, painting, and making dolls. These leisure activities were intended to teach daugh-ters middle-class skills and sensibilities, but that is not the way all girls wanted it to be. Catharine Beecher, who was a reluctant pupil, did not admire her mother's domestic accomplishments as a girl. Beecher recalled "the mournful, despairing hours when I saw the children at their sports, and was confined till I had picked out the bad stitches" (quoted in Sklar 1973, 7). For rebellious girls like Ellen Montgomery, the heroine in Susan Warner's best-selling "sentimental" novel, *The Wide, Wide World* (1850), domestic labor was as stultifying as it was arduous.

The lives of leisure, consumption, and display of the daughters of the well-to-do stood in sharp contrast to their urban neighbors'. Rural migrants and free blacks traveled to major American cities in the Northeast in search of employment. After 1847, they were joined by Irish refugees from the potato famine, many of whom were young women who traveled together and settled in poor, densely populated neighborhoods. Impoverished by persistent unemployment, the inevitable result of financial panics, economic depressions, and epidemic diseases, many families lived in overcrowded tenements and dilapidated shanties. In the 1820s and 1830s leisured, middle-class women with an evangelical mission established urban benevolent associations that provided poor girls and their families with clothing, firewood, food, and a religious tract but little else.

Because there was rarely enough cash on hand to acquire anything but immediate necessities, girls "earned their keep" by running errands, scavenging, and laboring. During good times and bad, the daughters of working-class families helped raise siblings, cook meals, and clean. Abandoned, orphaned, and runaway girls were joined by others on street corners, where they sold baked sweet potatoes and pears, tea cakes, fruit, candy, and hot corn. Peddling was the most reliable and legitimate form of employment available to working-class girls, whether they offered their wares on street corners or went door-to-door selling household supplies (e.g., scrub brushes, sponges, pins, matchsticks, fruits, and vegetables). Free black girls, who learned how to sew dresses and piece quilts from their wage-earning mothers, also sold the goods they made.

Girls relied on the street trades because children were in the process of being displaced by the cash economy. Although boy apprentices had been thrown out of work by the decline of the craft system and the rise of rural factories, they still found employment blacking boots, selling newspapers, and holding horses for people going into stores. Girls not old enough for domestic work typically worked as street sweepers, keeping crosswalks cleared and selling matchsticks on city streets. In Hans Christian Andersen's legendary tale about working-class life, deeply encoded with bourgeois cultural authority, the delirious "Little Match Girl" yearns for middle-class abundance, leisure, domestic tranquillity, and a feminized hereafter. In the many published works on the plight of street children, reformers often depicted the middle class as saintly and the poor as sinful.

Black and white teenage "outworkers" made artificial flowers, fringes, parasols, and other consumer goods in the "learning system." For pennies a day—or room and board—girls apprenticed to tailors, seamstresses, dressmakers, and milliners, who taught them the rudimentary skills of their trade. Also laboring as subordinates were immigrant and free black girls in their older teens and early twenties, who replaced the native-born girls who had abandoned domestic work by the middle of the nineteenth century. Some were graduates of industrial schools shaped by prevailing gender roles that taught girls vocational skills only useful for housekeeping. Yet working in the homes of middling and prosperous tradespeople, craftspeople, merchants, and professionals had its advantages for some. Irish girls from working-class backgrounds were more likely to appreciate the cash remuneration, the room, and also the opportunity to acquire the customs and master the codes of middle-class culture. Though they were not well paid, servant girls who boarded were often able to save money. However, for "bound" servants—provided with only room and board until they reached age eighteen or twenty-one—life could be intolerable. As bound servants, black girls were not only more likely to serve longer terms than white ones, but their status was also more like that of slaves. When they could, free girls preferred to assist their mothers, who often worked as self-employed laundresses.

Often girls too young to work as domestic servants scavenged instead. With friends and siblings, they pillaged tea, coffee, flour, and sugar from spilled sacks and overturned barrels. On the streets, at the docks, or at the lumberyards, girls collected coal, cotton, canvas, rags, cogs, rope, metal, bottles, paper, kitchen grease, and bad meat. "Wild ragged little girls" worked as petty thieves and pickpockets, exchanging the umbrellas and hats they acquired for much-needed cash at secondhand junkshops that lined waterfront areas in New York City (quoted in Stansell 1987, 205). Junk dealers, in turn, sold the things girls gathered to artisans and manufacturers. Despite the risks that their six- and seven-year-old daughters faced from the police, working-class parents throughout the nineteenth century depended upon their scavenging in order to help make ends meet.

Scavengers, seamstresses, sweepers, and others occasionally drifted into casual prostitution. In one hour, a girl who sold sex could earn the same shilling a seamstress in 1830 earned in a day. In 1853, a reporter for the *New York Herald* reported that four teenage girls who were in training in the garment industry prostituted themselves in order to pay the rent and buy clothes and food. Casual prostitution also provided a way to escape an abusive home life; girls suffered from a history of sexual abuse by workingmen, lodgers, grocers, soldiers, and fathers who groped with one hand and offered pennies and candy with the other. Stimulated by the eroticization of working-class girls in bourgeois Victorian culture, merchants, clerks, employees, workers, and sailors sought out girls and young women as prostitutes.

More than 100,000 working-class boys and girls from urban areas in the Northeast were transported on the orphan trains by reformers to "virtuous" homes in the rural Midwest between 1845 and 1929. Also on the frontier were other immigrant girls whose families had headed to agricultural areas in the Midwest instead of urban ones in the Northeast. Scandinavian, German, Bohemian, and Dutch families secured farms where girls' labor was so indispensable to family survival that many were prevented from attending school. On the Illinois prairie, as elsewhere, girls' full-time household chores included cooking, cleaning, caring for younger siblings, and feeding farmhands. For them and for their mothers, keeping a sod house clean was a challenge without running water and with limited domestic technology. In order to cook and clean, immigrant and native-born daughters in Nebraska and elsewhere in the Midwest hauled water and wood, washed, sewed, and mended the family's wardrobe. Girls also contributed to the family income by selling pies, chickens, eggs, milk, and butter to neighbors. In male-dominated mining towns in the Northwest, girls earned cash washing clothing, cooking meals, selling pies and vegetables, and running errands for prostitutes.

But whether they liked it or not, girls were expected to perform domestic chores by virtue of their sex. One girl recalled: "I was chore girl to help mother with domestic work, which I did not like, and often was slapped by my mother. I much preferred being outdoors, and was very curious, traits that brought much trouble to my relationship with my mother" (quoted in Schlissel, Gibbens, and Hampsten 1989, 218). However, innovations in farm technology that allowed those with less strength to operate heavy machinery would enable girls as young as eight to plow fields. One North Dakota pioneer recalled: "Our clan of growing girls were brought up to strict hard work, especially the oldest, Matilda and Ottilia, who became field workers. They were expected to do as much work as a man . . . hauling hay and pitching bundles for the threshing machine" (quoted in Schlissel, Gibbens, and Hampsten 1989, 218). Fears that farmwork was making Ántonia too rough and manly in Willa Cather's novel *My Ántonia* (1918), however, led her neighbors to find her a position as a "hired girl" so that she could acquire feminine, middle-class skills and sensibilities. "Determined to help in the struggle to clear the homestead from debt, they had no alternative but to go into service," Ántonia explained. "The girls I knew were always helping to pay for ploughs and reapers, brood-sows, or steers to fatten. One result of this family solidarity was that the foreign farmer fathers in our county were the first to become prosperous" (128).

The daughters of well-to-do Nebraska families were not unlike the adolescent daughters of wealthy plantation owners to the south. Largely shielded from work, southern girls learned little about how to raise a family and how to run a household. Their job was to absorb prevailing ideologies of race, class, and gender: southern white girls were to be proper, pure, and pious. Most elite white girls spent their adolescence frolicking with friends and flirting with beaus at home or at boarding school. Masking the violence of slavery—the widespread abuse of slave girls and women—was the *work* of the southern belle, a cultural construction of white supremacy, patriarchy, and gentility.

In nearby cabins with dirt floors and few furnishings, underfed and underclothed enslaved African American girls cooked calorie- and vitamin-deficient meals in fireplaces also used for heat and for laundering. From their mothers and other grownups, slave girls also learned domestic skills such as soap, candle, and basket making, as well as farming skills such as plowing fields and driving cattle. Although boys had a greater range of opportunities to acquire specialized skills (and purchase necessities and freedom), midwifery was the only option available to black girls, who apprenticed to their mothers who served both the black and the white plantation community. More typically, girls' work responsibilities began by age five, when they learned how to fan flies away from

Young textile workers in North Carolina, photograph by Lewis Hine (Library of Congress, 1909)

whites and haul food and water to slaves in the fields. Girls also fed the chickens, gathered eggs, milked cows, churned butter, gathered wood, swept yards, spun thread, hoed fields, and ran errands. The central task for slave girls and boys, however, was providing day care for slave children whose parents were field or house slaves; they also tended to the daughters and sons of their masters. Those workers perceived as slow, careless, or inattentive were whipped, beaten, and scalded. Adolescent girls joined pregnant women and older slaves on "trash gangs," where they acquired fieldwork skills from pregnant women and older slaves. From the more experienced workers, girls also learned how to fake illness or slow the pace of work, as well as other methods aimed at subverting the slave labor system. When they were older, they took their place in the fields along with other men and women, where there were few gender distinctions in regard to work; the ideology of domesticity largely applied to white women.

In the decades after the Civil War, hard work continued to dominate the daily lives of the daughters of rural sharecroppers in the war-torn "new South." During the last quarter of the nineteenth century, African American and white daughters of desperately poor families helped around the one-room shacks they called home. With no running water and limited household equipment, girls washed dishes and clothing in outdoor bins. Eldest daughters assisted their mothers in gathering wood and cooking three meals a day with food they were more likely to have purchased on credit than produced with crops. Girls were also needed in the fields, where they dropped cotton or tobacco seeds and toted water. The unrelenting crop-lien system kept them and their families starved for cash and forever in debt.

With access to southern markets, northern manufacturers ushered in a period of unprecedented industrial expansion that doubled the number of girls and young women in the labor force between 1870 and 1890 (Lichtenstein, Strasser, and Rosenzweig 2000, 34). More than one-quarter of the employees of southern cotton mills were children of failed white sharecroppers and tenant farmers, and half of them were twelve years old or younger. Girls hired as spinners brushed lint from machines and tied together broken threads twelve hours a day, six days a week. In 1890, 1.5 million girls and boys (ten to fifteen years old) worked for long hours earning pennies a day in dangerous textile mills, canneries, and tobacco-processing plants in the South and in hazardous sweatshops in the North. Many immigrants from Germany, Britain, and, increasingly, the countries in eastern and southern Europe settled in large industrial cities like Chicago and New York with easy access to jobs. Working-class girls and young women entered the workforce there in order to help sustain their families, who were easily impoverished by unemployment, accident, sickness, death, or desertion. By the end of the nineteenth century, "cash girls" who transported money and goods around department stores joined 4 million young, single women who worked for wages as domes-

tics, white-collar workers (e.g., retail stores and offices), factory workers, and industrial home workers (34).

1900 to the Present

Girls and adolescents were among the millions of migrants and "new immigrants" who fled poverty, overpopulation, and persecution on farms and in villages in Europe, the American South, and Mexico around the turn of the twentieth century. They often settled in urban neighborhoods close to sources of income (albeit unstable ones). Although the 1900 census revealed that nearly 2 million girls and boys between ten and sixteen worked for wages, that number did not include those under the age of ten or those who worked illegally (West 1989, 3). In order to shore up the family economy, girls of all ages and from a wide variety of ethnic and racial backgrounds peddled produce and flowers, sold newspapers, sewed goods, scavenged for junk, and bargained with urban storekeepers. Italian daughters from protective, patriarchal, working-class families assisted their mothers in making artificial flowers, sewing clothing, sorting and shelling nuts, and making dolls as industrial home workers. Many young women like Anzia Yezierska would document the trials of their girlhoods in memoirs and autobiographical novels.

Daughters, especially the eldest, were often forced to limit their education in order to serve as housekeeping assistants to their mothers, who were burdened with household chores. Although experts at the time recommended that chores assigned to children serve instructional purposes, Chinese American girls from working-class families shopped and cleaned, and others elsewhere in the country also cared for younger siblings.

Elizabeth Gurley Flynn, who championed the cause of working girls, inspired Industrial Workers of the World leader Joe Hill to compose "The Rebel Girl" in 1915. (Courtesy Industrial Workers of the World; from the Collection of the Labor Archives and Research Center, San Francisco State University)

Though they honored cultural traditions about filial duty, Jewish and Italian "little mothers" often resented the burdens that their brothers escaped by virtue of their sex. Some eldest daughters took pride in their maternal responsibilities, but others clearly resented the domestic expectations placed on them but not their siblings, who attended school, held jobs, and had fun.

In 1900, 13 percent of all textile workers were under sixteen years of age (Lichtenstein, Strasser, and Rosenzweig 2000, 222). As a girl, Pauline Newman recalled cutting threads from 7:30 in the morning until 9 at night in the garment factory where she worked. Immigrant Jewish and Italian young women often sewed shirtwaists, the ready-made blouses worn by working- and middle-class women around the turn of the century. Fierce market competition in the industry led to long hours, low wages, sexual harassment, and degraded and dangerous working conditions. Although work-related accidents were widespread, one of the worst industrial disasters occurred on March 25, 1911, when a fire engulfed the top floors of the Triangle Shirtwaist Company on New York's Lower East Side. Within half an hour, smoke inhalation and fatal injuries claimed the lives of 146 young women garment workers trapped by locked exits. The disaster galvanized many working girls and adolescents, who joined unions and charted new careers as labor activists.

Pauline Newman, an advocate for the Women's Trade Union League at age thirteen, had been drawn into the urban industrial economy by the expansion of "feminized" jobs that paid little and took a lot. Teenage Jewish girls, who accompanied fathers on the transatlantic journey, often labored in sweatshops and factories as operatives for the highest wage available in order to accumulate enough money to finance the travel of family members back home. Once here, they helped support unemployed or disabled fathers, widowed mothers, and younger siblings. English-speaking girls found jobs as sales clerks, but the hours were long and the wages low. Until they married and left the workforce, teenage Italian girls often worked for relatives and with other girls of the same ethnic background.

But the limited range of employment options, periodic unemployment, and economic downturns often drew young women into prostitution; adolescent girls were especially vulnerable to arrest and institutionalization. Chinese girls, sold by their desperately poor parents back home, worked as domestics in the homes of California's well-to-do Chinese. Many were forced into brothels, where they served a clientele of Chinese males who predominated among immigrants from that country.

Missionary women and Chinese social reformers led the crusade to stop the *mui-tsai* ("little sister") tradition. They were among other Progressive urban reformers who hoped to eliminate the pernicious effects of industrial capitalism. Many were middle-class graduates of recently established women's colleges with high expectations and limited professional opportunities. Politicizing their domestic role, "social housekeepers" aimed to clean up the new industrial order by helping girls and boys for whom they established day nurseries, baby clinics, health classes, and industrial schools. For example, the Little Mothers' Leagues served a clientele of 20,000 girls each week in 1912. In cities across the United States, Progressive reformers established numerous other organizations, including the Young Women's Christian Association, National Association of Colored Women, National Consumer's League, settlement houses, civic clubs, and municipal improvement societies, among many others. In an effort to protect girls from corruption and exploitation, these organizations offered vocational classes in working-class neighborhoods. But because they were unable to transcend their own backgrounds, reformers provided a curriculum largely limited to domestic science, cooking, child care, and sewing.

Elite reformers were influenced by profound fin-de-siècle social, cultural, economic, and political transformations: rising income, technological innovation, immigrant labor, and changing attitudes about gender, leisure, family life, and the "value" of children. As Viviana Zelizer has shown in *Pricing the Priceless Child* (1985), the social value of children among the middle class had changed to economically worthless but emotionally priceless. Reformers aimed to extend these changing ideals to the working class through legislation that mandated compulsory school attendance and prohibited child labor and industrial work at home. Despite their legislative efforts, factory bosses outmaneuvered child labor inspectors. The first federal child labor law was not passed by Congress until 1916 but was then declared unconstitutional by the conservative U.S. Supreme Court. By 1920, states enacted legislation that prohibited the employment of children under the age of fourteen, restricted girls and boys under sixteen to an eight-hour day, and mandated compulsory education.

In response to fears about the dangerous effects of industrialization, urbanization, and modernization on girls, reformers also established the Girl Scouts (1912), Girl Pioneers (1914), and Camp Fire Girls (1910). Through the official Girl Scout periodical *The American Girl* and the official Camp Fire Girls publication *Everygirls' Magazine* and in their outdoor programs, these girls' organizations taught the traditional craft skills associated with gender norms along with more feminist notions of womanhood to middle-class, minority, and disabled girls. For example, Girl Scouts were encouraged to contribute to the war effort by selling war bonds and Girl Scout cookies, seeding Victory gardens, and assisting in hospitals. Girls who joined the Junior Red Cross ran farms and "war gardens," held cake sales, and arranged garden parties to benefit European orphans of World War I.

In the 1920s, fewer girls worked for wages than in the previous period, but rural families continued to rely on their daughters' contributions, as they had since the previous century. With no child labor legislation restrictions on farm laborers, girls as young as three years of age helped out. In Texas in 1913, a four-year-old migrant worker photographed by National Child Labor Committee photojournalist Lewis Hine picked 8 pounds of cotton a day; her five-year-old sister picked 30 pounds. Farm families struggling with rising debts and falling prices relied on their daughters to can and churn, tend livestock, and feed fieldworkers. Their participation in fieldwork, however, depended on the availability of brothers and nonkin males, crop types, and farm technology. Navajo daughters assisted in sheepherding, which was the dominant form of farming among the Navajo. On the West Coast, Chinese, Japanese, Korean, and Asian Indian daughters picked and canned fruit and provided child care and housekeeping in the labor-intensive farms established by their fathers. Punjabi Mexican girls in California worked as migrant workers in vineyards, fields, and orchards. Other rural daughters provided their families with cash by working in canneries, though Americanized daughters of recent Mexican immigrants were more likely to hold on to a portion of their wages.

While others during the 1920s had enjoyed prosperity, farm girls and their families were among the first to experience the economic adversity that soon affected the rest of the country. During the Great Depression, adolescent girls responded to the needs of their families by working on farms, in factories, or at home. But the economic exigencies had forced teens out of the labor force and into high schools, where they could compete with each other and not with older workers. Though child labor diminished significantly in the 1930s, Depression-era girls (especially in immigrant families) nevertheless assumed a greater role in housework and child care, thus reinforcing girls' sense of responsibility and self-sacrifice. In middle-class families that reduced household expenditures to get through rough times, girls also did what they could to help. They used the wages earned from "minding the children" or from other jobs for personal expenses, school supplies, clothing, and social activities. In families pushed to the margins, girls swept porches and dusted the furniture for pennies, as did Anne Moody, who lived in the rural South. In some families, girls' wages were vital to basic household expenses, but in others girls took over housekeeping for their wage-earning mothers. Anne Moody was forced to quit her job so that she could babysit for her younger siblings.

With the money they earned, many girls went to the movies along with millions of other Americans eager to escape the harsh realities of their lives. There, they became fans of young female movie stars, a very recent profession open to girls and young women. In her numerous movies, Shirley Temple was typically parentless but never powerless. Teenager Judy Garland played an energetic and competent Dorothy in *The Wizard of Oz* (1939), triumphing over cataclysms that were more mythical and metaphorical than the Great Depression, yet just as devastating. Independent and intelligent, strong and skillful, Nancy Drew made her first appearance in books and movies during the Depression as a teenage detective who solved mysteries that puzzled male experts and supervised her motherless household.

Conditions changed for daughters of all ages when fathers joined the military, and mothers, inspired by patriotism and the promise of improved economic opportunities, found "man-sized" jobs in the World War II defense industries. That the federal government's day care appropriation was inadequate for the needs of the vast majority of families meant that many children were left unsupervised. That was not necessarily all bad for one girl, who assumed that if her father had been around, she would "not have been allowed so much personal freedom to roam the library, the city, the fields, neighborhoods, woods, and have a paper route" (Tuttle 1993, 28). Mothers who worked an eight-hour shift were nevertheless faulted for creating unsupervised "latchkey children."

Children were often cared for in parent-run nursery schools or by neighbors and older siblings. Wartime vocational courses in child care and homemaking for preadolescent girls (such as those offered by the Girl Scouts) instructed them in the essentials. Wartime mothers relied heavily upon junior high school children to run the household and feed the family. Relaxed attendance regulations enabled thirteen- and fourteen-year-old youngsters to get jobs. When not in school or at work, girls participated in the patriotic culture of Victory gardens, war bond campaigns, and scrap metal and paper drives. However they participated, many girls longed to play a more substantial role in war-related activities. Some dreamed of serving as uniformed "girl assistants" or soldiers or of joining their older sisters in defense plants. Until 1943, the National Youth Administration provided teenage girls with nontraditional apprenticeships and alternatives to pink-collar employment. Teenage graduates migrated from rural areas to defense plants, where they worked as defense workers in factories earning high wages. But some girls—such as teenage Mexican American girls—were also discriminated against by employers because of their age, sex, race, and ethnicity.

After World War II ended, white girls could ride their bikes to neighborhood parks in the newly available suburban neighborhoods, but wartime work opportunities dwindled with the rise of a new domestic ideal. In order to participate in the new teen culture, adolescent girls used their allowances or their earnings from babysitting (one of the few opportunities available to suburban girls) to purchase clothing, movie tickets, records, and magazines. The traditional sources of employment for younger girls (e.g., errand running) gave way in child-centered and car-dependent neighborhoods. There was also a growing fear of strangers of all kinds, as revealed in the urban legends that began to circulate in the early 1960s.

Not all girls in the postwar United States were raised in middle-class prosperity, despite the portrayals of family life in 1950s television sit-coms. In urban ghettos in the North and poor rural areas in the South, black girls attended poor schools and faced limited economic opportunities. In the 1960s, they were joined by Latinas from the Dominican Republic, Central America, and Mexico, especially after the passage of the Immigration and Naturalization Act of 1965. In order to help their families survive resettlement, Latina daughters (even as young as age six) spent thirty hours a week babysitting for younger siblings, taking care of ill or infirm kin, keeping house, running errands, and advocating

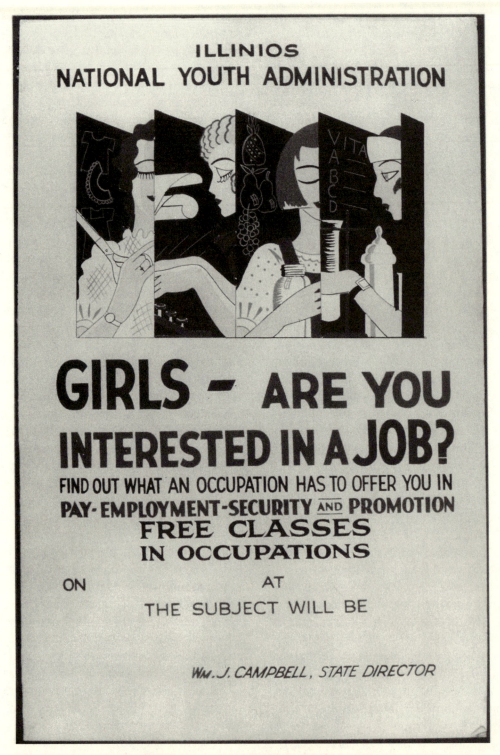

A National Youth Administration poster promotes educational opportunities for young women seeking training for employment. (Library of Congress, 1937)

and translating for Spanish-speaking family members (National Commission on Migrant Education 1992). The economic pressures that Latina adolescents faced, then as now, made them more likely to drop out of school to work.

Although some Latina's families settled in urban areas, others became seasonal migrant workers whose plight first came to national attention in the 1960s. White, black, and Latino migrant farmworkers spent each spring following the ripening crops northward from New York to Michigan to Washington. The approximately 409,000 children who accompanied their fathers, the principal farmworkers in 1989, were likely to shuttle back and forth between a residence in the United States (e.g., California, Texas, or Florida) and another in Mexico. Cynthia, who was born in the United States, along with 65 percent of other daughters of migrant workers, accompanied her father to the asparagus fields in Pasco, Washington, each year (Martin, 1). A smaller percentage of girl migrant workers are currently indigenous Mexicans and Central Americans who speak neither Spanish nor English.

In order to work in the fields, girls who are legally required to be sixteen often falsify papers. The wage they earn is often not their own but is turned over to parents whose total annual family earnings can hover around $5,000. Sixteen-year-old Cynthia gives her parents most of what she earns so that they can pay bills or buy necessities. She spends some on clothing for school. Although some girls will leave the field at midday to go to school, others will not attend school at all. The education of girls is often interrupted in order to contend with intermittent work schedules. "What I like least about being a migrant worker," explained

teenaged Cynthia, "is to change from school to school in different places. Also when you attend another school you don't know what's going on in the classes and you might not pass that class." When she grows up, Cynthia wants to be a teacher because it will not be as hard as working in the fields. But another migrant daughter, Iselda, recognizes that the obstacles in her path are formidable. She explains, "I have always dreamed of becoming a lawyer but the way things are going it's going to be a little hard."

Since the expansion of service-sector jobs in the 1970s, Mexican Americans, Puerto Ricans, and Dominicans have joined African Americans, Caucasians, Vietnamese, and Hmong girls in the new teen economy of fast food, convenience, and retail stores. Unfortunately, many working-class immigrant girls reside in economically depressed inner cities, where access to decent schools is as limited as employment opportunities. Because retail and fast-food stores locate in suburban neighborhoods, middle-class girls have had greater access to such employment. In 1996, the U.S. Bureau of the Census reported that rates of unemployment were the greatest among young African American and Latina women. Other studies have shown that compared to other adolescents in the workforce, Latinas and African American girls earn the least (Dodson 1998). Like other girls, many dream of fame and fortune as performers in the pop music industry, now no longer a male domain.

As the numbers of ten- to nineteen-year-old girls rose for the first time in fifteen years in the 1990s, new effort was made to train them to pursue "nontraditional" careers in science, math, and technology. Take Our Daughters to Work Day, created by the Ms. Foundation for Women

A female carpenter building a gazebo.
(Skjold Photographs)

Whether your first job is minding children, waiting tables, or selling jeans, you are learning more than you may realize. If you baby-sit, you're not only perfecting the art of putting on Pampers, you're learning about responsibility and punctuality and how to negotiate money with parents and bedtime with kids. If you're waiting tables, you're sharpening math, memory, and people skills. If you're selling clothes, you're mastering presentation, time management, and how to get along with customers and coworkers. You may also be learning that you don't want to baby-sit or wait on tables or ring up sales forever. (139)

With more mothers and fathers in the workplace working longer hours for less money, chores—often tied to allowances or privileges—play a renewed role in the work lives of most American girls. But because they are still seen as housework, girls' chores have yet to be calculated in the gross national product.

Miriam Forman-Brunell

in 1982 and celebrated on the fourth Thursday in April, aims to raise girls' career ambitions by having them spend the day interning at offices, studios, stations, and agencies. An unprecedented number of handbooks, manuals, and almanacs have similarly aimed to provide girls with advice on everything from eating disorders to employment options. Drawing upon a girl power ethos of "following your dreams," the self-help works emphasize the importance of persistence, determination, hard work, high standards, ambition, and achievement. In *For Girls Only: Wise Words, Good Advice* (1998), advice columnist Carol Weston explained to girls ten and older the benefits derived from the only jobs for which they qualify:

See also African American Girls in the Twentieth Century; Asian American Girls; Chicana Girls; Domestic Service; Domesticity; Enslaved Girls of African Descent; Indentured Servants; Latina Girls; Mennonite Girls; Mill Girls; Native American Girls

References and Further Reading
Ashby, Leroy. 1985. "Partial Promises and Semi-Visible Youths: The Depression and World War II." Pp. 489–532 in *American Childhood: A Research Guide and Historical Handbook.* Edited by Joseph M. Hawes and N. Ray Hiner. Westport, CT: Greenwood Press.
Atkin, S. Beth. 1993. *Voices from the Fields: Children of Migrant Farmworkers Tell Their Stories.* Boston: Little, Brown.
Axtell, James. 1981. *The Indian Peoples of Eastern America: A Documentary*

History of the Sexes. New York: Oxford University Press.

Berrol, Selma Cantor. 1995. *Growing Up American: Immigrant Children in America Then and Now.* New York: Twayne.

Boylan, Anne M. 1985. "Growing Up Female in America." Pp. 168–171 in *American Childhood: A Research Guide and Historical Handbook.* Edited by Joseph M. Hawes and N. Ray Hiner. Westport, CT: Greenwood Press.

Bremner, Robert A., et al., ed. 1970. *Children and Youth in America: A Documentary History.* Vol. 2. Cambridge, MA: Harvard University Press.

———. 1974. *Children and Youth in America: A Documentary History.* Vols. 2–3. Cambridge, MA: Harvard University Press.

Calvert, Karin. 1992. *Children in the House: The Material Culture of Early Childhood, 1600–1900.* Boston: Northeastern University Press.

Carr, Lois Green, and Lorena S. Walsh. 1977. "The Planter's Wife: The Experience of White Women in Seventeenth-Century Maryland." *William and Mary Quarterly* 34: 542–571.

Cather, Willa. 1918. *My Ántonia.* 1988. Reprint, Boston: Houghton Mifflin.

Clement, Priscilla F. 1997. *Growing Pains: Children in the Industrial Age, 1850–1890.* New York: Twayne.

Demos, John. 1970. *A Little Commonwealth: Family Life in Plymouth Colony.* New York: Oxford University Press.

Dodson, Lisa. 1998. *Don't Call Us out of Name: The Untold Lives of Women and Girls in Poor America.* Boston: Beacon Press.

Dublin, Thomas. 1979. *Women at Work: The Transformation of Work and Community.* New York: Columbia University Press.

———. 1981. *Farm to Factory: Women's Letters 1830–1860.* New York: Columbia University Press.

Dudden, Faye. 1983. *Serving Women: Household Service in Nineteenth-Century America.* Middletown, CT: Wesleyan University Press.

Earle, Alice Morse. 1899. *Child Life in Colonial Days.* New York: Macmillan, chap. 15.

Elder, Glen H. 1974. *Children of the Great Depression: Social Change in Life Experience.* Chicago: University of Chicago Press.

Fass, Paula, and Mary Ann Mason. 2000. *Childhood in America.* New York: New York University Press.

Fox-Genovese, Elizabeth. 1988. *Within the Plantation Household: Black and White Women in the Old South.* Chapel Hill: University of North Carolina Press.

Freedman, Russell. 1994. *Kids at Work: Lewis Hine and the Crusade against Child Labor.* New York: Clarion Books.

Greenberger, Ellen, and Lawrence Steinberg. 1986. *When Teenagers Work: The Psychological and Social Costs of Adolescent Employment.* New York: Basic Books.

Hawes, Joseph M. 1997. *Children between the Wars: American Childhood, 1920–1940.* New York: Twayne.

Hine, Thomas. 1999. *The Rise and Fall of the American Teenager.* New York: Avon.

Hyde, Mary Kendall. 1919. *Girls' Book of the Red Cross.* New York: Thomas Y. Crowell.

Jones, Jacqueline. 1986. *Labor of Love/Labor of Sorrow: Black Women, Work, and the Family from Slavery to the Present.* New York: Vintage.

Kamensky, Jane. 1995. *The Colonial Mosaic: American Women 1600–1760.* New York: Oxford University Press.

Kessler-Harris, Alice. 1982. *Out to Work.* New York: Oxford University Press.

King, Wilma. 1995. *Stolen Childhood: Slave Youth in Nineteenth-Century America.* Bloomington: Indiana University Press.

Larcom, Lucy. 1889. *A New England Girlhood: Outlined from Memory.* 1996. Reprint, Boston: Riverside Press.

Lichtenstein, Nelson, Susan Strasser, and Roy Rosenzweig. 2000. *Who Built America?* Vol. 2. New York: Worth.

Martin, Philip. *Migrant Farm Workers and Their Children.* Office of Educational Research and Improvement ED376. Washington, DC: Government Printing Office.

"Migrant Workers' Children." http://www.users.owt.com/rpeto/migrant/migrant.html.

Moody, Anne. 1976. *Coming of Age in Mississippi.* Reprint, New York: Dell.

Morgan, Edmund S. 1944. *The Puritan Family: Religion and Domestic Relations in Seventeenth Century New England.* 1966. Reprint, Harper and Row.

Nasaw, David. 1985. *Children of the City: At Work and at Play.* Garden City, NY: Anchor Press/Doubleday.

National Commission on Migrant Education (NCME). 1992. "Invisible Children: A Portrait of Migrant Education in the United States." Washington, DC: NCME (September 23).

Norton, Mary Beth. 1980. *Liberty's Daughters: The Revolutionary Experience of American Women, 1750–1800.* Ithaca, NY: Cornell University Press.

Palladino, Grace. 1996. *Teenagers: An American History.* New York: Basic Books.

Peiss, Kathy. 1986. *Cheap Amusements: Working Women and Leisure in Turn-of-the-Century New York.* Philadelphia: Temple University Press.

Robinson, Harriet. 1898. *Loom and Spindle or Life among the Early Mill Girls.* 1976. Reprint, Kailu, HI: Press Pacifica.

Rutman, Darrett B., and Anita H. Rutman. 1984. *A Place in Time: Middlesex County, Virginia, 1650–1750.* New York: W. W. Norton.

Sallquist, Sylvia Lea. 1984. "The Image of the Hired Girl in Literature: The Great Plains, 1860–WWI." *Great Plains Quarterly* 4, no. 3: 166–177.

Schlissel, Lillian, Bryd Gibbens, and Elizabeth Hampsten. 1989. *Far from Home: Families of the Westward Journey.* New York: Schocken Books.

Shaw, Stephanie J. 1997. "Mothering under Slavery in the Antebellum South." Pp. 297–318 in *Mothers and Motherhood: Readings in American History.* Edited by Rima D. Apple and Janet Golden. Columbus: Ohio State University Press.

Sklar, Kathryn Kish. 1973. *Catharine Beecher: A Study in American Domesticity.* New York: W. W. Norton, 7.

Smith, Abbot Emerson. 2000. "Kidnapping and White Servitude." Pp. 349–351 in *Childhood in America.* Edited by Paula S. Fass and Mary Ann Mason. New York: New York University Press.

Stansell, Christine. 1986. *City of Women: Sex and Class in New York, 1789–1860.* New York: Alfred A. Knopf.

Szasz, Margaret Connell. 1985. "Native-American Children." Pp. 311–342 in *American Childhood: A Research Guide and Historical Handbook.* Edited by Joseph M. Hawes and N. Ray Hiner. Westport, CT: Greenwood Press.

Tate, Thad W., and David L. Ammerman. 1979. *The Chesapeake in the Seventeenth Century: Essays on Anglo-American Society.* Chapel Hill: University of North Carolina Press.

Trattner, Walter I. 1970. *Crusade for the Children: A History of the National Child Labor Committee and Child Labor Reform in America.* Chicago: Quadrangle Books.

Tuttle, William, Jr. 1993. *"Daddy's Gone to War": The Second World War in the Lives of America's Children.* New York: Oxford University Press.

Weinberg, Sydney Stahl. 1997. "Jewish Mothers and Immigrant Daughters: Positive and Negative Role Models." P. 335 in *Mothers and Motherhood: Readings in American History.* Edited by Rima Apple and Janet Golden. Columbus: Ohio State University Press.

West, Elliott. 1989. *Growing Up with the Country: Childhood on the Far Western Frontier.* Albuquerque: University of New Mexico Press.

———. 1996. *Growing Up in Twentieth-Century America: A History and Reference Guide.* Westport, CT: Greenwood Press.

Weston, Carol. 1998. *For Girls Only: Wise Words, Good Advice.* New York: Avon.

Wilson, Harriet E. 1859. *"Our Nig"; or, Sketches from the Life of a Free Black, in a Two-story White House, North. Showing That Slavery's Shadows Fall Even There.* Edited by Henry Louis Gates, Jr. 1983. Reprint, New York: Random House.

Yezierska, Anzia. 1975. *Bread Givers.* Reprint, New York: Persea Books.

Zelizer, Viviana A. 1985. *Pricing the Priceless Child: The Changing Social Value of Children.* New York: Basic Books.

Z

Zines

Although quite diverse in form and content, zines can be defined generally as nonprofessional, noncommercial publications that are created, reproduced, and distributed by individuals wanting to create something different from mainstream forms of communication and entertainment. As alternative media, zines function as networking tools among people who otherwise may feel isolated in their homes, schools, jobs, and communities. In turn, zines often provide a considerable amount of information about issues, products, and communities that are ignored by or marginalized in the mass media. Traditionally, zine producers have been middle-class, white males, but in the last decade many females, working-class individuals, and people of color have joined what has become known as the "zine revolution." Since the late 1980s, an increasing number of girls have created zines in an effort to express themselves and connect with others who share their experiences and visions for the future.

Most zines contain handwritten or typewritten text, which often is supplemented with illustrations, clip art, or photographs. This material is arranged (pasted up) on various pages, which are then photocopied and folded or stapled together. With the wide availability of personal computers today, an increasing number of zine producers are using computers to create both paper zines and electronic publications known as "e-zines" or "webzines." Some zinemakers hand-color illustrations and photographic images, whereas others use colored paper or photocopies to enhance their zines' appeal. As free-form creations, zines typically have no table of contents, departments, or page numbers structuring their material. Because zines are not produced for profit, they carry no paid advertisements, although many promote other zines and alternative products.

Many zines exist as "one-offs," singular creations by individuals who, for whatever reason, do not produce or distribute other issues. Those zinemakers who are more committed to the zine community usually create multiple issues of a zine and develop a subscription list that requires a larger number of reproductions. However, even those zines that are produced by more committed individuals are rarely the same in form and content from issue to issue. They are normally produced at irregular intervals, between which their makers wait for either good copy or, more typically, enough capital to produce the next issue. Since zines are produced for pleasure, not for profit, they usually are printed in limited quantities. Typically, they are sold at alternative venues (such as concerts), traded for other zines or products, or distributed privately to subscribers. Some are distributed also by mainstream distributors like book and record stores or by alternative distributors like political collectives. In recent years, several zine directories (e.g., *Factsheet Five*) have emerged, which have provided zine readers with more knowledge about and better accessibility to these publications.

Most often, contemporary zines are traced back only as far as the punk fanzines of the late 1970s, which were created in opposition to the mainstream music industry and in celebration of alternate musical forms and artists. However, zines have a longer and more complex history in a variety of marginal subcultural groups, including science fiction fans of the late 1930s, the Beat poets of the 1950s, and underground presses of the 1960s and 1970s. As with earlier zinemakers, many contemporary zine producers feel alienated from dominant society and corporate culture, and thus advocate a do-it-yourself (DIY) philosophy. In an effort to resist or subvert mainstream culture, many producers rely on illicit means for creating their texts, using office time, equipment, and supplies (including postage) to produce and distribute their zines. In addition, many zinemakers create provocative juxtapositions between images appropriated from the mass media and their own text that critiques such representations. In order to avoid criminal prosecution and censorship for violating copyright laws, many producers do not reveal their real identities. In addition to using nicknames, zinemakers hide their identities and limit unwanted interference by using post office boxes as mailing addresses, changing the titles of their zines, and not accepting checks or credit cards as payment.

The disparate interests of individuals who make and consume zines have resulted in a wide variety of zine genres, including fanzines (created by fans of a particular cultural medium or genre such as music, film, sports); community/"scene" zines (e.g., punk, gays, feminists); topic/issue zines (e.g., work, politics, conspiracy theories); literary zines (e.g., poetry, short fiction, science fiction); and comix (underground comic books). Most girl zines (some of which are referred to as "grrrl zines" to indicate their producers' identification with feminism, lesbianism, or alternative politics) can be categorized under the genre of personal zines (or "perzines"), zines created by one individual and comprising mainly personal experiences and opinions.

Perhaps as a result of the integration of feminist and DIY philosophies in recent years, the number of zines created by female youth has increased phenomenally since the early 1990s. Although contemporary girl zines are associated often with Riot Grrrls, a pro-girl movement that emerged in 1991, many produced by girls are connected to other alternative communities. Most girl zine producers strongly prioritize their female identity and identify their zines as female-produced and female-oriented through titles like *Girl Germs*, *Bamboo Girl*, *Girlie Jones*, and *Angry Young Woman*. Several, such as *I, Amy Carter* and *Patti Smith*, reveal their pro-female stance by noting the producer's devotion to a specific female celebrity or public persona. Many girl zines are classifiable as perzines because of their individual creators, but some girl zines are produced through the collaborative effort of a community of female youth (e.g., *Housewife Turned . . . Assassin*).

Viable alternatives to commercial teen magazines that privilege consumerism, appearance improvement, and heterosexual romance over productivity, critical consciousness, and same-sex relationships, girl zines encourage their readers to publicly express their personal and political concerns as well as to develop their creative abilities and self-confidence. Girl zinemakers often focus on their experiences of being female in a misogynist society and counter patriarchy by filling their zines with information about powerful female figures in history and contemporary popular culture. In addition, many girl zines contain quotations from well-known feminist activists and provide lists of texts considered important for the development of girls' critical consciousness. Although the majority of girl zinemakers are white, several girl zines (e.g., *Gunk, Mamasita, Asian Take Over, Bamboo Girl*) are produced by nonwhite girls to explore racism in mainstream society as well as youth subcultures like punk. In turn, as adolescent lesbianism has received more public awareness, several girl zines have participated in the legitimation of homosexuality by printing coming-out stories and exploring issues of interest to young lesbians.

In the tradition of alternative forms of media, many girl zines disseminate information that is not made available in commercial publications. Female health and gynecology are topics given special attention in many girl zines: readers are provided with information about alternative forms of female hygiene, contraception, and abortion. Many girl zines encourage their readers to respect, value, and celebrate the female body, and a number are dedicated specifically to girls whose bodies do not meet the current standard of thinness privileged in mainstream culture. For those readers needing more specific information or assistance, many girl zines provide lists of resources and organizations dedicated to helping female youth.

Although girl zinemakers often pride themselves on their ability to create texts that bear no resemblance to commercial publications, many employ the textual and representational styles of teen magazines to disparage those texts and mock the stereotypes of females reproduced in them. For example, some girl zinemakers ridicule the patronizing morality apparent in teen magazines by creating parodic advice columns that include outlandish situations of reader frustration and humorous responses by advice columnists. Many girl zines reprint offensive advertisements from commercial magazines, often with critical comments about such ads' exploitation of female consumers and their damage to girls' self-esteem. Some zinemakers have devoted full issues of their publications to critiques of commercial magazines. For example, *Ben Is Dead* #23 uses *Sassy*'s layout and writing style in a parody issue that reveals its makers' conflicted pleasures in reading *Sassy* as well as their general distaste for mainstream teen magazines.

The expansion of personal computers, the Internet, and the World Wide Web into many homes, schools, and workplaces during the 1990s has introduced new ways for female youth to express themselves and reach out to others. Moreover, these new media have radically transformed zine culture. An increasing number of girls are becoming involved in the creation of e-zines, websites that combine the serial nature of magazines, the networking potential of the Web, and the personalized aspect of homepages (small websites that resemble perzines). Girl e-zines resemble girl-made paper zines in their pro-female stance and inclusion of issues of concern to girls and women. *Girls Can Do Anything, Cybergrrl,* and *NrrdGrrl* are some of the many girl e-zines that appear on the Web.

In contrast to paper zines, e-zines often follow the layout of commercially produced magazines because indexes and tables of contents allow for easier movement within websites. In addition, most e-zine producers favor the artistic advantages offered by computer technology (i.e., access to millions of colors, photographs, moving images, and sounds) over the amateur, handcrafted style typically associated with paper zines. Although many paper zinemakers are dubious about the political potential of e-zines, these online publications are widely praised for their ability to swiftly communicate with a large number of individuals. For that reason, many zinemakers produce electronic versions of their paper zines. Although several website producers have taken it upon themselves to create directories of e-zines (e.g., *E-zine List, Etext Archives*), unfortunately, they are often incomplete or out-of-date, and the various e-zines that are included are typically left uncategorized. Moreover, many of the creators of e-zine directories seem unwilling to include girl-made e-zines and thus reinforce the Web's stereotype as a male-dominated space. Fortunately, more substantial lists of girls' e-zines appear on many female-produced websites, such as *Femina, Grrrl Xchange,* and *Yahoo! Grrls Online.*

Mary Celeste Kearney

See also Girl Power; Girls' Magazines; Riot Grrrls

References and Further Reading
Carlip, Hillary. 1995. *Girl Power: Young Women Speak Out!* New York: Warner.
Duncombe, Stephen. 1997. *Notes from the Underground: Zines and the Politics of Alternative Culture.* New York: Verso.
Green, Karen, and Tristan Taormino, eds. 1997. *A Girl's Guide to Taking Over the World: Writings from the Girl Zine Revolution.* New York: St. Martin's Press.
Kearney, Mary Celeste. 1998. "Girls, Girls, Girls: Gender and Generation in Contemporary Discourses of Female Adolescence and Youth Culture." Ph.D. diss., University of Southern California.
Richardson, Angela. 1996. "Come on Join the Conversation: 'Zines as a Medium for Feminist Dialogue and Community Building." *Feminist Collections* 17, nos. 3–4 (Spring–Summer): 10–13.
Vale, V. 1996–1997. *Zines!* 2 vols. San Francisco: V/Search Publication.
Wertham, Frederic. 1973. *The World of Fanzines: A Special Form of Communication.* Carbondale: Southern Illinois University Press.

Bibliography

Ackerman, Lillian A. 1996. *A Song to the Creator: Traditional Arts of the Native American Women of the Plateau.* Norman: University of Oklahoma Press.

Acosta, Vivian, and Linda Jean Carpenter. 1994. *Women in Intercollegiate Sport.* Brooklyn: Brooklyn College Press.

Acosta-Alzuru, Maria Carolina. 1999. "The American Girl Dolls: Constructing American Girlhood through Representation, Identity, and Consumption." Ph.D. diss., University of Georgia.

Adams, David Wallace. 1995. *Education for Extinction: American Indians and the Boarding School Experience, 1875–1928.* Lawrence: University Press of Kansas.

Adler, Bill, ed. 1967. *Love Letters to the Monkees.* New York: Popular Library.

Adler, Freda. 1975. *Sisters in Crime.* Prospect Heights, IL: Waveland Press.

Agle, Nan Hayden. 1970. *My Animals and Me: An Autobiographical Story.* New York: Seabury Press.

Alcott, Louisa May. 1868. *Little Women.* 1989. Reprint, New York: Penguin.

Aldrich, Elizabeth. 1991. *From the Ballroom to Hell: Grace and Folly in Nineteenth-Century Dance.* Evanston, IL: Northwestern University Press.

Alexander, Ruth M. 1995. *The "Girl Problem": Female Delinquency in New York, 1900–1930.* Ithaca, NY: Cornell University Press.

Alsop, Gulielma Fell, and Mary F. McBride. 1940. *She's off to College: A Girl's Guide to College Life.* New York: Vanguard Press.

American Academy of Pediatrics. 1998. "Carrying Backpacks a Weighty Issue for Students." *AAP News* 14, no. 9: 31.

American Association of University Women. 1991. *Shortchanging Girls, Shortchanging America: Executive Summary.* Washington, DC: AAUW Educational Foundation.

———. 1992. *The AAUW Report: How Schools Shortchange Girls.* Washington, DC: AAUW Educational Foundation.

———. 1993. *Hostile Hallways. The AAUW Survey on Sexual Harassment in America's Schools.* Washington, DC: AAUW Educational Foundation.

———. 1999. *Gender Gaps.* New York: Marlowe.

———. 2000. *Tech-Savvy: Educating Girls for the New Computer Age.* Washington, DC: AAUW Educational Foundation.

American Psychological Association. 1994. *Diagnostic and Statistical Manual of Mental Disorders.* 4th ed. Washington, DC: American Psychological Association.

Ang, Ien. 1998. "*Dallas* and the Ideology of Mass Culture." Pp. 265–274 in *Cultural*

Theory and Popular Culture: A Reader. Edited by John Storey. Athens: University of Georgia Press.

Angelou, Maya. 1996. *I Know Why the Caged Bird Sings.* Reprint, New York: Random House.

Angold, Adrian, E. Jane Costello, Alaattin Erkanlli, and C. M. Worthman. 1999. "Pubertal Changes in Hormone Levels and Depression in Girls." *Psychological Medicine* 29, no. 5 (September): 1043–1053.

Aparicio, Frances R., and Susana Chavez-Silverman. 1997. *Tropicalizations: Transcultural Representations of Latinidad.* Hanover, NH: Dartmouth College Press.

Apple, Rima D. 1997. "Liberal Education or Vocational Training? Home Economics Education for Girls." Pp. 79–95 in *Rethinking Home Economics. Women and the History of a Profession.* Edited by Sarah Stage and Virginia Vincenti. Ithaca, NY: Cornell University Press.

ApRoberts, Allison. 2000. "About Face." *Sacramento Bee* (May 19): G1–G5.

Apter, Terri. 1990. *Altered Loves: Mothers and Daughters during Adolescence.* New York: Fawcett Columbine.

Archie Comics, "Katy's Korner," http://www.archiecomics.com/katy/allabout.html.

Arthur, T. S. 1848. *Advice to Young Ladies.* Boston: Putnam.

Ashby, Leroy. 1985. "Partial Promises and Semi-Visible Youths: The Depression and World War II." Pp. 489–532 in *American Childhood: A Research Guide and Historical Handbook.* Edited by Joseph M. Hawes and N. Ray Hiner. Westport, CT: Greenwood Press.

Ashton, Dianne. 1997. *Rebecca Gratz: Women and Judaism in Antebellum America.* Detroit: Wayne State University Press.

Atkin, S. Beth. 1993. *Voices from the Fields: Children of Migrant Farmworkers Tell Their Stories.* Boston: Little, Brown.

Austin, Joe. 2001. *Taking the Train: Youth, Urban Crisis, and Graffiti.* New York: Columbia University Press.

Austin, Joe, and Michael Willard. 1998. *Generations of Youth: Youth Cultures and History in Twentieth-Century America.* New York: New York University Press.

Avery, Gillian. 1994. *Behold the Child: American Children and Their Books 1621–1922.* Baltimore: Johns Hopkins University Press.

Axline, Virginia. 1947. *Play Therapy.* Boston: Houghton Mifflin.

Axtell, James. 1981. *The Indian Peoples of Eastern America: A Documentary History of the Sexes.* New York: Oxford University Press.

Baca-Zinn, Maxine. 1993. "Mexican-Heritage Families in the United States." Pp. 161–172 in *Handbook of Hispanic Cultures in the United States: Sociology.* Edited by Felix Padilla. Houston and Madrid: Arte Público Press and Instituto de Cooperación Iberoamericana.

Bacchilega, Cristina. 1997. *Postmodern Fairy Tales: Gender and Narrative Strategies.* Philadelphia: University of Pennsylvania Press.

Bacon, Jean. 1996. *Life Lines: Community, Family, and Assimilation Among Asian Indian Immigrants.* New York: Oxford University Press.

Bailey, Beth L. 1988. *From Front Porch to Back Seat: Courtship in Twentieth-Century America.* Baltimore: Johns Hopkins University Press.

———. 1999. *Sex in the Heartland.* Cambridge, MA: Harvard University Press.

Baker, Dale. 1998. "Equity Issues in Science Education." Pp. 868–895 in

International Handbook of Science Education. Edited by Barry Fraser and Kenneth Tobin. Dordrecht, the Netherlands: Kluwer Academic Publishers.

Baker, Dale, and Michael Piburn. 1997. *Constructing Science in Middle and Secondary School Classrooms.* Needham Heights, MA: Allyn and Bacon.

Banner, Lois W. 1983. *American Beauty.* Chicago: University of Chicago Press.

"Barbie Doll Set." 1964. *The Nation* (April 27): 407.

Basinger, Jeanine. 1975. *Shirley Temple: Pyramid Illustrated History of the Movie.* New York: Pyramid Publications.

———. 1999. *Silent Stars.* New York: Alfred A. Knopf.

Baskin, Barbara. 1977. *Notes from a Different Drummer: A Guide to Juvenile Fiction Portraying the Handicapped.* New York: R. R. Bowker.

———. 1984. *More Notes from a Different Drummer: A Guide to Juvenile Fiction Portraying the Disabled.* New York: R. R. Bowker.

Bataille, Gretchen M., and Kathleen Mullen Sands. 1984. *American Indian Women: Telling Their Lives.* Lincoln: University of Nebraska Press.

Bateson, David, and Sharon Parsons-Chatman. 1981. "Sex-related Difference in Science Achievement: A Possible Testing Artifact." *International Journal of Science Education* 11: 371–385.

Baumgardner, Jennifer, and Amy Richards. *Manifesta: Young Women, Feminism, and the Future.* New York: Farrar, Straus & Giroux.

Bayton, Mavis. 1998. *Frock Rock: Women Performing Popular Music.* New York: Oxford University Press.

Beach, Mark. 1971. "Fraternities and Sororities." Pp. 93–98 in *The Encyclopedia of Education.* Edited by Lee Deighton. New York: Macmillan.

Beals, Melba Patillo. 1995. *Warriors Don't Cry.* New York: Pocket Books.

Beard, Daniel Carter. 1882. *The American Boys Handy Book: What to Do and How to Do It.* 1983, 1890. Reprint, Boston: David R. Godine.

Beard, Lina, and Adelia B. Beard. 1887. *The American Girls Handy Book: How to Amuse Yourself and Others.* 1987. Reprint, Boston: David R. Godine.

———. 1902. *New Ideas for Work and Play: What a Girl Can Make and Do.* New York: Charles Scribner's Sons.

Beauchamp, Cari. 1997. *Without Lying Down: Frances Marion and the Powerful Women of Early Hollywood.* New York: Scribner.

Beauvoir, Simone de. 1971. *The Second Sex.* 1949. Reprint, New York: Alfred A. Knopf.

Becker, A. E. 1999. "Acculturation and Disordered Eating in Fiji." Paper presented at the Annual Meeting of the American Psychiatric Association, Washington, DC.

Bederman, Gail. 1995. *Manliness and Civilization: A Cultural History of Gender and Race in the United States, 1880–1917.* Chicago: University of Chicago Press.

Beecher, Catharine E. 1856. *Physiology and Calisthenics for Schools and Families.* New York: Harper and Brothers.

Beeson, Diana. 1994. "Translating Nancy Drew from Fiction to Film." *The Lion and the Unicorn* 18, no. 1: 37–47.

Begay, Shirley M. 1983. *Kinaaldá: A Navajo Puberty Ceremony.* Rough Rock,

AZ: Navajo Curriculum Center, Rough Rock Demonstration School.

Begos, Jane DuPree. 1987. "The Diaries of Adolescent Girls." *Women's Studies International Forum* 10: 69–74.

Beisel, David R. 1984. "Thoughts on the Cabbage Patch Kids." *Journal of Psychohistory* 12, no. 1: 133–142.

Belden, Louise. 1983. *The Festive Tradition: Table Decoration and Desserts in America, 1650–1900.* New York: W. W. Norton.

Belfrage, Sally. 1994. *Un-American Activities: A Memoir of the Fifties.* New York: HarperCollins.

Belk, Russell W. 1995. *Collecting in a Consumer Society.* London and New York: Routledge.

Belknap, Joanne. 1996. *The Invisible Woman: Gender, Crime, and Justice.* Cincinnati: Wadsworth Publishing.

Belknap, Joanne, and Kristi Holsinger. 1998. "An Overview of Delinquent Girls: How Theory and Practice Have Failed and the Need for Innovative Changes." Pp. 31–64 in *Female Crime and Delinquency: Critical Perspectives and Effective Interventions.* Edited by Ruth T. Zaplin. Gaithersburg, MD: Aspen Publishers.

Bellingham, Bruce. 1986. "Institution and Family: An Alternative View of Nineteenth-Century Child-Saving." *Social Problems* 33, no. 6: S33–S57.

Benedict, Helen. 1992. *Virgin or Vamp.* New York: Oxford University Press,

Bennett, Kay. 1964. *Kaibah: Recollections of a Navajo Childhood.* Los Angeles: Westerlore Press.

Benning, Sadie. 1989a. *Living Inside.* Black and white, 4 min.

———. 1989b. *Me and Rubyfruit.* Black and white, 4 min.

———. 1989c. *A New Year.* Black and white, 4 min.

———. 1990a. *If Every Girl Had a Diary.* Black and white, 6 min.

———. 1990b. *Jollies.* Black and white, 11 min.

———. 1990c. *A Place Called Lovely.* Black and white, 14 min.

Benson, Peter L. 1998. *Healthy Communities, Healthy Youth.* Minneapolis: Search Institute.

Benson, Susan Porter. 1998. "Gender, Generation, and Consumption in the United States: Working-Class Families in the Interwar Period." Pp. 223–240 in *Getting and Spending: European and American Consumer Societies in the Twentieth Century.* Edited by Susan Strasser, Charles McGovern, and Matthias Judt. Cambridge: Cambridge University Press.

Benton, Mike. 1989. *The Comic Book in America.* Dallas: Taylor Publishing.

Berenstain, Stan and Jan. 1990. *The Berenstain Bears and the Slumber Party.* New York: Random House.

Berkin, Carol. 1996. *First Generations: Women in Colonial America.* New York: Hill and Wang.

Berkin, Carol Ruth, and Mary Beth Norton. 1979. *Women of America: A History.* Boston: Houghton Mifflin.

Berman, Donna. 1996. "Bat Mitzvah." In *The Dictionary of Feminist Theologies.* Edited by Letty M. Russel and J. Shannon Clarkson. Louisville, KY: Westminster John Knox Press.

Bernat, Jeffrey, Karen Calhoun, and Stephanie Stolp. 1998. "Sexually Aggressive Men's Response to a Date Rape Analogue: Alcohol as a Disinhibiting Cue." *The Journal of Sex Research* 35, no. 4: 341–348.

Bernikow, Louise. 1997. *The American Women's Almanac*. New York: Berkley Books.

Berrol, Selma Cantor. 1995. *Growing Up American: Immigrant Children in America Then and Now*. New York: Twayne.

Best, Amy L. 2000. *Prom Night: Youth, Schools, and Popular Culture*. New York: Routledge.

Bettelheim, Bruno. 1977. *The Uses of Enchantment: The Meaning and Importance of Fairy Tales*. New York: Vintage.

Beyers, Christine, and Roberta Ogletree. 1998. "Sexual Coercion Content in 21 Sexuality Educational Curricula." *The Journal of School Health* 68, no. 9: 370–375.

Billman, Carol. 1986. *The Secret of the Stratemeyer Syndicate: Nancy Drew, the Hardy Boys, and the Million Dollar Fiction Factory*. New York: Ungar Publishing.

Birtha, Becky. 1987. *Lover's Choice*. Seattle: Seal Press.

Bishop, Robert, and Jacqueline Marx Atkins. 1995. *Folk Art in American Life*. New York: Viking Studio Books.

Bjerregaard, Beth, and Carolyn Smith. 1993. "Gender Differences in Gang Participation, Delinquency, and Substance Use." *Journal of Quantitative Criminology* 9, no. 4: 329–355.

Black, Shirley Temple. 1988. *Child Star: An Autobiography*. New York: McGraw-Hill Publishing Company.

Blake, M. E. M. 1891. "Literature and the Formation of Character." *Catholic World* 53 (July): 475–484.

Blake, Mabelle Babcock, et al. 1929, 1967. *The Education of the Modern Girl*. Freeport, NY: Books for Libraries Press.

Blankhorn, David. 1995. *Fatherless America: Confronting Our Most Urgent Social Problem*. New York: HarperCollins.

Block, Francesca Lia. 1989. *Weetzie Bat*. New York: HarperCollins.

Bodinger–de Uriarte, Cristina, and Gregory Austin. 1991. "Substance Abuse among Adolescent Females." *Prevention Research Update* 9 (Fall).

Bolton, Ethel S., and Eva J. Coe. 1921. *American Samplers*. 1973. Reprint, New York: Weathervane.

Boris, Eileen. 1986. *Art and Labor: Ruskin, Morris, and the Craftsman Ideal in America*. Philadelphia: Temple University Press.

Boston Public Library. 1890–1920. *Records of the Corporation*.

Boston Women's Health Book Collective. 1998. *Our Bodies, Ourselves for the New Century: A Book by and for Women*. Rev. ed. New York: Simon and Schuster.

Bosworth, K., D. L. Espelage, and T. R. Simon. 1999. "Factors Associated with Bullying Behavior in Middle School Students." *Journal of Early Adolescence* 19: 341–362.

Bottigheimer, Ruth B. 1986. *Fairy Tales and Society: Illusion, Allusion and Paradigm*. Philadelphia: University of Pennsylvania Press.

Bowser, Eileen. 1990. *The Transformation of Cinema, 1907–1915*. Vol. 2, *History of the American Cinema*. Berkeley: University of California Press.

Boy, Billy. 1987. *Barbie: Her Life and Times*. New York: Crown.

Boyd, Barbara. 1993. *In the Company of My Sisters: Black Women and Self-Esteem*. New York: Penguin Books.

Boydston, Jeanne. 1991. *Home and Work: Housework, Wages, and the Ideology of*

Labor in the Early Republic. New York: Oxford University Press.

Boyer, Paul, and Stephen Nissenbaum. 1974. *Salem Possessed: The Social Origins of Witchcraft.* Cambridge, MA: Harvard University Press.

———. 1993. *Salem Village Witchcraft: A Documentary Record of Local Conflict in Colonial New England.* Boston: Northeastern University Press.

Boylan, Anne M. 1985. "Growing Up Female in America." Pp. 168–171 in *American Childhood: A Research Guide and Historical Handbook.* Edited by Joseph M. Hawes and N. Ray Hiner. Westport, CT: Greenwood Press.

Brecher, Ruth, and Edward Brecher. 1966. "Every Sixth Teen-Age Girl in Connecticut." *New York Times Magazine* (May 29).

Breines, Wini. 1992. *Young, White and Miserable: Growing Up Female in the Fifties.* New York: Beacon Press.

Breitwieser, Mitchell. 1990. *American Puritanism and the Defense of Mourning: Religion, Grief and Ethnology in Mary White Rowlandson's Captivity Narrative.* Madison: University of Wisconsin Press.

Bremner, Robert A., John Barnard, Tamara K. Hareven, and Robert M. Mennel, eds. 1970–1974. *Children and Youth in America: A Documentary History.* 3 vols. Cambridge, MA: Harvard University Press.

Breuer, Joseph, and Sigmund Freud. 1895. "Studies in Hysteria." In *The Standard Edition of the Complete Psychological Works of Sigmund Freud.* Edited by James Strachey. London: Hogarth Press.

Briere, John, Lucy Berliner, Josephine A. Bulkley, Carole Jenny, and Theresa Reid, eds. 1996. *The APSAC Handbook on Child Maltreatment.* Thousand Oaks, CA: Sage.

Broderick, Patricia. 1998. "Early Adolescent Differences in the Use of Ruminative and Distracting Coping Strategies." *Journal of Early Adolescence* 18, no. 2: 173–191.

Brodie, Janet Farrell. 1994. *Contraception and Abortion in Nineteenth Century America.* Ithaca: Cornell University Press.

Brooks-Gunn, Jeanne, and Michelle P. Warren. 1989. "Biological and Social Contributions to Negative Affect in Young Adolescent Girls." *Child Development* 60: 40–55.

Brothers, Joyce. 1967. "On Becoming a Woman." *Good Housekeeping* (January).

Brotherton, David C. 1996. "'Smartness,' 'Toughness,' and 'Autonomy': Drug Use in the Context of Gang Female Delinquency." *Journal of Drug Issues* 26, no. 1: 261–277.

Broverman, I., D. Broverman, F. Clarkson, P. Rosenkrantz, and S. Vogel. 1970. "Sex-role Stereotypes and Clinical Judgments of Mental Health." *Journal of Consulting and Counseling Psychology* 43: 1–7.

Brown, Fern G. 1996. *Daisy and the Girl Scouts: The Story of Juliette Low.* Morton Grove, IL: Whitman.

Brown, Judith K. 1963. "A Cross-Cultural Study of Female Initiation Rites." *American Anthropologist* 65: 837–853.

Brown, Lyn Mikel. 1999. *Raising Their Voices: The Politics of Girls' Anger.* Cambridge, MA: Harvard University Press.

Brown, Lyn Mikel, and Carol Gilligan. 1992. *Meeting at the Crossroads: Women's Psychology and Girls' Development.* New York: Ballantine.

Brown, Rita Mae. 1988. *Rubyfruit Jungle.* New York: Daughters, Inc., 1973. Reprint, New York: Bantam.

Brownlow, Kevin. 1999. *Mary Pickford Rediscovered: Rare Pictures of a*

Hollywood Legend. New York: Harry N. Abrams, in association with the Academy of Motion Picture Arts and Sciences.

Brownmiller, Susan. 1975. *Against Our Will: Men, Women and Rape.* New York: Simon and Schuster.

Bruch, Hilde. 1978. *The Golden Cage: The Enigma of Anorexia Nervosa.* Cambridge, MA: Harvard University Press.

Brumberg, Joan Jacobs. 1988. *Fasting Girls: The Emergence of Anorexia Nervosa as a Modern Disease.* Cambridge, MA: Harvard University Press.

———. 1997. *The Body Project: An Intimate History of American Girls.* New York: Random House.

———. 1998. "It's Okay to Talk to Yourself." Chap. 17 in *33 Things Every Girl Should Know.* Edited by Tonya Bolden. New York: Crown.

Brumberg, Stephan F. 1986. *Going to America, Going to School: The Jewish Immigrant Public School Encounter in Turn-of-the-Century New York City.* New York: Praeger.

Bruns, Roger, ed. 1977. *Am I Not a Man and a Brother? The Antislavery Crusade of Revolutionary America, 1688–1788.* New York: Chelsea House.

Bryk, Anthony S., Valerie E. Lee, and Peter B. Holland. 1993. *Catholic Schools and the Common Good.* Cambridge, MA: Harvard University Press.

Buchwald, Emilie, Pamela Fletcher, and Martha Roth, eds. 1993. *Transforming a Rape Culture.* Minneapolis, MN: Milkweed Publications.

Buckler, Helen, Mary F. Fiedler, and Martha F. Allen. 1961. *Wo-he-lo: The Story of the Campfire Girls 1910–1960.* New York: Holt, Rinehart, and Winston.

Buckman, Peter. 1978. *Let's Dance: Social, Ballroom and Folk Dancing.* New York: Paddington Press.

Budgeon, Shelley. 1998. "'I'll Tell You What I Really, Really Want': Girl Power and Self-Identity in Britain." Pp. 115–144 in *Millennium Girls: Today's Girls around the World.* Edited by Sherrie A. Inness. Oxford: Rowman and Littlefield.

Budgeon, Shelley, and Dawn H. Currie. 1995. "From Feminism to Postfeminism: Women's Liberation in Fashion Magazines." *Women's Studies International Forum* 18, no. 2: 173–186.

Bureau of Justice Statistics. 1994. *Criminal Victimization in the United States.* Washington, DC: Bureau of Justice Statistics, U.S. Department of Justice.

Burgess, Ann, and Lynda Holmstrom. 1974. "Rape Trauma Syndrome." *American Journal of Psychiatry* 131, no. 9: 981–986.

Burk, Caroline Frear. 1900. "The Collecting Instinct." *Pedagogical Seminary* 7: 179–207.

Burnham, John C. 1993. *Bad Habits: Drinking, Smoking, Taking Drugs, Gambling, Sexual Misbehavior, and Swearing in American History.* New York: New York University Press.

Burnham, Michelle. 1997. *Captivity and Sentiment: Cultural Exchange in American Literature, 1682–1861.* Hanover, NH: University Press of New England.

Burris, Gladys Tolar. 1953. "Help Your Child Enjoy Writing Letters." *Parents' Magazine* 28 (December): 52–53.

Burton, Richard. 1898. "Literature for Our Children." *North American Review* 167: 278–286.

Byers, E. Sandra, and Lucia F. O'Sullivan, eds. 1996. *Sexual Coercion in Dating Relationships.* New York: Haworth Press.

Cahn, Susan. 1995. *Coming on Strong: Gender and Sexuality in Twentieth-Century Women's Sport*. Cambridge, MA: Harvard University Press.

Cain, Chelsea. 1999. *Wild Child: Girlhoods in the Counterculture*. Seattle, WA: Seal Press.

Caldwell, Doreen. 1981. *And All Was Revealed: Ladies Underwear 1907–1980*. New York: St. Martin's Press.

Calhoun, Arthur W. 1960. *A Social History of the American Family*. Vol. 1. New York: Barnes & Noble.

Callahan, Carolyn M., and Sally M. Reis. 1996. "Gifted Girls, Remarkable Women." In *Remarkable Women: Perspectives on Female Talent Development*. Edited by Karen D. Arnold, Kathleen Diane Noble, and Rena Faye Subotnik. Cresskill, NJ: Hampton Press.

Callicott, Catherine Dorris, and Lawson Holderness. 1978. *In Praise of Dollhouses: The Story of a Personal Collection*. New York: William Morrow.

Calloway, Colin G. 1999. *First Peoples: A Documentary Survey of American Indian History*. Boston: Bedford Books/St. Martin's Press.

Calvert, Karin. 1992. *Children in the House: The Material Culture of Early Childhood, 1600–1900*. Boston: Northeastern University Press.

Campbell, Anne. 1986. "Self-Report of Fighting by Females." *British Journal of Criminology* 26, no. 1: 28–46.

Campbell, Helen. 1888. *The American Girl's Home Book of Work and Play*. New York: G. P. Putnam's Sons.

Campbell, Patricia J. 1979. *Sex Education Books for Young Adults, 1892–1979*. New York: R. R. Bowker.

———. 1995. "Redefining the Girl Problem in Mathematics." Pp. 226–241 in *New Directions for Equity in Mathematics*. Edited by William Secada, Elizabeth Fenema, and Lisa Adajian. Cambridge, UK: Cambridge University Press.

Candelaria, Cordelia. 1980. "La Malinche: Feminist Prototype." *Frontiers: Journal of Women Studies* 5, no. 2 (Summer): 1–6.

———. 1993. "Latina Women Writers: Chicana, Cuban American, and Puerto Rican Voices." Pp. 134–162 in *Handbook of Hispanic Cultures in the United States: Literature and Art*. Edited by Francisco Lomeli et al. Houston, TX, and Madrid, Spain: Arte Público Press and Instituto de Cooperación Iberoamericana.

———. 1995. "La Malinche." P. 468 in *The Oxford Companion to Women's Writing in the United States*. Edited by Cathy N. Davidson and Linda Wagner-Martin. New York: Oxford University Press.

Canel, Annie, Ruth Oldenziel, and Karin Zachmann, eds. 2000. *Crossing Boundaries, Building Bridges: Comparing the History of Women Engineers, 1870s–1990*. London: Harwood Academic Publishers.

Canetto, Silvia Sara. 1998. "Meanings of Gender and Suicidal Behavior among Adolescents." *Suicide and Life Threatening Behaviors* 27: 339–351.

Canetto, Silvia Sara, and David Lester. 1995. "Gender and the Primary Prevention of Suicide Mortality." *Suicide and Life-Threatening Behavior* 25: 58–69.

Cantú, Norma Elia. 1995. *Canícula: Snapshots of a Girlhood en la Frontera*. Albuquerque: University of New Mexico Press.

———. 1999. "La Quinceañera: Towards an Ethnographic Analysis of a Life-Cycle Ritual." *Southern Folklore* 56, no. 1: 73–101.

Caprio, Betsy. 1992. *The Mystery of Nancy Drew: Girl Sleuth on the Couch.* Trabuco Canyon: Source Books.

Carlip, Hillary. 1995. *Girl Power: Young Women Speak Out!* New York: Warner.

Carp, E. Wayne. 1998. *Family Matters: Secrecy and Disclosure in the History of Adoption.* Cambridge, MA: Harvard University Press.

Carr, Lois Green, and Lorena S. Walsh. 1977. "The Planter's Wife: The Experience of White Women in Seventeenth-Century Maryland." *William and Mary Quarterly* 34: 542–571.

Carroll, Rebecca. 1997. *Sugar in the Raw: Voices of Young Black Girls in America.* New York: Crown Press.

Carter, Mia. 1998. "The Politics of Pleasure: Cross-Cultural Autobiographic Performance in the Video Works of Sadie Benning." *Signs: A Journal of Women in Culture and Society* 23, no. 3: 745–770.

Cassell, Justine, and Henry Jenkins. 1998. *From Barbie to Mortal Kombat: Gender and Computer Games.* Cambridge, MA: MIT Press.

Cassidy, Carol. 1999. *Girls in America: Their Stories, Their Words.* New York: TV Books.

Castiglia, Christopher. 1996. *Bound and Determined: Captivity, Culture-Crossing, and White Womanhood from Mary Rowlandson to Patty Hearst.* Chicago: University of Chicago Press.

Castle, Mr. and Mrs. Vernon. 1914. *Modern Dancing.* New York: Harper and Brothers.

Castleman, Craig. 1982. *Getting Up: Subway Graffiti in New York.* Boston: MIT Press.

Cather, Willa. 1896. "Tommy, the Unsentimental." Pp. 234–242 in *Chloe Plus Olivia: An Anthology of Lesbian Literature from the Seventeenth Century to the Present.* Edited by Lillian Faderman. 1994. Reprint, New York: Viking/Penguin.

———. 1905. "Paul's Case." Pp. 149–174 in *Willa Cather: Five Stories.* 1956. Reprint, New York: Vintage.

———. 1918. *My Ántonia.* 1988. Reprint, Boston: Houghton Mifflin.

Cavallo, Dominick. 1981. *Muscles and Morals: Organized Playgrounds and Urban Reform, 1880–1920.* Philadelphia: University of Pennsylvania Press.

Cecil, Lord David. 1957. "Letter Writing: A Private Talent of Women." *Vogue* 130 (August 1): 98–99.

Cervantes, Lorna Dee. 1980. "Beneath the Shadow of the Freeway" and "Uncle's First Rabbit." In *Emplumada.* Pittsburgh: University of Pittsburgh Press.

Chaiet, Donna. 1995. *Staying Safe while Shopping.* New York: Rose Publishing Group.

Chalfant, Henry, and Martha Cooper. 1984. *Subway Art.* New York: Henry Holt.

Chamberlain, Kathleen. 1994. "The Secrets of Nancy Drew: Having Their Cake and Eating It Too." *The Lion and the Unicorn* 18, no. 1: 1–12.

Chan, Sucheng. 1998. "Race, Ethnic Culture, and Gender in the Construction of Identities among Second-Generation Chinese Americans." Pp. 127–164 in *Claiming America: Constructing Chinese American Identities during the Exclusion Era.* Edited by K. Scott Wong and Sucheng Chan. Philadelphia: Temple University Press.

Chan, Sucheng, ed. 1994. *Hmong Means Free: Life in Laos and America.* Philadelphia: Temple University Press.

Chapman, Robert L., ed. 1997. *Dictionary of American Slang.* New York: HarperCollins.

Chappell, Linda Rae. 1997. *Coaching Cheerleading Successfully.* Champaign, IL: Human Kinetics.

Charsley, Simon. 1992. *Wedding Cakes and Cultural History.* London: Routledge.

Chauncey, George. 1994. *Gay New York: Gender, Urban Culture, and the Makings of the Gay Male World, 1890–1940.* New York: Basic Books.

Chávez, Denise. 1987. *The Last of the Menu Girls.* Houston: Arte Público.

Chavez, Leo. 1991. *Shadowed Lives: Undocumented Immigrants in American Society.* Fort Worth, TX: Harcourt Brace.

Chavira-Prado, Alicia. 1994. "Latina Experience and Latina Identity." Pp. 244–269 in *Handbook of Hispanic Cultures of the United States: Anthropology.* Edited by Thomas Weaver. Houston and Madrid: Arte Público Press and Instituto de Cooperación Iberoamericana.

Chen, Hsiang-shui. 1992. *Chinatown No More: Taiwan Immigrants in Contemporary New York.* Ithaca, NY: Cornell University Press.

Chen, Yong. 2000. *Chinese San Francisco, 1850–1943: A Trans-Pacific Community.* Palo Alto, CA: Stanford University Press.

Chernin, Kim. 1983. *In My Mother's House: A Daughter's Story.* New York: HarperCollins.

Chesney-Lind, Meda. 1973. "Judicial Enforcement of the Female Sex Role: The Family Court and the Female Delinquent." *Issues in Criminology* 8, no. 2: 51–69.

———. 1993. "Girls, Gangs and Violence: Anatomy of a Backlash." *Humanity and Society* 17, no. 3: 321–344.

———. 1997. *The Female Offender: Girls, Women, and Crime.* Thousand Oaks: Sage.

Chesney-Lind, Meda, and Marilyn Brown. 1998. "Girls and Violence: An Overview." Pp. 171–200 in *Youth Violence: Prevention, Intervention, and Social Policy.* Edited by Daniel J. Flannery and C. Ronald Huff. Washington, DC: American Psychiatric Association.

Chesney-Lind, Meda, and Randall G. Shelden. 1992. *Girls, Delinquency and Juvenile Justice.* Pacific Grove, CA: Brooks/Cole.

Child, Lydia Maria. 1833. *The Girls' Own Book.* New York: Clark Austin.

Choate, Ann Hyde, and Helen Ferris, eds. 1928. *Juliette Low and the Girl Scouts: The Story of an American Woman.* Garden City: Doubleday for the Girl Scouts.

Chodorow, Nancy J. 1978. *The Reproduction of Mothering: Psychoanalysis and the Sociology of Gender.* Berkeley: University of California Press.

Chun, Gloria Heyung. 2000. *Of Orphans and Warriors: Inventing Chinese American Culture and Identity.* New Brunswick, NJ: Rutgers University Press.

Cisneros, Sandra. 1991. *The House on Mango Street.* Houston: Arte Público, 1984. Reprint, New York: Vintage.

Clark, Beverly Lyon, and Margaret R. Higgonet. 1999. *Girls, Boys, Books, Toys: Gender in Children's Literature and Culture.* Baltimore: Johns Hopkins University Press.

Clark, James W., Jr. 1984. *Clover All Over: North Carolina 4-H in Action.* Raleigh: North Carolina State University Press.

Clark-Lewis, Elizabeth. 1994. *Living In, Living Out: African American Domestics* in Washington, D.C., 1910–1940. Washington, DC: Smithsonian Institution Press.

——. 1996. *Living In, Living Out: African American Domestics and the Great Migration.* New York: Kodansha International.

Clement, Priscilla F. 1997. *Growing Pains: Children in the Industrial Age, 1850–1890.* New York: Twayne.

Clinton, Catherine. 1982. *Plantation Mistress: Women's World in the Old South.* New York: Vintage.

Clover, Carol. 1993. *Men, Women and Chain Saws: Gender in the Modern Horror Film.* Princeton: Princeton University Press.

Coale, Ansley, and Melvin Zelnik. 1963. *New Estimates of Fertility and Population in the United States.* Princeton: Princeton University Press.

Coburn, Carol K., and Martha Smith. 1999. *Spirited Lives: How Nuns Shaped Catholic Culture and American Life, 1836–1920.* Chapel Hill: University of North Carolina Press.

Cogan, Frances. 1989. *All-American Girl: The Ideal of Real Womanhood in Mid-Nineteenth-Century America.* Athens: University of Georgia Press.

Cohen, Daniel. 1990. "For Happy Campers, Nothing Beats the Old Rites of Passage." *Smithsonian* 21 (August): 86–94.

Cohen, Larry. 1969. "The New Audience: From Andy Hardy to Arlo Guthrie." *Saturday Review* 27 (December): 9.

Cohen, Miriam. 1993. *Workshop to Office: Two Generations of Italian Women in New York City, 1900–1950.* Ithaca, NY: Cornell University Press.

Coleman, Michael C. 1993. *American Indian Children at School, 1850–1930.* Jackson: University of Mississippi Press.

——. 1994. "American Indian School Pupils as Cultural Brokers: Cherokee Girls at Brainerd Mission, 1828–1829." Pp. 122–136 in *Between Indian and White Worlds: The Cultural Broker.* Edited by Margaret Connell Szasz. Norman: University of Oklahoma Press.

Collins, Patricia Hill. 1993. "The Meaning of Motherhood in Black Culture and Black Mother-Daughter Relationships." Pp. 42–60 in *Double Stitch: Black Women Write about Mothers and Daughters.* Edited by Patricia Bell-Scott, Beverly Guy-Sheftall, Jacqueline Jones Royster, Janet Sims-Wood, Miriam DeCosta-Willis, and Lucille P. Fultz. New York: HarperPerennial.

——. 2000. *Black Feminist Thought.* Reprint, New York: Routledge.

Comas-Diaz, L., and B. Greene, eds. 1994. *Women of Color: Integrating Ethnic and Gender Identities in Psychotherapy.* New York: Guilford Press.

Comer, James P., and Alvin F. Poussaint. 1992. *Raising Black Children.* New York: Penguin Books.

Comer, Krista. Forthcoming, 2003. *From Gidget to Surfergrrrls: Cultural History and Gender Formation in an Era of Globalization.* (See for oral histories with Rosemari Reimers Rice, Linda Benson, and Jane Mackenzie.)

"The Comic Strip and Popular Culture." 1975. *Intellect* 104: 84–85.

Considine, David. 1985. *The Cinema of Adolescence.* Jefferson, NC: McFarland.

Coontz, Stephanie. 1992. *The Way We Never Were: American Families and the Nostalgia Trap.* New York: Basic Books/HarperCollins.

Coppolillo, Henry P. 1987. *Psychodynamic Psychotherapy of*

Children. Madison: International Universities Press.

Cornelius, Janet Duitsman. 1991. *"When I Can Read My Title Clear": Literacy, Slavery, and Religion in the Antebellum South.* Columbia: University of South Carolina Press.

Cornell, Betty. 1954. *Betty Cornell's Teen-Age Popularity Guide.* New York: Prentice-Hall.

Cott, Nancy. 1977. *The Bonds of Womanhood: "Women's Sphere" in New England, 1780–1835.* New Haven, CT: Yale University Press, chap. 2.

———. 1989. *The Grounding of Modern Feminism.* New Haven: Yale University Press.

Cowan, Ruth Schwartz. 1983. *More Work for Mother: The Ironies of Household Technology from the Open Hearth to the Microwave.* New York: Basic Books.

Cromley, Elizabeth Collins. 1992. "A History of American Beds and Bedrooms, 1890–1930." Pp. 120–144 in *American Home Life, 1880–1930: A Social History of Spaces and Services.* Edited by Jessica H. Foy and Thomas J. Schlereth. Knoxville: University of Tennessee Press.

Cross, Gary. 1997. *Kids' Stuff: Toys and the Changing World of American Childhood.* Cambridge, MA: Harvard University Press.

Crosson-Tower, Cynthia. 1999. *Understanding Child Abuse and Neglect.* 4th ed. Needham Heights, MA: Allyn and Bacon.

Croswell, T. R. 1899. "Amusements of Worcester School Children." *Pedagogical Seminary* 4 (September): 354.

Crow Dog, Mary, and Richard Erdoes. 1990. *Lakota Woman.* New York: HarperPerennial.

Crowther, Barbara. 1999. "Writing as Performance: Young Girls' Diaries." Pp.

197–220 in *Making Meaning of Narratives in the Narrative Study of Lives.* Edited by Ruthellen Josselson and Amia Lieblich. Thousand Oaks, CA: Sage.

Culley, Margo, ed. 1985. *A Day at a Time: The Diary Literature of American Women from 1764 to the Present.* New York: Feminist Press.

Cummings, Jeanne. 1992. "Election '92 TV's Starring Role." *Atlanta Journal and Constitution* (November 1): C4.

Currie, Dawn H. 1999. *Girl Talk: Adolescent Readers and Their Magazines.* Toronto: University of Toronto Press.

Curtin, Philip D. 1970. *The Atlantic Slave Trade: A Census.* Madison: University of Wisconsin Press.

Cutler, Martha. 1906. "Girls' Rooms." *Harper's Bazarre* 40 (October): 935–940.

Danbom, David B. 1979. "Rural Education Reform and the Country Life Movement, 1900–1920." *Agricultural History* 53, no. 2: 462–474.

Data File. 1992. *Vocational Education Journal* 67 (September): 37–39.

Davalos, Karen Mary. 1996. "La Quinceañera: Making Gender and Ethnic Identities." *Frontiers* 16, nos. 2–3: 101–127.

Davis, Lennard J., ed. 1997. *The Disabilities Studies Reader.* New York: Routledge.

Davis, Terry C., Gary Q. Peck, and John M. Storment. 1993. "Acquaintance Rape and the High School Student." *Journal of Adolescent Health* 14, no. 3 (May): 220–224.

Deboer, George. 1991. *A History of Ideas in Science Education.* New York: Teachers College Press.

Debold, Elizabeth, Marie Wilson, and Idelisse Malave. 1993. *Mother Daughter*

Revolution: From Betrayal to Power. Reading: Addison-Wesley.

Dee, Catherine. 1997. *The Girls' Guide to Life: How to Take Charge of the Issues That Affect You.* Boston: Little, Brown.

Dejong, David H. 1993. *Promises of the Past: A History of Indian Education in the United States.* Golden, CO: North American Press.

DeKeseredy, Walter. 1988. "Woman Abuse in Dating Relationships: The Relevance of Social Support Theory." *Journal of Family Violence* 3: 1–13.

DeKeseredy, Walter, and Martin Schwartz. 1993. "Male Peer Support and Woman Abuse: An Expansion of DeKeseredy's Model." *Sociological Spectrum* 13: 393–413.

Delaney, Lucy A. 1988. "From the Darkness Cometh the Light, or Struggles for Freedom." In *Six Women's Slave Narratives.* Edited by Henry Louis Gates, Jr. New York: Oxford University Press.

Deloria, Philip Joseph. 1998. *Playing Indian.* New Haven: Yale University Press.

DeMars, Christine. 1998. "Gender Differences in Mathematics and Science on a High School Proficiency Exam: The Role of Response Format." *Applied Measurement in Education* 11: 279–299.

D'Emilio, John, and Estelle B. Freedman. 1988. *Intimate Matters: A History of Sexuality in America.* New York: Harper and Row.

Demos, John. 1970. *A Little Commonwealth: Family Life in Plymouth Colony.* New York: Oxford University Press.

———. 1994. *The Unredeemed Captive: A Family Story from Early America.* New York: Alfred A. Knopf.

———. 1995. *The Tried and the True: Native American Women Confronting Colonization.* New York: Oxford University Press.

Denis, Christopher Paul, and Michael Denis. 1992. *Favorite Families of TV.* New York: Citadel Press.

Dennis, Charles. 1909. "Phoebe at the Fount." *The Soda Fountain* (May): 32.

Derounian-Stodola, Kathryn Zabelle, and James Arthur Levernier. 1993. *The Indian Captivity Narrative, 1550–1900.* New York: Twayne.

Devlin, Rachel. 1998. "Juvenile Delinquency and the Problem of Paternal Authority." Pp. 83–106 in *Delinquents and Debutantes: Twentieth-Century American Girls' Culture.* Edited by Sherrie A. Inness. New York: New York University Press.

Díaz-Stevens, Ana María. 1994. "Latinas in the Church" and "Latino Youth and the Church." Pp. 240–277 and 278–307 in *Hispanic Catholic Culture in the U.S.* Edited by Jay P. Dolan and Allan Figueroa Deck, S.J. Notre Dame: University of Notre Dame Press.

Dickens, Charles. 1842. *American Notes for General Circulation.* Leipzig: Bernard Tauchnitz.

Dietrich, Lisa C. 1998. *Chicana Adolescents: Bitches, 'Ho's, and Schoolgirls.* Westport, CT: Praeger.

Dill, Stephen H., and Clyde Burkholder, eds. 1966. *Current Slang.* Vol. 1. Vermillion: University of South Dakota.

Dodge, Kenneth A., John E. Bates, and Gregory S. Pettit. 1990. "Mechanisms in the Cycle of Violence." *Science* 250: 1678–1683.

Dodson, Lisa. 1998. *Don't Call Us out of Name: The Untold Lives of Women and Girls in Poor America.* Boston: Beacon Press.

Doherty, Thomas. 1988. *Teenagers and Teenpics: The Juvenilization of American Film*. Boston: Unwin Hyman.

Don Markestein's Cartoonpedia, "Little Lulu," http://www.stormloader.com/markstein/cartoonpedia/lulu.html.

Donley, Carol, and Sheryl Buckley, eds. 1996. *The Tyranny of the Normal: An Anthology*. Kent, OH: Kent State University Press.

Douglas, Deborah G. 1990. "United States Women in Aviation, 1940–1985." *Smithsonian Studies in Air and Space* no. 7. Washington, DC: Smithsonian Institution Press.

Douglas, Susan. 1994. *Where the Girls Are: Growing Up Female with the Mass Media*. New York: Times Books.

———. 1997. "Girls 'n' Spice: All Things Nice?" *The Nation* (August 25): 21–24.

Douglas, Theo, and Elizabeth Glazner. 1999. "The Real Gidget." *Wahine* 5, no. 2: 20–25.

Dowd, Gregory Evans. 1992. *A Spirited Resistance: The North American Indian Struggle for Unity, 1745–1815*. Baltimore: Johns Hopkins University Press.

Drinnon, Richard. 1972. *White Savage: The Case of John Dunn Hunter*. New York: Schocken.

Duberman, Martin, Fred Eggan, and Richard Clemmer. 1979. "Documents in Hopi Indian Sexuality: Imperialism, Culture, and Resistance." *Radical History Review* 20 (Spring–Summer): 99–130.

Dublin, Thomas. 1979. *Women at Work: The Transformation of Work and Community in Lowell, Massachusetts, 1826–1860*. New York: Columbia University Press.

———. 1981. *Farm to Factory: Women's Letters 1830–1860*. New York: Columbia University Press.

———. 1994. *Transforming Women's Work: New England Lives in the Industrial Revolution*. Ithaca, NY: Cornell University Press.

Dublin, Thomas, ed. 1996. *Becoming American, Becoming Ethnic: College Students Explore Their Roots*. Philadelphia: Temple University Press.

DuCille, Ann. 1999. "Barbie in Black and White." Pp. 127–142 in *The Barbie Chronicles: A Living Doll Turns Forty*. Edited by Yona Zeldis McDonough. New York: Touchstone.

Duclos, Jeff. 1999. "In Trim: Women of Malibu." *LongBoard Magazine* (May–June): 50–58.

Dudden, Faye E. 1983. *Serving Women: Household Service in Nineteenth-Century America*. Middletown, CT: Wesleyan University Press.

Duggan, Lisa. 1993. "The Trials of Alice Mitchell: Sensationalism, Sexology, and the Lesbian Subject in Turn-of-the-Century America." *Signs: A Journal of Women in Culture and Society* 18, no. 4: 791–814.

Duncombe, Stephen. 1997. *Notes from the Underground: Zines and the Politics of Alternative Culture*. New York: Verso.

———. 1998. "Let's All Be Alienated Together: Zines and the Making of Underground Community." Pp. 427–451 in *Generations of Youth: Youth Cultures and History in Twentieth-Century America*. Edited by Joe Austin and Michael Nevin Willard. New York: New York University Press.

Dunning, Jennifer. 1985. *"But First a School": The First Fifty Years of the*

School of American Ballet. New York: Viking.

Durost, Walter Nelson. 1932. *Children's Collecting Activity Related to Social Factors.* New York: Bureau of Publications, Teachers College, Columbia University.

Dushkin, Alexander M. 1918. *Jewish Education in New York City.* New York: Bureau of Jewish Education.

Dweck, C., and N. Repucci. 1973. "Learned Helplessness and Reinforcement Responsibility in Children." *Journal of Personality and Social Psychology* 25: 1090–1116.

Dyck, Cornelius J., ed. 1981. *An Introduction to Mennonite History: A Popular History of the Anabaptists and Mennonites.* Scottdale, PA: Herald Press.

Dyer, Carolyn Stewart, and Nancy Tillman Romalov. 1995. *Rediscovering Nancy Drew.* Iowa City: University of Iowa Press.

Earle, Alice Morse. 1899. *Child Life in Colonial Days.* New York: Macmillan.

Ebersole, Gary L. 1995. *Captured by Texts: Puritan to Post-Modern Images of Indian Captivity.* Charlottesville: University Press of Virginia.

Echols, Alice. 1989. *Daring to Be Bad: Radical Feminism in America, 1967–1975.* Minneapolis: University of Minnesota Press.

Edmonds, Mary Jaene. 1991. *Samplers and Samplermakers: An American Schoolgirl Art, 1700–1850.* New York: Rizzoli.

Edselas, F. M. 1895. "What Shall We Do with Our Girls?" *Catholic World* 61 (July): 538–545.

Edut, Ophira, ed. 1998. *Adios, Barbie: Young Women Write about Body Image and Identity.* Seattle, WA: Seal Press.

Edwards, Joan. 1983. *Sampler-making, 1540–1940.* Surrey, UK: Bayford Books.

Eells, Eleanor. 1986. *Eleanor Eells' History of Organized Camping: The First 100 Years.* Martinsville, IN: American Camping Association.

Ehle, John. 1988. *Trail of Tears: The Rise and Fall of the Cherokee Nation.* New York: Doubleday.

Ehrenreich, Barbara. 1983. *The Hearts of Men: American Dreams and the Flight from Commitment.* New York: Anchor Press.

Ehrenreich, Barbara, and Deirdre English. 1978. *For Her Own Good: 150 Years of the Experts' Advice to Women.* New York: Doubleday.

Ehrenreich, Barbara, Elizabeth Hess, and Gloria Jacobs. 1986. "Beatlemania: Girls Just Want to Have Fun." Pp. 84–106 in *The Adoring Audience: Fan Culture and Popular Media.* New York: Routledge.

Eisenmann, Linda, ed. 1998. *Historical Dictionary of Women's Education in the United States.* Westport, CT: Greenwood Press.

Eisenstein, Zillah. 1981. *The Radical Future of Liberal Feminism.* New York: Longman.

Eisler, Benita, ed. 1977. *The Lowell Offering: Writings by New England Mill Women (1840–1845).* New York: Harper Colophon.

Elder, Glen H. 1974. *Children of the Great Depression: Social Change in Life Experience.* Chicago: University of Chicago.

Eliot, Emily Marshall. Diaries for 1869–1871. Entry for March 2, 1869. In Schlesinger Library, Radcliffe College.

Elkind, David. 1998. *All Grown Up and No Place to Go.* Reading, MA: Addison-Wesley.

Ellis, A. C., and G. Stanley Hall. 1896. "Study of Dolls." *Pedagogical Seminary* 1, no. 2 (December).

Ellis, Ann. 1929. *The Life of an Ordinary Woman.* 1990. Reprint, Boston: Houghton Mifflin.

Emerson, Suzanne Gould. 1949. *Off to College.* Philadelphia: John C. Winston Company.

Emery, Lynne Fauley. 1980. *Black Dance in the United States from 1619 to 1970.* New York: Dance Horizons.

Equiano, Olaudah. 1995. *The Interesting Narrative of the Life of Olaudah Equiano: Written by Himself.* Edited by Robert J. Allison. Boston: Bedford Books of St. Martin's Press.

Erenberg, Lewis. 1981. *Steppin' Out: New York Nightlife and the Transformation of American Culture.* Chicago: University of Chicago Press.

Erevia, Sister Angela. 1980. *A Religious Celebration for the Quinceañera.* San Antonio, Texas: Mexican American Cultural Center.

Eschbach, Elizabeth. 1993. *The Higher Education of Women in England and America.* New York: Garland.

Espiritu, Yen Le. 1997. *Asian American Women and Men: Labor, Laws, and Love.* Thousand Oaks, CA: Sage.

Esquibel, Catrióna Rueda. 1998. "Memories of Girlhood: Chicana Lesbian Fictions." *Signs: A Journal of Women in Culture and Society* 23, no. 3: 645–682.

Estés, Clarissa Pinkola. 1992. *Women Who Run with the Wolves: Myths and Stories of the Wild Woman Archetype.* New York: Ballantine.

Evans, Sara. 1979. *Personal Politics: The Roots of Women's Liberation in the Civil Rights Movement and the New Left.* New York: Vintage Books.

Ewen, Elizabeth. 1985. *Immigrant Women in the Land of Dollars: Life and Culture on the Lower East Side, 1890–1925.* New York: Monthly Review Press.

Ewing, Elizabeth. 1977. *History of Children's Costume.* New York: Charles Scribner's Sons.

Eyman, Scott. 1990. *Mary Pickford: From Here to Hollywood.* New York: Donald I. Fine.

Factory Tracts. 1845. 1982. Reprint, Lowell, MA: Lowell Publishing Co.

Faderman, Lillian. 1981. *Surpassing the Love of Men: Romantic Friendship and Love between Women from the Renaissance to the Present.* New York: William Morrow.

Fahm, Esther Glover. 1990. "Home Economics: Our Roots, Our Present, Our Future." Pp. 190–252 in *Historically Black Land-Grant Institutions and the Development of Agriculture and Home Economics, 1890–1990.* By Leedell W. Neyland, with Esther Glover Fahm. Tallahassee: Florida A&M University Foundation.

Faragher, John Mack, and Florence Howe, eds. 1988. *Women and Higher Education in American History.* New York: W. W. Norton.

Farnham, Christie Anne. 1994. *The Education of the Southern Belle: Higher Education and Student Socialization in the Antebellum South.* New York: New York University Press.

Farrar, Eliza Ware. 1837. *The Young Lady's Friend.* Boston: American Stationers' Co.

Farrar, Mrs. n.d. *Mrs. Farrar's the Youth's Letter-Writer.* New York: Barlett and Raynor.

Fass, Paula S. 1977. *The Damned and the Beautiful: American Youth in the 1920s.* New York: Oxford University Press.

Fass, Paula, and Mary Ann Mason. 2000. *Childhood in America.* New York: New York University Press.

Faust, Drew Gilpin. 1982. *James Henry Hammond and the Old South: A Design for Mastery.* Baton Rouge: Louisiana State University Press.

Feinman, Claire. 1984. "An Historical Overview of the Treatment of Incarcerated Women: Myths and Realities of Rehabilitation." *The Prison Journal* 63: 12–26.

Felkenes, George T., and Harold K. Becker. 1995. "Female Gang Members: A Growing Issue for Policy Makers." *Journal of Gang Research* 2, no. 4: 1–10.

Ferris, William, ed. 1983. *Afro-American Folk Art and Crafts.* Boston: G. K. Hall.

Festle, Mary Jo. 1996. *Playing Nice: Politics and Apologies in Women's Sports.* New York: Columbia University Press.

Finders, Margaret J. 1997. *Just Girls: Hidden Literacies and Life in Junior High.* New York: Teachers College Press.

Findlen, Barbara, ed. 1995. *Listen Up! Voices from the Next Feminist Generation.* Seattle: Seal Press.

"Fine Feathers Make Fine Fans." 1935. *Time* (August 19): 26.

Fine, Michelle. 1993. "Sexuality, Schooling and Adolescent Females: The Missing Discourse of Desire." In *Beyond Silenced Voices: Class, Race and Gender in United States Schools.* Edited by Michelle Fine and Lois Weis. Albany: State University of New York Press.

Finkelhor, David. 1986. *A Sourcebook on Child Sexual Abuse.* Newbury Park, CA: Sage.

Finney, Ben, and James D. Houston. 1996. *Surfing: A History of the Ancient Hawaiian Sport.* San Francisco: Pomegranate Art Books.

Fischer, Claude S. 1992. *America Calling: A Social History of the Telephone to 1940.* Berkeley: University of California Press.

Fishman, Katherine. 1966. "Sex Becomes a Brand New Problem." *New York Times Magazine* (March 13).

Fiske, John. 1989. *Reading the Popular.* Boston: Unwin Hyman.

Fletcher, Alice C. 1896. "Glimpses of Indian Child Life." *The Outlook* (May 16): 891–892.

Fletcher, Alice C., and Francis La Flesche. 1911. *The Omaha Tribe.* Bureau of American Ethnology Twenty-Seventh Annual Report, 1905–1906. Washington, DC: Government Printing Office.

Foner, Philip S., ed. 1977. *The Factory Girls: A Collection of Writings on Life and Struggles in the New England Factories of the 1840s by the Factory Girls Themselves, and the Story, in Their Own Words, of the First Trade Unions of Women Workers in the United States.* Urbana: University of Illinois Press.

Foreman, Grant. 1932. *Indian Removal: The Emigration of the Five Civilized Tribes of Indians.* Norman: University of Oklahoma Press.

Forman-Brunell, Miriam. Forthcoming. *Sitting Pretty: Fears and Fantasies about Adolescent Girls.* New York: Routledge.

Formanek-Brunell, Miriam. 1998. *Made to Play House: Dolls and the Commercialization of American Girlhood, 1830–1930.* Baltimore: Johns Hopkins University Press.

Forrester, James. 1848. *Practical Morality.* Hartfort, CT: Andrews.

Foster, Shirley, and Judy Simons. 1995. *What Katy Read: Feminist Re-Readings of "Classic" Stories for Girls.* Iowa City: University of Iowa Press.

Foster, Vanda. 1982. *Bags and Purses.* Costume Accessories Series. Edited by Aileen Ribeiro. London: B. T. Batsford.

Foucault, Michel. 1978. *The History of Sexuality.* Trans. Robert Hurley. Vol. 1, *An Introduction.* New York: Pantheon.

Fox-Genovese, Elizabeth. 1988. *Within the Plantation Household: Black and White Women in the Old South.* Chapel Hill: University of North Carolina Press.

Fraiberg, Selma. 1987. *Selected Writings of Selma Fraiberg.* Columbus: Ohio State University Press.

Frank, Anne. 1952. *The Diary of a Young Girl.* Translated by B. M. Mooyart-Doubleday. Garden City, NY: Doubleday.

Frasko, Mary. 1994. *Daring Do: A History of Extraordinary Hair.* New York: Flammarion.

Freedman, Russell. 1994. *Kids at Work: Lewis Hine and the Crusade against Child Labor.* New York: Clarion Books.

Freeman, Elizabeth. 1994. "'What Factory Girls Had Power to Do': The Techno-logic of Working-Class Feminine Publicity in *The Lowell Offering.*" *Arizona Quarterly* 50, no. 2: 109–128.

Freeman, Jo. 1975. *The Politics of Women's Liberation: A Case Study of an Emerging Social Movement and Its Relation to the Political Process.* New York: Mayfield Publishing.

French, Laurence Armand. 2000. *Addictions and Native Americans.* Westport, CT: Praeger.

Freud, Anna. 1946. *The Psychoanalytical Treatment of Children.* London: Imago Publishing.

Freud, Sigmund. 1959. "Some Psychological Consequences of the Anatomical Distinction between the Sexes." Pp. 252–272 in *The Collected Papers of Sigmund Freud.* Edited by J. Strachey; translated by J. Riviere. Vol. 5. 1925. Reprint, New York: Basic Books.

Friends of Lulu, http://www. friendslulu. org/.

Frisch, Rose E. 1978. "Population, Food Intake, and Fertility." *Science* 199: 22–30.

Frith, Simon. 1981. *Sound Effects: Youth, Leisure, and the Politics of Rock 'n' Roll.* New York: Pantheon Books.

Fuller, Kathryn. 1996. *At the Picture Show: Small Town Audiences and the Creation of the Movie Fan.* Washington, DC: Smithsonian Institution Press.

Furness, Helen Kate Rogers. Letter to "Miss K. C. Brush" (the squirrel), dated April 25, 1850. Philadelphia: Historical Society of Pennsylvania.

Furnham, A., and N. Alibhai. 1983. "Cross-cultural Differences in the Perception of Female Body Shapes." *Psychological Medicine* 13: 829–837.

Gaar, Gillian. 1992. *She's a Rebel: The History of Women in Rock and Roll.* Seattle: Seal Press.

Gabbard, Andrea. 2000. *Girl in the Curl: A Century of Women's Surfing.* Seattle: Seal Press.

Gaitskill, Mary. 1992. *Two Girls Fat and Thin.* New York: Bantam.

Gannett, Cinthia. 1992. *Gender and the Journal: Diaries and Academic Discourse.* Albany: State University of New York Press.

———. 1995. "The Stories of Our Lives Become Our Lives: Journals, Diaries, and Academic Discourse." Pp. 109–136 in *Feminine Principles and Women's Experience in American Composition and Rhetoric.* Edited by Louise Wetherbee Phelps and Janet Emig. Pittsburgh: University of Pittsburgh Press.

Gardner, David M., and Paul E. Garfinkel, eds. 1997. *Handbook of Treatment for Eating Disorders.* 2d ed. New York: Guilford Press.

Gardner, Julia D. 1998. "'No Place for a Girl Dick': Mabel Maney and the Queering of Girls' Detective Fiction." Pp. 247–265 in *Delinquents and Debutantes: Twentieth-Century American Girls' Cultures.* Edited by Sherrie A. Inness. New York: New York University Press.

Garland, Ann F., and Edward Zigler. 1993. "Adolescent Suicide Prevention: Current Research and Social Policy Implications." *American Psychologist* 48: 169–182.

Garofalo, Reebee. 1997. *Rockin' Out: Popular Music in the USA.* Needham Heights, MA: Allyn and Bacon.

Garrod, Andrew, Janie Victoria Ward, Tracy L. Robinson, and Robert Kilkenny. 1999. *Souls Looking Back: Life Stories of Growing Up Black.* New York: Routledge.

Gaspar de Alba, Alicia. 1993. *The Mystery of Survival and Other Stories.* Tempe, AZ: Bilingual Review Press.

Gateward, Frances, and Murray Pomerance, eds. 2000. *Sugar and Spice: Cinemas of Adolescence.* Detroit: Wayne State University Press.

Gaunt, Kyra D. 1998. "Dancin' in the Streets to a Black Girl's Beat: Music, Gender, and the 'Ins and Outs' of Double-Dutch." Pp. 272–292 in *Generations of Youth: Youth Cultures and History in Twentieth-Century America.* Edited by Joe Austin and Michael Willard. New York: New York University Press.

Ge Xiaojia, Frederick Lorenz, Rand Conger, and Glen H. Elder. 1994. "Trajectories of Stressful Life Events and Depressive Symptoms during Adolescence." *Developmental Psychology* 30: 467–483.

Genovese, Eugene. 1969. *Roll, Jordan, Roll: The World the Slaves Made.* New York: Pantheon Books.

George, Nelson, Sally Banes, Susan Flinker, and Patty Romanowski. 1985. *Fresh, Hip Hop Don't Stop.* New York: Random House.

George, Sam. 1999. "500 Years of Women's Surfing." *Surfer* 40, no. 3: 112–113.

Gibbs, Jewelle Taylor. 1985. "City Girls: Psychological Adjustment of Urban Black Adolescent Females." *Sage: A Scholarly Journal on Black Women* 2, no. 2: 28–36.

Gibson, H. W. 1936. "The History of Organized Camping." *Camping* 7 (January–December).

Giddings, Paula. 1996. *When and Where I Enter.* New York: William Morrow.

Gil, Eliana. 1991. *The Healing Power of Play: Working with Abused Children.* New York: Guilford Press.

———. 1996. *Treating Abused Adolescents.* New York: Guilford Press.

Gillespie, Fern. 1991. "Black Dolls: The Christmas Wish of African-American Children?" *American Visions* 6, no. 5: 27–31.

Gilligan, Carol. 1982. *In a Different Voice.* Cambridge, MA: Harvard University Press.

———. 1993. *In a Different Voice: Psychological Theory and Women's*

Development. 2d ed. Cambridge: Harvard University Press.

Gilligan, Carol, Annie G. Rogers, and Deborah L. Tolman. 1991. *Women, Girls, and Psychotherapy: Reframing Resistance.* New York: Haworth Press.

Gilman, Wenona. 1891. *Val, the Tomboy.* Cleveland: A. Westbrook.

Gilmore, William J. 1989. *Reading Becomes a Necessity of Life: Material and Cultural Life in Rural New England, 1780–1835.* Knoxville: University of Tennessee Press.

Girl Scouts of the U.S.A. 1986. *Seventy-five Years of Girl Scouting.* New York: Girl Scouts of the USA.

———. 1997. *Highlights in Girl Scouting, 1912–1996.* New York: Girl Scouts of the USA.

Glenn, Evelyn Nakano. 1986. *Issei, Nisei, and War Bride: Three Generations of Japanese American Women in Domestic Service.* Philadelphia: Temple University Press.

Glenn, Evelyn Nakano, and Rachel Salazar Parreñas. 1996. "The Other Issei: Japanese Immigrant Women in the Pre–World War II Period." Pp. 110–124 in *Origins and Destinies: Immigration, Race, and Ethnicity in America.* Edited by Silvia Pedraza and Rubén G. Rumbaut. Belmont, CA: Wadsworth Publishing.

Goebel, Edmund J., Rev. 1937. *A Study of Catholic Secondary Education during the Colonial Period up to the First Plenary Council of Baltimore, 1852.* New York: Benziger Brothers Press.

Goldbert, Michael. 1994. *Breaking New Ground: American Women 1800–1848.* New York: Oxford University Press.

Goldin, Barbara Diamond. 1995. *Bat Mitzvah: A Jewish Girl's Coming of Age.* New York: Viking Press.

Goldstein, Ruth M., and Edith Zorrow. 1980. *The Screen Image of Youth: Movies about Children and Adolescents.* Metuchen, NJ: Scarecrow Press.

Gonzalez, Anita. 1998. "Powwow Dancing and Native Rap: American Indian Dance Patronage and the Politics of Spirituality." Society of Dance History Scholars Proceedings, 227–233.

Goodsell, Willystine. 1923. *The Education of Women: Its Social Background and Its Problems.* New York: Macmillan.

Gordon, Lynn D. 1990. *Gender and Higher Education in the Progressive Era.* New Haven, CT: Yale University Press.

Gordon, Michael. 1978. *The American Family in Social-Historical Perspective.* New York: St. Martin's Press.

Gorin, Arthur A. 1970. *New York Jews and the Quest for Community: The Kehillah Experiment, 1908–1922.* New York and Philadelphia: Columbia University Press/The Jewish Publication Society of America.

Gottlieb, Joanne, and Gayle Wald. 1994. "'Smells Like Teen Spirit': Riot Grrrls, Revolution, and Independent Rock." Pp. 250–274 in *Microphone Fiends: Youth Music and Youth Culture.* Edited by Andrew Ross and Tricia Rose. New York: Routledge.

Gottlieb, Lori. 2000. *Stick Figure: A Diary of My Former Self.* New York: Simon & Schuster.

Gould, Stephen Jay. 1981. *The Mismeasure of Man.* New York: W. W. Norton.

Gradler, Frank A. 1927. *Psychology and Technique of Cheer-leading: A Handbook for Cheer-leaders.* Menomonie, WI: Menomonie Athletic Book Supply.

"Graduate Course in Baby-Sitting." 1945. *Life* (April 12): 107–108.

Graham, Joe S., ed. 1991. *Hecho en Tejas: Texas-Mexican Folk Arts and Crafts.* Denton: University of North Texas Press.

Grant, Linda. 1984. "Black Females' 'Place' in Desegregated Classrooms." *Sociology of Education* 57 (April): 98–111.

Gray, Mary L. 1999. *In Your Face: Stories from the Lives of Queer Youth.* New York: Huntington Park Press.

Grayson, Alice Barr. 1944. *Do You Know Your Daughter?* New York: D. Appleton-Century Company.

Green, Hannah. 1964. *I Never Promised You a Rose Garden.* New York: Holt, Rinehart, and Winston.

Green, Harvey. 1983. *The Light of the Home: An Intimate View of the Lives of Women in Victorian America.* New York: Pantheon.

Green, Karen, and Tristan Taormino, eds. 1997. *A Girl's Guide to Taking Over the World: Writings from the Girl Zine Revolution.* New York: St. Martin's Press.

Green, Rayna. 1975. "The Pocahontas Perplex: The Image of Indian Women in American Culture." *The Massachusetts Review* 16 (Autumn).

Greenberger, Ellen, and Lawrence Steinberg. 1986. *When Teenagers Work: The Psychological and Social Costs of Adolescent Employment.* New York: Basic Books.

Greene, B. 1990. "Sturdy Bridges: The Role of African American Mothers in the Socialization of African American Children." *Women and Therapy: Motherhood, Feminist Perspectives* 10: 205–225.

Greenfield, Eloise. 1993. *Childtimes: A Three-Generation Memoir.* New York: Harper.

Greenhouse, Linda. 1999. "Sex Harassment in Class Is Ruled Schools' Liability." *New York Times* (May 25): A25.

Gregg, Edith E. W., ed. 1982. *The Letters of Ellen Tucker Emerson.* Kent, OH: Kent State University Press.

Greven, Philip J. 1979. *The Protestant Temperament: Patterns of Child-Rearing, Religious Experience, and the Self in Early America.* New York: Meridian.

Grier, Katherine C. 1995. "Animal House: Pet Keeping in Urban and Suburban Households in the Northeast, 1850–1900." Pp. 109–129 in *New England's Creatures: 1400–1900.* Dublin Center for New England Folklife Annual Proceedings, 1993. Edited by Peter Benes. Boston: Boston University Press.

———. Forthcoming. *Pets in America: A History.*

Grinstein, Hyman B. 1945. *The Rise of the Jewish Community of New York, 1654–1860.* Philadelphia: Jewish Publication Society of America.

Griswold, Robert. 1993. *Fatherhood in America.* New York: Basic Books.

Grossberg, Michael. 1985. *Governing the Hearth: Law and the Family in Nineteenth-Century America.* Chapel Hill: University of North Carolina Press.

Grover, Kathryn. 1992. *Hard at Play: Leisure in America, 1840–1940.* Amherst: University of Massachusetts Press.

Guevara, Nancy. 1985a. "Graffiti Talk: Words, Walls, Women." *Tabloid*, no. 9: 20–31.

———. 1985b. "Women Writin', Rappin', Breakin'." *Year Left* (London) 2, no. 2: 160–175.

Gutíerrez, David G. 1995. *Walls and Mirrors: Mexican Americans, Mexican Immigrants, and the Politics of Ethnicity.* Berkeley: University of California Press.

Gutiérrez, Ramón A. 1991. *When Jesus Came, the Corn Mothers Went Away: Marriage, Sexuality, and Power in New*

Mexico, 1500–1846. Palo Alto, CA: Stanford University Press.

Gutman, Herbert G. 1976. *The Black Family in Slavery and Freedom, 1725–1925.* New York: Random House.

Gutman, Richard J. S., and Kellie O. Gutman. 1983. *The Summer Camp Memory Book: A Pictorial Treasury of Everything, from Campfires to Color Wars, You Loved about Camp.* New York: Crown.

Guttmann, Allen. 1991. *Women's Sports: A History.* New York: Columbia University Press.

Haag, Pamela. 2000. *Voices of a Generation: Teenage Girls Report about Their Lives Today.* New York: Marlowe.

Habegger, Alfred. 1982. "Funny Tomboys." Pp. 172–183 in *Gender, Fantasy, and Realism in American Literature.* New York: Columbia University Press.

Haertig, Evelyn. 1983. *Antique Combs and Purses.* Carmel, CA: Gallery Graphics Press.

———. 1990. *More Beautiful Purses.* Carmel, CA: Gallery Graphics Press.

Hagan, Jacqueline Maria. 1994. *Deciding to Be Legal: A Maya Community in Houston.* Philadelphia: Temple University Press.

Hagedorn, John, and Mary L. Devitt. 1999. "Fighting Female: The Social Construction of Female Gangs." Pp. 256–276 in *Female Gangs in America: Essays on Girls, Gangs, and Gender.* Edited by Meda Chesney-Lind and John M. Hagedorn. Chicago: Lake View Press.

Hagedorn, John, and Joan Moore. 1996. "What Happens to Girls in the Gang?" Pp. 204–218 in *Gangs in America.* Edited by C. Ronald Huff. Thousand Oaks, CA: Sage.

Hagood, Margaret J. 1939. *Mothers of the South: Portraiture of the White Tenant Farm Woman.* Chapel Hill: University of North Carolina Press.

Haiken, Elizabeth. 1997. *Venus Envy: A History of Cosmetic Surgery.* Baltimore: Johns Hopkins University Press.

Haines, T. L., and L. W. Yaggy. 1876. *The Royal Path of Life.* Chicago: Western Publishing House.

Hale, Sarah Josepha. 1830. "Mary's Lamb." *Juvenile Miscellany* 4, no. 1 (September–October): 64.

———. 1868. "Pets and Their Uses." In *Manners; or, Happy Homes and Good Society All the Year Round.* 1972. Reprint, New York: Arno Press.

Hall, David D. 1991. *Witchcraft in Seventeenth-Century New England: A Documentary History, 1638–1692.* Boston: Northeastern University Press.

Hall, G. Stanley. 1907. *Aspects of Child Life and Education.* Boston: Ginn.

Hall, Radclyffe. 1928. *The Well of Loneliness.* 1990. Reprint, New York: Anchor Books.

Halperin, David. 1998. "Forgetting Foucault: Acts, Identities, and the History of Sexuality." *Representations* 63: 93–120.

Halpern, Sydney. 1988. *American Pediatrics: The Social Dynamics of Professionalism 1880–1980.* Berkeley: University of California Press.

Hampsten, Elizabeth. 1991. *Settlers' Children: Growing Up on the Great Plains.* Norman: University of Oklahoma Press.

Hankin, Benjamin, and Lynn Abramson. 1999. "Development of Gender Differences in Depression: Description and Possible Explanations." *Annals of Medicine* 31: 372–379.

Hanson, Mary Ellen. 1995. *Go! Fight! Win! Cheerleading in American Culture.* Bowling Green, OH: Bowling Green State University Popular Press.

Harbeson, Georgiana. 1938. *American Needlework.* New York: Bonanza Books.

Hareven, Tamara. 1982. *Family Time and Industrial Time.* Cambridge: Cambridge University Press.

Hargreaves, Mary W. M. 1979. "Rural Education on the Northern Plains Frontier." *Journal of the West* 18, no. 4: 25–32.

Harris, Mary G. 1988. *Cholas: Latina Girls and Gangs.* New York: AMS Press.

———. 1994. "Cholas, Chicano Girls and Gangs." *Sex Roles* 30: 289–431.

Harris, Susan K. 1990. *Nineteenth-Century American Women's Novels: Interpretative Strategies.* Cambridge: Cambridge University Press.

Harrison, Cynthia. 1989. *On Account of Sex: The Politics of Women's Issues, 1945–1968.* Berkeley: University of California Press.

Harrison, Kathryn. 1997. *The Kiss.* New York: Random House.

Hartocollis, Anemona. 1996. "She Drives Like a Man." *Life* (Winter).

Haskell, Molly. 1973. *From Reverence to Rape.* New York: Holt, Rinehart, and Winston.

Haug, Frigga et al. 1987. *Feminine Sexualisation: A Collective Work of Memory.* London: Verso.

Haugaard, Jeffrey J., and N. Dickon Reppucci. 1988. *The Sexual Abuse of Children.* San Francisco: Jossey-Bass.

Haupt, Enid A. 1957. *The Seventeen Book of Young Living.* New York: David McKay Company.

———. 1970. *The Seventeen Book of Etiquette and Young Living.* 2d ed. New York: David McKay Company.

Haviland, Virginia. 1973. *Children and Literature: Views and Reviews.* Glenview, IL: Scott, Foresman.

Hawes, Joseph M. 1997. *Children between the Wars: American Childhood 1920–1940.* New York: Twayne Publishers.

Hawkins, John. 1991. *Texas Cheerleaders: The Spirit of America.* New York: St. Martin's Press.

Hebdige, Dick. 1979. *Subculture: The Meaning of Style.* New York: Routledge.

Hemphill, C. Dallett. 1998. "Class, Gender, and the Regulation of Emotional Expression in Revolutionary-Era Conduct Literature." Pp. 33–51 in *Emotional History of the United States.* Edited by Peter N. Stearns and Jan Lewis. New York: New York University Press.

Herman, Judith. 1981. *Father-Daughter Incest.* Cambridge: Harvard University Press.

Heth, Charlotte, ed. 1992. *Native American Dance: Ceremonies and Social Traditions.* Washington, DC: National Museum of the American Indian, Smithsonian Institution, with Starwood Publishing.

Hilton, Kathleen C. 1987. "Growing Up Female: Girlhood Experiences and Social Feminism, 1890–1929." Ph.D. diss., Carnegie Mellon University, chap. 5.

Hine, Darlene Clark, ed. 1997. *Facts on File Encyclopedia of Black Women in America.* New York: Facts on File.

Hine, Darlene Clark, and Kathleen Thompson. 1998. *A Shining Thread of Hope: The History of Black Women in America.* New York: Broadway Books.

Hine, Darlene Clark, Elsa Barkley-Brown, and Rosalyn Terborg-Penn, eds. 1992. *Black Women in America: An Historical Encyclopedia*. Brooklyn: Carlson Publishing.

Hine, Thomas. 1999. *The Rise and Fall of the American Teenager*. New York: Avon.

Hiner, N. Ray, and Joseph M. Hawes, eds. 1985a. *Growing Up in America: Children in Historical Perspective*. Urbana: University of Illinois Press.

———. 1985b. *American Childhood: A Research Guide and Historical Handbook*. Westport, CT: Greenwood Press.

Hing, Bill Ong. 1993. *Making and Remaking Asian America through Immigration Policy, 1850–1990*. Stanford, CA: Stanford University Press.

Hoffman, M. 1997. "Sex Differences in Empathy and Related Behaviors." *Psychological Bulletin* 84, no. 4: 712–722.

Holden, George W., Robert Geffner, and Ernest N. Jouriles. 1998. *Children Exposed to Marital Violence*. Washington, DC: American Psychological Association.

Hollinger, Joan A., et al., eds. 1989. *Adoption Law and Practice*. New York: Matthew Bender Press.

Holsinger, Kristi. 1999. "Addressing the Distinct Experience of the Adolescent Female: Explaining Delinquency and Examining the Juvenile Justice System." Ph.D. diss., University of Michigan Dissertation Service.

Holt, Marilyn Irvin. 1993. *The Orphan Trains: Placing Out in America*. Lincoln: University of Nebraska Press.

Hondagneu-Sotelo, Pierette. 1994. *Gendered Transitions: Mexican Experiences of Immigration*. Berkeley: University of California Press.

hooks, bell. 1996. *Bone Black: Memories of Girlhood*. New York: Henry Holt.

Hopkins, Jerry. 1972. "The Fans." Pp. 161–172 in *Things in the Driver's Seat: Readings in Popular Culture*. Edited by Harry Russell Huebel. Chicago: Rand McNally.

Horn, Margo. 1989. *Before It's Too Late: The Child Guidance Movement in the United States, 1922–1945*. Philadelphia: Temple University Press.

Hornbacher, Marya. 1998. *Wasted: A Memoir of Anorexia and Bulimia*. New York: HarperCollins.

Horne, Esther Burnett, and Sally McBeth. 1998. *Essie's Story: The Life and Legacy of a Shoshone Teacher*. Lincoln: University of Nebraska Press.

Horno-Delgado, Asunción, Eliana Ortega, Nina M. Scott, and Nancy Saporta Sternbach, eds. 1989. *Breaking Boundaries: Latina Writing and Critical Readings*. Amherst: University of Massachusetts Press.

Horowitz, Daniel. 1998. *Betty Friedan and the Making of the Feminine Mystique: The American Left, the Cold War, and Modern Feminism*. Amherst: University of Massachusetts Press.

Horowitz, Helen Lefkowitz. 1984. *Alma Mater: Design and Experience in the Women's Colleges from Their Nineteenth Century Beginnings to the 1930s*. New York: Alfred A. Knopf.

———. 1987. *Campus Life: Undergraduate Cultures from the End of the Eighteenth Century to the Present*. New York: Alfred A. Knopf.

Horsman, Reginald. 1967. *Expansion and American Indian Policy, 1783–1812*. 1992. Reprint, Norman: University of Oklahoma Press.

Horton, James Oliver. 1976. "Generations of Protest: Black Families and Social Reform in Ante-Bellum Boston." *New England Quarterly* 49 (June): 51–76.

Houston, Jeanne Wakatsuki, and James D. Houston. 1973. *Farewell to Manzanar.* Boston: Houghton Mifflin.

Hoy, Suellen. 1995. *Chasing Dirt: The American Pursuit of Cleanliness.* New York: Oxford University Press.

Hubler, Angela E. 1998. "Can Anne Shirley Help 'Revive Ophelia'? Listening to Girl Readers." Pp. 266–284 in *Delinquents and Debutantes: Twentieth-Century American Girls' Cultures.* Edited by Sherrie A. Inness. New York: New York University Press.

Hunter, Jane. 1992. "Inscribing the Self in the Heart of the Family: Diaries and Girl hood in Late Victorian America." *American Quarterly* 44, no. 1 (March): 51–81.

Hurtado, Albert L. 1999. *Intimate Frontiers: Sex, Gender, and Culture in Old California.* Albuquerque: University of New Mexico Press.

Hustead, Alice M. 1944. *Strictly Confidential (for Young Girls).* Minneapolis: Augsburg Publishing House.

Hyde, Mary Kendall. 1919. *Girls' Book of the Red Cross.* New York: Thomas Y. Crowell.

Hyman, Paula E. 1990. "The Introduction of Bat Mitzvah in Conservative Judaism in Postwar America." *YIVO Annual* 19: 133–146.

———. 1995. *Gender and Assimilation in Modern Jewish History: The Roles and Representations of Women.* Seattle: University of Washington Press.

Hyman, Trina Schart. 1983. *Little Red Riding Hood.* New York: Holiday House.

Ingersoll, Thomas N. 1991. "Free Blacks in a Slave Society: New Orleans, 1718–1812." *William and Mary Quarterly* 48 (April): 173–200.

Inness, Sherrie A. 1993. "Girl Scouts, Campfire Girls and Woodcraft Girls: The Ideology of Girls' Scouting Novels 1910–1935." Pg. 229–240 in *Continuities in Popular Culture: The Present in the Past and the Past in the Present and Future.* Edited by Ray B. Browne and Ronald Ambrosetti. Bowling Green, OH: Bowling Green State University Popular Press.

———. 1995. *Intimate Communities: Representation and Social Transformation in Women's College Fiction, 1895–1910.* Bowling Green, OH: Bowling Green State University Popular Press.

———. 1998a. "'Anti-Barbies': The American Girls Collection and Political Ideologies." Pp. 164–183 in *Delinquents and Debutantes: Twentieth-Century American Girls' Cultures.* Edited by Sherrie A. Inness. New York: New York University Press.

———. 1998b. *Millennium Girls: Today's Girls around the World.* Lanham, MD: Rowman & Littlefield.

———. 2000. *Tough Girls.* Philadelphia: University of Pennsylvania Press.

Inness, Sherrie A., ed. 1997. *Nancy Drew and Company: Culture, Gender, and Girls' Series.* Bowling Green, OH: Bowling Green State University Popular Press.

———. 1998. *Delinquents and Debutantes: Twentieth-Century American Girls' Cultures.* New York: New York University Press.

Inscoe, John C. 1988. "Memories of a Presbyterian Mission Worker: An Interview with Rubie Ray Cunningham." *Appalachian Journal* 15, no. 2: 144–160.

Institute for Government Research. 1928. *The Problem of Indian Administration* (The Meriam Report). Baltimore: Johns Hopkins Press.

Irvine, Janice M., ed. 1994. *Sexual Cultures and the Construction of Adolescent Identities*. Philadelphia: Temple University Press.

Isaacs, Leora W. 1992. "What We Know about Enrollment." Pp. 61–70 in *What We Know about Jewish Education: A Handbook of Today's Research for Tomorrow's Jewish Education*. Edited by Stuart L. Kelman. Los Angeles: Torah Aura Publications.

Jackson, Kathy Merlock. 1986. *Images of Children in American Film*. Metuchen, NJ: Scarecrow Press.

Jackson, Valerie C. 1988. *Dolls' Houses and Miniatures*. London: John Murray.

Jacob, James E., Paul Rodenhauser, and Ronald J. Markert. 1987. "The Benign Exploitation of Human Emotions: Adult Women and the Marketing of Cabbage Patch Kids." *Journal of American Culture* 10, no. 3: 61–71.

Jacobs, Flora Gill. 1953, 1965. *A History of Dolls' Houses*. New York: Charles Scribner's Sons.

———. 1974. *Dolls' Houses in America: Historic Preservation in Miniature*. New York: Charles Scribner's Sons.

Jacobs, Harriet. 1861. *Incidents in the Life of a Slave Girl: Written by Herself*. Edited by Jean Fagin Yellin. 1987. Reprint, Cambridge, MA: Harvard University Press.

Jacobson, Lisa. Forthcoming. *Raising Consumers: Children, Childrearing, and the American Mass Market, 1890–1940*. New York: Columbia University Press.

Jeal, Tim. 1990. *The Boy-Man: The Life of Lord Baden-Powell*. New York: Morrow.

Jellison, Katherine. 1993. *Entitled to Power: Farm Women and Technology, 1913–1963*. Chapel Hill: University of North Carolina Press.

Jenkins, Henry. 1989. "Star Trek Rerun, Reread, Rewritten: Fan Writing as Textual Poaching." *Critical Studies in Mass Communication* 5: 85–107.

Jensen, Joan. 1986. *Loosening the Bonds: Mid-Atlantic Farm Women, 1750–1850*. New Haven: Yale University Press.

Joe, Karen A., and Meda Chesney-Lind. 1995. "'Just Every Mother's Angel': An Analysis of Gender and Ethnic Variations in Youth Gang Membership." *Gender and Society* 9, no. 4: 408–432.

Johnson, Deidre. 1993. *Edward Stratemeyer and the Stratemeyer Syndicate*. New York: Twayne.

Johnson Frisbie, Charlotte. 1967. *Kinaaldá: A Study of the Navaho Girl's Puberty Ceremony*. Middletown, CT: Wesleyan University Press.

Jones, Jacqueline. 1986. *Labor of Love, Labor of Sorrow: Black Women, Work and the Family from Slavery to the Present*. New York: Vintage.

Jones, Kathleen W. 1999. *Taming the Troublesome Child: American Families, Child Guidance and the Limits of Psychiatric Authority*. Cambridge: Harvard University Press.

Jordan, Judith. 1987. "Clarity in Connection: Empathic Knowing, Desire and Sexuality." *Work in Progress* no. 29. Wellesley, MA: Stone Center Work in Progress Series.

Jordan, Judith V., Alexandra G. Kaplan, Jean Baker Miller, Irene P. Stiver, and Janet L. Surrey. 1991. *Women's Growth in Connection: Writings from the Stone Center*. New York: Guilford Press.

Jordan, June. 2000. *Soldier: A Poet's Childhood.* New York: Basic Books.

Joselit, Jenna Weissman, ed., with Karen S. Mittelman. 1993. *A Worthy Use of Summer: Jewish Summer Camping in America.* Philadelphia: Museum of American Jewish History.

Jowett, Garth, Ian Jarvie, and Kathryn Fuller. 1996. *Children and the Movies: Media Influence and the Payne Fund Controversy.* New York: Cambridge University Press.

Juhnke, James C. 1989. *Vision, Doctrine, War: Mennonite Identity and Organization in America.* Scottdale, PA: Herald Press.

Juno, Andrea. 1996. *Angry Women in Rock.* Vol. 1. New York: Juno Books.

Kaestle, Carl F. 1983. *Pillars of the Republic: Common Schools and American Society, 1780–1860.* New York: Hill and Wang.

Kaestle, Carl F., Helen Damon-Moore, Lawrence C. Stedman, Katherine Tinsley, and William Vance Trollinger, Jr. 1991. *Literacy in the United States: Readers and Reading since 1880.* New Haven, CT: Yale University Press.

Kahn, Alice. 1991. "A Onetime Bimbo Becomes a Muse." *New York Times* (September 29): H24–H25.

Kamensky, Jane. 1995. *The Colonial Mosaic: American Women 1600–1760.* New York: Oxford University Press.

Kandall, Stephen R. 1996. *Substance and Shadow: Women and Addiction in the United States.* Cambridge, MA: Harvard University Press.

Kanellos, Nicolas, ed. 1997. *The Hispanic American Almanac: A Reference Work on Hispanics in the United States.* Detroit: Gale.

Kanin, Eugene. 1957. "Male Aggression in Dating-Courtship Relationships." *American Journal of Sociology* 63: 197–204.

———. 1967. "An Examination of Sexual Aggression as a Response to Sexual Frustration." *Journal of Marriage and the Family* 29: 428–433.

Kaplan, Elaine Bell. 1997. *Not Our Kind of Girl: Unraveling the Myths of Black Teenage Motherhood.* Berkeley: University of California Press.

Kaplan, Judy, and Linn Shapiro. 1985. *Red Diaper Babies: Children of the Left.* Edited Transcripts of Conferences Held at the World Fellowship Center, Conway, NH. Somerville, MA: Red Diaper Productions.

———. 1998. *Red Diapers: Growing Up in the Communist Left.* Urbana: University of Illinois Press.

Karlsen, Carol. 1987. *The Devil in the Shape of a Woman: Witchcraft in Colonial New England.* New York: W. W. Norton.

Kasson, Joy. 1990. *Marble Queens and Captives: Women in Nineteenth-Century American Sculpture.* New Haven: Yale University Press.

Katz, Michael. 1986. *In the Shadow of the Poor House.* New York: Basic Books.

Katzman, David M. 1981. *Seven Days a Week: Women and Domestic Service in Industrializing America.* Urbana: University of Illinois Press.

Kaysen, Susanna. 1993. *Girl, Interrupted.* City: Turtle Bay.

Kearney, Mary Celeste. 1997. "The Missing Links: Riot Grrrl—Feminism— Lesbian Culture." In *Sexing the Groove: Popular Music and Gender.* Edited by Sheila Whiteley. London: Routledge.

———. 1998a. "'Don't Need You': Rethinking Identity Politics and

Separatism from a Riot Grrrl Perspective." Pp. 148–188 in *Youth Culture: Identity in a Postmodern World*. Edited by Jonathan Epstein. Oxford: Blackwell.

———. 1998b. "Girls, Girls, Girls: Gender and Generation in Contemporary Discourses of Female Adolescence and Youth Culture." Ph.D. diss., University of Southern California.

———. 1998c. "Producing Girls: Rethinking the Study of Female Youth Culture." Pp. 285–310 in *Delinquents and Debutantes: Twentieth Century American Girls' Cultures*. Edited by Sherrie A. Inness. New York: New York University Press.

Keith, Anne. 1964. "The Navaho Girl's Puberty Ceremony." *E1 Palacio* 71: 27–36.

Kellogg, Alice M. 1910. "Decorations and Furnishings for the Home, IX—Furnishing a Young Girl's Room." *American Homes and Gardens* 7 (November): 420–423.

Kellogg, John. 1884. *Plain Facts for Old and Young*. Burlington, IA: I. F. Segner.

Kempf-Leonard, Kimberly, Elicka S. L. Peterson, and Lisa L. Sample. 1997. *Gender and Juvenile Justice in Missouri*. Jefferson City: Missouri Department of Public Safety.

Kenneally, James. 1990. *The History of American Catholic Women*. New York: Crossroad.

Kennedy, Pagan. 1990. "P.C. Comics." *The Nation* 250 (March 19): 386.

Kent, Kathryn R. 1996. "'No Trespassing': Girl Scout Camp and the Limits of the Counterpublic Sphere." *Women and Performance: A Journal of Feminist Theory* 8, no. 2: 185–203.

Kerber, Linda K. 1988. "'Why Should Girls Be Learn'd and Wise?' Two Centuries of Higher Education for Women as Seen through the Unfinished Work of Alice Mary Baldwin." Pp. 18–42 in *Women and Higher Education in American History: Essays from the Mount Holyoke College Sesquicentennial Symposia*. Edited by John Mack Faragher and Florence Howe. New York: W. W. Norton.

Kessler-Harris, Alice. 1982. *Out to Work*. New York: Oxford University Press.

Kett, Joseph. 1977. *Rites of Passage: Adolescence in America 1790 to the Present*. New York: Basic Books.

Kettlewell, Caroline. 1999. *Skin Game*. New York: St. Martin's.

Keyser, Elizabeth Lennox. 1999. *Little Women: A Family Romance*. New York: Twayne Publishers.

Kibria, Nazli. 1993. *Family Tightrope: The Changing Lives of Vietnamese Americans*. Princeton, NJ: Princeton University Press.

Kidwell, Clara Sue. 1995a. *Choctaws and Missionaries in Mississippi, 1818–1918*. Norman: University of Oklahoma Press.

———. 1995b. "Choctaw Women and Cultural Persistence in Mississippi." Pp. 114–134 in *Negotiators of Change: Historical Perspectives on Native American Women*. Edited by Nancy Shoemaker. New York: Routledge.

Kim, Elaine H., and Eui-Young Yu. 1996. *East to America: Korean American Life Stories*. New York: New Press.

Kimmage, Ann. 1996. *An Un-American Childhood*. Athens: University of Georgia Press.

King, Cheryl A. 1997. "Suicidal Behavior in Adolescence." Pp. 61–95 in *Review of Suicidology*. Edited by Ronald W. Maris, Morton M. Silverman, and Silvia Sara Canetto. New York: Guilford.

King, Constance Eileen. 1983. *The Collector's History of Dolls' Houses,*

Doll's House Dolls, and Miniatures. New York: St. Martin's Press.

King, Elizabeth. 1998. *Quinceañera: Celebrating Fifteen.* New York: Dutton.

King, Wilma. 1995. *Stolen Childhood: Slave Youth in Nineteenth-Century America.* Bloomington: Indiana University Press.

———. 1997. "Within the Professional Household: Slave Children in the Antebellum South." *The Historian* 59: 523–540.

Kinsey, Alfred C., Wardell B. Pomeroy, Clyde E. Martin, and Paul H. Gebhard. 1953. *Sexual Behavior in the Human Female.* Philadephia: W. B. Saunders.

Kiple, Kenneth L., and Virginia H. Kiple. 1977. "Slave Child Mortality: Some Nutritional Answers to a Perennial Puzzle." *Journal of Social History* 10: 284–309.

Kismaric, Carole, and Marvin Heiferman. 1998. *The Mysterious Case of Nancy Drew and the Hardy Boys.* New York: Simon and Schuster.

Klein, Ann G., and Debra Zehms. 1996. "Self-concept and Gifted Girls: A Cross-sectional Study of Intellectually Gifted Females in Grades 3, 5, 8." *Roeper Review* 19, no. 1: 30–34.

Klein, Herbert S. 1983. "African Women in the Atlantic Slave Trade." Pp. 29–38 in *Women and Slavery in Africa.* Edited by Claire Robinson and Martin C. Klein. Madison: University of Wisconsin Press.

Klein, Melanie. 1932. *The Psychoanalysis of Children.* London: Hogarth Press.

Kline, Bruce B., and Elizabeth B. Short. 1991. "Changes in Emotional Resilience: Gifted Adolescent Females." *Roeper Review* 13, no. 3: 118–121.

Kline, Stephen. 1993. *Out of the Garden: Toys, TV, and Children's Culture in the Age of Marketing.* New York: Verso.

Koller-Fox, Cherie. 1976. "Women and Jewish Education: A New Look at Bat Mitzvah." In *The Jewish Woman: New Perspectives.* Edited by Elizabeth Koltun. New York: Schocken Books.

Koppelman, Susan, ed. 1994. *Two Friends and Other Nineteenth-Century Lesbian Stories by American Women Writers.* New York: Meridian.

Koss, Mary. 1985. "The Hidden Rape Victim Personality, Attitudinal and Situational Characteristics." *Psychology of Women Quarterly* 9: 193–212.

———. 1989. "Hidden Rape: Sexual Aggression and Victimization in a National Sample of Students in Higher Education." Pp. 145–168 in *Violence in Dating Relationships: Emerging Social Issues.* Edited by M. A. Pirog-Good and J. Stets. New York: Praeger.

Koss, Mary, T. Dinero, C. Seibel, and S. Cox. 1988. "Stranger and Acquaintance Rape: Are There Differences in the Victim's Experiences?" *Psychology of Women Quarterly* 12: 1–24.

Koszarski, Richard. 1990. *An Evening's Entertainment: The Age of the Silent Feature Picture, 1915–1928.* Vol. 3, *History of the American Cinema.* Berkeley: University of California Press.

Kourany, Ronald F., et al. 1980. "Adolescent Babysitting: A 30-Year-Old Phenomenon." *Adolescence* 13, no. 60 (Winter): 939–945.

Kraybill, Donald B. 1987. "Mennonite Women's Veiling: The Rise and Fall of a Sacred Symbol." *Mennonite Quarterly Review* 61 (June): 298–320.

Kuznets, Simon. 1975. "Immigration of Russian Jews to the United States:

Background and Structure." *Perspectives in American History* 9: 35–124.

Ladner, Joyce A. 1971. *Tomorrow's Tomorrow: The Black Woman.* New York: Doubleday.

Lamphere, Louise. 1987. *From Working Daughters to Working Mothers: Immigrant Women in a New England Industrial Community.* Ithaca, NY: Cornell University Press.

Lander, Louise. 1988. *Images of Bleeding: Menstruation as Ideology.* New York: Orlando Press.

Larcom, Lucy. 1889. *A New England Girlhood Outlined from Memory.* 1996. Reprint, Boston: Riverside Press.

Larkin, Jack. 1988. *The Reshaping of Everyday Life 1790–1840.* New York: Harper and Row.

LaRossa, Ralph. 1997. *The Modernization of Fatherhood.* Chicago: University of Chicago Press.

Laumann, Edward. 1996. "Early Sexual Experiences: How Voluntary? How Violent?" In *Sexuality and American Social Policy: A Seminar Series.* Edited by M. D. Smith, et al. Menlo Park, CA: Henry J. Kaiser Family Foundation.

Lawton, Mary, ed. 1925. *A Lifetime with Mark Twain: The Memories of Katy Leary, for Thirty Years His Faithful and Devoted Servant.* New York: Harcourt, Brace.

Lazerson, Martin. 1971. *Origins of the Urban School: Public Education in Massachusetts, 1870–1915.* Cambridge: Harvard University Press.

Leach, William. 1993. "Child-World in the Promised Land." Pp. 209–238 in *The Mythmaking Frame of Mind: Social Imagination and American Culture.* Edited by James Gilbert, et al. Belmont, CA: Wadsworth Publishing.

Leadbetter, Bonnie, and Niobe Way, eds. 1996. *Urban Girls: Resisting Stereotypes, Creating Identities.* New York: New York University Press.

LeBlanc, Lauraine. 1999. *Pretty in Punk: Girls' Gender Resistance in a Boys' Subculture.* New York: Routledge.

Leder, Gerda. 1992. "Mathematics and Gender: Changing Perspectives." Pp. 597–622 in *Handbook of Research on Mathematics Teaching and Learning.* Edited by Douglas Grouws. New York: Macmillan.

Lee, Alfred McClung. 1955. *Fraternities without Brotherhood: A Campus Report on Racial and Religious Prejudice.* Boston: Beacon Press.

Lee, Mary Paik. 1990. *Quiet Odyssey: A Pioneer Korean Woman in America.* Edited by Sucheng Chan. Seattle: University of Washington Press.

Lee, Robert G. 1999. *Orientals: Asian Americans in Popular Culture.* Philadelphia: Temple University Press.

Lee, V. E., R. G. Croninger, E. Linn, and X. Chen. 1996. "The Culture of Sexual Harassment in Secondary Schools." *American Educational Research Association Journal* 33: 383–417.

Lees, Sue. 1989. "Learning to Love: Sexual Reputation, Morality and the Social Control of Girls." In *Growing Up Good: Policing the Behavior of Girls in Europe.* Edited by Maureen Cain. London: Sage.

Leibman, Nina C. 1995. *Living Room Lectures: The Fifties Family in Film and Television.* Austin: University of Texas Press.

Lemish, Dafna. 1998. "Spice Girls' Talk: A Case Study in the Development of Gendered Identity." Pp. 145–168 in *Millennium Girls: Today's Girls Around* the World. Edited by Sherrie A. Inness. Oxford: Rowman and Littlefield.

Leonard, Karen Isaksen. 1992. *Making Ethnic Choices: California's Punjabi Mexican Americans*. Philadelphia: Temple University Press.

———. 1997. *The South Asian Americans*. Westport, CT: Greenwood Publishing.

Leonard, Marion. 1997. "'Rebel Girl, You Are the Queen of My World': Feminism, 'Subculture' and Grrrl Power." In *Sexing the Groove: Popular Music and Gender*. Edited by Sheila Whiteley. London: Routledge.

———. 1998. "Paper Planes: Travelling the New Grrrl Geographies." In *Cool Places: Geographies of Youth Cultures*. Edited by Tracey Skelton and Gill Valentine. London: Routledge.

Lerman, Nina E., Arwen Mohun, and Ruth Oldenziel, guest eds. 1997. "Gender Analysis and the History of Technology." *Technology and Culture* 38, no. 1 (January).

Lerner, Gerda. 1993. "Sarah Mapps Douglass." In *Black Women in America: An Historical Encyclopedia*. Edited by Darlene Clark Hine, Elsa Barkley Brown, and Rosalyn Terborg-Penn. Brooklyn: Carlson Publishing.

Lerner, Gerda, ed. 1973. *Black Women in White America: A Documentary History*. New York: Vintage Books.

Lerner, Gerda, et al. 1992. *Black Women in White America: A Documentary History*. New York: Random House.

Lerner, Janet. 1985. *Learning Disabilities: Theories, Diagnosis and Teaching Strategies*. 4th ed. Boston: Houghton Mifflin.

Lesko, Nancy. 1988. "The Curriculum of the Body: Lessons from a Catholic High School." In *Becoming Feminine: The Politics of Popular Culture*. Edited by Leslie G. Roman and Linda Christian-Smith. London: Falmer Press.

Levenkron, Steven. 1978. *The Best Little Girl in the World*. New York: Warner Books.

Levenstein, Harvey. 1988. *Revolution at the Table*. New York: Oxford University Press.

Levinson, D. 1978. *The Seasons of a Man's Life*. New York: Alfred A. Knopf.

Lewinsohn, Peter M., Paul Rohde, and John R. Seeley. 1996. "Adolescent Suicidal Ideation and Attempts: Prevalence, Risk Factors, and Clinical Implications." *Clinical Psychology: Science and Practice* 3, no. 1: 25–46.

Lewis, Dio. 1862. *The New Gymnastics for Men, Women, and Children*. 3d ed. Boston: Ticknor and Fields.

Lewis, Heather. 1994. *House Rules*. New York: High Risk.

Lewis, Lisa. 1990. *Gender, Politics and MTV: Voicing the Difference*. Philadelphia: Temple University Press.

———. 1991. *The Adoring Audience*. New York: Routledge.

Lewis, Mary C. 1988. *Herstory: Black Female Rites of Passage*. Chicago: African American Images.

Lichtenstein, Nelson, Susan Strasser, and Roy Rosenzweig. 2000. *Who Built America?* Vol. 2. New York: Worth.

Lieberman, Robbie. 1989. *My Song Is My Weapon: People's Songs, American Communism, and the Politics of Culture, 1930–1950*. Urbana: University of Illinois Press.

Lincoln, Bruce. 1981. *Emerging from the Chrysalis: Studies in Rituals of Women's*

Initiation. Cambridge: Harvard University Press, pp. 17–33.

Lindstrom, David Edgar. 1946. *Rural Life and the Church.* Champaign, IL: Garrard Press.

Lipsitz, George. 1992. "The Meaning of Memory: Family, Class, and Ethnicity in Early Network Television." Pp. 71–108 in *Private Screenings: Television and the Female Consumer.* Edited by Lynn Spigel and Denise Mann. Minneapolis: University of Minnesota Press.

Littlefield, Valinda. 1997. "Introduction." In *Facts on File Encyclopedia of Black Women in America.* Edited by Darlene Clark Hine. New York: Facts on File.

Livingston, Lili Cockerille. 1997. *American Indian Ballerinas.* Norman: University of Oklahoma Press.

Lockridge, Kenneth A. 1974. *Literacy in Colonial New England: An Enquiry into the Social Context of Literacy in the Early Modern West.* New York: W. W. Norton.

Lomawaima, K. Tsianina. 1994. *They Called It Prairie Light: The Story of Chilocco Indian School.* Lincoln: University of Nebraska Press.

Lopez, Tiffany Ann, ed. 1993. *Growing Up Chicana/o.* Tucson: University of Arizona Press.

Lord, M. G. 1994. *Forever Barbie: The Unauthorized Biography of a Real Doll.* New York: William Morrow.

Lorde, Audre. 1992. *Zami: A New Spelling of My Name.* Freedom, CA: Crossing Press.

Lubs, Herbert A., et al. 1999. "Familial Dyslexia: Genetic, Behavioral and Imaging Studies." *Annals of Dyslexia.*

Luckett, Moya. 1997. "Girl Watchers: Patty Duke and Teen TV." Pp. 95–116 in *The Revolution Wasn't Televised: Sixties Television and Social Conflict.* Edited by

Lynn Spigel and Michael Curtin. New York: Routledge.

Luftig, Richard L., and Marci L. Nichols. 1991. "An Assessment of the Social Status and Perceived Personality and School Traits of Gifted Students by Non-gifted." *Roeper Review* 13, no. 3: 138–153.

Luker, Kristin. 1996. *Dubious Conceptions: The Politics of Teenage Pregnancy.* Cambridge, MA: Harvard University Press.

Lumet, Amy. 1994. "Sex Drive." *Seventeen* (March).

Lutes, Jean Marie. 1993. "Cultivating Domesticity: Labor Reform and the Literary Culture of the Lowell Mill Girls." *Works and Days* 11, no. 2: 7–26.

Lutzker, John R. 1998. *Handbook of Child Abuse Research and Treatment.* New York: Plenum Press.

Lynd, Robert S., and Helen Merrell Lynd. 1929. *Middletown: A Study in American Culture.* New York: Harcourt, Brace.

Lyness, Paul I. 1951. "Patterns in the Mass Communications Tastes of the Young Audience." *The Journal of Educational Psychology* 42, no. 8 (December): 449–467.

Maccoby, E. 1990. "Gender and Relationships: A Developmental Account." *American Psychologist:* 513–520.

———. 1998. *The Two Sexes: Growing Up Apart, Coming Together.* Cambridge, MA: Harvard University Press.

Macdonald, Anne L. 1988. *No Idle Hands: The Social History of American Knitting.* New York: Ballantine Books.

Maclean, P. 1958. "The Limbic System with Respect to Self-preservation and the Preservation of the Species." *Journal of Nervous and Mental Diseases* 127: 1–11.

MacLeod, Anne Scott. 1984. "The 'Caddie Woodlawn' Syndrome: American Girlhood in the Nineteenth Century." Pp. 97–120 in *A Century of Childhood, 1820–1920.* Edited by Mary Lynn Steven Heininger et al. Rochester, NY: Strong Museum.

———. 1994. *American Childhood: Essays on Children's Literature of the Nineteenth and Twentieth Centuries.* Athens: University of Georgia Press.

Macleod, David I. 1998. *The Age of the Child: Children in America, 1890–1920.* New York: Twayne Publishers.

Maggenti, Maria, director. 1995. *The Incredibly True Adventure of Two Girls in Love.* Smash Pictures.

Mahler, Sara J. 1995. *American Dreaming: Life on the Margins.* Princeton: Princeton University Press.

Maney, Mabel. 1993. *The Case of the Not-So-Nice Nurse: A Nancy Clue Mystery.* Pittsburgh: Cleis Press.

Manitowabi, Edna. 1971. *An Indian Girl in the City.* Buffalo, NY: Friends of Malatesta.

Mankiller, Wilma, and Michael Wallis. 1993. *Mankiller: A Chief and Her People.* New York: St. Martin's Press.

Manson-Burton, Marianne, comp. 1998. *Girls Know Best 2.* Hillsboro, OR: Beyond Worlds Publishing, 25–32.

Mara, Thalia. 1955. *First Steps in Ballet.* Garden City, NY: Doubleday.

———. 1956. *Second Steps in Ballet.* Garden City, NY: Doubleday.

———. 1959. *On Your Toes.* 1972. Reprint, Brooklyn, NY: Dance Horizons.

———. 1963. *Third Steps in Ballet.* London: Constable.

Marchalonis, Shirley. 1995. *College Girls: A Century of Fiction.* New Brunswick, NJ: Rutgers University Press.

Marcus, Greil. 1989. *Lipstick Traces: The Secret History of the Twentieth Century.* Cambridge, MA: Harvard University Press.

Margolin, Leslie. 1990. "Child Abuse by Baby-Sitters: An Ecological-Interactional Interpretation." *Journal of Family Violence* 5, no. 2 (June): 95–105.

Mark, Ted. 1967. *I Was a Teeny-Bopper for the CIA.* New York: Berkley.

Marsh, Peter, and Peter Collett. 1987. "Driving Passion: There Seems to Be No Slowing Down Our Ongoing Love Affair with the Car." *Psychology Today* (June).

Martin, Biddy. 1993. "Lesbian Identity and Autobiographical Difference[s]." Pp. 274–293 in *The Lesbian and Gay Studies Reader.* Edited by Henry Abelove, Michèle Barale, and David M. Halperin. New York: Routledge.

Martin, Carol. 1994. *Dance Marathons: Performing American Culture of the 1920s and 1930s.* Jackson: University Press of Mississippi.

Martin, Philip. *Migrant Farm Workers and Their Children.* Office of Educational Research and Improvement. ED376. Washington, DC: Government Printing Office.

Martin, William C. 1948. *The Church in the Rural Community.* New York: Board of Missions and Church Extension of the Methodist Church.

Mason, Bobbie Ann. 1995. *The Girl Sleuth.* Athens: University of Georgia Press.

Mason, Mary Ann. 1994. *From Father's Property to Children's Rights: The History of Child Custody in the United States.* New York: Columbia University Press.

Mather, Cotton. 1911–1912. "The Diary of Cotton Mather." Collections of the Massachusetts Historical Society. 7th series, vol. 7. Cited in Linda Pollock,

1987, *A Lasting Relationship: Parents and Children over Three Centuries*. Hanover: University Press of New England, 148.

Matson, Molly, ed. 1992. *An Independent Woman: The Autobiography of Edith Guerrier*. Amherst: University of Massachusetts Press.

Matsumoto, Valerie. 1993. *Farming the Home Place: A Japanese American Community in California*. Ithaca, NY: Cornell University Press.

Matthews, Glenda. 1987. *"Just a Housewife": The Rise and Fall of Domesticity in America*. New York: Oxford University Press.

May, Elaine Tyler. 1988. *Homeward Bound: American Families in the Cold War Era*. New York: Basic Books.

———. 1997. *Barren in the Promised Land: Childless Americans and the Pursuit of Happiness*. Cambridge, MA: Harvard University Press.

McBee, Randy D. 2000. *Dance Hall Days: Leisure and Intimacy among Working-Class Immigrants in the United States*. New York: New York University Press.

McCann, Carole. 1994. *Birth Control Politics in the United States, 1916–1945*. Ithaca, NY: Cornell University Press.

McCarthy, Kathleen D. 1991. *Women's Culture, American Philanthropy and Art, 1830–1930*. Chicago: University of Chicago Press.

McCaw, Jodee, and Charlene Senn. 1998. "Perception of Cues in Conflictual Dating Situations." *Violence against Women 4*, no. 5: 609–624.

McCracken, Grant. 1995. *Big Hair: A Journey into the Transformation of Self*. New York: Overlook Press.

McDonough, Yona Zeldis, ed. 1999. *The Barbie Chronicles: A Living Doll Turns Forty*. New York: Touchstone.

McElroy, Ann. 1989. "Ooleepeeka and Mina: Contrasting Responses to the Modernization of Two Baffin Island Inuit Women." Pp. 290–318 in *Being and Becoming Indian: Biographical Studies of North American Frontiers*. Edited by James A. Clifton. Chicago: Dorsey Press.

McGaw, Judith, ed. 1994. *Early American Technology: Making and Doing Things from the Colonial Era to 1850*. Chapel Hill: University of North Carolina Press.

McGee, Mark. 1995. *Faster and Furiouser: The Revised and Fattened Fable of American International Pictures*. Jefferson, NC: McFarland.

McGee, Mark, and R. J. Robertson. 1982. *The J.D. Films: Juvenile Delinquency in the Movies*. Jefferson, NC: McFarland.

McGreevy, Ann. 1990. "Treasures of Children: Collections Then and Now, or Treasures of Children Revisited." *Early Child Development and Care* 63: 33–36.

McMurry, Sally. 1987. *Farmhouses and Families*. New York: Oxford University Press, 178–185.

McNally, William P., Rev. 1942. "The Secondary School." Pp. 118–140 in *Essays on Catholic Education in the United States*. Edited by Roy J. Deferrari. Washington, DC: Catholic University of America Press.

McRobbie, Angela. 1991. *Feminism and Youth Culture: From Jackie to Just Seventeen*. Boston: Unwin Hyman.

———. 2000. *Feminism and Youth Culture*. 2d ed. New York: Routledge.

McRobbie, Angela, and Jenny Garber. 1975. "Girls and Subcultures." Pp. 209–222 in *Resistance through Rituals: Youth Subcultures in Post-War Britain*. Edited by Stuart Hall and Tony Jefferson. New York: Holmes and Meier.

Mechling, Jay. 1989. "The Collecting Self and American Youth Movements." Pp. 255–285 in *Consuming Visions: Accumulation and Display of Goods in America, 1889–1920.* Edited by Simon J. Bronner. New York: W. W. Norton.

Mediati, Ellen. 1997. "Hot Pink: An Interview with Lady Pink." *Siren* 2: 21.

Meredith, Robyn. 1999. "Hey, Nice Headlights: In Detroit, a Sex Change." *New York Times* (May 16).

Mergen, Bernard. 1980. "The Discovery of Children's Play." *American Quarterly* 32 (Fall): 399–420.

———. 1982. *Play and Playthings: A Reference Guide.* Westport, CT: Greenwood.

———. "Made, Bought, and Stolen: Toys and the Culture of Childhood." In *Small Worlds: Children and Adolescents in America, 1850–1950.* Edited by Elliott West and Paula Petrik. Lawrence: University of Kansas Press.

Merrell, James H. 1991. *The Indians' New World: Catawbas and Their Neighbors from European Contact through the Era of Removal.* New York: W. W. Norton.

Merrill, Marlene Deahl, ed. 1990. *Growing Up in Boston's Gilded Age: The Journal of Alice Stone Blackwell, 1872–1874.* New Haven: Yale University Press.

Metter, Bert. 1984. *Bar Mitzvah, Bat Mitzvah: How Jewish Boys and Girls Come of Age.* New York: Clarion Books.

Meusburger, Joanne. 1988. "Farm Girl." *The Palimpsest* 69, no. 1: 34–48.

Meyer, Michael A. 1988. *Response to Modernity: A History of the Reform Movement in Judaism.* New York: Oxford University Press.

Meyers, Joan. 1999. "Secret Lives: The Making of Feminist Red Diaper Daughters." Master's thesis, San Francisco State University.

Mickenberg, Julia. 2000. "Educating Dissent: Children's Literature and the Left, 1935–1965." Ph.D. diss., University of Minnesota.

"Migrant Workers' Children." http://www.users.owt.com/rpeto/migrant/html.

Miller, Ivor Lynn. 1993. "Aerosol Kingdom: The Indigenous Culture of the New York Subway." UMI 1349354. Master's thesis, Yale University.

Miller, Jean Baker. 1976. *Toward a New Psychology of Women.* Boston: Beacon Press.

———. 1986. *Toward a New Psychology of Women.* 2d ed. Boston: Beacon.

Miller, Lisa, Virginia Warner, Priya Wickramarane, and Myrna Weissman. 1997. "Self-esteem and Depression: Ten Year Follow-up of Mothers and Offspring." *Archives of General Psychiatry* 54: 932–942.

Millett, Kate. 1971. *Sexual Politics.* Garden City, NY: Doubleday.

Minard, Rosemary. 1975. *Womenfolk and Fairy Tales.* Boston: Houghton Mifflin.

Mintz, Sidney. 1985. *Sweetness and Power: The Place of Sugar in Modern History.* New York: Viking.

Mintz, Steven, and Susan Kellogg. 1988. *Domestic Revolutions: A Social History of American Family Life.* New York: The Free Press.

Minuchin, Salvador, Bernice L. Rosman, and Lester Baker. 1978. *Psychosomatic Families: Anorexia Nervosa in Context.* Cambridge: Harvard University Press.

Mirandé, Alfredo, and Evangelina Enríquez. 1979. *La Chicana: The Mexican-American Woman.* Chicago: University of Chicago Press.

Mishler, Paul C. 1999. *Raising Reds: The Young Pioneers, Radical Summer Camps, and Communist Political Culture in the United States.* New York: Columbia University Press.

Mitchell, Sally. 1995. *The New Girl: Girls' Culture in England, 1880–1915.* New York: Columbia University Press.

Moberg, David. 2001. "Bridging the Gap: Why Women Still Don't Get Equal Pay." *In These Times* (January 8): 24–26.

Modell, Judith S. 1994. *Kinship with Strangers: Adoption and Interpretation of Kinship in American Culture.* Berkeley: University of California Press.

Monaghan, E. Jennifer. 1989. "Literacy Instruction and Gender in Colonial New England." Pp. 53–80 in *Reading in America: Literature and Social History.* Edited by Cathy N. Davidson. Baltimore: Johns Hopkins University Press.

Monk, Katherine. 1997. "Resurgence of Bubblegum Pop Takes Music Industry by Surprise." *Ottawa Citizen* (April 7): D9.

Monroy, Douglas. 1999. *Rebirth: Mexican Los Angeles from the Great Migration to the Great Depression.* Berkeley: University of California Press.

Moody, Anne. 1976. *Coming of Age in Mississippi.* Reprint, New York: Dell.

Moon, Sarah. 1983. *Little Red Riding Hood.* Mankato: Creative Education.

Mooney, James. 1865; abridged 1976. *The Ghost-Dance Religion and the Sioux Outbreak.* Chicago: University of Chicago Press.

Moore, Kristin, and Barbara Sugland. 1999. "Piecing Together the Puzzle of Teenage Childbearing." *Policy and Practice of Public Human Services* 57, no. 2: 36–42.

Morales, Beatriz. 1994. "Latino Religion, Ritual, and Culture." Pp. 91–207 in

Handbook of Hispanic Cultures of the United States: Anthropology. Edited by Thomas Weaver. Houston and Madrid: Arte Público Press and Instituto de Cooperación Iberoamericana.

Morgan, Edmund S. 1944. *The Puritan Family: Religion and Domestic Relations in Seventeenth Century New England.* 1966. Reprint, New York: Harper and Row.

Morgan, Robin. 1970. *Sisterhood Is Powerful: An Anthology of Writings from the Women's Liberation Movement.* New York: Vintage.

———. 1978. *Going Too Far.* New York: Random House.

Morrow Nix, Elizabeth. 1996. "An Exuberant Flow of Spirits: Antebellum Adolescent Girls in the Writing of Southern Women." Ph.D. diss., Boston University.

"Most Popular Doll in Town." 1963. *Life* (August 21): 73–75.

Muehlenhard, C., and M. Linton. 1987. "Date Rape and Sexual Aggression in Dating Situations: Incidence and Risk Factors." *Journal of Counseling Psychology* 34: 186–196.

Mulvey, Laura. 1989. *Visual and Other Pleasures.* Bloomington: Indiana University Press.

Muncy, Robyn. 1991. *Creating a Female Dominion in American Reform, 1890–1935.* New York: Oxford University Press.

Munk, Nina. 1997. "Girl Power!" *Fortune* (December 8): 132–140.

Munsch, Robert. 1980. *The Paper Bag Princess.* New York: Annick Press.

Murphy, Patricia. 1996. "Assessment Practices and Gender in Science." Pp. 105–117 in *Gender Science and Mathematics.* Edited by Lesley Parker, Leonie Rennie, and Barry Fraser.

Dordrecht, the Netherlands: Kluwer Academic Publishers.

Murray, Gail Schmunk. 1998. *American Children's Literature and the Construction of Childhood.* New York: Twayne Publishers.

Murray, Pauli. 1987. *Proud Shoes: The Story of an American Family.* New York: Harper and Row.

Muzny, Charles C. 1989. *The Vietnamese in Oklahoma City: A Study of Ethnic Change.* New York: AMS Press.

Namias, June. 1993. *White Captives: Gender and Ethnicity on the American Frontier.* Chapel Hill: University of North Carolina Press.

Nasaw, David. 1985. *Children of the City at Work and at Play.* Garden City, NY: Anchor Press/Doubleday.

———. 1993. *Going Out: The Rise and Fall of Public Amusements.* New York: Basic Books.

Nash, Gary B. 1992. *Red, White, and Black: The People of Early North America.* 3d ed. Englewood Cliffs, NJ: Prentice-Hall.

Nass, Ruth. 1993. "Sex Differences in Learning Abilities and Disabilities." *Annals of Dyslexia* 43.

Nathanson, Constance A. 1991. *Dangerous Passage: The Social Control of Sexuality in Women's Adolescence.* Philadelphia: Temple University Press.

National Commission on Migrant Education (NCME). 1992. "Invisible Children: A Portrait of Migrant Education in the United States." Washington, DC: NCME, September 23.

National Committee to Prevent Child Abuse. 1994. *Current Trend in Child Abuse Reporting and Fatalities: The Results of the 1993 Annual Fifty State Survey.* Chicago: National Committee to Prevent Child Abuse.

National Council of Teachers of Mathematics. 1970. *A History of Mathematics Education. Thirty-Second Yearbook.* Washington, DC: National Council of Teachers of Mathematics.

National Research Council. 1993. *Understanding Child Abuse and Neglect.* Washington, DC: National Academy Press.

Nee, Victor G., and Brett de Bavy. 1972. *Longtime, California: A Documentary Study of an American Chinatown.* New York: Random House.

Neider, Charles, ed. 1985. *Papa: An Intimate Biography of Mark Twain by Suzy Clemens, His Daughter, Thirteen. With a Foreword and Copious Comments by Her Father.* Garden City, NY: Doubleday.

Neil, Randy. 1983. *The Official Pompon Girl's Handbook.* New York: St. Martin's Press/Marek.

Nelson, Claudia, and Lynne Vallone, eds. 1994. *The Girls' Own: Cultural Histories of the Anglo-American Girl, 1830–1915.* Athens: University of Georgia Press.

Nelson, Mariah Burton. 1991. *Are We Winning Yet? How Women Are Changing Sports and Sports Are Changing Women.* New York: Random House.

Neth, Mary. 1995. *Preserving the Family Farm: Women, Community, and the Foundations of Agribusiness in the Midwest, 1900–1940.* Baltimore: Johns Hopkins University Press.

Neupert, Alice Hughes. 1977. "In Those Days: Buffalo in the 1870's." *Niagara Frontier* 24, no. 4 (Winter): 77–89.

Neus, Margaret. 1990. *The Insider's Guide to Babysitting: Anecdotes and*

Advice from Babysitters for Babysitters. Master's thesis, Emerson College, Boston.

Newcomer, Mabel. 1959. *A Century of Higher Education for American Women.* New York: Harper and Brothers.

Nicholson, Joy. 1997. *The Tribes of Palos Verdes.* New York: St. Martin's Press.

Nichter, Mimi. 2000. *Fat Talk: What Girls and Their Parents Say about Dieting.* Cambridge, MA: Harvard University Press.

"No Question Now That Many Do—But with Whose Color?" 1963. *Printers' Ink* (August 16): 8.

Nolen-Hoeksema, Susan, and Joan S. Girgus. 1994. "The Emergence of Gender Differences in Depression during Adolescence." *Psychological Bulletin* 115: 424–443.

Nolen-Hoeksema, Susan, Judith Larson, and Carla Grayson. 1999. "Explaining the Gender Difference in Depressive Symptoms." *Journal of Personality and Social Psychology* 77, no. 5: 1061–1072.

Norden, Martin F. 1994. *The Cinema of Isolation: A History of Physical Disability in the Movies.* New Brunswick, NJ: Rutgers University Press.

North Bennet Street Industrial School (NBSIS) Archives. Manuscript Collection 269, Schlesinger Library, Radcliffe College, Cambridge, MA.

Norton, Mary Beth. 1980. *Liberty's Daughters: The Revolutionary Experience of American Women, 1750–1800.* Ithaca, NY: Cornell University Press.

———. 1997. *Founding Mothers and Fathers: Gendered Power and the Forming of American Society.* New York: Alfred A. Knopf.

Novak, Steven. 1977. *The Rights of Youth: American Colleges and Student Revolt.* Cambridge, MA: Harvard University Press.

Oak, Jacquelyn. 1994. *Sotheby's Guide to American Folk Art.* New York: Simon and Schuster.

Oakes, Jennie. 1990. "Opportunities, Achievement, and Choice: Women and Minority Students in Science and Mathematics." Pp. 153–237 in *Review of Education Research,* vol. 16. Edited by Courtney Cazden. Washington, DC: American Educational Research Association.

Obeidallah, Dawn A., Susan M. McHale, and Rainer K. Silbereisen. 1996. "Gender Role Socialization and Adolescents' Reports of Depression: Why Some Girls and Not Others." *Journal of Youth and Adolescence* 25, no. 6: 775–785.

Oboler, Suzanne. 1995. *Ethnic Labels, Latino Lives: Identity and the Politics of (Re)Presentation in the United States.* Minneapolis: University of Minnesota Press.

O'Brien, Lucy. 1999. "The Woman Punk Made Me." Pp. 186–198 in *Punk Rock: So What? The Cultural Legacy of Punk.* New York: Routledge.

O'Conner, Kevin John. 1991. *The Play Therapy Primer: An Integration of Theories and Techniques.* New York: John Wiley and Sons.

Odem, Mary E. 1995. *Delinquent Daughters: Protecting and Policing Adolescent Female Sexuality in the United States, 1885–1920.* Chapel Hill: University of North Carolina Press.

Office of Juvenile Justice and Delinquency Prevention. 1999. *1996 National Youth Gang Survey.* Washington, DC: U.S. Department of Justice.

O'Hara, Craig. 1999. *The Philosophy of Punk: More Than Noise!* San Francisco: AK Press.

Olweus, Dan. 1995. "Bullying or Peer Abuse at School: Facts and Intervention." *Current Directions in Psychological Science* 4: 196–200.

Ortner, Sherry. 1996. "Is Female to Male as Nature Is to Culture?" In *Anthropological Theory.* Edited by R. Jon McGee and Richard L. Warms. 1974. Mountain View, CA: Mayfield Publishing.

Oudshoorn, Nelly. 1994. *Beyond the Natural Body: An Archaeology of Sex Hormones.* London: Routledge.

Oxreider, J. W. 1977. "The Slumber Party: Transition into Adolescence." *Tennessee Folklore Society Bulletin* 43, no. 3: 128–134.

Page, Randy M. 1997. "Helping Adolescents Avoid Date Rape: The Role of Secondary Education." *High School Journal* 80, no. 2 (December–January): 75–80.

Page, Ruth. 1984. Class: *Notes on Dance Classes around the World 1915–1980.* Princeton: Princeton Book Co.

Palazzoli, Mara Selvini. 1978. *Self-Starvation.* New York: Jason Aronson.

Palladino, Grace. 1996. *Teenagers: An American History.* New York: Basic Books.

Palmieri, Patricia. 1995. *In Adamless Eden: The Community of Women Faculty at Wellesley.* New Haven: Yale University Press.

Pareles, Jon. 1985. "The Pop Life: Wham Facing Up to New Popularity." *New York Times* (February 13): C24.

Paris, Leslie. 1998. "Small Mercies: Colleen Moore and the National Doll House Tour, 1935–1939." In *Made to Play House: Dolls and the Commercialization of American Girlhood, 1830–1930.* Edited by Miriam Formanek-Brunell. Baltimore: Johns Hopkins University Press.

———. 2001. "The Adventures of Peanut and Bo: Summer Camps and Early Twentieth Century American Girlhood." *Journal of Women's History* 12, no. 4 (Winter).

———. Forthcoming, 2001. "'A Home Though Away from Home': Brooklyn Jews and Interwar Children's Summer Camps." In *The Jews of Brooklyn.* Edited by Ilana Abramovitch and Séan Galvin. Boston: University Press of New England/Brandeis University Press.

Parish, Peter J. 1989. *Slavery: History and Historians.* New York: Harper and Row.

Parker, Idella. 1991. *Idella: Marjorie Rawlings' "Perfect Maid."* With Mary Keating. Gainesville: University Press of Florida.

Parrot, Andrea, and Laurie Bechhofer, eds. 1991. *Acquaintance Rape: The Hidden Crime.* New York: Wiley.

Patterson, Gordon. 1994. "Color Matters: The Creation of the Sara Lee Doll." *Florida Historical Quarterly* 73, no. 2: 147–165.

Paul Revere Pottery Gallery File. Fine Arts Department, Boston Public Library.

Paulsen, Susan B. 1988. "Sociable Speech in the American Slumber Party: An Ethnographic Study." Ph.D. diss., University of Washington.

Pazicky, Diana Loercher. 1998. *Cultural Orphans in America.* Jackson: University of Mississippi Press.

Peavy, Linda, and Ursula Smith. 1999. *Frontier Children.* Norman: University of Oklahoma Press.

Peden, Margaret Sayers. 1982. *A Woman of Genius: The Intellectual Autobiography of Sor Juana Inés de la Cruz.* Translation of *La Respuesta* (i.e., *Response to Sor Filotea).* Salisbury, CT: Lime Rock Press.

Pedraza-Bailey, Sylvia. 1991. "Women and Migration: The Social Consequences of Gender." *Annual Review of Sociology* 17: 303–325.

Peffer, George Anthony. 1999. *If They Don't Bring Their Women Here: Chinese Female Immigration before Exclusion.* Urbana: University of Illinois Press.

Peiss, Kathy. 1986. *Cheap Amusements: Working Women and Leisure in Turn-of-the-Century New York.* Philadelphia: Temple University Press.

———. 1998. *Hope in a Jar: The Making of America's Beauty Culture.* New York: Owl Books.

Penner, Carol. 1991. "Mennonite Women's History: A Survey." *Journal of Mennonite Studies* 9: 122–135.

Perdue, Charles L., Jr., Thomas E. Barden, and Robert K. Phillips. 1980. *Weevils in the Wheat: Interviews with Virginia Ex-Slaves.* Bloomington: Indiana University Press.

Perdue, Theda. 1998. *Cherokee Women: Gender and Cultural Change, 1700–1835.* Lincoln: University of Nebraska Press.

Perdue, Theda, and Michael D. Green. 1995. *The Cherokee Removal: A Brief History with Documents.* Boston: Bedford Books.

Perebinossoff, Phillipe. 1974. "What Does a Kiss Mean? The Love Comic Formula and the Creation of the Ideal Teen-Age Girl." *Journal of Popular Culture* 8, no. 4: 825–835.

Perez Firmat, Gustavo. 1994. *Life on the Hyphen: The Cuban-American Way.* Austin: University of Texas.

Perrett, Antoinette R. 1910. "Girls' Rooms." *St. Nicholas* 37 (May): 595–596.

Pettitt, George A. 1946. *Primitive Education in North America.* Berkeley: University of California Press.

Phelps, Elizabeth Stuart. 1867. *Gypsy's Year at the Golden Crescent.* 1897. Reprint, New York: Dodd, Mead.

Phelps, Ethel Johnston. 1978. *Tatterhood and Other Tales.* New York: Feminist Press.

———. 1981. *The Maid of the North: Feminist Folk Tales from around the World.* New York: Holt, Rinehart and Winston.

Phillips, K. A. 1996. *The Broken Mirror: Understanding and Treating Body Dysmorphic Disorder.* New York: Oxford University Press.

———. 1998. "Body Dysmorphic Disorder: Clinical Aspects and Treatment Strategies." *Bulletin of the Menninger Clinic* 62, no. 4: A33–A48.

Pickford, Mary. 1956. *Sunshine and Shadow: The Autobiography of Mary Pickford.* London: William Heineman.

Pilch, Judah, ed. 1969. *A History of Jewish Education in America.* New York: Curriculum Research Institute of the American Association for Jewish Education.

Pipher, Mary. 1994. *Reviving Ophelia: Saving the Selves of Adolescent Girls.* New York: Ballantine Books.

Piran, N., M. P. Levine, and C. Steiner-Adair, eds. *Preventing Eating Disorders: A Handbook of Intervention and Special Challenges.* Philadelphia: Brunner-Routledge.

Planned Parenthood Federation of America. www.teenwire.com. Accessed January 11, 2001.

Pleck, Joseph. 1987. "American Fathering in Historical Perspective." Pp. 83–97 in *Changing Men: New Directions in Research on Masculinity.* Edited by Michael S. Kimmel. Newbury Park, CA: Sage.

Plunkett-Powell, Karen. 1993. *The Nancy Drew Scrapbook*. New York: St. Martin's Press.

Pollack, William. 1999. *Real Boys*. New York: Owl Books.

Pollock, Joycelyn M. 1999. *Criminal Women*. Cincinnati: Anderson Publishing.

Pollock, Kathryn M. 1943. "Helping the Mother-Aides." *Journal of Home Economics* 35, no. 1 (June): 31.

Pollock, Linda. 1987. *A Lasting Relationship: Parents and Children over Three Centuries*. Hanover, NH: University Press of New England.

Porweller, Amira. 1998. *Constructing Female Identities: Meaning-Making in an Upper Middle Class Youth Culture*. Albany: State University of New York Press.

Posadas, Barbara M. 1989. "Mestiza Girlhood: Interracial Families in Chicago's Filipino American Community since 1925." Pp. 273–282 in *Making Waves: An Anthology of Writings by and about Asian American Women*. Edited by Asian Women United of California. Boston: Beacon Press.

Post, Emily. 1922. *Etiquette in Society, in Business, in Politics and at Home*. New York: Funk and Wagnalls.

Potter, Eliza. 1991. *A Hairdresser's Experience in the High Life*. New York: Oxford University Press.

Powers, Jane Bernard. 1992. *The "Girl Question" in Education: Vocational Education for Young Women in the Progressive Era*. London: Falmer Press.

Powers, Sally, and Deborah P. Welsh. 1999. "Mother-Daughter Interactions and Adolescent Girls' Depression." Pp. 243–281 in *Conflict and Cohesion in Families*. Edited by Martha J. Cox and Jeanne Brooks-Gunn. Mahwah, NJ: Lawrence Erlbaum.

Prager, Arthur. 1971. *Rascals at Large; or, the Clue in the Old Nostalgia*. Garden City, NY: Doubleday.

Pratt, Joanne. 1961. "I'll Tell You a Letter." *Parents' Magazine* 36 (Fall): 54–55.

Prescott, Heather Munro. 1998. *"A Doctor of Their Own": The History of Adolescent Medicine*. Cambridge, MA: Harvard University Press.

Press, Joy. 1997. "Notes on Girl Power: The Selling of Softcore Feminism." *Village Voice* (September 23): 59–61.

Prince, Nancy. 1990. *A Black Woman's Odyssey through Russia and Jamaica*. New York: Markus Wiener Publishing.

Probyn, Elspeth. 1996. *Outside Belongings*. New York: Routledge.

Prucha, Francis Paul. 1984. *The Great Father: The United States Government and the American Indians*. 2 vols. Lincoln: University of Nebraska Press.

Pursell, Carroll W., Jr. 1979. "Toys, Technology, and Sex Roles in America, 1920–1940." In *Dynamos & Virgins Revisited: Women and Technological Change in History*. Edited by Martha Moore Trescott. Metuchen, NJ: Scarecrow Press.

Putnam, Catherine Bonney. 1871. Composition Book. In collection of Historic Cherry Hill, Albany, NY.

Qoyawayma, Polingaysi. 1964. *No Turning Back: A Hopi Indian Woman's Struggle to Live in Two Worlds*. 1992. Reprint, Albuquerque: University of New Mexico Press.

Quicker, John C. 1983. *Homegirls: Characterizing Chicana Gangs*. San Pedro, CA: International University Press.

Radner, Hillary. 1989. "'This Time's for Me': Making Up and Feminine Practice." *Cultural Studies* 3: 301–321.

Rameau, Pierre. 1725. *Le Maître à Danser.* Paris.

Ramirez, Roberto R. 2000. "The Hispanic Population in the United States." *Current Population Reports March 1999.* Washington, DC: U.S. Census Bureau.

Rand Youth Poll. 1999. Cited in Kathy Kristof, "Do Your Kids Know That Money Doesn't Grow on Christmas Trees?" *Los Angeles Times* (December 3, 2000): A1.

Rao, Uma, Constance Hammen, and Shannon Daley. 1999. "Continuity of Depression during the Transition to Adulthood: A 5-year Longitudinal Study of Young Women." *Journal of the American Academy of Child and Adolescent Psychiatry* 38, no. 7: 908–915.

Rawick, George P., ed. 1972. *The American Slave: A Composite Autobiography.* 19 vols. Westport, CT: Greenwood Press.

Read, Carolyn R. 1991. "Gender Distribution in Programs for the Gifted." *Roeper Review* 13, no. 3: 188–193.

Rebolledo, Tey Diana. 1995. *Women Singing in the Snow: A Cultural Analysis of Chicana Literature.* Tucson: University of Arizona Press.

Rebolledo, Tey Diana, and Eliana Rivero, eds. 1993. *Infinite Divisions: An Anthology of Chicana Literature.* Tucson: University of Arizona Press, 1.

Reck, Franklin M. 1951. *The 4-H Story: A History of 4-H Club Work.* Ames: Iowa State College Press.

Reisfeld, Randi, and Danny Fields. 1997. *Who's Your Fave Rave?* New York: Boulevard Books.

Reisner, Robert. 1971. *Graffiti: Two Thousand Years of Wall Writing.* New York: Cowles Book Company.

Rich, Adrienne. 1976. *Of Woman Born: Motherhood as Experience and Institution.* New York: W. W. Norton.

Richardson, Angela. 1996. "Come on Join the Conversation: 'Zines as a Medium for Feminist Dialogue and Community Building." *Feminist Collections* 17, nos. 3–4 (Spring–Summer): 10–13.

Richardson, Marilyn, ed. 1987. *Maria W. Stewart, America's First Black Woman Political Writer: Essays and Speeches.* Bloomington: Indiana University Press.

Richardson, Theresa. 1989. *The Century of the Child: The Mental Hygiene Movement and Social Policy in the United States and Canada.* Albany: State University of New York Press.

Richter, Daniel K. 1992. *The Ordeal of the Longhouse: The Peoples of the Iroquois League in the Era of European Colonization.* Chapel Hill: University of North Carolina Press.

Rierdan, Jill, and Elissa Koff. 1997. "Weight, Weight-related Aspects of Body Image, and Depression in Early Adolescent Girls." *Adolescence* 32, no. 127: 615–624.

Riesman, David. 1950. *The Lonely Crowd.* New Haven, CT: Yale University Press.

Ring, Betty. 1993. *Girlhood Embroidery, American Samplers and Pictorial Needlework, 1650–1850.* 2 vols. New York: Alfred A. Knopf.

Riordan, Cornelius. 1990. *Girls and Boys in School: Together or Separate?* New York: Teachers College Press.

Robbins, Trina. 1993. *A Century of Women Cartoonists.* Northampton, MA: Kitchen Sink Press.

———. 1996. *The Great Women Superheroes.* Northampton, MA: Kitchen Sink Press.

———. 1999. *From Girls to Grrlz*. San Francisco: Chronicle Books.

Roberts, Dorothy. 1997. *Killing the Black Body: Race, Reproduction, and the Meaning of Liberty*. New York: Pantheon Books.

Roberts, T., et al. 1997. *Am I the Last Virgin? Ten African American Reflections on Sex and Love*. New York: Aladdin Paperbacks.

Robinson, Harriet H. 1898. *Loom and Spindle or Life among the Early Mill Girls*. 1976. Reprint, Kailua, HI: Press Pacifica.

Robinson, T., and J. Ward. 1991. "A Belief in Self Far Greater Than Anyone's Disbelief: Cultivating Resistance among African American Female Adolescents." *Women and Therapy:* 81–103.

Rodriguez, Clara. 1989. *Puerto Ricans: Born in the U.S.A.* Boston: Unwin Hyman.

Roehm, Michelle, comp. 1997. *Girls Know Best: Advice for Girls from Girls on Just about Everything*. Hillsboro, OR: Beyond Words Publishing.

Romalov, Nancy Tillman. 1995. "Mobile Heroines: Early Twentieth Century Girls' Automobile Series." *Journal of Popular Culture* (Spring).

———. 1996. "Unearthing the Historical Reader, or, Reading Girls' Reading." *Primary Sources and Original Works* 4 (1–2): 87–101.

Roman, Leslie G., and Linda Christian-Smith, eds. 1988. *Becoming Feminine: The Politics of Popular Culture*. London: Falmer Press.

Romero, Mary. 1992. *Maid in the U.S.A.* New York: Routledge.

Romero, Mary, Pierette Hondagneu-Sotelo, and Vilma Ortiz, eds. 1997. *Challenging Fronteras: Structuring Latina and Latino Lives in the U.S.* New York: Routledge.

Rooks, Noliwe M. 1996. *Hair Raising: Beauty, Culture, and African American Women*. New Brunswick, NJ: Rutgers University Press.

Roscoe, Will. 1998. *Changing Ones: Third and Fourth Genders in Native North America*. New York: St. Martin's Press.

Rose, Elizabeth. 1999. *A Mother's Job: The History of Day Care, 1890–1960*. New York: Oxford University Press.

Rosenberg, Jessica, and Gitana Garofalo. 1998. "Riot Grrrl: Revolutions from Within." *Signs* 23, no. 3: 809–842.

Rosenthal, Michael. 1984. *The Character Factory: Baden-Powell and the Origins of the Boy Scout Movement*. New York: Pantheon.

Rosenzweig, Linda W. 1993. *The Anchor of My Life: Middle-Class American Mothers and Daughters, 1880–1920*. New York: New York University Press.

———. 1998. "'Another Self?': Middle-Class American Women and Their Friends, 1900–1960." Pp. 357–373 in *Emotional History of the United States*. Edited by Peter N. Stearns and Jan Lewis. New York: New York University Press.

Rossiter, Margaret W. 1997. "The Men Move In: Home Economics in Higher Education, 1950–1970." Pp. 96–117 in *Rethinking Home Economics: Women and the History of a Profession*. Edited by Sarah Stage and Virginia Vincenti. Ithaca, NY: Cornell University Press.

Roth, Rodris. 1988. "Tea-Drinking in Eighteenth-Century America: Its Etiquette and Equipage." Pp. 439–462 in *Material Life in America 1600–1860*. Edited by Robert Blair St. George. Boston: Northeastern University Press.

Rothman, David J. 1971. *The Discovery of the Asylum: Social Order and Disorder in the New Republic.* Boston: Little, Brown.

Rothman, Ellen K. 1984. *Hands and Hearts: A History of Courtship in America.* New York: Basic Books.

Rothman, Sheila. 1994. *Living in the Shadow of Death: Tuberculosis and the Social Experience of Illness in American History.* New York: Basic Books.

Roundtree, Helen C. 1990. *Pocahontas's People: The Powhatan Indians of Virginia through Four Centuries.* Norman: University of Oklahoma Press.

Rountree, Susan Hight. 1996. *Dollhouses, Miniature Kitchens and Shops.* Williamsburg: Colonial Williamsburg Foundation.

Rouse, Roger. 1992. "Making Sense of Settlement: Class Transformation, Cultural Struggle, and Transnationalism among Mexican Migrants in the United States." In *Towards a Transnational Perspective on Migration: Race, Class, and Nationalism Reconsidered.* Edited by Glick Schiller, Linda Basch, and Cristina Blanc-Szanton. New York: Annals of New York Academy of Sciences, vol. 645.

Rousseau, Jean-Jacques. 1762. *Emile.* 1974. Reprint, London: J. M. Dent & Sons, Ltd.

Ruiz, Vicki L. 1999. *From out of the Shadows: Mexican American Women in the Twentieth-Century America.* New York: Oxford University Press.

Rupp, Leila J. 1999. *A Desired Past: A Short History of Same-Sex Love in America.* Chicago: University of Chicago Press.

Rury, John. 1991. *Education and Women's Work.* Albany: State University of New York Press.

Ruskin, John. 1864. *Sesame and Lilies.* 1965. New York: Everyman's Library.

Russett, Cynthia Eagle. 1989. *Sexual Science: The Victorian Construction of Womanhood.* Cambridge, MA: Harvard University Press.

Rutman, Darrett B., and Anita H. Rutman. 1984. *A Place in Time: Middlesex County, Virginia, 1650–1750.* New York: W. W. Norton.

Ryan, Mary P. 1981. *Cradle of the Middle Class: The Family in Oneida County, New York, 1790–1865.* New York: Cambridge University Press.

S.E.G. News. November 1914–May 1917. Boston.

S.E.G. News, Cherry Tree Edition, 1899–1954. 1954. Boston.

S.E.G. News: 1899–1952. 1952. Boston.

Sadker, Myra, and David Sadker. 1994. *Failing at Fairness: How America's Schools Cheat Girls.* New York: Charles Scribner's Sons.

Sadler, A. W. 1964. "The Love Comics and American Popular Culture." *American Quarterly* 16, no. 3: 486–490.

Safford, Philip L., and Elizabeth J. Safford. 1996. *A History of Childhood and Disability.* New York: Teachers College Press.

Sahli, Nancy. 1979. "Smashing: Women's Relationships before the Fall." *Chrysalis* 8: 17–27.

Salcedo, Michele. 1997. *Quinceañera! The Essential Guide to Planning the Perfect Sweet Fifteen Celebration.* New York: Holt.

Sallquist, Sylvia Lea. 1984. "The Image of the Hired Girl in Literature: The Great Plains, 1860–WWI." *Great Plains Quarterly* 4, no. 3: 166–177.

Sánchez, George. 1990. "'Go after the Women': Americanization and the Mexican Immigrant Woman, 1915–1929."

In *A Multi-Cultural Reader in U.S. Women's History.* Edited by Ellen DuBois and Vicki L. Ruiz. New York: Routledge.

Sánchez-Korrol, Virginia. 1994. *From Colonia to Community: The History of Puerto Ricans in New York City.* Berkeley: University of California Press.

Sandmaier, Marian. 1980. *The Invisible Alcoholics: Women and Alcohol Abuse in America.* New York: McGraw-Hill.

Sawyer, Janet. 1994. "What Could You Possibly Learn by Studying Us? A Qualitative Study of the School Lives of High School Girls." Ph.D. diss., Hofstra University.

Saxon, Ruth O. 1998. *The Girl: Constructions of the Girl in Contemporary Fiction by Women.* New York: St. Martin's Press.

Schaefer, Charles, ed. 1976. *The Therapeutic Use of Child's Play.* New York: Jason Aronson.

Schafer, Judith Kelleher. 1981. "New Orleans Slavery in 1850 as Seen in Advertisements." *Journal of Southern History* 47: 33–56.

Scharff, Virginia. 1991. *Taking the Wheel: Women and the Coming of the Motor Age.* Albuquerque: University of New Mexico Press.

Scheiner, Georganne. 1998. "The Deanna Durbin Devotees: Fan Clubs and Spectatorship." Pp. 81–94 in *Generations of Youth: Youth Cultures and History in Twentieth Century America.* Edited by Michael Willard and Joe Austin. New York: New York University Press.

———. 2000. *Signifying Female Adolescence: Film Representations and Fans 1920–1950.* Westport, CT: Praeger.

Schilling, Peter, and Daniel Soyer. 1996. "Fraternities and Sororities." Pp. 1047–1052 in *Encyclopedia of African American Culture and History.* Edited by Jack Salzman, David Lionel Smith, and Cornel West. New York: Macmillan.

Schlissel, Lillian, Bryd Gibbens, and Elizabeth Hampsten. 1989. *Far from Home: Families of the Westward Journey.* New York: Schocken Books.

Schmidlapp, David, and Phase 2. 1996. *Style: Writing from the Underground, (R)evolution of Aerosol Linguistics.* Viterbo, Italy: Stampa Alternativa/Nuovi Equilibri.

Schmidt, Kimberly D., Steven D. Reschly, and Diane Zimmerman Umble. Forthcoming. *Insider/Outsider: Women of Anabaptist Traditions in Historical Perspective.* Baltimore: Johns Hopkins University Press.

Schneider, Eric C. 1992. *In the Web of Class: Delinquents and Reformers in Boston, 1810 to the 1930s.* New York: New York University Press.

Scholinski, Daphne, with Jane Meredith Adams. 1997. *The Last Time I Wore a Dress.* New York: Riverhead Books.

Schrecker, Ellen. 1994. *The Age of McCarthyism: A Brief History with Documents.* Boston and New York: Bedford Books of St. Martin's Press.

Schrum, Kelly. 1998. "'Teena Means Business': Teenage Girls' Culture and *Seventeen* Magazine, 1944–1950." Pp. 134–163 in *Delinquents and Debutantes: Twentieth-Century American Girls' Cultures.* Edited by Sherrie A. Inness. New York: New York University Press.

Schulenberg, John, Jennifer L. Maggs, and Klaus Hurrelmann. 1997. *Health Risks and Developmental Transitions during Adolescence.* New York: Cambridge University Press.

Schultz, Jerelyn. 1990. "Middle Schoolers Dig into Voc Ed If It's about Real Stuff: Home Economics Programs." *Vocational*

Education Journal 65 (November–December): 42.

Schultz, Lucille M. 1999. *The Young Composers: Composition's Beginnings in Nineteenth-Century Schools.* Carbondale: Southern Illinois University Press.

Schuster, B. 1996. "Mobbing, Bullying, and Peer Rejection." *Psychological Science Agenda* (July–August): 12–13.

Schwartz, Marie Jenkins. 1996. "One Thing, Then Another: The Work of Slave Children in Alabama." *Labor's Heritage* 7: 22–33, 56–61.

Schwartz, Martin, and Walter DeKeseredy. 1997. *Sexual Assault on the College Campus: The Role of Male Peer Support.* Thousand Oaks, CA: Sage Publications.

Scult, Mel. 1993. *Judaism Faces the Twentieth Century: A Biography of Mordecai M. Kaplan.* Detroit: Wayne State University Press.

Sedgwick, Eve Kosofsky. 1990. *Epistemology of the Closet.* Berkeley: University of California Press.

Seiter, Ellen. 1993. *Sold Separately: Children and Parents in Consumer Culture.* New Brunswick, NJ: Rutgers University Press.

Sekaquaptewa, Helen. 1969. *Me and Mine: The Life Story of Helen Sekaquaptewa.* Tucson: University of Arizona Press.

Serpell, James. 1996. *In the Company of Animals: A Study of Human-Animal Relationships.* 1986. Reprint, Cambridge University Press.

Settle, Shirley, and Richard Milich. 1999. "Social Persistence Following Failure in Boys and Girls with LD." *Journal of Learning Disabilities* 32, no. 3: 201–212.

Shandler, Sara, ed. 1999. *Ophelia Speaks: Adolescent Girls Write about Their Search for Self.* New York: HarperPerennial.

Shapiro, Brenda, and J. Conrad Schwarz. 1997. "Date Rape: Its Relationship to Trauma Symptoms and Sexual Self-esteem." *Journal of Interpersonal Violence* 12, no. 3: 407–419.

Shapiro, Laura. 1986. *Perfection Salad: Women and Cooking at the Turn of the Century.* New York: Farrar, Straus and Giroux.

Shaw, Anna Moore. 1974. *A Pima Past.* Tucson: University of Arizona Press.

Shaw, Stephanie J. 1996. *What a Woman Ought to Be and to Do: Black Professional Women Workers during the Jim Crow Era.* Chicago: University of Chicago Press.

———. 1997. "Mothering under Slavery in the Antebellum South." Pp. 297–318 in *Mothers and Motherhood: Readings in American History.* Edited by Rima D. Apple and Janet Golden. Columbus: Ohio State University Press.

Shaywitz, Sally E., Bennet A. Shaywitz, Jack Fletcher, and Michael D. Escobar. 1990. "Prevalence of Reading Disability in Boys and Girls: Results of the Connecticut Longitudinal Study." *Journal of the American Medical Association* 264: 998–1002.

Sheehan, Bernard W. 1973. *Seeds of Extinction: Jeffersonian Philanthropy and the American Indian.* Chapel Hill: University of North Carolina Press.

Sherman, Eric. 1987. "Frankie and Annette: Back to the Beach." *Ladies Home Journal* (July): 50.

Shmurak, Carol B. 1998. *Voices of Hope: Adolescent Girls at Single Sex and Coeducational Schools.* New York: Peter Lan Publishing.

Shoemaker, Nancy. 1995a. "Introduction." Pp. 1–25 in *Negotiators of Change: Historical Perspectives on Native American Women.* Edited by Nancy Shoemaker. New York: Routledge.

———. 1995b. "Kateri Tekakwitha's Tortuous Path to Sainthood." Pp. 49–71 in *Negotiators of Change: Historical Perspectives on Native American Women.* Edited by Nancy Shoemaker. New York: Routledge.

Shrimpton, Louise. 1912. "Furnishing the Girl's Own Room." *Woman's Home Companion* (May).

Shultz, Gladys Denny, and Daisy Gordon Lawrence. 1958. *Lady from Savannah: The Life of Juliette Low.* Philadelphia: Lippincott.

Shuman, Amy. 1986. *Storytelling Rights: The Uses of Oral and Written Texts by Urban Adolescents.* Cambridge: Cambridge University Press.

Sicherman, Barbara. 1995. "Reading *Little Women*: The Many Lives of a Text." Pp. 245–266 in *U.S. History as Women's History: New Feminist Essays.* Edited by Linda Kerber et al. Chapel Hill: University of North Carolina Press.

Siegel, Deborah L. 1997. "Nancy Drew as New Girl Wonder: Solving It All for the 1930s." Pp. 159–182 in *Nancy Drew and Company: Culture, Gender, and Girls' Series.* Edited by Sherrie A. Inness. Bowling Green: Bowling Green State University Popular Press.

Siegle, Del, and Sally M. Reis. 1998. "Gender Differences in Teacher and Student Perceptions of Gifted Students' Ability and Effort." *Gifted Child Quarterly* 42, no. 1: 101–110.

Silberg, Judy L., et al. 1999. "The Influence of Genetic Factors and Life Stress on Depression among Adolescent Girls." *Archives of General Psychiatry* 56, no. 3: 225–232.

Silverman, Linda Kreger. 1993. *Counseling the Gifted and Talented.* Denver: Love.

Simons, Elizabeth Radin. 1980. "The Slumber Party as Folk Ritual: An Analysis of the Informal Sex Education of Preadolescents." Master's thesis, University of California at Berkeley.

Simpson, J. A., and E. S. C. Weiner, eds. 1989. *The Oxford English Dictionary.* New York: Oxford University Press.

Singer, Bennett L. 1993. *Growing Up Gay: A Literary Anthology.* New York: New Press.

Sklar, Kathryn Kish. 1973. *Catharine Beecher: A Study in American Domesticity.* New York, W. W. Norton.

Sklover, Beverly. 1997. "Women/Sports." *AAUW Outlook* (Winter): 12–16.

Small, Sasha. 1937. *Heroines.* New York: Workers Library.

Smith, Abbot Emerson. 2000. "Kidnapping and White Servitude." Pp. 349–351 in *Childhood in America.* Edited by Paula S. Fass and Mary Ann Mason. New York: New York University Press.

Smith, Annie Curtis. 1877. "The Letter-Box." *St. Nicholas* 4, no. 11 (September): 765.

Smith, Danill Blake. 1980. *Inside the Great House: Planter Life in Eighteenth-Century Chesapeake Society.* Ithaca, NY: Cornell University Press.

Smith, Dianne. 2000. *Womanish Black Girls: Dancing Contradictions of Resistance.* New York: Peter Lang.

Smith, Jessie Carney, and Carrell P. Horten. 1997. *Statistical Record of Black America.* 4th ed. Detroit: Gale.

Smith, Patricia R. 1979. *Shirley Temple Dolls and Collectibles*, 2d series. Paducah, KY: Collectors Books.

Smith-Rosenberg, Caroll. 1975. "The Female World of Love and Ritual: Relations between Women in Nineteenth-Century America." *Signs: Journal of Women in Culture and Society* 1, no. 1: 1–29.

———. 1985. "The Female World of Love and Ritual: Relations between Women in Nineteenth-Century America." Pp. 53–76 in *Disorderly Conduct: Visions of Gender in Victorian America*. New York: Oxford University Press.

———. 1986. "The Female World of Love and Ritual: Relations Between Women in Nineteenth-Century America." Pp. 229–249 in *Feminist Frontiers II: Rethinking Sex, Gender, and Society*. Edited by Laurel Richardson and Verta Taylor. New York: Random House.

Snyder, Howard, and Melissa Sickmund. 1999. *Juvenile Offenders and Victims: 1999 National Report*. Washington, DC: Bureau of Justice Statistics and Office of Community Oriented Policing Services, U.S. Department of Justice, 29–30.

Snyder, Thomas. 1993. *120 Years of American Education: A Statistical Portrait*. Washington, DC: Government Printing Office.

Solinger, Rickie. 1992. *Wake Up Little Susie: Single Pregnancy and Race before Roe v. Wade*. New York: Routledge.

Solomon, Barbara Miller. 1985. *In the Company of Educated Women: A History of Women and Higher Education in America*. New Haven, CT: Yale University Press.

———. 1989. *Ancestors and Immigrants*. Boston: Northeastern University Press.

Soloveitchik, Haym. 1994. "Rupture and Reconstruction: The Transformation of Contemporary Orthodoxy." *Tradition* 28, no. 4: 64–130.

Sone, Monica. 1953. *Nisei Daughter*. Boston: Little, Brown.

Southworth, E. D. E. N. 1859. *The Hidden Hand, or, Capitola the Madcap*. Edited by Joanne Dobson. 1988. Reprint, New Brunswick, NJ: Rutgers University Press.

Spector, Janet. 1993. *What This Awl Means: Feminist Archaeology at a Wahpeton Dakota Village*. St. Paul: Minnesota Historical Society Press.

Spock, Benjamin, and Mary Morgan. *Spock on Spock: A Memoir of Growing Up with the Century*. New York: Pantheon Books.

St. Pierre, Mark. 1991. *Madonna Swan: A Lakota Woman's Story*. Norman: University of Oklahoma Press.

Stacey, Jackie. 1995. *Stargazing: Hollywood Cinema and Female Spectatorship*. London: Routledge.

Stage, Sarah, and Virginia Vincenti, eds. 1997. *Rethinking Home Economics: Women and the History of a Profession*. Ithaca, NY: Cornell University Press.

Stanley, Autumn. 1995. *Mothers and Daughters of Invention: Notes for a Revised History of Technology*. New Brunswick, NJ: Rutgers University Press.

Stansell, Christine. 1986. *City of Women: Sex and Class in New York, 1789–1860*. New York: Alfred A. Knopf.

Stearns, Lutie E. 1906. "The Problem of the Girl." *The Library Journal* 31: 103–106.

Stearns, Peter N. 1985. *Jealousy: The Evolution of an Emotion in American History*. New York: New York University Press.

———. 1993. "Girls, Boys and Emotions: Redefinitions and Historical Change."

Journal of American History 80 (June): 66–89.

———. 1994. *American Cool: Constructing a Twentieth-Century Emotional Style.* New York: New York University Press.

Stebbins, Genevieve. 1902. *Delsarte System of Expression.* 6th ed. 1997. Reprint, New York: Dance Horizons.

Steffensmeier, Darrell, and Emlie Allan. 1998. "The Nature of Female Offending: Patterns and Explanation." Pp. 5–29 in *Female Crime and Delinquency: Critical Perspectives and Effective Interventions.* Edited by Ruth T. Zaplin. Gaithersburg, MD: Aspen Publishers.

Stein, Nan. 1995. "Sexual Harassment in School: The Public Performance of Gendered Violence." *Harvard Educational Review* 65: 145–162.

———. 1999a. *Classrooms and Courtrooms: Facing Sexual Harassment in K–12 Schools.* New York: Teachers College Press.

———. 1999b. "Gender Violence in Elementary and Secondary Schools." *Women's Studies Quarterly* 27: 212–217.

Sterling, Dorothy. 1984. *We Are Your Sisters: Black Women in the Nineteenth Century.* New York: W. W. Norton.

Stern, Jane, and Michael Stern. 1990. *The Encyclopedia of Bad Taste.* New York: HarperCollins.

Stevenson, Brenda, ed. 1988. *The Journals of Charlotte Forten Grimké.* New York: Oxford University Press.

Stewart, Jack. 1989. *Subway Graffiti: An Aesthetic Study of Graffiti on the Subway System of New York City 1970–1978.* Ph.D. diss., New York University, UMI 9004328.

Stewart, Susan. 1993. *On Longing: Narratives of the Miniature, the Gigantic,* the Souvenir, the Collection. Durham, NC: Duke University Press.

Still, William. 1872. *The Underground Rail Road: A Record of Facts, Authentic Narratives, Letters, &c., Narrating the Hardships, Hairbreadth Escapes and Death Struggles of the Slaves in Their Efforts for Freedom, as Related by Themselves and Others, or the Largest Stockholders, and Most Liberal Aiders and Advisers, of the Road.* Philadelphia: Porter and Coats.

The Story of the Saturday Evening Girls' Reunion. 1929. Boston: Privately printed, December 12.

Stratyner, Barbara. 1996. *Ned Wayburn and the Dance Routine, from Vaudeville to the Ziegfield Follies.* Studies in Dance History no. 13. Minneapolis, MN: Society of Dance History Scholars.

Streatfeild, Noel. 1937. *Ballet Shoes.* New York: Random House.

———. 1945. *Theatre Shoes.* New York: Random House.

———. 1957. *Dancing Shoes.* New York: Random House.

Suarez-Orozco, Carola, and Marcelo Suarez-Orozco. 1995. *Transformations: Immigration, Family Life, and Achievement Motivation among Latino Adolescents.* Stanford: Stanford University Press.

Suettinger, Sue Jean Lee. 1992. "West Side Story." Pp. 38–44 in *Asian Americans: Oral Histories of First to Fourth Generation Americans from China, the Philippines, Japan, India, the Pacific Islands, Vietnam, and Cambodia.* Edited by Joann Faung Jean Lee. New York: New Press.

Swan, Susan Burrows. 1977. *Plain and Fancy: American Women and Their Needlework, 1700–1850.* New York: Routledge.

Sweet, Ellen. 1985. "Date Rape: The Story of an Epidemic and Those Who Deny It." *Ms.* 14, no. 4 (October).

Szasz, Margaret Connell. 1974. *Education and the American Indian: The Road to Self-Determination since 1928.* 3d ed. 1999. Albuquerque: University of New Mexico Press.

———. 1985. "Native American Children." Pp. 311–342 in *American Childhood: A Research Guide and Historical Handbook.* Edited by Joseph M. Hawes and N. Ray Hiner. Westport, CT: Greenwood Press.

———. 1988. *Indian Education in the American Colonies, 1607–1783.* Albuquerque: University of New Mexico Press.

Tachau, Nina. 1915. "The Girl's Room." *House Beautiful* 38 (June): 10–12.

Tagudin, Catherine. 1996. "My Experience with Immigration/ Assimilation in America." Pp. 193–197 in *Becoming American, Becoming Ethnic: College Students Explore Their Roots.* Edited by Thomas Dublin. Philadelphia: Temple University Press.

Tanenbaum, Leora. 1999. *Slut! Growing Up Female with a Bad Reputation.* New York: Seven Stories Press.

Tanner, James Mourilyan. 1981. *A History of the Study of Human Growth.* New York: Cambridge University Press.

Tarbox, Katherine. 2000. *Katie.com: My Story.* New York: Dutton.

Tate, Thad W., and David L. Ammerman. 1979. *The Chesapeake in the Seventeenth Century: Essays on Anglo-American Society.* Chapel Hill: University of North Carolina Press.

Taylor, Ella. 1989. *Prime-Time Families: Television Culture in Postwar America.* Berkeley: University of California Press.

Taylor, Susie King. 1968. *Reminiscences of My Life in Camp.* New York: Arno Press and *New York Times.*

Tedesco, Lauren. 1998. "Making a Girl into a Scout: Americanizing Scouting for Girls." Pp. 19–39 in *Delinquents and Debutantes: Twentieth-Century American Girls' Cultures.* Edited by Sherrie A. Inness. New York: New York University Press.

Temple, Judy Nolte, and Suzanne L. Bunkers. 1995. "Mothers, Daughters, Diaries: Literacy, Relationship, and Cultural Context." In *Nineteenth-Century Women Learn to Write.* Edited by Catherine Hobbs. Charlottesville: University of Virginia Press.

Thomas, Yvonne. 1992. "Untitled." Pp. 99–100 in *Rising Voices: Writings of Young Native Americans.* Selected by Arlene B. Hirschfelder and Beverly R. Singer. New York: Charles Scribner's Sons.

Thompson, Roger. 1984. "Adolescent Culture in Colonial Massachusetts." *Journal of Family History* (Summer): 127–144.

Thompson, Sharon. 1995. *Going All the Way: Teenage Girls' Tales of Sex, Romance, and Pregnancy.* New York: Hill and Wang.

Thorne, Barry. 1993. *Gender Play: Girls and Boys in School.* New Brunswick, NJ: Rutgers University Press.

Thrasher, Frederic M. 1927. *The Gang: A Study of 1,313 Gangs.* Chicago: University of Chicago Press.

Tjaden, Patricia, and Nancy Thoennes. 1998. *Prevalence, Incidence and Consequences of Violence against Women: Findings from the National Violence against Women Survey.* Washington, DC: National Institute of Justice, U.S. Department of Justice.

Tolman, Deborah L. 1994. "Doing Desire: Adolescent Girls' Struggle for/with Sexuality." *Gender and Society* 8, no. 3: 324–342.

Tomko, Linda J. 1999. *Dancing Class: Gender, Ethnicity, and Social Divides in American Dance, 1890–1920.* Bloomington: Indiana University Press.

Tompkins, Jane. 1987. "Afterword." Pp. 584–608 in *The Wide, Wide World.* By Susan Warner. New York: Feminist Press.

Tong, Benson. 1994. *Unsubmissive Women: Chinese Prostitutes in Nineteenth-Century San Francisco.* Norman: University of Oklahoma Press.

———. 1999. *Susan La Flesche Picotte, M.D.: Omaha Reformer and Tribal Leader.* Norman: University of Oklahoma Press.

———. 2000. *The Chinese Americans.* Westport, CT: Greenwood Press.

Trambley, Estela Portillo. 1975. "The Paris Gown" and "If It Weren't for the Honeysuckle." In *Rain of Scorpions and Other Writings.* Berkeley, CA: Tonatiuh International.

Trattner, Walter I. 1970. *Crusade for the Children: A History of the National Child Labor Committee and Child Labor Reform in America.* Chicago: Quadrangle Books.

———. 1994. *From Poor Law to Welfare State: A History of Social Welfare in America.* 5th ed. New York: Free Press.

Trennert, Robert A. 1982. "Educating Indian Girls at Nonreservation Boarding Schools, 1878–1920." *Western Historical Quarterly* 13 (July): 271–290.

"Tricks for Teens: Fashion Fads That Hit High School Fancies." 1941. *Parents' Magazine* (April): 108.

Triplett, Ruth, and Laura B. Myers. 1995. "Evaluating Contextual Patterns of Delinquency: Gender-Based Differences." *Justice Quarterly* 12, no. 1: 59–84.

True, Alfred Charles. 1969. *A History of Agricultural Extension Work in the United States, 1785–1923.* New York: Arno Press and the *New York Times.*

Tucker, Susan. 1988. *Telling Memories among Southern Women: Domestic Workers and Their Employers in the Segregated South.* Baton Rouge: Louisiana State University Press.

Tudor, Tasha. 1965. *Tasha Tudor Book of Fairy Tales.* New York: Platt and Munk.

Turk, Diana. 1999. "Bound by a Mighty Vow: Sisterhood in Kappa Alpha Theta, 1870–1920." *Kappa Alpha Theta Magazine* (Summer): 6–7.

Tuttle, William, Jr. 1993. *"Daddy's Gone to War": The Second World War in the Lives of America's Children.* New York: Oxford University Press.

Twain, Mark. 1897. "Hellfire Hotchkiss." Pp. 88–133 in *Mark Twain's Satires and Burlesques.* Edited by Franklin R. Rogers. 1967. Reprint, Berkeley: University of California Press.

Tyack, David B., and Elizabeth Hansot. 1990. *Learning Together: A History of Coeducation in American Public Schools.* New Haven, CT: Yale University Press.

Uchida, Yoshiko. 1982. *Desert Exile: The Uprooting of a Japanese-American Family.* Seattle: University of Washington Press.

Ulrich, Laurel. 1980. *Good Wives: Image and Reality in the Lives of Women in Northern New England, 1650–1750.* New York: Vintage.

Ulrich, Laurel Thatcher. 1990. *A Midwife's Tale: The Life of Martha Ballard, Based on Her Diary, 1785–1812.* New York: Alfred A. Knopf.

———. 1998. "Wheels, Looms, and the Gender Division of Labor in Eighteenth-

Century New England." *William and Mary Quarterly* 55: 3–38.

UNICEF (United Nations Children's Fund). 2000. "Intercountry Adoption Information Portfolio." http://old.unicef-icdc.org/information/portfolios/intercountry-adoption/.

U.S. Bureau of the Census. 1864. *Population of the United States in 1860: Compiled from Original Returns of the Eighth Census by Joseph C. G. Kennedy.* Washington, DC: Government Printing Office.

———. 1975. *Historical Statistics of the United States, Colonial Times to 1970.* Washington, DC: Government Printing Office.

U.S. Department of Agriculture. *Annual Report of the Secretary of Agriculture.* 1910–1999. Washington, DC: Government Printing Office.

U.S. Department of State. 2000. "1999 Country Reports on Human Rights Practices: China." http://www.state.gov/global/human_rights/1999_hrp_report/china.html.

Vale, V. 1996–1997. *Zines!* 2 vols. San Francisco: V/Search Publication.

Vale, V., ed. 1996. *Search and Destroy #1–6, The Complete Reprint.* San Francisco: V/Search Publications.

Valenzuela, Abel. 1998. "Gender Roles and Settlement Activities among Children and Their Immigrant Families." *American Behavioral Scientist* 42, no. 4: 720–742.

Vallone, Lynne. 1995. *Disciplines of Virtue: Girls' Culture in the Eighteenth and Nineteenth Centuries.* New Haven, CT: Yale University Press.

Van Kirk, Sylvia. 1984. "The Role of Native Women in the Fur Trade Society of Western Canada, 1670–1830." *Frontiers* 7, no. 3: 9–13.

Vaughan, Alden T., and Edward W. Clark. 1981. *Puritans among the Indians: Accounts of Captivity and Redemption, 1620–1675.* Cambridge: Belknap Press of Harvard University Press.

Velez-Ibanez, Carlos. 1980. "Se me acabo la canción: An Ethnography of Non-Consenting Sterilizations among Mexican Women in Los Angeles." In *Mexican Women in the United States: Struggles Past and Present.* Edited by Magdelana Mora and Adelaida Del Castillo. Los Angeles: Chicano Studies Research Center, UCLA.

Vermorel, Fred, and Judy Vermorel. 1985. *Starlust: The Secret Life of Fans.* London: Comet Books.

Vicinus, Martha. 1982. "'One Life to Stand Beside Me': Emotional Conflicts in First-Generation College Women in England." *Feminist Studies* 8, no. 3: 603–628.

Vigil, Angel. 1998. *Una Linda Raza: Cultural and Artistic Traditions of the Hispanic Southwest.* Golden, CO: Fulcrum.

Villarreal, Cindy. 1994. *The Cheerleader's Guide to Life.* New York: HarperPerennial.

Vincenti, Virginia. 1997. "Chronology of Events and Movements Which Have Defined and Shaped Home Economics." Pp. 321–330 in *Rethinking Home Economics: Women and the History of a Profession.* Edited by Sarah Stage and Virginia Vincenti. Ithaca, NY: Cornell University Press.

Viorst, Judith. 1986. "And Then the Prince Knelt Down and Tried to Put the Glass Slipper on Cinderella's Foot." P. 73 in *Don't Bet on the Prince: Contemporary Feminist Fairy Tales in North America and England.* Edited by Jack Zipes. New York: Methuen.

Vortex, Women's Issue. 1970. Lawrence: University of Kansas Libraries.

Wade-Gayles, Gloria Jean. 1995. *Pushed Back to Strength: A Black Woman's Journey Home.* New York: Avon Books.

———. 1998. *Father Songs: Testimonies by African-American Sons and Daughters.* Boston: Beacon Press.

Wagner, Ann. 1997. *Adversaries of Dance: From the Puritans to the Present.* Urbana: University of Illinois Press.

Wald, Gayle. 1997. "Just a Girl? Rock Music, Feminism, and the Cultural Construction of Female Youth." *Signs* 23, no. 3: 585–610.

Walkerdine, Valerie. 1990. *Schoolgirl Fictions.* London: Verso.

———. 1997. *Daddy's Girl: Young Girls and Popular Culture.* Cambridge, MA: Harvard University Press.

Wallace, Anthony F. C. 1969. *The Death and Rebirth of the Seneca.* New York: Vintage Books.

Walsh, Lorena. 1979. "Till Death Do Us Part: Marriage and Family in Seventeenth Century Maryland." In *The Chesapeake in the Seventeenth Century: Essays in Anglo-American Society.* Edited by Thad W. Tate and David L. Ammerman. Chapel Hill: University of North Carolina Press.

Walsh, Lorena, and Lois G. Carr. 1977. "The Planter's Wife: The Experience of White Women in 17th Century Maryland." *William and Mary Quarterly* 34, 3d series.

Walters, Suzanna Danuta. 1992. *Lives Together/Worlds Apart: Mothers and Daughters in Popular Culture.* Berkeley: University of California Press.

Ward, S., K. Chapman, E. Cohen, S. White, and K. Williams. 1991. "Acquaintance Rape and the College Social Scene." *Family Relations* 40: 65–71.

Ware, Caroline F. 1931. *The Early New England Cotton Manufacture: A Study in Industrial Beginnings.* Boston: Houghton Mifflin.

Ware, Leonard. 1970. *Helen Osborne Storrow, 1864–1944: A Memoir.* Northhampton, MA: Privately printed.

Ware, Susan. 1989. *Modern American Women: A Documentary History.* Belmont: Wadsworth Publishing Company.

Warner, Marina. 1994. *From the Beast to the Blonde: On Fairy Tales and Their Tellers.* New York: Farrar, Straus and Giroux.

Warner, Susan. 1850. *The Wide, Wide World.* 1987. Reprint, New York: Feminist Press.

Warren, Donna, to John Lair, November 30, 1941. John Lair Papers, Southern Appalachian Collection, Berea College, Berea, KY.

Warshaw, Matt. 1997. *Surfriders: In Search of the Perfect Wave.* New York: HarperCollins.

Way, Niobe. 1998. *Everyday Courage: The Lives and Stories of Urban Teenagers.* New York: New York University Press.

Weate, Gwen M. 1995. "Suffer the Children." *Vocational Education Journal* 70 (April): 24–25, 45.

Weaver, Thomas. 1994. *Handbook of Hispanic Cultures of the United States: Anthropology.* Houston and Madrid: Arte Público Press and Instituto de Cooperación Iberoamericana.

Weigand, Kathleen A. 2001. *Red Feminism: American Communism and the Making of Women's Liberation.* Baltimore: Johns Hopkins University Press.

Weinberg, Sydney Stahl. 1988. *World of Our Mothers: Lives of Jewish Immigrant*

Women. Chapel Hill: University of North Carolina Press.

———. 1997. "Jewish Mothers and Immi grant Daughters: Positive and Negative Role Models." P. 335 in *Mothers and Motherhood: Readings in American History.* Edited by Rima Apple and Janet Golden. Columbus: Ohio State University Press.

Weiner, Lynn. 1985. *From Working Girl to Working Mother: The Female Labor Force in the United States, 1820–1980.* Chapel Hill: University of North Carolina Press.

Weiss, Erica, James Longhurst, and Carolyn M. Mazure. 1999. "Childhood Sexual Abuse as a Risk Factor for Depression in Women: Psychosocial and Neurobiological Correlates." *American Journal of Psychiatry* 156, no. 6: 816–828.

Weissman, Myrna, Roger Bland, Peter R. Joyce, and Stephen Newman. 1993. "Sex Differences in Rates of Depression: Cross-national Perspectives." *Journal of Affective Disorders* 29, nos. 2–3: 77–84.

Wells, Ruth Herman. 1994. "America's Delinquent Daughters Have Nowhere to Turn for Help." *Corrections Compendium* 19, no. 11: 4–6.

Welter, Barbara. 1966. "The Cult of True Womanhood, 1820–1860." *American Quarterly* 18: 151–174.

Werne, J., ed. 1996. *Treating Eating Disorders.* San Francisco: Jossey-Bass.

Werner, Emmy. 1995. *Pioneer Children on the Journey West.* Boulder, CO: Westview Press.

Wertham, Frederic. 1954. *Seduction of the Innocent.* New York: Rinehart.

———. 1973. *The World of Fanzines: A Special Form of Communication.* Carbondale: Southern Illinois University Press.

Wertheimer, Jack. 1999. "Jewish Education in the United States: Recent Trends and Issues." Pp. 3–115 in *American Jewish Year Book, 1999.* Edited by David Singer and Ruth R. Seldin. New York: American Jewish Committee.

Wessel, Thomas, and Marilyn Wessel. 1982. *4-H: An American Idea, 1900–1980.* Chevy Chase, MD: National 4-H Council.

West, Elliott. 1989. *Growing Up with the Country: Childhood on the Far Western Frontier.* Albuquerque: University of New Mexico Press.

———. 1996. *Growing Up in the Twentieth Century: A History and Reference Guide.* Westport, CT: Greenwood Press.

West, Elliott, and Paula Petrik, eds. 1992. *Small Worlds: Children and Adolescents in America, 1850–1950.* Lawrence: University of Kansas Press.

Weston, Carol. 1998. *For Girls Only: Wise Words, Good Advice.* New York: Avon.

Wharton, Linda F. 1983. "The Significance of Black American Children's Singing Games in an Educational Setting." *The Journal of Negro Education* 52, no. 1 (Winter): 46–56.

White, Barbara A. 1985. *Growing Up Female: Adolescent Girlhood in America.* Westport, CT: Greenwood Press.

White, Julia C. [Meyna Hahn-a'ae]. 1996. *The Pow Wow Trail.* Summertown, TN: Book Publishing Company.

White, Renee T. 1999. *Putting Risk in Perspective: Black Teenage Lives in the Era of AIDS.* Lanham, MD: Rowman and Littlefield.

Whitfield, Eileen. 1997. *Pickford: The Woman Who Made Hollywood.* Lexington: University Press of Kentucky.

Whitley, Mary T. 1929. "Children's Interest in Collecting." *Journal of Educational Psychology* 20: 249–261.

Whitney, Catherine. 1999. *The Calling: A Year in the Life of an Order of Nuns.* New York: Crown Publishers.

Whitney, I., and P. K. Smith. 1993. "A Survey of the Nature and Extent of Bullying in Junior/Middle and Secondary Schools." *Educational Research* 35: 3–25.

Wichstrom, Lars. 1999. "The Emergence of Gender Differences in Depressed Mood during Adolescence: The Role of Intensified Gender Socialization." *Developmental Psychology* 35: 232–245.

Widom, Cathy Spatz. 1989. "The Cycle of Violence." *Science* 244: 160–166.

Wiggins, David K. 1980. "The Play of Slave Children in the Plantation Communities of the Old South, 1820–1960." *Journal of Sport History* 7: 21–39.

———. 1985. "The Play of Slave Children in Plantation Communities of the Old South, 1820–1860." In *Growing Up in America: Children in Historical Perspective.* Edited by N. Ray Hiner and Joseph M. Hawes. Urbana: University of Illinois Press.

Wilder, Laura Ingalls. 1941. *Little Town on the Prairie.* New York: Harper and Row.

Wilkinson, Doris Y. 1987. "The Doll Exhibit: A Psycho-Cultural Analysis of Black Female Role Stereotypes." *Journal of Popular Culture* 21, no. 2: 19–29.

Wilson, Harriet. 1859. *"Our Nig"; or, Sketches from the Life of a Free Black, in a Two-Story White House, North. Showing That Slavery's Shadows Fall Even There.* Edited by Henry Louis Gates, Jr. 1983. Reprint, New York: Random House.

Wilson, James. 1998. *The Earth Shall Weep: A History of Native America.* 1983. Reprint, New York: Grove Press.

Wilson, Lisa. 1999. *Ye Heart of a Man: The Domestic Life of Men in Colonial New England.* New Haven: Yale University Press.

Winnicott, D. W. 1977. *The Piggle.* New York: International Universities Press.

Wishy, Bernard. 1972. *The Child and the Republic: The Dawn of Modern American Nurture.* Philadelphia: University of Pennsylvania Press.

Witty, Paul A., and Harvey C. Lehman. 1930. "Further Studies of Children's Interest in Collecting." *Journal of Educational Psychology* 21: 112–127.

———. 1931. "Sex Differences: Collecting Interests." *Journal of Educational Psychology* 22: 221–228.

———. 1933. "The Collecting Interests of Town Children and Country Children." *Journal of Educational Psychology* 24: 170–184.

Wolf, Eric, ed. 1976. *The Valley of Mexico: Studies in Pre-Hispanic Ecology and Society.* Albuquerque: University of New Mexico Press.

Wolf, Naomi. 1991. *The Beauty Myth.* New York: William Morrow.

Woloch, Nancy. 1996. *Women and the American Experience: A Concise History.* New York: McGraw-Hill.

Woloson, Wendy. Forthcoming. *Refined Tastes: Sugar, Confections, and the Cultural Use of an American Commodity in the Nineteenth Century:* Baltimore, MD: Johns Hopkins University Press.

Women's Sports Foundation. 1989. "Minorities in Sports: The Effect of Varsity Sports Participation on the Social, Educational, and Career Mobility of Minority Students." New York: Women's Sports Foundation.

Wonderland—the Ultimate Wonder Woman Site, http://www.lacosa.sion.com/ww.

Wong, Jade Snow. 1945. *Fifth Chinese Daughter.* New York: Harper and Row.

Wood, Abigail. 1972. *The Seventeen Book of Answers to What Your Parents Don't Talk About and Your Best Friends Can't Tell You.* New York: David McKay Company.

Woodson, Carter G., ed. 1969. *The Mind of the Negro as Reflected in Letters Written during the Crisis, 1800–1860.* New York: Russell and Russell.

Woodward, Grace Steele. 1969. *Pocahontas.* Norman: University of Oklahoma Press.

Woody, Thomas. 1929. *A History of Women's Education in the United States.* New York: Science Press.

Wooley, S. C., and A. Kearney-Cooke. 1986. "Intensive Treatment of Bulimia and Body Image Disturbance." In *Handbook of Eating Disorders: Physiology, Psychology, and Treatment of Obesity, Anorexia, and Bulimia.* Edited by K. D. Brownell and J. P. Foreyt. New York: Basic Books.

Worrell, Estelle Ansley. 1980. *Children's Costume in America 1607–1910.* New York: Charles Scribner's Sons.

www.4h-usa.org

www.campfire.org.

www.cybergrrl.com.

www.laca.org/Johnstown/Cornell/states.html (one-room rural schools).

www.mum.org.

www.Promisekeepers.com

www.proms.net (accessed March 1999).

Yans-McLaughlin, Virginia. 1977. *Family and Community: Italian Immigrants in Buffalo, 1880–1930.* Ithaca, NY: Cornell University Press.

Yezierska, Anzia. 1975. *Bread Givers.* Reprint, New York: Persea Books.

Yolen, Jane. 1986. "The Moon Ribbon." In *Don't Bet on the Prince: Contemporary Feminist Fairy Tales in North America and England.* Edited by Jack Zipes. New York: Methuen.

———. 1995. *Sleeping Ugly.* New York: Houghton Mifflin.

Yoo, David K. 2000. *Growing Up Nisei: Race, Generation, and Culture among Japanese Americans of California, 1924–1949.* Urbana: University of Illinois Press.

Youcha, Geraldine. 1995. *Minding the Children: Child Care in America from Colonial Times to the Present.* New York: Scribner.

Young, Philip. 1962. "The Mother of Us All." *Kenyon Review* 24 (Summer): 391–441.

Yung, Judy. 1996. *Unbound Feet: A Social History of Chinese Women in San Francisco.* Berkeley: University of California Press.

Zelizer, Viviana A. 1985. *Pricing the Priceless Child: The Changing Social Value of Children.* New York: Basic Books.

Zerbe, Kathryn J. 1993. *The Body Betrayed: Women, Eating Disorders and Treatment.* Washington, DC: American Psychiatric Press.

———. 1999. *Women's Mental Health and Primary Care.* Philadelphia: W. B. Saunders.

Zesiger, Sue. 1995. "Velocity Girl: In Tomorrow's High-Performance

Automobiles, Speed Becomes Sexier—and Safer." *Harper's Bazaar* (September).

Zierold, Norman J. 1965. *The Child Stars.* New York: Coward-McCann.

Zillner, Dian, and Patty Cooper. 1998. *Antique and Collectible Dollhouses and Their Furnishings.* Atglen, PA: Shiffer Publishing.

Zinsser, William K. 1964. "Barbie Is a Million-Dollar Doll." *Saturday Evening Post* (December 12): 72–73.

Zipes, Jack. 1986. *Don't Bet on the Prince: Contemporary Feminist Fairy Tales in North America and England.* New York: Methuen.

———. 1993. *The Trials and Tribulations of Red Riding Hood: Versions of the Tale in a Sociohistorical Context.* 2d ed. New York: Routledge.

Zitkala-Ša. 1921. *American Indian Stories.* 1985. Reprint, Lincoln: University of Nebraska Press.

Zonderman, David A. 1992. *Aspirations and Anxieties: New England Workers and the Mechanized Factory System 1815–1850.* New York: Oxford University Press.

Index

Abortion, 14, 72, 77, 647, 650
Abstinence, 72, 76, 80, 285–286, 650, 651
Academic achievement, 306–307
Acne, 13, 160
Acquaintance rape, **1–9**
  drugs and, 3, 615
  See also Sexual assault; Sexual harassment
Adams, Abigail, 137, 577
Adolescence, as stage, 14, 74, 560, 596, 646
Adolescent health and medicine, **9–15**, 701
Adoption, **15–22**
  history of, 15–17, 647
  as Native American retribution, 513
  transracial, transnational, 19, 21, 488–489
Adoption law, 17–18
Advertisement. *See* Consumer culture
Advice books and columns, **22–26**, 145, 148, 150, 256, 257, 334–335, 336, 499, 593, 696, 701
Aerosol art, 344, 347
African American girls in the twentieth century, 25, **26–34**, 117, 196, 553
  activities and play of, 25, 67, 229, 287, 289, 318, 509
  and beauty standards, 160
  and Birmingham church bombing, 31
  clubs and sororities of, 29, 30, 287, 289, 318, 597
  education of, 27–28, 29–30, 31, 139, 249, 253, 265, 293–295, 597
  and Little Rock nine, 31

northward migration of, 28, 29, 685
and school desegregation, 31, 249, 253
self-esteem of, 229, 562
sexual activity of, 77, 285, 646, 649, 650
and sexual harassment, 588
in sports, 607
television portrayals of, 663, 664
work of, 28, 233, 695
See also Enslaved girls of African descent; Free girls of African descent
Age-of-consent laws, 73, 74, 283, 646
Agricultural workers
  African American, 28, 264–265, 636, 688
  Asian American, 49, 50
  on family farms, 375, 568, 687, 692
  4-H youth as, 287–288, 289, 290
  migrant, 692, 695
  Native American, 680, 681
AIDS (acquired immunodeficiency syndrome), 186
Alcohol, 6, 117, 178, 181, 599, 611–613, 614
  medicinal use of, 612, 615
Alcott, Louisa May, 23, 134, 208, 328, 545
Allowances and spending money, **32–38**, 156, 159
Amenorrhea, 447
American Girl, 154, 317, 334, 551
American Girls dolls, **38–42**, 136, 231, 332–333, 551
Amphetamines, 615
Anger, 256, 257, 258, 259

Animals. *See* Pets
Anorexia, 67, 81, 241, 242, 245, 246–247, 447
Arts and crafts, **42–48**
  instruction in, 44, 45, 47, 691
  See also Samplers
Asian American girls, **48–57**, 185, 228, 689
  and cultural tensions, 51, 52, 53, 54, 55, 185
  media portrayals of, 51, 664
  work of, 48, 49, 50, 53, 692
Assertiveness, 523, 560
Athletic participation. *See* Cheerleaders; Sports
Autograph collecting, 134
Autonomy. *See* Independence
Aviation, 641

Babysitting, **59–63**
  in film, 62, 63, 463
  See also Little mothers
Backpacks, 359, 361
Ballet, 170, 171
Barbie, **63–68**, 157, 231, 232, 442
Baseball, 607
Basketry, 43, 45
Bat Mitzvah, **68–71**, 389
Bathing. *See* Hygiene
Beach bunnies, 355–356, 461
Beadwork, 45
Beanie Babies, 136
Beauty, ideal of, 244, 515, 517
Beauty pageants, 66, 104, 161, 543
Bedroom culture, 657
Beecher, Catharine, 17, 23, 167, 225, 237, 252, 362–363, 685
Beepers, 151–152
Behavioral therapies, 123, 247, 523. *See also* Child guidance; Psychotherapy

Biculturalism, 53, 54, 55, 410, 412, 413, 480. *See also* Multiculturalism
Binge eating disorder. *See* Eating disorders
Bipolar illness. *See* Depression
Birth control, **71–80**, 285, 286
    and age and marital status, 78, 80
    contraceptives for, 72, 76, 78, 79, 185, 285, 411, 650
    cultural views on, 410
    legislation and courts on, 74, 76, 77, 78, 411, 650
    See also Abstinence
Birth control pills. *See* Birth control, contraceptives for
Bisexual girls, 620
Blue Birds, 87
Bobby-soxers, 459, 509, 653
Body care. *See* Hygiene
Body dysmorphic disorder, 83
Body image, 64, 65, **80–84**, 203
    and prom preparation, 515–518
Body piercing, 529, 564
Boys' participation, in girls' activities, 62, 66, 89–90, 103, 104, 178–179, 336, 366, 434
Brassieres, 66, 371
Break dancing, 172, 343, 348
Bride capture, 5
Brown v. Board of Education, 229
Bubblegum music, 654–655, 657
Bulimia, 81, 241, 242, 243, 245, 246–247
Bullying, 587
Bundling, 183, 281–282

Calling All Girls, 144, 335, 336
Camp Fire Girls, 45, **85–90**, 334, 507, 623–624, 691
Camps. *See* Summer camps
Candy. *See* Girls and sweets
Captivity, and Native Americans, **90–95**
Career development, 307, 330, 498, 499, 524
Cars, **95–98**, 184
Cash girls, 689
Catholic girls, **98–103**, 110, 535
Cell 16, 542, 543

Cell phones, 151, 152
Chaperones, 3–4, 184, 602
Character development, 207, 208, 239, 504
Charcot, Jean-Martin, 242, 520
Chat rooms, 152
Cheerleaders, **103–107**
Chesapeake Bay colonies, 379–380
Chicana girls, 46, **107–114**, 411, 420
    coming-of-age ceremony for, 535–539
    feminista representations for, 111–113
    See also Latina girls
Child abuse, **114–119**, 311. *See also* Incest; Sexual abuse
Child care, 29, 433, 601, 688, 692, 693. *See also* Babysitting; Little mothers
Child development. *See* Child guidance
Child guidance, **119–126**, 520, 523
    in juvenile justice system, 120–122
    psychoanalytic theory in, 119, 121, 123–124
Child labor, 685, 686, 692
Child labor law, 591
Child, Lydia Maria, 17, 24, 545
Child maltreatment. *See* Child abuse
Child neglect, 115, 116, 117, 118, 459
Child pornography, 116, 285, 593
Child prostitution, 116
Child protection movement, 115
Child savers. *See* Social reform
Childbearing, 72–73, 400, 401, 615–616
Childhood
    depictions of, 91, 92–93, 426
    and sexual identity, 417, 422
Childrearing. *See* Child guidance
Children as property, 114
Chinese Americans, 48, 49, 51, 282, 689, 691
Christian morality, 24–25, 503
Cinderella, 274, 275, 483, 515

Civil rights movement, 30–32, 160, 161, 217, 249, 253, 332, 597
    for lesbians and gays, 419
Class, sex as, 541, 542
Cleanliness. *See* Hygiene
Clitoris, 286
Clothing, 37, 43, 87, **126–132**, 266
    doll-inspired, 39, 66–67
    of Mennonites, 445–446
    for play, 502, 503, 504
    for prom, 516–518
    of punk rock, 530, 564
Clothwork, 43, 451–452, 637, 638
Clubs
    African American, 29, 30, 287, 289, 318
    See also Camp Fire Girls; 4-H; Girl Scouts; Saturday Evening Girls; Sororities; Young Pioneers
Cocaine, 615
Cock rock, 655
Cold War, 148, 355, 556, 557
Collecting, **132–136**, 506
    of Nancy Drew mysteries, 468, 469–470
College girls, **136–141**, 249, 253, 344
    female friendships in, 139
    and home economics education, 362, 363, 365
    and radical feminism, 543–544
    See also Cheerleaders; Sports
Comadrazgo, 420
Comic books, **141–146**, 335, 508
Coming-of-age
    in Latina literature, 411–413
    See also Bat Mitzvah; Kinaaldá; La Quinceañera
Communication, **146–153**
Communist Party (CP), 552, 554, 555–556, 557
Community self-government, 580
Community service projects, 88, 289, 290, 445
Compadrazgo, 110
Complexion, 13
Computer technology, 643–644
Condoms, 72, 76, 186

Connectedness. *See* Emotions; Relational theory

Consciousness raising, radical feminist, 542, 543, 544

Consumer culture, 135–136, 150, **153–158**, 314, 325, 508, 509
  brand loyalty in, 153–154, 156, 157
  and collecting, 41, 64, 65, 135
  rebellion against, 157–158, 509
  and technological advance, 638–639
  See also Allowances and spending money; Girls' culture

Consumer education, 35, 36, 290

Contraception. *See* Birth control

Cooties game, 587

Cosmetics, **158–163**, 266, 371

Cotton production, 451, 638, 689

Counterculture, 96, 145, 333, 509, 543, 577, 700, 701

Courtship. *See* Dating and courtship

Crack babies, 616

Crafts. *See* Arts and crafts

Crocheting, 44

Cross-dressing, 671

Cross-gender identification, 281

Crushes, 139, 418

Crying, 259

Cuban Americans, 407, 409, 412–413

Cultural instruction, of Native Americans, 472, 473–474

Cultural tensions, in Asian American families, 51, 52, 53, 54, 55

Custody rights, 18

Cybersex, 186

Cyberspace. *See* Internet

Dame schools, 137, 248, 249, 250, 383, 425, 575

Dance classes, **165–174**

Dance halls and palaces, 174–176, 177–179

Dance marathons, 176

Dances and dancing, 104, **174–182**

African American, 165, 167, 171, 172
ballet, 170, 171
ballroom, 170
Broadway, 170
Charleston, 177
country and western, 182
disco, 180, 181
freestyle, 174, 180, 181, 182
group (line), 180, 181, 182
immigrant, 165, 167, 174
Lindy, jitterbug, 177, 181
minuet, 165, 166(illus.), 167
modern, 170–171
Native American, 168–169, 171–172
pivoting, spieling, 176–177
raves and tripping out, 180, 182
rock and roll, 180
shadow, 176
shimmy, black bottom, 177
statue posing, 168
step, 170, 173
tap, 170
tough, 177
twist, 180
waltz, 177
See also Dance classes; Dance halls and palaces

Date rape. *See* Acquaintance rape

Date rape drugs, 3, 615

Dating and courtship, 123, **182–186**, 189, 266, 282, 303, 323, 332, 334, 506
  and cars, 95–96, 184

Daughters and fathers, **186–194**, 602

Daughters and mothers, 17, 124, **195–201**, 204, 463

Death and dying, 214

Defiance. *See* Rebelliousness

Dependent children. *See* Orphans and orphanages

Depression, 117, **201–206**, 259, 397
  and suicidal behavior, 617, 620
  types and symptoms of, 201–202

Depression (1929–1939). *See* Great Depression

Diabetes, 13

Diaries, **206–211**, 426, 504

Dickens, Charles, 454–455

Diets and dieting, 82, 243, 244–245. *See also* Eating disorders

Disabilities. *See* Girls with disabilities

Discotheques, 180–181

Divining games, 502, 679

Divorce, 498–499

DIY (do-it-yourself) ethic
  in music, 525, 530, 531, 563, 564
  in writing, 563, 564–565, 700

Dobbins, Peggy, 543

Dodge, Mary Mapes, 24, 134, 545

Dollhouses, **219–224**, 501, 504

Dolls, 64, **224–233**, 501, 502–503, 504, 508
  black, 226, 227, 229, 231
  of frontier girls, 301–302
  industry of, 224, 225, 226, 227–229
  of Native Americans, 474
  paper, 145, 299
  in psychotherapy, 523
  See also American Girls Series; Barbie

Domestic being, 577

Domestic containment, 148

Domestic service, **233–237**, 256, 638, 683, 686
  of African Americans, 28, 29, 233, 234, 236, 264, 295, 686
  of Asian Americans, 49, 50
  bound and putting out, 187, 223, 236, 295, 381, 478, 485, 487, 682, 686
  of Native Americans, 478
  See also Indentured servants

Domestic sphere, 148, 150, 188, 237, 354, 356, 363, 473, 600

Domestic violence, 118, 589

Domesticity, 196, 197, 219, 222–223, **237–240**, 504
  in film and literature, 327, 328, 331, 498–499, 545, 546, 673
  reflected in samplers, 576–577
  of southern girls, 600–602
  See also Communication; Domestic sphere; Home economics education;

Homemaking, household economy; Motherhood
Dominican Americans, 408, 413
Dressmaking, 43, 296, 637, 638, 685
Dress-up play, 360
Drill teams, 104–105
Drugs. *See* Substance abuse
Dyslexia. *See* Learning disabilities, reading disorders, and girls

Eating disorders, 81, 82, **241–248**, 599, 620
  biological factors in, 246–247
  history of, 242–243
Economic dependence. *See* Allowances and spending money
Education, **248–255**, 424–425
  of African American girls, 27–28, 29–30, 31, 139, 249, 252, 253, 265, 293–295, 363, 424, 427–428, 597
  of Asian American girls, 50, 51, 52
  Catholic-run, 98–103, 110, 250, 252–253
  of disabled, 212–213, 214, 217
  elementary and dame schools in, 137, 248, 249, 250, 383, 425, 435–436, 575–576
  female academies and seminaries in, 137, 251, 252, 437–438, 602, 684
  frontier, 250, 253, 302–303
  gender discrimination in, 24, 435, 438, 442–443, 448–449, 560
  of gifted girls, 305–308
  in home economics, 362–367, 640
  of immigrant girls, 251, 373, 375, 377, 378, 385, 386, 387, 388, 578, 579, 580, 581, 582, 584
  of Jewish girls, 68, 383–391
  of Latina girls, 99, 101–102, 110, 112, 408
  in mathematics and science, 435–444
  on money management, 35, 36
  for motherhood, 137, 248, 251, 252, 253
  ornamental, 137, 602
  of rural girls, 568–569
  and school desegregation, 31, 249, 253
  secondary, 248, 251, 252, 436–439
  teacher training, 251
  through specimen collection, 133–134
  vocational, 29, 45, 100, 253, 363, 365, 387–388, 427, 440, 582, 640, 641, 691
  on women's issues, 543–544
  See also College girls; Literacy; Reading
Elders, Native American, 473–474
E-mail, 151, 152
Embroidery, 43, 573, 574–575, 576–577
Emotional abuse, 117
Emotional dysfunction. *See* Girls with Disabilities
Emotional problems. *See* Adolescent health; Child guidance; Psychotherapy
Emotions, **255–261**
  gender differentiation in, 255–260, 558, 559
Empathy, 200, 559, 560
Employment. *See* Work
Empowerment. *See* Girl power; Power relations
Enslaved girls of African descent, 40, 188–189, **261–267**
  education of, 252, 427–428
  leisure activities of, 43, 165, 326, 505–506
  orphaned, 485
  protective mask of, 265, 295–296
  sexual activity of, 184, 265–266, 282, 420, 646
  work of, 233, 236, 256, 264–265, 636, 687–688
Equal Rights Amendment, 319
Eroticism, 285, 352, 353
Estrogen therapy, 12
Etiquette, 22, 23, 149, 150, 256, 257, 602, 633. *See also* Advice books and columns
Eugenics, 77, 214
Everygirls' Magazine, 87, 88, 154, 333

Exercise, 24
  compulsive, 82, 242
  See also Physical education; Sports

Factory workers. *See* Mill girls
Fairy tales, **269–276**
Fan clubs, 66, 148, **276–279**, 656, 657
Farm girls. *See* Agricultural workers; 4-H; Rural girls
Fashion. *See* Clothing; Cosmetics; Hair; Handbags
Fasting, 242, 243
Fathers. *See* Daughters and fathers
Feeblemindedness, 77, 122, 214
Female objectification, by males, 559, 561
Female sexual development, 12–13, 284, 286
  precocious, 10–11, 448
  See also Menstruation; Puberty
Female sexuality, **279–287**, 518
  African American, 77, 184, 265–266, 282, 285, 420, 646, 649, 650
  and candy, 324–325
  as delinquent, 13, 120, 122, 283–284, 392, 394–395, 411, 458–461
  and double standard, 4, 74, 282, 311, 394–395, 615
  fantasy, 654, 655, 656, 658
  in film and literature, 332, 458, 459–460, 461, 509
  Latina, 410–411
  Native American, 77, 183, 281
  premarital, 71, 72, 76, 95, 284–285, 410
  and prior sexual abuse, 117, 394, 395
  and procreation, 72, 76, 410
  psychoanalytic theories on, 520, 521
  and substance use, 612, 613, 615
  working-class, 73–74, 179, 184, 282, 283, 284, 646
  See also Abstinence; Dating and courtship; Female sexual development; Femininity; Gender identity and role development; Pregnancy,

out-of-wedlock; Sexual
barter; Teen pregnancy
Female socialization. *See*
Gender identity and role
development
Feminine power and influence.
See Power relations
Feminine strength, 327,
330–331
Femininity, 155, 157, 224, 503,
515, 576, 683
of Barbie, 64, 65, 66, 67, 157
and prom preparation,
515–519
of radical feminism, 542
and sugar, 320, 322–323
and suicidal behavior, 618,
620
technology of, 641
See also Body image;
Domesticity; Gender
identity and role
development; Girls'
fiction; Motherhood;
Southern belles
Feminism, feminist
movement, 94, 140–141,
161, 344, 365, 469, 700
in advice literature, 25
on birth control, 78
in comics, 144, 146
on delinquency, 396–397
domestic, 317, 363
on father's role, 193
second/third-wave, 145–146,
541, 557, 564
and girl power, 312–313, 315
in Girl Scouts, 317, 319
on mother's role, 197, 200
music of, 528, 531
politicos in, 541–542, 556
in psychotherapy, 523
on sexual development, 14,
284, 286
youth movement of,
563–566
See also Girl power;
Postfeminism; Radical
feminism
Fertility rates, 405–406, 601
Fiction. *See* Girls' fiction
Fieldworkers. *See* Agricultural
workers
Figure. *See* Body image
Filipino Americans, 52, 54
Film. *See* Movies
Fitness, 24. *See also* Physical
education; Sports

Flappers, 354, 458, 508, 612
Flirting, 184, 602–603
Folk dancing, 169
Folk music, 527
Foreign student exchanges, 290
Forten, Charlotte, 207, 291,
293, 296
Foster care, 17, 488
4-H, **287–291**
Frank, Anne, 209
Free girls of African descent,
167, **291–298**
education of, 252, 293–295,
363, 424
protective mask of, 295–296
work of, 43, 295, 433, 685,
686, 688, 695
Free love, 185, 186
Freud, Sigmund, 121, 123, 198,
215, 242, 272, 284,
418–419, 520–521. *See
also* Psychoanalytic
theory
Friendship, 259
of girl power, 315
romantic same-sex, 139,
282–283, 417–419, 420,
672
See also Emotions; Lesbians;
Relational theory
Frontier girls, **299–303**, 331
education of, 250, 253,
302–303
play of, 226, 301–302, 506
work of, 299, 686–687

Games. *See* Play
Gangs. *See* Girl gangs
Garland, Judy, 459, 692
Garment work. *See* Sewing;
Textile work
Gender identity and role
development, 197–198,
200, 204, 306, 560–561
adolescence as stage in, 14,
74, 560, 596, 646
and childhood, 417, 422
reactions to, 325–326, 509,
673
samplers reflecting, 576–577
through play, 224, 225,
502–505
See also Communication;
Domesticity; Female
sexuality; Femininity;
Gender relationships;
Girls' culture; Girls'
fiction; Independence;

Relational theory; Self-
esteem; Selfhood;
Separation; Tomboys
Gender relationships, 3–5, 203
female objectification in,
559, 561
in graffiti culture, 344–348
radical feminist view of,
541, 542
Gifted girls, **305–308**, 442
Girdles, 371, 550
Girl bonding, 315. *See also*
Friendship
Girl gangs, **308–312**, 461
Girl Pioneers, 45, 507, 691
"Girl poisoning" culture, 509.
See also Gender identity
and role development;
Girl power
Girl power, 63, **312–316**, 510,
631, 665, 696. *See also*
Power relations
Girl Scouts, 45, **316–320**, 334,
495, 507, 508, 570, 625,
691
Girl, use of term, 313, 547, 564
Girls and sweets, **320–325**
Girls' culture, **325–327**, 509,
547
in film, 458, 459, 463
Girls' fiction, **327–333**,
465–466, 505, 508,
545–550. *See also* Fairy
tales; Literacy; Reading
Girls' magazines, 134, 154,
334–338, 410, 550–551,
656
19th c., 545, 547
See also Advice books and
columns; Comic books;
Consumer culture; Zines
Girls' rooms, **338–342**
Girls with disabilities, **211–218**
hearing, 212–213
hidden, 216
vision, 87, 212, 213
Goddess cultures, 200
Godparents, 110
Going steady, 182, 185, 284,
334
Graffiti, **342–350**
Grandmothers, 32, 45, 46
Great Depression, 30, 37, 59,
197, 290, 340, 354–355,
459, 692
Great Migration, 29, 30
Grooming. *See* Hygiene
Groupie, 279

Grrrl zines. See *Zines*
Grrrls' comix, 146
Guerrilla theater, 543
Gymnastics, 167. *See also*
　Sports

Habit training and clinics, 119,
　123
Hair, 32, **351–358**, 503, 504,
　530
Hall, G. Stanley, 121, 135, 227,
　284, 339, 622
Hallucinogens, 615
Handbags, **358–361**
Handicaps. *See* Girls with
　Disabilities
Hanging out, 182–183
Hanging together, 185
Haunting, 588
Health care. *See* Adolescent
　health
Helplessness, 205, 416
Hip-hop culture, 172, 343, 348
Hippies, 96. *See also*
　Counterculture
Hispanic Americans, 67, 77,
　168. *See also* Chicana
　girls; Latina girls
Hmong Americans, 53
Home economics education,
　362–367, 582
Homelessness, 419
Homemaking, household
　economy, 340
　18th–19th c., 22, 23, 42–43,
　　299, 533
　immigrant girls in, 35, 375,
　　377, 378, 689
　Latinas in, 111, 405, 406,
　　408, 409–410, 695
　Native Americans in,
　　472–473
　rural club projects in,
　　287–291
　rural girls in, 567–568, 692
　technology affecting,
　　635–637, 638–639
　work of, 451, 681–683,
　　686–687, 691, 692
　working girls in, 37
　See also Arts and crafts;
　　Domestic service;
　　Domesticity; Home
　　economics education;
　　Little mothers
Homosexuality. *See* Lesbians
Hooking up, 182
Hope chest, 135

Horizon Club, 88
Hormonal change, 245
Hormonal therapy, 12
Horney, Karen, 124, 422, 522
Horses, 495
Hunting, 301
Hygiene, **367–371**
　menstrual, 447, 449–450
Hymen, 11, 450
Hysteria, 242, 243, 520, 679

Ice cream socials, 39, 42
Identity formation. *See* Gender
　identity and role
　development
Illegitimacy, 16, 71. *See also*
　Birth control; Pregnancy,
　out-of-wedlock; Teen
　pregnancy
Immigrant girls, 16, 189, 260,
　373–379, 553, 646
　Americanization of, 580,
　　581–582
　Asian American, 48–49, 51,
　　53
　dance of, 165, 167, 174
　education of, 252, 373, 375,
　　377, 378, 385, 386, 387,
　　388, 578, 579, 580, 581,
　　582, 584
　Italian American, 376–377,
　　578, 584, 690
　Jewish, 377–378, 385, 578,
　　584, 690
　Latina, 405–408, 409,
　　411–412
　leisure activities for, 578,
　　579, 580, 581, 582–583
　work of, 35, 227, 233, 375,
　　377, 378, 456, 685–686,
　　689–691, 693–695
　See also Migrant workers;
　　Saturday Evening Girls
Incest, 117, 192–193
Indentured servants, **379–381**,
　484, 487, 637, 681–682.
　　See also Domestic service
Independence, 120, 123, 124,
　208–209, 341–342, 458
　film portrayals of, 458, 459,
　　463, 498
　in literature, 327, 328, 329,
　　333, 550
　and selfhood, 198, 246, 558,
　　559, 561
Individualism, 315, 340, 427,
　558, 559, 561
Industrialization, 637–641, 689

Infanticide, 114
Inferiority complex, 12, 13
Information age, 642–644
Inhalants, 615
Inheritance rights, 16, 534
Innocence, 93, 285, 330, 426,
　487
Insanity. *See* Mental illness
Instant messaging, 152
Intelligence, abstract, 305, 561
International student
　exchanges, 290
Internationalism, 317, 318. *See*
　also Multiculturalism
Internet, 151, 152, 158, 186,
　286, 337, 509, 701–702
Interpersonal relationships. *See*
　Relational theory
Invalids, 214, 329
IQ (intelligence quotient) tests,
　305
Iranian Americans, 185
Irish Americans, 100, 233, 456,
　686
Italian Americans, 99, 189,
　376–377, 578, 584, 690

Jamestown colony, 379,
　681–682
Japanese Americans, 49, 51, 52
Jealousy, 257, 258
Jewelry, 324
Jewish girls, 189, 625
　bat mitzvah of, 68–71
　education of, **383–392**
　immigrant, 377–378, 385,
　　578, 584, 690
　and political culture, 553,
　　555
　work of, 690
Jordanian Americans, 185
Junior Bazaar, 336
Juvenile delinquents, **392–398**
　and child abuse, 117, 395,
　　396
　and fathers, 190–192
　in gangs, 308–312
　and gender differences,
　　396–397
　rehabilitation of, 29,
　　120–122, 235
　self-injurious behavior of,
　　397
　and sexual behavior, 13,
　　120, 122, 283–284, 392,
　　394–395, 411, 458–461
　and status offenses, 394–396

Juvenile justice system, 120–121, 122, 283, 392, 394, 395, 397–398
ethnic minorities in, 411
The Juvenile Miscellany, 24, 545

Kin keeper, 433
Kinaaldá, **399–403**
Kindness, 491
Knitting, 44
Korean Americans, 50, 51

Labor. *See* Work; Working-class girls
Labor movement, 455–456, 684, 690, 691
Ladies' Home Journal, Sub-Deb column, 334–335, 508
Laotian Americans, 53
Latina girls, 102, 231, **405–414**, 693–695
education of, 99, 101–102, 110, 112, 408
immigration of, 405–408, 409, 411–412
work of, 405, 406, 408, 409–410, 695
See also Chicana girls
Learning disabilities, reading disorders, and girls, 216, **414–417**
Lesbianism, as political, 543
Lesbians, 7, 113, 139, 282, 284, 285, 411, **417–423**, 564, 620, 700, 701
protection of, 587
Letter writing, 146–147, 148–150, 426, 428
Library clubs, 578, 579, 582
Literacy, 343, **423–431**. *See also* Girls' fiction; Reading
Little mothers, **431–434**
Little Red Riding Hood, 269, 270(illus.), 271–273
Little Rock nine, 31
Little Women (Alcott), 328, 505, 545, 546, 671, 673–674
Lolita (Nabokov), 66, 324
Love and sex, 259
Low, Juliette Gordon, 220, 316, 624
Lowell Offering, 24, 453(illus.), 454–455

LSD (lysergic acid diethylamide), 613

Mademoiselle, 3
Magazines. *See* Girls' magazines
Male dominance, 4–5, 6. *See also* Patriarchy
Malnutrition, 241
Manic depression. *See* Depression
Manners. *See* Etiquette
Marijuana, 613
Marriage, 49, 73, 99, 138, 183, 476, 534
father's role in, 187–188, 189, 534
Masturbation, 24, 284, 285, 320
Maternal kinship, 183, 399
Maternal overprotection, 124, 204
Maternal rejection, 124
Mathematics and science, 306, 307, **435–444**
Matriarchal core, 102
Matrophobia, 195, 197
McCarthyism, 556, 557
Media. *See* Movies; Television
Mennonite girls, **444–447**
Menstruation, 203, 241, 368, 370–371, **447–451**
onset of, 11, 13, 447–448, 449, 474
rite at onset of, 399–403
Mental hygiene movement, 12, 119
Mental illness and impairment, 214, 215, 216, 333. *See also* Adolescent health; Child guidance; Depression; Psychotherapy
Mental retardation, 122, 214
Mentoring, 139, 200
Mexican American girls. *See* Chicana girls
Midwifery, 687
Migrant workers, 691, 692, 693–695
Migration, of African Americans, 28, 29, 685
Mill girls, **451–457**, 505, 684
Minute Girl Program, 87, 88
Miss America pageant, 161, 543
Modern dance, 170–171
Momism, 197

Money management, 35–38
Monroe, Marilyn, 160
Motherhood, 98, 101–102, 123–124, 198, 259, 363
education for, 137, 248, 251, 252, 253
Latina, 405, 411
republican, 137, 207, 423, 426
See also Single motherhood
Mothers. *See* Daughters and mothers
Movies, adolescent girls in, 62–63, **457–464**, 470. *See also* Fan clubs; Pickford, Mary; Pocahontas; Temple, Shirley
Movies, drive-in, 96
Ms. magazine, 3
Mui-tsai, 49, 691
Multiculturalism, 40, 41, 290, 318, 332–333. *See also* Biculturalism
Museums, 133–134
Music, 30, 314, 525–532, 563–564, 565. *See also* Teenybopper

Nabokov, Vladimir, 66, 324
Name calling, 587
Nancy Drew mysteries, 330, **465–472**, 550, 692
Narcissism, 80–81
Native American girls, **472–482**, 501, 636
arts and crafts of, 45–46, 228
cultural revitalization of, 476
dance of, 168–169, 171–172
displacement of, 476–478, 479, 480
education of, 252, 424, 427, 428, 476–477, 478–480
and Euro-Americans, 472, 474–480, 512–514
Latin American, 535–536
play of, 224, 226, 228, 472, 474, 501
sexual activity of, 77, 183, 281
work of, 86–87, 472–473, 475, 680, 681, 692
See also Camp Fire Girls; Captivity; Kinaaldá; Pocahontas
Nature study, 133–134, 136. *See also* Outdoor activity
Necking, 12, 96, 284

Needlework, 43, 359–360, 577
New woman, 196, 604–605
New York Radical Feminists, 542
Night walking, 502
Norplant, 79, 410
Note-passing, 148, 150, 430
Novels. *See* Girls' fiction
Nutrition, 11
Nuyorican women, 412
Nymphet, 66

Obesity, 83, 241
Oedipal conflict, 190, 192
Olympic games, 604, 609
Opiates, 615
Orgasm, 285
Orphans and orphanages, 249, 330, **483–489**
    transports of, 488, 686
Othermothering, 197
Outdoor activity, 44, 45, 316, 622–623, 625
Overactivity disorder, 242

Parent education, 118, 119–120, 122–123, 124, 335, 555–556
Parent-daughter relations. *See* Daughters and fathers; Daughters and mothers; Parent education
Parental consent, for medical procedures, 14
Parenting, shared, 198
Parents' Magazine, Tricks for Teens column, 335, 336
Patriarchy, 4, 5, 6, 148, 193, 198
    of immigrants, 49, 109–110, 189
    and political activism, 554, 557
    of Puritans, 533, 534
    of southern society, 600
Patriotism, 87–88, 100, 101, 148, 149, 207, 290, 317, 426, 692, 693
PCP (phencyclidine), 615
Peddling, 685
Peer pressure, 13, 158, 160, 306, 309, 334
Pelvic examinations, 11, 13
Pen pals, 149
Penmanship, 425–426
Pep clubs, 104, 105

Personality development. *See* Gender identity and role development
Perzines, 700
Pets, **491–496**
Petting, 12, 96, 182, 185, 284, 334, 508
Phi Beta Kappa, 595
Photograph collecting, 134
Physical abuse. *See* Child abuse; Sexual abuse
Physical appearance. *See* Body image
Physical deformity, 214
Physical development. *See* Female sexual development; Puberty
Physical education, 139, 449, 604–605, 608. *See also* Sports
Physical fitness, 24. *See also* Physical education; Sports
Pickford, Mary, 457–458, **496–501**
Pickups, 284
Pinned, 185
Planned Parenthood, 76
Play, 326, **501–511**
    conflict in, 560
    dress-up, 360
    of enslaved girls, 265, 326
    of frontier girls, 301–302, 506
    history of Euro-American, 501–510
    of Native Americans, 472, 474
    of rural girls, 570
    and technology, 639, 642–643
    of working girls, 505, 507
    See also Dollhouses; Dolls; Tea parties
Play therapy, 522–523
Playing house, 220–221, 228
Pocahontas, 281, **512–514**
Poetry, on samplers, 576–577
Political activism, 532, 552–557, 564–566. *See also* Civil rights movement
Poor. *See* Poverty
Pop music, 655, 658
Pornography, 116, 285, 593
Postfeminism, 63, 313, 315
Posttraumatic stress disorder, 7

Pottery works, 579, 580–581, 584
Poverty, 118, 409, 488
    and teen pregnancy, 79, 650, 651, 652
Powder puff derbies, 641
Power relations, 4–5, 97, 559, 561, 562, 563, 564
    and feminine influence, 328, 330, 545
    in sexual harassment, 587, 589
    See also Girl power
Pregnancy, out-of-wedlock
    in 17th–19th c., 73, 183, 282, 380, 502, 534, 646
    See also Female sexuality, premarital; Sterilization; Teen pregnancy
Prejudice. *See* Racism
Premarital sexual activity. *See* Female sexuality, premarital; Pregnancy, out-of-wedlock
Private sphere of women. *See* Domestic sphere
Prohibition, 612, 613
Prom, **514–519**
    resistance to, 518–519
Promiscuity, 77, 120–122, 283, 285, 410
Property ownership, 346
Prostitution, 49, 160, 282, 283, 394, 475, 612, 691
    casual, 686
    child, 116
    and tomboys, 670
Psychedelics, 613
Psychiatric treatment. *See* Psychotherapy
Psychoanalytic theory, 119, 121, 123–124, 190, 197–198, 201, 520–522. *See also* Freud, Sigmund
Psychological problems. *See* Adolescent health; Body image; Child abuse; Child guidance; Eating disorders; Emotions; Psychotherapy; Relational theory
Psychotherapy, **520–525**. *See also* Psychoanalytic theory
Puberty, 10, 195, 203, 245–246
    and fear of growing up, 246

See also Female sexual
   development;
   Menstruation
Puberty rites, 399–403, 474
Puerto Rican Americans, 407,
   408, 409, 410, 412
Punjabi Mexicans, 50, 52, 692
Punk rock, 337, **525–532**, 563,
   700
   precursors of, 526–528
Puritan girls, 90–92, 186,
   187–188, 225, 501–502,
   532–534
Purity, 74, 242, 504, 600, 603
   and hygiene, 368, 370
   and sweets, 320, 324
Purses, 358–361

Queers. *See* Lesbians
Quilting, 43–44, 46
La Quinceañera, 101, 110,
   535–539

Racism, 26, 30, 31, 32, 51–52,
   293, 295, 467
   reactions against, 529, 701
   in sexual development, 11,
   447–448
Radical feminism, **541–544**
Rape, 1, 2, 3, 4–5, 7, 29, 272.
   See also Acquaintance
   rape
Rapping, 343, 348
Reading, 138, **545–552**. *See
   also* Girls' fiction;
   Literacy
Reading disorders. *See*
   Learning disabilities,
   reading disorders, and
   girls
Rebelliousness, 123, 124, 497,
   518
   19th c., 505–507, 546,
   549–550, 602
   in music, 526, 529, 563–564
   See also Counterculture;
   Girls' culture; Graffiti;
   Slumber parties
Red diaper girls, **552–558**
Redstockings, 542
Reformers. *See* Social reform
Relational theory, **558–562**
   and interpersonal relations,
   200, 204, 522, 523
   See also Friendship
Relational therapies, 522

Religious development,
   110–111, 133–134,
   206–207
Religious groups. *See* Catholic
   girls; Jewish girls;
   Mennonite girls; Puritan
   girls
Religious vocations, 99, 101
Riot grrrls, 313, 337, 531–532,
   563–566, 700
Rites of passage. *See* Coming-
   of-age
Rock and roll, 180, 527
Rosie the Riveter, 641
Rousseau, Jean-Jacques, 225,
   502, 503
Running away, 311, 395, 397
Rural girls, **566–571**, 692
   homemaking clubs for,
   287–291
   play of, 504, 570, 571
   work of, 567–568, 692
   See also Frontier girls;
   Mennonite girls

Sadness. *See* Depression
Safe sex, 186, 286
St. Nicholas, 24, 134, 153, 154,
   545
Samplers, 43, **573–578**
Sassy, 336, 551, 701
Saturday Evening Girls (SEG),
   578–585
Scavenging, 686
Schizophrenia, 333
Science. *See* Mathematics and
   science
Séances, 592
Self-esteem, 7, 101, 620, 658
   of African American girls,
   229, 562
   and family interactions, 204
   and objectification of girls,
   559, 561
   and physical appearance, 13,
   82, 203
   and schoolwork, 305–306,
   441
Selfhood, 198, 246, 558, 559,
   561
Separation, 325, 326, 341–342,
   552, 558, 559
Separation anxiety, 523
Servants. *See* Domestic service
Service sector employment, 50,
   695
Seton, Ernest Thompson, 86

Seventeen, 25, 38, 149, 150,
   156, 160, 335–336, 550,
   587
Sewing, 42–43, 45, 296, 573,
   637, 638, 683, 685
Sex crimes. *See* Acquaintance
   rape
Sex delinquency. *See* Juvenile
   delinquents
Sex differences, in relational
   theory, 558–559
Sex education, 8, 24, 79–80,
   122
Sexism, reactions to, 529, 542,
   543
Sexual abuse, 116–117, 119,
   204, 394, 395, 523, 620
   known perpetrators of, 283
   See also Incest
Sexual arousal, 11, 286
Sexual assault, 1, 2, 3, 272
   culture of, 4–5, 6, 7, 28–29,
   32, 49, 589
   prevention of, 3, 5–6, 7
   See also Sexual harassment
Sexual barter, 179, 283, 615
Sexual delinquency. *See*
   Female sexuality, as
   delinquent
Sexual harassment in schools,
   585–590, 599
Sexual identity, and childhood,
   417, 422. *See also* Gender
   identity and role
   development
Sexuality, sexual behavior. *See*
   Female sexuality
Shacking up, 185
Sibling rivalry, 258
Single motherhood, 32, 650,
   651
Sissies and tomboys, 672
16 Magazine, 655
Skin disorders, 13, 160
Slumber parties, **591–594**
Sluts, 588
Smashes, 139, 418
Smoking. *See* Marijuana;
   Tobacco
Smotherhood, 259
Social change, 531, 554, 563
Social reform, 120–121, 239,
   392–393, 488, 685, 691
Social welfare, 597
Socialization, gender
   differences in. *See*
   Relational theory

Soda fountain, 323
Softball, 607
Song girls, 104
Sororities, 140, **594–600**
Southeast Asian Americans, 53
Southern belles, 503, **600–603**,
    682–683, 687
Spanking, 116
Spending money. *See*
    Allowances and spending
    money
Spinning, 43, 44, 451, 637, 683,
    688
Spock, Benjamin, 120, 434
Sports, **603–611**
    community, 604, 605, 606,
        607, 609
    partnership model of, 610
    professional, 607, 609
    school-based, 139, 604–605,
        607, 608–609
"Squaw" dresses, 86, 131
Starvation, 241, 243
Step-parents, 192
Sterilization, 77, 78, 410
Stowe, Harriet Beecher, 23, 93,
    226, 237, 239, 252
Street trades, 685
Stress, 204–205
Studs, 588
Substance abuse, 117, 181, 311,
    611–616, 620
    and crack babies, 616
    See also Acquaintance rape;
    Alcohol
Subway painting, 346
Sugar, 320, 322–325
Suicidal behavior in girls, 419,
    616–621
    crisis services for, 621
Summer camps, 70, 85, 555,
    580, **621–627**, 625
Sunday schools, 384–385, 386
Supernatural powers, 502, 678,
    679
Supreme Court
    on reproductive autonomy,
    650
    on sexual harassment, 585,
    587
Surfer girls, **627–631**
Surrogate motherhood, 21
Sweets. *See* Girls and sweets

Take Our Daughters to Work
    Day, 193, 696
Talented girls, 305–308
Tampons, 370, 449–450

Tea parties, 39, 42, **633–635**
Teaching, as occupation, 252,
    303, 378, 383, 388, 389,
    684
Teasing, 587
Technology, **635–645**
Teen, 25
Teen pregnancy, 4, 77, 78–79,
    117, 509, **645–653**
    of married girls, 648
    and poverty, 79, 650, 651,
    652
    use of term, 645, 649
Teenager, use of term, 159,
    645, 649
Teenbeat, 66
Teenybopper, **653–659**
Telephone, 148, 150
Television, 5, 82–83, 105, 156,
    314, 470, **659–666**
Temple, Shirley, 129, 229,
    666–669, 692
Test-taking, 307
Textile work, 43, 44, 451–452,
    638, 690. *See also* Mill
    girls
Thinness, 81, 82–83, 244, 245,
    614, 615, 701
    and fear of growing up, 246
Title IX, 106, 141, 253, 585,
    608
Tobacco, 508, 611, 612, 613,
    614
Today's Girl, 89
Tomboys, 329, **669–675**
    and sissies, 672
Toy (graffiti writer), 344
Toys. *See* Dollhouses; Dolls;
    Play
Treating, 179, 283
True womanhood, 94, 196, 239
Tuberculosis, 10, 13

Uncle Tom's Cabin (Stowe),
    93, 226, 237, 239, 485,
    487, 672
Underground culture. *See*
    Counterculture
Uterine atrophy, 24

Vamp, virgin portrayals of
    women, 5
Vietnamese Americans, 53
Violence, 564
    and child abuse, 396
    in gangs, 308, 310, 311
    gender differences in,
    396–397, 491, 493

Virgin of Guadalupe, 111
Virgin Mary, as cultural ideal,
    98, 110–111
Vomiting, 242, 243

Warner, Susan, 134, 327, 545
Weaving, 43, 44, 637
Websites. *See* Internet
Weight control and loss. *See*
    Thinness
Weight gain. *See* Obesity
Welfare benefits, 650, 652
Western frontier. *See* Frontier
    girls
Wheatley, Phillis, 137, 297
The Wide, Wide World
    (Warner), 134, 327–328,
    333, 487, 545, 546, 671,
    672, 674
Wilder, Laura Ingalls, 148, 331
Willard, Emma, 252, 363, 437
WITCH (Women's
    International Terrorist
    Conspiracy from Hell),
    542, 543
Witchcraft, **677–680**
Wizard of Oz, 270, 692
Woman's Christian
    Temperance Union
    (WCTU), 74
Women as property, 4–5, 28
Women's clubs
    African American, 29
    See also Sororities
Women's movement, 140–141,
    344, 365, 541, 542, 543,
    544. *See also* Feminism,
    feminist movement;
    Radical feminism
Womyn, 145
Womyn's music, 528
Woodworking, 44
Work, **680–698**
    of African American
        enslaved girls, 236,
        264–265, 636, 687–688
    of African American girls in
        20th c., 28, 233, 695
    of Asian American girls, 48,
        50, 53
    feminized, 680, 690, 696
    of frontier girls, 299, 301
    of immigrant girls, 35, 227,
        233, 375, 377, 378, 456,
        685–686, 689–691,
        693–695
    of Latina girls, 406, 407,
        408, 409

of Native American girls,
475
of orphans, 483–486, 487
See also Agricultural
workers; Child care;
Domestic service;
Homemaking, household
economy; Indentured
servants; Mill girls; Street
trades; Working-class
girls
Working-class girls, 73–74, 122,
497, 664, 685, 689–695
education of, 99, 100,
454–455
and family economy, 35, 37,
196

leisure activities of,
174–176, 178–179, 336,
343, 505, 507, 578–579,
604
political activism of, 378,
555
sexual activity of, 73–74,
179, 184, 282, 283, 284,
646
See also Immigrant girls;
Mill girls; Saturday
Evening Girls
World War I, 87, 289–290, 317,
692
World War II, 52, 197, 229, 290,
317, 340, 354, 508, 641,
693

Writing (graffiti art), 343–349
Writing instruction, 425–427.
See also Literacy

Yearbook signing, 430
Young and Modern (YM), 25,
551
Young Miss, 336, 551
Young Pioneers, 555
Young Women's Christian
Association (YWCA), 74,
648
Youth as stage. *See*
Adolescence, as stage

Zines, 146, 158, 337, 509, 563,
564–565, **699–702**

About the Editor

Miriam Forman-Brunell is associate professor of history and former director of the Women's and Gender Studies Program at the University of Missouri, Kansas City. She is the author of *Made to Play House: Dolls and the Commercialization of American Girlhood, 1830–1930* and *Sitting Pretty: Fears and Fantasies about Adolescent Girls.*